Merriam-Webster's COMPACT VISUAL Dictionary

Jean-Claude **Corbeil**
Ariane **Archambault**

Merriam-Webster, Incorporated
Springfield, Massachusetts
USA

Merriam-Webster Inc.

www.Merriam-Webster.com
www.LearnersDictionary.com
www.VisualDictionaryOnline.com

Merriam-Webster's Compact Visual Dictionary
was created and produced by

QA International
329 Rue de la Commune West, 3rd Floor
Montreal (Quebec) H2Y 2E1 Canada
T 514.499.3000 F 514.499.3010
www.qa-international.com

Published by Merriam-Webster Inc. 2008
Copyright © QA International 2008

ISBN: 978-0-87779-290-1

Printed and bound in Singapore

12340908

ACKNOWLEDGEMENTS

**We would like to extend our deepest thanks to the individuals, organizations
and companies who generously agreed to review the definitions and, when
needed, suggested changes that helped to clarify them.**

Arcand, Denys (motion picture director); Audet, Nathalie (Radio Canada);
Beaudouin, Yves (Université du Québec à Montréal); Beaudry, Jean (Longeuil Police
Department); Beaulieu, Jacques (Sainte-Thérèse Automotive Vocational Training
Center); Bordeleau, André (astronomer); Bugnet-Buchwalter, Marie-Odile (Music
Librarian, Université de Montréal); Butler, Philip (Stewart Museum); Christian, Ève
(meteorology consultant); Delorme, Michel (Montreal Biodôme); Deschamps,
Laurent; Desjardins, Jean-Pierre (Université du Québec à Montréal); Doray, Francine
(Hydro- Québec); Doyon, Philippe (Ministry of Natural Resources, Wildlife, and
Parks); Dupré, Céline (terminologist); Dupuis, Laval (Montreal Trade School of
Motorized Equipment); Faucher, Claude (Communications Transcript); Fournier,
Jacques (Éditions Roselin); Gagnon, Roger (astronomer); Garceau, Gaétan (Sainte-
Thérèse Automotive Vocational Training Center); Harou, Jérôme (Montreal School of
Construction Trades); Lachapelle, Jacques (School of Architecture, Université de
Montréal); Lafleur, Claude (science journalist); Lapierre, Robert (chief machinist); Le
Tirant, Stéphane (Montreal Insectarium); Lemay, Lucille (Leclerc Weaving Center);
Lemieux-Bérubé, Louise (Montreal Center of Contemporary Textiles); Lévesque,
Georges (ER doctor); Marc, Daniel (Montreal School of Construction Trades);
Marchand, Raymond G. (Université Laval); Martel, Félix (information technology
consultant); McEvoy, Louise (Air Canada Linguistic Services); Michotte, Pierre
(Maritime Institute of Quebec); Morin, Nadia (Montreal Fire Department Training
Center); Mosimann, François (Université de Sherbrooke); Neveu, Bernard
(Université du Québec à Trois-Rivières); Normand, Denis (telecommunications
consultant); Ouellet, Joseph (Montreal School of Construction Trades); Ouellet,
Rosaire (Cowansville Vocational Education Training Center); Papillon, Mélanie
(aeronautical engineer); Paquette, Luc (Montreal Trade School of Motorized
Equipment); Paradis, Serge (Pratt & Whitney); Parent, Serge (Montreal Biodôme);
Prichonnet, Gilbert (Université du Québec à Montréal); Rancourt, Claude (Montreal
Trade School of Motorized Equipment); Revéret, Jean-Pierre (Université du Québec à
Montréal); Robitaille, Jean-François (Laurentian University, Ontario); Ruel, Jean-
Pierre (Correctional Service Canada); Thériault, Joël.

EDITORIAL STAFF
Editor: Jacques Fortin
Authors: Jean-Claude Corbeil and
Ariane Archambault
Editorial Director: François Fortin
Editor-in-Chief: Anne Rouleau
Graphic Designer: Anne Tremblay

PRODUCTION
Nathalie Fréchette
Josée Gagnon

TERMINOLOGICAL RESEARCH
Jean Beaumont
Catherine Briand
Nathalie Guillo

ENGLISH DEFINITIONS
Nancy Butchart
Rita Cloghesy
Tom Donovan
Diana Halfpenny
John Woolfrey
Kathe Roth

ILLUSTRATIONS
Artistic Direction: Jocelyn Gardner
Jean-Yves Ahern
Rielle Lévesque
Alain Lemire
Mélanie Boivin
Yan Bohler
Claude Thivierge
Pascal Bilodeau
Michel Rouleau
Anouk Noël
Carl Pelletier
Raymond Martin

LAYOUT
Pascal Goyette
Danielle Quinty
Émilie Corriveau
Preliminary layout: Émilie Bellemare
Sonia Charette

DOCUMENTATION
Gilles Vézina
Kathleen Wynd
Stéphane Batigne
Sylvain Robichaud
Jessie Daigle

DATA MANAGEMENT
Programmer: Éric Gagnon
Josée Gagnon

REVISION
Veronica Schami
Jo Howard
Marie-Nicole Cimon
Liliane Michaud

PREPRESS
Karine Lévesque
Kien Tang

MERRIAM-WEBSTER EDITORS
Anne Bello
Daniel B. Brandon
Christopher C. Connor
Ilya A. Davidovich
Anne Eason
Daniel J. Hopkins
Neil S. Serven
Peter A. Sokolowski
Paul S. Wood

CONTRIBUTIONS
QA International wishes to extend a special thank you to the following people for their contribution to this book:
Jean-Louis Martin, Marc Lalumière, Jacques Perrault, Stéphane Roy, Alice Comtois, Michel Blais, Christiane Beauregard, Mamadou Togola, Annie Maurice, Charles Campeau, Mivil Deschênes, Jonathan Jacques, Martin Lortie, Frédérick Simard, Yan Tremblay, Mathieu Blouin, Sébastien Dallaire, Hoang Khanh Le, Martin Desrosiers, Nicolas Oroc, François Escalmel, Danièle Lemay, Pierre Savoie, Benoît Bourdeau, Marie-Andrée Lemieux, Caroline Soucy, Yves Chabot, Anne-Marie Ouellette, Anne-Marie Villeneuve, Anne-Marie Brault, Nancy Lepage, Daniel Provost, François Vézina, Guylaine Houle, Daniel Beaulieu, Sophie Pellerin, Tony O'Riley, Mac Thien Nguyen Hoang, Serge D'Amico.

INTRODUCTION

Merriam-Webster's Compact Visual Dictionary is an abridgement of Merriam-Webster's Visual Dictionary designed to present the most essential parts of the larger book in a compact and convenient form. It is intended for the general public and designed to meet a wide range of personal and professional needs: finding an unknown term, checking the meaning of a word, or being a handy resource for writers, teachers, and translators. The aim has been to bring together in one book the specialized vocabulary that is required and encountered in the wide range of fields that shape our daily experience.

EDITORIAL POLICY

Like Merriam-Webster's Visual Dictionary, upon which this work is based, each word in Merriam-Webster's Compact Visual Dictionary has been chosen after consulting the authoritative information sources containing the appropriate level of specialization. In some instances, the sources consulted revealed that different words are used to name the same concept. In such cases, the most authoritative sources were used in selecting the term.

Words are usually referred to in the singular, even if the illustration shows a number of individual examples. The word refers the concept, not the illustration.

DEFINITIONS

Within the hierarchical format of the Compact Visual Dictionary's presentation, the definitions fit together like a Russian doll. For example, the information within the term insect at the top of the page does not have to be repeated for each of the insects illustrated. Instead, the text concentrates on defining the distinguishing characteristics of each insect (the louse is a parasite, the female yellow jacket stings, and so forth).

Since the definition leaves out what is obvious, the illustrations and the definitions complement one another.

The vast majority of the terms in the Compact Visual Dictionary are defined and can be found in the index. Terms are not defined when the illustration makes the meaning absolutely clear, or when the illustration suggests the usual meaning of the word (for example, the numerous tool handles).

STRUCTURE

The dictionary has three sections: the introductory pages, including the table of contents; the body of the text (i.e., the detailed treatment of each theme); and the index.

The order of presentation is from the abstract to the concrete: theme, subtheme, title, subtitle, illustration, terminology, definition.

HOW TO CONSULT THIS DICTIONARY

Users may gain access to the contents of the Compact Visual Dictionary in a variety of ways:

From the table of contents, the user can locate the section that is of interest.

The index can be consulted to locate a specific term, and by examining the illustration cited, one can see what corresponds to the word and how it is defined.

One can examine the illustrations in the relevant sections of the book. The great strength of the Compact Visual Dictionary is the fact that the illustrations enable the user to find a word even if he or she has only a vague idea of what it is.

AUTHORS

Jean-Claude Corbell is an expert in linguistic planning, with a world-wide reputation in the fields of comparative terminology and socio-linguistics. He serves as a consultant to various international organizations and governments.

Ariane Archambault, a specialist in applied linguistics, has taught foreign languages and is now a terminologist and editor of dictionaries and reference books.

TITLE

Its definition is found below. If the title refers to information that continues over several pages, after the first page it is shown in a shaded tone with no definition.

THEME

These are shown at the end of the preliminary pages. They are then repeated on each page of the section.

TERM

Each term appears in the index with a reference to the pages on which it appears.

SUB-THEME

They are repeated on each page of a section, but without the definition.

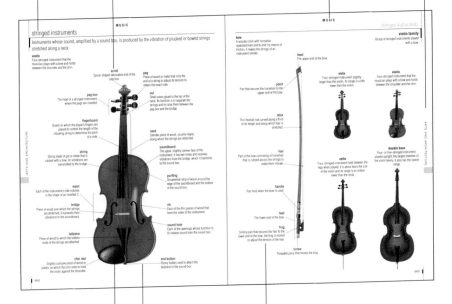

stringed instruments
Instruments whose sound, amplified by a sound box, is produced by the vibration of plucked or bowed strings stretched along a neck.

violin
Four-stringed instrument that the musician plays with a bow and holds between the shoulder and the chin.

scroll
Spiral-shaped decorative end of the peg box.

peg
Piece of wood or metal that rolls the end of a string to adjust its tension to obtain the exact note.

peg box
The head of a stringed instrument, where the pegs are inserted.

nut
Small piece glued to the top of the neck; its function is to separate the strings and to raise them between the peg box and the bridge.

fingerboard
Board on which the player's fingers are placed to control the length of the vibrating string to determine the pitch of a note.

neck
Slender piece of wood, usually maple, along which the strings are stretched.

string
String made of gut or metal that is rubbed with a bow; its vibrations are transmitted to the bridge.

soundboard
The upper, slightly convex face of the instrument; it has two holes and receives vibrations from the bridge, which it transmits to the sound box.

purfling
Ornamental strip of wood around the edge of the soundboard and the bottom of the sound box.

waist
Each of the instrument's side notches in the shape of an inverted C.

bridge
Piece of wood over which the strings are stretched; it transmits their vibrations to the soundboard.

rib
Each of the thin pieces of wood that form the sides of the instrument.

tailpiece
Piece of wood to which the bottom ends of the strings are attached.

sound hole
Each of the openings whose function is to release sound from the sound box.

chin rest
Slightly concave piece of wood or plastic on which the chin rests to hold the violin against the shoulder.

end button
Ebony button used to attach the tailpiece to the sound box.

bow
A wooden stick with horsehair stretched from end to end; by means of friction, it makes the strings of an instrument vibrate.

head
The upper end of the bow.

point
Part that secures the horsehair to the upper end of the bow.

stick
Thin flexible rod curved along a third of its length and along which hair is stretched.

hair
Part of the bow consisting of horsehair that is rubbed across the strings to make them vibrate.

handle
Part held when the bow is used.

heel
The lower end of the bow.

frog
Sliding part that secures the hair to the lower end of the bow; the frog is moved to adjust the tension of the hair.

screw
Threaded piece that moves the frog.

violin family
Group of stringed instruments played with a bow.

viola
Four-stringed instrument slightly larger than the violin; its range is a fifth lower than the violin.

violin
Four-stringed instrument that the musician plays with a bow and holds between the shoulder and the chin.

cello
Four-stringed instrument held between the legs when played; it is about twice the size of the violin and its range is an octave lower than the viola.

double bass
Four- or five-stringed instrument, played upright, the largest member of the violin family; it also has the lowest range.

MUSIC

ARTS AND ARCHITECTURE

662

663

ILLUSTRATION

It is an integral part of the visual definition for each of the terms that refer to it.

DEFINITION

It explains the inherent qualities, function, or characteristics of the element depicted in the illustration.

NARROW LINES

These link the word to the item indicated. Where too many lines would make reading difficult, they have been replaced by color codes with captions or, in rare cases, by numbers.

CONTENTS

UNIVERSE AND EARTH

2   CELESTIAL BODIES
14   ASTRONOMICAL OBSERVATION
20   ASTRONAUTICS
28   GEOGRAPHY
36   GEOLOGY
62   METEOROLOGY
76   ENVIRONMENT

PLANTS AND GARDENING

84   PLANTS
138 GARDENING

ANIMAL KINGDOM

158 SIMPLE ORGANISMS AND ECHINODERMS
164 INSECTS AND ARACHNIDS
176 MOLLUSKS
178 CRUSTACEANS
180 FISHES
184 AMPHIBIANS
188 REPTILES
196 BIRDS
212 RODENTS AND LAGOMORPHS
215 INSECTIVOROUS MAMMALS
216 UNGULATE MAMMALS
223 CARNIVOROUS MAMMALS
233 MARINE MAMMALS
238 PRIMATE MAMMALS
240 MARSUPIAL MAMMALS
242 FLYING MAMMAL

THE HUMAN BEING

244 HUMAN BODY
252 ANATOMY
298 SENSE ORGANS

FOOD AND KITCHEN

312 FOOD
378 KITCHEN

HOUSE AND DO-IT-YOURSELF

430 LOCATION
432 STRUCTURE OF A HOUSE
444 ELEMENTS OF A HOUSE
448 HEATING
450 AIR CONDITIONING
452 PLUMBING
464 ELECTRICITY
472 HOUSE FURNITURE
514 DO-IT-YOURSELF

CLOTHING AND PERSONAL ACCESSORIES

544 CLOTHING
602 PERSONAL ACCESSORIES
622 PERSONAL ARTICLES

ARTS AND ARCHITECTURE

644 FINE ARTS
646 PERFORMING ARTS
650 VISUAL ARTS
658 MUSIC
684 ARCHITECTURE

COMMUNICATIONS AND OFFICE AUTOMATION

696 COMMUNICATIONS
740 OFFICE AUTOMATION

TRANSPORTATION

792 ROAD TRANSPORT
836 RAIL TRANSPORT
850 MARITIME TRANSPORT
866 AIR TRANSPORT

SCIENCE AND ENERGY

876 CHEMISTRY
881 PHYSICS: MECHANICS
883 PHYSICS: ELECTRICITY AND MAGNETISM
889 PHYSICS: OPTICS
900 MEASURING DEVICES
912 SCIENTIFIC SYMBOLS
924 GEOTHERMAL AND FOSSIL ENERGY
934 HYDROELECTRICITY
940 NUCLEAR ENERGY
946 SOLAR ENERGY
948 WIND ENERGY

SPORTS AND GAMES

952 TRACK AND FIELD
954 BALL SPORTS
966 RACKET SPORTS
974 GYMNASTICS
976 AQUATIC AND NAUTICAL SPORTS
984 COMBAT SPORTS
992 STRENGTH SPORTS
996 PRECISION AND ACCURACY SPORTS
1003 CYCLING
1007 MOTOR SPORTS
1010 WINTER SPORTS
1027 SPORTS ON WHEELS
1030 OUTDOOR LEISURE
1042 GAMES

LIST OF CHAPTERS

UNIVERSE AND EARTH 2

PLANTS AND GARDENING 84

ANIMAL KINGDOM 158

THE HUMAN BEING 244

FOOD AND KITCHEN 312

HOUSE AND DO-IT-YOURSELF 430

CLOTHING AND PERSONAL ACCESSORIES 544

ARTS AND ARCHITECTURE 644

COMMUNICATIONS AND OFFICE AUTOMATION 696

TRANSPORTATION 792

SCIENCE AND ENERGY 876

SPORTS AND GAMES 952

INDEX 1049

solar system

Region of our galaxy under the influence of the Sun; includes eight planets and their natural satellites as well as dwarf planets, asteroids and comets.

outer planets
Planets located beyond the asteroid belt; these are known as the gas giants.

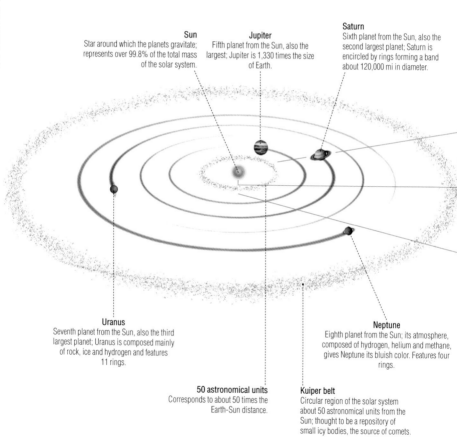

Sun
Star around which the planets gravitate; represents over 99.8% of the total mass of the solar system.

Jupiter
Fifth planet from the Sun, also the largest; Jupiter is 1,330 times the size of Earth.

Saturn
Sixth planet from the Sun, also the second largest planet; Saturn is encircled by rings forming a band about 120,000 mi in diameter.

Uranus
Seventh planet from the Sun, also the third largest planet; Uranus is composed mainly of rock, ice and hydrogen and features 11 rings.

Neptune
Eighth planet from the Sun; its atmosphere, composed of hydrogen, helium and methane, gives Neptune its bluish color. Features four rings.

50 astronomical units
Corresponds to about 50 times the Earth-Sun distance.

Kuiper belt
Circular region of the solar system about 50 astronomical units from the Sun; thought to be a repository of small icy bodies, the source of comets.

inner planets
Rocky planets closest to the Sun;
located inside the asteroid belt.

asteroid belt
Circular region between Mars and Jupiter
containing the greatest number of
asteroids; marks the boundary between the
inner and outer planets.

1 astronomical unit
Unit of distance equal to the mean
distance between Earth and the Sun,
equivalent to about 93 million mi.

Earth
Third planet from the Sun, inhabited by
humankind; up to now, the only planet with
evidence of life.

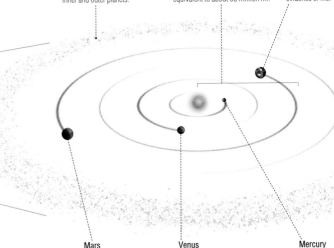

Mars
Fourth planet from the Sun; its crust
contains iron oxide, giving Mars its
reddish color.

Venus
Second planet from the Sun; its density
and chemical composition are similar
to those of Earth.

Mercury
The planet closest to the Sun; devoid of
atmosphere, heavily cratered and
marked by extreme variations in
temperature (-300°F to 800°F).

planets and satellites

Planets and dwarf planets orbit the Sun, satellites orbit the planets. They are represented from left to right from the Sun, based on their relative sizes.

Venus
Second planet from the Sun; its density and chemical composition are similar to those of Earth.

Moon
Earth's only natural satellite; devoid of water and atmosphere and characterized by a highly uneven surface.

Earth
Third planet from the Sun, inhabited by humankind; up to now, the only planet with evidence of life.

Mars
Fourth planet from the Sun; its crust contains iron oxide, giving Mars its reddish color.

Jupiter
Fifth planet from the Sun, also the largest; Jupiter is 1,330 times the size of Earth.

Ceres
Discovered in 1801, it was promoted to status of dwarf planet in 2006.

Io
Satellite of Jupiter; the celestial body with the greatest number of active volcanoes.

Mercury
The planet closest to the Sun; devoid of atmosphere, heavily cratered and marked by extreme variations in temperature (-300°F to 800°F).

Callisto
Satellite of Jupiter; its heavily cratered surface indicates that Callisto is very old.

Europa
Satellite of Jupiter; displays a surface layer of ice that might cover liquid water.

Ganymede
Satellite of Jupiter; the largest natural satellite in the solar system; its glacial surface is thought to cover an ocean and a mantle.

Sun
Star around which the planets gravitate; represents over 99.8% of the total mass of the solar system.

Eris
Dwarf planet discovered in 2005, with a diameter bigger than Pluto's. It has a satellite, Dysnomia.

Saturn
Sixth planet from the Sun, also the second largest planet; Saturn is encircled by rings forming a band about 120,000 mi in diameter.

Charon
Pluto's only satellite; almost equal in size and mass to the planet itself.

Uranus
Seventh planet from the Sun, also the third largest planet; Uranus is composed mainly of rock, ice and hydrogen and features 11 rings.

Neptune
Eighth planet from the Sun; its atmosphere, composed of hydrogen, helium and methane, gives Neptune its bluish color. Features four rings.

Ariel
Satellite of Uranus; its cratered surface is composed of numerous long valleys and extremely high escarpments.

Triton
Neptune's largest satellite; together with Pluto, Triton is the coldest object in the solar system.

Tethys
Satellite of Saturn thought to be composed of ice; visible on its surface is an immense impact crater named Odysseus.

Titan
Saturn's largest satellite, 1.5 times the diameter of the Moon.

Pluto
Discovered in 1930, it was long considered the ninth planet of the solar system. Since 2006, it has been classified as a dwarf planet.

Dione
Satellite of Saturn; its cratered surface features ice deposits.

Rhea
Satellite of Saturn; its cratered surface is covered with ice as hard as rock.

Titania
The largest satellite of Uranus; its surface displays numerous valleys and faults.

5

Sun

Star composed of 92.1% hydrogen atoms and 7.8% helium atoms, around which the planets gravitate; represents more than 99.8% of the solar system's total mass.

structure of the Sun
From the center to the periphery are the core, the radiation and convection zones, the photosphere, the chromosphere and the corona.

flare
Violent projection of extremely hot gas into space, provoking polar auroras on Earth a few days later.

sunspot
A dark, slightly cooler zone of the photosphere where the magnetic field is more intense.

spicules
A narrow jet of gas in the form of a plume observed in the solar chromosphere.

chromosphere
The lowest level of the solar atmosphere, with a temperature of 18,000°F.

core
The innermost part of the Sun where hydrogen is converted into helium by nuclear fusion; core temperatures reach 27,000,000°F.

radiation zone
Region where energy produced in the core cools before migrating in the form of light and heat.

prominence
Gas that erupts from the chromosphere and solar corona, contrasting with the darkness of space.

faculae
Luminous region of the photosphere.

corona
The outermost layer of the solar atmosphere, visible in the form of a halo during a total eclipse; corona temperatures can reach 1,800,000°F.

convection zone
Region where hot gas currents circulate between the hot regions of the core and the cool surface.

photosphere
Visible surface of the Sun, with a temperature of 10,000°F.

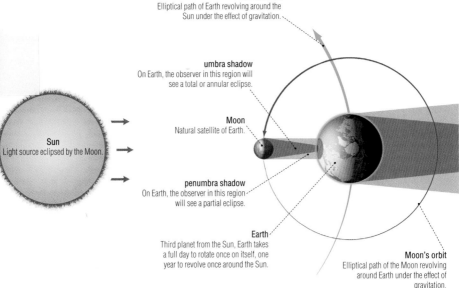

solar eclipse
Obscuration of the Sun brought about by the passage of the Moon between Earth and the Sun.

Earth's orbit
Elliptical path of Earth revolving around the Sun under the effect of gravitation.

umbra shadow
On Earth, the observer in this region will see a total or annular eclipse.

Moon
Natural satellite of Earth.

Sun
Light source eclipsed by the Moon.

penumbra shadow
On Earth, the observer in this region will see a partial eclipse.

Earth
Third planet from the Sun, Earth takes a full day to rotate once on itself, one year to revolve once around the Sun.

Moon's orbit
Elliptical path of the Moon revolving around Earth under the effect of gravitation.

types of eclipses
There are three types of solar eclipse, based on the degree of obscuration.

annular eclipse
Occurs when the Moon comes between Earth and the Sun, reducing the latter to a luminous ring.

partial eclipse
Observed by anyone within the penumbra zone during an eclipse.

total eclipse
Occurs when the lunar disk completely covers the solar disk and only the Sun's corona remains visible.

Moon

Earth's only natural satellite; devoid of water and atmosphere, it displays a highly uneven surface.

lunar features
Aspect of the Moon determined by past volcanic activity,
meteorite impact and soil fractures.

highland
Designates bright regions riddled with
craters; these oldest regions cover
85% of the surface.

lake
Small isolated plain of hardened lava.

sea
Designates the vast plains of hardened
lava forming the dark regions; younger
than the highlands, these cover 15% of
the surface.

cliff
Steep rock face shaped by a sea.

bay
Small plain of hardened lava located
along the edges of a sea.

mountain range
Vestiges of the walls of a once-large
crater; semicircular in shape, it can
span hundreds of miles.

crater
Circular basin dug out by the impact of
a meteorite.

ocean
A very large sea.

cirque
Vast crater characterized by remarkable
relief; varies between 12 and 120 mi in
diameter.

crater ray
Band that radiates from a young crater,
the result of matter ejected during a
meteorite impact.

wall
Mountain usually surrounding a cirque.

lunar eclipse
Eclipse during which the Moon enters Earth's umbra shadow in part or in full.

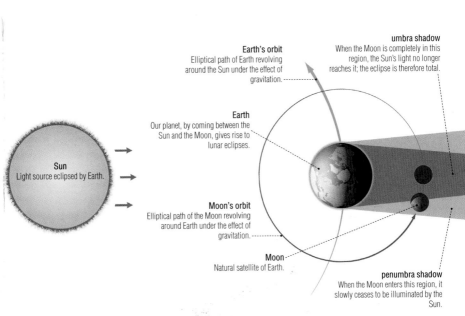

umbra shadow
When the Moon is completely in this region, the Sun's light no longer reaches it; the eclipse is therefore total.

Earth's orbit
Elliptical path of Earth revolving around the Sun under the effect of gravitation.

Earth
Our planet, by coming between the Sun and the Moon, gives rise to lunar eclipses.

Sun
Light source eclipsed by Earth.

Moon's orbit
Elliptical path of the Moon revolving around Earth under the effect of gravitation.

Moon
Natural satellite of Earth.

penumbra shadow
When the Moon enters this region, it slowly ceases to be illuminated by the Sun.

types of eclipses
There are two types of eclipse based on the degree of obscuration: partial or total.

total eclipse
Occurs when the Moon is completely within the umbra shadow and takes on a reddish appearance.

partial eclipse
When the Moon enters the umbra shadow, its bright side diminishes little by little.

Moon

phases of the Moon

Changes in the Moon's appearance over the course of a month; result from the movement of the Moon in relation to the Sun, as seen from Earth.

new moon

The Moon lies directly between Earth and the Sun; it is not visible, as the Sun's light is too brilliant.

first quarter

The visible face of the Moon grows increasingly bright; the lunar crescent gradually changes until it forms a semi-circle after one week.

new crescent
The Moon is visible in the early evening in the shape of a thin crescent.

waxing gibbous
As the Moon moves away from the Sun, its shadow gradually recedes.

comet

Small icy body that partially evaporates as it approaches the Sun; made up of a head with a solid core and tails composed of gas and dust.

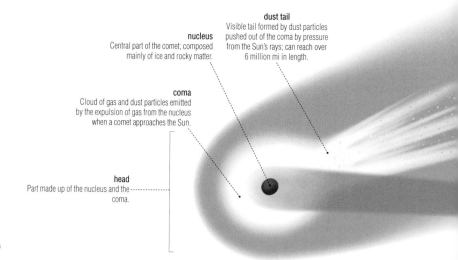

dust tail
Visible tail formed by dust particles pushed out of the coma by pressure from the Sun's rays; can reach over 6 million mi in length.

nucleus
Central part of the comet; composed mainly of ice and rocky matter.

coma
Cloud of gas and dust particles emitted by the expulsion of gas from the nucleus when a comet approaches the Sun.

head
Part made up of the nucleus and the coma.

full moon
The visible face of the Moon is completely illuminated by the Sun's rays.

last quarter
The bright side gradually recedes until it becomes a half-moon.

waning gibbous
As the Moon moves closer to the Sun, its shadow begins to obscure the Sun's disk.

old crescent
The Moon lies to the right of the Sun and appears in the sky at dawn in the form of a thin crescent.

comet

ion tail
Almost invisible tail formed by the gas of the coma pushed back by the solar wind; can reach several hundreds of millions of miles in length.

galaxy

Grouping of stars and interstellar matter linked together by gravitation; each galaxy comprises an average of 100 billion stars.

Milky Way

Spiral galaxy composed of 200 to 300 billion stars, including the Sun; thought to be 10 billion years old.

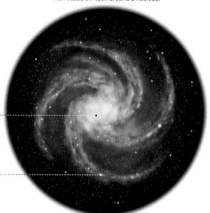

Milky Way (seen from above)
From above, the Milky Way appears as a spiral that rotates on itself around a nucleus.

nucleus
Central region of the bulge; the densest and most luminous region.

spiral arm
Curved grouping of stars influenced by the rotation of the galaxy around its nucleus.

halo
Region surrounding the galaxy, inhabited by isolated stars or groupings called globular clusters; the halo has a radius of about 50,000 light-years.

Milky Way (side view)
From the side, the Milky Way appears as a disk because its spiral arms are seen from the same angle.

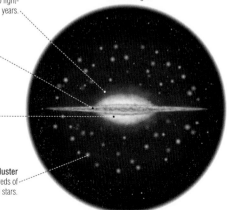

disk
The main part of the galaxy, made up of a bulge and attaching arms.

bulge
The central bulge of the Milky Way's disk; the densest region of the Milky Way, with a depth of 15,000 light-years.

globular cluster
Cluster made up of hundreds of thousands of old stars.

Hubble's classification

Classification of galaxies according to their form, devised by astronomer Edwin Hubble in the 1920s; it is still used today.

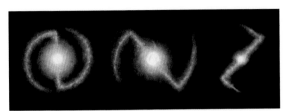

barred spiral galaxy
Galaxy crossed by a bar of stars and interstellar matter; the spiral arms emerge from the ends of the bar.

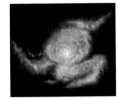

type I irregular galaxy
Rare type of galaxy that seems to possess spiral arms without displaying a specific symmetry.

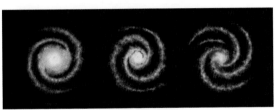

normal spiral galaxy
Galaxy composed of a large nucleus from which spiral arms emerge.

type II irregular galaxy
Rare type of galaxy whose structure obeys no specific symmetry.

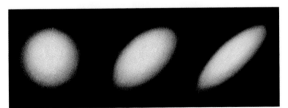

elliptical galaxy
Spherical or oval galaxy with no spiral arms.

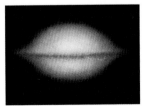

lenticular galaxy
Flat, lens-shaped galaxy with a large bulge but no arms.

reflecting telescope

Optical instrument that uses an objective mirror to observe celestial bodies.

UNIVERSE AND EARTH

eyepiece
Lens or system of lenses meant to magnify the image when placed before the eye.

right ascension setting scale
Graduated disk indicating the right ascension of the observed celestial body.

finderscope
Small low-magnification telescope with a wide field of view; serves to locate celestial bodies.

main tube
The barrel of the telescope through which light rays travel; houses the optical system.

focusing knob
Adjusting device that makes it possible to obtain a clear image of the object.

declination setting scale
Graduated disk indicating the declination of the celestial body observed.

azimuth clamp
Clamp serving to lock the telescope along its horizontal axis.

altitude clamp
Clamp serving to lock the telescope along its vertical axis.

altitude fine adjustment
Fine-tuning device that serves to position the telescope vertically.

azimuth fine adjustment
Fine-tuning device that serves to position the telescope horizontally.

refracting telescope

Optical instrument that uses an objective lens to observe celestial bodies.

UNIVERSE AND EARTH

eyepiece
Lens or system of lenses meant to magnify the image when placed before the eye.

finderscope
Small low-magnification telescope with a wide field of view; serves to locate celestial bodies.

main tube
The barrel of a telescope housing the optical system; light rays travel through the main tube.

declination setting scale
Graduated disk indicating the declination of the celestial body observed.

azimuth clamp
Clamp serving to lock the telescope along its horizontal axis.

altitude clamp
Clamp serving to lock the telescope along its vertical axis.

right ascension setting scale
Graduated disk indicating the right ascension of the observed celestial body.

tripod
Stable three-legged stand of variable height.

azimuth fine adjustment
Fine-tuning device serving to position the telescope horizontally.

altitude fine adjustment
Fine-tuning device serving to position the telescope vertically.

astronomical observatory

Building specially designed to house a large telescope.

cross section of an astronomical observatory

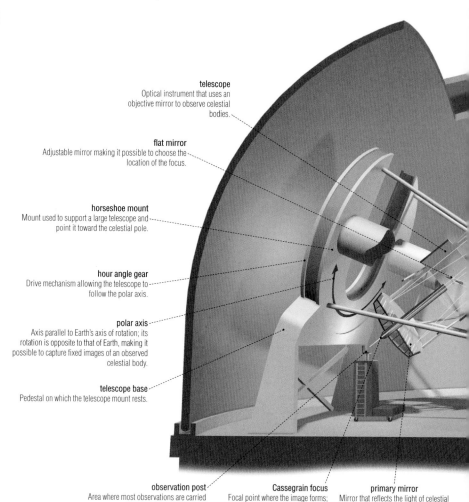

telescope
Optical instrument that uses an objective mirror to observe celestial bodies.

flat mirror
Adjustable mirror making it possible to choose the location of the focus.

horseshoe mount
Mount used to support a large telescope and point it toward the celestial pole.

hour angle gear
Drive mechanism allowing the telescope to follow the polar axis.

polar axis
Axis parallel to Earth's axis of rotation; its rotation is opposite to that of Earth, making it possible to capture fixed images of an observed celestial body.

telescope base
Pedestal on which the telescope mount rests.

observation post
Area where most observations are carried out.

Cassegrain focus
Focal point where the image forms; located behind the primary mirror.

primary mirror
Mirror that reflects the light of celestial bodies, directing it toward the prime focus.

secondary mirror
Mirror that intercepts light and redirects it toward the Cassegrain focus through a hole in the center of the primary mirror.

light
Emitted by the celestial body, light is sent back toward the Cassegrain focus by the primary and secondary mirrors.

observatory

dome shutter
Upper part of the dome that opens so that light can enter the telescope.

rotating dome
Roof of the observatory that pivots on itself so that all parts of the sky can be observed.

prime focus observing capsule
Area where astronomers once gathered to monitor the exposure time of photographic plates.

prime focus
Focal point of the primary mirror where the light rays concentrate.

interior dome shell
Regulates the temperature of the telescope so as to avoid air turbulence and prevent the mirror from becoming deformed.

coudé focus
Focal point located at a distance from the telescope, obtained using a series of mirrors; stationary, it is used to conduct complex analyses and experiments.

laboratory
Area where the chemical composition of observed celestial bodies is studied using spectroscopy.

exterior dome shell
Protects against foul weather.

Hubble space telescope

Telescope placed in orbit above Earth's atmosphere (370 mi), making it possible to observe the universe as never before.

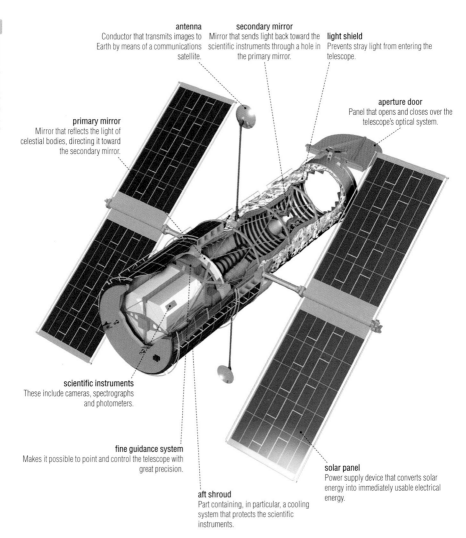

antenna
Conductor that transmits images to Earth by means of a communications satellite.

secondary mirror
Mirror that sends light back toward the scientific instruments through a hole in the primary mirror.

light shield
Prevents stray light from entering the telescope.

aperture door
Panel that opens and closes over the telescope's optical system.

primary mirror
Mirror that reflects the light of celestial bodies, directing it toward the secondary mirror.

scientific instruments
These include cameras, spectrographs and photometers.

fine guidance system
Makes it possible to point and control the telescope with great precision.

aft shroud
Part containing, in particular, a cooling system that protects the scientific instruments.

solar panel
Power supply device that converts solar energy into immediately usable electrical energy.

celestial coordinate system

Imaginary horizontal and vertical lines used to describe the position of an object on the celestial sphere.

UNIVERSE AND EARTH

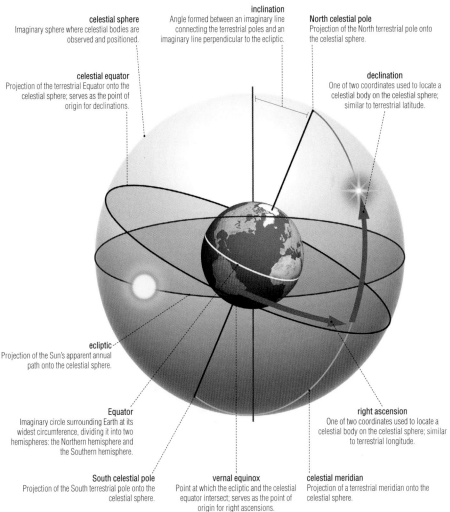

celestial sphere
Imaginary sphere where celestial bodies are observed and positioned.

inclination
Angle formed between an imaginary line connecting the terrestrial poles and an imaginary line perpendicular to the ecliptic.

North celestial pole
Projection of the North terrestrial pole onto the celestial sphere.

celestial equator
Projection of the terrestrial Equator onto the celestial sphere; serves as the point of origin for declinations.

declination
One of two coordinates used to locate a celestial body on the celestial sphere; similar to terrestrial latitude.

ecliptic
Projection of the Sun's apparent annual path onto the celestial sphere.

Equator
Imaginary circle surrounding Earth at its widest circumference, dividing it into two hemispheres: the Northern hemisphere and the Southern hemisphere.

right ascension
One of two coordinates used to locate a celestial body on the celestial sphere; similar to terrestrial longitude.

South celestial pole
Projection of the South terrestrial pole onto the celestial sphere.

vernal equinox
Point at which the ecliptic and the celestial equator intersect; serves as the point of origin for right ascensions.

celestial meridian
Projection of a terrestrial meridian onto the celestial sphere.

spacesuit

A pressurized watertight suit that provides the astronaut with oxygen and protects against solar rays and meteorites during space walks.

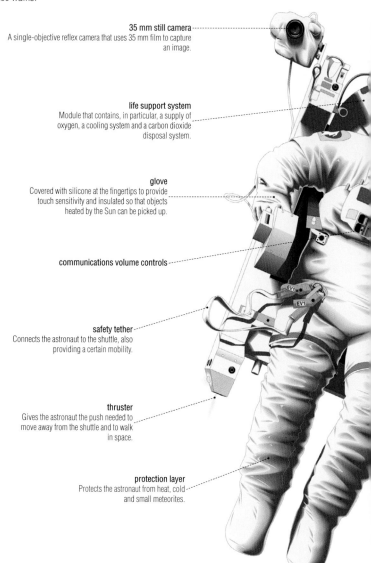

35 mm still camera
A single-objective reflex camera that uses 35 mm film to capture an image.

life support system
Module that contains, in particular, a supply of oxygen, a cooling system and a carbon dioxide disposal system.

glove
Covered with silicone at the fingertips to provide touch sensitivity and insulated so that objects heated by the Sun can be picked up.

communications volume controls

safety tether
Connects the astronaut to the shuttle, also providing a certain mobility.

thruster
Gives the astronaut the push needed to move away from the shuttle and to walk in space.

protection layer
Protects the astronaut from heat, cold and small meteorites.

spacesuit

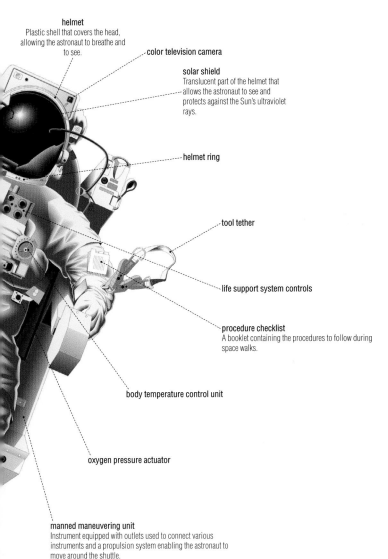

helmet
Plastic shell that covers the head, allowing the astronaut to breathe and to see.

color television camera

solar shield
Translucent part of the helmet that allows the astronaut to see and protects against the Sun's ultraviolet rays.

helmet ring

tool tether

life support system controls

procedure checklist
A booklet containing the procedures to follow during space walks.

body temperature control unit

oxygen pressure actuator

manned maneuvering unit
Instrument equipped with outlets used to connect various instruments and a propulsion system enabling the astronaut to move around the shuttle.

international space station

Complex made up of some 10 modules in orbit around Earth; built and assembled by 15 countries, it is used to conduct scientific and technological research on weightlessness.

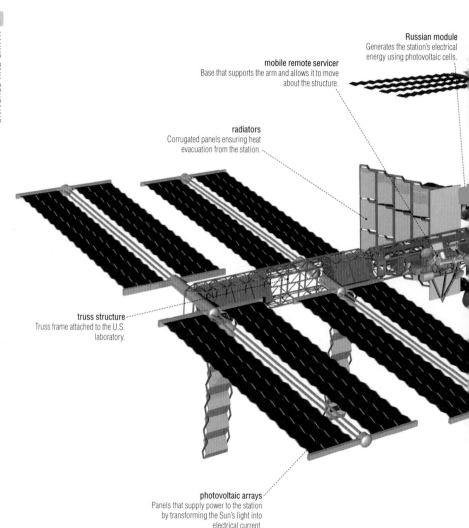

Russian module
Generates the station's electrical energy using photovoltaic cells.

mobile remote servicer
Base that supports the arm and allows it to move about the structure.

radiators
Corrugated panels ensuring heat evacuation from the station.

truss structure
Truss frame attached to the U.S. laboratory.

photovoltaic arrays
Panels that supply power to the station by transforming the Sun's light into electrical current.

remote manipulator system
This mechanical arm is used to lift heavy loads during the assembly of the station and to perform maintenance work.

centrifuge module
Module used to create variable artificial gravity, making it possible to study the effect of gravity levels on living organisms.

Japanese experiment module
Designed to conduct research in the life sciences and in the science of matter; also equipped with a platform for outside experiments.

remote manipulator system
Mechanical arm designed to conduct scientific experiments on the Japanese platform.

mating adaptor
Connector on which the space shuttle orbiter docks during most of the station's supply and assembly missions.

U.S. laboratory
Designed to carry out scientific activities, particularly in the life sciences and in physics.

European experiment module
Designed to conduct research in the life and materials sciences, in physics and in numerous other technologies.

crew return vehicle
Vehicle used to bring the crew back to Earth in case of emergency.

U.S. habitation module
Designed to accommodate six persons; contains a kitchen, roomettes, a bathroom and first-aid equipment.

space shuttle

Reusable manned space vehicle composed of an orbiter, two rockets and a fuel tank.

orbiter
The only part of the shuttle to fly in orbit; can transport 13 tons of material and five to seven astronauts.

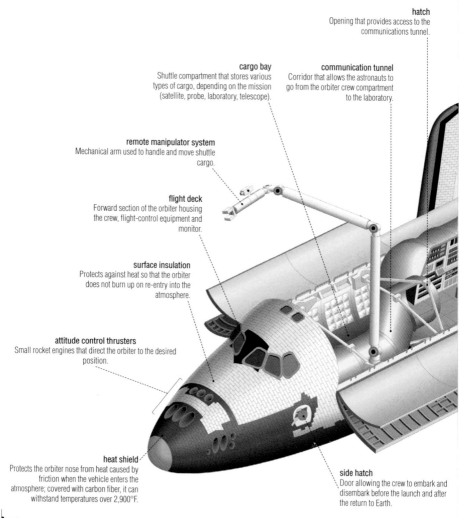

hatch
Opening that provides access to the communications tunnel.

cargo bay
Shuttle compartment that stores various types of cargo, depending on the mission (satellite, probe, laboratory, telescope).

communication tunnel
Corridor that allows the astronauts to go from the orbiter crew compartment to the laboratory.

remote manipulator system
Mechanical arm used to handle and move shuttle cargo.

flight deck
Forward section of the orbiter housing the crew, flight-control equipment and monitor.

surface insulation
Protects against heat so that the orbiter does not burn up on re-entry into the atmosphere.

attitude control thrusters
Small rocket engines that direct the orbiter to the desired position.

heat shield
Protects the orbiter nose from heat caused by friction when the vehicle enters the atmosphere; covered with carbon fiber, it can withstand temperatures over 2,900°F.

side hatch
Door allowing the crew to embark and disembark before the launch and after the return to Earth.

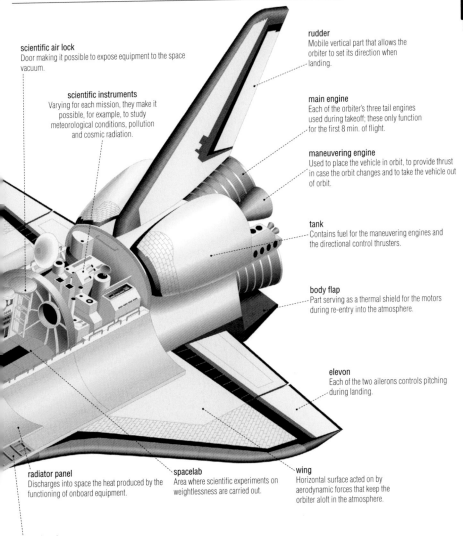

scientific air lock
Door making it possible to expose equipment to the space vacuum.

scientific instruments
Varying for each mission, they make it possible, for example, to study meteorological conditions, pollution and cosmic radiation.

rudder
Mobile vertical part that allows the orbiter to set its direction when landing.

main engine
Each of the orbiter's three tail engines used during takeoff; these only function for the first 8 min. of flight.

maneuvering engine
Used to place the vehicle in orbit, to provide thrust in case the orbit changes and to take the vehicle out of orbit.

tank
Contains fuel for the maneuvering engines and the directional control thrusters.

body flap
Part serving as a thermal shield for the motors during re-entry into the atmosphere.

elevon
Each of the two ailerons controls pitching during landing.

radiator panel
Discharges into space the heat produced by the functioning of onboard equipment.

spacelab
Area where scientific experiments on weightlessness are carried out.

wing
Horizontal surface acted on by aerodynamic forces that keep the orbiter aloft in the atmosphere.

cargo bay door
Remains open in orbit so as to expose the content of the cargo bay to space.

space shuttle

space shuttle at takeoff
On takeoff, the space shuttle is made up of an orbiter, two rockets and an external fuel tank.

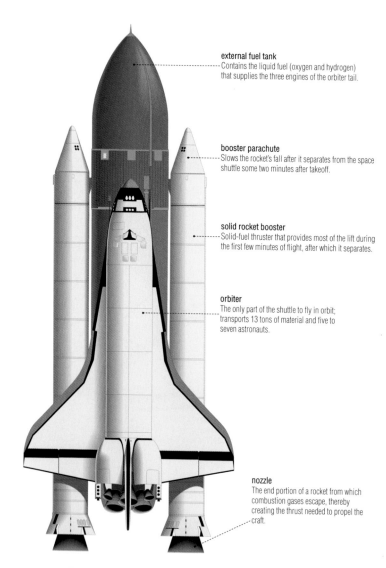

external fuel tank
Contains the liquid fuel (oxygen and hydrogen) that supplies the three engines of the orbiter tail.

booster parachute
Slows the rocket's fall after it separates from the space shuttle some two minutes after takeoff.

solid rocket booster
Solid-fuel thruster that provides most of the lift during the first few minutes of flight, after which it separates.

orbiter
The only part of the shuttle to fly in orbit; transports 13 tons of material and five to seven astronauts.

nozzle
The end portion of a rocket from which combustion gases escape, thereby creating the thrust needed to propel the craft.

space launcher

Rocket that serves to place satellites in Earth's orbit or to send probes into the solar system.

examples of space launchers

Ariane IV
European Space Agency launcher; in service from 1989 to 1997.

Saturn V
In service from 1967 to 1973, the most powerful rocket ever built served to launch the Apollo missions; the only launcher never to have failed.

Titan IV
In service since 1989, this U.S. launcher serves, in particular, to launch large military satellites.

Delta II
In service since 1989, this highly versatile launcher places meteorological and communications satellites in orbit.

configuration of the continents

The continents are vast tracts of land surrounded by water; they cover about 30% of the Earth's surface.

planisphere
Map depicting the Earth's two hemispheres.

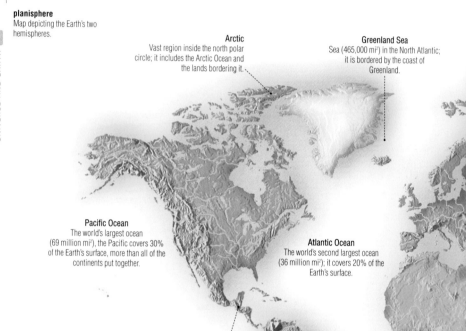

Arctic
Vast region inside the north polar circle; it includes the Arctic Ocean and the lands bordering it.

Greenland Sea
Sea (465,000 mi²) in the North Atlantic; it is bordered by the coast of Greenland.

Pacific Ocean
The world's largest ocean (69 million mi²), the Pacific covers 30% of the Earth's surface, more than all of the continents put together.

Atlantic Ocean
The world's second largest ocean (36 million mi²); it covers 20% of the Earth's surface.

Central America
Extends from the Isthmus of Tehuantepec in Mexico to the Isthmus of Panama.

Antarctica
The only uninhabited continent (5 million mi²), located inside the south polar circle; 98% of its surface is covered with an ice cap. Antarctica holds 90% of the Earth's freshwater reserves.

Arctic Ocean
The smallest of the oceans
(5.8 million mi²), bordered by the northern
coasts of Asia, America and Europe; it is
largely covered with pack ice.

Bering Sea
Northern part of the Pacific between
Kamchatka (in Asia) and Alaska; it is
deepest in its southern portion.

Eurasia
Composed of Europe and Asia, Eurasia represents
about 39% of the world's land; it forms a true continent
that geographers have distinguished for historical and
ethnographic reasons.

North America
Its area (9.3 million mi²) represents
about 16% of the world's land; the
Central American isthmus is an
extension of North America.

South America
Represents 12% of the world's land; linked to
North America by Central America; it includes
the Andes in the west and plains and plateaus
in east and central regions.

Oceania
Continent that represents 6% of the world's land and
features a great many islands in the Pacific and
Indian oceans; Australia is its true continent.

Indian Ocean
Relatively small ocean (29 million mi²)
located between Africa, Asia and Australia;
it has high water temperatures and is dotted
with numerous islands.

Europe
Western extremity of the vast Eurasian continent
that, by convention, is separated from Asia by
the Ural Mountains; it covers a relatively small
area.

Asia
The largest and most populous
continent, Asia represents 32% of the
world's land; it is dominated by
imposing mountain ranges.

Australia
The world's largest island (3 million mi²) is
sparsely inhabited in spite of its size;
because of its isolation, Australia's wildlife
is unique.

Africa
Continent that represents about 20% of the world's land;
two-thirds of its surface lies north of the Equator.
Characterized by very hot climates, Mediterranean in the
north and south, tropical and arid elsewhere.

cartography

A collective term for the techniques and graphic arts used to develop and produce maps based on direct observation or documentation.

Earth coordinate system
The intersection of two imaginary lines, longitude and latitude, makes it possible to locate a precise point on the Earth's surface.

North Pole
Point on the Earth's surface at the northern extremity of the axis of rotation, where the meridians converge.

Arctic Circle
Parallel of latitude 66°34' N; it marks the polar zone, where days and nights last 24 hours during solstices.

Equator
Imaginary line encircling the Earth at its greatest circumference and perpendicular to the polar axis; its latitude, 0, serves as a reference point for calculating other latitudes.

Tropic of Cancer
Parallel located at 23°26' N latitude (a distance of about 1,600 mi from the Equator).

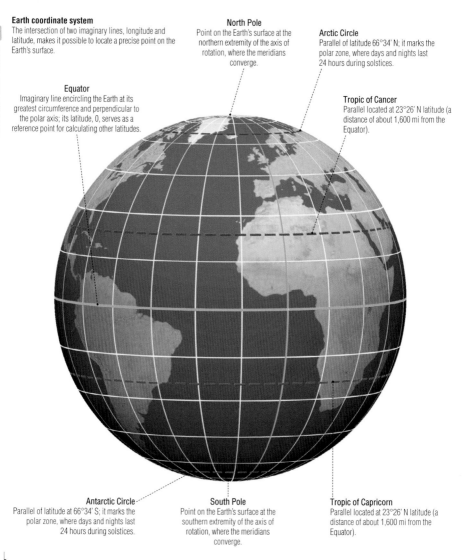

Antarctic Circle
Parallel of latitude at 66°34' S; it marks the polar zone, where days and nights last 24 hours during solstices.

South Pole
Point on the Earth's surface at the southern extremity of the axis of rotation, where the meridians converge.

Tropic of Capricorn
Parallel located at 23°26' N latitude (a distance of about 1,600 mi from the Equator).

hemispheres

The globe is divided by convention into four half spheres, using the Greenwich meridian or the Equator as a reference point.

Northern Hemisphere
Northern half of the globe in relation to the Equator.

Southern Hemisphere
Southern half of the globe in relation to the Equator.

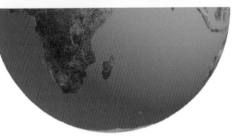

Western Hemisphere
Western half of the globe in relation to the prime meridian.

Eastern Hemisphere
Eastern half of the globe in relation to the prime meridian.

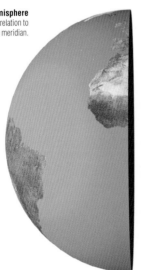

cartography

grid system
Collective term for the parallels and meridians that form an imaginary grid over the Earth's surface, making it possible to locate a specific point.

line of latitude
Coordinate of a point on the Earth's surface indicating, in degrees, its distance from the Equator.

Arctic Circle
Parallel of latitude 66°34' N; it marks the polar zone, where days and nights last 24 hours during solstices.

Equator
Imaginary line encircling the Earth at its greatest circumference and perpendicular to the polar axis; its latitude, 0, serves as a reference point for calculating other latitudes.

Tropic of Cancer
Parallel located at 23°26' N latitude (a distance of about 1,600 mi from the Equator).

Tropic of Capricorn
Parallel located at 23°26' N latitude (a distance of about 1,600 mi from the Equator).

parallel
Imaginary circle whose plane is parallel to the Equator.

Antarctic Circle
Parallel of latitude at 66°34' S; it marks the polar zone, where days and nights last 24 hours during solstices.

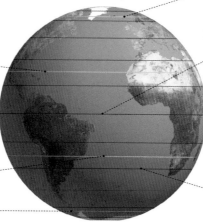

line of longitude
Coordinate of a point on the Earth's surface indicating, in degrees, its distance from the prime meridian.

Eastern meridian
Imaginary line connecting the poles and perpendicular to the Equator; located east of the Greenwich meridian.

prime meridian
Chosen by convention as the meridian of origin; its longitude, 0, divides the Eastern and Western hemispheres.

Western meridian
Imaginary line connecting the poles and perpendicular to the Equator; located west of the Greenwich meridian.

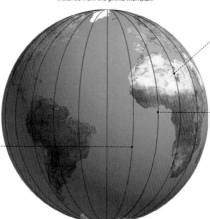

map projections
Representations of the Earth's surface on a plane.

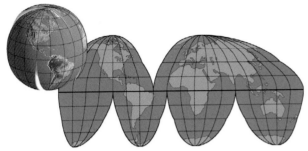

interrupted projection
Results in a map that is not continuous but cut off, the divisions often placed in the middle of the oceans; it is used to represent the continents.

cylindrical projection
Obtained by projecting the Earth's surface onto a cylinder; the meridians and parallels are thus straight lines intersecting at right angles.

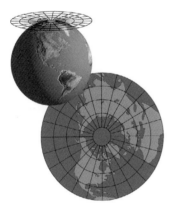

plane projection
Produced on a plane placed in such a way that it is tangent to a point on the Earth's surface; it can represent only one hemisphere.

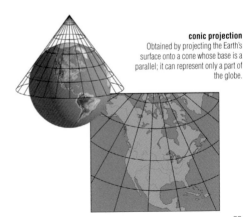

conic projection
Obtained by projecting the Earth's surface onto a cone whose base is a parallel; it can represent only a part of the globe.

cartography

physical map
Type of map representing the Earth's surface (topography, watercourses, aquatic areas) using various techniques (contour lines, colors).

mountain range
A row of connected mountains characterized by high summits and deep valleys.

prairie
Vast expanse of relatively flat land that is characterized by grasses and is naturally devoid of trees.

mountain mass
Group of closely spaced mountains.

river
Natural watercourse of minor or intermediate size that empties into another watercourse.

plateau
Vast expanse of relatively flat land, higher than the surrounding region and bounded by deep valleys with sheer cliffs.

gulf
Long curvature in a coastline; it reaches far inland and is more or less open.

cape
Massive elevated headland extending into the sea or a river estuary.

plain
Vast, relatively flat expanse of land, lower than the surrounding landscape; its valleys are wide and shallow.

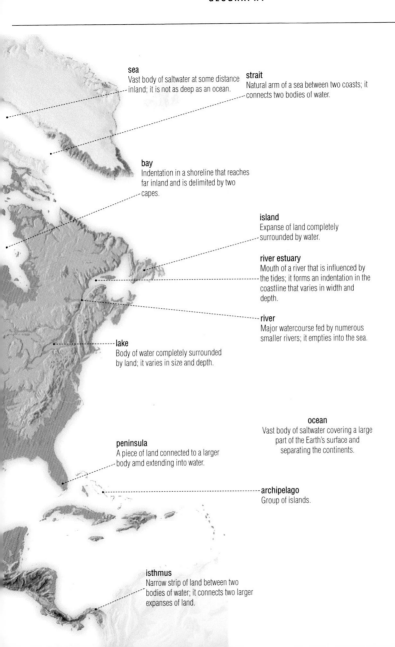

sea
Vast body of saltwater at some distance inland; it is not as deep as an ocean.

strait
Natural arm of a sea between two coasts; it connects two bodies of water.

bay
Indentation in a shoreline that reaches far inland and is delimited by two capes.

island
Expanse of land completely surrounded by water.

river estuary
Mouth of a river that is influenced by the tides; it forms an indentation in the coastline that varies in width and depth.

river
Major watercourse fed by numerous smaller rivers; it empties into the sea.

lake
Body of water completely surrounded by land; it varies in size and depth.

ocean
Vast body of saltwater covering a large part of the Earth's surface and separating the continents.

peninsula
A piece of land connected to a larger body amd extending into water.

archipelago
Group of islands.

isthmus
Narrow strip of land between two bodies of water; it connects two larger expanses of land.

section of the Earth's crust

The Earth's crust, continental and oceanic, is composed mainly of sedimentary, metamorphic and igneous rock.

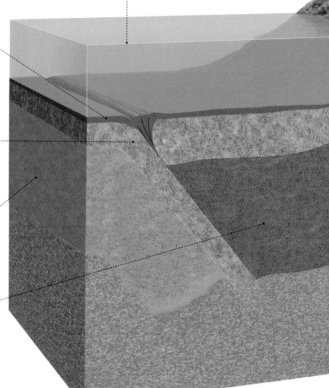

sea level
Average height of seawater observed for a given time (day, month, year); it is used as a reference point to define coastal features and measure land elevations.

deep-sea floor
Part of the Earth's surface beneath the seas and the oceans; its topography is highly variable.

sedimentary rocks
Rocks formed by the accumulation, compaction and cementation of fragments of eroded rock and debris left by living organisms.

basaltic layer
Layer of basalt, a rock denser than granite, that forms the deep-sea floor and is covered with various types of debris.

metamorphic rocks
Rocks made from igneous or sedimentary rocks that have been subjected to high pressure and very high temperatures.

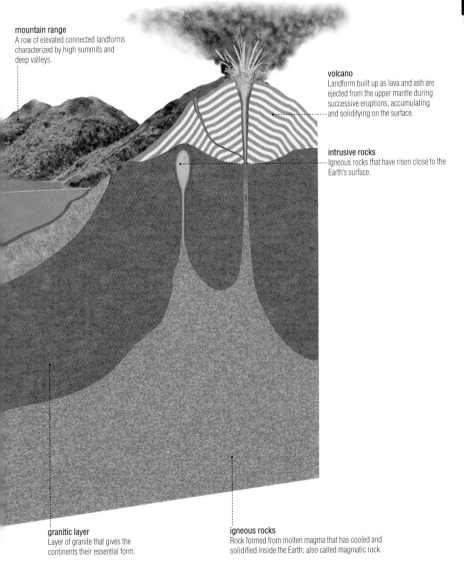

mountain range
A row of elevated connected landforms characterized by high summits and deep valleys.

volcano
Landform built up as lava and ash are ejected from the upper mantle during successive eruptions, accumulating and solidifying on the surface.

intrusive rocks
Igneous rocks that have risen close to the Earth's surface.

granitic layer
Layer of granite that gives the continents their essential form.

igneous rocks
Rock formed from molten magma that has cooled and solidified inside the Earth; also called magmatic rock.

UNIVERSE AND EARTH

structure of the Earth

The Earth is formed of three concentric layers: the core, the mantle and the crust; these are separated by transition zones called discontinuities.

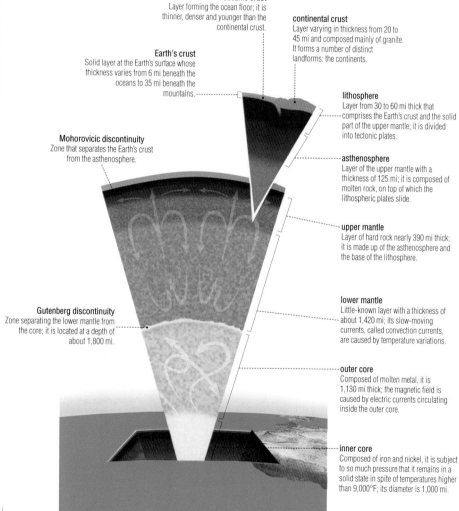

oceanic crust
Layer forming the ocean floor; it is thinner, denser and younger than the continental crust.

continental crust
Layer varying in thickness from 20 to 45 mi and composed mainly of granite. It forms a number of distinct landforms: the continents.

Earth's crust
Solid layer at the Earth's surface whose thickness varies from 6 mi beneath the oceans to 35 mi beneath the mountains.

lithosphere
Layer from 30 to 60 mi thick that comprises the Earth's crust and the solid part of the upper mantle; it is divided into tectonic plates.

Mohorovicic discontinuity
Zone that separates the Earth's crust from the asthenosphere.

asthenosphere
Layer of the upper mantle with a thickness of 125 mi; it is composed of molten rock, on top of which the lithospheric plates slide.

upper mantle
Layer of hard rock nearly 390 mi thick; it is made up of the asthenosphere and the base of the lithosphere.

lower mantle
Little-known layer with a thickness of about 1,420 mi; its slow-moving currents, called convection currents, are caused by temperature variations.

Gutenberg discontinuity
Zone separating the lower mantle from the core; it is located at a depth of about 1,800 mi.

outer core
Composed of molten metal, it is 1,130 mi thick; the magnetic field is caused by electric currents circulating inside the outer core.

inner core
Composed of iron and nickel, it is subject to so much pressure that it remains in a solid state in spite of temperatures higher than 9,000°F; its diameter is 1,000 mi.

earthquake

Sudden tremor in a region of the Earth's crust caused by one rock mass sliding against another.

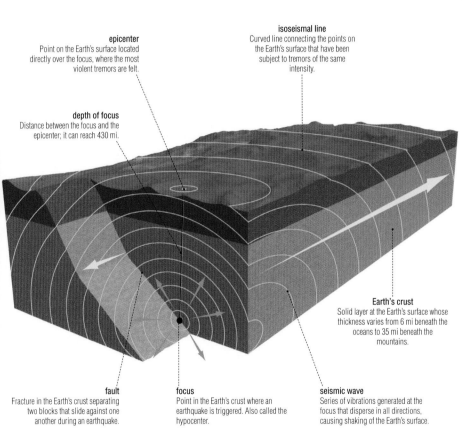

epicenter
Point on the Earth's surface located directly over the focus, where the most violent tremors are felt.

isoseismal line
Curved line connecting the points on the Earth's surface that have been subject to tremors of the same intensity.

depth of focus
Distance between the focus and the epicenter; it can reach 430 mi.

Earth's crust
Solid layer at the Earth's surface whose thickness varies from 6 mi beneath the oceans to 35 mi beneath the mountains.

fault
Fracture in the Earth's crust separating two blocks that slide against one another during an earthquake.

focus
Point in the Earth's crust where an earthquake is triggered. Also called the hypocenter.

seismic wave
Series of vibrations generated at the focus that disperse in all directions, causing shaking of the Earth's surface.

tectonic plates

Immense portions of the lithosphere that slide over the asthenosphere; this shifting movement shapes the Earth's topography.

North American Plate
Together with the Pacific Plate, this plate creates the San Andreas Fault (750 mi), which extends from the Gulf of California to San Francisco.

Cocos Plate
Plate along the coast of Mexico and Central America; it is sinking beneath the North American Plate and the Caribbean Plate.

Caribbean Plate
Plate subducting under the American plates; the Caribbean Plate created the islands of the Lesser Antilles.

Pacific Plate
The only entirely oceanic plate, it is also among the most rapidly shifting plates (4 in per year).

Nazca Plate
One of the most rapidly shifting plates, moving 3 in per year.

Scotia Plate
Small plate under which the Antarctic Plate and part of the South American Plate are sliding.

South American Plate
Plate that forms the Andes cordillera by means of subduction with the Nazca Plate.

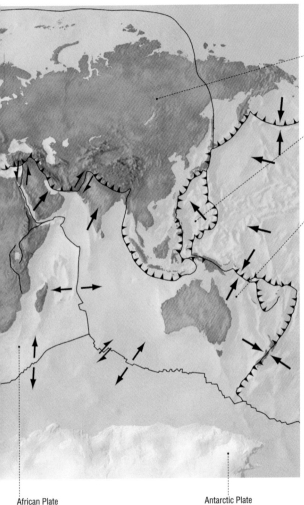

Eurasian Plate
Plate converging with the Australian-Indian Plate; it created the Himalayas.

Philippine Plate
Plate that forms the Philippines archipelago by means of subduction with the Eurasian Plate.

Australian-Indian Plate
Plate that is moving north 3 in per year; it forms the Red Sea by means of divergence from the African Plate.

subduction
Phenomenon by which an oceanic plate slides under a continental plate or under another oceanic plate, resulting in a trench.

transform plate boundaries
Plates that slide against each other, triggering earthquakes along faults of the same name.

convergent plate boundaries
Plates that collide, triggering either subduction or folding, which results in the creation of mountains.

divergent plate boundaries
Plates that are moving apart, causing magma to appear, which solidifies to generate a new crust.

African Plate
Plate that, diverging from the South American Plate, forms an underwater mountain chain.

Antarctic Plate
The largest plate; it is stationary.

volcano

Landform built up as lava and ash are ejected from the upper mantle during successive eruptions, accumulating and solidifying on the surface.

volcano during eruption
Eruption of magmatic matter (molten rock, ash, gas) from the upper mantle; it can last several years.

cloud of volcanic ash
Ash is formed of particles less than 0.08 in in diameter; it is composed of pulverized magma and ground rock.

fumarole
Regular emission of gas from a fissure on the Earth's surface.

laccolith
Mass of magma that enters the Earth's crust and then solidifies, causing a deformation on the Earth's surface.

geyser
Hot water spring that ejects sporadic jets of water and vapor.

dike
Mass of magma that enters the Earth's crust and then solidifies in the form of bladelike shafts that are vertical or oblique to the layers of the Earth.

sill
Layer of magma that has solidified between the layers of the Earth's crust; it is about 30 feet thick and several miles long.

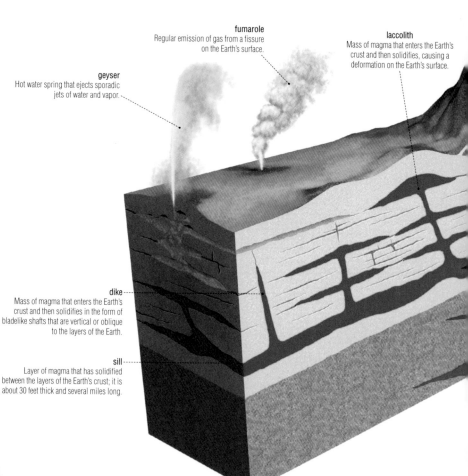

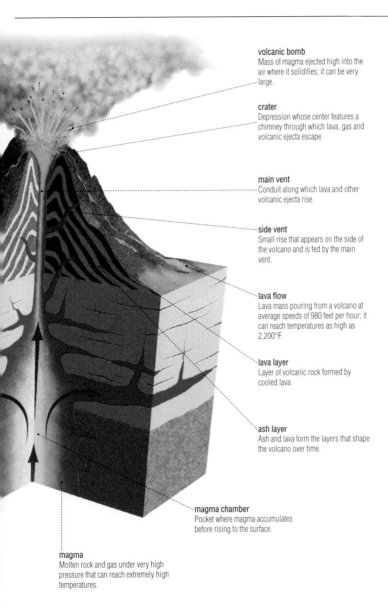

volcanic bomb
Mass of magma ejected high into the air where it solidifies; it can be very large.

crater
Depression whose center features a chimney through which lava, gas and volcanic ejecta escape.

main vent
Conduit along which lava and other volcanic ejecta rise.

side vent
Small rise that appears on the side of the volcano and is fed by the main vent.

lava flow
Lava mass pouring from a volcano at average speeds of 980 feet per hour; it can reach temperatures as high as 2,200°F.

lava layer
Layer of volcanic rock formed by cooled lava.

ash layer
Ash and lava form the layers that shape the volcano over time.

magma chamber
Pocket where magma accumulates before rising to the surface.

magma
Molten rock and gas under very high pressure that can reach extremely high temperatures.

mountain

Elevated landform characterized by steep slopes; it is usually part of a chain.

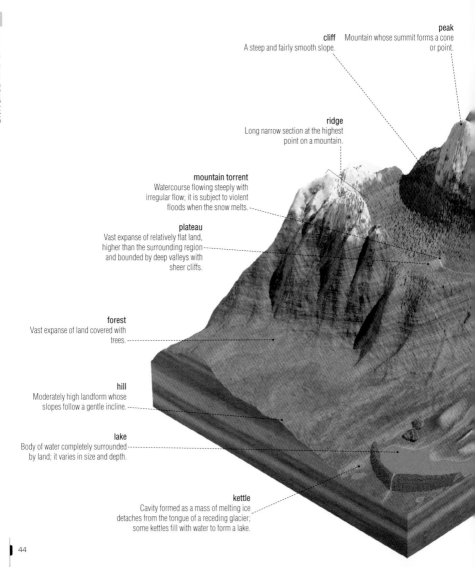

peak
Mountain whose summit forms a cone or point.

cliff
A steep and fairly smooth slope.

ridge
Long narrow section at the highest point on a mountain.

mountain torrent
Watercourse flowing steeply with irregular flow; it is subject to violent floods when the snow melts.

plateau
Vast expanse of relatively flat land, higher than the surrounding region and bounded by deep valleys with sheer cliffs.

forest
Vast expanse of land covered with trees.

hill
Moderately high landform whose slopes follow a gentle incline.

lake
Body of water completely surrounded by land; it varies in size and depth.

kettle
Cavity formed as a mass of melting ice detaches from the tongue of a receding glacier; some kettles fill with water to form a lake.

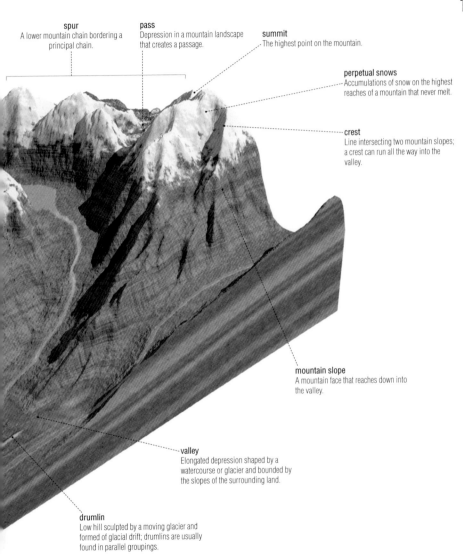

spur
A lower mountain chain bordering a principal chain.

pass
Depression in a mountain landscape that creates a passage.

summit
The highest point on the mountain.

perpetual snows
Accumulations of snow on the highest reaches of a mountain that never melt.

crest
Line intersecting two mountain slopes; a crest can run all the way into the valley.

mountain slope
A mountain face that reaches down into the valley.

valley
Elongated depression shaped by a watercourse or glacier and bounded by the slopes of the surrounding land.

drumlin
Low hill sculpted by a moving glacier and formed of glacial drift; drumlins are usually found in parallel groupings.

glacier

Mass of ice resulting from the accumulation and compression of snow; it moves under its own weight.

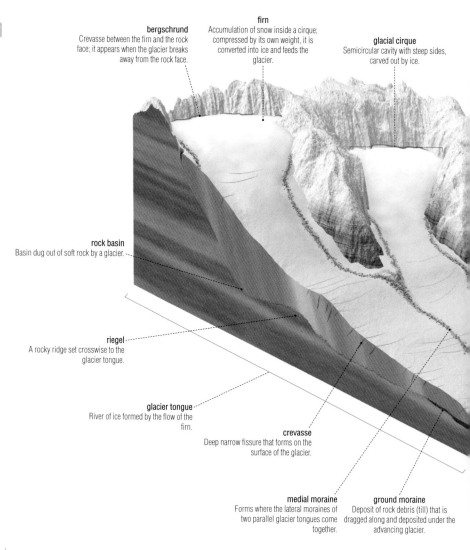

bergschrund
Crevasse between the firn and the rock face; it appears when the glacier breaks away from the rock face.

firn
Accumulation of snow inside a cirque; compressed by its own weight, it is converted into ice and feeds the glacier.

glacial cirque
Semicircular cavity with steep sides, carved out by ice.

rock basin
Basin dug out of soft rock by a glacier.

riegel
A rocky ridge set crosswise to the glacier tongue.

glacier tongue
River of ice formed by the flow of the firn.

crevasse
Deep narrow fissure that forms on the surface of the glacier.

medial moraine
Forms where the lateral moraines of two parallel glacier tongues come together.

ground moraine
Deposit of rock debris (till) that is dragged along and deposited under the advancing glacier.

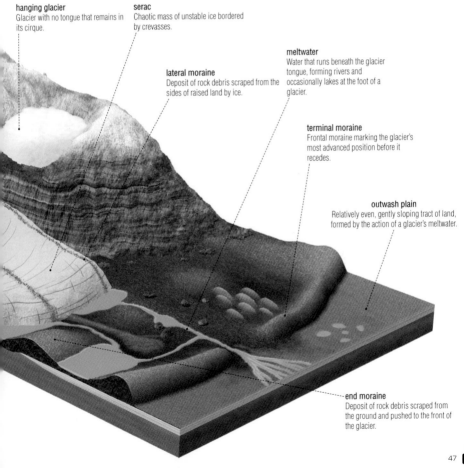

hanging glacier
Glacier with no tongue that remains in its cirque.

serac
Chaotic mass of unstable ice bordered by crevasses.

lateral moraine
Deposit of rock debris scraped from the sides of raised land by ice.

meltwater
Water that runs beneath the glacier tongue, forming rivers and occasionally lakes at the foot of a glacier.

terminal moraine
Frontal moraine marking the glacier's most advanced position before it recedes.

outwash plain
Relatively even, gently sloping tract of land, formed by the action of a glacier's meltwater.

end moraine
Deposit of rock debris scraped from the ground and pushed to the front of the glacier.

cave

Natural underground cavity that results from the slow dissolution and erosion of rock by water.

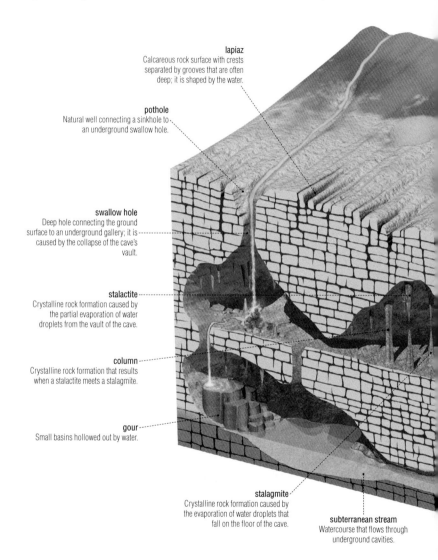

lapiaz
Calcareous rock surface with crests separated by grooves that are often deep; it is shaped by the water.

pothole
Natural well connecting a sinkhole to an underground swallow hole.

swallow hole
Deep hole connecting the ground surface to an underground gallery; it is caused by the collapse of the cave's vault.

stalactite
Crystalline rock formation caused by the partial evaporation of water droplets from the vault of the cave.

column
Crystalline rock formation that results when a stalactite meets a stalagmite.

gour
Small basins hollowed out by water.

stalagmite
Crystalline rock formation caused by the evaporation of water droplets that fall on the floor of the cave.

subterranean stream
Watercourse that flows through underground cavities.

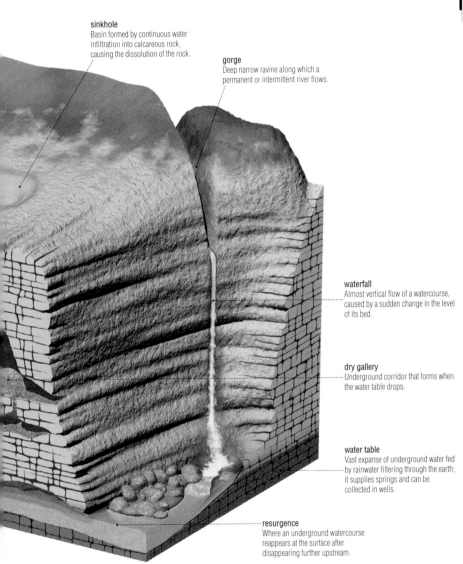

sinkhole
Basin formed by continuous water infiltration into calcareous rock, causing the dissolution of the rock.

gorge
Deep narrow ravine along which a permanent or intermittent river flows.

waterfall
Almost vertical flow of a watercourse, caused by a sudden change in the level of its bed.

dry gallery
Underground corridor that forms when the water table drops.

water table
Vast expanse of underground water fed by rainwater filtering through the earth; it supplies springs and can be collected in wells.

resurgence
Where an underground watercourse reappears at the surface after disappearing further upstream.

watercourse

Natural flow of water that varies in size, depending on the ground slope and the number of tributaries.

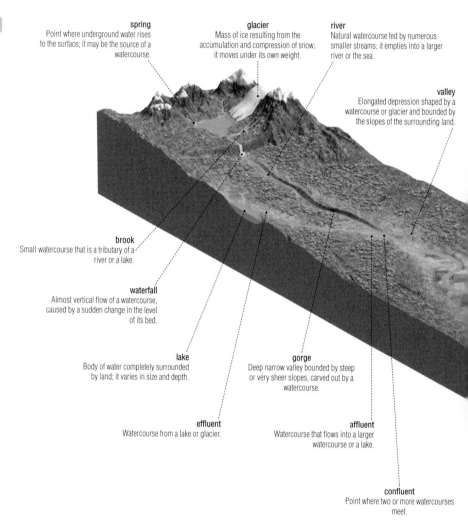

spring
Point where underground water rises to the surface; it may be the source of a watercourse.

glacier
Mass of ice resulting from the accumulation and compression of snow; it moves under its own weight.

river
Natural watercourse fed by numerous smaller streams; it empties into a larger river or the sea.

valley
Elongated depression shaped by a watercourse or glacier and bounded by the slopes of the surrounding land.

brook
Small watercourse that is a tributary of a river or a lake.

waterfall
Almost vertical flow of a watercourse, caused by a sudden change in the level of its bed.

lake
Body of water completely surrounded by land; it varies in size and depth.

gorge
Deep narrow valley bounded by steep or very sheer slopes, carved out by a watercourse.

effluent
Watercourse from a lake or glacier.

affluent
Watercourse that flows into a larger watercourse or a lake.

confluent
Point where two or more watercourses meet.

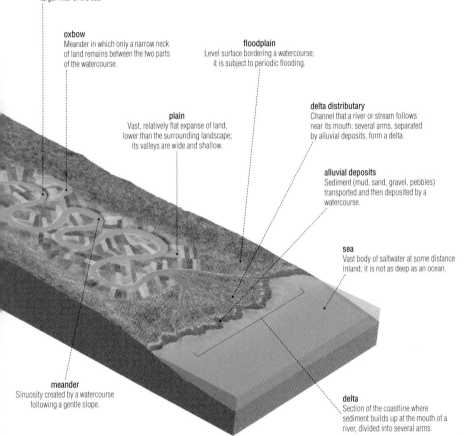

river
Natural watercourse fed by numerous
smaller streams; it empties into a
larger river or the sea.

oxbow
Meander in which only a narrow neck
of land remains between the two parts
of the watercourse.

floodplain
Level surface bordering a watercourse;
it is subject to periodic flooding.

plain
Vast, relatively flat expanse of land,
lower than the surrounding landscape;
its valleys are wide and shallow.

delta distributary
Channel that a river or stream follows
near its mouth; several arms, separated
by alluvial deposits, form a delta.

alluvial deposits
Sediment (mud, sand, gravel, pebbles)
transported and then deposited by a
watercourse.

sea
Vast body of saltwater at some distance
inland; it is not as deep as an ocean.

meander
Sinuosity created by a watercourse
following a gentle slope.

delta
Section of the coastline where
sediment builds up at the mouth of a
river, divided into several arms.

wave

Undulation caused by the wind on the surface of a sea or lake.

UNIVERSE AND EARTH

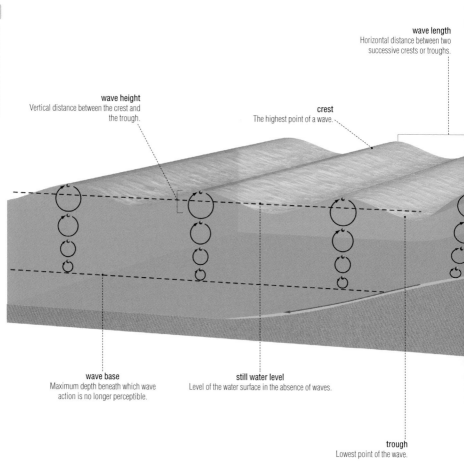

wave length
Horizontal distance between two successive crests or troughs.

wave height
Vertical distance between the crest and the trough.

crest
The highest point of a wave.

wave base
Maximum depth beneath which wave action is no longer perceptible.

still water level
Level of the water surface in the absence of waves.

trough
Lowest point of the wave.

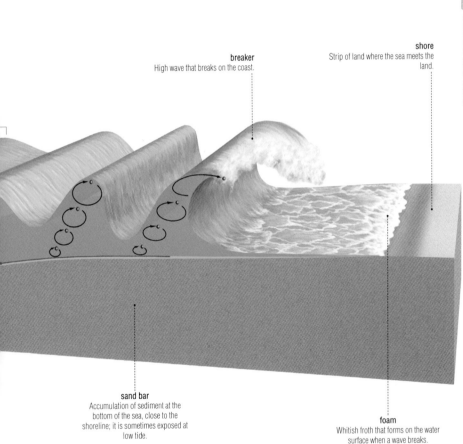

breaker
High wave that breaks on the coast.

shore
Strip of land where the sea meets the land.

sand bar
Accumulation of sediment at the bottom of the sea, close to the shoreline; it is sometimes exposed at low tide.

foam
Whitish froth that forms on the water surface when a wave breaks.

ocean floor

Part of the Earth's surface beneath the seas and the oceans; its topography is highly variable.

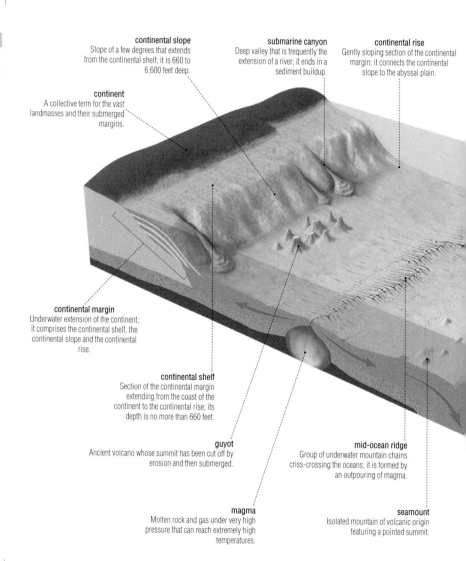

continental slope
Slope of a few degrees that extends from the continental shelf; it is 660 to 6,600 feet deep.

submarine canyon
Deep valley that is frequently the extension of a river; it ends in a sediment buildup.

continental rise
Gently sloping section of the continental margin; it connects the continental slope to the abyssal plain.

continent
A collective term for the vast landmasses and their submerged margins.

continental margin
Underwater extension of the continent; it comprises the continental shelf, the continental slope and the continental rise.

continental shelf
Section of the continental margin extending from the coast of the continent to the continental rise; its depth is no more than 660 feet.

guyot
Ancient volcano whose summit has been cut off by erosion and then submerged.

mid-ocean ridge
Group of underwater mountain chains criss-crossing the oceans; it is formed by an outpouring of magma.

magma
Molten rock and gas under very high pressure that can reach extremely high temperatures.

seamount
Isolated mountain of volcanic origin featuring a pointed summit.

abyssal plain
Zone located at a depth of 6,600 to
20,000 feet; it covers most of the ocean floor.

sea level
Mean water level observed for a given duration (day,
month, year); it is used as a reference to define
coastal features and calculate the elevation of
topographical elements.

abyssal hill
Rounded underwater rise of low elevation.

trench
Extremely deep elongated depression
bordering a continent or island arc; it
occurs when one tectonic plate moves
under another.

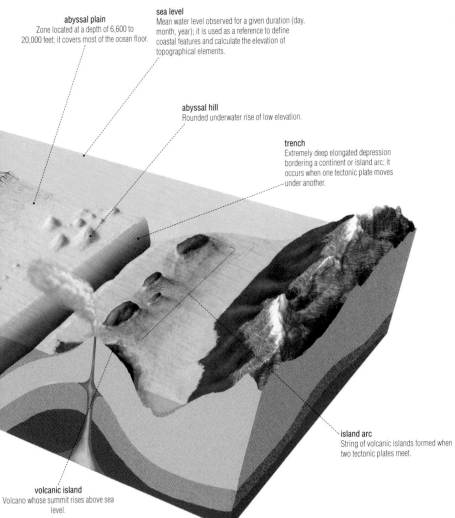

island arc
String of volcanic islands formed when
two tectonic plates meet.

volcanic island
Volcano whose summit rises above sea
level.

common coastal features

Area where the land meets the sea; its features vary depending on climate, wind, sea and the type of rocks of which it is composed.

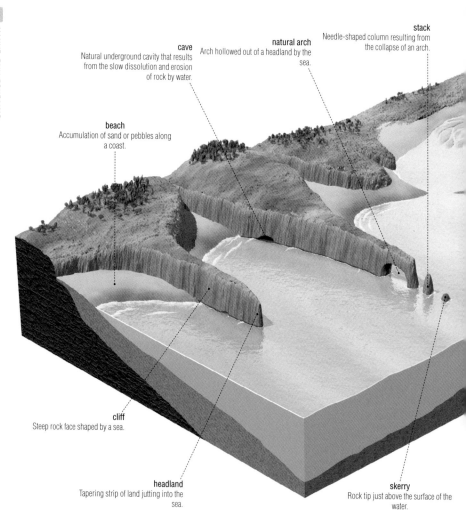

cave
Natural underground cavity that results from the slow dissolution and erosion of rock by water.

natural arch
Arch hollowed out of a headland by the sea.

stack
Needle-shaped column resulting from the collapse of an arch.

beach
Accumulation of sand or pebbles along a coast.

cliff
Steep rock face shaped by a sea.

headland
Tapering strip of land jutting into the sea.

skerry
Rock tip just above the surface of the water.

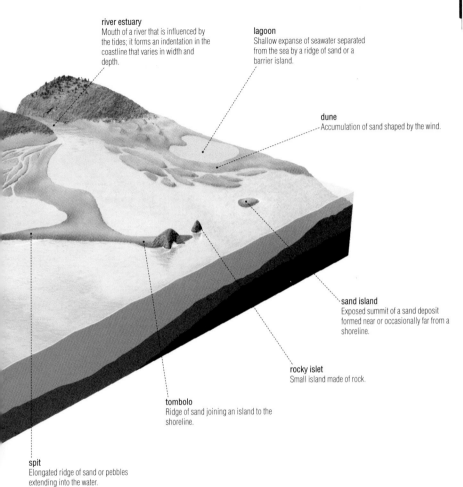

river estuary
Mouth of a river that is influenced by the tides; it forms an indentation in the coastline that varies in width and depth.

lagoon
Shallow expanse of seawater separated from the sea by a ridge of sand or a barrier island.

dune
Accumulation of sand shaped by the wind.

sand island
Exposed summit of a sand deposit formed near or occasionally far from a shoreline.

rocky islet
Small island made of rock.

tombolo
Ridge of sand joining an island to the shoreline.

spit
Elongated ridge of sand or pebbles extending into the water.

UNIVERSE AND EARTH

common coastal features

UNIVERSE AND EARTH

examples of shorelines
Shoreline: strip of land where the sea meets the land.

rias
Coastal valleys that are filled by the sea and get shallower inland.

shore cliff
Steep rock-faced shoreline shaped by the sea.

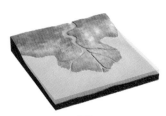

delta
Section of the coastline where sediment builds up at the mouth of a river, divided into several arms.

barrier beach
Usually narrow ridge of sand or pebbles bordering the shoreline.

lagoon
Shallow expanse of water separated from the sea by a coral reef.

atoll
Ring-shaped coral-reef island enclosing a lagoon and often a central island.

fjords
Deep glacial valleys filled with seawater and cutting into the shoreline.

desert

Hot region where aridity (less than 4 in of annual rainfall) is such that plant and animal life is almost nonexistent.

examples of dunes

Dune: accumulation of sand transported by the wind, found in deserts and along coasts.

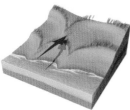

parabolic dune
Crescent-shaped coastal dune whose arms point into the wind; vegetation often keeps it in place.

complex dune
Star-shaped dune that forms where winds blowing in various directions meet.

crescentic dune
Moving crescent-shaped dune whose arms extend in the same direction as the wind.

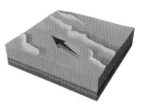

chain of dunes
Dunes aligned in the same direction, parallel to the wind.

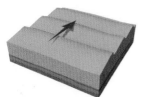

transverse dunes
Dunes that form perpendicular to the direction of the wind.

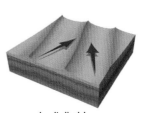

longitudinal dunes
Narrow elongated dunes that form when the wind blows in two convergent directions.

—

desert

dune
Accumulation of sand transported by the
wind, found in deserts and along coasts.

sandy desert
Desert where minuscule grains of rock
(sand) form dunes by wind action.

rocky desert
Most common type of desert, where
rock fragments fracture due to
temperature variations between night
and day.

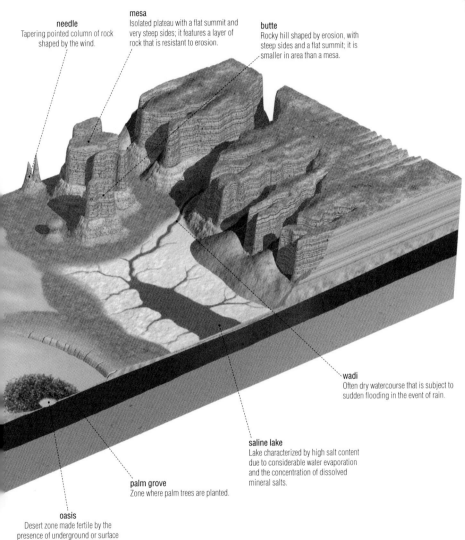

needle
Tapering pointed column of rock shaped by the wind.

mesa
Isolated plateau with a flat summit and very steep sides; it features a layer of rock that is resistant to erosion.

butte
Rocky hill shaped by erosion, with steep sides and a flat summit; it is smaller in area than a mesa.

wadi
Often dry watercourse that is subject to sudden flooding in the event of rain.

saline lake
Lake characterized by high salt content due to considerable water evaporation and the concentration of dissolved mineral salts.

palm grove
Zone where palm trees are planted.

oasis
Desert zone made fertile by the presence of underground or surface water.

profile of the Earth's atmosphere

Atmosphere: layer of air that surrounds the Earth and is composed mainly of nitrogen (78%) and oxygen (21%); its density decreases with altitude.

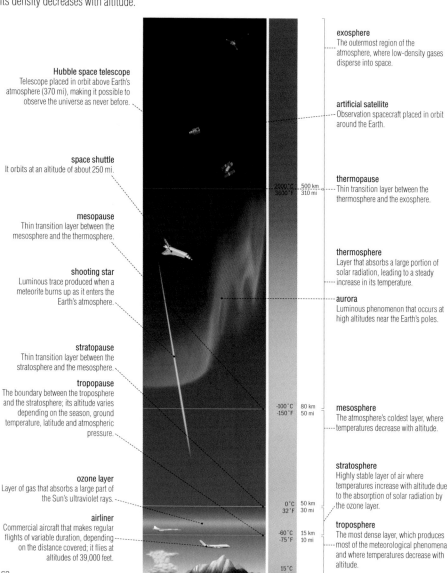

Hubble space telescope
Telescope placed in orbit above Earth's atmosphere (370 mi), making it possible to observe the universe as never before.

space shuttle
It orbits at an altitude of about 250 mi.

mesopause
Thin transition layer between the mesosphere and the thermosphere.

shooting star
Luminous trace produced when a meteorite burns up as it enters the Earth's atmosphere.

stratopause
Thin transition layer between the stratosphere and the mesosphere.

tropopause
The boundary between the troposphere and the stratosphere; its altitude varies depending on the season, ground temperature, latitude and atmospheric pressure.

ozone layer
Layer of gas that absorbs a large part of the Sun's ultraviolet rays.

airliner
Commercial aircraft that makes regular flights of variable duration, depending on the distance covered; it flies at altitudes of 39,000 feet.

exosphere
The outermost region of the atmosphere, where low-density gases disperse into space.

artificial satellite
Observation spacecraft placed in orbit around the Earth.

thermopause
Thin transition layer between the thermosphere and the exosphere.

thermosphere
Layer that absorbs a large portion of solar radiation, leading to a steady increase in its temperature.

aurora
Luminous phenomenon that occurs at high altitudes near the Earth's poles.

mesosphere
The atmosphere's coldest layer, where temperatures decrease with altitude.

stratosphere
Highly stable layer of air where temperatures increase with altitude due to the absorption of solar radiation by the ozone layer.

troposphere
The most dense layer, which produces most of the meteorological phenomena and where temperatures decrease with altitude.

2000°C / 3600°F — 500 km / 310 mi

-100°C / -150°F — 80 km / 50 mi

0°C / 32°F — 50 km / 30 mi

-60°C / -75°F — 15 km / 10 mi

15°C / 60°F

seasons of the year

Periodic climate changes over the course of a year; they are a function of the Earth's inclination toward the Sun and its rotation around it.

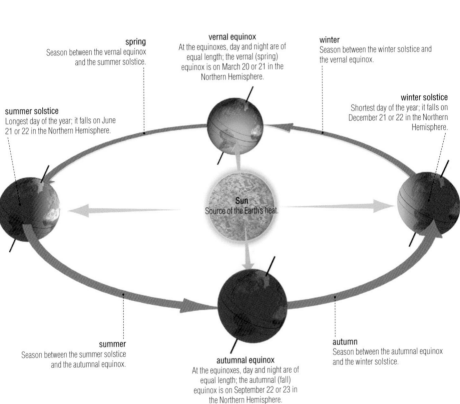

spring
Season between the vernal equinox and the summer solstice.

vernal equinox
At the equinoxes, day and night are of equal length; the vernal (spring) equinox is on March 20 or 21 in the Northern Hemisphere.

winter
Season between the winter solstice and the vernal equinox.

summer solstice
Longest day of the year; it falls on June 21 or 22 in the Northern Hemisphere.

winter solstice
Shortest day of the year; it falls on December 21 or 22 in the Northern Hemisphere.

Sun
Source of the Earth's heat.

summer
Season between the summer solstice and the autumnal equinox.

autumnal equinox
At the equinoxes, day and night are of equal length; the autumnal (fall) equinox is on September 22 or 23 in the Northern Hemisphere.

autumn
Season between the autumnal equinox and the winter solstice.

climates of the world

Climate is a collective term for the atmospheric conditions (temperature, humidity, air pressure, wind, precipitation) that characterize a given region.

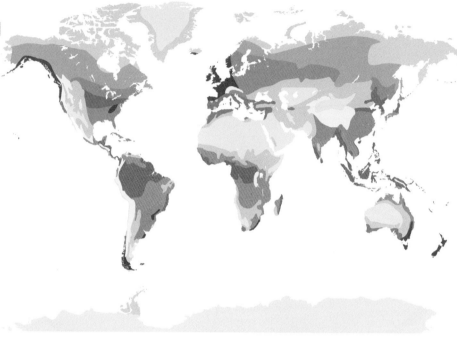

tropical climates

Climates that are hot year-round and are characterized by alternating dry and rainy seasons.

highland climates

Climates where temperatures decrease and precipitation increases with altitude.

tropical rain forest
Tropical, typically humid marine climate that fosters luxuriant vegetation and dense forests.

highland

tropical wet-and-dry (savanna)
Tropical continental climate, with an extended dry season and vegetation composed of tall grasses and scattered trees.

cold temperate climates
Climates with four clearly defined seasons, with cold winters and cool summers.

humid continental-hot summer
Climate characterized by a large annual range of temperature and relatively low rainfall. Summers are quite hot in these regions.

humid continental-warm summer
Climate characterized by a large annual range of temperature and relatively low annual rainfall. Summers are quite cool in these regions.

subarctic
Climate characterized by long, very cold winters and short cool summers; precipitation falls mainly in the summer.

warm temperate climates
Climates with four clearly defined seasons, including a mild winter and a hot or cool summer.

humid subtropical
Climate characterized by hot summers and mild winters, with precipitation distributed evenly throughout the year.

Mediterranean subtropical
Climate characterized by hot dry summers, intermediary seasons and mild rainy winters.

marine
Climate characterized by a limited annual range of temperature and by precipitation distributed throughout the year.

polar climates
Extremely cold dry climates.

polar tundra
Region where the thaw lasts only four or five months and where only mosses, lichen and a few shrubs survive the cold.

polar ice cap
The Earth's coldest region (as cold as -130°F), where the temperature, always below 32°F, creates a permanent ice cover.

dry climates
Climates characterized by very low precipitation.

steppe
Region with hot summers and very cold winters; it is devoid of trees and covered with herbaceous plants adapted to arid climates.

desert
Hot region where aridity (less than 4 in of annual rainfall) is such that plant and animal life is almost nonexistent.

clouds

Fine droplets of water or ice crystal suspended in the atmosphere; the World Meteorological Organization classifies them according to 10 types.

high clouds

Clouds at an altitude higher than 20,000 feet and composed of ice crystals; these clouds do not generate precipitation.

cirrostratus
Whitish layer that can completely cover the sky and that creates a halo around the Sun.

middle clouds

Clouds at an altitude of 6,500 to 20,000 feet and composed of water droplets and ice crystals.

altostratus
Gray sheet that can completely cover the sky but allows the Sun to be seen without a halo phenomenon; it can trigger heavy precipitation.

altocumulus
Cloud composed of large white or gray flecks that sometimes form parallel layers; it foreshadows the arrival of a depression.

low clouds

Clouds that do not exceed 6,500 feet in altitude and are composed of water droplets occasionally mixed with ice crystals; they sometimes generate continuous precipitation.

stratocumulus
Gray and white cloud arranged in more or less continuous rolled layers; it does not usually trigger precipitation.

nimbostratus
Cloud in the form of a dark layer sufficiently thick to block out the Sun; it triggers continuous precipitation.

stratus
Gray cloud forming a continuous veil that is similar to fog, though it never touches the ground; it can trigger light precipitation.

cirrocumulus
Cloud formed of white or gray flecks or strips, often arranged in rows.

cirrus
Cloud in the form of wisps or separate strips; it usually appears in advance of a depression.

clouds of vertical development
Clouds whose base is at low altitude but extend very high; the two types are cumulus and cumulonimbus.

cumulonimbus
Very imposing cloud that can reach a thickness of 6 mi and whose base is very dark; it can trigger violent precipitation.

cumulus
Fair-weather cloud with very clear contours; it has a gray, flat base and a white top with rounded protuberances.

tropical cyclone

Low-pressure zone that forms in the intertropical region and is marked by violent precipitation and swirling winds of 74 to 185 mph.

prevailing wind
It moves the cyclone forward at an average speed of 15 mph.

subsiding cold air
Cool air that reaches the top of the clouds and once again descends, becoming warmer as it becomes more compressed.

spiral cloud band

heavy rainfall

eye
Relatively calm zone in the center of the cyclone, with light winds and very few clouds; it is about 20 mi in diameter.

high-pressure area
Column of ascending air that causes a rise in upper air pressure, at the top of the most developed clouds.

eye wall
Thick layer of cloud that swirls around the eye; it has the most powerful winds (up to 185 mph) and the most intense precipitation.

convective cell
Phenomenon formed by hot humid air that rises and condenses to form a cloud, and a descending current of cold air.

rising warm air
A hot air column forms when the ocean's surface is warmed by the Sun.

low-pressure area
A rising column of air causes a decrease in air pressure on the ocean's surface.

tornado and waterspout

waterspout
Tornado that occurs over the sea and is not as violent as a tornado on land.

tornado
Swirling column of air that extends from the ground to the base of a cumulonimbus; it produces violent winds that can reach 300 mph.

wall cloud
Ring-shaped cloud mass, usually the first sign that a tornado is imminent.

funnel cloud
Cloud that extends from another cloud's base and reaches the ground; extremely high winds whirl around it.

debris
Cloud of dust and debris swept up from the ground.

precipitation

Collective term for water particles in the atmosphere that fall or are deposited on the ground in solid or liquid form.

rain forms
By international convention, precipitation in the form of rain is classified according to the quantity that falls.

drizzle
Uniform continuous precipitation of slow-falling water droplets between 0.008 and 0.02 in in diameter.

light rain
Precipitation of water drops over 0.02 in in diameter; it results in accumulations of 0.1 in per hour.

moderate rain
Precipitation that results in 0.1 to 0.3 in accumulation per hour.

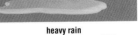

heavy rain
Precipitation that results in over 0.3 in accumulation per hour.

precipitation

snow crystals

Ice crystals whose form depends on temperature and humidity; they fall separately or in agglomerations of flakes.

stellar crystal
Star-shaped crystal with six branches.

hail
Hard, usually spherical ice crystal that varies between 0.2 and 2 in in diameter; it is formed of concentric layers of clear opaque ice.

sleet
Ice crystal less than 0.2 in diameter that results from rain drops or snow flakes freezing before they touch the ground.

snow pellet
Opaque ice crystal less than 0.2 in diameter that froze inside a cloud.

winter precipitations

During the winter, water can fall in various forms, depending on the air temperature.

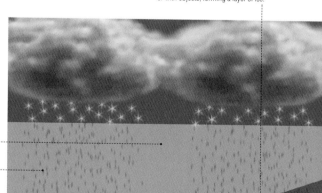

freezing rain
Precipitation in the form of raindrops that freeze on impact with the ground or with objects, forming a layer of ice.

warm air

rain
Precipitation of water droplets produced when the air temperature is higher than 32°F.

capped column
Ice crystal that is identical to the column, except for the thin hexagon-shaped cap at each extremity.

irregular crystal
Ice crystal with no defined shape resulting from the agglomeration of several crystals.

spatial dendrite
Ice crystal characterized by complex branches similar to those of a tree.

plate crystal
Ice crystal in the form of a thin hexagonal plate that is occasionally hollow.

column
Short translucent ice crystal with flat extremities; it is prism-shaped and occasionally hollow.

needle
Translucent prism-shaped ice crystal; it is long and narrow and has pointed ends.

sleet
Precipitation in the form of water droplets or wet snow that freezes before it touches the ground.

cold air

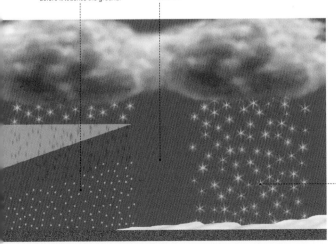

snow
Precipitation of ice crystals produced when the air temperature is below 32°F.

precipitation

UNIVERSE AND EARTH

stormy sky
A thunderstorm is characterized by
lightning, thunder and gusts of wind,
usually accompanied by rain showers
or hail.

lightning
Brief but intense luminous phenomenon
caused by an electrical discharge
between two clouds or between a cloud
and the ground.

cloud
The very imposing cloud that generates
thunderstorms is the cumulonimbus; it can
reach a thickness of 6 mi and its base is
very dark.

rain
Precipitation of water droplets
produced when the air temperature is
higher than 32°F.

rainbow
Luminous arc formed of bands of
color; during a shower, it is visible in
the opposite direction to the Sun.

dew
Condensation of water vapor in the air that settles on cold surfaces in droplet form.

rime
Deposit of ice crystals on surfaces whose temperature is close to 32°F; it is caused by the condensation of water vapor in the air.

mist
Light fog that does not limit visibility to 0.6 mi.

fog
Condensation of water vapor resulting in the suspension of microscopic droplets that reduce visibility to less than 0.6 mi.

frost
Layer of ice on the ground or on an object; it is caused by the condensation of fine rain when the temperature is hovering around 32°F.

hydrologic cycle

Continuous circulation of water in its different states (liquid, solid and gaseous) between the oceans, the atmosphere and the Earth's surface.

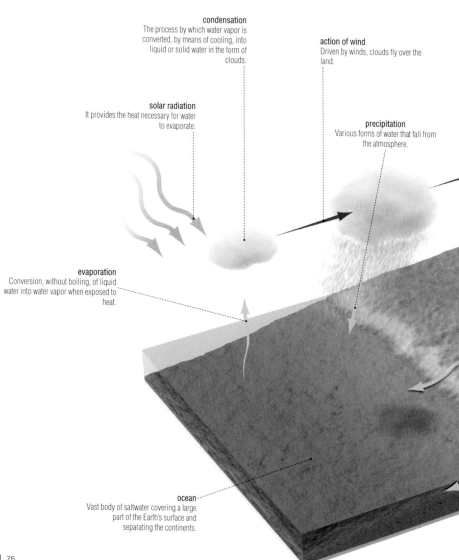

condensation
The process by which water vapor is converted, by means of cooling, into liquid or solid water in the form of clouds.

action of wind
Driven by winds, clouds fly over the land.

solar radiation
It provides the heat necessary for water to evaporate.

precipitation
Various forms of water that fall from the atmosphere.

evaporation
Conversion, without boiling, of liquid water into water vapor when exposed to heat.

ocean
Vast body of saltwater covering a large part of the Earth's surface and separating the continents.

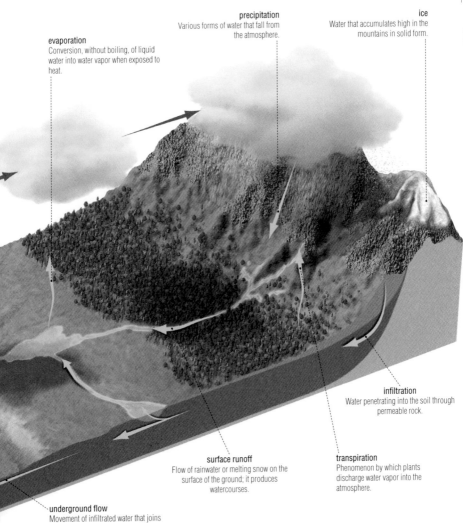

precipitation
Various forms of water that fall from the atmosphere.

ice
Water that accumulates high in the mountains in solid form.

evaporation
Conversion, without boiling, of liquid water into water vapor when exposed to heat.

infiltration
Water penetrating into the soil through permeable rock.

surface runoff
Flow of rainwater or melting snow on the surface of the ground; it produces watercourses.

transpiration
Phenomenon by which plants discharge water vapor into the atmosphere.

underground flow
Movement of infiltrated water that joins a watercourse on the surface or flows directly into lakes or the ocean.

greenhouse effect

Warming of the atmosphere that occurs when certain gases absorb part of the solar radiation reflected by the Earth.

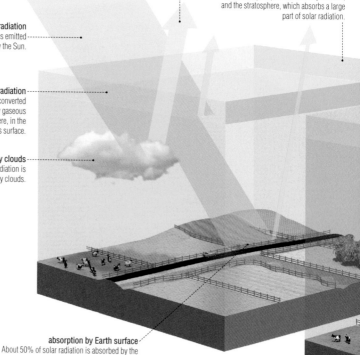

natural greenhouse effect
The greenhouse effect is an indispensable natural phenomenon; without it, the average temperature, currently 59°F, would be no higher than 0°F.

reflected solar radiation
Thirty percent of solar radiation is sent back into space by clouds, by particles suspended in the atmosphere and by the Earth's surface.

tropopause
Boundary between the troposphere, where meteorological phenomena are produced, and the stratosphere, which absorbs a large part of solar radiation.

solar radiation
All the electromagnetic waves emitted by the Sun.

absorbed solar radiation
A portion of solar radiation is converted into thermal energy by gaseous constituents in the atmosphere, in the clouds and on the Earth's surface.

absorption by clouds
About 25% of solar radiation is absorbed by clouds.

absorption by Earth surface
About 50% of solar radiation is absorbed by the Earth's surface.

heat loss
Part of the infrared rays reflected by the Earth's surface is not absorbed and dissipates in space.

infrared radiation
The Earth's surface reflects infrared radiation, part of which is retained in the atmosphere by greenhouse gases and clouds.

greenhouse gas
Gas that traps heat in the atmosphere; composed mainly (60%) of carbon dioxide (CO_2), methane (15%) and CFCs (12%).

heat energy
Infrared radiation carries heat energy, which increases the temperature of the atmosphere.

greenhouse effect

enhanced greenhouse effect
Human activity constantly emits greenhouse gases, which trap ever more heat in the atmosphere.

air conditioning system
Air conditioning systems use chlorofluorocarbons (CFCs) that absorb infrared rays and damage the ozone layer.

fossil fuel
The combustion of wood and fossil fuels (coal, oil, natural gas) emits carbon dioxide and methane into the atmosphere.

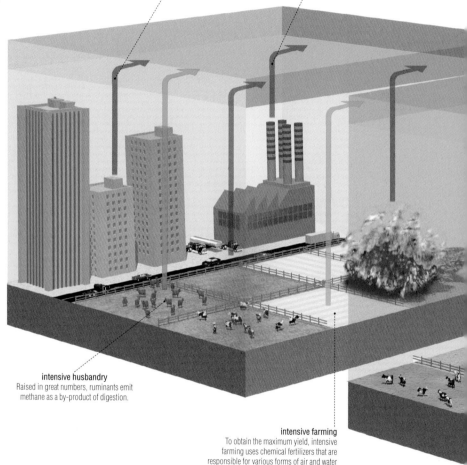

intensive husbandry
Raised in great numbers, ruminants emit methane as a by-product of digestion.

intensive farming
To obtain the maximum yield, intensive farming uses chemical fertilizers that are responsible for various forms of air and water pollution.

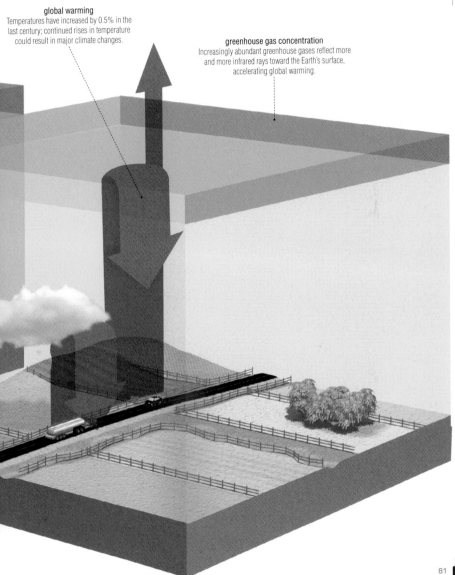

global warming
Temperatures have increased by 0.5% in the last century; continued rises in temperature could result in major climate changes.

greenhouse gas concentration
Increasingly abundant greenhouse gases reflect more and more infrared rays toward the Earth's surface, accelerating global warming.

acid rain

Rain that contains abnormally high concentrations of sulfuric acid and nitric acid.

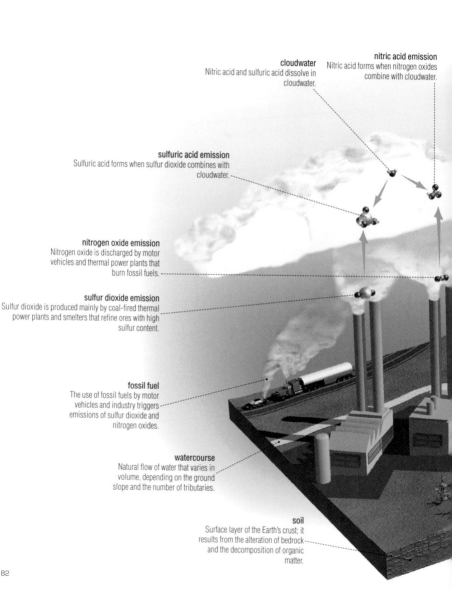

cloudwater
Nitric acid and sulfuric acid dissolve in cloudwater.

nitric acid emission
Nitric acid forms when nitrogen oxides combine with cloudwater.

sulfuric acid emission
Sulfuric acid forms when sulfur dioxide combines with cloudwater.

nitrogen oxide emission
Nitrogen oxide is discharged by motor vehicles and thermal power plants that burn fossil fuels.

sulfur dioxide emission
Sulfur dioxide is produced mainly by coal-fired thermal power plants and smelters that refine ores with high sulfur content.

fossil fuel
The use of fossil fuels by motor vehicles and industry triggers emissions of sulfur dioxide and nitrogen oxides.

watercourse
Natural flow of water that varies in volume, depending on the ground slope and the number of tributaries.

soil
Surface layer of the Earth's crust; it results from the alteration of bedrock and the decomposition of organic matter.

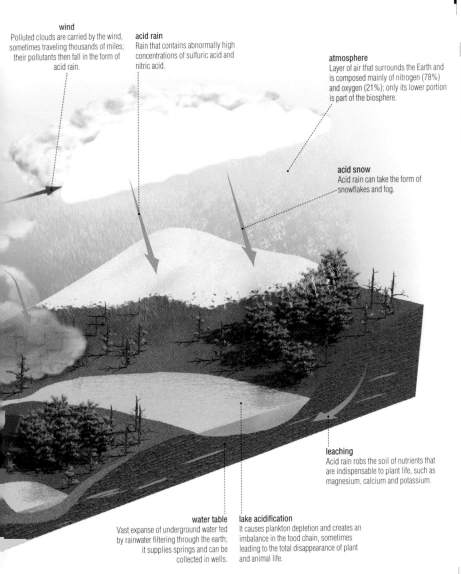

wind
Polluted clouds are carried by the wind, sometimes traveling thousands of miles; their pollutants then fall in the form of acid rain.

acid rain
Rain that contains abnormally high concentrations of sulfuric acid and nitric acid.

atmosphere
Layer of air that surrounds the Earth and is composed mainly of nitrogen (78%) and oxygen (21%); only its lower portion is part of the biosphere.

acid snow
Acid rain can take the form of snowflakes and fog.

leaching
Acid rain robs the soil of nutrients that are indispensable to plant life, such as magnesium, calcium and potassium.

water table
Vast expanse of underground water fed by rainwater filtering through the earth; it supplies springs and can be collected in wells.

lake acidification
It causes plankton depletion and creates an imbalance in the food chain, sometimes leading to the total disappearance of plant and animal life.

plant cell

Smallest living structure and the constituent element of all vegetables; it varies in size and shape depending on its function.

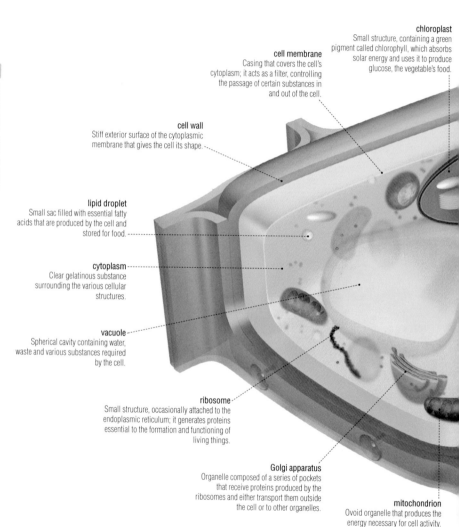

chloroplast
Small structure, containing a green pigment called chlorophyll, which absorbs solar energy and uses it to produce glucose, the vegetable's food.

cell membrane
Casing that covers the cell's cytoplasm; it acts as a filter, controlling the passage of certain substances in and out of the cell.

cell wall
Stiff exterior surface of the cytoplasmic membrane that gives the cell its shape.

lipid droplet
Small sac filled with essential fatty acids that are produced by the cell and stored for food.

cytoplasm
Clear gelatinous substance surrounding the various cellular structures.

vacuole
Spherical cavity containing water, waste and various substances required by the cell.

ribosome
Small structure, occasionally attached to the endoplasmic reticulum; it generates proteins essential to the formation and functioning of living things.

Golgi apparatus
Organelle composed of a series of pockets that receive proteins produced by the ribosomes and either transport them outside the cell or to other organelles.

mitochondrion
Ovoid organelle that produces the energy necessary for cell activity.

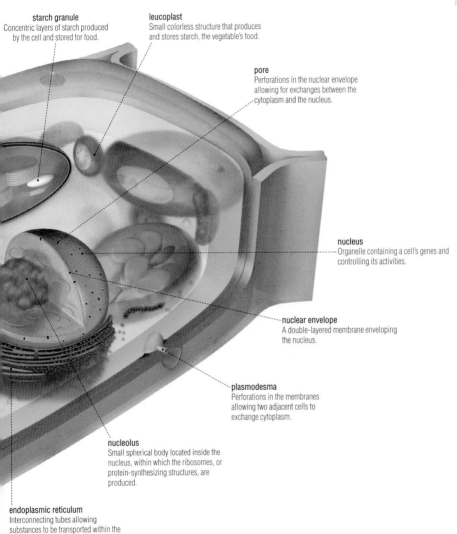

starch granule
Concentric layers of starch produced by the cell and stored for food.

leucoplast
Small colorless structure that produces and stores starch, the vegetable's food.

pore
Perforations in the nuclear envelope allowing for exchanges between the cytoplasm and the nucleus.

nucleus
Organelle containing a cell's genes and controlling its activities.

nuclear envelope
A double-layered membrane enveloping the nucleus.

plasmodesma
Perforations in the membranes allowing two adjacent cells to exchange cytoplasm.

nucleolus
Small spherical body located inside the nucleus, within which the ribosomes, or protein-synthesizing structures, are produced.

endoplasmic reticulum
Interconnecting tubes allowing substances to be transported within the cell or between the cell and its exterior environment.

lichen

Vegetable formed from the symbiotic association of an alga and a fungus.

structure of a lichen

apothecium
Reproductive organ of the fungus that is a part of the lichen.

thallus
Lichen's main structure formed by the imbrication of fungal filaments and alga cells.

examples of lichens
There are more than 20,000 species of lichen, found growing out of the soil, on tree trunks or on rocks; they grow in all climatic zones.

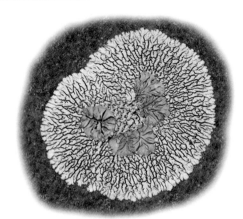

crustose lichen
Lichen whose thallus forms a crust that is firmly attached to its substrate.

fruticose lichen
Lichen whose thallus resembles a small tree; it is attached to its substrate at a single point.

foliose lichen
Lichen whose thallus resembles leaves or lobes that are loosely attached to their substrate and can be easily removed.

moss

Flowerless vegetable, usually small in size, that grows in large tightly packed tufts to create a veritable soft carpet.

structure of a moss

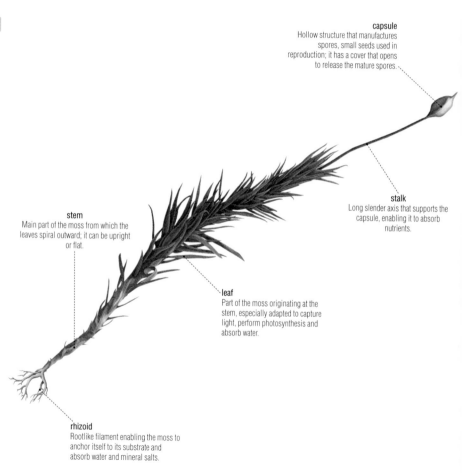

capsule
Hollow structure that manufactures spores, small seeds used in reproduction; it has a cover that opens to release the mature spores.

stalk
Long slender axis that supports the capsule, enabling it to absorb nutrients.

stem
Main part of the moss from which the leaves spiral outward; it can be upright or flat.

leaf
Part of the moss originating at the stem, especially adapted to capture light, perform photosynthesis and absorb water.

rhizoid
Rootlike filament enabling the moss to anchor itself to its substrate and absorb water and mineral salts.

examples of mosses
There are more than 13,000 species of moss; they generally grow in damp soil, on rocks or tree trunks and occasionally in fresh water.

prickly sphagnum
Bog moss that has no rhizoid and rarely bears a capsule; it has a high water content and its decomposition helps to form peat.

common hair cap moss
Ground moss with an erect stem and stiff leaves that grows in tufts, mostly in wooded areas; the capsule emerges from the end of a very long stalk.

alga

Flowerless vegetable that usually lives in aquatic environments; it produces oxygen and is at the base of the food chain.

structure of an alga

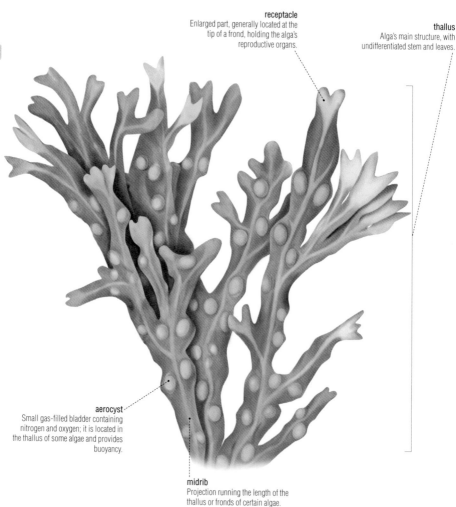

receptacle
Enlarged part, generally located at the tip of a frond, holding the alga's reproductive organs.

thallus
Alga's main structure, with undifferentiated stem and leaves.

aerocyst
Small gas-filled bladder containing nitrogen and oxygen; it is located in the thallus of some algae and provides buoyancy.

midrib
Projection running the length of the thallus or fronds of certain algae.

PLANTS AND GARDENING

examples of algae

More than 25,000 species of algae live in aquatic environments or in some regions with damp soil; they vary in size from microscopic to 60 ft in length.

lamina
Part of the thallus that is shaped like a blade; it is quite wide and looks like a leaf.

hapteron
Small, occasionally branched disk, located at the base of certain thalli, enabling their attachment to a substrate.

red alga
Red-pigmented alga that generally lives in salt water and at greater depths than other algae; there are 4,000 species of red algae.

brown alga
Brown-pigmented alga that usually lives in the sea, often in cold water; there are more than 1,500 species of brown algae.

green alga
Alga often found in freshwater, but also in seas and some nonaquatic environments; there are 6,000 species of green algae.

fern

Flowerless vegetable that grows mainly in the tropics; it also grows in temperate climates in rich damp soil.

structure of a fern

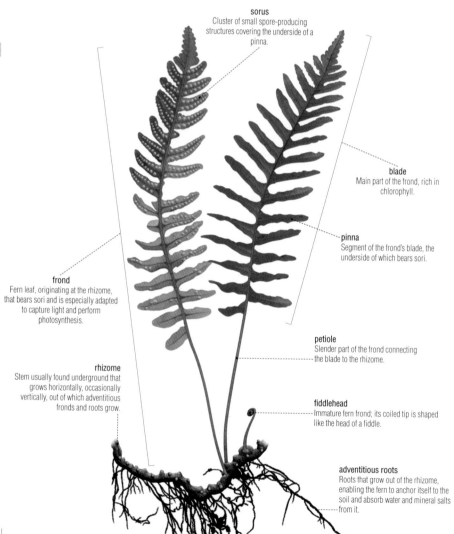

sorus
Cluster of small spore-producing structures covering the underside of a pinna.

blade
Main part of the frond, rich in chlorophyll.

pinna
Segment of the frond's blade, the underside of which bears sori.

frond
Fern leaf, originating at the rhizome, that bears sori and is especially adapted to capture light and perform photosynthesis.

petiole
Slender part of the frond connecting the blade to the rhizome.

rhizome
Stem usually found underground that grows horizontally, occasionally vertically, out of which adventitious fronds and roots grow.

fiddlehead
Immature fern frond; its coiled tip is shaped like the head of a fiddle.

adventitious roots
Roots that grow out of the rhizome, enabling the fern to anchor itself to the soil and absorb water and mineral salts from it.

fern

examples of ferns
There are more than 10,000 species of fern, varying in height from a a fraction of an inch to several feet.

tree fern
Large fern that resembles a tree and can reach heights of up to 65 ft; it grows mainly in the tropics.

trunk
Main part of the fern, composed of a vertical rhizome covered with the stubs of old fronds and, often, with aboveground adventitious roots.

common polypody
Fern with fronds up to a foot long; it is usually found in damp overgrown soil, on rocks or tree trunks.

bird's nest fern
Fern that usually grows out of another plant without deriving nourishment from it; its fronds grow in a rosette around a central rhizome, hence its name.

mushroom

Organism that exists parasitically or symbiotically with other living things or grows on dead organic matter.

structure of a mushroom
The mushroom is composed of an underground part (mycelium) and an aboveground, often edible part that is also the reproductive organ.

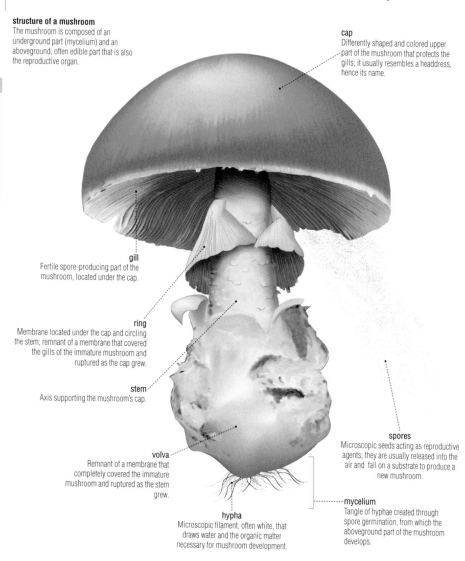

cap
Differently shaped and colored upper part of the mushroom that protects the gills; it usually resembles a headdress, hence its name.

gill
Fertile spore-producing part of the mushroom, located under the cap.

ring
Membrane located under the cap and circling the stem; remnant of a membrane that covered the gills of the immature mushroom and ruptured as the cap grew.

stem
Axis supporting the mushroom's cap.

volva
Remnant of a membrane that completely covered the immature mushroom and ruptured as the stem grew.

hypha
Microscopic filament, often white, that draws water and the organic matter necessary for mushroom development.

spores
Microscopic seeds acting as reproductive agents; they are usually released into the air and fall on a substrate to produce a new mushroom.

mycelium
Tangle of hyphae created through spore germination, from which the aboveground part of the mushroom develops.

deadly poisonous mushroom
Mushroom containing a toxin that, following contact or ingestion, produces serious effects on humans, generally resulting in death.

poisonous mushroom
Mushroom containing a toxin that, following contact or ingestion, produces a range of usually nonfatal effects on humans.

destroying angel
White ground mushroom with an unpleasant smell, growing in wooded areas; the effects of its often-deadly toxin act in a delayed manner, mainly attacking the liver.

fly agaric
The cap of this woodland mushroom is covered with white warts; its toxin primarily attacks the nervous system, causing hallucinations, among other symptoms.

edible mushrooms
Mushrooms that can be eaten without danger by human beings.

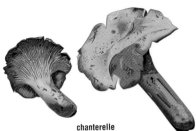

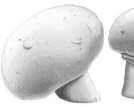

chanterelle
Pleasantly fragrant and valued by gourmets, especially those in Europe; it is served most often with meat or omelettes.

cultivated mushroom
The most widely cultivated and consumed mushroom; it is eaten raw, in salads or with dips, or cooked, primarily in sauces and on pizza.

plant

Vegetable rooted in the soil, the upper part of which grows aboveground or in freshwater; it produces oxygen and is at the bottom of the food chain.

structure of a plant

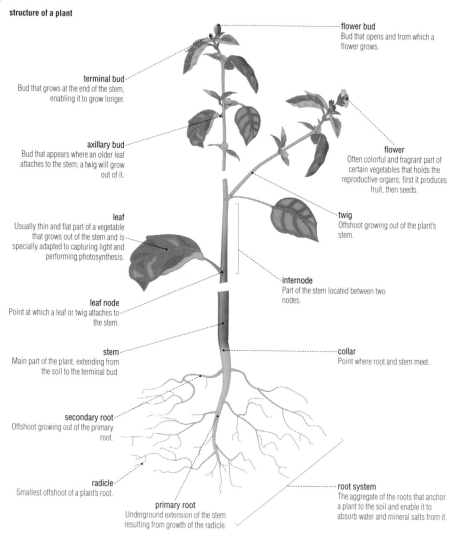

flower bud
Bud that opens and from which a flower grows.

terminal bud
Bud that grows at the end of the stem, enabling it to grow longer.

axillary bud
Bud that appears where an older leaf attaches to the stem; a twig will grow out of it.

flower
Often colorful and fragrant part of certain vegetables that holds the reproductive organs; first it produces fruit, then seeds.

leaf
Usually thin and flat part of a vegetable that grows out of the stem and is specially adapted to capturing light and performing photosynthesis.

twig
Offshoot growing out of the plant's stem.

internode
Part of the stem located between two nodes.

leaf node
Point at which a leaf or twig attaches to the stem.

stem
Main part of the plant, extending from the soil to the terminal bud.

collar
Point where root and stem meet.

secondary root
Offshoot growing out of the primary root.

radicle
Smallest offshoot of a plant's root.

primary root
Underground extension of the stem resulting from growth of the radicle.

root system
The aggregate of the roots that anchor a plant to the soil and enable it to absorb water and mineral salts from it.

PLANTS AND GARDENING

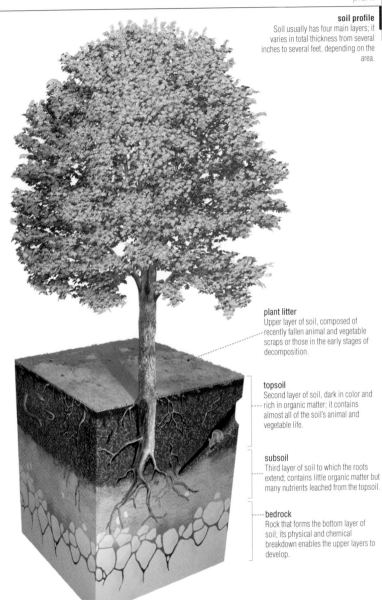

soil profile
Soil usually has four main layers; it varies in total thickness from several inches to several feet, depending on the area.

plant litter
Upper layer of soil, composed of recently fallen animal and vegetable scraps or those in the early stages of decomposition.

topsoil
Second layer of soil, dark in color and rich in organic matter; it contains almost all of the soil's animal and vegetable life.

subsoil
Third layer of soil to which the roots extend; contains little organic matter but many nutrients leached from the topsoil.

bedrock
Rock that forms the bottom layer of soil; its physical and chemical breakdown enables the upper layers to develop.

plant

photosynthesis
Phenomenon by which the plant, helped by
solar energy, obtains its food (glucose)
from the air and the soil and releases
oxygen into the atmosphere.

solar energy
Energy derived from sunlight and
absorbed through the chlorophyll, the
green pigment found in plant leaves.

leaf
Part of the plant where photosynthesis
takes place; it also helps oxygenate the
ambient air and reduce carbon dioxide.

stem
Main part of the plant, extending from
the soil to the terminal bud.

glucose
Organic food produced through
photosynthesis and used by the plant to
ensure growth; it is transported throughout
the plant by the sap.

absorption of water and mineral salts
Water and mineral salts are absorbed through the
roots and carried up to the leaves by the stem and its
offshoots.

release of oxygen
The process of photosynthesis
releases oxygen, a gas essential to life.

carbon dioxide absorption
The carbon dioxide in the atmosphere required for
photosynthesis is absorbed by the leaf.

section of a bulb
Bulb: underground structure of certain plants where nutrients are stored; it ensures seasonal regrowth of the aboveground part of the plant.

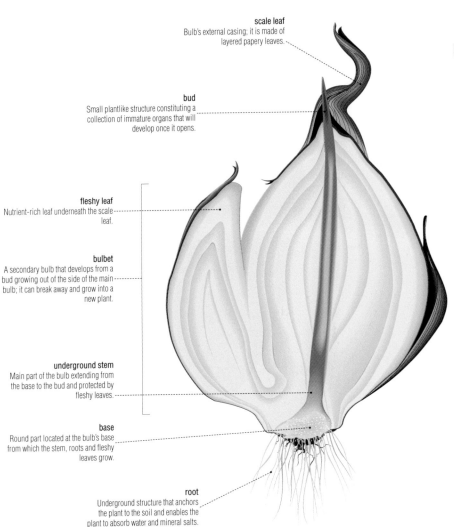

scale leaf
Bulb's external casing; it is made of layered papery leaves.

bud
Small plantlike structure constituting a collection of immature organs that will develop once it opens.

fleshy leaf
Nutrient-rich leaf underneath the scale leaf.

bulbet
A secondary bulb that develops from a bud growing out of the side of the main bulb; it can break away and grow into a new plant.

underground stem
Main part of the bulb extending from the base to the bud and protected by fleshy leaves.

base
Round part located at the bulb's base from which the stem, roots and fleshy leaves grow.

root
Underground structure that anchors the plant to the soil and enables the plant to absorb water and mineral salts.

leaf

Usually thin and flat part of a vegetable that grows out of the stem and is specially adapted to capturing light and performing photosynthesis.

structure of a leaf

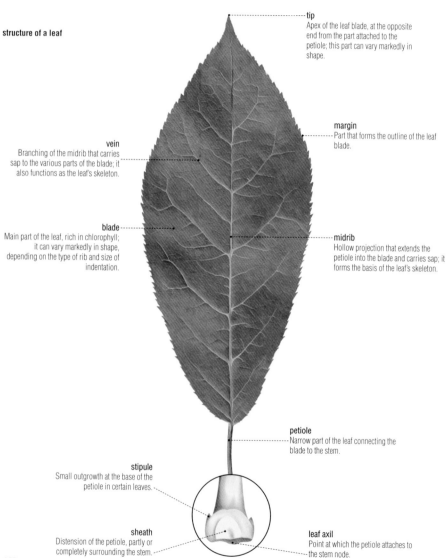

tip
Apex of the leaf blade, at the opposite end from the part attached to the petiole; this part can vary markedly in shape.

margin
Part that forms the outline of the leaf blade.

vein
Branching of the midrib that carries sap to the various parts of the blade; it also functions as the leaf's skeleton.

blade
Main part of the leaf, rich in chlorophyll; it can vary markedly in shape, depending on the type of rib and size of indentation.

midrib
Hollow projection that extends the petiole into the blade and carries sap; it forms the basis of the leaf's skeleton.

petiole
Narrow part of the leaf connecting the blade to the stem.

stipule
Small outgrowth at the base of the petiole in certain leaves.

sheath
Distension of the petiole, partly or completely surrounding the stem.

leaf axil
Point at which the petiole attaches to the stem node.

compound leaves

Leaves with blades divided into several distinct sections, called folioles, the arrangement of which determines the leaf type.

abruptly pinnate
Compound feathered leaf ending in two folioles on each side of the main petiole.

odd pinnate
Compound feathered leaf with a main petiole ending in a single foliole.

pinnatifid
Compound leaf with folioles on both sides of a common petiole.

trifoliolate
Leaf having three distinct folioles.

palmate
Compound leaf with all its folioles attached at the same point, at the apex of the petiole.

simple leaves

Leaves with an undivided blade; there
are many types, grouped according to
shape.

orbiculate
Simple leaf with a somewhat rounded
blade.

spatulate
Simple leaf in which the blade widens,
taking the shape of a spatula.

cordate
Simple leaf with a heart-shaped blade.

reniform
Simple leaf with a kidney-shaped
blade.

hastate
Simple leaf with a spear-shaped blade.

lanceolate
Simple leaf with a narrow blade that is
longer than it is wide, ending in a
point.

peltate
Simple leaf with a petiole attached
perpendicularly to the center of the
blade's underside.

ovate
Simple leaf with an egg-shaped blade.

linear
Simple leaf with a long and very
narrow blade and almost parallel
margins.

flower

Often colorful and fragrant part of certain vegetables that holds the reproductive organs; first it produces fruit, then seeds.

structure of a flower

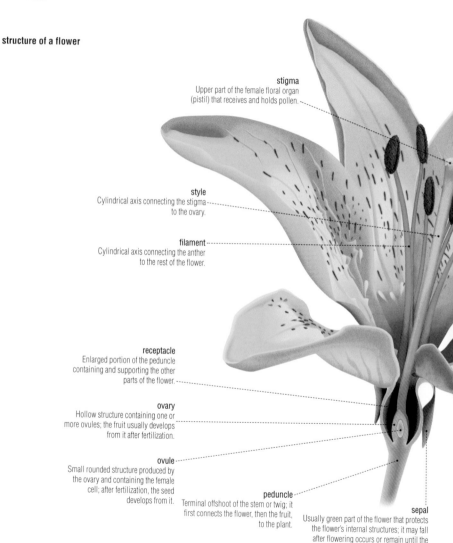

stigma
Upper part of the female floral organ (pistil) that receives and holds pollen.

style
Cylindrical axis connecting the stigma to the ovary.

filament
Cylindrical axis connecting the anther to the rest of the flower.

receptacle
Enlarged portion of the peduncle containing and supporting the other parts of the flower.

ovary
Hollow structure containing one or more ovules; the fruit usually develops from it after fertilization.

ovule
Small rounded structure produced by the ovary and containing the female cell; after fertilization, the seed develops from it.

peduncle
Terminal offshoot of the stem or twig; it first connects the flower, then the fruit, to the plant.

sepal
Usually green part of the flower that protects the flower's internal structures; it may fall after flowering occurs or remain until the fruit has ripened.

anther
Upper part of the male floral organ (stamen) that produces pollen grains; at maturity, it splits to release them.

petal
Usually colorful and scented part of the flower that surrounds the male and female reproductive organs; it often helps attract pollinators.

pistil
Each of the female floral organs at the flower's center, consisting of an ovary, a stylus and a stigma.

corolla
Part of the flower composed of all its petals.

stamen
Each of the male floral organs, consisting of a filament and an anther.

calyx
Part of the flower composed of all its sepals.

examples of flowers

Flowers: there are more than 250,000
varieties of flowers, prized for their shapes,
colors and great range of scents.

poppy
Bright red wildflower, related to the
domestic poppy.

carnation
Strongly scented flower of various
colors; it is sometimes worn as a
boutonniere on special occasions.

orchid
Flower prized for the variety of its delicate
shapes and colors; there are more than
15,000 species.

tulip
Flower whose petals grow in the shape
of a rounded vase; there are
approximately 100 differently colored
species.

violet
Small flower with several ornamental
varieties; it is also cultivated for
perfume production and cooking.

lily of the valley
Small strongly scented bell-shaped
white flower that grows in clusters.

begonia
Decorative flower that is native to
South America and prized for its
vibrant colors.

lily
Large flower of various colors, prized
for its beauty; the white lily is the
symbol of French royalty and the
emblem of Quebec.

flower

rose
Flower cultivated for its beauty, scent and range of colors; it is used in floral arrangements.

crocus
Small white flower that blooms with the first warm rays of spring sunshine.

daffodil
Fairly tall bright yellow flower that blooms in the spring.

buttercup
Wildflower with usually bright-yellow petals, widespread in fields and prairies.

sunflower
Tall flower whose seeds provide a high-quality cooking oil. The head always turns toward the Sun, hence its name.

primrose
Small decorative flower in various
colors that blooms early in the spring.

daisy
Flower with a yellow center and usually
white petals, common in fields and
woodlands.

dandelion
Very common flower composed of
dozens of small, tightly bunched
florets.

thistle
Wildflower whose receptacle is
covered with modified leaves covered
with spines.

fruits

Vegetable structures usually resulting from the development of one or several floral ovaries that, once mature, contain seeds; they are often edible.

stone fleshy fruit

Fruit whose seed is surrounded by three distinct layers: an exocarp, a fleshy mesocarp and an extremely hard stone, or endocarp.

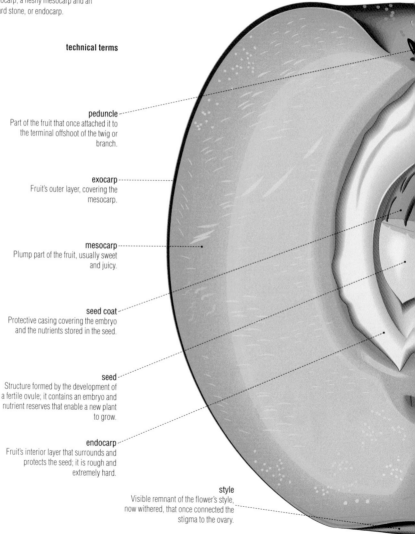

technical terms

peduncle
Part of the fruit that once attached it to the terminal offshoot of the twig or branch.

exocarp
Fruit's outer layer, covering the mesocarp.

mesocarp
Plump part of the fruit, usually sweet and juicy.

seed coat
Protective casing covering the embryo and the nutrients stored in the seed.

seed
Structure formed by the development of a fertile ovule; it contains an embryo and nutrient reserves that enable a new plant to grow.

endocarp
Fruit's interior layer that surrounds and protects the seed; it is rough and extremely hard.

style
Visible remnant of the flower's style, now withered, that once connected the stigma to the ovary.

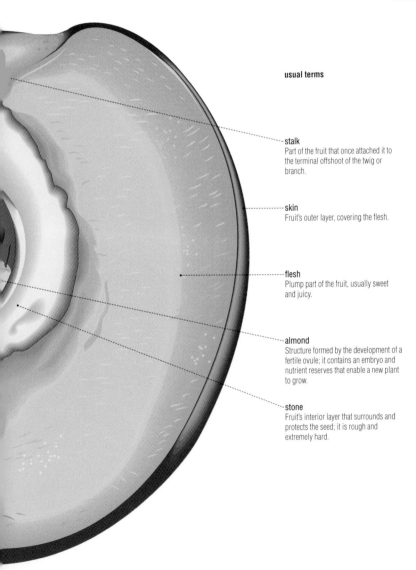

section of a peach

usual terms

stalk
Part of the fruit that once attached it to the terminal offshoot of the twig or branch.

skin
Fruit's outer layer, covering the flesh.

flesh
Plump part of the fruit, usually sweet and juicy.

almond
Structure formed by the development of a fertile ovule; it contains an embryo and nutrient reserves that enable a new plant to grow.

stone
Fruit's interior layer that surrounds and protects the seed; it is rough and extremely hard.

fruits

fleshy fruit: citrus fruit

Fruit composed of several segments, each one enclosing
seeds that are in direct contact with the pulp.

technical terms

wall
Thin membrane separating the citrus
fruit into segments.

seed
Structure formed by the development of a
fertile ovule; it contains an embryo and
nutrient reserves that enable a new plant
to grow.

juice sac
Each of the small juice-filled pockets
that combine to make up the fruit's
pulp.

mesocarp
Designates the whitish part of the rind
of a citrus fruit.

exocarp
Fruit's outer layer, covering the
mesocarp.

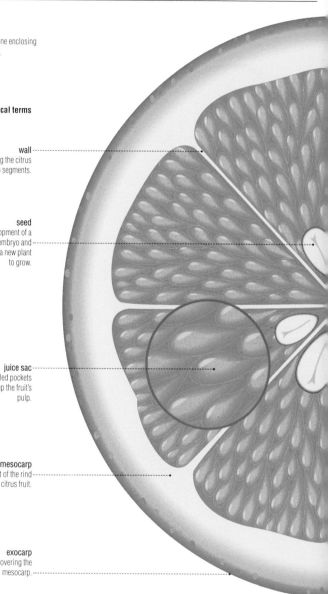

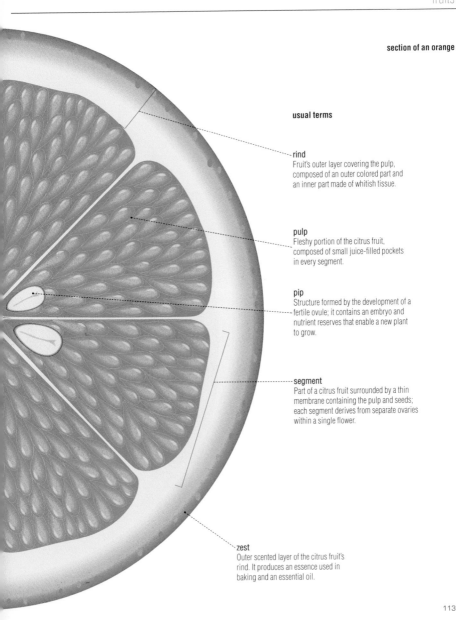

section of an orange

usual terms

rind
Fruit's outer layer covering the pulp, composed of an outer colored part and an inner part made of whitish tissue.

pulp
Fleshy portion of the citrus fruit, composed of small juice-filled pockets in every segment.

pip
Structure formed by the development of a fertile ovule; it contains an embryo and nutrient reserves that enable a new plant to grow.

segment
Part of a citrus fruit surrounded by a thin membrane containing the pulp and seeds; each segment derives from separate ovaries within a single flower.

zest
Outer scented layer of the citrus fruit's rind. It produces an essence used in baking and an essential oil.

fleshy fruit: berry fruit

Fruit in which the seed is surrounded by two distinct layers: an exocarp and a fleshy mesocarp that is in direct contact with the seed.

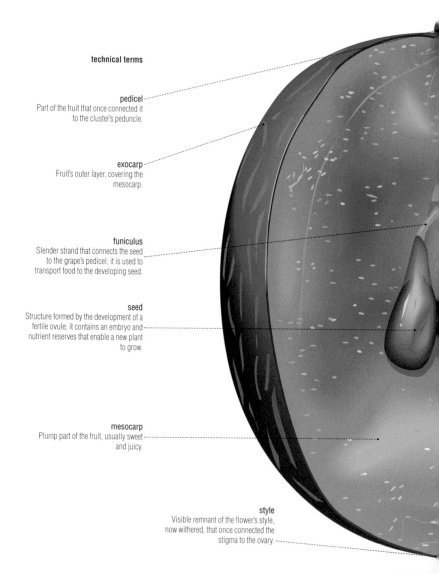

technical terms

pedicel
Part of the fruit that once connected it to the cluster's peduncle.

exocarp
Fruit's outer layer, covering the mesocarp.

funiculus
Slender strand that connects the seed to the grape's pedicel; it is used to transport food to the developing seed.

seed
Structure formed by the development of a fertile ovule; it contains an embryo and nutrient reserves that enable a new plant to grow.

mesocarp
Plump part of the fruit, usually sweet and juicy.

style
Visible remnant of the flower's style, now withered, that once connected the stigma to the ovary.

section of a grape

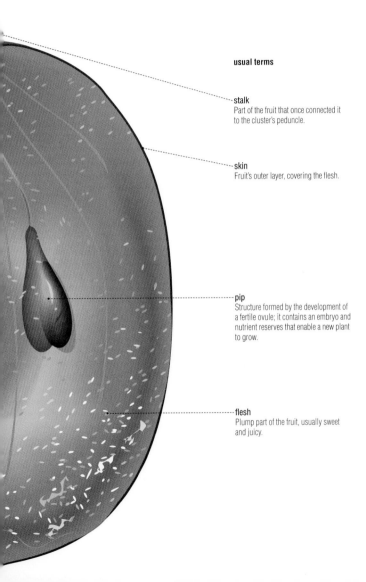

usual terms

stalk
Part of the fruit that once connected it
to the cluster's peduncle.

skin
Fruit's outer layer, covering the flesh.

pip
Structure formed by the development of
a fertile ovule; it contains an embryo and
nutrient reserves that enable a new plant
to grow.

flesh
Plump part of the fruit, usually sweet
and juicy.

PLANTS AND GARDENING

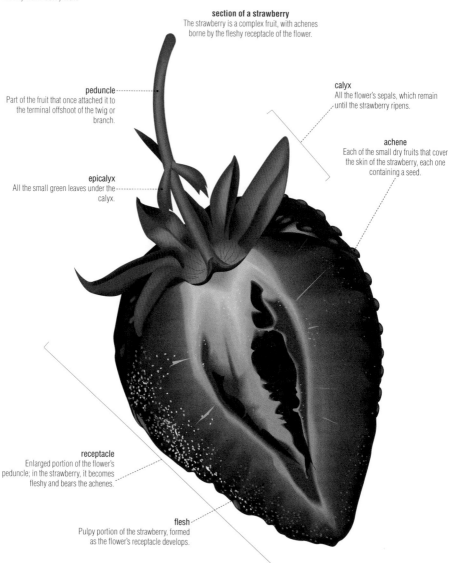

section of a strawberry
The strawberry is a complex fruit, with achenes
borne by the fleshy receptacle of the flower.

peduncle
Part of the fruit that once attached it to
the terminal offshoot of the twig or
branch.

calyx
All the flower's sepals, which remain
until the strawberry ripens.

achene
Each of the small dry fruits that cover
the skin of the strawberry, each one
containing a seed.

epicalyx
All the small green leaves under the
calyx.

receptacle
Enlarged portion of the flower's
peduncle; in the strawberry, it becomes
fleshy and bears the achenes.

flesh
Pulpy portion of the strawberry, formed
as the flower's receptacle develops.

section of a raspberry
The raspberry is an aggregate fruit; it consists of a
number of small fleshy fruits attached to a common
receptacle.

peduncle
Part of the fruit that once attached it to
the terminal offshoot of the twig or
branch.

sepal
The flower's sepal remains until the
raspberry ripens.

seed
Structure formed by the development of a
fertile ovule; it contains an embryo and
nutrient reserves that enable a new plant
to grow.

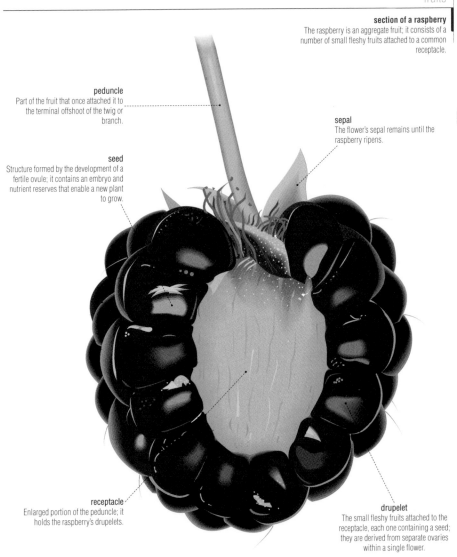

receptacle
Enlarged portion of the peduncle; it
holds the raspberry's drupelets.

drupelet
The small fleshy fruits attached to the
receptacle, each one containing a seed;
they are derived from separate ovaries
within a single flower.

fruits

pome fleshy fruit
Fruit with a seed, or pip, surrounded by three distinct layers: an exocarp, a fleshy mesocarp and a stiff endocarp containing loculi.

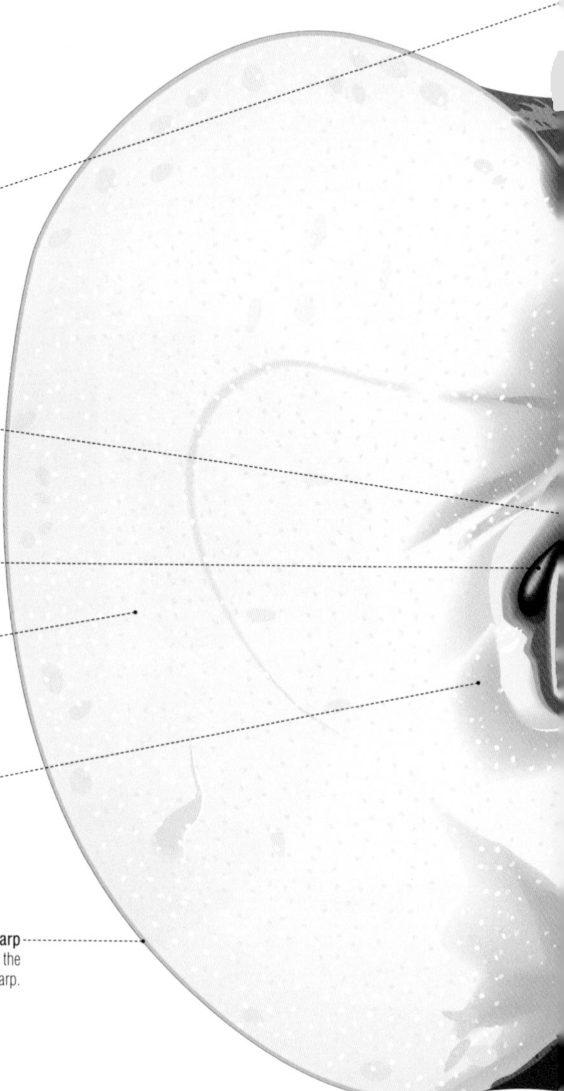

technical terms

peduncle
Part of the fruit that once attached it to the terminal offshoot of the twig or branch.

loculus
Small cavity located under the endocarp, usually containing two seeds.

seed
Structure formed by the development of a fertile ovule; it contains an embryo and nutrient reserves that enable a new plant to grow.

mesocarp
Plump part of the fruit, usually sweet and juicy.

endocarp
The stiff inner layer of the fruit, surrounding and protecting the seed and covering the loculi.

exocarp
Fruit's outer layer, covering the mesocarp.

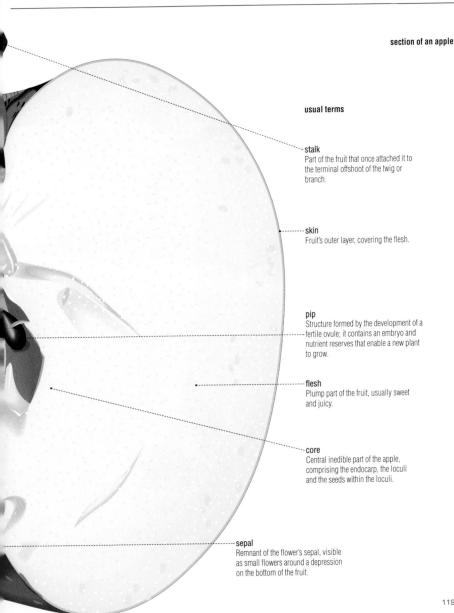

section of an apple

usual terms

stalk
Part of the fruit that once attached it to
the terminal offshoot of the twig or
branch.

skin
Fruit's outer layer, covering the flesh.

pip
Structure formed by the development of a
fertile ovule; it contains an embryo and
nutrient reserves that enable a new plant
to grow.

flesh
Plump part of the fruit, usually sweet
and juicy.

core
Central inedible part of the apple,
comprising the endocarp, the loculi
and the seeds within the loculi.

sepal
Remnant of the flower's sepal, visible
as small flowers around a depression
on the bottom of the fruit.

fruits

dry fruits
Fruits with usually edible seeds, surrounded by
a single dry, somewhat rigid layer.

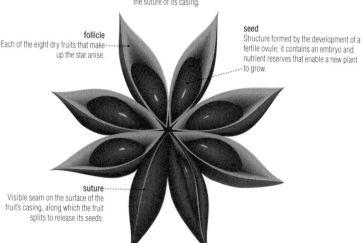

section of a hazelnut
The fruit of the hazelnut tree, the hazelnut is an
achene; its pericarp is covered by a cupule.

cupule
Thin scaly or prickly casing made of
fused bracts; it partially or completely
covers the hazelnut.

bract
Little leaf, smaller than the plant's other
leaves, attached to the peduncle of the
flower or fruit.

seed
Structure formed by the development of a
fertile ovule; it contains an embryo and
nutrient reserves that enable a new plant
to grow.

pericarp

stigma
Visible remnant of the flower's stigma,
now withered, forming a point at the
fruit's base.

achene
Small dry fruit containing a single seed
not fused to the pericarp; when ripe,
the achene cannot split unaided to
release its seed.

section of a follicle: star anise
Follicle: dry single-chambered fruit that, when ripe, splits along
the suture of its casing.

follicle
Each of the eight dry fruits that make
up the star anise.

seed
Structure formed by the development of a
fertile ovule; it contains an embryo and
nutrient reserves that enable a new plant
to grow.

suture
Visible seam on the surface of the
fruit's casing, along which the fruit
splits to release its seeds.

section of a silique: mustard
Silique: dry fruit with two valves that, when the fruit is ripe, split to release seeds.

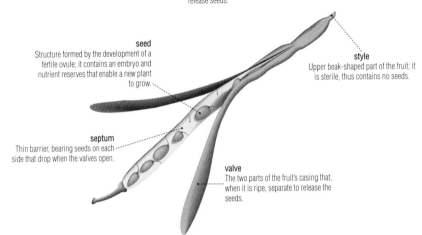

seed
Structure formed by the development of a fertile ovule; it contains an embryo and nutrient reserves that enable a new plant to grow.

style
Upper beak-shaped part of the fruit; it is sterile, thus contains no seeds.

septum
Thin barrier, bearing seeds on each side that drop when the valves open.

valve
The two parts of the fruit's casing that, when it is ripe, separate to release the seeds.

section of a capsule: poppy
Capsule: dry many-chambered fruit that opens laterally or at the apex when ripe; it contains a great many seeds.

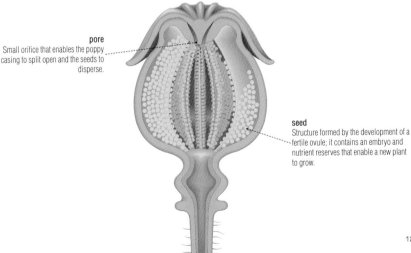

pore
Small orifice that enables the poppy casing to split open and the seeds to disperse.

seed
Structure formed by the development of a fertile ovule; it contains an embryo and nutrient reserves that enable a new plant to grow.

cereals

Plants that are often cultivated on a large scale; their grains have been a major food staple for humans and certain domestic animals for centuries.

section of a grain of wheat
A grain of wheat is a small dry fruit whose single grain is fused to its casing; the varieties differ in size, shape and color.

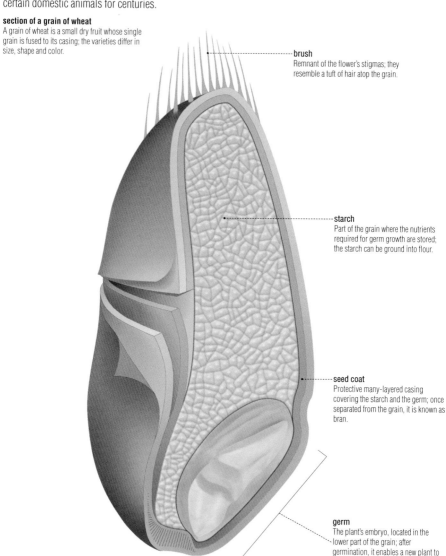

brush
Remnant of the flower's stigmas; they resemble a tuft of hair atop the grain.

starch
Part of the grain where the nutrients required for germ growth are stored; the starch can be ground into flour.

seed coat
Protective many-layered casing covering the starch and the germ; once separated from the grain, it is known as bran.

germ
The plant's embryo, located in the lower part of the grain; after germination, it enables a new plant to grow.

wheat: spike
The spike is composed of a main axis bearing seeds without a pedicel; the seeds are clustered at the stem's apex.

wheat
Cereal cultivated for its grain, important in producing food, especially foodstuffs such as flour, bread and semolina.

barley: spike
The spike is composed of a main axis bearing seeds without a pedicel; the seeds are clustered at the stem's apex.

barley
Cereal cultivated for its grain; it is used mainly to produce malt for brewing beer and as cattle fodder.

cereals

rye
Highly resistant cereal whose grain is
used mainly to feed cattle; it is used to
produce flour that can be mixed with
wheat flour to make bread.

rye: spike
The spike is composed of a main axis
bearing seeds without a pedicel; the
seeds are clustered at the stem's apex.

corn
Native American cereal cultivated for its
grains and used for human and animal
food; it is also used to produce a sweet
syrup and a cooking oil.

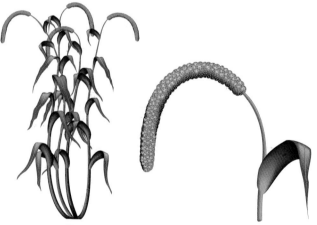

millet
Cereal cultivated as fodder or for its
grain; it is used mainly to make
unleavened bread and to feed
domesticated birds.

millet: spike
The spike is composed of a main axis
bearing seeds without a pedicel; the
seeds are clustered at the stem's apex.

corn: cob

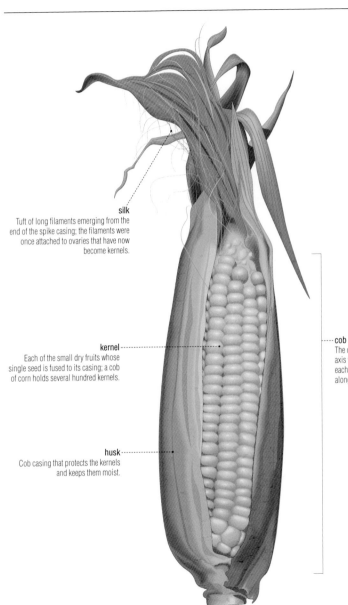

silk
Tuft of long filaments emerging from the end of the spike casing; the filaments were once attached to ovaries that have now become kernels.

kernel
Each of the small dry fruits whose single seed is fused to its casing; a cob of corn holds several hundred kernels.

cob
The cob is composed of a wide main axis with rows of tightly packed kernels; each cob grows in the axil of a leaf along the stem.

husk
Cob casing that protects the kernels and keeps them moist.

cereals

oats
Cereal cultivated for its grain; although it
is mainly used to feed horses, humans
also eat it, mostly in the form of flakes
(rolled oats).

oats: panicle
The panicle is composed of a main
axis with offshoots, each stem bearing
grains that have a pedicel.

buckwheat
Cereal cultivated for its grain, mainly
ground into flour; it is also used to feed
cattle and some domesticated birds.

buckwheat: raceme
The raceme is composed of a main
axis and grains that have a pedicel,
clustered at the stem's apex.

rice
Cereal whose grain is a major food staple in many parts of the world; rice is generally grown in flooded fields.

rice: panicle
The panicle is composed of a main axis with offshoots, each stem bearing grains that have a pedicel.

sorghum
Cereal cultivated for the sugar in its sap and for its grain; it is also used as fodder, to make unleavened bread and certain kinds of beer.

sorghum: panicle
The panicle is composed of a main axis with offshoots; at its apex, each stem bears a cluster of grains that have a pedicel.

tree

Large vegetable whose root system and aboveground part are well developed; it produces oxygen and provides wood.

structure of a tree
The tree is composed of an underground part, the roots, and two aboveground parts, the trunk and the crown.

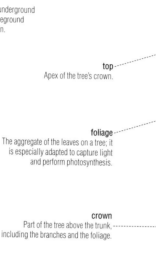

top
Apex of the tree's crown.

foliage
The aggregate of the leaves on a tree; it is especially adapted to capture light and perform photosynthesis.

crown
Part of the tree above the trunk, including the branches and the foliage.

limb
Offshoot growing directly out of a tree trunk, subsequently dividing into branches and twigs.

bole
Part of the tree trunk extending between the stump and the first lower limbs; it has no offshoots.

trunk
Main part of the tree extending between the soil and the lower branches.

taproot
First root growing out of the seed that grows vertically into the soil; it usually has few offshoots, its main function being to anchor the tree in the ground.

branches
The aggregate of larger and smaller branches that provide support for the tree's leaves, flowers and fruit.

branch
Offshoot of one of the tree's limbs.

twig
The most slender offshoot of a tree branch.

stump
Lower part of the trunk that remains in place, with its roots, when the tree is cut down.

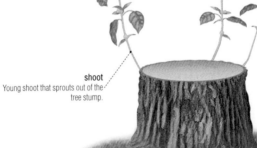

shoot
Young shoot that sprouts out of the tree stump.

shallow root
Root, often having many offshoots, growing somewhat horizontally into the rich moist topsoil.

radicle
The most slender offshoot of a tree root.

root-hair zone
Part of the radicle covered in small absorbent hairs that ensure the tree is supplied with mineral salts and water.

examples of broadleaved trees

Broadleaved trees have mainly large flat leaves; in temperate zones, these usually fall as winter approaches.

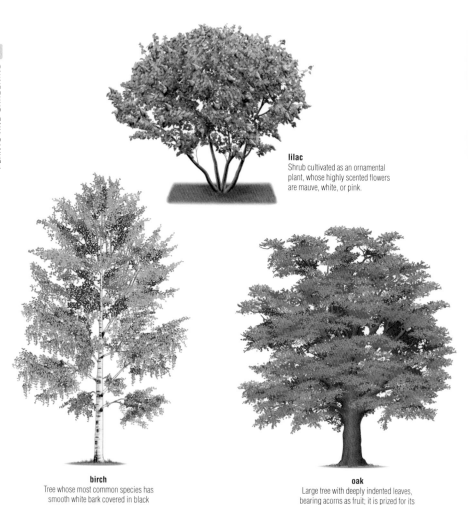

lilac
Shrub cultivated as an ornamental plant, whose highly scented flowers are mauve, white, or pink.

birch
Tree whose most common species has smooth white bark covered in black markings; the bark readily peels off the trunk in large sections.

oak
Large tree with deeply indented leaves, bearing acorns as fruit; it is prized for its hard and extremely resistant wood.

beech
Smooth-barked tree, prized for its ornamental value and its wood; it is used especially in woodworking and for heating.

weeping willow
Tree with long flexible hanging branches; it is often used for ornamental purposes and generally grows near water.

palm tree
Tree native to tropical regions; among its various species are date- and coconut-bearing kinds.

tree

examples of broadleaved trees

poplar
Tall slender fast-growing tree; its soft wood is used especially in woodworking and to make pulp for papermaking.

walnut
Large tree that produces an edible fruit, the walnut; its hard compact wood is prized especially by carpenters for its use in making furniture.

maple
Tree producing the samara, a small dry winged fruit; its wood is prized by cabinetmakers. The sugar maple tree's sap can be made into a syrup.

conifer

Tree that usually retains its needle- or scalelike leaves all winter long; it bears cones, hence its name, and produces a sticky sap known as resin.

structure of a conifer
Conifers, like other trees, have an underground part, the roots, and two aerial parts, the trunk and the crown.

crown
Part of the tree above the trunk, including the branches and the foliage.

foliage
The aggregate of the leaves on a tree; it is especially adapted to capture light and perform photosynthesis.

trunk
Main part of the tree extending between the soil and the lower branches.

shallow root
Root, often having many offshoots, growing somewhat horizontally into the rich moist topsoil.

conifer

examples of conifers

There are 550 conifer species; because they are
well adapted to harsh climates, they often form
the tree line on mountains and in subpolar
regions.

umbrella pine
Conifer native to the Mediterranean area
whose branches form a flattened crown,
hence its name; it produces an edible
seed, the pine nut.

larch
One of the few conifers that sheds its
needles in the fall; its scented, resistant
wood is used in construction and
carpentry.

cedar of Lebanon
Conifer of Middle Eastern origin with a
large, flattened top; now rare, former
civilizations made abundant use of its
wood.

spruce
Conifer with small cylindrical needles
encircling the branch; it has reddish-
brown bark and can grow to 180 ft.

fir
Scented conifer with flat needles arranged
on each side of the branch; it has grayish
bark, flecked with resin. Fir is commonly
used as a Christmas tree.

vegetation and biosphere

vegetation regions
Vegetation plays an essential role in maintaining
biospheric equilibrium; it varies depending on
climate and soil characteristics.

desert
Hot region where aridity (less than 4 in
of annual rainfall) is such that plant
and animal life is almost nonexistent.

maquis
Vast expanse of degenerated
vegetation composed of shrubs with
evergreen leaves; it is adapted to
summer drought.

tropical rain forest
Dense forest whose biodiversity is
among the richest; its growth is
fostered by abundant and regular
precipitation.

savanna
Vast expanse of herbaceous plants,
dominated by tall grasses and shrubs; it
is typical of hot regions that have a rainy
season.

temperate forest
Forest composed mainly of deciduous
trees, including oak, ash and beech.

grassland
Vast expanse of herbaceous plants,
mostly grasses; virtually devoid of trees,
these regions are characterized by
relatively cold, dry winters.

tundra
Plant formation that grows in relatively
arid regions; it includes mosses,
lichens, grasses, bushes and dwarf
trees.

boreal forest
Vast expanse of forest composed
mainly of conifers, although certain
deciduous trees also grow here.

PLANTS AND GARDENING

pleasure garden

Private plot reserved for cultivating ornamental plants where one strolls and relaxes.

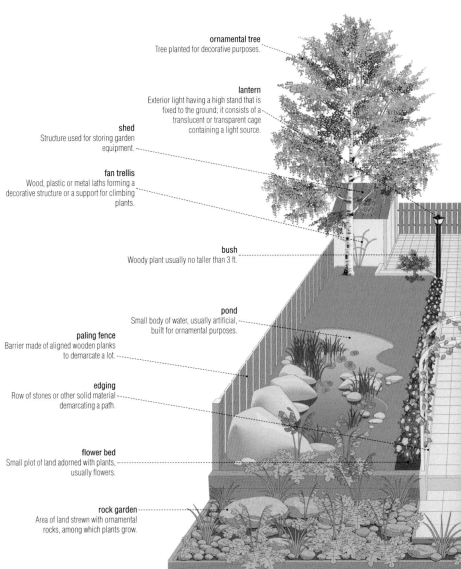

ornamental tree
Tree planted for decorative purposes.

lantern
Exterior light having a high stand that is fixed to the ground; it consists of a translucent or transparent cage containing a light source.

shed
Structure used for storing garden equipment.

fan trellis
Wood, plastic or metal laths forming a decorative structure or a support for climbing plants.

bush
Woody plant usually no taller than 3 ft.

pond
Small body of water, usually artificial, built for ornamental purposes.

paling fence
Barrier made of aligned wooden planks to demarcate a lot.

edging
Row of stones or other solid material demarcating a path.

flower bed
Small plot of land adorned with plants, usually flowers.

rock garden
Area of land strewn with ornamental rocks, among which plants grow.

climbing plant
Plant growing upward using a nearby structure as support.

pergola
Small structure with horizontal girders supported by posts, used as a support for baskets or climbing plants.

patio
Outdoor surface of various sizes usually covered with flagstone.

hanging basket
Hanging container for ornamental plants.

hedge
Bushes planted in a row to demarcate a lot.

clump of flowers
Grouping of flowers planted in a decorative manner.

lawn
Short thick grass requiring regular mowing.

arbor
Decorative doorway with rounded apex.

stake
Stick for training a stem or for supporting a fragile one.

tub
Container for ornamental or edible plants.

path
Walkway bordered by plants.

seeding and planting tools

garden line
Cord stretched between two stakes and used as a guide for marking straight furrows and edges for a border or a hedge, or for demarcating sections of a vegetable garden.

dibble
Pointed tool for digging a small hole in the ground in which to plant seeds or bulbs.

seeder
Small shovel fitted with a distribution device for sowing seeds without touching them.

bulb dibble
Tool with a cylindrical container for removing a core of soil to create a hole in which plant bulbs or young plants are planted.

stake
Stick for training a stem or for
supporting a fragile one.

spreader
Small handcart with a reservoir and
distribution mechanism for evenly
spreading seeds or fertilizer on an area.

wheel
Circular instrument rotating around an
axle so that the device can be moved.

tools for loosening the earth

PLANTS AND GARDENING

lawn edger
Tool with a semicircular blade for trimming the edge of the lawn, usually along a driveway, a patio or flower bed.

shovel
Tool used for digging holes and manipulating various objects, such as soil, sand and compost.

spading fork
Tool with metal tines, which make it easier to loosen soil that is hard or contains many stones or roots.

spade
Tool with a flat or slightly concave blade, used mainly for turning over soil.

hoe
Tool with a thick sturdy blade attached directly to the handle; it is used especially for loosening and weeding dense soil.

rake
Tool with tines perpendicular to the handle, for leveling the soil, removing pebbles and gathering debris.

hook
Tool with curved tines, used to handle fertilizer and compost, pull up root vegetables and loosen or weed the soil.

pick
Tool whose head is pointed on one end and has a cutting edge on the other; it is used to break up hard or rocky soil.

hoe-fork
Tool with a blade, which serves as a hoe, and tines; it is used especially for making furrows.

draw hoe
Tool whose blade loosens, weeds and aerates the soil; it is also used to groom the soil around a plant.

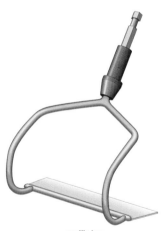

scuffle hoe
Tool whose blade, more slanted that that of the draw hoe, loosens, weeds and aerates the soil; it is also used for harvesting root vegetables.

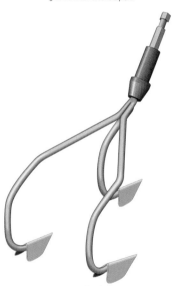

weeding hoe
Tool with claws designed mainly for loosening and weeding soil.

tiller
Motorized machine that uses its
rotating tines to turn over and loosen
the soil and mix fertilizer into it.

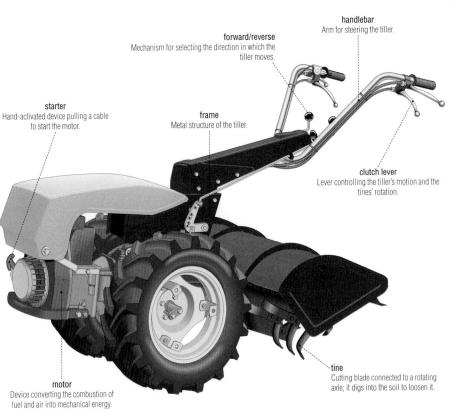

handlebar
Arm for steering the tiller.

forward/reverse
Mechanism for selecting the direction in which the
tiller moves.

starter
Hand-activated device pulling a cable
to start the motor.

frame
Metal structure of the tiller.

clutch lever
Lever controlling the tiller's motion and the
tines' rotation.

motor
Device converting the combustion of
fuel and air into mechanical energy.

tine
Cutting blade connected to a rotating
axle; it digs into the soil to loosen it.

watering tools

hose trolley
Reel mounted on a cart, for transporting and storing a garden hose.

reel
Spool for quickly rolling and unrolling a garden hose.

tap connector
Threaded part receiving a hose connected to a tap.

garden hose
Circular pipe, flexible or semirigid, conducting water from a tap to a watering device such as a nozzle, gun or sprinkler.

trolley crank
Handle for rolling up the garden hose on the reel.

hose nozzle
Detachable instrument attached to the end of a garden hose, for adjusting the shape and flow of the water spray.

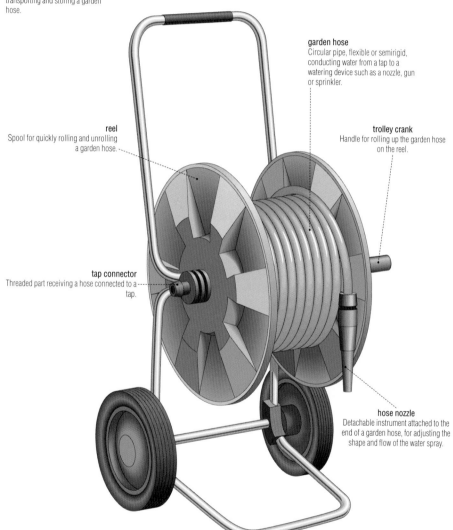

PLANTS AND GARDENING

watering can
Container fitted with a long neck,
usually with a rose at its end, used for
sprinkling plants with water or
treatment products.

handle
Part shaped like a semicircle for
gripping the can.

rose
Detachable perforated part causing
water or a liquid to pour in a shower.

tank sprayer
Device with a tank and a wand that sprays
fine droplets of water or treatment products
on plants and soil.

sprinkler hose
Hose with small openings through
which water flows; placed on the
ground, it deeply waters large areas.

watering tools

PLANTS AND GARDENING

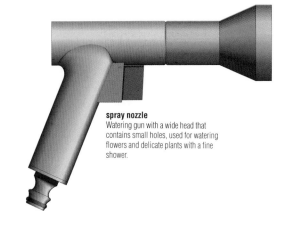

spray nozzle
Watering gun with a wide head that
contains small holes, used for watering
flowers and delicate plants with a fine
shower.

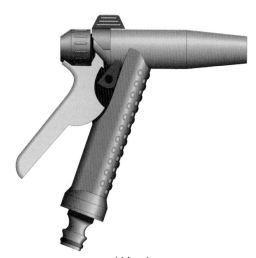

sprayer
Small atomizer used mainly for
spraying plant foliage and seedlings.

pistol nozzle
Watering nozzle activated by means of
a trigger flow switch.

revolving sprinkler
Watering device with rotating arms that
distribute water in a full circle.

arm
Part attached to the sprinkler's pivot for
distributing water.

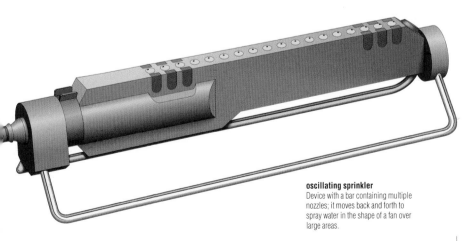

oscillating sprinkler
Device with a bar containing multiple
nozzles; it moves back and forth to
spray water in the shape of a fan over
large areas.

watering tools

impulse sprinkler

Watering device whose single nozzle is mounted on a pivot that rotates in jerks, emitting a powerful spray to distribute water in a circle or arc.

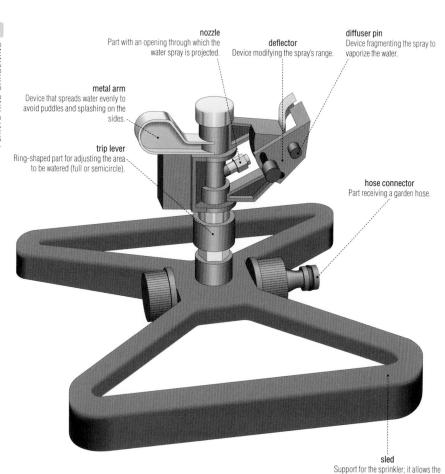

nozzle
Part with an opening through which the water spray is projected.

deflector
Device modifying the spray's range.

diffuser pin
Device fragmenting the spray to vaporize the water.

metal arm
Device that spreads water evenly to avoid puddles and splashing on the sides.

trip lever
Ring-shaped part for adjusting the area to be watered (full or semicircle).

hose connector
Part receiving a garden hose.

sled
Support for the sprinkler; it allows the device to be moved by pulling on the hose, which avoids treading on watered areas.

pruning and cutting tools

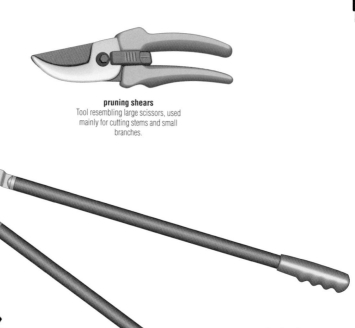

pruning shears
Tool resembling large scissors, used mainly for cutting stems and small branches.

lopping shears
Long-handled pruning shears, used to cut medium-sized branches.

axe
Tool with a thick blade attached to a handle, used especially to fell small trees and chop wood.

pruning and cutting tools

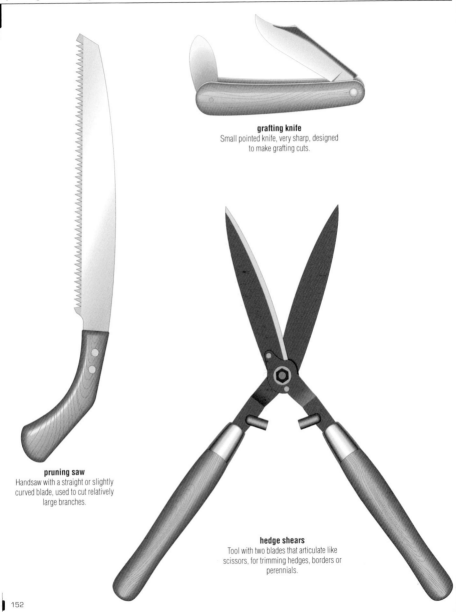

grafting knife
Small pointed knife, very sharp, designed
to make grafting cuts.

pruning saw
Handsaw with a straight or slightly
curved blade, used to cut relatively
large branches.

hedge shears
Tool with two blades that articulate like
scissors, for trimming hedges, borders or
perennials.

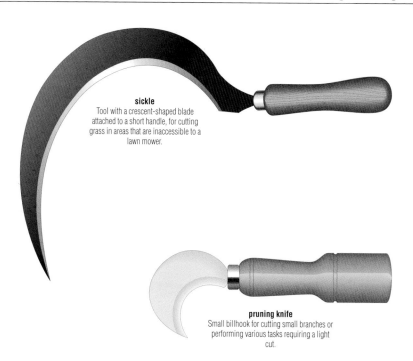

sickle
Tool with a crescent-shaped blade attached to a short handle, for cutting grass in areas that are inaccessible to a lawn mower.

pruning knife
Small billhook for cutting small branches or performing various tasks requiring a light cut.

billhook
Tool with a powerful hooked blade, used especially to cut branches and undergrowth.

pruning and cutting tools

chainsaw

Portable motorized saw with a cutting chain; it is manipulated with two hands to cut tree limbs, fell trees and saw wood.

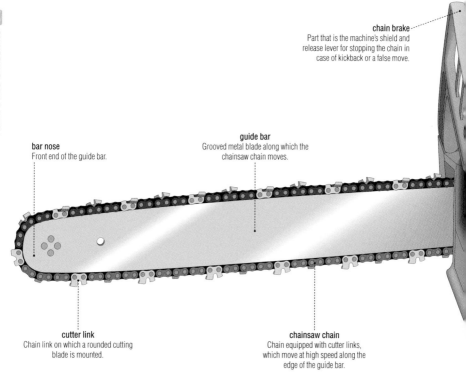

chain brake
Part that is the machine's shield and release lever for stopping the chain in case of kickback or a false move.

bar nose
Front end of the guide bar.

guide bar
Grooved metal blade along which the chainsaw chain moves.

cutter link
Chain link on which a rounded cutting blade is mounted.

chainsaw chain
Chain equipped with cutter links, which move at high speed along the edge of the guide bar.

antivibration handle
Auxiliary handle, insulated from the housing by rubber shock absorbers that dampen the vibrations produced by the tool.

engine housing

air filter
Device that removes dust from the air entering the engine.

stop button
Button for instantly stopping the engine.

security trigger
Device blocking the accelerator control to prevent the chain from being activated accidentally.

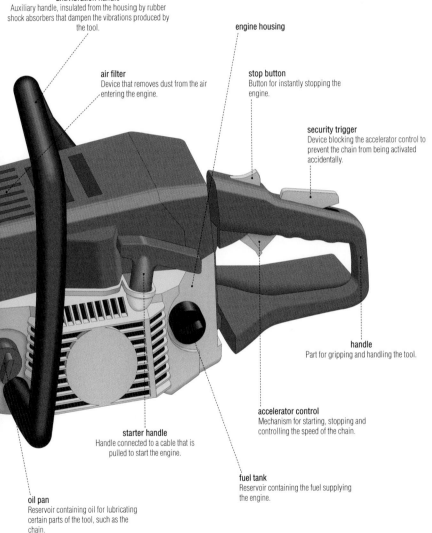

handle
Part for gripping and handling the tool.

accelerator control
Mechanism for starting, stopping and controlling the speed of the chain.

starter handle
Handle connected to a cable that is pulled to start the engine.

fuel tank
Reservoir containing the fuel supplying the engine.

oil pan
Reservoir containing oil for lubricating certain parts of the tool, such as the chain.

lawn care

lawn trimmer
Portable motorized tool, equipped with nylon yarn rotating at high speed, used for cutting grass in places inaccessible to a lawn mower.

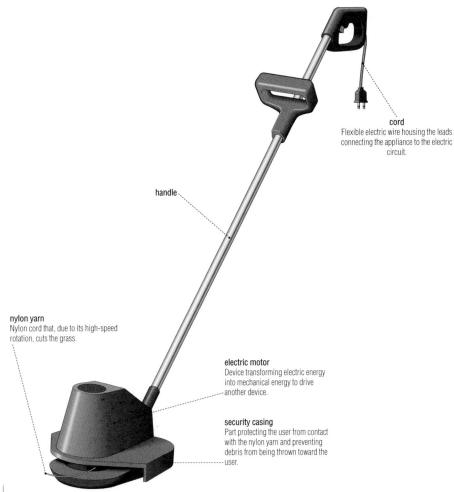

cord
Flexible electric wire housing the leads connecting the appliance to the electric circuit.

handle

nylon yarn
Nylon cord that, due to its high-speed rotation, cuts the grass.

electric motor
Device transforming electric energy into mechanical energy to drive another device.

security casing
Part protecting the user from contact with the nylon yarn and preventing debris from being thrown toward the user.

PLANTS AND GARDENING

power mower
Motorized device using a rotating horizontal
blade to cut grass over large areas.

handle
Bar for moving and guiding the mower.

filler cap
Cylindrical part plugging a tank's filler opening.

safety handle
Lever controlling both the blade
rotation and the wheel motion.

starter
Hand-activated device pulling a cable
to start the motor.

motor
Device converting the combustion of fuel
and air into mechanical energy.

grassbox
Detachable container collecting the cut
grass.

casing
Part supporting and covering a rotating
blade for cutting the grass.

deflector
Part deflecting the cut grass toward the
grassbox.

animal cell

Smallest living structure and constituent unit of all animals, including human beings; its size and shape vary according to function.

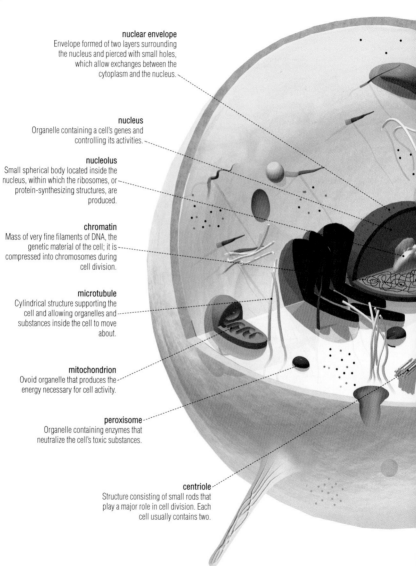

nuclear envelope
Envelope formed of two layers surrounding the nucleus and pierced with small holes, which allow exchanges between the cytoplasm and the nucleus.

nucleus
Organelle containing a cell's genes and controlling its activities.

nucleolus
Small spherical body located inside the nucleus, within which the ribosomes, or protein-synthesizing structures, are produced.

chromatin
Mass of very fine filaments of DNA, the genetic material of the cell; it is compressed into chromosomes during cell division.

microtubule
Cylindrical structure supporting the cell and allowing organelles and substances inside the cell to move about.

mitochondrion
Ovoid organelle that produces the energy necessary for cell activity.

peroxisome
Organelle containing enzymes that neutralize the cell's toxic substances.

centriole
Structure consisting of small rods that play a major role in cell division. Each cell usually contains two.

animal cell

ribosome
Organelle, free or attached to the
endoplasmic reticulum, producing
proteins essential to the constitution and
functioning of living beings.

lysosome
Small spheroid organ containing enzymes
that break down food, spent cell
components and other harmful substances
that have been absorbed.

Golgi apparatus
Organelle composed of a series of pockets that
receive proteins produced by the ribosomes
and either transport them outside the cell or to
other organelles.

endoplasmic reticulum
Organelle formed of walls to which the
ribosomes are attached.

microfilament
Rod-shaped structure supporting the
cell and giving it its shape.

cytoplasm
Clear gelatinous substance
surrounding the various cellular
structures.

vacuole
Spherical cavity containing water,
waste and various substances required
by the cell.

cell membrane
The cell's flexible outer casing; it separates the
cell from the surrounding environment and
works as a filter to control the entry and exit of
certain substances.

cilium
Filament-like extension of the
cytoplasmic membrane allowing the
cell and certain substances on its
surface to move about.

unicellulars

Single-cell organisms living in freshwater or salt water, in humid soil or as parasites of other organisms (plants or animals).

ANIMAL KINGDOM

amoeba
Variably shaped one-cell organism, found in freshwater or salt water, in humid soil or, sometimes, as a parasite of animals. It moves about and feeds with the help of pseudopodia.

plasma membrane
The cell's flexible outer casing; it separates the cell from the surrounding environment and works as a filter to control the entry and exit of certain substances.

contractile vacuole
Spheroid cavity acting as a pump to evacuate excess water and waste from the cell.

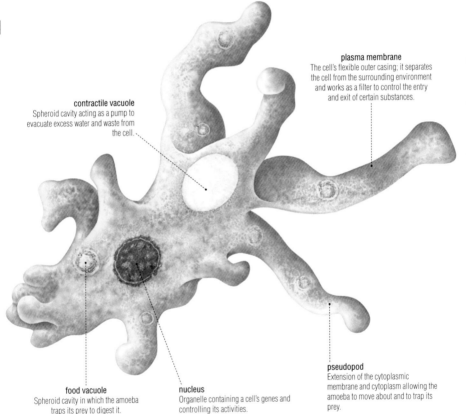

food vacuole
Spheroid cavity in which the amoeba traps its prey to digest it.

nucleus
Organelle containing a cell's genes and controlling its activities.

pseudopod
Extension of the cytoplasmic membrane and cytoplasm allowing the amoeba to move about and to trap its prey.

paramecium
Ovoid-shaped one-cell organism generally found in freshwater and covered with cilia, which allow it to move about and to feed, mainly on bacteria.

cilium
Filament-like extension of the cytoplasmic membrane allowing the cell and certain substances on its surface to move about.

food vacuole
Spheroid cavity in which food particles from the cytopharynx are digested.

plasma membrane
The cell's flexible outer casing; it separates the cell from the surrounding environment and works as a filter to control the entry and exit of certain substances.

micronucleus
Small nucleus ensuring cell reproduction.

peristome
Depression lined with cilia, which undulate to direct food particles toward the cytostome.

cytostome
Opening corresponding to the mouth and allowing ingestion of food and rejection of undesirable elements.

macronucleus
Large nucleus controlling cellular activities.

cytopharynx
Fold of the plasma membrane; food particles originating in the cytostome are directed toward it.

cytoplasm
Clear gelatinous substance surrounding the various cellular structures.

forming food vacuole
The paramecium continually produces food vacuoles out of cytoplasmic membrane. Each food vacuole traps food particles accumulated in the bottom of the cytopharynx.

contractile vacuole
Spheroid cavity acting as a pump to evacuate excess water and waste from the cell.

cytoproct
Orifice corresponding to the anus; the food vacuole opens into it, allowing waste to be eliminated.

sponge

Porous multicell organism, mostly marine (currently about 5,000 species); it anchors itself to a support and filters water to take in food particles.

calcareous sponge
Marine sponge with a skeleton composed of small calcareous needles (spicules).

anatomy of a sponge

pinacocyte
Flat ectodermal cell forming the outer covering of the sponge.

mesohyl
Gelatinous substance, rich in water, located between the ectoderm and the endoderm.

choanocyte
Inner cell having a filament (flagellum), which allows water to circulate and food particles to be caught and digested.

spongocoel
Hollow portion of the sponge covered with choanocytes, in which water circulates before exiting through the osculum.

osculum
Large opening protected by spicules, through which the sponge discharges water from the gastric cavity.

water flow
Choanocyte flagella allow water to move inside the sponge, carrying oxygen and food particles to it.

incurrent pore
Opening into the gastric cavity, through which water enters the sponge.

endoderm
Inner layer of the sponge formed of cells (choanocytes) whose role is mainly to feed the organism.

ectoderm
Outer layer of the sponge formed of cells (pinacocytes) whose role is mainly to protect the organism.

echinoderms

Marine invertebrates (currently more than 6,000 species) covered with calcareous plates; an ambulacral ossicle runs along the body, helping the organism to move, anchor itself to a support and capture its prey.

morphology of a starfish
Starfish: carnivorous echinoderm found in the ocean depths; it generally has five arms, which allow it to crawl slowly along surfaces.

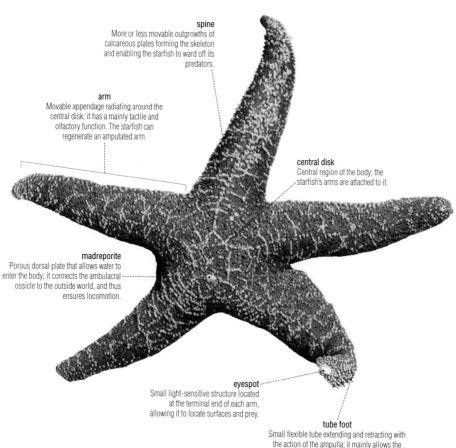

spine
More or less movable outgrowths of calcareous plates forming the skeleton and enabling the starfish to ward off its predators.

arm
Movable appendage radiating around the central disk; it has a mainly tactile and olfactory function. The starfish can regenerate an amputated arm.

central disk
Central region of the body; the starfish's arms are attached to it.

madreporite
Porous dorsal plate that allows water to enter the body; it connects the ambulacral ossicle to the outside world, and thus ensures locomotion.

eyespot
Small light-sensitive structure located at the terminal end of each arm, allowing it to locate surfaces and prey.

tube foot
Small flexible tube extending and retracting with the action of the ampulla; it mainly allows the organism to move about, anchor itself to a support and capture its prey.

butterfly

Adult insect having two pairs of wings and three pairs of legs; it emerges after the first three stages of metamorphosis: the egg, the caterpillar and the chrysalis.

morphology of a butterfly

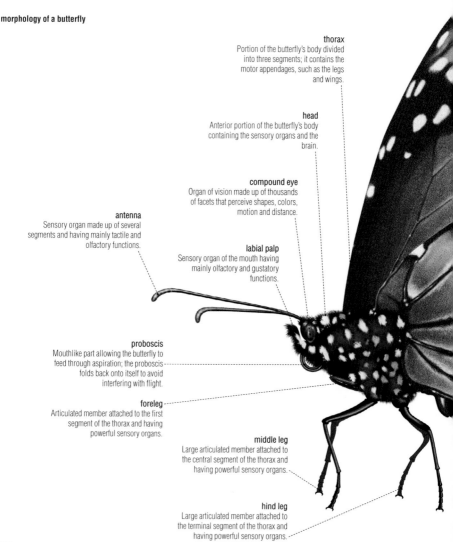

thorax
Portion of the butterfly's body divided into three segments; it contains the motor appendages, such as the legs and wings.

head
Anterior portion of the butterfly's body containing the sensory organs and the brain.

compound eye
Organ of vision made up of thousands of facets that perceive shapes, colors, motion and distance.

antenna
Sensory organ made up of several segments and having mainly tactile and olfactory functions.

labial palp
Sensory organ of the mouth having mainly olfactory and gustatory functions.

proboscis
Mouthlike part allowing the butterfly to feed through aspiration; the proboscis folds back onto itself to avoid interfering with flight.

foreleg
Articulated member attached to the first segment of the thorax and having powerful sensory organs.

middle leg
Large articulated member attached to the central segment of the thorax and having powerful sensory organs.

hind leg
Large articulated member attached to the terminal segment of the thorax and having powerful sensory organs.

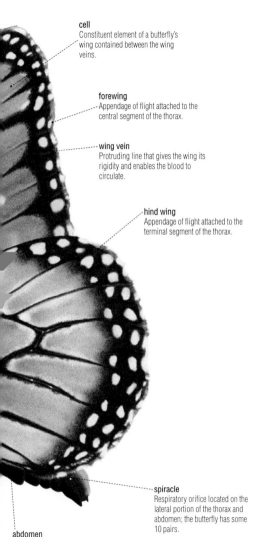

cell
Constituent element of a butterfly's wing contained between the wing veins.

forewing
Appendage of flight attached to the central segment of the thorax.

wing vein
Protruding line that gives the wing its rigidity and enables the blood to circulate.

hind wing
Appendage of flight attached to the terminal segment of the thorax.

hind leg
Large articulated member attached to the terminal segment of the thorax and having powerful sensory organs.

coxa
Anterior segment of the leg articulating with the thorax and the trochanter.

trochanter
Segment of the leg between the hip and the femur.

femur
Segment of the leg between the trochanter and the tibia.

tibia
Segment of the leg between the femur and the tarsus.

tarsus
Terminal segment of the leg, divided into five parts and having two claws.

spiracle
Respiratory orifice located on the lateral portion of the thorax and abdomen; the butterfly has some 10 pairs.

claw
Pointy fang-shaped structure attached to the tarsus and enabling the butterfly to cling to things and feed itself.

abdomen
Posterior portion of the butterfly's body made up of 10 segments and containing the major vital organs, such as the heart, the intestines and the genital organs.

ANIMAL KINGDOM

honeybee

Insect living in a highly complex social order; it instinctively produces honey as a food reserve.

morphology of a honeybee: worker

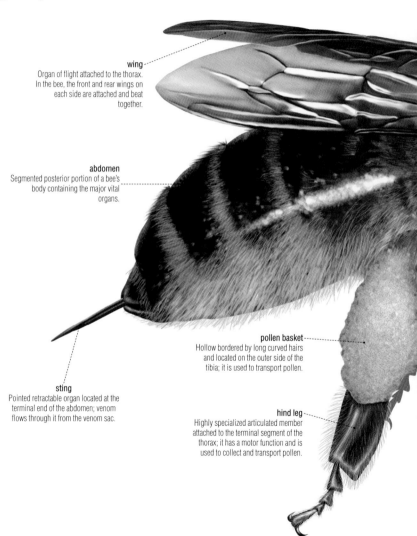

wing
Organ of flight attached to the thorax. In the bee, the front and rear wings on each side are attached and beat together.

abdomen
Segmented posterior portion of a bee's body containing the major vital organs.

pollen basket
Hollow bordered by long curved hairs and located on the outer side of the tibia; it is used to transport pollen.

sting
Pointed retractable organ located at the terminal end of the abdomen; venom flows through it from the venom sac.

hind leg
Highly specialized articulated member attached to the terminal segment of the thorax; it has a motor function and is used to collect and transport pollen.

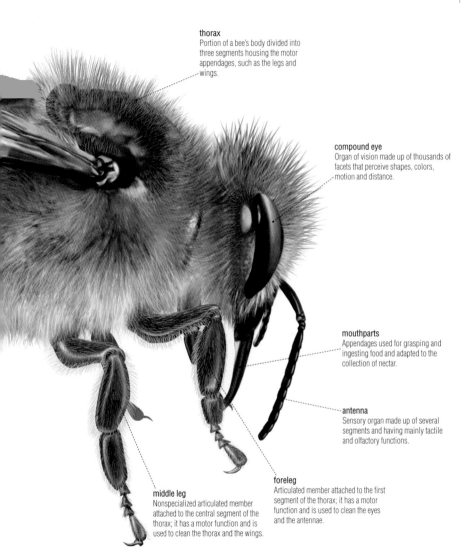

thorax
Portion of a bee's body divided into three segments housing the motor appendages, such as the legs and wings.

compound eye
Organ of vision made up of thousands of facets that perceive shapes, colors, motion and distance.

mouthparts
Appendages used for grasping and ingesting food and adapted to the collection of nectar.

antenna
Sensory organ made up of several segments and having mainly tactile and olfactory functions.

middle leg
Nonspecialized articulated member attached to the central segment of the thorax; it has a motor function and is used to clean the thorax and the wings.

foreleg
Articulated member attached to the first segment of the thorax; it has a motor function and is used to clean the eyes and the antennae.

ANIMAL KINGDOM

honeycomb section

honey cell
Cell in which workers store the honey
they produced as larva food and winter
reserves.

pupa
Intermediary stage between the larva
and the adult bee, lasting between four
and 10 days.

larva
Intermediary stage between the egg
and the pupa.

pollen cell
Cell in which workers store the pollen
used to feed the colony.

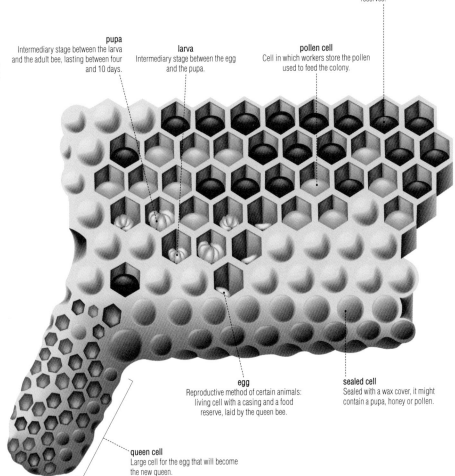

egg
Reproductive method of certain animals:
living cell with a casing and a food
reserve, laid by the queen bee.

sealed cell
Sealed with a wax cover, it might
contain a pupa, honey or pollen.

queen cell
Large cell for the egg that will become
the new queen.

examples of insects

Insects: invertebrates with bodies divided into three parts; they usually have three pairs of legs, two pairs of wings and antennae.

tsetse fly
Stinging African insect, a parasite of mammals, birds and humans; it is best known for transmitting sleeping sickness.

termite
Social insect that lives in hill colonies; it eats away at wood with its crushing mouthparts.

flea
Extremely small, wingless leaping insect, a parasite of certain mammals, birds and humans; it stings them to feed off their blood.

louse
Small wingless insect, a parasite of humans, mammals, birds and certain plants.

mosquito
Insect with two wings and long antennae; the female stings humans and animals to feed off their blood.

fly
Stocky insect of drab or metallic coloring and having a proboscis, two wings and short antennae; there are numerous species.

ant
Small social insect living in a highly complex colony; it has developed jaws and might or might not have wings. It consumes mainly insect pests.

furniture beetle
Small insect, common throughout Europe; its larva feeds on lumber and dead wood.

examples of insects

burying beetle
Insect that lays its eggs on dead animals or decomposing matter, which it buries; the egg cache gives off a strong musky smell.

ladybug
Brightly colored round-bodied insect that preys on aphids and mealybugs.

shield bug
Small flat-bodied land insect that stings and sucks, a parasite of humans, animals and plants; it releases an unpleasant odor as a defense.

horsefly
Large fly found in warm countries; the female stings animals and occasionally humans to feed off their blood.

hornet
Large wasp with a painful and dangerous sting; it feeds mainly on insects and fruit.

yellowjacket
Social insect; the female has a venomous sting that is painful.

bumblebee
Plump hairy insect related to the bee; it lives in colonies and produces honey.

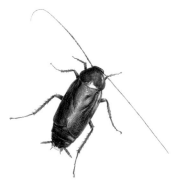

oriental cockroach
Scurrying flat-bodied nocturnal insect that is widely dispersed; some species live in human dwellings, feeding on waste matter. It emits an unpleasant odor.

cicada
Large sap-sucking insect; the male produces a shrill monotone sound in hot weather.

cockchafer
Common garden insect with fringed antennae; it eats leaves and tree roots. Infestations of this pest can cause serious damage.

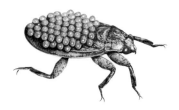

water bug
Large carnivorous insect with a lean flat body; it is widely dispersed and lives in aquatic environments.

bow-winged grasshopper
Hopping insect with short antennae and powerful hind legs; it lives especially in hot climates and emits an intense lively song.

great green bush-cricket
Carnivorous leaping insect with long antennae, growing to 1 to 2 in in length; the male produces a shrill sound.

mantid
Long-bodied carnivorous insect found in tropical regions and blending in with its surroundings; its pincer-shaped front legs have spines.

examples of insects

monarch butterfly
Large diurnal migratory butterfly with spotted wings; in North America, thousands of monarchs migrate southward in the autumn, sometimes more than 1,800 miles, and return north in spring.

peppered moth
Large butterfly with delicate wings, active at night or at dawn; its caterpillar lives in birch trees, causing major damage.

dragonfly
Long-bodied carnivorous insect found near water, having four rigid wings and the largest compound eyes of any insect.

water strider
Widespread carnivorous insect with a long thin body and six legs, of which the four longest help it to move across water.

atlas moth
Large nocturnal butterfly with colored wings and a wingspan that can reach more than 1 foot; it is found mainly in Southeast Asia.

ANIMAL KINGDOM

examples of arachnids

Arachnids: invertebrates usually with four pairs of legs and two pairs of appendages attached to their heads.

crab spider
Widespread small arachnid that moves sideways and has powerful front legs; it changes color to catch its prey.

garden spider
Arachnid with a bulging stomach that weaves large webs and is commonly found in fields and gardens; its various species can be found around the world.

water spider
Aquatic arachnid found in Eurasia; to live in the water, it weaves a kind of bell that it fills with air and carries along on the hairs of its abdomen.

tick
Extremely small arachnid, parasite of animals and occasionally humans; it can transmit infectious diseases.

scorpion
Relatively large carnivorous arachnid with spines, usually found on land; it has pincers and its abdomen ends in a tail with a poisonous sting.

red-kneed tarantula
Large hairy arachnid found in Mexico, having a painful but usually innocuous bite; it lives underground in a closed compartment or cocoon.

spider

Articulated arachnid with fangs and silk-producing glands; its body ranges in size from less than an inch to 3.5 in.

morphology of a spider

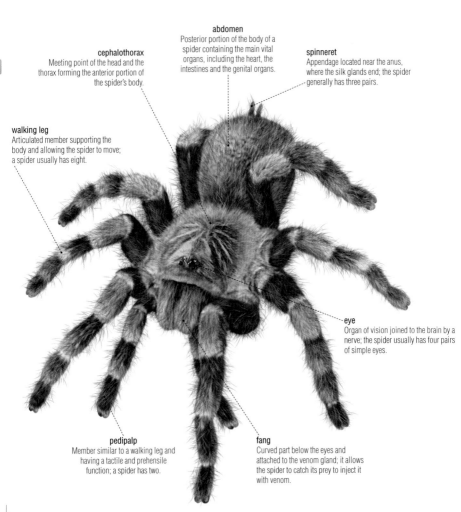

abdomen
Posterior portion of the body of a spider containing the main vital organs, including the heart, the intestines and the genital organs.

cephalothorax
Meeting point of the head and the thorax forming the anterior portion of the spider's body.

spinneret
Appendage located near the anus, where the silk glands end; the spider generally has three pairs.

walking leg
Articulated member supporting the body and allowing the spider to move; a spider usually has eight.

eye
Organ of vision joined to the brain by a nerve; the spider usually has four pairs of simple eyes.

pedipalp
Member similar to a walking leg and having a tactile and prehensile function; a spider has two.

fang
Curved part below the eyes and attached to the venom gland; it allows the spider to catch its prey to inject it with venom.

ANIMAL KINGDOM

spider web
Network of silk threads woven by a
spider; it solidifies in the air.

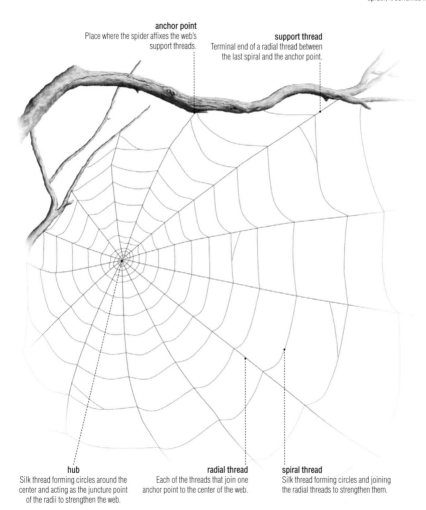

anchor point
Place where the spider affixes the web's
support threads.

support thread
Terminal end of a radial thread between
the last spiral and the anchor point.

ANIMAL KINGDOM

hub
Silk thread forming circles around the
center and acting as the juncture point
of the radii to strengthen the web.

radial thread
Each of the threads that join one
anchor point to the center of the web.

spiral thread
Silk thread forming circles and joining
the radial threads to strengthen them.

octopus

Carnivorous marine mollusk with a head bearing eight powerful arms covered with suckers; the octopus can change color to camouflage itself. Certain species are edible.

morphology of an octopus

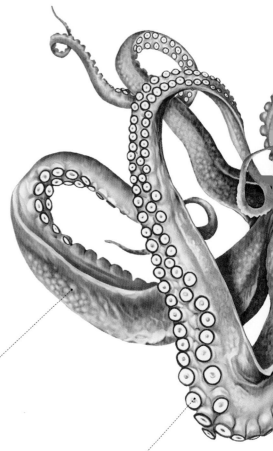

tentacle
Long powerful muscular appendage located around the mouth and used for locomotion and grasping.

sucker
Adhesive disk surrounded by a flexible ring located on the ventral surface of the tentacle and used for suction and anchoring.

eye
Developed organ of sight used to make out light intensity, motion, shapes and certain colors.

mantle
Thick fold of tissue enveloping the body of the octopus and secreting the shell, which is hidden inside.

siphon
Tubular muscular organ, conical at its opening at the dorsal mantle cavity; the octopus discharges water through it to move quickly and to oxygenate itself.

ANIMAL KINGDOM

lobster

Large marine crustacean having a carapace and five large pairs of legs, the first of which bears powerful claws; its meat is highly prized.

morphology of a lobster

ANIMAL KINGDOM

thoracic legs
Articulated limbs attached to the cephalothorax and having a prehensile and motor function; the first three legs bear pincer claws while the last two bear claws.

cephalothorax
Meeting of the head and the thorax that forms the anterior portion of the body of the lobster.

abdomen
Posterior portion of the body formed of six segments and bearing the pleopods, articulated appendages used for swimming, circulating water over the gills and holding the eggs.

telson
Terminal end of the body having no appendages; the anus is located on its ventral surface. It comprises the central part of the tail.

tail
Swimming organ formed of the telson and the two uropods.

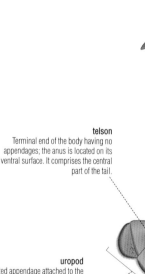

uropod
Articulated appendage attached to the last abdominal segment before the telson; it is formed of two lobes and helps the lobster to swim.

ANIMAL KINGDOM

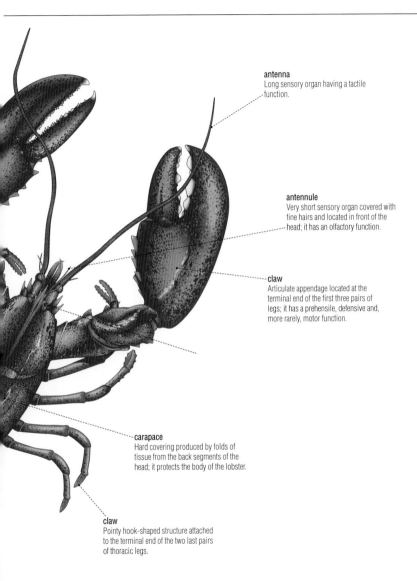

antenna
Long sensory organ having a tactile function.

antennule
Very short sensory organ covered with fine hairs and located in front of the head; it has an olfactory function.

claw
Articulate appendage located at the terminal end of the first three pairs of legs; it has a prehensile, defensive and, more rarely, motor function.

carapace
Hard covering produced by folds of tissue from the back segments of the head; it protects the body of the lobster.

claw
Pointy hook-shaped structure attached to the terminal end of the two last pairs of thoracic legs.

cartilaginous fish

Fish whose skeleton is made of cartilage rather than bone; its skin is covered in hard scales called denticles.
There are currently 700 species.

morphology of a shark

Shark: large cartilaginous carnivorous fish with a tapered body and
extremely powerful toothed jaws; it rarely attacks humans.

snout
Pointy anterior protruding portion of
the head located above the mouth and
bearing the nostrils on each side.

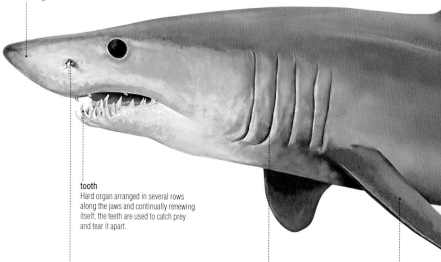

tooth
Hard organ arranged in several rows
along the jaws and continually renewing
itself; the teeth are used to catch prey
and tear it apart.

nostril
External orifice of the nasal cavity
located above the mouth with a highly
developed olfactory function.

gill slits
Respiratory organs (five pairs) shaped like
long narrows channels between the buccal
cavity and the outside of the body; the shark
uses them to circulate water.

pectoral fin
Swimming appendage made of firm
cartilage that ensures stability,
orientation, stopping and
thermoregulation.

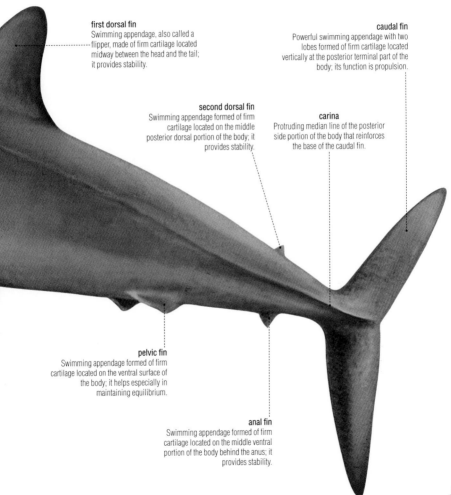

first dorsal fin
Swimming appendage, also called a flipper, made of firm cartilage located midway between the head and the tail; it provides stability.

caudal fin
Powerful swimming appendage with two lobes formed of firm cartilage located vertically at the posterior terminal part of the body; its function is propulsion.

second dorsal fin
Swimming appendage formed of firm cartilage located on the middle posterior dorsal portion of the body; it provides stability.

carina
Protruding median line of the posterior side portion of the body that reinforces the base of the caudal fin.

pelvic fin
Swimming appendage formed of firm cartilage located on the ventral surface of the body; it helps especially in maintaining equilibrium.

anal fin
Swimming appendage formed of firm cartilage located on the middle ventral portion of the body behind the anus; it provides stability.

ANIMAL KINGDOM

bony fish

Fish with a rigid skeleton and smooth flat scales; the 20,000 present-day species make up the largest group of fish.

morphology of a perch
Perch: bony carnivorous freshwater fish with an oval body and a spiny dorsal fin; its flesh is highly prized.

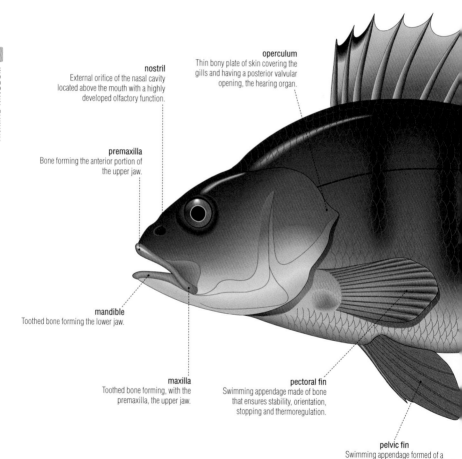

nostril
External orifice of the nasal cavity located above the mouth with a highly developed olfactory function.

operculum
Thin bony plate of skin covering the gills and having a posterior valvular opening, the hearing organ.

premaxilla
Bone forming the anterior portion of the upper jaw.

mandible
Toothed bone forming the lower jaw.

maxilla
Toothed bone forming, with the premaxilla, the upper jaw.

pectoral fin
Swimming appendage made of bone that ensures stability, orientation, stopping and thermoregulation.

pelvic fin
Swimming appendage formed of a membrane and rays located on the ventral surface of the body; it helps especially in maintaining equilibrium.

ANIMAL KINGDOM

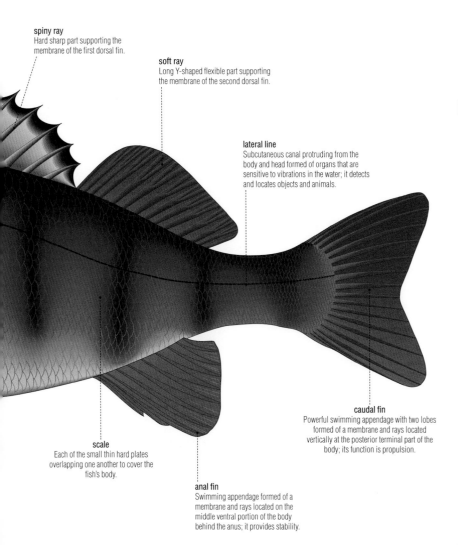

spiny ray
Hard sharp part supporting the membrane of the first dorsal fin.

soft ray
Long Y-shaped flexible part supporting the membrane of the second dorsal fin.

lateral line
Subcutaneous canal protruding from the body and head formed of organs that are sensitive to vibrations in the water; it detects and locates objects and animals.

caudal fin
Powerful swimming appendage with two lobes formed of a membrane and rays located vertically at the posterior terminal part of the body; its function is propulsion.

scale
Each of the small thin hard plates overlapping one another to cover the fish's body.

anal fin
Swimming appendage formed of a membrane and rays located on the middle ventral portion of the body behind the anus; it provides stability.

frog

Cold-blooded freshwater amphibian with smooth moist skin and powerful back legs for hopping and swimming.

morphology of a frog

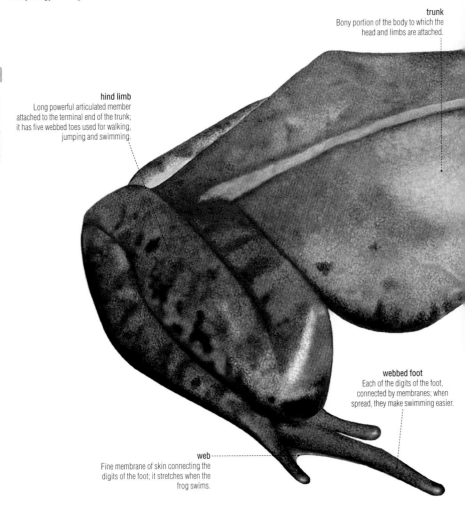

trunk
Bony portion of the body to which the head and limbs are attached.

hind limb
Long powerful articulated member attached to the terminal end of the trunk; it has five webbed toes used for walking, jumping and swimming.

webbed foot
Each of the digits of the foot, connected by membranes; when spread, they make swimming easier.

web
Fine membrane of skin connecting the digits of the foot; it stretches when the frog swims.

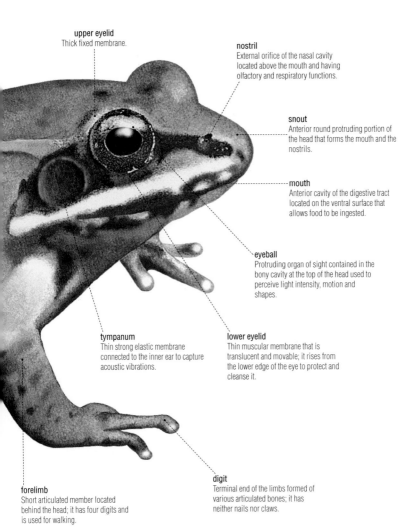

upper eyelid
Thick fixed membrane.

nostril
External orifice of the nasal cavity located above the mouth and having olfactory and respiratory functions.

snout
Anterior round protruding portion of the head that forms the mouth and the nostrils.

mouth
Anterior cavity of the digestive tract located on the ventral surface that allows food to be ingested.

eyeball
Protruding organ of sight contained in the bony cavity at the top of the head used to perceive light intensity, motion and shapes.

tympanum
Thin strong elastic membrane connected to the inner ear to capture acoustic vibrations.

lower eyelid
Thin muscular membrane that is translucent and movable; it rises from the lower edge of the eye to protect and cleanse it.

forelimb
Short articulated member located behind the head; it has four digits and is used for walking.

digit
Terminal end of the limbs formed of various articulated bones; it has neither nails nor claws.

ANIMAL KINGDOM

frog

ANIMAL KINGDOM

life cycle of the frog
The stages of development are the egg, the tadpole and the adult; each stage usually lasts several weeks, but can last up to two years in some species.

eggs
Embryonic stage of the frog resulting when the egg is fertilized by the sperm.

tadpole
Aquatic larva of the frog having a large head and a slender body ending in a tail; it breathes through gills.

external gills
Respiratory organs that filter water and take in food particles; they are later replaced by internal gills.

hind limb
The hind limbs appear after the gills.

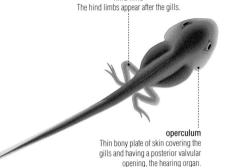

operculum
Thin bony plate of skin covering the gills and having a posterior valvular opening, the hearing organ.

forelimb
The forelimbs appear during the last stage of the tadpole's metamorphosis.

examples of amphibians

There are about 4,000 species of amphibians divided into three main groups, depending on whether or not they have a tail and limbs.

newt
Amphibian with a flat tail found mainly in freshwater and usually feeding on insects.

wood frog
Tailless amphibian found mostly in the woods of North America; it feeds on various small animals.

common toad
Tailless nocturnal insectivorous amphibian usually found on land and not very adept at jumping; its body is covered with small outgrowths.

tree frog
Small tailless, usually insectivorous amphibian found mostly in trees near water; its digits are fitted with suction cups.

common frog
Squat tailless amphibian usually found on land, mostly in Europe; it feeds on various small animals.

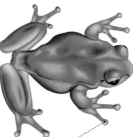

Northern leopard frog
Tailless, mostly nocturnal amphibian with a spotted body that is covered with ridges; it lives mainly in North America.

adhesive disk
Adhesive disk surrounded by a ring; it is located at the terminal end of the limbs and used for anchoring.

salamander
Nocturnal amphibian, mainly insectivorous, with a tail; there are land and aquatic species.

snake

Legless reptile with a very long cylindrical body and tail, moving by undulation; there are about 2,700 species.

ANIMAL KINGDOM

anatomy of a venomous snake

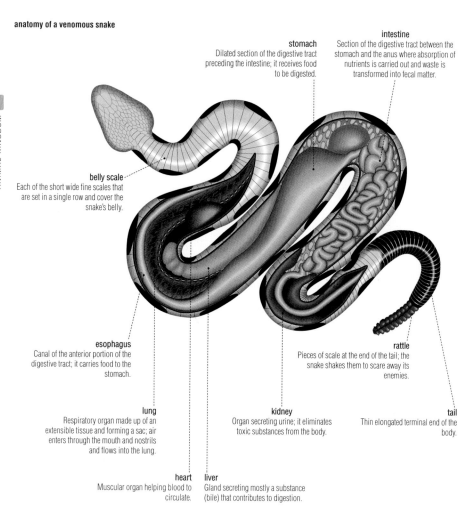

stomach
Dilated section of the digestive tract preceding the intestine; it receives food to be digested.

intestine
Section of the digestive tract between the stomach and the anus where absorption of nutrients is carried out and waste is transformed into fecal matter.

belly scale
Each of the short wide fine scales that are set in a single row and cover the snake's belly.

esophagus
Canal of the anterior portion of the digestive tract; it carries food to the stomach.

rattle
Pieces of scale at the end of the tail; the snake shakes them to scare away its enemies.

lung
Respiratory organ made up of an extensible tissue and forming a sac; air enters through the mouth and nostrils and flows into the lung.

kidney
Organ secreting urine; it eliminates toxic substances from the body.

tail
Thin elongated terminal end of the body.

heart
Muscular organ helping blood to circulate.

liver
Gland secreting mostly a substance (bile) that contributes to digestion.

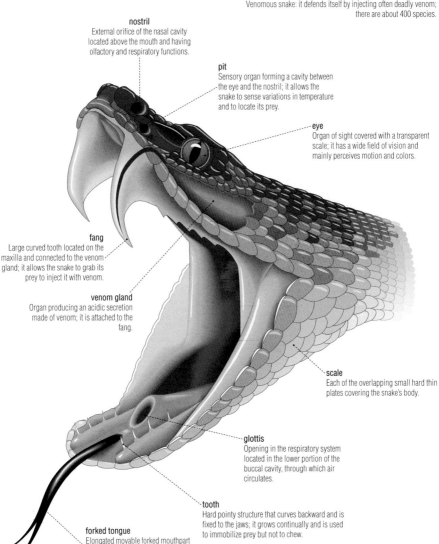

morphology of a venomous snake: head
Venomous snake: it defends itself by injecting often deadly venom; there are about 400 species.

nostril
External orifice of the nasal cavity located above the mouth and having olfactory and respiratory functions.

pit
Sensory organ forming a cavity between the eye and the nostril; it allows the snake to sense variations in temperature and to locate its prey.

eye
Organ of sight covered with a transparent scale; it has a wide field of vision and mainly perceives motion and colors.

fang
Large curved tooth located on the maxilla and connected to the venom gland; it allows the snake to grab its prey to inject it with venom.

venom gland
Organ producing an acidic secretion made of venom; it is attached to the fang.

scale
Each of the overlapping small hard thin plates covering the snake's body.

glottis
Opening in the respiratory system located in the lower portion of the buccal cavity, through which air circulates.

tooth
Hard pointy structure that curves backward and is fixed to the jaws; it grows continually and is used to immobilize prey but not to chew.

forked tongue
Elongated movable forked mouthpart having olfactory, tactile and gustatory functions; it is not used to ingest food.

turtle

Squat land or aquatic reptile with short legs and bearing a carapace into which it retracts; there are about 250 species.

morphology of a turtle

vertebral shield
Large corneous scales set in a row on the middle portion of the back shell.

eyelid
Each of the three movable muscular membranes protecting the anterior surface of the eye.

eye
Organ of sight located on the head and having poor vision; it can make out motion and colors.

horny beak
Thick cutaneous formation covering toothless jaws; its sharp edges allow the turtle to feed.

neck
Long flexible portion of the body covered in small scales; the turtle folds it back to retract its head into the carapace.

scale
Each of the small hard thin overlapping plates covering the body of the turtle.

claw
Slightly curved, rigid pointy structure; the forelegs have five while the hind legs have four.

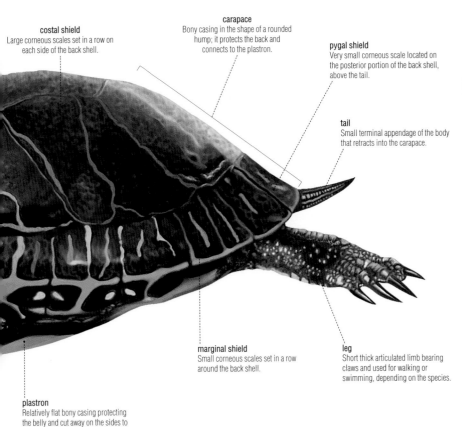

costal shield
Large corneous scales set in a row on each side of the back shell.

carapace
Bony casing in the shape of a rounded hump; it protects the back and connects to the plastron.

pygal shield
Very small corneous scale located on the posterior portion of the back shell, above the tail.

tail
Small terminal appendage of the body that retracts into the carapace.

marginal shield
Small corneous scales set in a row around the back shell.

leg
Short thick articulated limb bearing claws and used for walking or swimming, depending on the species.

plastron
Relatively flat bony casing protecting the belly and cut away on the sides to allow the legs to move.

ANIMAL KINGDOM

ANIMAL KINGDOM

anatomy of a turtle

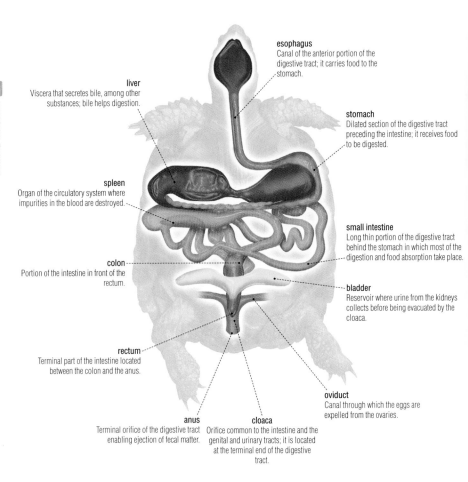

esophagus
Canal of the anterior portion of the digestive tract; it carries food to the stomach.

liver
Viscera that secretes bile, among other substances; bile helps digestion.

stomach
Dilated section of the digestive tract preceding the intestine; it receives food to be digested.

spleen
Organ of the circulatory system where impurities in the blood are destroyed.

small intestine
Long thin portion of the digestive tract behind the stomach in which most of the digestion and food absorption take place.

colon
Portion of the intestine in front of the rectum.

bladder
Reservoir where urine from the kidneys collects before being evacuated by the cloaca.

rectum
Terminal part of the intestine located between the colon and the anus.

oviduct
Canal through which the eggs are expelled from the ovaries.

anus
Terminal orifice of the digestive tract enabling ejection of fecal matter.

cloaca
Orifice common to the intestine and the genital and urinary tracts; it is located at the terminal end of the digestive tract.

examples of reptiles

Reptiles: cold-blooded vertebrates covered in scales (about 6,000 species) having limbs that are sometimes atrophied or absent.

viper
Venomous snake found in hot arid regions of Eurasia and Africa with a flat triangular head and short tail; its bite can be fatal.

cobra
Venomous snake found in tropical regions of Asia and Africa; it inflates its neck when threatened.

garter snake
Widespread nonvenomous snake with a slightly flat oval head; its tail is longer than that of the viper.

rattlesnake
Venomous land snake of the Americas; it rattles its scaly tail to warn off enemies.

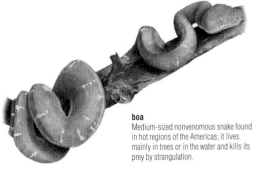

boa
Medium-sized nonvenomous snake found in hot regions of the Americas; it lives mainly in trees or in the water and kills its prey by strangulation.

ANIMAL KINGDOM

examples of reptiles

coral snake
Slender venomous snake of the
Americas living under rocks or hidden
in the ground; its bite can be fatal.

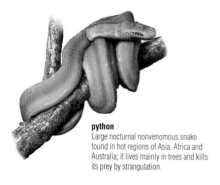

python
Large nocturnal nonvenomous snake
found in hot regions of Asia, Africa and
Australia; it lives mainly in trees and kills
its prey by strangulation.

lizard
Widespread diurnal and mainly
insectivorous land reptile with a long
brittle tail.

chameleon
Insectivorous lizard of Africa and India
with a prehensile tail; it lives in trees
and can change color to hide itself.

iguana
Giant lizard found in tropical regions of
the Americas and the Pacific islands
and having a spiny dorsal crest; it lives
mainly in trees.

monitor lizard
Large diurnal carnivorous lizard with an
elongated head found in hot regions of
Africa, Asia and Australia; there are land
and aquatic species.

alligator
Short-legged aquatic reptile found in
North America and China; its head is
shorter and wider than that of the
crocodile.

crocodile
Aquatic and land reptile found in hot
regions; it has an elongated head,
strong jaws, short legs and a powerful
tail.

caiman
Medium-sized aquatic reptile found in
Central and South America; it is less
aggressive than the crocodile and the
alligator.

bird

Vertebrate with a feather-covered body and a toothless bill; its forelimbs (wings) are usually adapted for flight.

morphology of a bird

wing
Flight appendage made of hollow bones and feathers, and comprising the forelimb; in some species, it is not adapted for flight.

back
Upper posterior portion of the body between the head and the tail.

upper tail covert
Short feather covering the upper portion of the base of the tail; it maintains the body's internal temperature.

rump
Posterior portion of the body formed by the last vertebrae and bearing the tail feathers.

tail feather
Long stiff tail feather carried on the rump; it controls direction during flight.

under tail covert
Short feather covering the lower portion of the base of the tail; it maintains the body's internal temperature.

flank
Lateral portion of the body between the wing and the abdomen.

thigh
Long bone fused to the fibula between the femur and the tarsus.

tarsus
Portion of the limb formed of long bones and covered in scales; it connects the tibia to the toes.

hind toe
First articulated toe of the foot, usually made of a single phalange and pointing toward the back; it is also called the thumb.

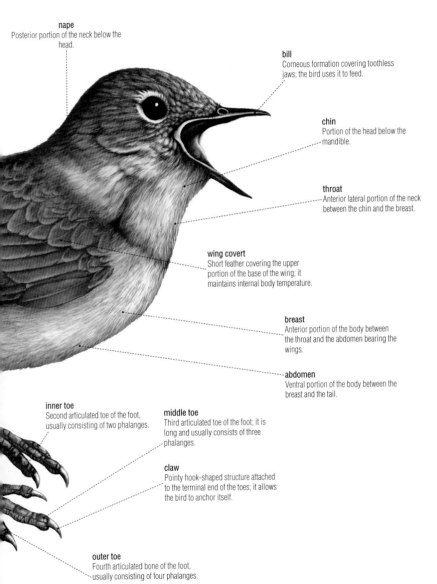

nape
Posterior portion of the neck below the head.

bill
Corneous formation covering toothless jaws; the bird uses it to feed.

chin
Portion of the head below the mandible.

throat
Anterior lateral portion of the neck between the chin and the breast.

wing covert
Short feather covering the upper portion of the base of the wing; it maintains internal body temperature.

breast
Anterior portion of the body between the throat and the abdomen bearing the wings.

abdomen
Ventral portion of the body between the breast and the tail.

inner toe
Second articulated toe of the foot, usually consisting of two phalanges.

middle toe
Third articulated toe of the foot; it is long and usually consists of three phalanges.

claw
Pointy hook-shaped structure attached to the terminal end of the toes; it allows the bird to anchor itself.

outer toe
Fourth articulated bone of the foot, usually consisting of four phalanges.

bird

ANIMAL KINGDOM

wing
Appendage of flight formed of hollow
bones and feathers, and comprising the
forelimb; in certain species, the wing is
not adapted for flight.

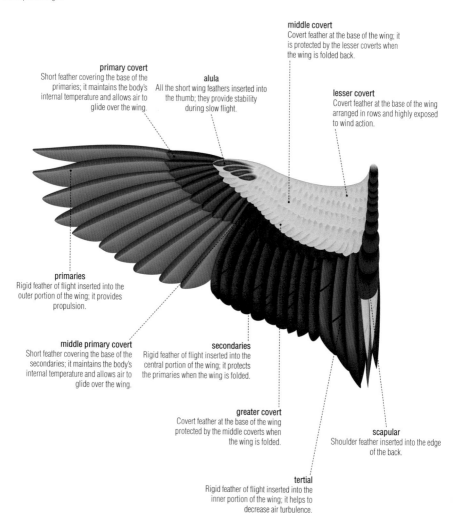

middle covert
Covert feather at the base of the wing; it
is protected by the lesser coverts when
the wing is folded back.

primary covert
Short feather covering the base of the
primaries; it maintains the body's
internal temperature and allows air to
glide over the wing.

alula
All the short wing feathers inserted into
the thumb; they provide stability
during slow flight.

lesser covert
Covert feather at the base of the wing
arranged in rows and highly exposed
to wind action.

primaries
Rigid feather of flight inserted into the
outer portion of the wing; it provides
propulsion.

middle primary covert
Short feather covering the base of the
secondaries; it maintains the body's
internal temperature and allows air to
glide over the wing.

secondaries
Rigid feather of flight inserted into the
central portion of the wing; it protects
the primaries when the wing is folded.

greater covert
Covert feather at the base of the wing
protected by the middle coverts when
the wing is folded.

scapular
Shoulder feather inserted into the edge
of the back.

tertial
Rigid feather of flight inserted into the
inner portion of the wing; it helps to
decrease air turbulence.

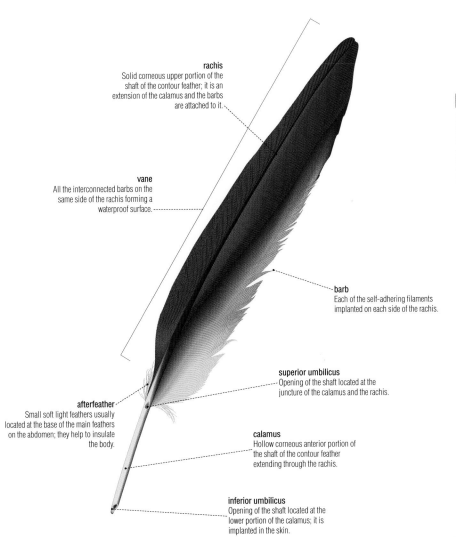

contour feather
Large rigid feather of the wings and tail enabling flight.

rachis
Solid corneous upper portion of the shaft of the contour feather; it is an extension of the calamus and the barbs are attached to it.

vane
All the interconnected barbs on the same side of the rachis forming a waterproof surface.

barb
Each of the self-adhering filaments implanted on each side of the rachis.

superior umbilicus
Opening of the shaft located at the juncture of the calamus and the rachis.

afterfeather
Small soft light feathers usually located at the base of the main feathers on the abdomen; they help to insulate the body.

calamus
Hollow corneous anterior portion of the shaft of the contour feather extending through the rachis.

inferior umbilicus
Opening of the shaft located at the lower portion of the calamus; it is implanted in the skin.

ANIMAL KINGDOM

ANIMAL KINGDOM

skeleton of a bird

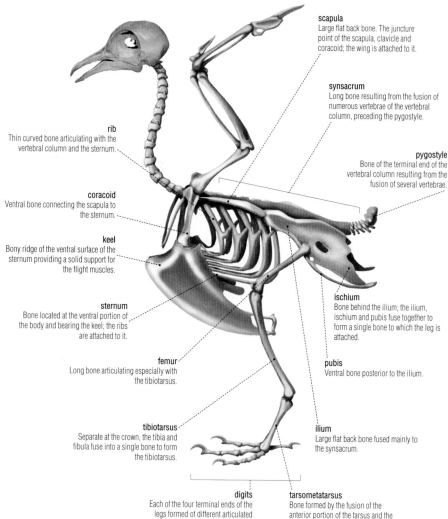

scapula
Large flat back bone. The juncture point of the scapula, clavicle and coracoid; the wing is attached to it.

synsacrum
Long bone resulting from the fusion of numerous vertebrae of the vertebral column, preceding the pygostyle.

pygostyle
Bone of the terminal end of the vertebral column resulting from the fusion of several vertebrae.

rib
Thin curved bone articulating with the vertebral column and the sternum.

coracoid
Ventral bone connecting the scapula to the sternum.

keel
Bony ridge of the ventral surface of the sternum providing a solid support for the flight muscles.

sternum
Bone located at the ventral portion of the body and bearing the keel; the ribs are attached to it.

ischium
Bone behind the ilium; the ilium, ischium and pubis fuse together to form a single bone to which the leg is attached.

femur
Long bone articulating especially with the tibiotarsus.

pubis
Ventral bone posterior to the ilium.

tibiotarsus
Separate at the crown, the tibia and fibula fuse into a single bone to form the tibiotarsus.

ilium
Large flat back bone fused mainly to the synsacrum.

digits
Each of the four terminal ends of the legs formed of different articulated bones called phalanges; most birds have four digits.

tarsometatarsus
Bone formed by the fusion of the anterior portion of the tarsus and the metatarsus; the digits articulate with it. It is also called the tarsus.

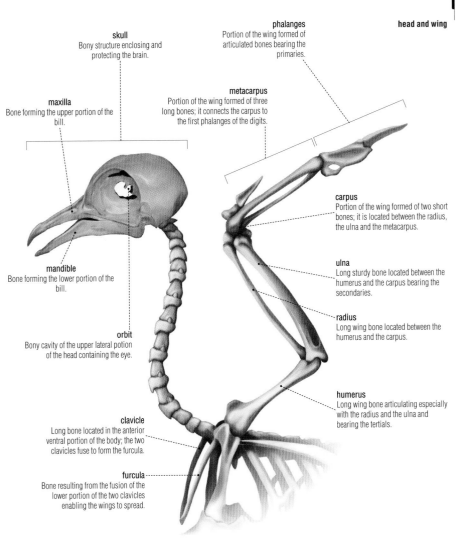

head and wing

skull
Bony structure enclosing and protecting the brain.

phalanges
Portion of the wing formed of articulated bones bearing the primaries.

maxilla
Bone forming the upper portion of the bill.

metacarpus
Portion of the wing formed of three long bones; it connects the carpus to the first phalanges of the digits.

carpus
Portion of the wing formed of two short bones; it is located between the radius, the ulna and the metacarpus.

mandible
Bone forming the lower portion of the bill.

ulna
Long sturdy bone located between the humerus and the carpus bearing the secondaries.

radius
Long wing bone located between the humerus and the carpus.

orbit
Bony cavity of the upper lateral potion of the head containing the eye.

humerus
Long wing bone articulating especially with the radius and the ulna and bearing the tertials.

clavicle
Long bone located in the anterior ventral portion of the body; the two clavicles fuse to form the furcula.

furcula
Bone resulting from the fusion of the lower portion of the two clavicles enabling the wings to spread.

ANIMAL KINGDOM

bird

ANIMAL KINGDOM

examples of bills

A bill's shape is characteristic of the lifestyle of the bird species. Its main function is to allow the bird to feed, to construct its nest and to defend itself.

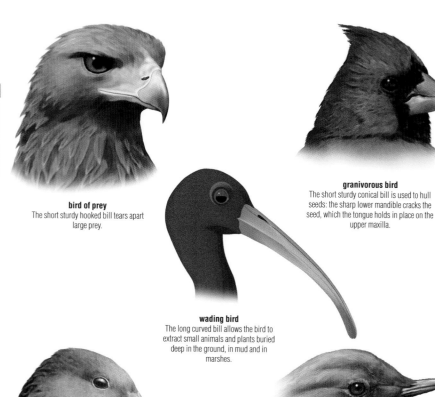

bird of prey
The short sturdy hooked bill tears apart large prey.

granivorous bird
The short sturdy conical bill is used to hull seeds: the sharp lower mandible cracks the seed, which the tongue holds in place on the upper maxilla.

wading bird
The long curved bill allows the bird to extract small animals and plants buried deep in the ground, in mud and in marshes.

aquatic bird
The large flat bill, with corneous lateral plates, filters water and mud to extract food.

insectivorous bird
The long thin pointed bill allows the bird to catch insects in flight.

There are more than 9,000 species of birds scattered around the world.

hummingbird
Tiny brightly colored bird with a long thin bill found on the North American continent; it can hover and fly backward.

finch
Widespread bird with a melodious song.

sparrow
Bird that feeds mainly on seeds and insects; it is widespread in cities and in the countryside.

European robin
European perching bird found in woods and gardens characterized by a bright red throat and chest and emitting a fairly loud, lively melodious song.

kingfisher
Colorful fish-eating bird that spends most of its time perched by the water's edge.

swallow
Widespread in the Northern hemisphere and found in highly diverse habitats; it usually feeds on insects caught in flight.

goldfinch
Brightly plumed songbird feeding mainly on the seeds of the thistle.

examples of birds

magpie
Noisy omnivore found in trees and
bushes in temperate regions of the
Northern hemisphere.

starling
Straight-billed omnivorous bird with
dark plumage; it lives in trees.

swift
Widespread and very swift insectivore;
it is usually airborne since its toes
make it difficult to perch.

oystercatcher
Swift long-billed bird found in Eurasia;
it feeds mainly on shellfish.

raven
Strong-billed scavenger with usually
black plumage; it sometimes damages
crops.

nightingale
Bird with a melodious song that feeds
on insects and fruit; it is found in the
bushes of forests and parks.

jay
Usually noisy, brightly colored bird
found in forests; it feeds mainly on fruit
and insects.

northern saw-whet owl
Nocturnal bird of prey found in the
forests of North America.

tern
Widespread web-footed aquatic bird
with long wings and a forked tail; it
dives for the fish it feeds on.

lapwing
Mainly insectivorous bird found in the
wetlands and marshes of Eurasia and
Africa; it has a tuft of upright feathers
on its head.

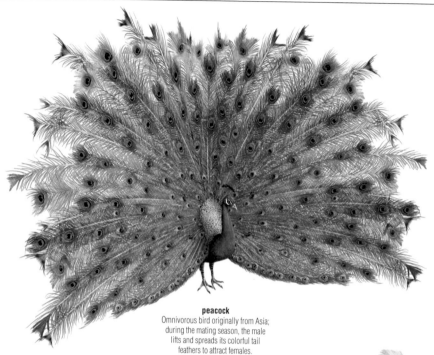

peacock
Omnivorous bird originally from Asia;
during the mating season, the male
lifts and spreads its colorful tail
feathers to attract females.

albatross
Web-footed aquatic bird of the south
seas; its wingspan can reach 10 ft,
allowing it to glide for hours.

toucan
Large yet gentle bird found in the
forests of the Americas; its dentate bill
allows it to feed especially on fruits
and insects.

heron
Widespread wading bird found in
shallow waters and marshes, mostly
piscivorous, with a neck that folds into
an S when it is at rest.

ANIMAL KINGDOM

penguin
Piscivorous marine bird living in colonies in the Southern hemisphere; it has webbed feet and wings that have evolved into fins.

pelican
Web-footed bird with a lower jaw featuring an extensible pouch for catching fish.

ostrich
Flightless bird of Africa reaching over 7 ft in height, with powerful two-toed legs; it is raised for its feathers and meat.

stork
Wading bird found in marshes and fields; two species are threatened with extinction.

flamingo
Bird with webbed feet and usually pink plumage living in colonies in brackish or salt water; it feeds by filtering water through its bill.

examples of birds

condor
Diurnal scavenger of the Americas, with a bald head and neck; one California species is facing extinction.

vulture
Diurnal raptor of the Americas and Eurasia, mainly a scavenger, with a bald head and neck, powerful beak and weak talons.

eagle
Widely prevalent raptor with piercing eyes, a hooked beak and sharp talons allowing it to catch live prey.

great horned owl
Nocturnal raptor found in the forests of North America, with a protruding tuft of feathers on each side of its head.

falcon
Diurnal bird of prey with piercing eyes and powerful talons and beak; it captures its prey in flight and is sometimes trained to hunt.

guinea fowl
Wild terrestrial bird with a bald head and horned comb originally from Africa and domesticated in Europe for its meat.

chick
Newly hatched bird covered in down.

rooster
Domestic bird (male of the hen) with a large serrated comb and a long-plumed tail.

hen
Domestic fowl (female of the rooster) with a small serrated comb raised in captivity for its eggs and meat.

turkey
Bird originating in the Americas with a bald head and neck covered with outgrowths; it is raised in captivity for its meat.

ANIMAL KINGDOM

examples of birds

pheasant
Bird originally from Asia and characterized by its long tail; its meat is highly prized. Certain pheasants are raised solely for hunting.

pigeon
Generally grain-eating bird prized for its meat and its keen sense of direction (carrier pigeon).

quail
Bird found in fields and meadows and much prized as game; certain species are domesticated.

goose
Web-footed bird of the Northern hemisphere better adapted to land than water; certain species are raised mainly for the production of foie gras.

duck
Web-footed aquatic bird spending most of its time on water; the domestic duck is raised for its meat and for the production of foie gras.

bullfinch
Red-breasted bird found in the woods and parks of Eurasia and the Americas; it feeds mainly on seeds and insects.

cardinal
Brightly colored bird with a tuft of upright feathers on its head; it is found mostly in North American woods and gardens.

partridge
Land-based bird that flies with difficulty.

ANIMAL KINGDOM

cockatoo
Noisy perching bird with drab plumage and a tuft of upright feathers on its head, found mainly in Australia; it can mimic human speech.

woodpecker
Widespread insectivore that pecks at the bark of trees to find food and to nest.

macaw
Noisy brightly colored perching bird found in the tropical forests of the Americas; it feeds mainly on seeds and fruit.

examples of rodents

ANIMAL KINGDOM

hamster
Rodent of the Eurasian steppes
sometimes domesticated and used for
laboratory experiments; it stores its food
in its cheek pouches.

chipmunk
Small, mainly vegetarian North
American rodent found in hardwood
forests and bushes.

jerboa
Rodent found in the deserts of Asia and
Africa adapted for hopping and able to
survive without drinking water.

guinea pig
Rodent originating in South America,
sometimes domesticated but mainly
used in laboratory experiments.

field mouse
Rodent found in woods and fields; it
moves about by hopping and can
cause serious crop damage.

rat
Omnivorous rodent characterized by its intelligence; it can transmit certain viruses and bacteria to humans. Some species are domesticated.

groundhog
Rodent of the Northern hemisphere prized for its fur; it hibernates six months a year and emits a high-pitched whistle when in danger.

squirrel
Mostly vegetarian rodent found in woods and forests around the world, except in Australia; some squirrels move about by gliding from tree to tree.

beaver
Amphibious rodent found in Eurasia and North America prized for its fur; it uses branches to build lodges and dams in streams.

porcupine
Rodent found on land and in trees in warm and temperate regions; its body is covered with long sharp quills, which it raises to defend itself.

examples of lagomorphs

Lagomorphs: small four-legged herbivorous vertebrates (about 60 species) with dense fur, a short or absent tail and three pairs of incisors.

pika
Tailless lagomorph living in the wild in the mountains of Central Asia and North America.

rabbit
Widespread and extremely prolific lagomorph living in the wild in burrows; it is also raised for its meat and fur.

hare
Widespread lagomorph with strong hind limbs adapted for swift running; it lives in the wild and is valued especially for its meat.

mole
Insectivorous mammal (about 20 species) found in Eurasia and the Americas; it digs underground tunnels with its front limbs to reach its food.

ANIMAL KINGDOM

hedgehog
Insectivorous mammal of Eurasia (about 10 species) with a body usually covered with stiff hairs or barbs, which stand on end when it rolls itself into a ball for protection.

shrew
Widespread insectivorous mammal (about 200 species); it occasionally digs tunnels and emits a fetid secretion for protection.

horse

Maned ungulate mammal domesticated for riding and for use as a draft animal.

morphology of a horse

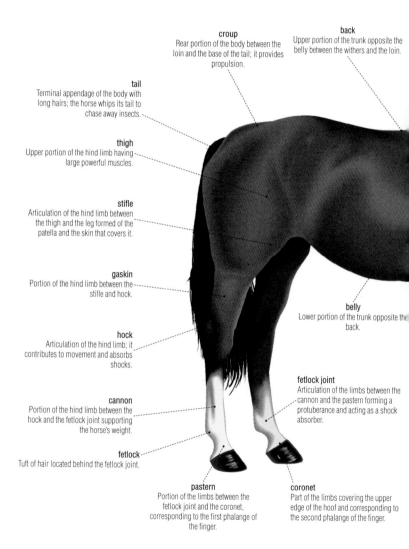

croup
Rear portion of the body between the loin and the base of the tail; it provides propulsion.

back
Upper portion of the trunk opposite the belly between the withers and the loin.

tail
Terminal appendage of the body with long hairs; the horse whips its tail to chase away insects.

thigh
Upper portion of the hind limb having large powerful muscles.

stifle
Articulation of the hind limb between the thigh and the leg formed of the patella and the skin that covers it.

gaskin
Portion of the hind limb between the stifle and hock.

belly
Lower portion of the trunk opposite the back.

hock
Articulation of the hind limb; it contributes to movement and absorbs shocks.

fetlock joint
Articulation of the limbs between the cannon and the pastern forming a protuberance and acting as a shock absorber.

cannon
Portion of the hind limb between the hock and the fetlock joint supporting the horse's weight.

fetlock
Tuft of hair located behind the fetlock joint.

pastern
Portion of the limbs between the fetlock joint and the coronet, corresponding to the first phalange of the finger.

coronet
Part of the limbs covering the upper edge of the hoof and corresponding to the second phalange of the finger.

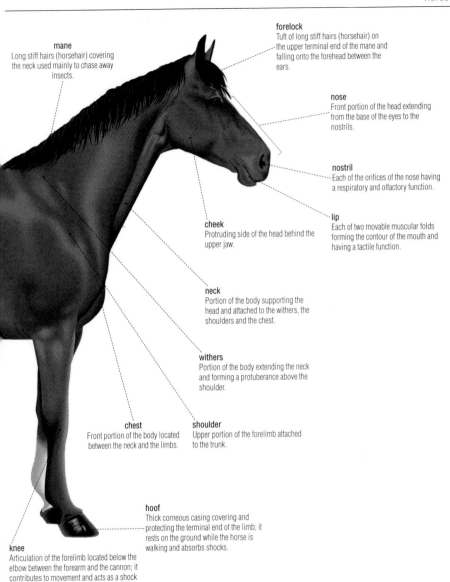

forelock
Tuft of long stiff hairs (horsehair) on the upper terminal end of the mane and falling onto the forehead between the ears.

mane
Long stiff hairs (horsehair) covering the neck used mainly to chase away insects.

nose
Front portion of the head extending from the base of the eyes to the nostrils.

nostril
Each of the orifices of the nose having a respiratory and olfactory function.

cheek
Protruding side of the head behind the upper jaw.

lip
Each of two movable muscular folds forming the contour of the mouth and having a tactile function.

neck
Portion of the body supporting the head and attached to the withers, the shoulders and the chest.

withers
Portion of the body extending the neck and forming a protuberance above the shoulder.

chest
Front portion of the body located between the neck and the limbs.

shoulder
Upper portion of the forelimb attached to the trunk.

hoof
Thick corneous casing covering and protecting the terminal end of the limb; it rests on the ground while the horse is walking and absorbs shocks.

knee
Articulation of the forelimb located below the elbow between the forearm and the cannon; it contributes to movement and acts as a shock absorber.

examples of ungulate mammals

There are many species of ungulate mammals; some are wild, some are domesticated and some are both.

peccary
Wild ungulate found in the forests of
the Americas having a dorsal gland
that emits a nauseous secretion; it is
prized for its hide.

wild boar
Wild ungulate found in forests and
marshes with sharp canines that it uses
to defend itself; it is hunted for its hide.

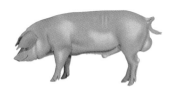

pig
Domestic omnivororous ungulate raised
mainly for its meat and its hide.

sheep
Ungulate ruminant covered with a thick
wooly coat domesticated for its milk,
meat and wool.

antelope
Ungulate ruminant with hollow horns
found throughout Africa and Asia; it
runs very fast and is prized for its meat
and hide.

mouflon
Extremely agile ungulate ruminant
found in the wild in mountainous
regions.

ass
Wild maned ungulate originally from
Africa domesticated as a pack animal.

mule
Sterile male, a cross between an ass
and a mare (female of the horse); it is
very hardy and can carry heavy loads.

ANIMAL KINGDOM

ox
Castrated bovine (male of the cow) domesticated for its meat and sometimes used as a draft animal.

cow
Ungulate ruminant with horns (female of the bull); it is raised for its milk and meat, and for reproduction.

goat
Ungulate ruminant with hollow horns able to jump and climb; it is domesticated for its milk and meat.

calf
Baby cow, male or female, up to the age of one year raised for its meat.

zebra
Maned ungulate that runs very fast; it is found in herds in the forests and steppes of Africa.

horse
Maned ungulate mammal domesticated for riding and for use as a draft animal.

examples of ungulate mammals

caribou
Ungulate ruminant found in cold regions of
the Northern hemisphere; it is raised in
captivity by some peoples for its meat, hide
and milk, and as a draft animal.

white-tailed deer
Wild ungulate ruminant of North America; it
runs very fast and is highly prized as game.

elk
Wild ungulate ruminant of Canada; a
good swimmer and runner, it is prized
for its meat and antlers and is
sometimes raised in captivity.

buffalo
Ungulate ruminant found in the tropical
regions of Africa and Asia; it is wild or
raised in captivity for its meat and milk,
and as a draft animal.

llama
Ungulate ruminant found in the
mountains of South America; it can be
wild or domesticated and is highly
prized for its wool.

okapi
Ungulate ruminant of Africa with an
extensible and prehensile tongue; only
the male has small horns.

dromedary camel
Single-humped ruminant ungulate of
Africa adapted to arid climates; it is
used especially as a pack animal and
for riding.

bactrian camel
Two-humped ruminant ungulate of Asia
adapted to arid climates; it is
domesticated especially for its meat, milk
and hide, and as a pack animal.

bison
Ungulate ruminant of North America
and Europe, usually wild, sometimes
raised for its meat.

yak
Ruminant ungulate of Central Asia
domesticated in Tibet for its milk and
its hide, and as a pack animal.

moose
Ruminant ungulate found in the cold regions of
the Northern hemisphere with wide hooves that
allow it to wade through marshes and ponds.

examples of ungulate mammals

rhinoceros
Ungulate found in the savannas and marshy areas of Africa and Asia with a one-horned or two-horned muzzle; it is threatened with extinction.

giraffe
Ruminant ungulate found in African savannas that can reach 23 feet in height; it has a prehensile tongue and small horns.

hippopotamus
Amphibious ungulate of Africa that can weigh up to 6 tons; it defends itself with its canine teeth, which grow constantly.

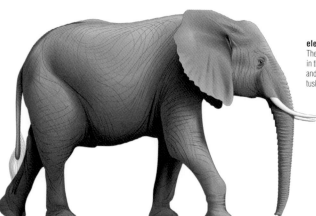

elephant
The largest land mammal today, found in the forests and savannas of Africa and Asia; it is hunted for its ivory tusks.

dog

Carnivorous mammal with an excellent sense of smell; it has been domesticated since prehistoric times and trained to perform a number of tasks: guarding and protecting, detecting, carrying and hunting.

dog's forepaw
Articulated limb ending in four toes allowing the dog to move about, dig and scratch.

claw
Nonretractable corneous structure that is not very sharp; the dog digs with it and it provides stability and grip.

digital pad
Thick cutaneous bulge, elastic and resistant to wear upon which the toe rests; it contributes to locomotion and absorbs shocks.

toe
Terminal end of the limb supporting the body; it is formed of various articulated bones and ends in a claw.

dewclaw
Pointy corneous appendage, the remnant of a thumb; it does not touch the ground and is often absent on the hind limb.

palmar pad
Thick cutaneous bulge, elastic and resistant to wear supporting the metacarpus; the dog uses it to move about and it absorbs shocks.

dew pad
Thick elastic cutaneous bulge located at the base of the dewclaw; it does not touch the ground.

carpal pad
Thick cutaneous bulge, elastic and resistant to wear; it does not touch the ground but prevents the dog from sliding as it lands after a jump.

ANIMAL KINGDOM

223

dog

morphology of a dog

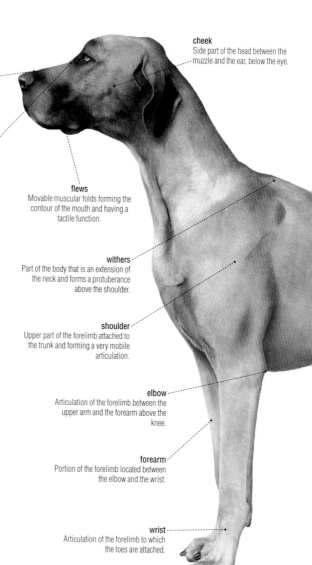

cheek
Side part of the head between the
muzzle and the ear, below the eye.

muzzle
Elongated front part of the head usually
covered with sensory hairs (mustaches) that
has a highly developed tactile and olfactory
function.

stop
Part between the top of the head and
the muzzle.

flews
Movable muscular folds forming the
contour of the mouth and having a
tactile function.

withers
Part of the body that is an extension of
the neck and forms a protuberance
above the shoulder.

shoulder
Upper part of the forelimb attached to
the trunk and forming a very mobile
articulation.

elbow
Articulation of the forelimb between the
upper arm and the forearm above the
knee.

forearm
Portion of the forelimb located between
the elbow and the wrist.

wrist
Articulation of the forelimb to which
the toes are attached.

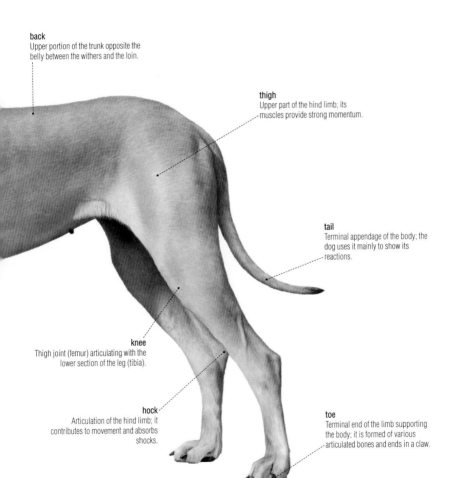

back
Upper portion of the trunk opposite the belly between the withers and the loin.

thigh
Upper part of the hind limb; its muscles provide strong momentum.

tail
Terminal appendage of the body; the dog uses it mainly to show its reactions.

knee
Thigh joint (femur) articulating with the lower section of the leg (tibia).

hock
Articulation of the hind limb; it contributes to movement and absorbs shocks.

toe
Terminal end of the limb supporting the body; it is formed of various articulated bones and ends in a claw.

cat

Carnivorous mammal with a supple muscular body and paws ending in retractable claws; it is a very common pet.

cat's head
Anterior portion of the body containing the main sensory organs and the brain.

pupil
Central opening of the eye where light enters; it is particularly well adapted to the dark.

eyelashes
Hairs implanted on the free edge of the eyelid preventing dust and other particles from landing on the eye.

whiskers
Highly sensitive long stiff hairs located above the eyes and having a tactile function.

upper eyelid
Thin muscular membrane lowering from the upper edge of the eye to protect and clean it.

lower eyelid
Thin muscular membrane that is translucent and movable; it rises from the lower edge of the eye to protect and cleanse it.

nictitating membrane
Thin muscular membrane extending sideways from the inside corner of the eye to protect and moisten it.

whiskers
Extremely sensitive long stiff hairs (vibrissae) located on the muzzle having a tactile function.

nose leather
Terminal end of the muzzle bearing the nostrils made of strong damp tissue; it has an olfactory and respiratory function.

muzzle
Short round front part of the head with whiskers; it has a highly developed tactile and olfactory function.

lip
Movable muscular part forming the contour of the mouth; a cat has two upper lips lined with whiskers.

morphology of a cat

eye
Organ of sight especially adapted to darkness; it mainly perceives light intensity, motion and certain colors.

ear
Highly mobile organ of hearing, also contributing to equilibrium; cats have a highly developed sense of hearing.

tail
Terminal appendage of the body providing equilibrium when the cat jumps.

fur
Hair covering the body, mainly for maintaining internal body temperature and providing protection from insect bites.

ANIMAL KINGDOM

examples of carnivorous mammals

Carnivorous mammals (about 270 species) that have strong canines (fangs) and sharp molars (carnassials) adapted for eating flesh.

ANIMAL KINGDOM

weasel
Very agile carnivorous mammal common in Eurasia; it is capable of attacking large prey (rats, voles, rabbits) in spite of its size.

mink
Carnivorous amphibious and mostly nocturnal mammal with webbed feet found in Eurasia and the Americas; it is hunted and raised in captivity for its highly prized fur.

stone marten
Mostly nocturnal carnivorous mammal of Eurasia; it is a good swimmer and climber and often catches fowl, domestic rabbits and rats.

fox
Very common carnivorous mammal living in a den and hunting at night (mostly rodents); its fur is highly prized.

fennec
Nocturnal carnivorous mammal found in the deserts of Arabia and North Africa; it is easily tamed and capable of going without water for long periods.

mongoose
Very agile carnivorous mammal of Africa and Asia; it is easily tamed and is used to destroy harmful pests (snakes, rats).

ANIMAL KINGDOM

badger
Mostly nocturnal carnivorous mammal of the Northern hemisphere digging complex tunnels; its hairs are used to make hairbrushes and paintbrushes.

marten
Mostly nocturnal agile carnivorous mammal of Eurasia and North America prized for its silky fur; it is a good climber.

river otter
Widespread carnivorous amphibious and usually nocturnal mammal with webbed feet feeding mainly on fish and prized for its fur.

raccoon
Mostly nocturnal carnivorous mammal of the Americas.

skunk
Carnivorous mammal of the Americas, whose fur is prized; when threatened, it releases a nauseous and irritating secretion from its anal glands.

examples of carnivorous mammals

ANIMAL KINGDOM

hyena
Carnivorous scavenger of Africa and
Asia; hyenas live alone or in packs and
will attack live prey.

lynx
Very agile and powerful carnivorous mammal
found in the forests of the Northern hemisphere;
it is a night hunter with piercing eyes and its fur
is highly prized.

cougar
Carnivorous mammal of the Americas
living in various habitats (mountains,
forests); it hunts only at night and is
famed for its ability to leap.

lion
Large carnivorous mammal common
mainly in Africa that lives in groups
called prides; only the male has a
mane.

cheetah
Carnivorous mammal of Africa and the Middle East with nonretractable claws; it is the fastest of the land mammals, reaching speeds of 62 mph.

leopard
Carnivorous mammal of Africa and Asia with yellow fur and black spots; it mostly lives in trees and usually hunts at night.

ANIMAL KINGDOM

jaguar
Carnivorous mammal of Central and South America with spotted fur; it is an excellent swimmer and hunts at night.

tiger
Large and very powerful carnivorous mammal of Asia; it hunts at night.

examples of carnivorous mammals

ANIMAL KINGDOM

wolf
Nocturnal carnivorous mammal of
Eurasia and North America; it lives in
packs and hunts large mammals
(deer).

black bear
Mostly nocturnal carnivorous mammal of
North America; it is a good swimmer, is an
excellent climber and feeds mainly on fruit
and nuts.

polar bear
Carnivorous mammal of arctic regions; a
good swimmer, it feeds mainly on seals
and fish, and is the largest carnivorous
land mammal.

examples of marine mammals

Marine mammals: many actively hunted species (more than 110 out of 116) are protected or are subject to hunting restrictions.

killer whale
Widespread swift aggressive marine mammal reaching up to 30 feet in length; it attacks mainly young whales and dolphins.

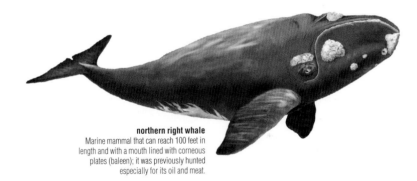

northern right whale
Marine mammal that can reach 100 feet in length and with a mouth lined with corneous plates (baleen); it was previously hunted especially for its oil and meat.

sperm whale
Mammal found in tropical and subtropical waters reaching up to 65 feet in length; hunted mainly for its meat and blubber, it is now a protected species.

examples of marine mammals

ANIMAL KINGDOM

sea lion
Amphibious marine mammal with external ear flaps that moves about on land with the help of its four limbs; it is hunted mainly for its fur.

walrus
Amphibious marine mammal of arctic regions; it is hunted for its hide, blubber and ivory tusks.

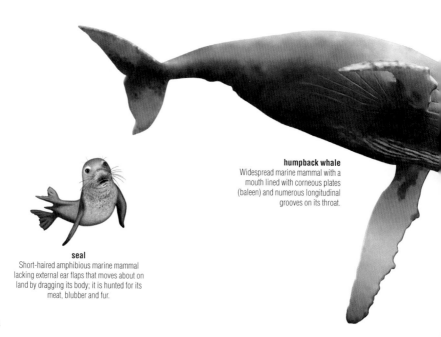

seal
Short-haired amphibious marine mammal lacking external ear flaps that moves about on land by dragging its body; it is hunted for its meat, blubber and fur.

humpback whale
Widespread marine mammal with a mouth lined with corneous plates (baleen) and numerous longitudinal grooves on its throat.

porpoise
Mammal found in cold and temperate waters whose flesh is highly prized; it is a protected species.

dolphin
Mammal of warm and temperate waters famed for its intelligence; it is a swift swimmer (about 28 mph).

narwhal
Mammal of arctic waters; the male, whose spiraled tusk can reach 10 feet in length, is hunted for its ivory.

beluga whale
Marine mammal of the polar and subarctic regions emitting various whistles to communicate, hence its nickname "sea canary".

examples of primates

Many species are protected, especially because of deforestation (destruction of their habitat) and hunting.

tamarin
Small hopping primate of South America with elongated claws instead of nails that allow it to move about and to feed.

baboon
Mainly terrestrial African primate with colored ischial callosities and large cheek pouches in which it stores food.

orangutan
Primate found in Sumatra and Borneo with long powerful arms; it moves slowly and carefully between the trees in which it lives.

macaque
Common primate of Asia with a nonprehensile tail living on the ground and in trees; it is often used for laboratory experiments.

marmoset
Small South American primate with strong claws instead of nails that it uses to cling to the trees it lives in.

lemur
Tree-dwelling agile primate of Madagascar with a long tail; it is mainly nocturnal and feeds on insects and fruit.

chimpanzee
Primate of equatorial Africa whose genetic makeup is very close to that of humans; it is used mainly in medical research.

gibbon
Tailless tree-dwelling primate of Asia; it swings from branch to branch with agility, using its hands as hooks.

gorilla

Mainly terrestrial vegetarian primate of the equatorial forests of Africa; the largest of the primates, it can reach 7 feet in height.

morphology of a gorilla

ANIMAL KINGDOM

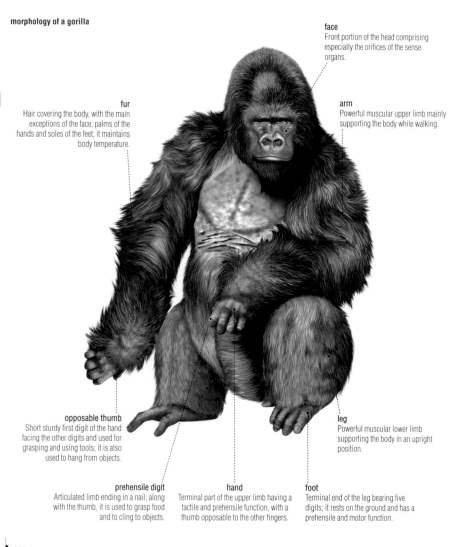

face
Front portion of the head comprising especially the orifices of the sense organs.

fur
Hair covering the body, with the main exceptions of the face, palms of the hands and soles of the feet; it maintains body temperature.

arm
Powerful muscular upper limb mainly supporting the body while walking.

opposable thumb
Short sturdy first digit of the hand facing the other digits and used for grasping and using tools; it is also used to hang from objects.

leg
Powerful muscular lower limb supporting the body in an upright position.

prehensile digit
Articulated limb ending in a nail; along with the thumb, it is used to grasp food and to cling to objects.

hand
Terminal part of the upper limb having a tactile and prehensile function, with a thumb opposable to the other fingers.

foot
Terminal end of the leg bearing five digits; it rests on the ground and has a prehensile and motor function.

examples of marsupials

The 260 or so species live on land or in trees in Oceania and the Americas.

ANIMAL KINGDOM

Tasmanian devil
Carnivorous scavenging nocturnal marsupial with powerful jaws that allow it to devour its prey whole (flesh, bones, fur, feathers).

opossum
Omnivorous nocturnal marsupial of the Americas and Australia without a pouch; its fur is highly prized.

kangaroo
Herbivorous marsupial with a highly developed tail; it lives in groups in Australia and Tasmania and moves rapidly by leaping.

wallaby
Marsupial closely related to the kangaroo and living in Australia, Tasmania and New Guinea; certain species are prized for their fur.

koala
Tailless nocturnal marsupial of Australia; this solitary tree-dweller lives in eucalyptus forests and feeds on the tree's leaves.

kangaroo

Herbivorous marsupial with a highly developed tail; it lives in groups in Australia and Tasmania and moves rapidly by leaping.

morphology of a kangaroo

pinna
Movable outer portion of the ear made of cartilage and located on the side of the head to capture sounds.

snout
Long front portion of the head having mainly a highly developed olfactory function.

forelimb
Poorly developed articulated limb ending in five clawed digits; the kangaroo uses it to feed and to defend itself.

claw
Pointy sharp corneous structure used especially to scratch and claw adversaries during combat.

foot
Powerful terminal end of the limb bearing four digits; it supports the body and has a motor function.

digit
Articulated limb at the end of the foot. The kangaroo does not usually have a thumb. The 2nd and 3rd digits are fused, while the 4th digit ends in a strong sharp claw.

fur
Hair covering the body, mainly for
maintaining body temperature; the fur
insulates against cold and heat.

thigh
Upper portion of the hind limb; its
muscles provide the kangaroo with
strong propulsion.

pouch
Located on the female's belly and having
nipples; the newborn continues to develop
inside it. In some species, the pouch is
dorsal or absent.

tail
Very muscular terminal appendage; it
helps maintain equilibrium while
jumping and, with the back legs,
supports the body at rest.

hind limb
Extremely muscular articulated limb
ending in four digits allowing the
kangaroo to move swiftly by powerful
bounds and to strike its enemies.

bat

Usually insectivorous nocturnal flying mammal using echoes of the sounds it produces (echolocation) to orient itself and to find its prey.

morphology of a bat

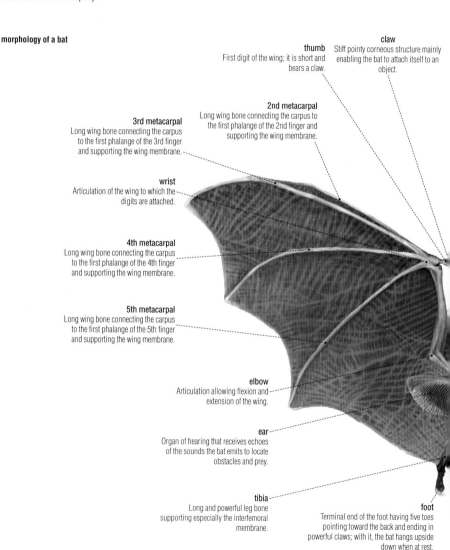

thumb
First digit of the wing; it is short and bears a claw.

claw
Stiff pointy corneous structure mainly enabling the bat to attach itself to an object.

2nd metacarpal
Long wing bone connecting the carpus to the first phalange of the 2nd finger and supporting the wing membrane.

3rd metacarpal
Long wing bone connecting the carpus to the first phalange of the 3rd finger and supporting the wing membrane.

wrist
Articulation of the wing to which the digits are attached.

4th metacarpal
Long wing bone connecting the carpus to the first phalange of the 4th finger and supporting the wing membrane.

5th metacarpal
Long wing bone connecting the carpus to the first phalange of the 5th finger and supporting the wing membrane.

elbow
Articulation allowing flexion and extension of the wing.

ear
Organ of hearing that receives echoes of the sounds the bat emits to locate obstacles and prey.

tibia
Long and powerful leg bone supporting especially the interfemoral membrane.

foot
Terminal end of the foot having five toes pointing toward the back and ending in powerful claws; with it, the bat hangs upside down when at rest.

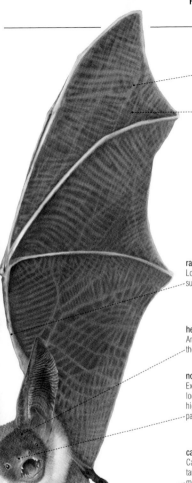

blood vessels
Channels in which blood circulates; they regulate the body's temperature.

wing membrane
Smooth fold of skin stretching between the digits of the wings and extending to the feet; it is used mainly for flight and thermoregulation.

radius
Long and powerful wing bone supporting the wing membrane.

head
Anterior portion of the body containing the main sensory organs and the brain.

nose leaf
External opening of the nasal cavity located above the mouth and having a highly developed olfactory function in particular.

calcar
Cartilaginous structure attached to the tarsus and supporting the interfemoral membrane.

interfemoral membrane
Fold of smooth skin between the legs and the tail; it provides stability when the bat is in flight and capturing prey.

tail
Terminal appendage of the body supporting especially the interfemoral membrane.

wings
Appendages of flight comprised of a cutaneous membrane supported by four very long fingers (only the thumb remains free); the bat folds its wings when resting.

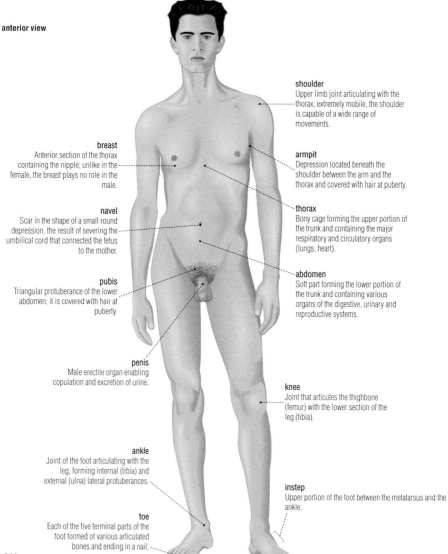

man

Male human being producing cells able to fertilize the ovum (egg); the male's skeleton is generally larger and heavier than that of the female.

anterior view

THE HUMAN BEING

shoulder
Upper limb joint articulating with the thorax; extremely mobile, the shoulder is capable of a wide range of movements.

breast
Anterior section of the thorax containing the nipple; unlike in the female, the breast plays no role in the male.

armpit
Depression located beneath the shoulder between the arm and the thorax and covered with hair at puberty.

thorax
Bony cage forming the upper portion of the trunk and containing the major respiratory and circulatory organs (lungs, heart).

navel
Scar in the shape of a small round depression, the result of severing the umbilical cord that connected the fetus to the mother.

abdomen
Soft part forming the lower portion of the trunk and containing various organs of the digestive, urinary and reproductive systems.

pubis
Triangular protuberance of the lower abdomen; it is covered with hair at puberty.

penis
Male erectile organ enabling copulation and excretion of urine.

knee
Joint that articutes the thighbone (femur) with the lower section of the leg (tibia).

ankle
Joint of the foot articulating with the leg, forming internal (tibia) and external (ulna) lateral protuberances.

instep
Upper portion of the foot between the metatarsus and the ankle.

toe
Each of the five terminal parts of the foot formed of various articulated bones and ending in a nail.

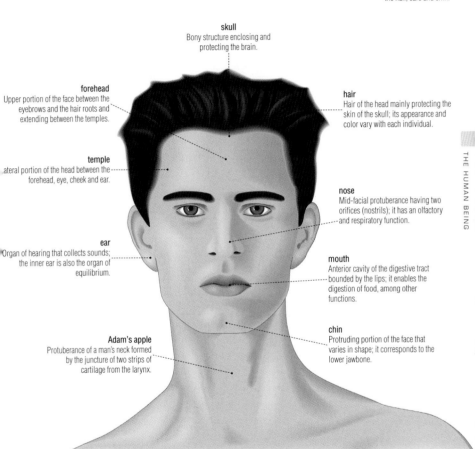

face
Front portion of the head bounded by the hair, ears and chin.

skull
Bony structure enclosing and protecting the brain.

forehead
Upper portion of the face between the eyebrows and the hair roots and extending between the temples.

hair
Hair of the head mainly protecting the skin of the skull; its appearance and color vary with each individual.

temple
Lateral portion of the head between the forehead, eye, cheek and ear.

nose
Mid-facial protuberance having two orifices (nostrils); it has an olfactory and respiratory function.

ear
Organ of hearing that collects sounds; the inner ear is also the organ of equilibrium.

mouth
Anterior cavity of the digestive tract bounded by the lips; it enables the digestion of food, among other functions.

Adam's apple
Protuberance of a man's neck formed by the juncture of two strips of cartilage from the larynx.

chin
Protruding portion of the face that varies in shape; it corresponds to the lower jawbone.

THE HUMAN BEING

posterior view

hair
Hair of the head mainly protecting the skin of the skull; its appearance and color vary with each individual.

shoulder blade
Slender flat back bone articulating especially with the humerus (arm bone) and forming the posterior section of the shoulder.

nape
Posterior section of the neck formed mainly of vertebrae and muscles.

back
Posterior portion of the trunk extending from the shoulders to the kidneys on each side of the vertebral column.

arm
Section of the upper limb between the shoulder and the elbow and articulating especially with the scapula.

elbow
Arm joint (humerus) articulating with the forearm (radius and ulna); it protrudes when the limb is flexed.

waist
Narrowed section of the body between the base of the thorax and the hips.

forearm
Section of the upper limb between the elbow and the wrist; its muscles control the movements of the hand and fingers.

hip
Leg joint articulating with the pelvis (base of the trunk).

wrist
Joint of the hand (carpus) articulating with the forearm (radius).

loin
Lower portion of the back; it is located on each side of the vertebral column.

posterior rugae
Deep slender ridge between the two buttocks through which the anus opens.

hand
Terminal part of the upper limb having a tactile and prehensile function, with a thumb opposable to the other fingers.

buttock
Fleshy section made up mostly of muscles; it is located at the base of the back.

thigh
Section of the leg between the hip and the knee; it contains many powerful muscles.

calf
Fleshy section formed by the muscles at the back of the leg between the knee and the ankle.

heel
Posterior section of the foot; it rests on the ground when walking.

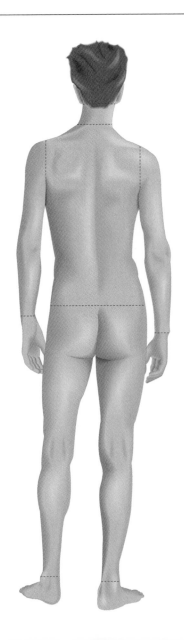

head
Upper portion of the body supported by the neck and made up essentially of the main sensory organs and the brain.

neck
Portion of the body connecting the head to the trunk; the respiratory tract, nerve centers and blood vessels, in particular, pass through it.

trunk
Portion of the body to which the head and limbs are attached; it is made up of the thorax, abdomen and pelvis.

leg
Lower limb attached to the trunk; it supports the body in an upright position and during locomotion.

foot
Terminal part of the lower limb enabling upright stance and walking.

woman

Human being of the female sex capable of conceiving children from an ovum (egg) fertilized by a spermatozoon (sperm, the reproductive male cell).

THE HUMAN BEING

anterior view

shoulder
Upper limb joint articulating with the thorax; extremely mobile, the shoulder is capable of a wide range of movements.

nipple
Cone-shaped or cylindrical erectile protuberance of the breast surrounded by the areola; the lactiferous ducts open into it.

armpit
Depression located beneath the shoulder between the arm and the thorax and covered with hair at puberty.

breast
Female milk-secreting glandular organ; it develops at puberty and increases in size during pregnancy.

thorax
Bony cage making up the upper portion of the trunk; it contains the major respiratory and circulatory organs (lungs, heart).

navel
Scar in the shape of a small round depression, the result of severing the umbilical cord that connected the fetus to the mother.

abdomen
Soft part forming the lower portion of the trunk and containing various organs of the digestive, urinary and reproductive systems.

pubis
Triangular protuberance of the lower abdomen; it is covered with hair at puberty.

groin
Depression resulting from the juncture of the lower abdomen and the thigh.

vulva
All the external female genital organs enabling functions such as copulation (vaginal orifice) and the evacuation of urine.

knee
Joint that articules the thighbone (femur) with the lower section of the leg (tibia).

toe
Each of the five terminal parts of the foot formed of various articulated bones and ending in a nail.

ankle
Joint of the foot articulating with the leg, forming internal (tibia) and external (ulna) lateral protuberances.

face
Front portion of the head bounded by
the hair, ears and chin.

skull
Bony structure enclosing and
protecting the brain.

forehead
Upper portion of the face between the
eyebrows and the hair roots and
extending between the temples.

hair
Hair of the head mainly protecting the
skin of the skull; its appearance and
color vary with each individual.

eye
Organ of sight used to make out
shapes, distances, colors and
movements; the human being is
endowed with good eyesight.

temple
Lateral portion of the head between the
forehead, eye, cheek and ear.

nose
Mid-facial protuberance having two
orifices (nostrils); it has an olfactory
and respiratory function.

ear
Organ of hearing that collects sounds;
the inner ear is also the organ of
equilibrium.

mouth
Anterior cavity of the digestive tract
bounded by the lips; it enables the
digestion of food, among other
functions.

cheek
Lateral portion of the face containing
muscles capable of producing many
different expressions.

chin
Protruding portion of the face that
varies in shape; it corresponds to the
lower jawbone.

neck
Portion of the body connecting the head
to the trunk; the respiratory tract, nerve
centers and blood vessels, in particular,
pass through it.

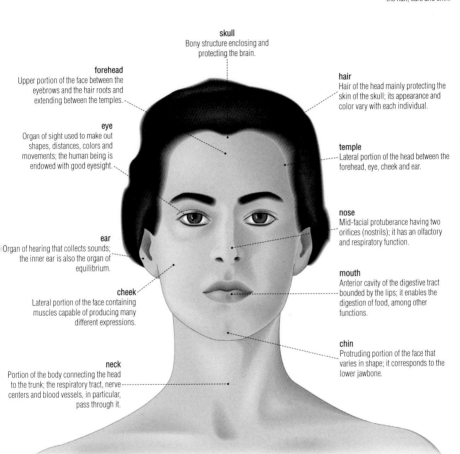

THE HUMAN BEING

woman

posterior view

shoulder blade
Slender flat back bone articulating especially with the humerus (arm bone) and forming the posterior section of the shoulder.

nape
Posterior section of the neck formed mainly of vertebrae and muscles.

back
Posterior portion of the trunk extending from the shoulders to the kidneys on each side of the vertebral column.

arm
Section of the upper limb between the shoulder and the elbow and articulating especially with the scapula.

waist
Narrowed section of the body between the base of the thorax and the hips.

elbow
Arm joint (humerus) articulating with the forearm (radius and ulna); it protrudes when the limb is flexed.

forearm
Section of the upper limb between the elbow and the wrist; its muscles control the movements of the hand and fingers.

hip
Leg joint articulating with the pelvis (base of the trunk).

wrist
Joint of the hand (carpus) articulating with the forearm (radius).

loin
Lower portion of the back; it is located on each side of the vertebral column.

hand
Terminal part of the upper limb having a tactile and prehensile function, with a thumb opposable to the other fingers.

posterior rugae
Deep slender ridge between the two buttocks through which the anus opens.

buttock
Fleshy section made up mostly of muscles; it is located at the base of the back.

thigh
Section of the leg between the hip and the knee; it contains many powerful muscles.

calf
Fleshy section formed by the muscles at the back of the leg between the knee and the ankle.

heel
Posterior section of the foot; it rests on the ground when walking.

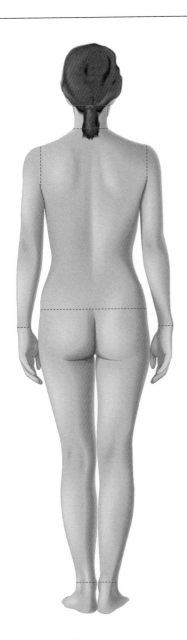

head
Upper portion of the body supported
by the neck and made up essentially of
the main sensory organs and the brain.

neck
Portion of the body connecting the head to
the trunk; the respiratory tract, nerve
centers and blood vessels, in particular,
pass through it.

trunk
Portion of the body to which the head
and limbs are attached; it is made up of
the thorax, abdomen and pelvis.

leg
Lower limb attached to the trunk; it
supports the body in an upright
position and during locomotion.

foot
Terminal part of the lower limb
enabling upright stance and walking.

THE HUMAN BEING

muscles

Contractile organs made of fibers allowing the body to move and maintain its posture; the human body has over 600 muscles.

anterior view

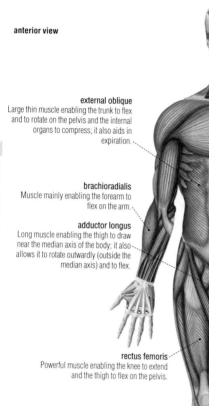

biceps of arm
Muscle allowing the forearm to flex and to rotate outwardly (palm of the hand toward the front); the biceps contracts while the triceps relaxes.

external oblique
Large thin muscle enabling the trunk to flex and to rotate on the pelvis and the internal organs to compress; it also aids in expiration.

rectus abdominis
Flat muscle enabling the trunk to flex frontward; it protects and enables compression of the internal organs, and aids in expiration.

brachioradialis
Muscle mainly enabling the forearm to flex on the arm.

brachialis
Powerful muscle enabling the forearm to flex on the arm.

adductor longus
Long muscle enabling the thigh to draw near the median axis of the body; it also allows it to rotate outwardly (outside the median axis) and to flex.

long palmaris
Muscle enabling various hand movements, including flexing it and drawing it away from the median axis of the body; it also helps to stabilize the wrist.

sartorius
Long narrow ribbon-shaped muscle enabling the thigh to flex and to rotate outwardly (outside the median axis); it also allows the leg to flex.

rectus femoris
Powerful muscle enabling the knee to extend and the thigh to flex on the pelvis.

gastrocnemius
Large thick muscle forming the curve of the calf and allowing the foot to extend; it also helps the knee to extend.

peroneus longus
Muscle attached to the fibula enabling the foot to extend and to draw away from the median axis of the body; it also supports the plantar arch.

soleus
Thick muscle enabling the foot to extend, the heel to lift off the ground and the body to rise; it is a major muscle involved in walking, running and jumping.

anterior tibialis
Thick muscle enabling the foot to flex on the leg and to draw near the median axis of the body; the posterior tibial allows the foot to extend.

extensor digitorum longus
Long muscle allowing all the toes, except the big toe, to extend; it also helps the foot to flex on the leg.

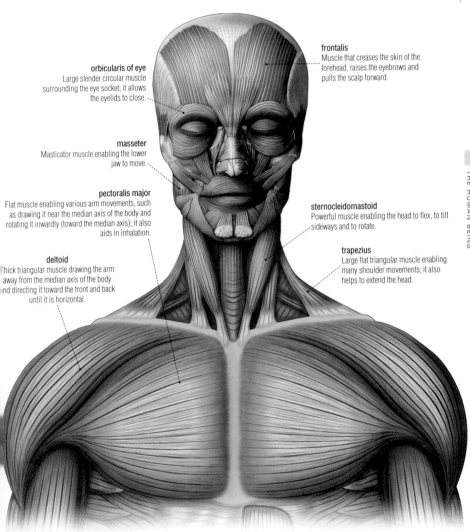

frontalis
Muscle that creases the skin of the forehead, raises the eyebrows and pulls the scalp forward.

orbicularis of eye
Large slender circular muscle surrounding the eye socket; it allows the eyelids to close.

masseter
Masticator muscle enabling the lower jaw to move.

pectoralis major
Flat muscle enabling various arm movements, such as drawing it near the median axis of the body and rotating it inwardly (toward the median axis); it also aids in inhalation.

sternocleidomastoid
Powerful muscle enabling the head to flex, to tilt sideways and to rotate.

trapezius
Large flat triangular muscle enabling many shoulder movements; it also helps to extend the head.

deltoid
Thick triangular muscle drawing the arm away from the median axis of the body and directing it toward the front and back until it is horizontal.

muscles

posterior view

latissimus dorsi
Large flat muscle especially enabling the arm to draw near the median axis of the body, to extend and to rotate inwardly.

external oblique
Large thin muscle enabling the trunk to flex and to rotate on the pelvis and the internal organs to compress; it also aids in expiration.

triceps of arm
Powerful muscle enabling the forearm to extend on the arm; it contracts whereas the biceps relaxes.

anconeus
Short muscle reinforcing the action of the triceps; it allows the forearm to extend on the arm and also stabilizes the elbow joint.

gluteus maximus
Thick muscle enabling the hip to extend and to rotate outwardly (outside the median axis); it also allows the trunk to return to a vertical position.

common extensor of fingers
Muscle enabling all the fingers, except the thumb, to extend; it also helps the hand to extend on the forearm.

ulnar flexor of wrist
Muscle enabling the hand to flex and to draw near the median axis of the body.

ulnar extensor of wrist
Muscle enabling the hand to extend and to draw near the median axis of the body.

adductor magnus
Powerful muscle enabling the thigh to draw near the median axis of the body, to rotate outwardly (outside the median axis), to flex and to extend.

semitendinosus
Long muscle enabling the thigh to extend on the pelvis, the knee to flex, and the thigh and the leg to rotate inwardly (toward the median axis).

vastus lateralis
Large outer thigh muscle mainly allowing the knee to extend; it also stabilizes the knee.

biceps of thigh
Large muscle enabling the leg to flex on the thigh and to rotate outwardly (outside the median axis) and the thigh to extend on the pelvis.

short peroneus
Muscle attached to the fibula enabling the foot to extend and to draw away from the median axis of the body.

gracilis
Muscle enabling the thigh to draw near the median axis of the body, and the leg to flex on the thigh and to rotate inwardly (toward the median axis).

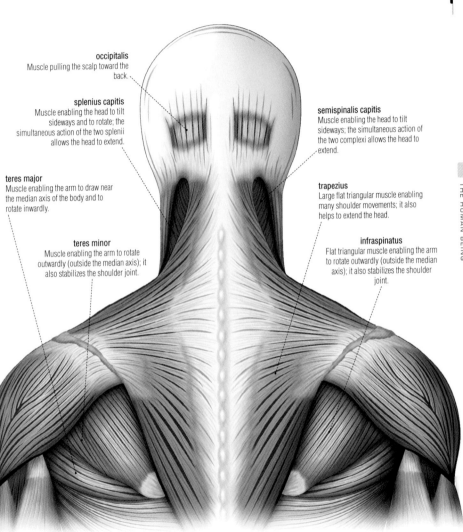

occipitalis
Muscle pulling the scalp toward the back.

splenius capitis
Muscle enabling the head to tilt sideways and to rotate; the simultaneous action of the two splenii allows the head to extend.

semispinalis capitis
Muscle enabling the head to tilt sideways; the simultaneous action of the two complexi allows the head to extend.

teres major
Muscle enabling the arm to draw near the median axis of the body and to rotate inwardly.

trapezius
Large flat triangular muscle enabling many shoulder movements; it also helps to extend the head.

teres minor
Muscle enabling the arm to rotate outwardly (outside the median axis); it also stabilizes the shoulder joint.

infraspinatus
Flat triangular muscle enabling the arm to rotate outwardly (outside the median axis); it also stabilizes the shoulder joint.

THE HUMAN BEING

skeleton

All the articulated bones (about 200), of varying sizes and shapes, forming the frame of the body, supporting the muscles and protecting the vital organs.

anterior view

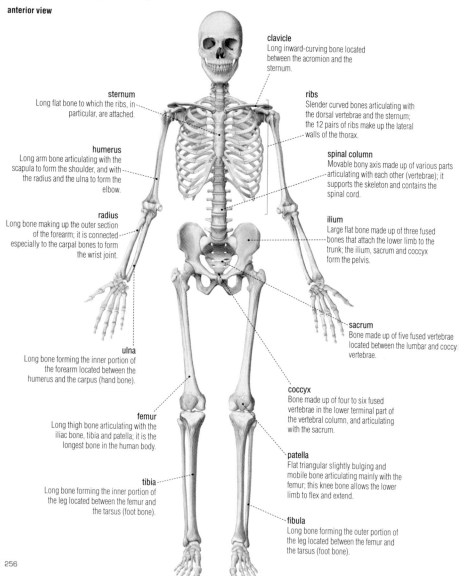

clavicle
Long inward-curving bone located between the acromion and the sternum.

sternum
Long flat bone to which the ribs, in particular, are attached.

ribs
Slender curved bones articulating with the dorsal vertebrae and the sternum; the 12 pairs of ribs make up the lateral walls of the thorax.

humerus
Long arm bone articulating with the scapula to form the shoulder, and with the radius and the ulna to form the elbow.

spinal column
Movable bony axis made up of various parts articulating with each other (vertebrae); it supports the skeleton and contains the spinal cord.

radius
Long bone making up the outer section of the forearm; it is connected especially to the carpal bones to form the wrist joint.

ilium
Large flat bone made up of three fused bones that attach the lower limb to the trunk; the ilium, sacrum and coccyx form the pelvis.

sacrum
Bone made up of five fused vertebrae located between the lumbar and coccy vertebrae.

ulna
Long bone forming the inner portion of the forearm located between the humerus and the carpus (hand bone).

coccyx
Bone made up of four to six fused vertebrae in the lower terminal part of the vertebral column, and articulating with the sacrum.

femur
Long thigh bone articulating with the iliac bone, tibia and patella; it is the longest bone in the human body.

patella
Flat triangular slightly bulging and mobile bone articulating mainly with the femur; this knee bone allows the lower limb to flex and extend.

tibia
Long bone forming the inner portion of the leg located between the femur and the tarsus (foot bone).

fibula
Long bone forming the outer portion of the leg located between the femur and the tarsus (foot bone).

THE HUMAN BEING

posterior view

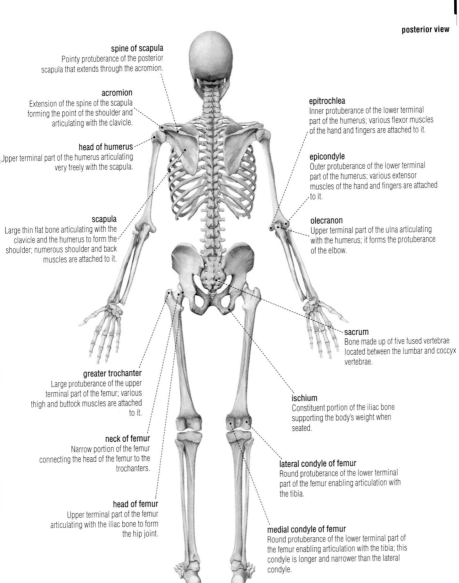

spine of scapula
Pointy protuberance of the posterior
scapula that extends through the acromion.

acromion
Extension of the spine of the scapula
forming the point of the shoulder and
articulating with the clavicle.

head of humerus
Upper terminal part of the humerus articulating
very freely with the scapula.

scapula
Large thin flat bone articulating with the
clavicle and the humerus to form the
shoulder; numerous shoulder and back
muscles are attached to it.

epitrochlea
Inner protuberance of the lower terminal
part of the humerus; various flexor muscles
of the hand and fingers are attached to it.

epicondyle
Outer protuberance of the lower terminal
part of the humerus; various extensor
muscles of the hand and fingers are attached
to it.

olecranon
Upper terminal part of the ulna articulating
with the humerus; it forms the protuberance
of the elbow.

sacrum
Bone made up of five fused vertebrae
located between the lumbar and coccyx
vertebrae.

greater trochanter
Large protuberance of the upper
terminal part of the femur; various
thigh and buttock muscles are attached
to it.

neck of femur
Narrow portion of the femur
connecting the head of the femur to the
trochanters.

head of femur
Upper terminal part of the femur
articulating with the iliac bone to form
the hip joint.

ischium
Constituent portion of the iliac bone
supporting the body's weight when
seated.

lateral condyle of femur
Round protuberance of the lower terminal
part of the femur enabling articulation with
the tibia.

medial condyle of femur
Round protuberance of the lower terminal part of
the femur enabling articulation with the tibia; this
condyle is longer and narrower than the lateral
condyle.

THE HUMAN BEING

skeleton

hand
Terminal part of the forearm with a tactile and prehensile function and a thumb opposable to the other fingers. The skeleton of the hand has 27 bones.

carpus
All eight short articulated bones, laid out in two rows, forming the wrist and giving it a wide range of motion; it connects the radius to the metacarpus.

hamate
Bone of the anterior row of the carpus, articulating especially with the metacarpal bones of the third and little fingers.

pisiform
Bone of the posterior row of the carpus; it is the smallest of the carpal bones.

triquetral
Last bone in the posterior row of the carpus, set opposite the thumb.

ulna
Long bone forming the inner portion of the forearm, and articulating especially with the radius.

lunate
Bone of the posterior row of the carpus articulating especially with the radius to form the wrist.

radius
Long bone making up the outer section of the forearm; it is connected especially to the carpal bones to form the wrist joint.

scaphoid
The largest bone in the posterior row of the carpus articulating with the radius to form the wrist.

capitate
Bone of the anterior row of the carpus articulating especially with the metacarpal bone of the middle finger.

trapezoid
Bone of the anterior row of the carpus articulating especially with the metacarpal bone of the index finger.

trapezium
Bone of the anterior row of the carpus articulating especially with the metacarpal bone of the thumb.

metacarpal
Each of the five bones forming the metacarpus. The metacarpal bone of the thumb is very mobile.

THE HUMAN BEING

metacarpus
All five long bones forming the palm of the hand; they link the anterior row of the carpus to the proximal phalanges.

phalanges
Articulated bones forming the skeleton of the fingers; each finger has three, while the thumb has two.

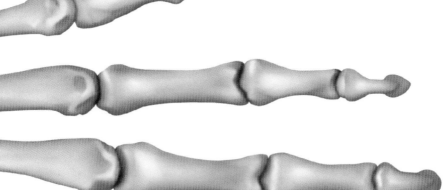

middle phalange
Second phalange of the finger between the proximal and distal phalanges. The thumb does not have a middle phalange.

proximal phalange
First phalange of the finger; it is connected to the metacarpus.

distal phalange
Last phalange of the finger bearing a nail.

proximal phalange
First phalange of the finger; it is connected to the metacarpus.

distal phalange
Last phalange of the finger bearing a nail.

foot
Terminal part of the leg enabling upright stance and walking. The skeleton of the foot is made up of 26 bones.

tarsus
All seven short articulated bones, laid out in two rows, making up the heel and the ankle; it connects the tibia and the fibula to the metatarsus.

2nd cuneiform
Bone of the anterior row of the tarsus articulating especially with the metatarsal bone of the second toe and the scaphoid bone.

tibia
Long bone forming the inner portion of the leg; it is connected especially to the tarsus to form the ankle joint.

talus
Short bone of the tarsus that, with the calcaneus, ensures rotation of the ankle and, with the tibia and fibula, flexion and extension of the foot.

navicular
Bone of the posterior row of the tarsus articulating especially with the talus and the three cuneiforms.

fibula
Long bone forming the outer portion of the leg; it is connected especially to the bones of the tarsus to form the ankle joint.

calcaneus
Bone of the posterior row of the tarsus forming the protuberance of the heel and supporting a large portion of the body's weight; the Achilles tendon is attached to it.

cuboid
Bone of the anterior row of the tarsus articulating especially with the metatarsal bones of the two last toes.

lateral cuneiform
Bone of the anterior row of the tarsus articulating especially with the metatarsal bone of the third toe.

THE HUMAN BEING

metatarsus
All five long bones that make up the
sole of the foot; it connects the anterior
row of the tarsus to the proximal
phalanges.

proximal phalange
First phalange of the toe; it is joined to
the metatarsus.

1st cuneiform
Bone of the anterior row of the tarsus
articulating especially with the
metatarsal bone of the big toe and the
scaphoid bone.

phalanges
Articulated bones forming the skeleton
of the toes. Each toe has three, while
the big toe has only two.

distal phalange
Last phalange of the toe bearing a nail.

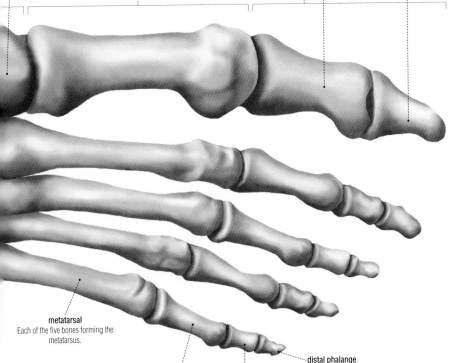

THE HUMAN BEING

metatarsal
Each of the five bones forming the
metatarsus.

distal phalange
Last phalange of the toe bearing a nail.

proximal phalange
First phalange of the toe; it is joined to
the metatarsus.

middle phalange
Second phalange of the toe between
the proximal and distal phalanges. The
big toe does not have a middle
phalange.

skeleton

lateral view of skull
Skull: bony structure enclosing and
protecting the brain. The eight cranial bones
in an adult are fused to each other by means
of sutures.

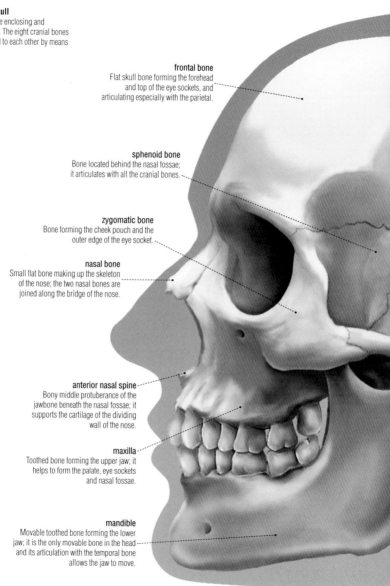

frontal bone
Flat skull bone forming the forehead
and top of the eye sockets, and
articulating especially with the parietal.

sphenoid bone
Bone located behind the nasal fossae;
it articulates with all the cranial bones.

zygomatic bone
Bone forming the cheek pouch and the
outer edge of the eye socket.

nasal bone
Small flat bone making up the skeleton
of the nose; the two nasal bones are
joined along the bridge of the nose.

anterior nasal spine
Bony middle protuberance of the
jawbone beneath the nasal fossae; it
supports the cartilage of the dividing
wall of the nose.

maxilla
Toothed bone forming the upper jaw; it
helps to form the palate, eye sockets
and nasal fossae.

mandible
Movable toothed bone forming the lower
jaw; it is the only movable bone in the head
and its articulation with the temporal bone
allows the jaw to move.

coronal suture
Immobile joint made of fibrous tissue connecting the frontal bone and the two parietal bones.

parietal bone
Flat cranial bone articulating with the frontal, occipital, temporal and sphenoid bones; the two parietal bones form the largest portion of the dome of the skull.

squamous suture
Immobile joint made of fibrous tissue connecting the parietal and temporal bones.

lambdoid suture
Immovable joint made of fibrous tissue connecting the occipital and the two parietal bones.

temporal bone
Flat skull bone that protects mainly the organs responsible for hearing and equilibrium.

occipital bone
Flat skull bone articulating with the parietal bone and atlas (first cervical vertebra), among others; it makes up the largest portion of the base of the skull.

external auditory meatus
Canal through which sounds collected by the auricle (outer section of the ear) reach the tympanic cavity, a hollow in the temporal bone.

mastoid process
Protruding cone-shaped part of the temporal bone located behind the outer ear. Certain neck muscles, such as the sternocleidomastoid, are attached to it.

styloid process
Elongated protuberance of the temporal bone; several tongue muscles are attached to it.

skeleton

spinal column

The vertebral column is made up of different kinds of articulated bones (vertebrae) supporting the skeleton and protecting the spinal cord.

atlas
First cervical vertebra supporting the head and supported by the axis.

axis
Second cervical vertebra supporting the atlas; it allows the head to rotate.

cervical vertebra (7)
Bony part of the neck forming the upper terminal part of the spinal column.

intervertebral foramen
Orifice located between two contiguous vertebrae on each side of the column allowing nerves to pass through.

intervertebral disk
Flat rounded cartilaginous structure separating two vertebrae; its elasticity allows the vertebral column to move.

thoracic vertebra (12)
Bony part supporting the ribs located between the cervical and lumbar vertebrae.

vertebral body
Anterior bony cylinder of a vertebra surrounded by two transverse processes.

transverse process
Bony protuberance extending laterally from each side of the vertebra; the muscles are attached to it.

lumbar vertebra (5)
Bony part larger than the other vertebrae located between the dorsal vertebrae and the sacrum; it supports a major portion of the body's weight.

sacrum
Bone made up of five fused vertebrae located between the lumbar and coccyx vertebrae.

coccyx
Bone made up of four to six fused vertebrae in the lower terminal part of the spinal column, and articulating with the sacrum.

THE HUMAN BEING

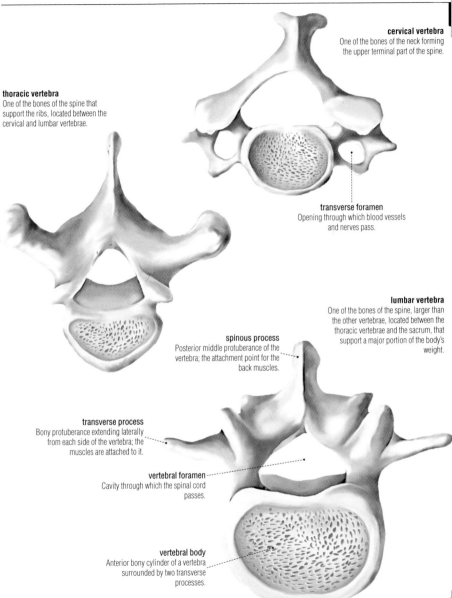

cervical vertebra
One of the bones of the neck forming
the upper terminal part of the spine.

thoracic vertebra
One of the bones of the spine that
support the ribs, located between the
cervical and lumbar vertebrae.

transverse foramen
Opening through which blood vessels
and nerves pass.

lumbar vertebra
One of the bones of the spine, larger than
the other vertebrae, located between the
thoracic vertebrae and the sacrum, that
support a major portion of the body's
weight.

spinous process
Posterior middle protuberance of the
vertebra; the attachment point for the
back muscles.

transverse process
Bony protuberance extending laterally
from each side of the vertebra; the
muscles are attached to it.

vertebral foramen
Cavity through which the spinal cord
passes.

vertebral body
Anterior bony cylinder of a vertebra
surrounded by two transverse
processes.

teeth

Hard organs implanted in maxillae and used for masticating food; a child usually has 20 and an adult 32 (16 per jaw).

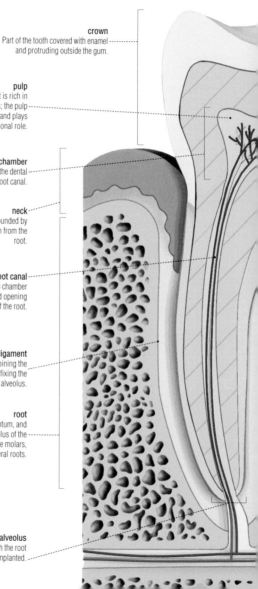

cross section of a molar
Teeth are formed of two main parts: the crown (the visible protruding part) and one or several roots (the part inserted into the maxilla).

crown
Part of the tooth covered with enamel and protruding outside the gum.

pulp
Soft conjunctive tissue that is rich in blood vessels and nerves; the pulp gives the tooth its sensitivity and plays an essential nutritional role.

pulp chamber
Central chamber of the crown enclosing the dental pulp and extending through the root canal.

neck
Narrow part of the tooth surrounded by the gum separating the crown from the root.

root canal
Extension of the pulp chamber containing the dental pulp and opening at the apex of the root.

periodontal ligament
Fibrous connective tissue joining the cementum to the bone, thus fixing the tooth into its alveolus.

root
Part of the tooth covered with cementum, and implanted into the dental alveolus of the maxilla; certain teeth, such as the molars, have several roots.

dental alveolus
Bony maxillary cavity in which the root of the tooth is implanted.

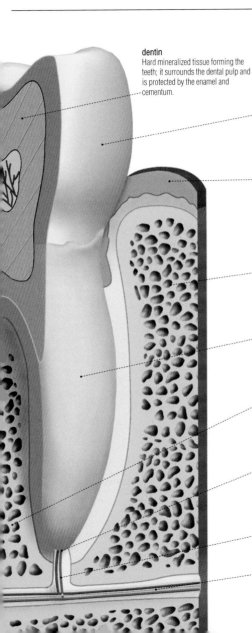

dentin
Hard mineralized tissue forming the teeth; it surrounds the dental pulp and is protected by the enamel and cementum.

enamel
Highly mineralized tissue covering and protecting the dentin of the crown; it is the hardest tissue in the organism.

gum
Thick section of the mucous membrane of the mouth that is rich in blood vessels and nerves; it covers the edge of the dental alveolus and adheres to the neck.

maxillary bone
Jawbone into which the teeth are inserted.

cementum
Hard mineralized tissue comparable to bone covering and protecting the dentin of the root.

alveolar bone
Section of the maxilla bone surrounding the dental alveola; its presence depends on the presence of teeth: it forms and disappears when they do.

apex
Terminal part of the dental root whose opening (apical foramen) allows blood vessels and nerves to pass through.

apical foramen
Narrow orifice located at the terminal part of the apex allowing blood vessels and nerves to pass into the tooth.

plexus of nerves
Grouping of blood vessels and nerves that enters the pulp through the apical foramen to nourish the tooth.

THE HUMAN BEING

teeth

human denture
The set of teeth placed symmetrically at the edge of the two maxillae; each maxilla has four incisors, two canines, four premolars and six molars.

central incisor
Each of the two incisors in the middle section of the maxilla.

canine
Pointy tooth between the incisors and the premolars having only one root and used to tear apart food; each maxilla has two.

incisors
Each of the four flat cutting teeth of the anterior part of the maxilla having just one root; they are used to cut up food.

lateral incisor
Each of the two incisors of the maxilla located between the central incisors and the canines.

premolars
Each of four teeth between the canines and the molars; they have one or two roots and are used to grind food.

first premolar

wisdom tooth
Third molar, which appears about the age of 20 and occasionally must be extracted (if it is poorly positioned); each maxilla has two.

second premolar

first molar

molars
Each of six large teeth of the posterior section of the maxilla; it has several roots and is used to grind food.

second molar

blood circulation

Propelled by the contractions of the heart, blood travels through the blood vessels of the body bringing oxygen and nutrients and removing waste.

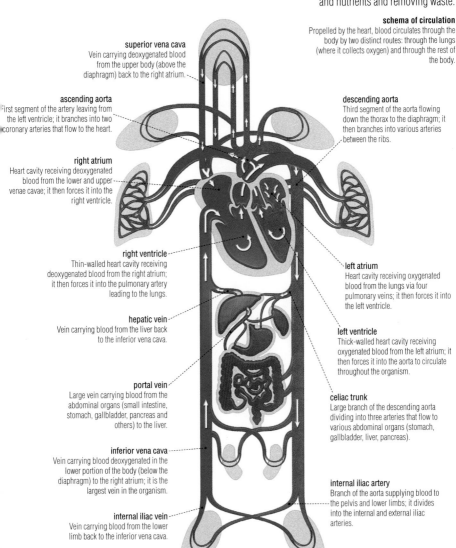

schema of circulation
Propelled by the heart, blood circulates through the body by two distinct routes: through the lungs (where it collects oxygen) and through the rest of the body.

superior vena cava
Vein carrying deoxygenated blood from the upper body (above the diaphragm) back to the right atrium.

ascending aorta
First segment of the artery leaving from the left ventricle; it branches into two coronary arteries that flow to the heart.

descending aorta
Third segment of the aorta flowing down the thorax to the diaphragm; it then branches into various arteries between the ribs.

right atrium
Heart cavity receiving deoxygenated blood from the lower and upper venae cavae; it then forces it into the right ventricle.

right ventricle
Thin-walled heart cavity receiving deoxygenated blood from the right atrium; it then forces it into the pulmonary artery leading to the lungs.

left atrium
Heart cavity receiving oxygenated blood from the lungs via four pulmonary veins; it then forces it into the left ventricle.

hepatic vein
Vein carrying blood from the liver back to the inferior vena cava.

left ventricle
Thick-walled heart cavity receiving oxygenated blood from the left atrium; it then forces it into the aorta to circulate throughout the organism.

portal vein
Large vein carrying blood from the abdominal organs (small intestine, stomach, gallbladder, pancreas and others) to the liver.

celiac trunk
Large branch of the descending aorta dividing into three arteries that flow to various abdominal organs (stomach, gallbladder, liver, pancreas).

inferior vena cava
Vein carrying blood deoxygenated in the lower portion of the body (below the diaphragm) to the right atrium; it is the largest vein in the organism.

internal iliac artery
Branch of the aorta supplying blood to the pelvis and lower limbs; it divides into the internal and external iliac arteries.

internal iliac vein
Vein carrying blood from the lower limb back to the inferior vena cava.

THE HUMAN BEING

blood circulation

principal arteries
The arteries (except for the pulmonary arteries) distribute oxygenated blood throughout the body.

common carotid artery
Branch of the aorta flowing to the head and upper portion of the neck; it is divided into internal and external carotid arteries.

arch of aorta
Second segment of the aorta, which branches into the arteries flowing to the head and upper limbs; with the ascending aorta, it forms the arch of the aorta.

subclavian artery
Main artery of the upper limb passing through the clavicle and extending through the axillary artery; it also flows to the lower section of the neck.

axillary artery
Artery crossing the hollow of the armpit and extending through the brachial artery; it also circulates through the thoracic wall and the shoulder.

brachial artery
Artery flowing along the humerus and supplying the flexor muscles of the arm; it divides into the radial and ulnar arteries at the bend in the elbow.

pulmonary artery
Artery carrying blood that is poor in oxygen and rich in carbon dioxide to the lungs; it is the only artery that transports oxygen-poor blood.

renal artery
Branch of the abdominal aorta circulating blood to the kidney.

superior mesenteric artery
Branch of the abdominal aorta that supplies blood to the ascending colon and half of the transverse colon.

common iliac artery
Branch of the abdominal aorta that circulates blood to the pelvis and the lower limbs; it divides into the internal and external iliac arteries.

abdominal aorta
Fourth segment of the aorta circulating to all the organs and to the walls of the abdomen; it branches into the common iliac arteries.

internal iliac artery
Branch of the common iliac artery flowing to the pelvis, the genital organs and the inner thigh.

femoral artery
Main artery of the lower limb; it is a continuation of the external iliac artery and runs along the femur.

anterior tibial artery
Artery running along the front of the leg and supplying blood to the extensor muscles; it extends through the dorsal artery of the foot.

dorsalis pedis artery
Artery flowing to the ankle and the back of the foot.

arch of foot artery
Continuation of the dorsalis pedis artery; it divides into the arteries of the metatarsus.

principal veins
The veins (except for the pulmonary veins) carry deoxygenated blood toward the heart.

superior vena cava
Vein carrying deoxygenated blood from the upper body (above the diaphragm) back to the right atrium.

external jugular vein
Vein carrying blood from the cranial walls, deep regions of the face and outer walls of the neck to the subclavian vein.

internal jugular vein
Vein collecting blood from the encephalon and from one portion of the face and neck; it is the largest vein in the neck.

pulmonary vein
Vein that returns blood to the heart after it has been oxygenated in the lungs; unlike other veins, the pulmonary veins carry oxygen-rich blood.

subclavian vein
Vein collecting blood from the arm and part of the neck and face; it passes beneath the clavicle and receives the flow of the external jugular vein, among others.

inferior vena cava
Vein carrying blood deoxygenated in the lower portion of the body (below the diaphragm) to the right atrium; it is the largest vein in the organism.

axillary vein
Deep vein running through the hollow of the armpit and ending at the subclavian vein; it receives the flow of the shoulder and thorax veins, among others.

superior mesenteric vein
Vein collecting blood from a section of the intestine (small intestine, right colon); it is one of the veins that flows into the portal vein.

cephalic vein
Superficial vein of the outer arm emptying into the axillary vein; it also receives blood from the superficial veins of the shoulder.

renal vein
Large vein collecting blood from the kidney; it flows into the inferior vena cava.

basilic vein
Large superficial vein of the inner surface of the arm; it connects to the humeral vein in the armpit to form the axillary vein.

femoral vein
Vein collecting blood from the deep structures of the thighs and receives blood from the great saphenous vein, among others.

great saphenous vein
Superficial vein collecting blood from the inner leg and thigh and receiving blood from certain veins of the foot; it is the longest vein in the body.

blood circulation

heart
Muscular organ divided into four chambers; its regular rhythmic contractions cause blood to circulate throughout the organism.

oxygenated blood
Blood enriched with oxygen in the lungs; it leaves the left section of the heart and flows through the arteries to distribute oxygen and nutrients to the organism.

deoxygenated blood
Blood whose oxygen is depleted; the veins carry it to the right portion of the heart, after which it is re-oxygenated in the lungs.

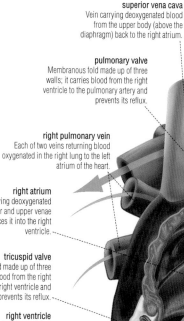

superior vena cava
Vein carrying deoxygenated blood from the upper body (above the diaphragm) back to the right atrium.

pulmonary valve
Membranous fold made up of three walls; it carries blood from the right ventricle to the pulmonary artery and prevents its reflux.

right pulmonary vein
Each of two veins returning blood oxygenated in the right lung to the left atrium of the heart.

right atrium
Heart cavity receiving deoxygenated blood from the lower and upper venae cavae; it then forces it into the right ventricle.

tricuspid valve
Membranous fold made up of three walls; it carries blood from the right atrium to the right ventricle and prevents its reflux.

right ventricle
Thin-walled heart cavity receiving deoxygenated blood from the right atrium; it then forces it into the pulmonary artery leading to the lungs.

endocardium
Smooth thin inner casing of the heart attached to the myocardium.

inferior vena cava
Vein carrying blood deoxygenated in the lower portion of the body (below the diaphragm) to the right atrium; it is the largest vein in the organism.

aorta
Main artery of the body that originates in the left ventricle of the heart and is made up of four segments; it distributes oxygenated blood throughout the body.

arch of aorta
Second segment of the aorta, which branches
into the arteries flowing to the head and upper
limbs; with the ascending aorta, it forms the
arch of the aorta.

pulmonary artery
Artery carrying blood that is poor in
oxygen and rich in carbon dioxide to the
lungs; this is the only artery that
transports oxygen-poor blood.

left pulmonary vein
Each of two veins returning blood,
oxygenated in the left lung, to the left
atrium of the heart.

left atrium
Heart cavity receiving oxygenated
blood from the lungs via four
pulmonary veins; it then forces it into
the left ventricle.

aortic valve
Membranous fold made up of three
walls; it carries blood from the left
ventricle to the aorta and prevents its
reflux.

mitral valve
Membranous fold made up of two walls; it
carries blood from the left atrium to the left
ventricle and prevents its reflux.

left ventricle
Thick-walled heart cavity receiving
oxygenated blood from the left atrium; it
then forces it into the aorta to circulate
throughout the organism.

papillary muscle
Internal ventricular muscle restraining the
mitral or tricuspid valve and preventing it
from being pushed back into the atrium
during contraction of the ventricle.

interventricular septum
Mostly muscular partition separating the
right and left ventricles of the heart.

myocardium
Thick muscular casing around the
heart; its contraction is involuntary and
depends on the autonomous nervous
system.

respiratory system

It causes gaseous exchanges to take place in the lungs by ensuring that oxygen is carried to the blood through inspiration, and carbon dioxide is eliminated from the blood through expiration.

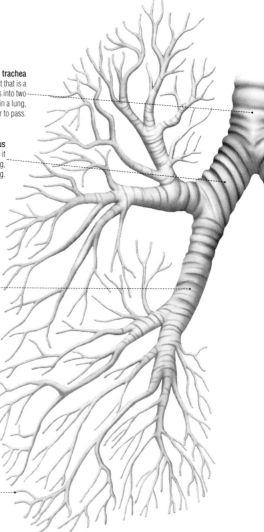

lungs
Respiratory organs formed of extensible tissue, in which air from the nasal and oral cavities is carried, ensuring oxygenation of the blood.

trachea
Muscular cartilaginous tract that is a continuation of the larynx; it divides into two main bronchi, each of which ends in a lung, and allows air to pass.

main bronchus
Channel leading from the trachea; it allows air to enter and exit the lung, and branches out inside the lung.

lobe bronchus
Branch of the main bronchus ending in a pulmonary lobe and dividing into smaller and smaller bronchi.

terminal bronchiole
Final branch of the bronchus having no cartilage and ending in small air pockets (alveolae) where gases are exchanged with the blood.

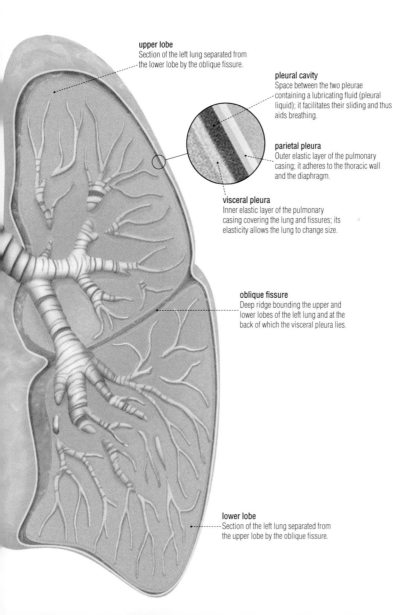

upper lobe
Section of the left lung separated from the lower lobe by the oblique fissure.

pleural cavity
Space between the two pleurae containing a lubricating fluid (pleural liquid); it facilitates their sliding and thus aids breathing.

parietal pleura
Outer elastic layer of the pulmonary casing; it adheres to the thoracic wall and the diaphragm.

visceral pleura
Inner elastic layer of the pulmonary casing covering the lung and fissures; its elasticity allows the lung to change size.

oblique fissure
Deep ridge bounding the upper and lower lobes of the left lung and at the back of which the visceral pleura lies.

lower lobe
Section of the left lung separated from the upper lobe by the oblique fissure.

THE HUMAN BEING

main respiratory organs

nasal cavity
Place where air inhaled through the nostrils is filtered and humidified; it also plays an olfactory role.

oral cavity
Secondary entry point of the respiratory system (physical effort, partial obstruction of the nose); it also helps the ingestion of food.

epiglottis
Movable cartilaginous plate ensuring that the larynx closes during ingestion of food so that food cannot enter the respiratory tract.

larynx
Muscular cartilaginous duct at the upper terminal part of the trachea; it contains the vocal cords and plays a role in speech and respiration.

right lung
Respiratory organ divided into three lobes in which blood from the pulmonary artery is cleansed of carbon dioxide and enriched with oxygen.

vocal cord
Muscular fold aiding speech; the vocal cords close and vibrate when air is expelled from the lungs, thereby producing sound.

upper lobe
Section of the right lung separated from the middle lobe by a horizontal fissure and from the lower lobe by an oblique fissure.

middle lobe
Section of the right lung separated from the upper lobe by a horizontal fissure and from the lower lobe by an oblique fissure.

pericardium
Exterior casing of the heart formed of an inner layer adhering to the myocardium and a thick fibrous outer layer.

lower lobe
Section of the right lung separated from the middle and upper lobes by an oblique fissure.

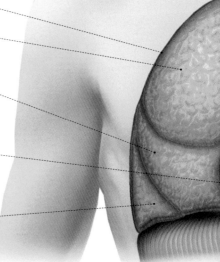

pharynx
Muscular membranous channel connecting the
nasal cavity to the larynx and the oral cavity to the
esophagus; it enables breathing, ingestion of
food and speech.

esophagus
Muscular membranous channel of the
anterior section of the digestive tract; it
allows food to reach the stomach.

trachea
Muscular cartilaginous tract that is a
continuation of the larynx; it divides into two
main bronchi, each of which ends in a lung,
and allows air to pass.

aorta
Main artery of the body that originates in the
left ventricle of the heart and is made up of
four segments; it distributes oxygenated
blood throughout the body.

upper lobe
Section of the left lung separated from
the lower lobe by the oblique fissure.

left lung
Respiratory organ divided into two lobes
where blood from the pulmonary artery is
cleansed of carbon dioxide and enriched
with oxygen.

pulmonary artery
Artery carrying blood that is poor in
oxygen and rich in carbon dioxide to the
lungs; it is the only artery that transports
oxygen-poor blood.

heart
Muscular organ divided into four
chambers; its regular rhythmic
contractions cause blood to circulate
throughout the organism.

lower lobe
Section of the left lung separated from
the upper lobe by the oblique fissure.

diaphragm
Main muscle of inspiration separating the
thorax from the abdomen; its contraction
increases the size of the thoracic cage and
lungs, into which inhaled air is carried.

digital system

digestive system

Formed of the mouth, digestive tract and appended glands, it converts ingested food so that it can be assimilated by the organism.

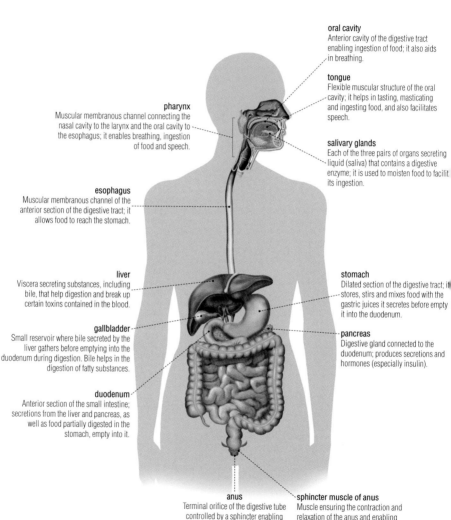

oral cavity
Anterior cavity of the digestive tract enabling ingestion of food; it also aids in breathing.

tongue
Flexible muscular structure of the oral cavity; it helps in tasting, masticating and ingesting food, and also facilitates speech.

pharynx
Muscular membranous channel connecting the nasal cavity to the larynx and the oral cavity to the esophagus; it enables breathing, ingestion of food and speech.

salivary glands
Each of the three pairs of organs secreting liquid (saliva) that contains a digestive enzyme; it is used to moisten food to facilit its ingestion.

esophagus
Muscular membranous channel of the anterior section of the digestive tract; it allows food to reach the stomach.

liver
Viscera secreting substances, including bile, that help digestion and break up certain toxins contained in the blood.

stomach
Dilated section of the digestive tract; it stores, stirs and mixes food with the gastric juices it secretes before empty it into the duodenum.

gallbladder
Small reservoir where bile secreted by the liver gathers before emptying into the duodenum during digestion. Bile helps in the digestion of fatty substances.

pancreas
Digestive gland connected to the duodenum; produces secretions and hormones (especially insulin).

duodenum
Anterior section of the small intestine; secretions from the liver and pancreas, as well as food partially digested in the stomach, empty into it.

anus
Terminal orifice of the digestive tube controlled by a sphincter enabling ejection of fecal matter.

sphincter muscle of anus
Muscle ensuring the contraction and relaxation of the anus and enabling defecation.

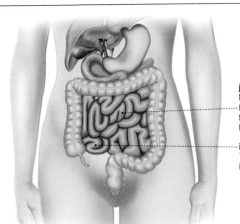

small intestine
Narrow section of the digestive tract, about 20 ft long, between the stomach and cecum, where a part of digestion and food absorption occurs.

jejunum
Middle section of the small intestine between the duodenum and the ileum; the majority of nutrients are absorbed here.

ileum
Terminal part of the small intestine between the jejunum and cecum.

large intestine
Last wide section of the digestive tract, about 5 ft long, where the final stage of digestion and elimination of waste occurs; it includes the colon and the rectum.

descending colon
Third segment of the colon; it stores waste before it is eliminated.

transverse colon
Second segment of the colon (middle section of the large intestine). The right colon (the ascending colon plus half the transverse colon) mainly enables absorption of water.

ascending colon
First segment of the colon; it absorbs water from food residue before it is excreted.

cecum
Anterior part of the large intestine; it receives food particles from the ileum.

vermiform appendix
Tubular extension of the cecum; this appendage is occasionally the site of appendicitis, a severe inflammation.

rectum
Terminal section of the large intestine preceding the anus.

sigmoid colon
Fourth segment of the colon; it carries waste to the rectum.

urinary system

Eliminates the organism's waste through secretion and evacuation of urine; it also regulates the quantity of water and salt in the body.

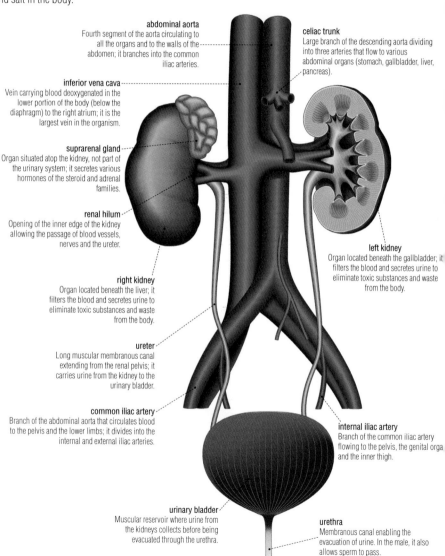

abdominal aorta
Fourth segment of the aorta circulating to all the organs and to the walls of the abdomen; it branches into the common iliac arteries.

celiac trunk
Large branch of the descending aorta dividing into three arteries that flow to various abdominal organs (stomach, gallbladder, liver, pancreas).

inferior vena cava
Vein carrying blood deoxygenated in the lower portion of the body (below the diaphragm) to the right atrium; it is the largest vein in the organism.

suprarenal gland
Organ situated atop the kidney, not part of the urinary system; it secretes various hormones of the steroid and adrenal families.

renal hilum
Opening of the inner edge of the kidney allowing the passage of blood vessels, nerves and the ureter.

left kidney
Organ located beneath the gallbladder; it filters the blood and secretes urine to eliminate toxic substances and waste from the body.

right kidney
Organ located beneath the liver; it filters the blood and secretes urine to eliminate toxic substances and waste from the body.

ureter
Long muscular membranous canal extending from the renal pelvis; it carries urine from the kidney to the urinary bladder.

common iliac artery
Branch of the abdominal aorta that circulates blood to the pelvis and the lower limbs; it divides into the internal and external iliac arteries.

internal iliac artery
Branch of the common iliac artery flowing to the pelvis, the genital orga and the inner thigh.

urinary bladder
Muscular reservoir where urine from the kidneys collects before being evacuated through the urethra.

urethra
Membranous canal enabling the evacuation of urine. In the male, it also allows sperm to pass.

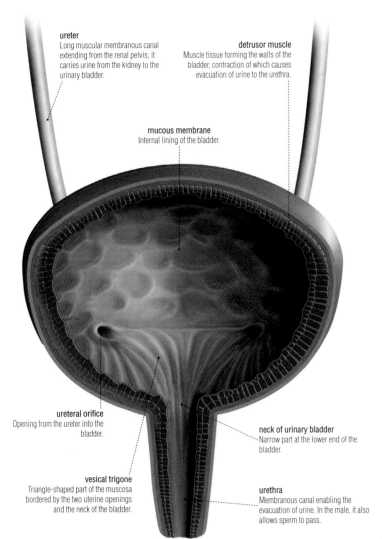

urinary bladder
Muscular reservoir where urine from the kidneys collects before being evacuated through the urethra.

ureter
Long muscular membranous canal extending from the renal pelvis; it carries urine from the kidney to the urinary bladder.

detrusor muscle
Muscle tissue forming the walls of the bladder, contraction of which causes evacuation of urine to the urethra.

mucous membrane
Internal lining of the bladder.

ureteral orifice
Opening from the ureter into the bladder.

neck of urinary bladder
Narrow part at the lower end of the bladder.

vesical trigone
Triangle-shaped part of the muscosa bordered by the two uterine openings and the neck of the bladder.

urethra
Membranous canal enabling the evacuation of urine. In the male, it also allows sperm to pass.

THE HUMAN BEING

nervous system

It directs the movements of the organs and muscles and receives and interprets sensory messages coming from the body.

peripheral nervous system
Part of the nervous system formed by all the motor or sensory nerves (43 pairs) connecting the central nervous system to the organism.

brachial plexus
Network formed of the last four cervical nerves and the first dorsal nerve whose branches ensure motion and feeling in the upper limb.

median nerve
Branch of the brachial plexus providing nerve sensation to various muscles in the lower part of the forearm and part of the hand, where it divides into five branches.

ulnar nerve
Branch of the brachial plexus providing nerve sensation, with the median nerve, especially to the flexor muscles of the hand and toes.

lumbar plexus
Network formed of the first four lumbar nerves whose six branches ensure movement and sensation in the lower limb.

obturator nerve
Branch of the lumbar plexus providing nerve sensation especially to the abductor muscles of the inner thigh.

femoral nerve
Large branch of the lumbar plexus ensuring nerve sensation especially in the flexor muscles of the thigh and the extensor muscles of the leg.

sacral plexus
Network formed of several nerves whose branches ensure movement and sensation in the buttock and part of the thigh.

iliohypogastric nerve
Branch of the lumbar plexus ensuring nerve sensation in one section of the abdominal wall and in the genital organs.

common peroneal nerve
Branch of the sciatic nerve ensuring nerve sensation especially in the muscles of the anterior and external parts of the leg.

superficial peroneal nerve
Branch of the common peroneal nerve ensuring nerve sensation mainly in the lateral peroneal muscles of the outer leg and the back of the foot.

sciatic nerve
The organism's largest nerve, originating in the sacral plexus, ensuring nerve and motor sensation in a large portion of the lower limb.

saphenous nerve
Branch of the femoral nerve ensuring nerve sensation in the inner leg and knee.

deep peroneal nerve
Branch of the common peroneal nerve ensuring nerve sensation mainly in the muscles of the anterior part of the leg and the back of the foot.

THE HUMAN BEING

cranial nerves
Each of 12 pairs of nerves connected to the brain providing nerve sensation to the head and neck; they serve a motor or sensory function.

axillary nerve
Branch of the brachial plexus providing nerve sensation especially in the deltoid and small round muscles; it also ensures sensitivity in the shoulder joint.

radial nerve
Branch of the brachial plexus providing nerve sensation especially in the extensor muscles of the upper limb and fingers.

intercostal nerve
Nerve ensuring motor function and sensation in the muscles between the ribs, as well as in a portion of the diaphragm and the abdominal wall.

gluteal nerve
The lower gluteal nerve (originating in the posterior cutaneous nerve of thigh) and the upper gluteal nerve (branch of the sacral plexus) provide nerve sensation to the greatest, medium and small gluteal muscles.

digital nerve
Nerve originating in the brachial plexus ensuring nerve sensation in the fingers of the hand.

tibial nerve
Branch of the sciatic nerve extending through the posterior tibial nerve and providing nerve sensation to certain muscles of the leg and the sole of the foot.

sural nerve
Branch of the tibial nerve ensuring nerve sensation especially to the outer part of the calf, the ankle and the heel.

THE HUMAN BEING

nervous system

central nervous system
Part of the nervous system connected to the peripheral nervous system formed by the brain and the spinal cord; it controls and deciphers nerve information.

cerebrum
Large part of the brain formed of two hemispheres; it contains the control center of the higher nerve functions (motor activities, language and others).

cerebellum
Part of the brain that mainly controls motor coordination, equilibrium, muscle tone and posture.

spinal column
Movable bony axis made up of various parts articulating with each other (vertebrae); it supports the skeleton and contains the spinal cord.

spinal cord
Part of the central nervous system located in the spinal column; it receives and transmits nerve information and releases the reflexes.

internal filum terminale
Terminal part of the dura mater extending to the second sacral vertebra.

dura mater
Thick and resistant outer meninx fusing with the tissue covering the spinal nerves; it does not adhere directly to the bony vertebral wall.

filum terminale
Thin fibrous cord that is a continuation of the spinal cord between the second lumbar vertebra and the coccyx.

structure of the spinal cord
The spinal cord, protected by several solid and liquid membranes, is the source of 31 pairs of spinal nerves; it connects them to the brain.

posterior horn
Each of the terminal parts of the two masses of gray matter enclosing the associative neurons through which the sensory root enters the spinal cord.

sensory root
Bundle of sensory nerve fibers (axons) communicating information from the periphery of the body to the spinal cord.

white matter
Section of the spinal cord made up of nerve fibers (axons) and surrounding the gray matter.

spinal cord
Part of the central nervous system located in the spinal column; it receives and transmits nerve information and releases the reflexes.

gray matter
Central part of the spinal cord primarily made of the cell bodies of neurons.

spinal nerve
Nerve formed by the union of the sensory and motor roots; it communicates nerve messages between the spinal cord and the various parts of the organism.

spinal ganglion
Bulge of the posterior sensory root of the spinal nerve; it encloses the cell bodies of the neuron sensors.

motor root
Bundle of motor nerve fibers (axons) communicating information from the spinal cord to the periphery of the body, especially the muscles.

anterior horn
Each of the terminal parts of two masses gray matter enclosing the cell bodies of motor neurons and from which the motor root originates.

arachnoid
Meninx located between the dura mater and the pia mater.

dura mater
Thick and resistant outer meninx fusing with the tissue covering the spinal nerves; it does not adhere directly to the bony vertebral wall.

meninges
Each of three fibrous membranes surrounding and protecting the central nervous system (spinal cord, brain).

pia mater
Thin and highly veined inner meninx directly covering the spinal cord and the roots of the spinal nerves.

sympathetic ganglion
Bulge made up of nerve cell bodies forming a chain on both sides of the spinal cord; it mainly controls contraction of the visceral muscles.

THE HUMAN BEING

brain
Part of the central nervous system located in the skull, made up of the cerebrum, cerebellum, and brainstem.

cerebrum
Large part of the brain formed of two hemispheres; it contains the control center of the higher nerve functions (motor activities, language and others).

corpus callosum
Thin plate of a white substance formed by a bundle of nerve fibers that connect the two cerebral hemispheres.

pineal gland
Gland secreting a hormone (melatonin) that mainly influences the biological rhythms.

cerebellum
Part of the brain that mainly controls motor coordination, equilibrium, muscle tone and posture.

medulla oblongata
Part of the brain stem that is a continuation of the spinal cord; it mainly controls breathing, blood circulation and cardiac rhythm.

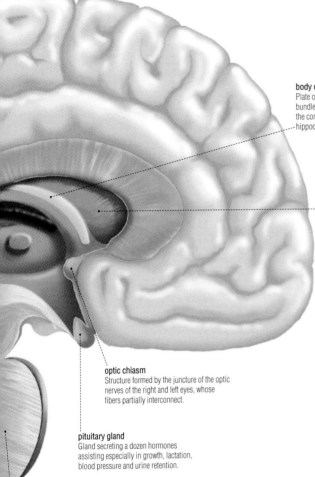

body of fornix
Plate of a white substance formed by a bundle of nerve fibers and located below the corpus callosum; it connects the hippocampus to the hypothalamus.

septum pellucidum
Thin double membrane separating the anterior part of the two cerebral hemispheres and extending from the corpus callosum to the body of fornix.

optic chiasm
Structure formed by the juncture of the optic nerves of the right and left eyes, whose fibers partially interconnect.

pituitary gland
Gland secreting a dozen hormones assisting especially in growth, lactation, blood pressure and urine retention.

pons
Part of the cerebral trunk made up of nerve fibers; it serves as a bridge between the brain, the cerebellum and the medulla oblongata, and aids breathing.

chain of neurons
All the interconnected complex nerve cells receiving, communicating and transmitting messages in the form of nerve impulses.

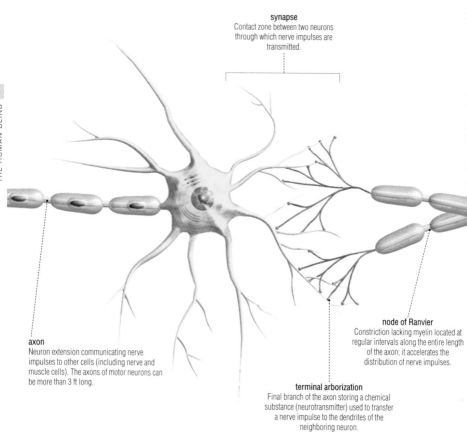

synapse
Contact zone between two neurons through which nerve impulses are transmitted.

axon
Neuron extension communicating nerve impulses to other cells (including nerve and muscle cells). The axons of motor neurons can be more than 3 ft long.

node of Ranvier
Constriction lacking myelin located at regular intervals along the entire length of the axon; it accelerates the distribution of nerve impulses.

terminal arborization
Final branch of the axon storing a chemical substance (neurotransmitter) used to transfer a nerve impulse to the dendrites of the neighboring neuron.

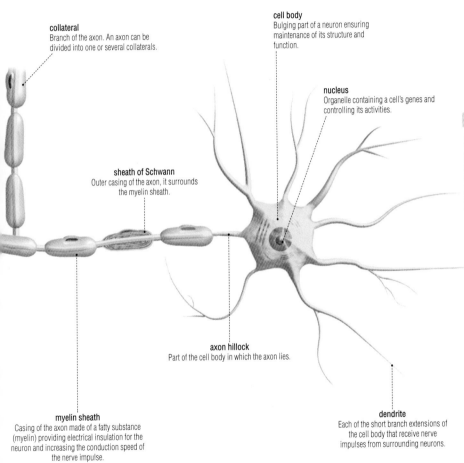

collateral
Branch of the axon. An axon can be divided into one or several collaterals.

cell body
Bulging part of a neuron ensuring maintenance of its structure and function.

nucleus
Organelle containing a cell's genes and controlling its activities.

sheath of Schwann
Outer casing of the axon, it surrounds the myelin sheath.

axon hillock
Part of the cell body in which the axon lies.

myelin sheath
Casing of the axon made of a fatty substance (myelin) providing electrical insulation for the neuron and increasing the conduction speed of the nerve impulse.

dendrite
Each of the short branch extensions of the cell body that receive nerve impulses from surrounding neurons.

nervous system

cranial nerves
Each of 12 pairs of nerves connected to the brain providing nerve sensation to the head and neck; they serve a motor or sensory function.

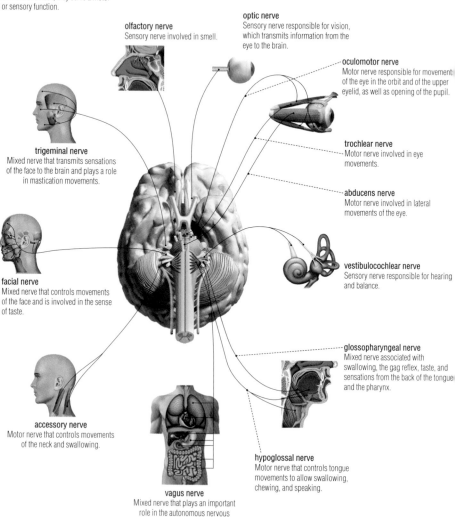

olfactory nerve
Sensory nerve involved in smell.

optic nerve
Sensory nerve responsible for vision, which transmits information from the eye to the brain.

oculomotor nerve
Motor nerve responsible for movement of the eye in the orbit and of the upper eyelid, as well as opening of the pupil.

trochlear nerve
Motor nerve involved in eye movements.

abducens nerve
Motor nerve involved in lateral movements of the eye.

trigeminal nerve
Mixed nerve that transmits sensations of the face to the brain and plays a role in mastication movements.

vestibulocochlear nerve
Sensory nerve responsible for hearing and balance.

facial nerve
Mixed nerve that controls movements of the face and is involved in the sense of taste.

glossopharyngeal nerve
Mixed nerve associated with swallowing, the gag reflex, taste, and sensations from the back of the tongue and the pharynx.

accessory nerve
Motor nerve that controls movements of the neck and swallowing.

hypoglossal nerve
Motor nerve that controls tongue movements to allow swallowing, chewing, and speaking.

vagus nerve
Mixed nerve that plays an important role in the autonomous nervous system by innervating all of the viscera.

THE HUMAN BEING

breast

Female milk-secreting glandular organ; it develops at puberty and increases in size during pregnancy.

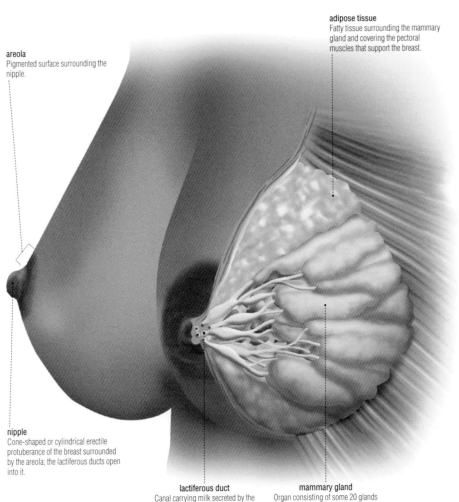

adipose tissue
Fatty tissue surrounding the mammary gland and covering the pectoral muscles that support the breast.

areola
Pigmented surface surrounding the nipple.

nipple
Cone-shaped or cylindrical erectile protuberance of the breast surrounded by the areola; the lactiferous ducts open into it.

lactiferous duct
Canal carrying milk secreted by the mammary gland to the nipple.

mammary gland
Organ consisting of some 20 glands (lobes) ensuring secretion of milk.

female reproductive organs

Mainly internal, they enable fertilization of the egg by the spermatozoon and the development of the embryo and fetus.

sagittal section
Front-to-back vertical section on the median line of the body.

abdominal cavity
Lower portion of the trunk containing the majority of the organs of the digestive, urinary and genital systems.

peritoneum
Resistant membrane covering the internal walls and organs of the abdominal cavity and maintaining its shape.

fallopian tube
Canal through which the egg travels from the ovary to the uterus. Fertilization of the egg by the spermatozoon normally takes place in the upper section of the tube.

ovary
Female genital gland that produces eggs and the sex hormones estrogen and progesterone.

uterus
Hollow muscular organ receiving the egg and, once fertilized, enabling its development and expulsion at the end of pregnancy.

urinary bladder
Muscular reservoir where urine from the kidneys collects before being evacuated through the urethra.

mons pubis
Middle protuberance of the pubis made of adipose tissues and covered with hair at puberty.

symphysis pubis
Slightly movable fibrocartilaginous joint connecting the two pubes (anterior part of the two iliac bones).

clitoris
Small erectile organ at the anterior section of the vulva constituting a major erogenous zone.

urethra
Membranous canal enabling evacuation of urine from the bladder.

labia minora
Mucous folds of the vulva located between the labia majora.

labia majora
Thick cutaneous hairy folds of the vulva protecting the vaginal orifice.

THE HUMAN BEING

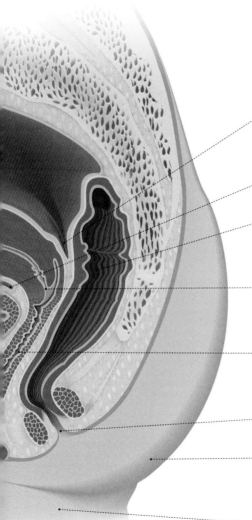

pouch of Douglas
Small pouch formed by the fold of the peritoneum between the rectum and the uterus.

uterovesical pouch
Small pouch formed by the fold of the peritoneum between the uterus and the bladder.

rectum
Terminal section of the large intestine preceding the anus.

cervix of uterus
Lower narrow section of the uterus through which it connects with the vagina.

vagina
Muscular canal located between the neck of the uterus and the vulva enabling copulation.

anus
Terminal orifice of the digestive tract enabling ejection of fecal matter.

buttock
Fleshy part consisting mostly of muscles located at the base of the back.

thigh
Section of the leg between the hip and the knee; it contains many powerful muscles.

female reproductive organs

posterior view

broad ligament of uterus
Peritoneal fold connecting the lateral edge of the uterus to the abdominal cavity wall.

isthmus of fallopian tube
Narrow section of the fallopian tube opening into the uterus.

infundibulum of fallopian tube
Largely flat section of the fallopian tube through which the egg enters.

ovary
Female genital gland that produces eggs and the sex hormones estrogen and progesterone.

uterus
Hollow muscular organ receiving the egg and, once fertilized, enabling its development and expulsion at the end of pregnancy.

ampulla of fallopian tube
Widened section of the fallopian tube located between the infundibulum and the isthmus.

labia minora
Mucous folds of the vulva located between the labia majora.

vagina
Muscular canal located between the neck of the uterus and the vulva enabling copulation.

labia majorum
Thick cutaneous hairy folds of the vulva protecting the vaginal orifice.

THE HUMAN BEING

fallopian tubes
Canals transporting the egg from the ovary to the uterus; fertilization of the egg by the spermatozoon generally takes place in the upper part of the tube.

vulva
External female genital organs consisting mainly of the labia and the clitoris.

female reproductive organs

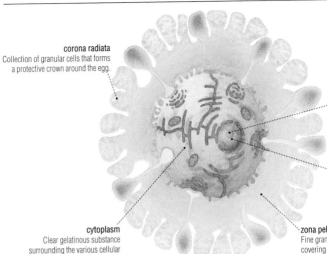

egg
Mature female reproductive cell produced by the ovary, which, after fertilization by a spermatozoon, enables the embryo to develop.

corona radiata
Collection of granular cells that forms a protective crown around the egg.

nucleolus
Small spherical body located inside the nucleus, within which the ribosomes, or protein-synthesizing structures, are produced.

nucleus
Organelle containing a cell's genes and controlling its activities.

cytoplasm
Clear gelatinous substance surrounding the various cellular structures.

zona pellucida
Fine granular coat composed of mucopolysaccharides covering the egg; it allows a single spermatozoon to penetrate the egg, which then becomes impermeable to others.

male reproductive organs

The male genitalia ensure reproduction; they produce spermatozoa and eject them into the female genital tract during copulation.

spermatozoon
Mature and mobile reproductive male cell produced by the testicle; the main constituent of the sperm used to fertilize an egg.

head
Anterior section of the spermatozoon formed of a nucleus (organelle containing genetic information) and the acrosome (structure aiding in penetration of the egg).

middle piece
Part surrounding the base of the tail where the mitochondria, small organelles that supply the energy needed for the spermatozoon to move, concentrate.

tail
Filament whose oscillations enable the movement of the spermatozoon.

end piece
Terminal end of the spermatozoon's tail.

neck
Narrow part connecting the head to the intermediary section; it contains the centrioles, structures that aid in cell division.

THE HUMAN BEING

male reproductive organs

sagittal section
Front-to-back vertical section on the
median line of the body.

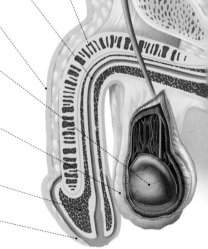

abdominal cavity
Lower portion of the trunk containing
the majority of the organs of the
digestive, urinary and genital systems.

symphysis pubis
Slightly movable fibrocartilaginous
joint connecting the two pubes
(anterior part of the two iliac bones).

cavernous body
Erectile tissue of the back of the penis
extending to the gland.

male urethra
Membranous duct enabling evacuation
of urine and carrying sperm to the
terminal part of the penis.

penis
Organ enabling copulation as well as the
evacuation of urine and sperm; during
sexual arousal, it fills with blood and
forms an erection.

testicle
Male genital gland that produces
spermatozoa and the sex hormone
testosterone.

scrotum
Cutaneous muscular pouch containing
the testicles and regulating their
temperature.

glans penis
Bulging anterior terminal portion of the
penis consisting of a spongy body; it is
surrounded by the prepuce and is where
the meatus of the urethra opens.

foreskin
Cutaneous fold covering the glans
penis.

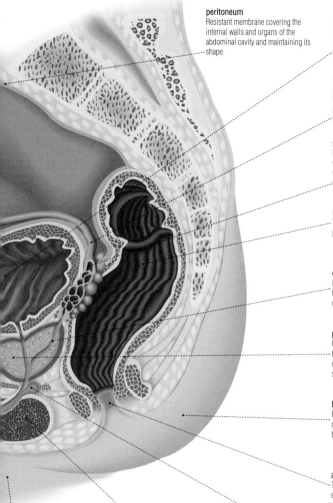

peritoneum
Resistant membrane covering the internal walls and organs of the abdominal cavity and maintaining its shape.

urinary bladder
Muscular reservoir where urine from the kidneys collects before being evacuated through the urethra.

deferent duct
Muscular membranous duct channeling the sperm of the epididymis to the prostate gland; it extends through the ejaculator duct.

seminal vesicle
Enlargement of the deferent duct whose glands secrete a protein-rich viscous liquid that makes up about 60% of the sperm.

rectum
Terminal section of the large intestine preceding the anus.

ejaculatory duct
Muscular membranous duct extending the deferent canal and opening into the urethra in the prostrate gland.

prostate
Gland secreting a thick whitish liquid that aids in the formation of sperm and contributes to the mobility of the spermatozoa.

buttock
Fleshy part consisting mostly of muscles located at the base of the back.

anus
Terminal orifice of the digestive tract enabling ejection of fecal matter.

thigh
Section of the leg between the hip and the knee; it contains many powerful muscles.

bulbocavernous muscle
Muscle contributing to erection and to the evacuation of urine and sperm.

Cowper's gland
Organ secreting a viscous substance emptying out into the urethra just before ejaculation to lubricate and to neutralize the acidity of residual traces of urine.

touch

Sense enabling the skin to detect sensations (contact, heat, pain and others) due to specialized receptors spread widely over the surface of the body.

skin
Outer covering of the body consisting of three layers; it has a role in protection, tactile sensation and thermoregulation.

hair
Threadlike epidermal outgrowth present on almost the entire body having a sebaceous gland and an arrector pili muscle; it plays a protective role.

stratum corneum
Layer of the epidermis consisting of dead cells rich in keratin (the protein that protects the skin); it is shed as a new layer is formed.

stratum lucidum
Layer of the epidermis usually present only in the thick skin of the palms of the hands and soles of the feet.

stratum granulosum
Layer of the epidermis whose cells help to form keratin, which renders the skin impermeable.

stratum basale
Layer of the epidermis whose cells divide and migrate toward the surface to form the upper layers, thus ensuring renewal of the epidermis.

sebaceous gland
Organ connected to a hair follicle secreting a fatty substance (sebum) that lubricates the hair and skin, making them impermeable to air and water.

arrector pili muscle
Muscle attached to a hair follicle and whose contraction raises the hair on end as a result of cold or fear.

nerve fiber
Structure formed of neuron extensions along which the skin's sensory information travels.

hair follicle
Small cavity of the dermis and hypodermis in which the hair root is implanted and which receives secretions from the sebaceous and sweat glands.

apocrine sweat gland
Sweat-secreting organ whose excretory duct opens into the hair follicle.

blood vessel
Membranous canal through which blood circulates in the organism, bringing in oxygen and nutrients and carrying away waste.

skin surface
Surface portion of the skin in contact with the air from which dead cells are regularly shed and replaced by new cells of the stratum basale.

pore
Orifice in which the sweat duct opens, allowing excretion of sweat onto the surface of the skin.

epidermis
Surface layer of the skin covering and protecting the dermis; it contains proteins that make the skin impermeable and block ultraviolet rays.

sudoriferous duct
Duct carrying sweat produced by the sweat gland to the surface of the skin.

connective tissue
Tissue rich in veins and nerves made up especially of collagen and elastin fibers that give the skin its elasticity and resistance.

dermis
Layer of skin enclosing tactile receptors ensuring nutrition and support of the epidermis.

capillary blood vessel
Very fine blood vessel connected to the arterial and venal networks; through it the blood and cells of the organism are exchanged.

adipose tissue
Tissue enclosing numerous fat cells, thermally insulating the organism and providing an energy reserve.

subcutaneous tissue
Tissue rich in veins and nerves at the base of the dermis enabling especially the absorption of shocks.

eccrine sweat gland
Sweat-secreting organ whose excretory duct opens onto the surface of the skin; the sweat glands help especially in the elimination of waste.

THE HUMAN BEING

touch

finger
Each of the five terminal parts of the hand containing numerous Meissner's corpuscles, giving them great sensitivity.

middle phalanx
Second phalange of the finger between the proximal and distal phalanges.

epidermis
Surface layer of the skin covering and protecting the dermis; it contains proteins that make the skin impermeable and block ultraviolet rays.

dermis
Layer of skin enclosing tactile receptors ensuring nutrition and support of the epidermis.

nail matrix
Section of the epidermis from which the nail grows.

root of nail
Base of the nail implanted in the matrix and protected by a fold of skin (cuticle).

lunula
Whitish section between the root and the body of the nail corresponding to the visible front portion of the matrix.

body of nail
Central pinkish section of the nail adhering to the nail bed.

free margin
Whitish terminal part of the nail extending beyond the finger.

digital pulp
Fleshy terminal part of the inner finger.

distal phalanx
Last phalange of the finger bearing a nail.

nail bed
Portion of the finger upon which the nail sits containing numerous blood vessels, thus nourishing the nail.

THE HUMAN BEING

hearing

Sense that perceives sounds and maintains balance; the human ear is capable of distinguishing almost 400,000 sounds.

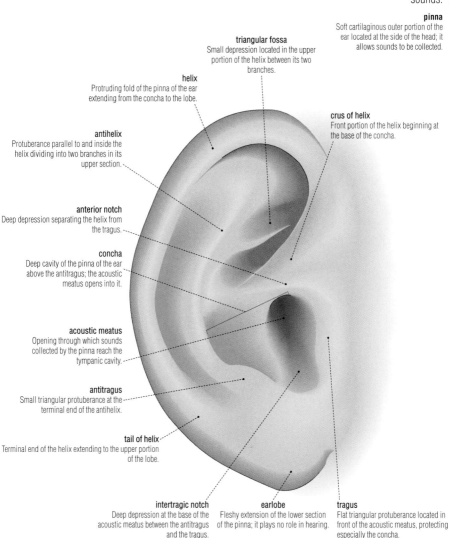

pinna
Soft cartilaginous outer portion of the ear located at the side of the head; it allows sounds to be collected.

triangular fossa
Small depression located in the upper portion of the helix between its two branches.

helix
Protruding fold of the pinna of the ear extending from the concha to the lobe.

crus of helix
Front portion of the helix beginning at the base of the concha.

antihelix
Protuberance parallel to and inside the helix dividing into two branches in its upper section.

anterior notch
Deep depression separating the helix from the tragus.

concha
Deep cavity of the pinna of the ear above the antitragus; the acoustic meatus opens into it.

acoustic meatus
Opening through which sounds collected by the pinna reach the tympanic cavity.

antitragus
Small triangular protuberance at the terminal end of the antihelix.

tail of helix
Terminal end of the helix extending to the upper portion of the lobe.

intertragic notch
Deep depression at the base of the acoustic meatus between the antitragus and the tragus.

earlobe
Fleshy extension of the lower section of the pinna; it plays no role in hearing.

tragus
Flat triangular protuberance located in front of the acoustic meatus, protecting especially the concha.

THE HUMAN BEING

hearing

structure of the ear

The ear is made up of three distinct parts; hearing is controlled by the inner ear, which contains the sensory organs.

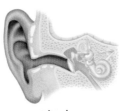

external ear
Visible portion of the ear enabling sounds to be collected and directed to the middle ear through the acoustic meatus.

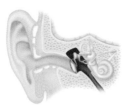

middle ear
Air-filled cavity hollowed out of the temporal bone; it receives sounds from the external ear, amplifies them through the auricles and transmits them to the internal ear.

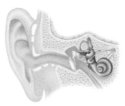

internal ear
Liquid-filled cavity hollowed out of the temporal bone that transforms sound vibrations into nerve influxes to be interpreted by the brain.

pinna
Soft cartilaginous outer portion of the ear located at the side of the head; it allows sounds to be collected.

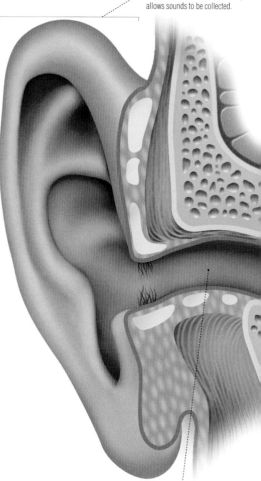

acoustic meatus
Canal carrying the sounds collected by the pinna to the eardrum. It is lined with hair and covered with cerumen, a waxy substance that retains dust particles.

eardrum
Slender resistant elastic membrane; it vibrates when sound waves are received from the auditory canal, then transmits the waves to the ossicles.

posterior semicircular canal
Vertical canal parallel to the temporal bone; it monitors head movements to ensure that equilibrium is maintained.

superior semicircular canal
Vertical canal perpendicular to the temporal bone; it monitors head movements to ensure that equilibrium is maintained.

auditory ossicles
The smallest bones in the human body, held in place by several muscles and ligaments; they amplify the vibrations of the eardrum.

lateral semicircular canal
Horizontal canal; it monitors head movements to ensure that equilibrium is maintained.

vestibular nerve
Nerve transmitting messages related to equilibrium to the brain; it emanates from the vestibule and the semicircular canals.

cochlear nerve
Nerve transmitting auditory messages collected in the cochlea to the brain. The cochlear and vestibular nerves join to form the auditory nerve.

vestibule
Bony structure into which the three semicircular canals open; with these canals, it is responsible for equilibrium.

cochlea
Bony structure intended for hearing; it receives vibrations from the ossicles and transforms them into nervous impulses before transmitting them to the brain.

auditory ossicles
Each of the three small interarticulated bones of the middle ear that amplify the vibrations of the eardrum and transmit them to the internal ear.

Eustachian tube
Tube connecting the middle ear to the nasopharynx; it allows outside air to pass through, thus equalizing air pressure on both sides of the eardrum.

incus
Auricle of the middle ear articulating with the malleus and the stapes.

stapes
Auricle of the middle ear transmitting vibrations from the incus to the internal ear; at about .15 in long, the stapes is the smallest bone in the body.

malleus
Auricle of the middle ear transmitting vibrations to the incus from the ear drum (to which it is attached).

smell and taste

Since the oral and nasal cavities are connected, the olfactory sense affects taste. The human being can distinguish four basic flavors and almost 10,000 odors.

mouth
Anterior cavity of the digestive tract; it has a role in ingesting food, tasting, breathing and speaking.

soft palate
Muscular membranous section of the wall separating the mouth from the nasal cavity; it has a role especially in ingesting food and speaking.

superior dental arch
Arch formed by the set of teeth of the maxilla.

gum
Thick section of the mucous membrane of the mouth that is rich in blood vessels and nerves; it covers the edge of the dental alveolus and adheres to the neck.

upper lip
Movable muscular fold forming the upper contour of the mouth; the main roles of the lips are protecting the teeth and helping in speech.

hard palate
Bony section of the wall dividing the mouth from the nasal cavity; it is extended by the soft palate.

isthmus of fauces
Orifice by which the mouth connects with the pharynx (meeting point of the respiratory and digestive tracts) enabling food to reach the esophagus.

palatoglossal arch
Muscular lateral fold of the posterior edge of the soft palate.

uvula
Fleshy movable appendage that is an extension of the posterior edge of the soft palate; it aids in ingesting food and speaking.

tonsil
Lymphoid structure (rich in white blood cells) involved in protecting the respiratory tract by fighting bacterial infections.

tongue
Flexible muscular structure of the oral cavity; it helps in tasting, masticating and ingesting food, and also facilitates speech.

inferior dental arch
Arch formed by the set of teeth of the mandible.

lower lip
Movable muscular fold forming the lower contour of the mouth.

commissure of lips of mouth
Each of the two juncture points of the upper and lower lips.

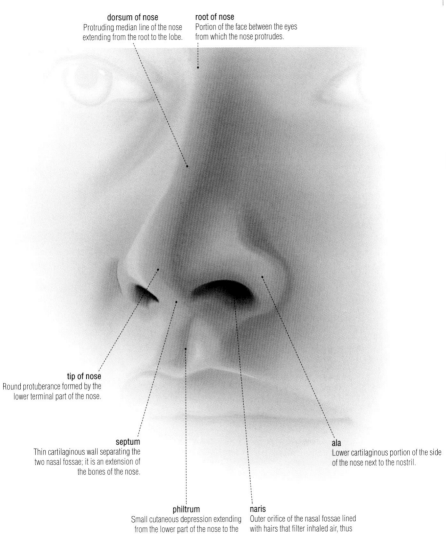

dorsum of nose
Protruding median line of the nose extending from the root to the lobe.

root of nose
Portion of the face between the eyes from which the nose protrudes.

tip of nose
Round protuberance formed by the lower terminal part of the nose.

septum
Thin cartilaginous wall separating the two nasal fossae; it is an extension of the bones of the nose.

ala
Lower cartilaginous portion of the side of the nose next to the nostril.

philtrum
Small cutaneous depression extending from the lower part of the nose to the upper lip.

naris
Outer orifice of the nasal fossae lined with hairs that filter inhaled air, thus preventing the penetration of foreign bodies.

smell and taste

nasal fossae
Each of two cavities separated by a middle partition; they assist in olfaction, respiration and speech.

olfactory bulb
Nerve structure where fibers of the olfactory nerve end; it receives nervous impulses from the mucous membrane and transmits them to the olfactory tract.

olfactory tract
Nerve structure containing the axons; it enables nerve impulses from the bulb to be carried to the brain, where they are interpreted.

frontal sinus
Cavity hollowed out of the frontal bone of the skull; it connects with the nasal fossae and warms inhaled air.

olfactory nerve
Bundle of nerve fibers formed by the axons of the mucous membrane's olfactory cells, which transmit nerve impulses to the brain.

superior nasal concha
Curved bony plate resting on the ethmoid and contributing to olfaction by bringing inhaled air into contact with the mucous membrane.

nasal bone
Small flat bone forming the skeleton of the root of the nose; the two nasal bones join along the bridge of the nose.

septal cartilage of nose
Plate of resistant elastic tissue; it extends the bones of the nose and separates the nasal fossae.

middle nasal concha
Curved bony plate resting on the ethmoid. Among its functions, the nasal chamber warms inhaled air by increasing the mucous surface.

greater alar cartilage
Thin plate of resistant elastic tissue supporting the bridge of the nose and delimiting the contour of the nostril.

inferior nasal concha
Curved bony plate attached to the lateral wall of the nasal fossae.

olfactory mucosa
Tissue lining a portion of the nasal fossae and containing olfactory cells, which detect odors and release nerve impulses.

hard palate
Bony section of the wall dividing the mouth from the nasal cavity; it is extended by the soft palate.

tongue
Flexible muscular structure of the oral cavity; it helps in tasting, masticating and ingesting food, and also facilitates speech.

sphenoidal sinus
Cavity hollowed out of the sphenoid bone of the skull; it connects with the nasal fossae and warms inhaled air.

olfactory bulb
Nerve structure where fibers of the olfactory nerve end; it receives nervous impulses from the mucous membrane and transmits them to the olfactory tract.

nasopharynx
Section of the pharynx (meeting point of the respiratory and digestive tracts) through which the mouth connects with the nasal fossae and where the Eustachian tube opens.

axon
Extension of olfactory cell, communicating nerve impulses to the olfactory bulb.

Eustachian tube
Tube connecting the middle ear to the nasopharynx; it allows outside air to pass through, thus equalizing air pressure on both sides of the ear drum.

Bowman's gland
Gland of the olfactory mucosa that secretes mucus.

olfactory cell
Neuron one end of which has cilia that convert chemical stimuli into nerve impulses, which will be transmitted to the olfactory bulb.

soft palate
Muscular membranous section of the wall separating the mouth from the nasal cavity; it has a role especially in ingesting food and speaking.

uvula
Fleshy movable appendage that is an extension of the posterior edge of the soft palate; it aids in ingesting food and speaking.

mucus
Runny secretion produced by the Bowman's glands, which moistens the cilia at the end of the olfactory cells to dissolve odorous molecules.

smell and taste

dorsum of tongue

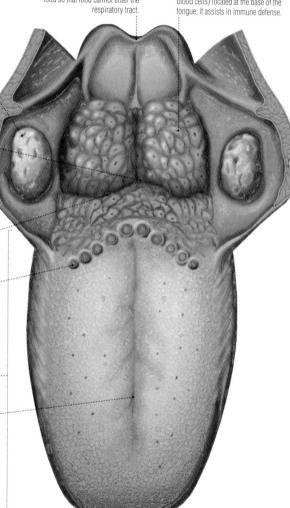

epiglottis
Movable cartilaginous plate ensuring that the larynx closes during ingestion of food so that food cannot enter the respiratory tract.

lingual tonsil
Lymphoid structure (rich in white blood cells) located at the base of the tongue; it assists in immune defense.

palatine tonsil
Lymphoid structure (rich in white blood cells) located on each side of the base of the tongue; it protects the respiratory tract by fighting bacteria.

foramen cecum
Small depression located at the base of the tongue, at the top of the sulcus terminalis.

root
Part that fixes the tongue to the mandible and the hyoid bone of the skull; it is also joined on each side to the walls of the pharynx.

sulcus terminalis
Inverted V-shaped depression separating the base of the body of the tongue, topped by the foramen cecum.

circumvallate papilla
Each of the large taste buds (about 10) forming a lingual V at the back of the body of the tongue ensuring the taste function; they mostly perceive bitter flavors.

body
Free mobile portion of the tongue composed mostly of mucous-covered muscles and bearing the taste buds.

median lingual sulcus
Depression extending over the entire length of the body of the tongue and separating it into two symmetrical halves.

apex
Mobile terminal end of the tongue; it mostly perceives sweet flavors.

taste receptors
The mucous membrane of the tongue is composed of small protuberances, lingual taste buds, distinguished by their particular sensitivity to one of the basic flavors: sweet, salty, sour, bitter.

fungiform papilla
Mushroom-shaped taste bud occurring in large numbers at the apex and on the sides of the tongue and having a taste function; it reacts mainly to sweet and salty flavors.

foliate papilla
Taste bud located mainly on the posterior lateral edges of the tongue and having a taste function; it is most sensitive to sour flavors.

filiform papilla
Cone-shaped taste bud covering the rear of the tongue; its function is solely tactile. These taste buds give the tongue its velvety appearance.

circumvallate papilla
Each of the large taste buds (about 10) forming a lingual V at the back of the body of the tongue ensuring the taste function; they mostly perceive bitter flavors.

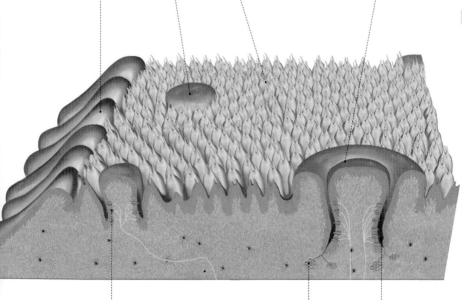

THE HUMAN BEING

taste bud
Organ of taste formed of sensory cells that, in contact with saliva, detect flavors and transmit them to the brain in the form of nerve impulses.

salivary gland
Each of the three pairs of saliva-secreting organs responsible for moistening food so that the taste buds can perceive its taste.

furrow
Saliva-filled depression delimiting the lingual taste buds.

sight

The human being possesses a highly developed visual sensitivity, far superior to that of the other senses.

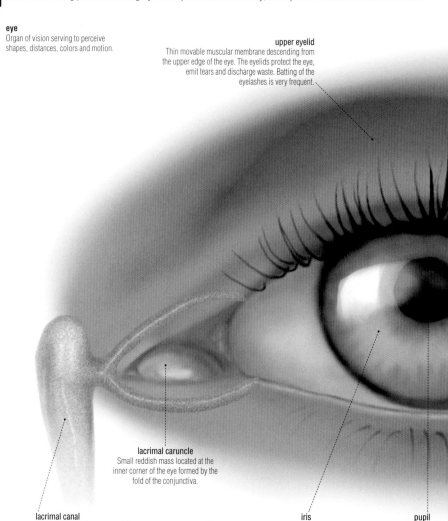

eye
Organ of vision serving to perceive shapes, distances, colors and motion.

upper eyelid
Thin movable muscular membrane descending from the upper edge of the eye. The eyelids protect the eye, emit tears and discharge waste. Batting of the eyelashes is very frequent.

lacrimal caruncle
Small reddish mass located at the inner corner of the eye formed by the fold of the conjunctiva.

lacrimal canal
Duct opening out into the nasal fossae through which tears produced by the tear glands are discharged.

iris
Colored central portion of the eyeball composed of muscles whose dilation or contraction controls the opening of the pupil.

pupil
Central orifice of the eye whose opening varies to regulate the amount of light entering the eye; light causes the pupil to contract.

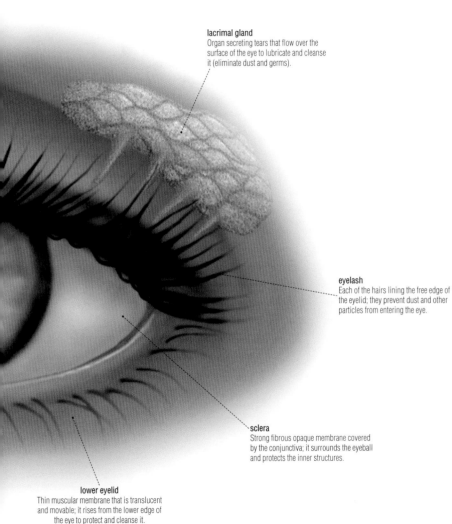

lacrimal gland
Organ secreting tears that flow over the surface of the eye to lubricate and cleanse it (eliminate dust and germs).

eyelash
Each of the hairs lining the free edge of the eyelid; they prevent dust and other particles from entering the eye.

sclera
Strong fibrous opaque membrane covered by the conjunctiva; it surrounds the eyeball and protects the inner structures.

lower eyelid
Thin muscular membrane that is translucent and movable; it rises from the lower edge of the eye to protect and cleanse it.

mushrooms

Vegetable that grows in damp cool places; its edible varieties are served as condiments or as an ingredient in a variety of foods.

royal agaric
Equally flavorful raw or cooked, it has been famous since ancient times; it is not to be confused with the poisonous fly agaric, which it resembles.

delicious lactarius
Secretes an orange milk when broken open; it is used primarily in spicy sauces, especially in Spain and the south of France.

enoki mushroom
Long-stemmed, soft-fleshed resistant mushroom very popular in Asia; it is eaten raw, in salads, or cooked, in soups and Oriental dishes.

green russula
Its white brittle flesh has an aroma of hazelnut; it can be eaten raw or cooked, preferably grilled.

morel
The darker the specimen, the more flavorful its thin fragrant flesh; it should be thoroughly cooked to eliminate toxic substances.

edible boletus
Squat, it can grow up to 10 in in height and diameter; it is usually cooked in oil, braised or served in an omelette.

truffle
Underground mushroom hard to find
and perceived as a luxury food; it is
usually associated with game and
poultry.

wood ear
Its tasteless gelatinous flesh is popular
in Asia; it is usually eaten in soups or
with vegetables.

oyster mushroom
Grows on trees or on dead wood; its soft
white flesh is a valued ingredient in sauces,
where it can substitute for the cultivated
mushroom.

cultivated mushroom
The most widely cultivated and consumed
mushroom; it is eaten raw, in salads or with dips,
or cooked, primarily in sauces and on pizza.

shiitake mushroom
The equivalent of the cultivated mushroom
in Japan, where it is widely grown for use
in Oriental dishes and sauces and for its
therapeutic value.

chanterelle
Pleasantly fragrant and valued by
gourmets, especially those in Europe; it
is served most often with meat or
omelettes.

FOOD AND KITCHEN

seaweed

Usually aquatic vegetables used in cooking or as dietary supplements; they are primarily produced and eaten by the Japanese.

arame
Milder and less crunchy than hijiki, it is used mainly in salads and soups or served fried as a side vegetable.

wakame
Popular with the Japanese, it is rich in calcium and has a delicate texture and flavor; among its many uses, it is a often served with legume dishes.

spirulina
Microscopic freshwater alga, rich in nutrients (protein, iron, magnesium); it is used mainly as a dietary supplement.

Irish moss
Plentiful in the North Atlantic, it can only be eaten cooked; also produces carrageen, a substance used to thicken certain dishes.

agar-agar
Translucent strips derived from red algae, which is melted to produce a jelly that can replace gelatin in numerous recipes.

hijiki
These dried twigs expand when soaked, resembling black, somewhat crunchy noodles; they are often served as a vegetable.

kombu
Eaten since ancient times, it is sold in large blackish strips; it is used primarily as an ingredient in broth or to make a kind of tea.

sea lettuce
Resembles lettuce leaves in taste and appearance; its soft leaves are eaten raw in salads or cooked in soups.

nori
Purplish alga that turns black when dried; usually sold in thin dried sheets, it is used mainly to make sushi.

dulse
Iron-rich, it has long been eaten by people living along Europe's coasts; it enhances soups and salads with its soft texture and strong flavor.

vegetables

Plants used as foodstuffs; a simple way to classify vegetables is to group them according to their edible part. The sweet fruit category of plants constitutes another food category (fruits).

bulb vegetables

The main edible part of these vegetables is their bulb, the underground structure where the plant's nutrient reserves are stored.

red onion
The sweetest of the onions, it is often eaten raw, in salads or sandwiches.

yellow onion
The most common onion, widely used as a flavoring ingredient, either raw or cooked; it is also the essential ingredient in onion soup.

leek
The white part is the most popular, but the green part adds flavor to puréed soups and stews; it is often combined with potatoes in a cold soup called vichyssoise.

pearl onion
Small white onion picked before fully ripe; it is primarily used to make pickles or as an ingredient in stews such as boeuf bourguignon.

white onion
Mild and sweet, this onion is widely used as a flavoring ingredient; it is often eaten raw or deep-fried in rings.

vegetables

green onion
Mild onion picked before fully ripe; it is usually sold with the stem, in bunches. It is often eaten raw in salads or cooked in sautéed dishes.

shallot
It has a more subtle flavor than the onion or the chive; it is eaten raw or cooked and often used as a flavoring ingredient in sauces.

scallion
Its bulb is less developed than that of the green onion; the white part is used like the onion and the green is used to season a variety of dishes.

water chestnut
The aquatic bulb of a Chinese plant; its white crunchy flesh is an important ingredient in many Asian dishes.

garlic
The bulb is composed of bulblets called cloves; the germ at its center can make garlic difficult to digest.

chive
Smallest member of the onion family; its stem is used primarily to season various hot and cold dishes.

tuber vegetables

Tubers that are eaten like vegetables; they consist of underground growths containing the plant's nutrient reserves.

crosne
Native to Asia, where it is very popular although little known elsewhere; it has a slightly sweet flavor and is used and prepared like the potato.

cassava
The sweet variety is eaten like the potato; the bitter one is used to make tapioca.

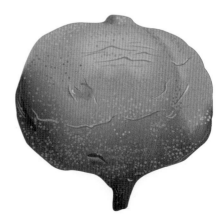

taro
Its starchy, sweet flesh is a staple in several tropical countries; eaten raw, preferably very hot and prepared like the potato.

jicama
Its flesh is sweet, crunchy and juicy; it is eaten raw in salads, as an hors d'oeuvre or with dips; it adds a crunchy element to cooked dishes.

vegetables

tuber vegetables

FOOD AND KITCHEN

yam
A staple food in many countries, especially in South America and the West Indies, where it is eaten cooked, prepared like the potato.

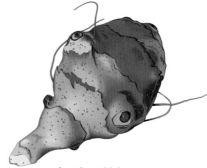

Jerusalem artichoke
Eaten raw, cooked or marinated; it has sweet, crunchy, juicy flesh.

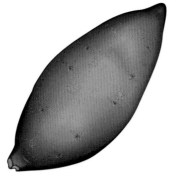

sweet potato
Sweeter than the potato and not of the same family; a staple of Creole cooking.

potato
The best-known tuber; eaten especially as a vegetable side dish, either steamed, deep-fried or mashed.

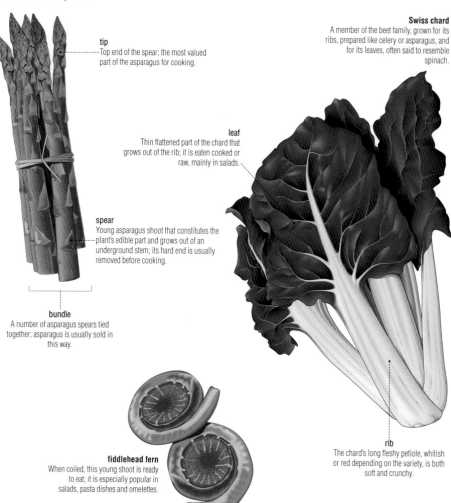

stalk vegetables
Edible plants whose stems are consumed like vegetables; the leaves of some varieties are also edible.

asparagus
Often thought of as a luxury, it is picked before fully ripe; whether served hot or cold, it is always cooked.

tip
Top end of the spear; the most valued part of the asparagus for cooking.

Swiss chard
A member of the beet family, grown for its ribs, prepared like celery or asparagus, and for its leaves, often said to resemble spinach.

leaf
Thin flattened part of the chard that grows out of the rib; it is eaten cooked or raw, mainly in salads.

spear
Young asparagus shoot that constitutes the plant's edible part and grows out of an underground stem; its hard end is usually removed before cooking.

bundle
A number of asparagus spears tied together; asparagus is usually sold in this way.

fiddlehead fern
When coiled, this young shoot is ready to eat; it is especially popular in salads, pasta dishes and omelettes.

rib
The chard's long fleshy petiole, whitish or red depending on the variety, is both soft and crunchy.

fennel
Mainly associated with Italian cooking; the bulb is eaten as a vegetable while the leaves and seeds are used to season a variety of dishes.

stalk
Part of the fennel growing out of the bulb and bearing small feathery dark-green leaves; it is traditionally used to flavor fish dishes.

bulb
Fleshy edible part of the fennel, composed of the overlapping enlarged parts at the base of the stems.

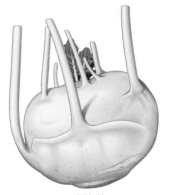

kohlrabi
Very popular in Central and Eastern Europe, where its bulbous stem is eaten raw or cooked like turnip; its cabbage-flavored leaves can also be eaten.

bamboo shoot
Very popular in Asia, this plant can only be eaten once cooked; it is an essential ingredient in sukiyaki, a typical Japanese dish.

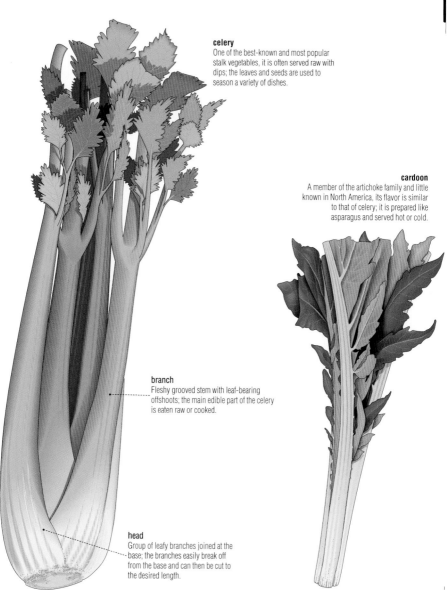

celery
One of the best-known and most popular stalk vegetables, it is often served raw with dips; the leaves and seeds are used to season a variety of dishes.

cardoon
A member of the artichoke family and little known in North America, its flavor is similar to that of celery; it is prepared like asparagus and served hot or cold.

branch
Fleshy grooved stem with leaf-bearing offshoots; the main edible part of the celery is eaten raw or cooked.

head
Group of leafy branches joined at the base; the branches easily break off from the base and can then be cut to the desired length.

FOOD AND KITCHEN

vegetables

FOOD AND KITCHEN

leaf vegetables
Leaves of edible plants consumed as vegetables.

leaf lettuce
Lettuce having soft wavy leaves with curly edges; like most types of lettuce, it is usually eaten raw, in salads or sandwiches.

romaine lettuce
Lettuce with firm crisp leaves used especially to make Caesar salad.

celtuce
A celerylike vegetable that is derived from lettuce; it combines the flavors of celery and lettuce.

escarole
Its leaves are less bitter than those of the curled endive, to which it is related; it is usually eaten raw, in salads.

butterhead lettuce
Formed in a loosely compacted ball, its large soft leaves break off easily; Boston lettuce is a well-known variety of this species.

iceberg lettuce
The most widely sold lettuce in North America, it was initially covered with ice during transport, hence its name.

radicchio
Red endive native to northern Italy and having a somewhat bitter taste; it is often served with other types of lettuce.

ornamental kale
Related to the curled kale; its differently colored leaves are added to salads, soups and rice, or used to garnish serving platters.

sea kale
Widely used in Europe, its leaves and wide fleshy stems are prepared like asparagus.

collards
It has thick, strongly flavored leaves and tough central ribs; it is eaten like spinach, either raw or cooked.

curled kale
Its very curly, stringy tough leaves have a strong flavor; it is almost always eaten cooked.

Brussels sprouts
The smallest member of the cabbage family is only eaten cooked and whole as a vegetable side dish.

red cabbage
Milder-tasting than other cabbages, it is usually eaten raw and finely chopped in salads.

white cabbage
After fermentation, it is used to make sauerkraut; it is also used as an ingredient in stews.

savoy cabbage
Cabbage with somewhat flexible leaves, making it well suited to preparing cabbage rolls.

green cabbage
When finely chopped, it is the main ingredient in coleslaw; it is also added to soups and stews.

FOOD AND KITCHEN

vegetables

nettle
When cooked or dried, the leaves lose their sting; it has a somewhat spicy flavor and can be prepared more or less like spinach.

watercress
Tender and juicy, it is mostly eaten raw, in salads; the delicate leaves have a slight mustardlike flavor.

dandelion
The leaves of this common plant are excellent in salads; when cooked, they can be prepared like spinach.

purslane
Both the stems and the tender fleshy leaves are eaten; it has a slightly acidic, spicy flavor.

grape leaf
Associated with Mediterranean cooking, it is used to prepare dolmades (stuffed grape leaves) and as a garnish for fruit and salad platters.

celery cabbage
A crunchy refreshing Chinese cabbage, mostly eaten cooked.

bok choy
The stems of this Chinese cabbage are juicy and crunchy; it is served in soups, with rice and in many Chinese dishes.

corn salad
Also called lamb's lettuce; its soft, mild-tasting leaves are primarily eaten raw, in salads.

arugula
Especially popular in southern France and Italy; whether raw or cooked, it should be used in moderation because of its strong flavor.

garden sorrel
Its slightly lemon-flavored leaves are traditionally served with fish and veal; it is also used in a puréed soup that is a classic in a number of European countries.

spinach
The vegetable used to make dishes à la Florentine. It is also eaten raw, in salads, and cooked, as a side dish or a stuffing ingredient.

curled endive
The very frilly, somewhat bitter leaves are primarily eaten raw, in salads.

garden cress
Picked while very young and sold in bunches; its tiny leaves add a hint of spice especially to salads, sandwiches and sauces.

Belgian endive
Its crunchy, slightly bitter leaves are much in demand for salads (used raw) or for such classic recipes as endive and ham au gratin.

FOOD AND KITCHEN

vegetables

FOOD AND KITCHEN

inflorescent vegetables
The flowers or flower buds of edible plants eaten as vegetables.

Gai-lohn
Also called Chinese broccoli, its delicately flavored leaves and stems can be eaten raw or cooked, prepared in the same manner as broccoli.

broccoli rabe
Its slightly bitter stems, leaves and flowers can all be eaten, prepared like broccoli.

artichoke
Especially valued for its soft fleshy heart, it is often served with a dipping sauce; the leaves surrounding the heart can also be eaten.

cauliflower
The head, composed of immature buds, is either white or purple; it is eaten raw or cooked.

broccoli
Native to Italy, it is often green and occasionally white or purple; it is chosen primarily for its flower buds but the stem and leaves are also eaten.

fruit vegetables

Fruits of edible plants consumed as vegetables.

hot pepper
Cutting it or removing the seeds moderates its spicy burning taste.

okra
Vegetable containing a substance used to thicken soups and ragouts, it is used in many Creole dishes.

tomatillo
Picked when green, this berry is used to make sauces and is an essential ingredient in many Mexican dishes.

olive
Inedible when raw, the olive is treated to reduce its bitter taste, then cured in brine or sometimes in oil.

green sweet pepper
Mild pepper picked before fully ripe, it is used in many typical Mexican and Portuguese dishes.

red sweet pepper
Mild pepper picked when ripe, it is very sweet and has a higher vitamin C content than the green sweet pepper.

yellow sweet pepper
Mild pepper picked when ripe, it is strongly scented and has a sweet taste; it is often used in salads.

avocado
Fruit of the avocado tree; its smooth greenish flesh is eaten raw, in salads or mashed.

currant tomato
Very flavorful tomato characterized by its sweetness and long shelf life.

tomato
Native to Central America, this fruit is essential to Italian, Provençal, Greek and Spanish cooking.

FOOD AND KITCHEN

vegetables

cucumber
Related to squash and melons, it bears
seeds and is usually eaten raw.

gherkin
Picked when not yet ripe, it is often
pickled in vinegar and eaten as a
condiment; it is also served raw in
salads.

wax gourd
Its firm flavorful flesh is often used in
puréed soups or spicy dishes.

eggplant
Yellowish and spongy-fleshed
vegetable that is sometimes sweated
with salt to alleviate its bitter taste.

zucchini
Small white-fleshed squash picked
before fully ripe; it is an essential
ingredient in ratatouille.

seedless cucumber
European variety grown exclusively in
greenhouses without fertilization.

summer squash
Picked when ripe, the seeds are
removed and the flesh eaten raw or
cooked; it bears edible flowers.

bitter melon
Too bitter to be eaten raw, it is an
ingredient in various kinds of Asian
cooking, such as soups or steamed
dishes.

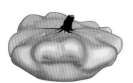

pattypan squash
When very ripe the flesh turns hard and white; its firm flesh has a flavor similar to the artichoke.

crookneck squash
The soft edible rind is covered in small ridges; best if picked very early, it can be eaten raw or cooked.

straightneck squash
The result of genetically altering the crookneck squash to eliminate the thin crooked neck; it is eaten raw or cooked.

spaghetti squash
Derives its name from its cooked flesh, resembling spaghetti, which it can replace in most recipes.

acorn squash
Its smooth hard skin turns orange when fully ripe; the delicate, slightly fibrous flesh tastes of pepper and hazelnuts.

pumpkin
Used primarily in North America, it can be recognized by its hard fibrous pedicel; its flesh is widely used in soups and desserts and its edible seeds are dried.

autumn squash
The rind can be yellow, orange or green; often confused with the pumpkin, it can be recognized by its pedicel, which is soft and enlarged where it attaches to the vegetable.

chayote
This squash, grown mainly in tropical countries, is used in Creole cooking; the central stone can be eaten once cooked.

FOOD AND KITCHEN

root vegetables
The fleshy roots of edible plants consumed as vegetables.

black radish
Popular in Eastern Europe, although less juicy than the red radish; it can be cooked or sweated with salt to alleviate its bitter taste.

radish
Juicy and crunchy, it is eaten raw, as an hors d'oeuvre or in salads; it is also popular served cooked or pickled, especially in Asia.

horseradish
Often used as a flavoring ingredient, especially in sauces; its strong flavor becomes milder when mixed with cream or mayonnaise.

daikon
Its somewhat mild-tasting flesh, leaves and sprouted seeds are prepared in various ways; in Japan, it is served with sashimi.

carrot
Eaten in a variety of ways: plain, in salads, in deserts, as a vegetable side dish or a juice.

salsify
Its sweet mild flavor is often said to resemble the oyster's; its young leaves are also edible.

parsnip
The yellowish flesh of this little-known vegetable has a slightly nutty taste and a texture similar to the turnip; it can be eaten raw or cooked.

black salsify
Closely related to salsify, its cream-colored flesh is less stringy and more flavorful; it is an ingredient in dishes such as soups and ragouts.

burdock
Root of a plant harvested before the floral stem develops; it is used as a vegetable or as a flavoring ingredient.

turnip
Often confused with the rutabaga, this white-fleshed vegetable is eaten raw or cooked and prepared like carrots.

rutabaga
Larger and stronger-tasting than the turnip, it can be recognized by its usually yellow flesh and by the bump on its top.

beet
Its usually red flesh contains a juice that stains readily; it is eaten raw, pickled or cooked, most famously in borscht, a hearty soup from Eastern Europe.

malanga
A staple in the West Indies, where it is grated and used to make fried doughnuts called acras; its strong taste hints of hazelnuts.

celeriac
A slightly spicy kind of celery; the raw vegetable, combined with mustard mayonnaise, becomes the classic celeriac remoulade.

legumes

The main edible part of these pod-shaped fruits is their seeds, consumed fresh, dried or sprouted; if dried, they often require soaking before they can be cooked.

lupine
Protein-rich seed, prepared and served plain or sprinkled with lemon juice.

alfalfa
The sprouted seeds are added raw to sandwiches or used in various cooked dishes.

peanut
Often served as a snack, it is also made into a butter and a vegetable oil and, in some countries, into a spicy sauce served with a variety of dishes.

lentils
A main ingredient of hearty soups, they can also be puréed and made into croquettes; in India, they are often paired with rice.

broad beans
Starchy and strong-tasting, they are typically puréed; they are also eaten whole and added to soups and stews.

peas

The rounded seeds are called "green peas" when they are fresh and "dried peas" when they are dried.

chick peas
Basic ingredient of hummus and falafel and found in couscous; they are also used to make various southern French dishes such as estouffade.

split peas
These pea seeds, dried and split in two, are generally puréed and used in various kinds of soups.

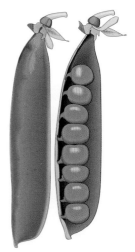

green peas
Delicious freshly picked, they are also available frozen or canned; a component of mixed vegetables and of dishes labeled "à la jardinière".

sweet peas
Eaten freshly picked with the sweet and crunchy pod, hence their name; they are especially popular in Chinese dishes.

legumes

dolichos beans
Fruit of a member of the bean family; the seeds are somewhat elongated and ovoid.

black-eyed pea
This flavorful seed has a black spot that resembles an eye, hence its name; it is typical especially of southern American cooking.

lablab bean
Characterized by a white ridge; it can be sprouted or ground into flour.

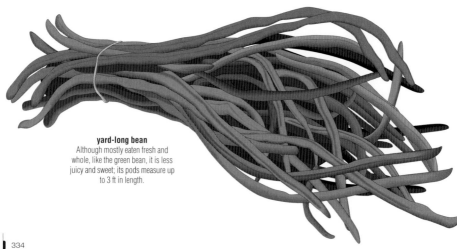

yard-long bean
Although mostly eaten fresh and whole, like the green bean, it is less juicy and sweet; its pods measure up to 3 ft in length.

beans

Fruits of plants native to Central and South America, the seeds are oval or kidney-shaped; before they are fully ripe, the pods are often edible.

green bean
The young green pod is usually served as a vegetable side dish, sometimes with sauce or butter.

wax bean
Somewhat juicier than the green bean, it is sometimes eaten raw but mostly cooked, as a vegetable side dish.

roman bean
A staple of Italian cooking, it resembles the pinto bean, although often larger and darker; it absorbs the flavor of the foods it is cooked with.

adzuki bean
Has a delicate flavor and is often served with rice; in Asian countries, the paste made from these beans can replace tomato paste.

scarlet runner bean
The seeds are eaten fresh or dried, in which case they are prepared like the red kidney bean; a favorite accompaniment to onions, tomatoes and tuna.

mung bean
In Asia they are either puréed or ground into flour; in the West they are more commonly eaten sprouted, especially in chop suey.

Lima bean
Has a mild flavor and a starchy texture and is generally green- or cream-colored; when puréed, it can replace the potato.

pinto bean
When cooked, their spots disappear and they turn pink; because of their creamy texture, they are mostly used to make purées.

legumes

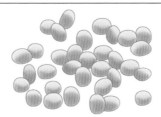

soybeans
Produces a kind of milk used mainly to make tofu and also a vegetable oil;
when fermented, it is the main ingredient in soy sauce.

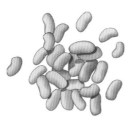

flageolet
Thin flat and less starchy than most other legumes, this bean is a
favorite in France, where it is traditionally served with leg of
lamb.

soybean sprouts
After sprouting for a few days they are ready to be eaten, either raw or
lightly cooked; they are characteristic of Chinese cooking.

red kidney bean
One of the best-known beans, it is used to
make the Mexican dish called chili con
carne; it retains its shape when cooked so
is often canned.

black gram
A favorite in Asia, where it is used to
make a popular black sauce; in India, it is
mixed with rice to make pancakes and a
spicy purée.

black bean
Available mainly in Central and North
America, it is a staple of Mexican
cooking.

fruits

Usually sweet vegetables, primarily consumed at breakfast, as a snack or for dessert, and used extensively in pastry and candy making.

stone fruits

Fruits whose somewhat juicy flesh surrounds a hard, usually inedible stone.

plum
Of various colors and sizes, it is excellent either raw or cooked and is used especially to make chutney; the dried plum is called a prune.

cherry
An essential ingredient in Black Forest cake and, candied, in fruitcake; when artificially colored and flavored, it is used as a cocktail garnish.

date
Has a high sugar content and is often sold dried; in North America, it is primarily associated with baked goods, such as squares, muffins and cakes.

apricot
Often eaten dried or candied, its orange flesh can be mushy if picked before fully ripe; the kernel inside the stone contains a toxic substance.

peach
A velvety skin covers its juicy fragrant flesh; it is especially enjoyed plain, in juice and in various desserts, such as the classic peach melba.

nectarine
Differentiated from the peach by its smooth, more colorful skin and by its more flavorful flesh; like the peach, it is eaten raw or used in certain desserts.

FOOD AND KITCHEN

fruits

berries

Small fleshy fruits containing one or several usually edible seeds; when they grow together in clusters, each fruit is called a seed.

black currant
Black berry primarily used to make coulis, jellies, wine and liqueurs such as crème de cassis, an ingredient in kir.

currant
Small red or white currant primarily eaten cooked due to its sour taste; its juice can replace vinegar in salad dressing.

gooseberry
Larger than the clustered berries, it is especially popular in Europe; the British use it to make a chutney that is served with mackerel.

blueberry
Little known outside its native North America, it is primarily eaten plain or in desserts; the lowbush variety is the sweetest.

bilberry
Although not related to it, this berry of Europe and Asia resembles the blueberry and is used like it.

red whortleberry
Closely related to the cranberry, this small tart berry is somewhat bitter and rarely eaten raw; it is used instead to make sauces, jams and desserts.

alkekengi
Covered in a thin, inedible membrane, it is slightly tart and not very sweet; it is often used to make jams and jellies because of its high pectin content.

grape
This variously colored fruit of the vine is enjoyed worldwide, either plain, cooked, dried or in juice; it is also the main ingredient in wine.

cranberry
Too tart to be eaten raw, it is primarily used for making desserts, sauces or juice; a traditional accompaniment to turkey in North America.

blackberry
Grows on canes as does the raspberry, and is used like that fruit; the several trailing species are comminly called dewberries.

strawberry
The cultivated strawberry was bred from the smaller and more fragrant wild strawberry; it is very flavorful and is used raw or cooked, primarily in desserts.

raspberry
Generally red, there are also different-colored varieties; slightly tart and very fragrant, it makes an excellent coulis that can be incorporated into desserts.

fruits

dry fruits

Often called nuts, these fruits usually have a hard dry
covering called the shell that encloses an edible
kernel.

ginkgo nut
Extensively used in Japanese cooking
but little known in the West, this nut is
either eaten as is or is used in Asian
dishes.

pistachio nut
Its greenish kernel is covered with a
brown skin; it is extensively used in
Mediterranean and Asian cooking, as well
as in pastry and candy making.

macadamia nut
A popular candy ingredient, it is often sold
coated in chocolate or honey; it is also a
popular ingredient in mixed vegetables,
curries, salads and desserts.

pine nut
Edible seed inside the cone of certain
species of pine that is often used in
cooking and baking.

cola nut
Used in drink preparations such as
Coca-Cola™; it contains stimulants
that are slightly less potent than those
in coffee.

pecan nut
Native to North America, it is used to
make certain savory dishes and
numerous desserts, such as the
traditional pecan pie.

cashew
This fruit of the cashew tree is always
sold shelled; its shell is covered by a
juicy fleshy edible layer known as the
cashew apple.

almond
Primarily used to garnish chicken and fish, and
to make almond paste, candies (nougat and
pralines) and an essence that flavors Amaretto
and a variety of foodstuffs.

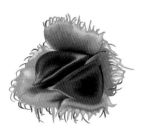

hazelnut
Primarily used to make paste, butter or a kind of flour used in cakes and cookies; in candy making, it is often combined with chocolate.

walnut
A green covering, the husk, covers the shell; the walnut is served as an appetizer, or added to a variety of desserts, salads, sauces and main dishes.

beechnut
Fruit of the common beech tree, its flavor resembles the hazelnut's; more flavorful toasted than raw, it also yields a cooking oil.

chestnut
Designates the fruit of the chestnut tree; Europeans often serve it with game and poultry. When puréed, it is the main ingredient in the dessert known as Mont Blanc.

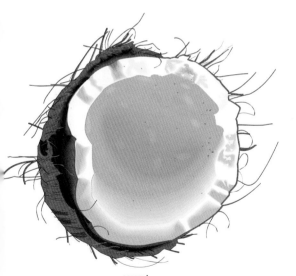

coconut
The whitish meat, known as copra, surrounds a cavity containing a refreshing liquid, not to be confused with coconut milk, which is derived from the grated flesh.

Brazil nut
Often served as an appetizer; it is also made into candy, such as when chocolate-coated. It replaces coconut in some recipes.

FOOD AND KITCHEN

FOOD AND KITCHEN

citrus fruits
Somewhat acidic fruits with a high vitamin C content comprising numerous sections and covered with a rind that has an external layer called zest.

lime
Intensely fragrant and used like the lemon; it is an essential ingredient in ceviche, a raw marinated fish dish.

kumquat
Small citrus fruit, .75 to 2 in long with a sweet tender rind that can be eaten unpeeled; its flavor is enhanced through light steeping.

mandarin
Similar to a small, slightly flattened orange, it is less acidic than most citrus fruits and is often eaten as is; it peels easily.

bergamot
Because its greenish flesh is inedible, it is primarily used for the zest and essential oil derived from its rind, especially in Earl Grey tea.

orange
Widely available, it is often eaten plain or in juice, and it goes well with duck; it yields a flavor essence and an essential oil.

lemon
Highly acidic, it is especially used to flavor various recipes and enhance the flavor of certain foods; it is the main ingredient in lemonade.

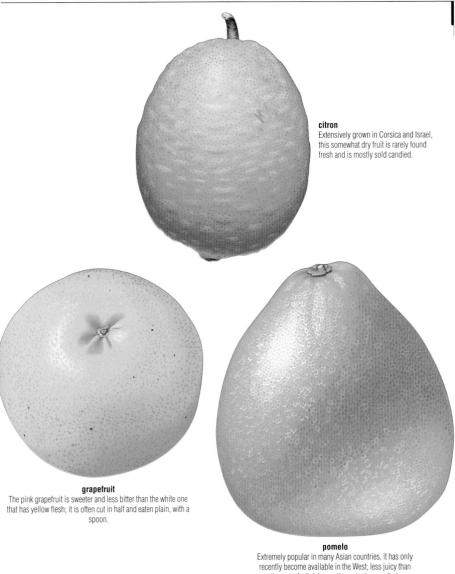

citron
Extensively grown in Corsica and Israel, this somewhat dry fruit is rarely found fresh and is mostly sold candied.

grapefruit
The pink grapefruit is sweeter and less bitter than the white one that has yellow flesh; it is often cut in half and eaten plain, with a spoon.

pomelo
Extremely popular in many Asian countries, it has only recently become available in the West; less juicy than the grapefruit, it is mostly cooked or candied.

fruits

melons

Related to squash and cucumbers, these tender fruits are juicy sweet and refreshing; they are
primarily consumed raw.

casaba melon
The flavor of its creamy white flesh,
often less fragrant than that of other
melons, can be enhanced with lemon
or lime juice.

honeydew melon
Owes its name to its very sweet, green
flesh; its smooth firm rind turns
creamy-yellow as it ripens.

muskmelon
Named for the characteristic musky
smell of its flesh; it has a textured rind
and its flavorful flesh is pink or orange.

cantaloupe
This orange-fleshed melon is
characterized by its patterned textured
ribs; the most widely cultivated variety
is the charentais.

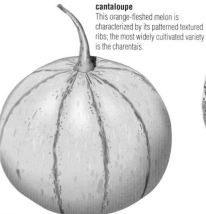

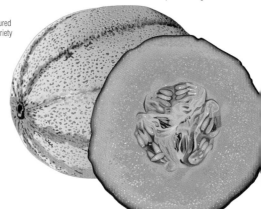

Ogen melon
Small round melon with a hard smooth ribbed rind; its very juicy flesh is either dark pink or pale green.

canary melon
Has sweet whitish flesh that is rose-tinted near the central cavity; it becomes very fragrant when ripe.

watermelon
This thirst-quenching fruit, named for its high water content, is primarily eaten plain, in slices.

pome fruits

Fruits where the flesh covers an inedible central part, the core, comprising a certain number of seeds called pips.

quince
Fruit of the quince tree, native to warm climates; inedible raw, it is traditionally made into jams and jellies.

pear
Among its many and varied uses, it forms the basis for a fruit brandy; it is picked before fully ripe to prevent the flesh from acquiring a granular texture.

apple
There are 7,500 known varieties; it is used to make cider and is also eaten raw or made into juice, jelly, compote or desserts, such as pie or strudel.

Japanese plum
Has thin skin, sometimes covered in fine hairs, that envelops juicy, somewhat sour flesh; whether raw or cooked, it tastes somewhat like cherries or plums.

tropical fruits

A variety of fruits, usually of exotic origin, more or less available in the West.

kiwi
Its juicy, slightly acidic green flesh has a high vitamin C content; delicious plain, its downy skin is generally discarded, although it can be eaten.

tamarillo
Within the inedible skin there is a firm, slightly acidic flesh. If very ripe, it can be eaten raw; otherwise, it is often cooked like a vegetable.

longan
Stone fruit, related to the litchi, whose whitish translucent flesh is sweet and juicy; the peeled and stoned fruit is often eaten plain.

horned melon
Its green flesh contains soft edible seeds, similar to those of the cucumber; it is often peeled and then made into juice.

mangosteen
Within the inedible skin that hardens as the fruit ages, there is a sweet juicy white flesh that is divided into sections; it is eaten as is, like an orange.

pineapple
Once the inedible rind has been removed, it is eaten raw, cooked or in juice; in North America, it is traditionally served with ham.

banana
Eaten as is, sautéed, fried or flambéed with rum; it is a classic garnish for ice-cream dishes and is also used in muffins and cakes.

jackfruit
This very large fruit has edible seeds than can be boiled or roasted; the starchy flesh is eaten as a fruit or vegetable, either raw or cooked.

plantain
Nicknamed the "cooking banana", this staple of African and West Indian cooking is inedible when raw; it is primarily eaten as a vegetable, either steamed, roasted or fried.

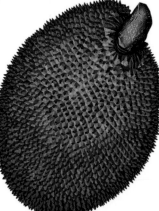

FOOD AND KITCHEN

jujube
Somewhat dry stone fruit, eaten fresh or dried, raw or cooked, like the date.

jaboticaba
Little known outside Brazil, it is eaten as is, like grapes, or made into jelly, jam, juice or wine; its translucent flesh is either white or pink.

litchi
Its juicy crunchy translucent flesh is more fragrant than the longan's; it is often eaten raw and the Chinese serve it with fish or meat.

sapodilla
Has juicy fragrant, slightly granular flesh that tastes like honey and apricots; it is easy to peel and is eaten raw or cooked.

guava
Very popular in South America, its fragrant, slightly acidic flesh is eaten raw or cooked, with or without the skin and seeds.

Japanese persimmon
This national fruit of Japan is often eaten plain, with a spoon; the fuyu variety is eaten like an apple.

rambutan
The shell, covered in soft spikes, splits easily to reveal flesh like the litchi's but less fragrant; it is used like the litchi.

fig
Among its many varieties are the black, the green and the purple fig; whether fresh or dried, it is mostly eaten raw, but can also be cooked.

passion fruit
Within its inedible skin that wrinkles when ripe, there is a highly aromatic gelatinous pulp; delicious plain, it is used to flavor fruit punches and cocktails.

pomegranate
The edible part is the small, very juicy berries enclosed within the fruit's membranes; it is used to make grenadine syrup, an ingredient in drinks and desserts.

prickly pear
Fruit of a member of the cactus family;
the spines and skin should be removed
before eating the flesh, plain or sprinkled
with lemon or lime juice.

carambola
Within the delicate edible skin is a
juicy, slightly acidic flesh that can be
eaten raw or cooked, as a fruit or
vegetable.

Asian pear
Most popular Asian fruit, primarily eaten
plain; its flesh is sweet and juicy, like the
pear's, and crunchy, like the apple's.

mango
Fruit with a flattened stone and a skin that
should be discarded, as it irritates the
mouth; it is mostly eaten ripe, but
sometimes used green, as a vegetable.

feijoa
Has sweet fragrant, slightly granular
flesh; after peeling, it is eaten raw or
cooked, plain or in various desserts.

cherimoya
The skin and the seeds inside the slightly
granular flesh are inedible; the flesh is
sprinkled with orange juice and eaten with a
spoon.

papaya
Its usually orange, juicy flesh is eaten like the
melon and contains spicy, edible seeds; when
green, it is eaten like winter squash.

pepino
The orange or yellow flesh is slightly
starchy. Before fully ripe, it is often cooked
and prepared like a squash; once ripe, it is
eaten like a melon.

durian
Large fruit that emits a disagreeable odor
when ripe; its sweet creamy flesh is often
eaten plain while the seeds are used like
nuts.

herbs

Aromatic fresh or dried plants used separately or mixed to bring out the flavor of recipes; they often make excellent infusions.

dill
Used primarily for its leaves and seeds, it imparts flavor to vinegar and pickles as well as to salmon and herring.

anise
Extensively used in making candy (licorice) and liqueurs (pastis), its edible leaves and seeds can flavor savory as well as sweet dishes.

sweet bay
The dried leaves must be used sparingly; it is an ingredient in bouquets garnis and is used to flavor soups and stews.

oregano
Wild, slightly more flavorful variety of marjoram; extensively used in Mediterranean cooking, it goes especially well with tomato dishes.

basil
A popular choice for seasoning tomato and pasta dishes, it is also one of the main ingredients in pistou and Italian pesto.

sage
Its pungent flavor complements a variety of dishes; it is often used with pork, duck and goose, as well as in Italian veal dishes.

tarragon
Has a slightly bitter, peppery anise flavor that complements bland foods; it is often used with chicken and is always used in béarnaise sauce.

thyme
Used with parsley and sweet bay to make bouquets garnis; because it withstands lengthy cooking, it is a popular choice for flavoring soups and stews.

mint
Gives a refreshing taste to numerous sweet and savory dishes, such as lamb; its aromatic essential oil is used to flavor candy, liqueurs and many other types of food.

parsley
The smooth flat-leafed parsley is less bitter and more fragrant than curly-leafed parsley; it is used to flavor numerous recipes, such as tabbouleh.

chervil
Has a subtle delicate taste and is used like parsley; it is often included with tarragon, parsley and chives in a traditional blend known as fines herbes.

savory
Reminiscent of thyme, its flavor enhances legumes, meat and stuffing; it is also used to flavor vinegar and goat's milk cheeses.

coriander
Its leaves are used like parsley and it has edible musk- and lemon-scented seeds; the roots can be substituted for garlic.

hyssop
The highly aromatic leaves are mostly used in salads, soups, ragouts and fruit platters, as well as in some liqueurs, such as Chartreuse and Benedictine.

borage
Delicious in yogurt, cream cheese or salad dressing; the young leaves can be used in salads.

rosemary
Its fairly pungent, aromatic flavor is very popular in southern France and in Italy, where it is used especially in sauces and marinades, and with roast meat.

lovage
Resembles celery but with a stronger flavor; it is particularly tasty with potatoes and also goes well with ragouts, sauces and salads.

lemon balm
Its lemon-scented leaves are used extensively in Asian cooking; it goes well with bitter foods.

cereal products

Cereals that have been processed in various ways to make ground (flour, semolina), unground (rice) or manufactured products (bread, pasta, noodles).

bread

Food made from flour, water and salt, often containing an agent (leaven or yeast) that makes it rise.

bagel
Jewish ring-shaped roll traditionally coated in sesame seeds; it is usually served warm, with cream cheese.

croissant
A small roll of layered or puffed dough, frequently eaten as a plain or stuffed pastry; it is also used to make hors d'oeuvres and sandwiches.

ear loaf
Baguette made so it can be easily broken into pieces by hand.

black rye bread
Made from rye flour, this dense strong-tasting bread goes particularly well with seafood and smoked foods.

baguette
This light crusty, typically French bread is often served with a meal and also goes well with cheese and pâté; it must be eaten fresh.

French bread
Long crusty loaf resembling an oversized baguette; it stays fresh somewhat longer than the typical baguette.

Greek bread
Round loaf with a golden crust, sometimes sprinkled with sesame seeds; olive bread is one of its many variants.

Indian chapati bread
Flat crusty, slightly puffy bread, eaten
warm with vegetables and rice or used as
a spoon to scoop up food.

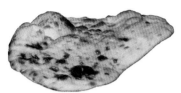

Indian naan bread
The yogurt in the dough of this soft
light sweetish bread helps it rise; it is
eaten plain or stuffed.

phyllo dough
Flexible wafer-thin dough of Greek
origin, used to prepare hors d'oeuvres
and pastries, such as baklava.

unleavened bread
Light and crusty unleavened bread,
eaten mainly during Jewish Passover;
it is easily digested and has a long
shelf life.

pita bread
Flat bread originally from the Middle
East; its crust forms a pocket that can
be filled with hot or cold kinds of
stuffing.

tortilla
Disk of unleavened bread made with corn
flour that is the basis for many Latin-
American dishes; it can be eaten plain,
with a filling or cooked.

FOOD AND KITCHEN

353

cereal products

bread
Food made from flour, water and salt, often containing an agent
(leaven or yeast) that makes it rise.

Russian pumpernickel
Made with a mixture of wheat and rye
flour, it has a thin but resilient crust; it
goes well with soups and ragouts.

German rye bread
Dark dense bread with a strong, slightly acidic taste, made
with rye and wheat flour; it has a long shelf life.

cracked rye bread
Thin crusty flat bread made with rye
flour, usually eaten with cheese.

Danish rye bread
This bread is usually sweeter and lighter than German rye
bread; it often contains molasses.

Jewish hallah
Light soft sweetish bread traditionally
served on the Sabbath and other
Jewish festivals; it is usually braided.

Scandinavian cracked bread
Thin crusty flat bread usually made with wheat or rye flour; it is generally
served with soup, salad or cheese.

Irish bread
The crust of this bread is marked with a cross; it is made with baking powder, which gives it a cakelike consistency.

American corn bread
The crumb of this corn flour-based bread is golden in color; it is easy to make and very popular in the southern United States.

English loaf
Thin-crusted, round or rectangular bread of British origin; it is primarily used to make toast, canapés, croque-monsieurs and sandwiches.

white bread
Bread made with white flour that comes in a variety of shapes, thickness and textures; it is less nutritious than wholemeal bread.

multigrain bread
Usually contains 80% white flour, whole wheat flour or a mixture of the two, to which other cereals (oats, rye, etc.) are added.

FOOD AND KITCHEN

farmhouse bread
Its thick, often floury crust and slightly acidic-tasting interior can last a long time without becoming stale; it can be used in a variety of ways.

wholemeal bread
Because it is made with whole wheat flour, it is highly nutritious and contains more minerals and protein than white bread.

FOOD AND KITCHEN

pasta

Made from hard wheat semolina and water, shaped into various forms and dried; it is an essential ingredient in Italian cooking that is bought ready-made.

rigatoni
This fairly large tubular pasta is suitable for serving with all kinds of sauces because they cling to it readily.

rotini
Because of its spiral grooves, it readily holds meat, cheese and vegetable sauces; it is also ideal for salads.

conchiglie
Small shell-shaped pasta that can be served with a sauce or added to soup or pasta salads.

fusilli
This spiral-shaped pasta is thinner and longer than rotini, but can replace it in most recipes.

ditali
Short tube-shaped pasta that resemble fat macaroni, used especially in broth and vegetable soups.

tortellini
Pasta stuffed with meat or cheese and sometimes colored with tomato or spinach; it is delicious with tomato or cream sauce.

gnocchi
Often made from a potato or semolina dough with eggs and cheese; it is usually served au gratin, as an appetizer.

elbows
Sometimes used in a salad, this type of macaroni is also served with tomato or cheese sauce.

penne
Tube-shaped pasta with diagonally cut ends, often served with a spicy tomato sauce in a dish called penne all'arrabiata.

spaghetti
One of the best-known forms of pasta and the most extensively used; it is traditionally served with tomato or meat sauce.

fettucine
Thicker but not as wide as tagliatelle, this pasta is often served with Alfredo sauce.

ravioli
Pasta stuffed with meat, cheese or vegetables; a classic way to serve it is with tomato sauce, sprinkled with grated Parmesan.

spaghettini
Thinner than spaghetti but thicker than angel hair pasta or vermicelli noodles; it is particularly well suited to delicate sauces.

cannelloni
This fairly large tubular pasta is usually stuffed with meat or cheese, covered with tomato sauce and baked au gratin.

spinach tagliatelle
Flat ribbonlike pasta made with spinach and eggs, traditionally served with meat sauce.

lasagna
These wide strips, green if spinach-flavored, are combined with a filling in alternate layers to create the eponymous dish.

dairy products

Foods produced by processing fresh milk; they are used daily in Western countries, where they are known for their high calcium content.

soft cheeses

Ripened but neither pressed nor cooked, these cheeses have a soft, creamy texture and a somewhat velvety rind, which is often edible.

Coulommiers
Native to the area around Paris, it is similar to Brie but smaller; it contains from 45% to 50% milk fat.

Camembert
Soft and easy to spread, France's most famous cheese is smaller and slightly firmer than Brie.

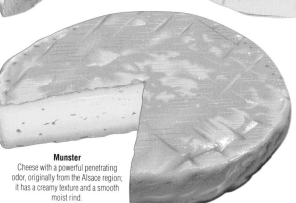

Munster
Cheese with a powerful penetrating odor, originally from the Alsace region; it has a creamy texture and a smooth moist rind.

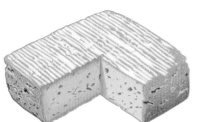

Pont-l'Évêque
Somewhat soft cheese with a pronounced odor; its name derives from the town in Normandy where it is made.

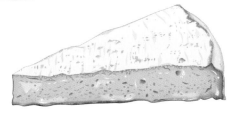

Brie
Native to Brie, near Paris, it is one of the best-known French cheeses; among its many varieties is the one from Meaux.

goat's-milk cheeses
Cheeses made from goat's milk, which is sometimes mixed with cow's milk; these medium-strong cheeses have a smooth texture and a high water content.

Chèvre cheese
Fresh rindless cheese that has a tangy, mild taste; it is sometimes flavored with herbs.

Crottin de Chavignol
Soft French cheese with a rind that is covered in mold; it is eaten fresh or dried and, as it dries, its flavor becomes more pronounced.

fresh cheeses
Nonripened cheeses that contain up to 80% water; they are smooth and mild or slightly tangy; they spoil quickly.

cottage cheese
Low in fat and grainy in texture; it works well as a spread or can be added to salads, desserts and sauces.

mozzarella
This native Italian cheese has a rubbery texture and is firmer than other cheeses; it is the garnish of choice for pizza.

cream cheese
Made with cream, which is sometimes mixed with milk; it is smooth and spreads easily, and is used as a spread or as a dessert ingredient (e.g., in cheesecake).

ricotta
Granular cheese with a smooth moist rind; it is used in Italian cooking, primarily for stuffed foods and desserts.

dairy products

pressed cheeses

Ripened cheeses that are also cooked and pressed and contain less than 35% moisture; they usually have a firm compact texture and a hard rind.

Emmenthal
Characterized by large holes, this mild Swiss cheese is very popular in fondues and au gratin dishes.

Romano
Native to Rome, this dry granular cheese is made from cow, ewe or goat's milk or a mixture of all three; it is mostly used in grated form.

Raclette
Cheese specifically made to be used in a traditional eponymous dish that originated in the Valais region of Switzerland.

Gruyère
Swiss cheese with small holes called "eyes" and a medium-sweet taste; extensively used in cooking, either as is, grated or melted.

Jarlsberg
Norwegian cheese with large holes that has a characteristic nutty taste.

Parmesan
Strong-smelling Italian cheese with a grainy texture, sold in rounds or grate is a popular flavoring ingredient, especially for pasta dishes.

blue-veined cheeses
Also called "blue cheese", it usually has a crumbly texture, is veined with mold and has a pungent peppery taste.

Gorgonzola
Native to Italy and recognizable by its textured gray rind, spotted with red.

Danish Blue
Native to Denmark, it has a pungent flavor, a creamy texture and a milk fat content of up to 60%.

Roquefort
The best-known blue cheese, originally from Roquefort, France; it is made from ewe's milk and goes well with pears, cream and butter.

Stilton
English cheese with a firm but creamy texture; it is often served with crackers and port.

variety meat

Edible parts of slaughter animals, apart from the meat.

sweetbreads
Designates the tender, delicately flavored thymus gland of calves, lambs and kids; veal sweetbreads are especially prized.

heart
Cooked in ragouts and casseroles, it can also be sautéed, roasted, braised or simmered; veal, lamb and chicken heart are the most popular.

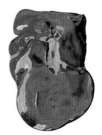

liver
People eat the liver of slaughter animals, poultry, game and some fish (cod); it has a high iron content.

tripe
Ruminants' stomach lining, made ready for cooking; the main ingredient in many regional dishes, the best known being tripes à la mode de Caen.

marrow
Soft fatty tissue found in the centre of bones; it is served mainly with roast beef and cardons and can also be used to add flavor to soups.

tongue
Covered with a thick skin that lifts off easily once cooked; calf tongue is the most tender.

kidney
Young slaughter animals such as calves tend to have more tender kidneys; there is an unpleasant aftertaste if they are not prepared carefully.

brains
Lamb, sheep and veal brains are the most prized, served in salads, au gratin, in croquettes, stuffings and sauces.

delicatessen

Foodstuff made from the meat (usually pork) or offal of various animals; among the many different varieties, some can be consumed as is, some are cooked.

rillettes
Often made with pork or goose meat and cooked in fat until the meat disintegrates; they are always served cold.

foie gras
Goose or duck liver, abnormally enlarged by force-feeding; considered a gourmet item, it is sold raw or ready to eat.

prosciutto
Raw dried ham native to the Parma region of Italy; it is mostly eaten thinly sliced and served with melon or fresh figs.

cooked ham
Salt-cured and cooked pork meat, usually served thinly sliced; it is eaten hot or cold, especially in sandwiches, and on croque-monsieurs and canapés.

pancetta
Rolled Italian bacon, sometimes spiced; it is an essential ingredient in pasta alla carbonara and also flavors sauces, soups and meat dishes.

American bacon
Salted and smoked side pork, cut into thin slices; in North America, it is traditionally served with eggs, for breakfast.

Canadian bacon
Piece of salted, usually smoked, meat from the pork loin; it goes well with eggs and in dishes such as quiches and omelets.

delicatessen

chorizo
Semidry Spanish sausage seasoned with red chiles, available in several versions that vary in spiciness; it is often added to paella.

pepperoni
This dry, somewhat spicy Italian sausage is a favorite pizza topping; diced, it is added to certain dishes to give them more flavor.

kielbasa sausage
Native to Poland, it is made with coarsely ground pork and beef, seasoned with garlic and spices.

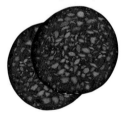

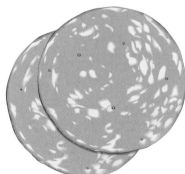

mortadella
Italian sausage made with meat and fat and flavored with peppercorns and pistachios.

Genoa salami
Dry Italian sausage made with a mixture of pork, veal and fat; the thin slices are often served as an hors d'oeuvre.

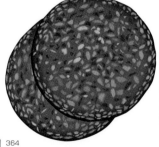

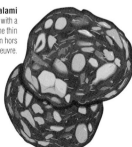

German salami
Made with finely ground beef and pork, it is usually served sliced, as an hors d'oeuvre, but also on pizza and canapés and in sandwiches.

chipolata sausage
Raw pork, or pork and beef, sausage characteristically flavored with cloves; it is often grilled or fried.

merguez sausage
Small, highly spiced sausage made with lamb, beef or mutton; popular in North Africa and Spain, it is usually eaten fried or grilled.

Toulouse sausage
Raw sausage, native to France, made with coarsely ground pork and pepper; often added to cassoulet.

andouillette
Cooked sausage made from pig or calf intestines; it can be grilled or fried and served with mustard.

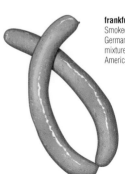

frankfurter
Smoked precooked sausage that is native to Germany and made from a pastelike pork mixture; among its many versions is the American hot dog.

blood sausage
The main ingredients in blood pudding are blood and suet (from pigs or other animals) packed into a casing; white pudding is made from white meat and milk.

meat

Flesh of slaughter animals, consumed as food; a distinction is usually made between red meat, such as beef and lamb, and white meat, such as veal and pork.

cuts of beef

Bovine carcasses are divided into quarters, then into pieces of meat that are ready to prepare.

ground beef
Made from various parts of the steer; when lean and taken from the tenderloin, it is the basis for steak tartare.

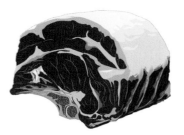

rib roast
Piece of meat intended for roasting, taken from the animal's rib section; this tender and tasty cut is one of the most popular kinds of roast beef.

steak
Strip of meat that can be grilled or sautéed; in general, the most tender steaks, loin, sirloin and rib, come from the central section of the carcass.

beef cubes
Their tenderness varies, depending on the section from which they were cut; they are mainly used to make brochettes or ragouts, such as boeuf bourguignon.

shank
Comes from a section of the front or hind leg of a steer; somewhat tough, it is primarily used in stews.

tenderloin roast
Taken from the back, along the spine, it is prized for its tenderness and is excellent when grilled; tournedos and châteaubriand come from it.

back ribs
They comprise sections of rib taken from the back and the attached muscles; they are delicious with a sweet-and-sour sauce.

FOOD AND KITCHEN

cuts of pork

Pieces taken from a pig carcass, the most tender of which come from the loin (back); the side (belly), leg (butt) and shoulder are the least tender parts.

hock
Also called "shank end", it comes from the lower section of the pig's front or hind leg; it is used to make the traditional pork hock stew.

ground pork
It is made from various parts of the pig and is very tender; it is used especially to make stuffed vegetables and meat loaf.

loin chop
Piece composed of a bone from the rib section and the attached muscles; some, like the butterfly chop, are sold boned.

spareribs
They comprise sections of rib taken from the back and the attached muscles; North American-style Chinese cooking usually serves them with sweet-and-sour sauce.

smoked ham
Taken from the pig's legs, this cut is preserved by smoking; it is sold as is, boned or sliced and can be prepared in numerous ways.

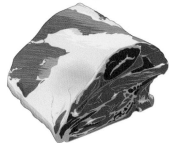

roast
Piece of meat intended for roasting, usually from the loin, leg or shoulder.

mollusks

Usually marine-dwelling, soft-bodied invertebrates; some have shells and are sold live.

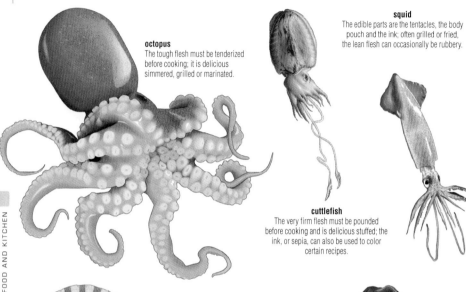

squid
The edible parts are the tentacles, the body pouch and the ink; often grilled or fried, the lean flesh can occasionally be rubbery.

octopus
The tough flesh must be tenderized before cooking; it is delicious simmered, grilled or marinated.

cuttlefish
The very firm flesh must be pounded before cooking and is delicious stuffed; the ink, or sepia, can also be used to color certain recipes.

great scallop
Related to the scallop, the delicately flavored flesh is prized by Europeans; the shells are resistant to heat and are often used as cooking and serving dishes.

abalone
The muscle, also called the "foot", is delicious raw or cooked; it must be pounded before cooking.

hard-shell clam
Mollusk with a very hard shell whose flesh can be eaten raw or cooked; they are used to make chowder, a popular New England recipe.

scallop
The main edible part is the nut (the muscle that opens and shuts the shells) and sometimes the coral (the orange part); excellent raw or cooked, it can be prepared in numerous ways.

soft-shell clam
Primarily harvested in the Atlantic, this large soft mollusk of the clam family can replace the latter in recipes.

snail
Snails are often sold canned, frozen or ready-cooked; served with garlic butter, they constitute a classic appetizer.

limpet
It has a single shell and is eaten raw with lemon juice or vinegar, or grilled, with butter.

common periwinkle
Its flesh resembles the snail's, which it can replace in most recipes; whether eaten hot or cold, it is always cooked first.

clam
Related to the hard-shell clam, it is as tasty raw (with or without lemon juice) as it is cooked (in soups, or stuffed, like the blue mussel).

cockle
Generally designates the European variety, although others exist; it has a firmer texture and a more pronounced flavor than oysters and mussels.

blue mussel
Fresh mussels are usually poached in broth or steamed until they open; those that fail to open should be discarded.

whelk
Resembles a large periwinkle; the flesh will toughen if it is cooked too long and it is often eaten sprinkled with lemon juice.

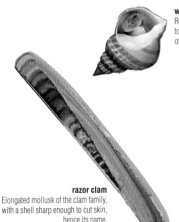

cupped Pacific oyster
Juicy and meaty, with a well-developed lower shell; like all oysters, it is often eaten raw, either plain or with lemon juice.

razor clam
Elongated mollusk of the clam family, with a shell sharp enough to cut skin, hence its name.

flat oyster
Less common than the cupped oyster, with a completely flat lower shell; the belon variety is particularly prized.

FOOD AND KITCHEN

crustaceans

Aquatic invertebrates having a carapace over their bodies; they are sold live, frozen (raw or cooked) or canned.

crayfish
Small freshwater crustacean usually prepared like lobster; only the tail is eaten and its pinkish-white flesh is lean and delicate.

scampi
Rarely sold live, it resembles a small lobster but has more delicate flesh; it is often served with garlic butter.

lobster
To ensure maximum freshness, the lobster should be cooked live, by plunging it into boiling liquid.

shrimp
Delicious hot or cold; although many prefer them deveined, the intestine (the dark vein running along the back) is edible.

crab
Sometimes sold live and cooked like the lobster, its lean stringy flesh, its liver and the creamy substance under the shell can all be eaten.

spiny lobster
Spiny-shelled crustacean whose flesh is slightly less flavorful than the lobster's; the tail is the only part that is commonly found for sale, either raw or cooked.

cartilaginous fishes

Fish with skeletons made of cartilage rather than bones; their flesh usually contains no bones.

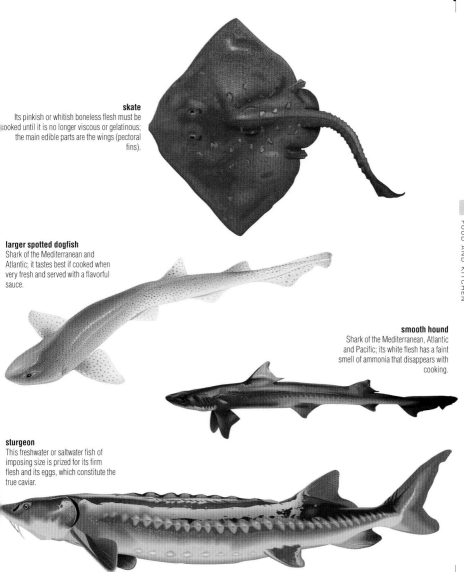

skate
Its pinkish or whitish boneless flesh must be cooked until it is no longer viscous or gelatinous; the main edible parts are the wings (pectoral fins).

larger spotted dogfish
Shark of the Mediterranean and Atlantic; it tastes best if cooked when very fresh and served with a flavorful sauce.

smooth hound
Shark of the Mediterranean, Atlantic and Pacific; its white flesh has a faint smell of ammonia that disappears with cooking.

sturgeon
This freshwater or saltwater fish of imposing size is prized for its firm flesh and its eggs, which constitute the true caviar.

FOOD AND KITCHEN

bony fishes

Fish with smooth flat scales and a rigid skeleton; the various species make up the largest group of fish.

sardine
Related to the herring, it is often canned (in oil, tomato sauce or white wine) and is eaten with bread, as is or with lemon juice.

anchovy
Very popular in Mediterranean countries, this highly perishable fish is often preserved in brine, oil or salt and sold in cans or jars.

sea bream
Its delicate lean white flesh can be prepared in many ways although the simplest are the best; it is delicious smoked, in sashimi or in ceviche.

herring
One of the world's most harvested species, it is sold fresh as well as canned, marinated, salted and smoked; it can replace mackerel in most recipes.

goatfish
In spite of its many bones, it is highly prized, especially in southern France, for its particularly delicate flavor.

smelt
The somewhat oily cucumber-scented flesh is the main part eaten, but the head, bones, tail and eggs are also considered edible; it is most often simply gutted and fried.

swordfish
The highly prized flesh becomes easier to digest if it is poached before being prepared; the tail and fins are also edible.

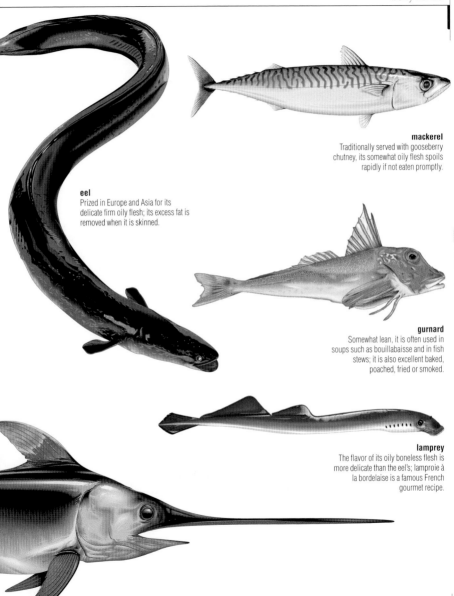

mackerel
Traditionally served with gooseberry chutney, its somewhat oily flesh spoils rapidly if not eaten promptly.

eel
Prized in Europe and Asia for its delicate firm oily flesh; its excess fat is removed when it is skinned.

gurnard
Somewhat lean, it is often used in soups such as bouillabaisse and in fish stews; it is also excellent baked, poached, fried or smoked.

lamprey
The flavor of its oily boneless flesh is more delicate than the eel's; lamproie à la bordelaise is a famous French gourmet recipe.

FOOD AND KITCHEN

bony fishes

mullet
Excellent hot or cold, it is well suited to all cooking methods; its eggs are used to make boutargue provençale and the Greek taramosalata (a creamy spread).

bass
Rarely found for sale, this sport fishing species has lean flaky flesh that is well suited to all cooking methods.

pike
The flesh sometimes has a slightly muddy taste that disappears with soaking; because it has many bones, it is often made into pâtés or quenelles.

carp
Soaking in vinegar water will make the sometimes muddy taste of the wild varieties disappear; it is especially prized for its tongue and lips.

perch
Related to the pike perch, it is often poached, steamed or floured and fried in butter; its bony flesh has a delicate flavor.

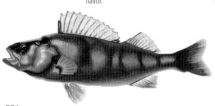

shad
Acidic ingredients such as sorrel and rhubarb are often used to prepare its somewhat oily, tender flesh; the bones of the female are more easily removed.

pike perch
Freshwater fish with a lean firm delicate flesh that can be cooked in many ways; whole and filleted, it is prepared like perch or pike.

bluefish
Very popular in the U.S., this lean fish is often grilled, braised or poached; it is prepared like mackerel.

sea bass
Its firm lean flesh has few bones and withstands cooking well; it is best cooked simply, to avoid overpowering the delicate taste.

monkfish
Also called "angler fish", only its tail is eaten and the taste is said to be similar to lobster; it is delicious cold, served with a dressing.

tuna
Often canned in oil or water, it is one of the main ingredients in the Italian dish vitello tonnato; it is also used to make salads, sushi and sashimi.

FOOD AND KITCHEN

375

bony fishes

redfish
Excellent raw, cooked or smoked; if cooked in broth or grilled, it is best to leave the skin on to prevent its flaky flesh from falling apart.

trout
Freshwater fish with medium-oily delicate and fragrant flesh that is delicious smoked; rainbow trout is the species most often raised in captivity.

whiting
Its delicate flaky flesh is similar to cod's and is easy to digest; it is often wrapped in tinfoil or cooked in a flavored broth.

haddock
Related to cod but with flesh that is sweeter and more delicate; it is often smoked.

brook trout
Native to Canada, it resembles the trout and is greatly prized for its delicate flesh, which is best when simply prepared.

black pollock
Especially popular in England, it is also used in Canada to make surimi, a paste from which imitation seafood is made.

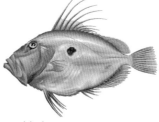

Atlantic cod
It is often dried or salted and its liver yields an oil that is rich in vitamin D; it is fished extensively off the Canadian and American coasts.

John dory
Usually prepared like sole or turbot, its medium-firm flesh contains gelatinous bones that make an excellent fish stock.

Pacific salmon
King salmon (or chinook) has the oiliest flesh and is greatly prized; the leaner and less oily varieties are often canned.

Atlantic salmon
The only species of salmon inhabiting the Atlantic; it is prized for its pink, somewhat oily and fragrant flesh and is sold fresh, frozen and smoked.

turbot
One of the tenderest saltwater fish, with lean white flavorful flesh; sold whole or filleted, it is usually poached or grilled.

common plaice
Because it has so many bones, it is often sold filleted and is one of the varieties used in fish-and-chips; it is found primarily off the European coast.

FOOD AND KITCHEN

halibut
The largest of the flatfish family, it is commonly cooked in wine or served with anchovy butter; its lean flaky flesh has few bones.

sole
Often confused with plaice, it is only found in waters off the European coast; the most highly prized variety is the common or Dover sole.

kitchen

Room where meals are prepared.

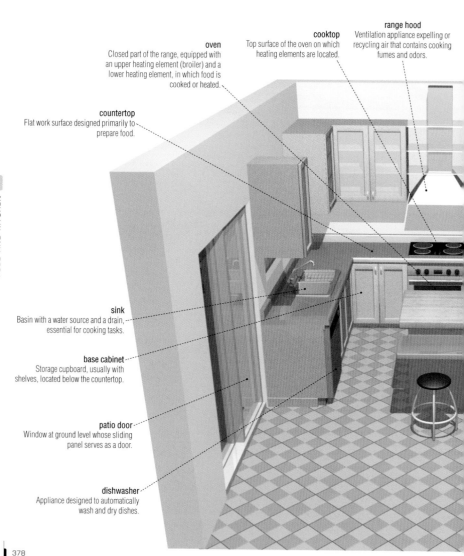

oven
Closed part of the range, equipped with an upper heating element (broiler) and a lower heating element, in which food is cooked or heated.

cooktop
Top surface of the oven on which heating elements are located.

range hood
Ventilation appliance expelling or recycling air that contains cooking fumes and odors.

countertop
Flat work surface designed primarily to prepare food.

sink
Basin with a water source and a drain, essential for cooking tasks.

base cabinet
Storage cupboard, usually with shelves, located below the countertop.

patio door
Window at ground level whose sliding panel serves as a door.

dishwasher
Appliance designed to automatically wash and dry dishes.

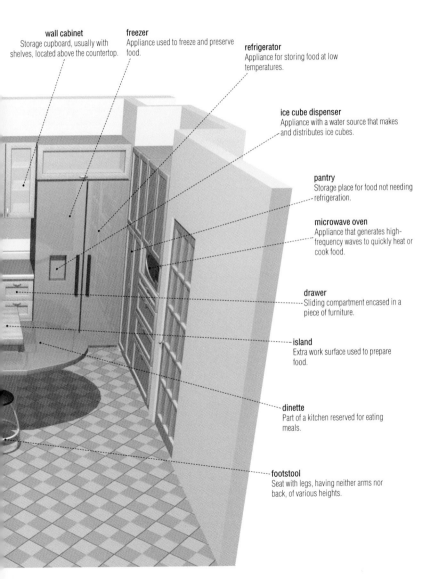

wall cabinet
Storage cupboard, usually with shelves, located above the countertop.

freezer
Appliance used to freeze and preserve food.

refrigerator
Appliance for storing food at low temperatures.

ice cube dispenser
Appliance with a water source that makes and distributes ice cubes.

pantry
Storage place for food not needing refrigeration.

microwave oven
Appliance that generates high-frequency waves to quickly heat or cook food.

drawer
Sliding compartment encased in a piece of furniture.

island
Extra work surface used to prepare food.

dinette
Part of a kitchen reserved for eating meals.

footstool
Seat with legs, having neither arms nor back, of various heights.

FOOD AND KITCHEN

glassware

Drinking receptacles; some are used to measure volume for cooking.

liqueur glass
Very small stemmed glass used for drinking liqueurs with a high alcohol content.

port glass
Small rounded stemmed glass used to serve port and dessert wines.

brandy snifter
Short-stemmed glass whose pear shape allows the cognac to warm up, and whose narrow lip concentrates the aroma.

white wine glass
Somewhat narrow stemmed glass usually used for white wines.

Alsace glass
Glass with a long stem, usually green, used to serve Alsatian white wines.

sparkling wine glass
Stemmed glass, wider than it is tall, used to serve champagne and sparkling wines.

bordeaux glass
Tulip-shaped stemmed glass, mainly used for Bordeaux; tapering slightly at the top, it concentrates the aroma.

burgundy glass
Stemmed glass whose wide mouth ensures maximum oxygenation of the wine; it is used mainly for Burgundies.

cocktail glass
Conical stemmed glass used to serve certain cocktails; before serving, the rim of the glass can be frosted or decorated with fruit.

champagne flute
Tall and very thin stemmed glass used for champagne and sparkling wines; because the air bubbles break more slowly, the wine retains its effervescence longer.

water goblet
Large stemmed glass used to serve water at the table; taller and wider than wine glasses.

highball glass
Tall narrow straight glass used for serving liquor such as gin, often over ice or sometimes mixed with water, soda, etc.

old-fashioned glass
Wide short straight glass with a thick bottom primarily used for serving whiskey.

decanter
Glass or crystal carafe with a wide base and a narrow neck used to serve water or wine.

beer mug
Large cylindrical vessel with a handle used to serve beer; it is usually made of thick glass, ceramic or stoneware.

small decanter
Small carafe used in restaurants to serve wine.

FOOD AND KITCHEN

dinnerware

Receptacles of various sizes, shapes and materials used to present food and for eating it.

demitasse
Small cup for serving coffee.

coffee mug
Large cup used to serve café au lait.

creamer
Small jug used to serve cream at the table.

cup
Cup, larger than the demitasse, used to serve tea.

sugar bowl
Small pot used to serve sugar at the table.

teapot
Receptacle used for steeping and serving tea.

bread and butter plate
Small flat plate used to serve desserts.

soup bowl
Deep round container used to serve
individual portions of soup.

salad plate
Flat plate commonly used to serve salads or
appetizers.

rim soup bowl
Shallower round container used to
serve individual portions of soup.

dinner plate
Large piece of flat or shallow dinnerware,
usually containing individual portions of
solid food.

butter dish
Flat covered receptacle from which
guests serve themselves butter.

FOOD AND KITCHEN

dinnerware

platter
Large oval plate used to present and serve various solid foods, such as cuts of meat, roasts, grilled meat and omelettes.

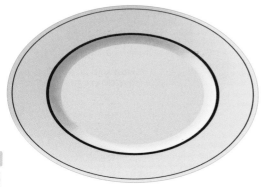

salt shaker
Small receptacle used to serve salt at the table, often paired with the pepper shaker.

pepper shaker
Small receptacle used to serve pepper at the table, often paired with the salt shaker.

fish platter
Large oval plate used to serve a whole cooked fish.

vegetable bowl
Large receptacle used to bring side vegetables to the table.

hors d'oeuvre dish
Serving platter divided into sections used to serve several complementary foods.

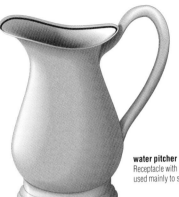

gravy boat
Receptacle used to serve sauces at the table.

water pitcher
Receptacle with a handle and a spout used mainly to serve juice and water.

soup tureen
Large bowl with a removable lid used for bringing soup to the table and serving it.

ramekin
Small containers, suitable for oven and table, used to cook and serve individual portions.

salad bowl
Container of medium depth used to toss and serve salad.

salad dish
Small container used to serve individual portions of salad.

FOOD AND KITCHEN

silverware

Utensils used at the table, generally knives, forks and spoons, to which other utensils may be added, depending on the menu.

fork

Utensil with tines used to spear food and carry it to the mouth.

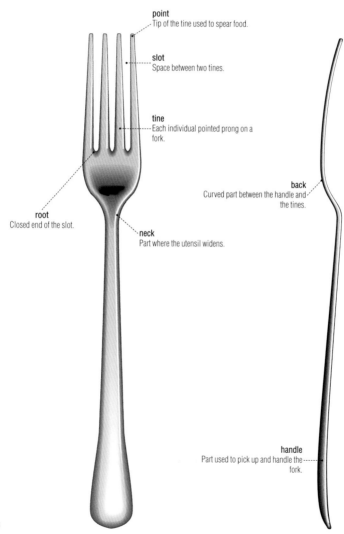

point
Tip of the tine used to spear food.

slot
Space between two tines.

tine
Each individual pointed prong on a fork.

back
Curved part between the handle and the tines.

root
Closed end of the slot.

neck
Part where the utensil widens.

handle
Part used to pick up and handle the fork.

examples of forks

There are many different kinds of forks, each one intended for eating a specific kind of food.

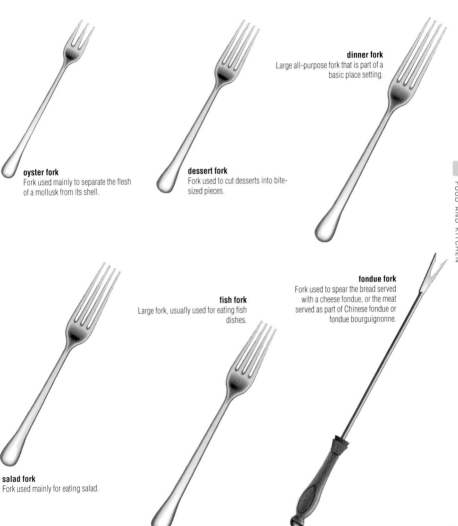

dinner fork
Large all-purpose fork that is part of a basic place setting.

oyster fork
Fork used mainly to separate the flesh of a mollusk from its shell.

dessert fork
Fork used to cut desserts into bite-sized pieces.

fondue fork
Fork used to spear the bread served with a cheese fondue, or the meat served as part of Chinese fondue or fondue bourguignonne.

fish fork
Large fork, usually used for eating fish dishes.

salad fork
Fork used mainly for eating salad.

silverware

spoon
Utensil consisting of a handle and a hollow part used to eat
liquid or semisolid foods.

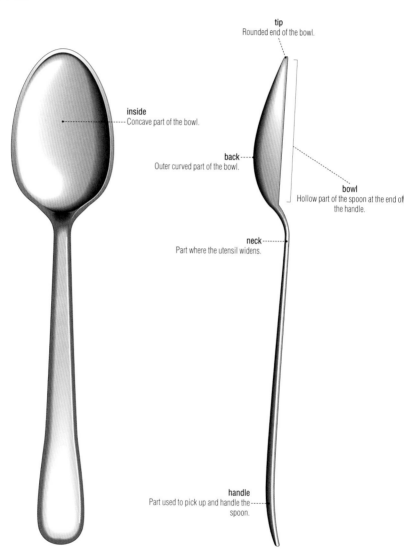

tip
Rounded end of the bowl.

inside
Concave part of the bowl.

back
Outer curved part of the bowl.

bowl
Hollow part of the spoon at the end of
the handle.

neck
Part where the utensil widens.

handle
Part used to pick up and handle the
spoon.

examples of spoons
There are many different kinds of spoons, each with a specific use.

soup spoon
Spoon used for eating liquid or semiliquid foods; it is part of a basic place setting.

teaspoon
Somewhat larger spoon, with a capacity of 1/6 oz or 1/3 tablespoon.

coffee spoon
The smallest utensil in this category, hence sometimes called a small spoon.

tablespoon
Largest spoon, with a capacity of .5 oz.

sundae spoon
Long-handled spoon used for mixing drinks or eating desserts served in a sundae glass.

dessert spoon
Spoon used for eating liquid or semiliquid desserts.

silverware

knife
Piece of silverware consisting of a handle and a
sharp blade used to cut food into bite-sized pieces.

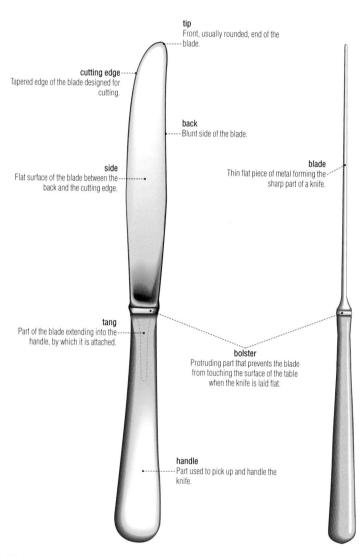

tip
Front, usually rounded, end of the
blade.

cutting edge
Tapered edge of the blade designed for
cutting.

back
Blunt side of the blade.

side
Flat surface of the blade between the
back and the cutting edge.

blade
Thin flat piece of metal forming the
sharp part of a knife.

tang
Part of the blade extending into the
handle, by which it is attached.

bolster
Protruding part that prevents the blade
from touching the surface of the table
when the knife is laid flat.

handle
Part used to pick up and handle the
knife.

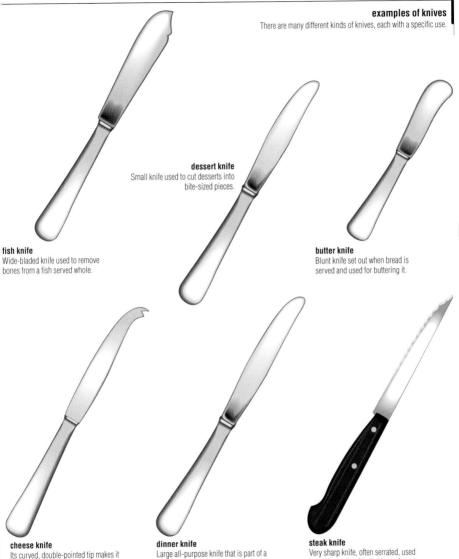

examples of knives
There are many different kinds of knives, each with a specific use.

dessert knife
Small knife used to cut desserts into bite-sized pieces.

fish knife
Wide-bladed knife used to remove bones from a fish served whole.

butter knife
Blunt knife set out when bread is served and used for buttering it.

cheese knife
Its curved, double-pointed tip makes it easier to spear individual pieces of cheese.

dinner knife
Large all-purpose knife that is part of a basic place setting.

steak knife
Very sharp knife, often serrated, used to cut firm, often fried, pieces of meat.

kitchen utensils

Accessories or simple mechanical devices used for preparing food.

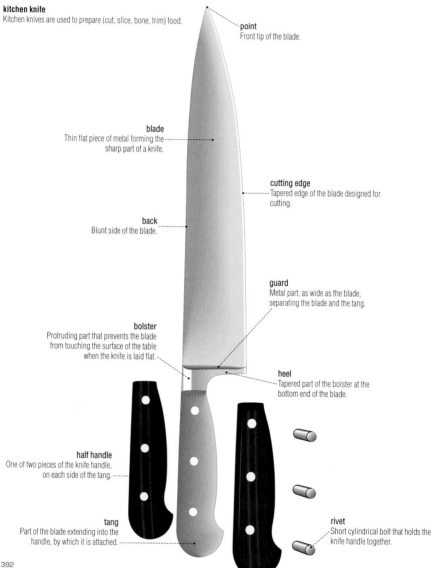

kitchen knife
Kitchen knives are used to prepare (cut, slice, bone, trim) food.

point
Front tip of the blade.

blade
Thin flat piece of metal forming the
sharp part of a knife.

cutting edge
Tapered edge of the blade designed for
cutting.

back
Blunt side of the blade.

guard
Metal part, as wide as the blade,
separating the blade and the tang.

bolster
Protruding part that prevents the blade
from touching the surface of the table
when the knife is laid flat.

heel
Tapered part of the bolster at the
bottom end of the blade.

half handle
One of two pieces of the knife handle,
on each side of the tang.

tang
Part of the blade extending into the
handle, by which it is attached.

rivet
Short cylindrical bolt that holds the
knife handle together.

examples of kitchen knives

The shape and size of kitchen knives vary depending on their use and the type of food for which they are intended.

grapefruit knife
Knife used to detach citrus fruit pulp.

filleting knife
Knife with a long pointed blade used for separating fish into fillets.

boning knife
Small pointed knife with a tapered blade used to separate the meat from the bones.

paring knife
Miniature version of the cook's knife, it is used to clean, scrape and slice small pieces of food.

cleaver
Knife with a wide rigid blade heavy enough to break bones.

ham knife
Knife with a ridged blade used to cut whole cooked ham.

carving knife
Knife with a narrow blade used to slice pieces of cooked meat into portions.

bread knife
Serrated knife used for cutting fresh bread.

cook's knife
Knife with a wide range of uses, from cutting large pieces of meat to chopping fresh herbs.

FOOD AND KITCHEN

393

zester
Knife whose blade curves at the end
and has five small cutting holes; it is
used to remove thin strips of rind from
citrus fruits.

peeler
Its pivoting blade follows the contours
of the fruits and vegetables it is used to
peel.

carving fork
Fork used to hold a piece of meat in
place when it is being cut into
portions.

oyster knife
Double-edged knife with a guard used
to open oyster shells by severing the
muscle that holds them closed.

butter curler
Utensil with a serrated hook that
creates butter curls when scraped
across cold butter.

sharpening steel
Cylindrical steel rod with narrow
grooves used for honing a knife edge.

sharpening stone
Abrasive stone used to sharpen knife
edges.

cutting board
Made of plastic or wood and used for
cutting up foods.

groove
Furrow where cooking juices collect.

for opening

Instruments that remove lids, caps or corks from containers in order to provide access to their contents.

can opener
Tool used to open cans by cutting along the inside edge of the lid.

bottle opener
Instrument used to remove caps from bottles.

lever corkscrew
Instrument with a screw and two wings that rise as the screw penetrates the cork; they then act as levers to open the bottle.

wine waiter corkscrew
Instrument with a screw and a lever that open wine bottles by leverage, a blade for cutting the hood around the top, and a bottle opener.

kitchen utensils

for grinding and grating
Instruments that can reduce food to fine particles, shavings, powder, purées, etc.

nutcracker
Tongs used to break nutshells and release the kernel inside.

garlic press
Utensil used to finely crush garlic cloves.

nutmeg grater
Small conical grater used to reduce nutmeg seeds to a powder.

mortar
Hemispheric receptacle made of marble, porcelain or hardwood in which certain foods can be ground with a pestle.

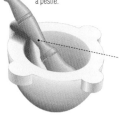

pestle
Usually heavy instrument whose short handle extends into a head; it is used mainly to grind seeds, dry ingredients and garlic.

food mill
Instrument used to reduce cooked fruit and vegetables to a purée, the consistency of which depends on the disk used.

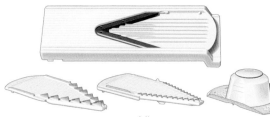

mandoline
Instrument comprising interchangeable cutting blades inserted in a frame; it slices vegetables in different ways, depending on the blade used.

citrus juicer
Instrument used to extract juice from citrus fruits, usually lemons or oranges.

meat grinder
Instrument with a knife and
interchangeable disks used to grind meat;
the perforations in the disks determine the
size of the grind.

rotary cheese grater
Instrument used to grate cheese by
scraping it against the teeth of a
rotating drum.

pusher
Bent part of the handle that presses the
piece of cheese against the drum.

crank
Angled lever that makes the drum
rotate.

drum
Cylindrical part of the utensil that
grates the cheese.

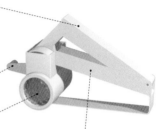

handle
Part enabling the user to hold the
grater and exert pressure on the
pusher.

FOOD AND KITCHEN

pasta maker
Instrument that can roll out and cut pasta dough into
different shapes with its removable blades.

grater
Instrument used to reduce food such
as vegetables, cheese and nuts into
fine particles or a powder.

kitchen utensils

for measuring
Instruments designed to measure the volume or weight of ingredients, food temperature, and cooking or preparation time.

egg timer
Device with two glass vials, one of which is filled with sand; the flow of the sand between the vials measures a precise time period.

kitchen timer
Device used to measure a period of time; once that time has elapsed, the timer rings.

measuring cups
Receptacles used to measure the exact quantity of an ingredient.

measuring spoons
The bowls on these spoons correspond to an exact quantity of an ingredient, and are used to measure it.

measuring cup
Graduated container with a pouring spout used for measuring liquids.

measuring beaker
Graduated container used to measure dry and liquid ingredients.

meat thermometer
Thermometer inserted into a roast to
check its degree of doneness.

candy thermometer
Thermometer that is placed in hot
liquid sugar mixtures to measure their
exact temperature.

FOOD AND KITCHEN

oven thermometer
Thermometer that is placed inside an
oven to check the exact temperature.

kitchen scale
Instruments used to weigh dry
ingredients (e.g., flour, sugar, rice).

instant-read thermometer
Digital thermometer that, when inserted into a roast, instantly
indicates the meat's internal temperature.

kitchen utensils

for straining and draining
Instruments used to filter dry or liquid foods, or to remove the liquid used to wash, blanch, cook or fry certain foods.

chinois
Finely meshed cone-shaped strainer used to filter broth and sauces, and to reduce food to a purée.

mesh strainer
Instrument used to sift dry ingredients or filter liquid ones.

fry basket
Metal mesh receptacle designed to hold foods during frying and drain them afterward.

colander
Instrument used to drain food.

funnel
Cone-shaped instrument ending in a tube used to pour liquid into a narrow-necked container.

muslin
Cloth woven into a fine loose mesh and used to strain creamed soups and sauces so they become finer and smoother.

salad spinner
Apparatus that uses centrifugal force to remove water from freshly washed lettuce leaves.

sieve
Strainer made of woven nylon, metal or silk strands and attached to a wooden frame; it is used to strain dry and liquid ingredients.

FOOD AND KITCHEN

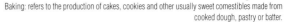

baking utensils
Baking: refers to the production of cakes, cookies and other usually sweet comestibles made from cooked dough, pastry or batter.

egg beater
Mechanical device with two whisks activated by a crank handle; it is used to beat liquid and semiliquid ingredients.

icing syringe
Fitted with interchangeable nozzles that are filled with icing, it is used to decorate baked goods and molded desserts.

pastry cutting wheel
Device used for cutting dough; the indented wheel gives it a fluted edge.

cookie cutters
Hollow metal molds used to cut dough into soft shapes that will be retained after baking.

sifter
Device used to sieve flour; it has a spring-loaded handle that moves the flour about and makes it lighter.

pastry bag and nozzles
Leakproof bag into which interchangeable nozzles are inserted; it is used to decorate dishes, baked goods and molded desserts, or to make pastries.

whisk
Utensil made of several curved and intersecting steel wires used to blend, beat or whip liquid and semiliquid ingredients.

pastry brush
Device with silk or nylon bristles at one end, used to coat, brush or glaze pastries, or to grease baking pans.

baking sheet
Rectangular pan with low sides, usually made of aluminum, used for baking cookies, cakes and other pastries that do not require molding.

dredger
Container with a perforated lid used for sprinkling food with flour, sugar or grated cheese.

pastry blender
Utensil used to blend fatty ingredients with flour.

rolling pin
Wooden cylinder that rolls freely between two lateral handles; it is used to roll out pastry.

muffin pan
Baking pan with indentations used to give muffins their distinctive shape.

mixing bowls
Round containers of various sizes used to prepare or mix food and ingredients.

cake pan
Relatively deep metal baking pan with
enough room to allow the cake to rise.

soufflé dish
Deep porcelain dish that prevents the
rising soufflé from overflowing as it
cooks.

pie pan
Metal pan used to make a pie crust and
to bake a pie in the oven.

quiche plate
Metal baking pan with a scalloped
edge that makes the crust of the quiche
more attractive.

FOOD AND KITCHEN

removable-bottomed pan
Metal baking pan whose bottom, and sometimes its side,
come apart so the contents can be removed more easily.

charlotte mold
Deep metal pan shaped like a pail and
used to cook a cream-based sweet
dessert surrounded by biscuits.

set of utensils
Main kitchen utensils, often matching, stored in a stand.

spatula
Long blade of variable width used to turn food over during cooking.

draining spoon
Large elongated slightly concave spoon with perforations; it is used to remove small pieces of food from their cooking liquid.

skimmer
Large round slightly concave spoon with perforations; it is used to skim broth and sauce, or to remove food from its cooking liquid.

potato masher
Utensil used to manually purée cooked fruits and vegetables.

turner
Utensil used to handle cooked food without breaking it.

ladle
Spoon with a deep bowl and a long handle; it is used to decant liquid or semiliquid food.

stoner
Tonglike device used to remove stones from olives and cherries without damaging the flesh.

melon baller
Spoon used to cut small round pieces from the flesh of fruits or vegetables.

apple corer
Utensil used to remove the core from apples and pears.

vegetable brush
Utensil used to clean certain vegetables, such as potatoes.

trussing needle
Tool used to thread pieces of string through poultry or to tie a roast.

larding needle
Tool used to insert strips of lard, ham or truffles into cuts of meat.

tasting spoon
Wooden spoon consisting of two bowls joined by a shallow groove used to take and taste liquids.

ice cream scoop
Spoon used to remove a serving of ice milk or ice cream from a container.

kitchen utensils

kitchen shears
Multipurpose utensil used for cutting fresh herbs, trimming meat and vegetables.

poultry shears
Utensil used to cut poultry into pieces.

snail tongs
Utensil used to hold snail shells so the snail can be extracted.

tea ball
Hollow sphere that holds dried tea leaves during steeping.

egg slicer
Device that uses taut steel wires to slice a hard-boiled egg.

baster
Utensil with a graduated tube and a rubber bulb; it is used to suck up cooking liquid and drizzle it over the meat.

tongs
Utensil used for holding, turning and serving food.

spaghetti tongs
Two-armed utensil with teeth at the end that facilitate serving long strips of pasta.

snail dish
Has several indentations for holding snails when they are served.

cooking utensils

Utensils used for cooking food, especially in the oven or on the stove.

rack
Perforated sheet; the hooks allow it to be lifted so that, once cooked, the fish can be drained and removed.

fish poacher
Oblong receptacle that has a rack and a cover; it is used to cook whole fish.

lid
Removable part that covers the fish poacher during cooking.

wok set
Cooking utensil native to Asia used for rapidly cooking food in very little fat.

FOOD AND KITCHEN

lid
Removable part that covers the wok during cooking.

rack
Half-moon-shaped grating used to drain or set aside food.

wok
Large cone-shaped frying pan; food collects at the center of the rounded bottom, where the heat is most intense.

burner ring
Metal base used to balance the wok over the burner or hot plate.

cooking utensils

fondue set
Utensil designed to prepare and serve
various kinds of fondue, such as meat,
cheese or chocolate.

fondue pot
Container with one or two side handles
used for cooking fondue.

stand
Metal base designed to hold the
fondue pot and the burner.

burner
Compartment containing a flammable
liquid that keeps the fondue pot warm
throughout the meal.

tajine
Varnished earthenware dish with a
cone-shaped airtight lid used in
northwestern Africa to cook an
eponymous dish.

pressure cooker
Stock pot with a screw-on, airtight lid
designed to cook food rapidly using
pressurized steam.

pressure regulator
Device maintaining the pressure at a
constant level.

safety valve
Device that regulates escaping steam
when the stock pot is under pressure.

terrine
Container with a perforated lid that allows steam to escape; it is designed for cooking recipes with or without jelly.

dripping pan
Slightly concave rectangular pan used to roast meat or to catch the meat's cooking juices.

roasting pans
Somewhat deep large-capacity utensils used to roast meat in the oven.

FOOD AND KITCHEN

FOOD AND KITCHEN

Dutch oven
Somewhat deep stock pot used for
cooking food in a liquid.

stock pot
Container used for cooking large
quantities of food in a liquid.

steamer
Utensil comprising two saucepans; the
steam from the boiling water in the
bottom one cooks the food in the top
one.

steamer basket
Perforated receptacle that is placed in a saucepan
above the water level and filled with food to be steam-
cooked.

couscous kettle
Double container in which steam from the
broth in which the food in the bottom part
is simmering cooks and flavors the
semolina in the top part.

egg poacher
Device used to poach eggs by placing them in indentations in
a tray suspended over a hot liquid.

frying pan
Utensil used to fry, sauté or brown food.

sauté pan
Similar to a frying pan but with a straight edge, used to cook food in fat, over high heat.

pancake pan
Round thick-bottomed skillet with a shallow edge that allows a spatula to loosen and flip the pancake.

diable
Utensil composed of two skillets of porous clay that fit tightly together; it is used for braising food.

saucepan
Low-sided receptacle commonly used to heat liquids or cook food in a liquid.

small saucepan
Deeper than a frying pan, this utensil is used to simmer or braise dishes.

double boiler
Utensil comprising two saucepans; the bottom one contains boiling water, which cooks or heats the food in the top one.

FOOD AND KITCHEN

domestic appliances

Domestic appliances operating on electricity.

for mixing and blending
Appliances used for stirring, for blending several ingredients together or for changing the appearance of an ingredient.

cap
Part that gives the container an airtight seal.

blender
Electric appliance comprising a motor unit with a container on top, in which raw or cooked food is mixed, crushed or puréed.

container
Glass jug in which food or ingredients are placed.

cutting blade
Propeller blade that mixes or grinds food as it turns.

push button
Buttons used to start the appliance and select blade speed.

motor unit
Part containing the motor and the various circuits making the appliance work.

FOOD AND KITCHEN

table mixer
Electric appliance comprising a powerful motor unit, two beaters and a stand used to beat or mix liquid or semiliquid foods.

beater
Device used to beat or mix food; the beaters are inserted into cogwheels that turn in opposite directions.

beater ejector
Button pressed to remove the beaters.

tilt-back head
The motor unit rotates on an axis so the beaters can be lowered into the bowl and lifted out of it.

mixing bowl
Round container of various sizes used to mix food in.

turntable
Enables the mixing bowl to be rotated so the contents will be beaten or mixed uniformly.

stand
Base that holds the mixing bowl and the tilt-back head.

speed control
Device for selecting the speed at which the beaters rotate.

FOOD AND KITCHEN

413

domestic appliances

hand mixer
Electric appliance comprising two beaters and a motor unit used to beat or mix liquid or semiliquid food.

beater ejector
Button pressed to remove the beaters.

speed selector
Device for selecting the speed at which the beaters rotate.

handle
Part used to pick up and handle the mixer.

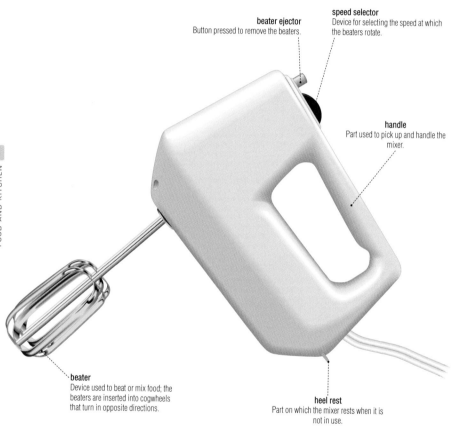

beater
Device used to beat or mix food; the beaters are inserted into cogwheels that turn in opposite directions.

heel rest
Part on which the mixer rests when it is not in use.

beaters

Instruments used to mix, beat or knead liquid or
semiliquid foods.

four blade beater
All-purpose beater used to mix, beat or
whisk various ingredients.

spiral beater
Beater used primarily to mix and knead
light dough.

wire beater
Beater used to mix, emulsify or beat
many different ingredients or to
incorporate air into a mixture.

dough hook
Beater used to mix and knead dough.

domestic appliances

hand blender
Electric appliance with a handheld motor unit; less powerful than the blender, it is used for mixing liquids and grinding soft foods.

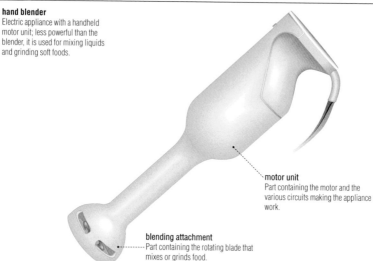

motor unit
Part containing the motor and the various circuits making the appliance work.

blending attachment
Part containing the rotating blade that mixes or grinds food.

for juicing
Device designed to extract juice from fruit, especially citrus fruit, when pressure is exerted upon it.

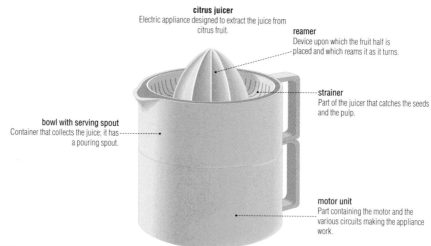

citrus juicer
Electric appliance designed to extract the juice from citrus fruit.

reamer
Device upon which the fruit half is placed and which reams it as it turns.

strainer
Part of the juicer that catches the seeds and the pulp.

bowl with serving spout
Container that collects the juice; it has a pouring spout.

motor unit
Part containing the motor and the various circuits making the appliance work.

for cutting
Appliances used primarily for separating elements into small parts or portions.

food processor
Electric appliance comprising a motor unit, a blade and a set of disks used for cutting, chopping, slicing, grating, mixing, kneading, etc.

feed tube
Conduit in which food is placed.

spindle
Shaft that transmits the motor's movement to the blade or disks.

lid
Removable part covering the bowl.

bowl
Container in which food or ingredients are placed.

handle
Part used to pick up and move the bowl.

blade
Propeller blade that mixes or grinds food as it turns.

motor unit
Part containing the motor and the various circuits making the appliance work.

Dough

Pulse

domestic appliances

for cooking
Appliances that bring raw food into
contact with a heat source in order to
cook them.

deep fryer
Container with a heating element that
raises the temperature of fat high
enough to deep-fry food.

basket
Wire mesh container with a detachable
handle designed to hold foods during
frying and drain them once cooked.

rack
Notched device used to raise or lower
the basket.

timer
Device used to monitor cooking time.

filter
Device that absorbs the steam from
hot fat.

thermostat
Device used to regulate fat
temperature.

signal lamp
Light indicating when the desired
temperature has been reached.

lid
Removable part that covers the deep
fryer during cooking.

microwave oven
Appliance that generates high-frequency waves to quickly heat or cook food.

sensor probe
Instrument that is inserted into food and used to check internal temperature and monitor cooking.

door
Movable part that closes the microwave oven.

latch
Device that opens the door when pushed.

clock timer
Displays either real time or the programmed cooking time.

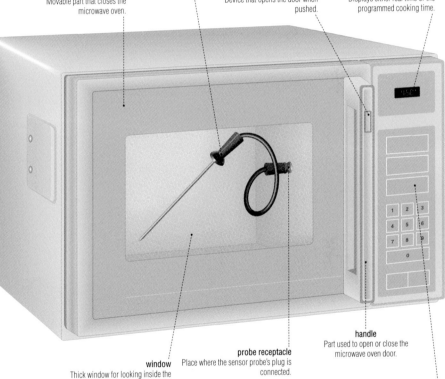

window
Thick window for looking inside the oven.

probe receptacle
Place where the sensor probe's plug is connected.

handle
Part used to open or close the microwave oven door.

control panel
Panel containing the programming keys.

domestic appliances

FOOD AND KITCHEN

raclette with grill
Appliance with covered heating elements used to melt cheese or grill meat and side vegetables.

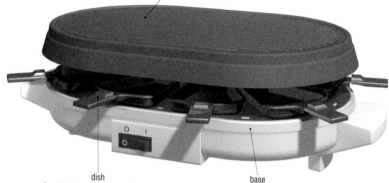

cooking plate
Ribbed cooking surface covering the heating elements; it is used for grilling food.

dish
Small shallow nonstick container used for cooking individual servings of food.

base
Stand supporting the raclette with grill; it contains the heating elements that cook the food.

indoor electric grill
Electric appliance comprising a metal grill and a heating element used to cook food.

cooking surface
Metal grill on which the food is cooked.

insulated handle
Part used to pick up and move the grill without burning oneself.

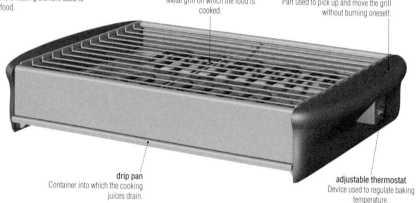

drip pan
Container into which the cooking juices drain.

adjustable thermostat
Device used to regulate baking temperature.

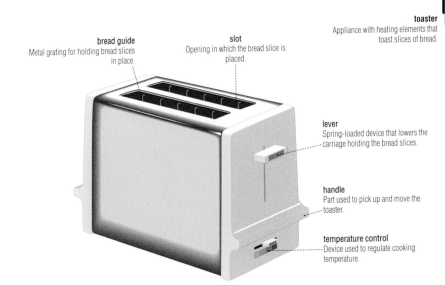

toaster
Appliance with heating elements that toast slices of bread.

bread guide
Metal grating for holding bread slices in place.

slot
Opening in which the bread slice is placed.

lever
Spring-loaded device that lowers the carriage holding the bread slices.

handle
Part used to pick up and move the toaster.

temperature control
Device used to regulate cooking temperature.

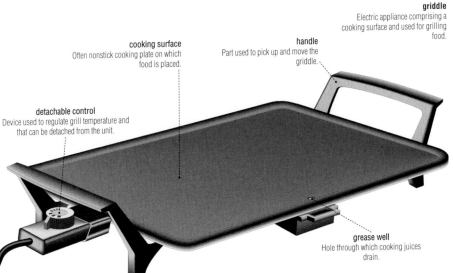

griddle
Electric appliance comprising a cooking surface and used for grilling food.

cooking surface
Often nonstick cooking plate on which food is placed.

handle
Part used to pick up and move the griddle.

detachable control
Device used to regulate grill temperature and that can be detached from the unit.

grease well
Hole through which cooking juices drain.

FOOD AND KITCHEN

waffle iron
Appliance comprising two indented plates, each one covering a heating element; it is used to cook waffles or grill food.

handle
Part used to raise and lower the lid.

lid
Movable part that closes the waffle iron.

plate
Indented cooking surface that, because it is attached to the inside of the lid, can be raised and lowered.

temperature selector
Device used to regulate plate temperature.

hinge
Jointed part that makes it possible to raise and lower the lid.

plate
Indented cooking surface designed to receive waffle batter or food intended for grilling.

Utensils used to brew coffee; each of the various models produces coffee that has a distinctive flavor.

automatic drip coffee maker
Electric coffee maker that allows hot water to drain into a paper filter containing the ground beans, and coffee to drip into the carafe below.

lid
Removable part covering the reservoir and under which the basket is located.

reservoir
Container holding the water to be heated.

basket
Removable container that holds the filter with the ground beans.

water level
Indicates how many cups of coffee can be made.

signal lamp
Light showing that the appliance is on.

on-off switch
Button for turning the device on or off.

warming plate
Surface used to keep the coffee warm.

carafe
Container with a spout into which the coffee drips and that is used to pour it.

FOOD AND KITCHEN

coffee makers

Neapolitan coffee maker

Coffee maker that is placed on a heat source to boil the water; it is then turned over so the boiling water filters through the ground beans into the serving compartment.

plunger

Coffee maker that allows hot water to be poured over ground beans; once the grounds have steeped, the plunger is depressed to push the grounds to the bottom of the carafe.

espresso coffee maker

Coffee maker that allows boiling water from the lower compartment to be forced through the ground beans into the upper compartment.

coffee makers

espresso machine
Electric coffee maker that allows hot
water to be forced under pressure
through the ground beans.

filter holder
Removable part with a handle into
which the metal filter containing the
ground beans is inserted.

on-off switch
Button for turning the device on or off.

steam control knob
Device used to regulate the steam
coming out of the nozzle.

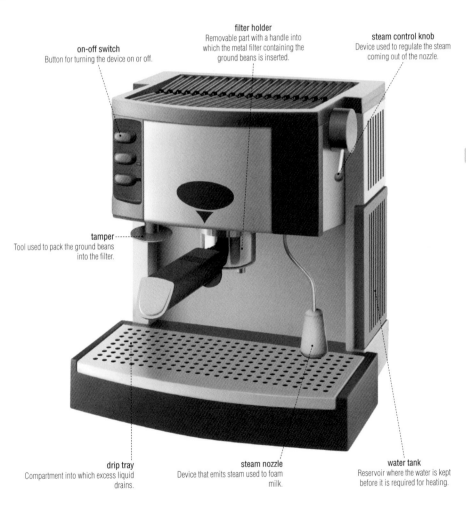

tamper
Tool used to pack the ground beans
into the filter.

drip tray
Compartment into which excess liquid
drains.

steam nozzle
Device that emits steam used to foam
milk.

water tank
Reservoir where the water is kept
before it is required for heating.

coffee makers

vacuum coffee maker
Coffee maker that brews coffee by causing the water to pass through the ground beans twice.

upper bowl
Compartment into which the brewed coffee rises and from which it drains into the lower bowl as the heat source cools.

stem
Conduit through which the hot water rises.

lower bowl
Compartment from which boiling water rises under pressure into the upper bowl, passing through the ground beans; the brewed coffee drains into it for serving.

percolator
Electric coffee maker that allows the hot water to rise several times through a tube to percolate through ground beans.

spout
Tube-shaped part through which the coffee is poured.

signal lamp
Light showing that the appliance is on.

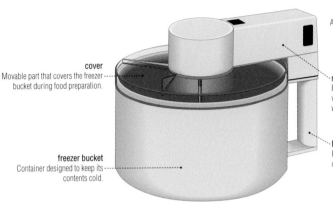

ice cream freezer
Appliance comprising a freezer bucket in which revolving paddles make sherbet and ice cream.

cover
Movable part that covers the freezer bucket during food preparation.

motor unit
Part containing the motor and the various circuits making the appliance work.

freezer bucket
Container designed to keep its contents cold.

handle
Part used to pick up and move the ice cream freezer.

coffee mill
Appliance that uses a rotating blade to finely grind coffee beans or other items, such as spices.

lid
Removable part that covers the coffee mill when it is in use.

blade
Instrument used to grind coffee beans or other items.

on-off button
Device that turns the appliance on or off.

motor unit
Part containing the motor and the various circuits making the appliance work.

FOOD AND KITCHEN

427

miscellaneous domestic appliances

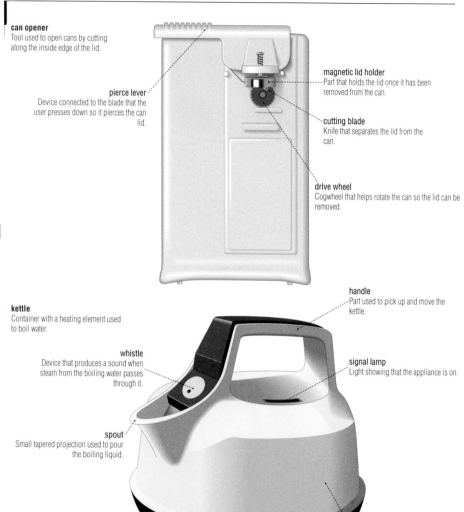

can opener
Tool used to open cans by cutting along the inside edge of the lid.

magnetic lid holder
Part that holds the lid once it has been removed from the can.

pierce lever
Device connected to the blade that the user presses down so it pierces the can lid.

cutting blade
Knife that separates the lid from the can.

drive wheel
Cogwheel that helps rotate the can so the lid can be removed.

handle
Part used to pick up and move the kettle.

kettle
Container with a heating element used to boil water.

whistle
Device that produces a sound when steam from the boiling water passes through it.

signal lamp
Light showing that the appliance is on.

spout
Small tapered projection used to pour the boiling liquid.

base
Stand supporting the kettle; it contains the heating element that boils the water.

body
Part of the kettle that holds the water to be boiled.

juicer
Appliance that uses centrifugal force to extract the juice from vegetables and fruit, except citrus fruits, which must be reamed.

strainer
Device that allows only the fruit or vegetable juice to pass through.

pusher
Device that pushes the fruits or vegetables into the appliance.

lid
Movable part that covers the juicer when it is in operation.

feed tube
Conduit into which fruit or vegetables are placed to extract their juice.

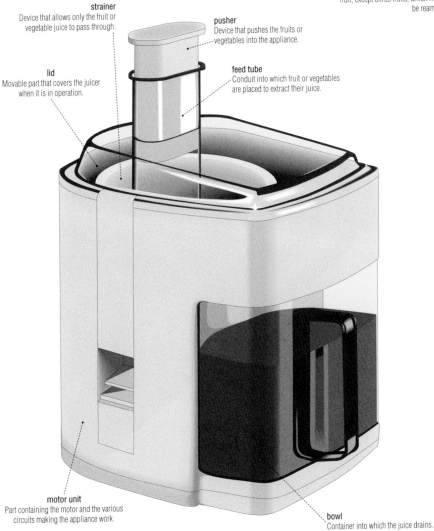

motor unit
Part containing the motor and the various circuits making the appliance work.

bowl
Container into which the juice drains.

FOOD AND KITCHEN

exterior of a house

View of a house on its site with the components of its exterior structure.

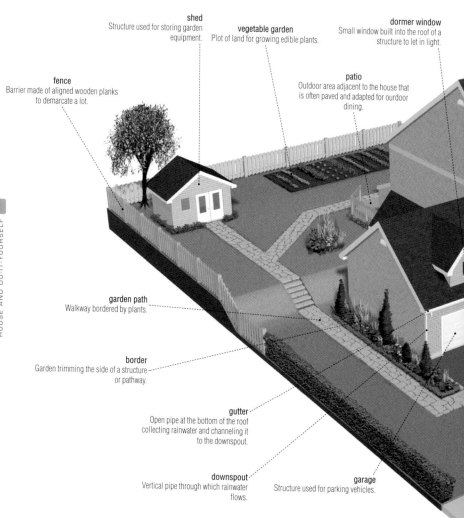

shed
Structure used for storing garden equipment.

vegetable garden
Plot of land for growing edible plants.

dormer window
Small window built into the roof of a structure to let in light.

fence
Barrier made of aligned wooden planks to demarcate a lot.

patio
Outdoor area adjacent to the house that is often paved and adapted for ourdoor dining.

garden path
Walkway bordered by plants.

border
Garden trimming the side of a structure or pathway.

gutter
Open pipe at the bottom of the roof collecting rainwater and channeling it to the downspout.

downspout
Vertical pipe through which rainwater flows.

garage
Structure used for parking vehicles.

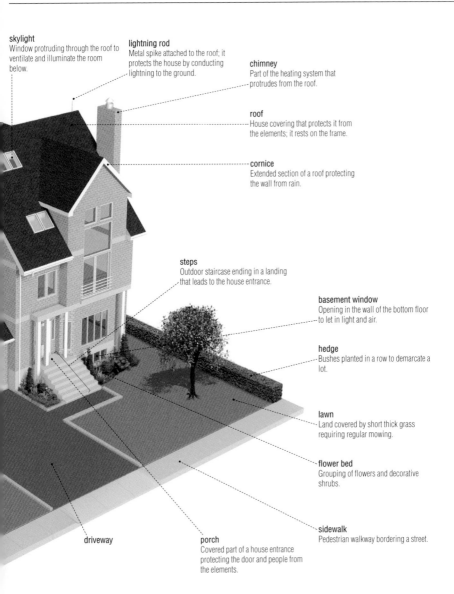

skylight
Window protruding through the roof to ventilate and illuminate the room below.

lightning rod
Metal spike attached to the roof; it protects the house by conducting lightning to the ground.

chimney
Part of the heating system that protrudes from the roof.

roof
House covering that protects it from the elements; it rests on the frame.

cornice
Extended section of a roof protecting the wall from rain.

steps
Outdoor staircase ending in a landing that leads to the house entrance.

basement window
Opening in the wall of the bottom floor to let in light and air.

hedge
Bushes planted in a row to demarcate a lot.

lawn
Land covered by short thick grass requiring regular mowing.

flower bed
Grouping of flowers and decorative shrubs.

sidewalk
Pedestrian walkway bordering a street.

driveway

porch
Covered part of a house entrance protecting the door and people from the elements.

HOUSE AND DO-IT-YOURSELF

main rooms

HOUSE AND DO-IT-YOURSELF

elevation
Vertical representation of the
projection of the house.

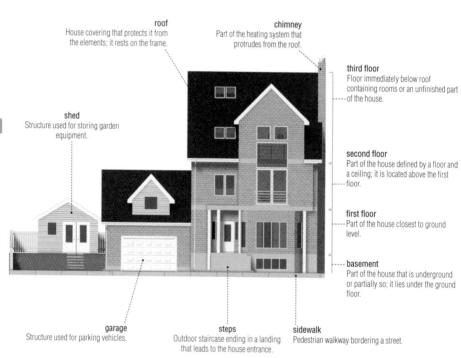

roof
House covering that protects it from
the elements; it rests on the frame.

chimney
Part of the heating system that
protrudes from the roof.

third floor
Floor immediately below roof
containing rooms or an unfinished part
of the house.

shed
Structure used for storing garden
equipment.

second floor
Part of the house defined by a floor and
a ceiling; it is located above the first
floor.

first floor
Part of the house closest to ground
level.

basement
Part of the house that is underground
or partially so; it lies under the ground
floor.

garage
Structure used for parking vehicles.

steps
Outdoor staircase ending in a landing
that leads to the house entrance.

sidewalk
Pedestrian walkway bordering a street.

loft
An upper room or space immediately
the roof.

railing
Handrail at support level bordering the
open side of a room.

study
Room intended for intellectual work; it
usually contains a worktable.

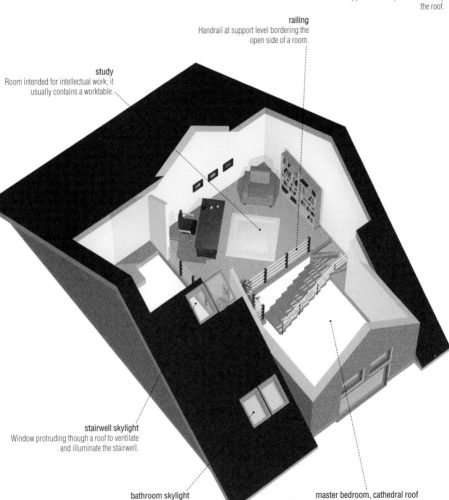

stairwell skylight
Window protruding though a roof to ventilate
and illuminate the stairwell.

bathroom skylight
Window protruding though a roof to ventilate and
illuminate the bathroom.

master bedroom, cathedral roof
The largest room for sleeping. This one is enclosed by
a high ceiling having two slopes.

main rooms

second floor
Part of the house defined by a floor and a ceiling; it is
located above the first floor.

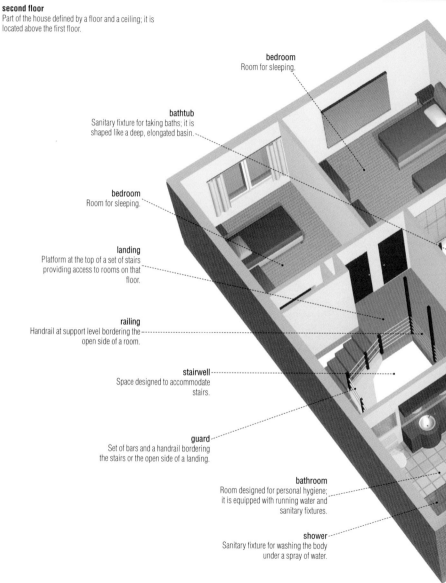

bedroom
Room for sleeping.

bathtub
Sanitary fixture for taking baths; it is
shaped like a deep, elongated basin.

bedroom
Room for sleeping.

landing
Platform at the top of a set of stairs
providing access to rooms on that
floor.

railing
Handrail at support level bordering the
open side of a room.

stairwell
Space designed to accommodate
stairs.

guard
Set of bars and a handrail bordering
the stairs or the open side of a landing.

bathroom
Room designed for personal hygiene;
it is equipped with running water and
sanitary fixtures.

shower
Sanitary fixture for washing the body
under a spray of water.

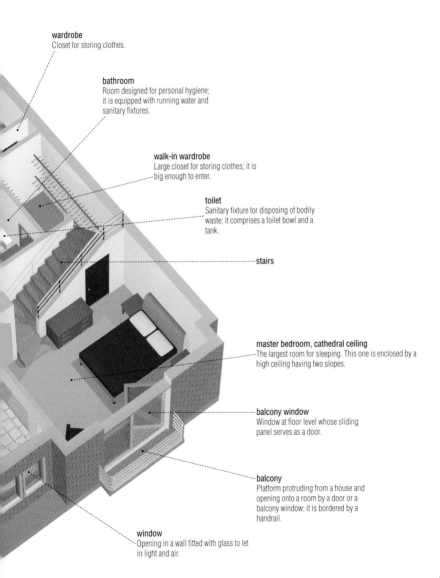

wardrobe
Closet for storing clothes.

bathroom
Room designed for personal hygiene;
it is equipped with running water and
sanitary fixtures.

walk-in wardrobe
Large closet for storing clothes; it is
big enough to enter.

toilet
Sanitary fixture for disposing of bodily
waste; it comprises a toilet bowl and a
tank.

stairs

master bedroom, cathedral ceiling
The largest room for sleeping. This one is enclosed by a
high ceiling having two slopes.

balcony window
Window at floor level whose sliding
panel serves as a door.

balcony
Platform protruding from a house and
opening onto a room by a door or a
balcony window; it is bordered by a
handrail.

window
Opening in a wall fitted with glass to let
in light and air.

HOUSE AND DO-IT-YOURSELF

main rooms

first floor
Part of the house closest to ground level.

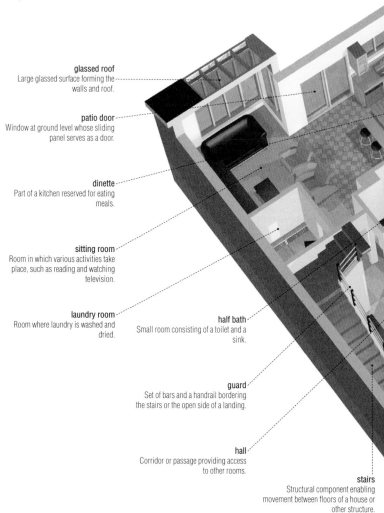

glassed roof
Large glassed surface forming the walls and roof.

patio door
Window at ground level whose sliding panel serves as a door.

dinette
Part of a kitchen reserved for eating meals.

sitting room
Room in which various activities take place, such as reading and watching television.

laundry room
Room where laundry is washed and dried.

half bath
Small room consisting of a toilet and a sink.

guard
Set of bars and a handrail bordering the stairs or the open side of a landing.

hall
Corridor or passage providing access to other rooms.

stairs
Structural component enabling movement between floors of a house or other structure.

HOUSE AND DO-IT-YOURSELF

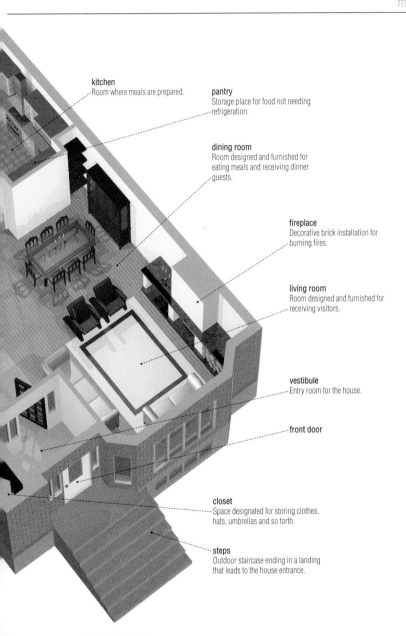

kitchen
Room where meals are prepared.

pantry
Storage place for food not needing refrigeration.

dining room
Room designed and furnished for eating meals and receiving dinner guests.

fireplace
Decorative brick installation for burning fires.

living room
Room designed and furnished for receiving visitors.

vestibule
Entry room for the house.

front door

closet
Space designated for storing clothes, hats, umbrellas and so forth.

steps
Outdoor staircase ending in a landing that leads to the house entrance.

HOUSE AND DO-IT-YOURSELF

frame

Assembly of members that consists of the load-bearing structure of a building and that provides stability to it.

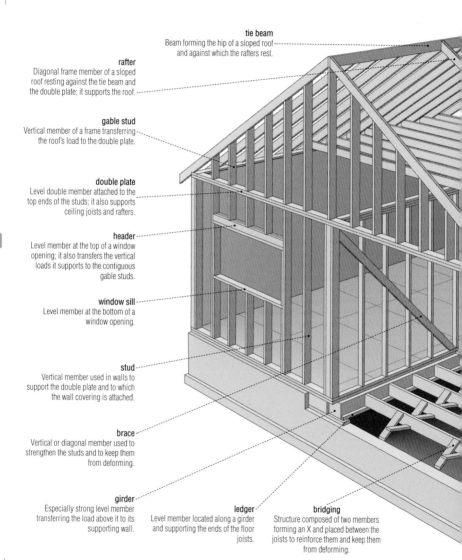

tie beam
Beam forming the hip of a sloped roof and against which the rafters rest.

rafter
Diagonal frame member of a sloped roof resting against the tie beam and the double plate; it supports the roof.

gable stud
Vertical member of a frame transferring the roof's load to the double plate.

double plate
Level double member attached to the top ends of the studs; it also supports ceiling joists and rafters.

header
Level member at the top of a window opening; it also transfers the vertical loads it supports to the contiguous gable studs.

window sill
Level member at the bottom of a window opening.

stud
Vertical member used in walls to support the double plate and to which the wall covering is attached.

brace
Vertical or diagonal member used to strengthen the studs and to keep them from deforming.

girder
Especially strong level member transferring the load above it to its supporting wall.

ledger
Level member located along a girder and supporting the ends of the floor joists.

bridging
Structure composed of two members forming an X and placed between the joists to reinforce them and keep them from deforming.

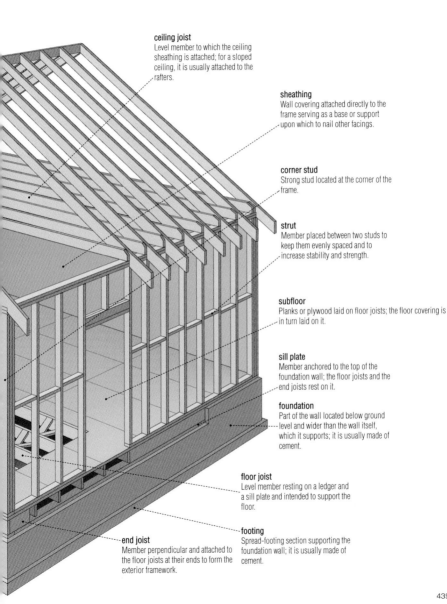

ceiling joist
Level member to which the ceiling sheathing is attached; for a sloped ceiling, it is usually attached to the rafters.

sheathing
Wall covering attached directly to the frame serving as a base or support upon which to nail other facings.

corner stud
Strong stud located at the corner of the frame.

strut
Member placed between two studs to keep them evenly spaced and to increase stability and strength.

subfloor
Planks or plywood laid on floor joists; the floor covering is in turn laid on it.

sill plate
Member anchored to the top of the foundation wall; the floor joists and the end joists rest on it.

foundation
Part of the wall located below ground level and wider than the wall itself, which it supports; it is usually made of cement.

floor joist
Level member resting on a ledger and a sill plate and intended to support the floor.

footing
Spread-footing section supporting the foundation wall; it is usually made of cement.

end joist
Member perpendicular and attached to the floor joists at their ends to form the exterior framework.

HOUSE AND DO-IT-YOURSELF

foundation

Work done on-site in cement or masonry; it supports a structure's load and transfers it to the ground, thus providing stability.

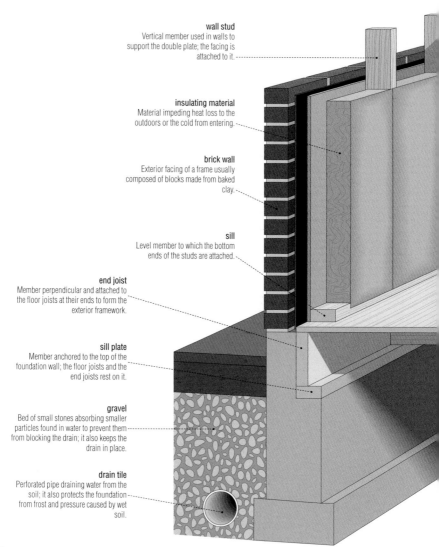

wall stud
Vertical member used in walls to support the double plate; the facing is attached to it.

insulating material
Material impeding heat loss to the outdoors or the cold from entering.

brick wall
Exterior facing of a frame usually composed of blocks made from baked clay.

sill
Level member to which the bottom ends of the studs are attached.

end joist
Member perpendicular and attached to the floor joists at their ends to form the exterior framework.

sill plate
Member anchored to the top of the foundation wall; the floor joists and the end joists rest on it.

gravel
Bed of small stones absorbing smaller particles found in water to prevent them from blocking the drain; it also keeps the drain in place.

drain tile
Perforated pipe draining water from the soil; it also protects the foundation from frost and pressure caused by wet soil.

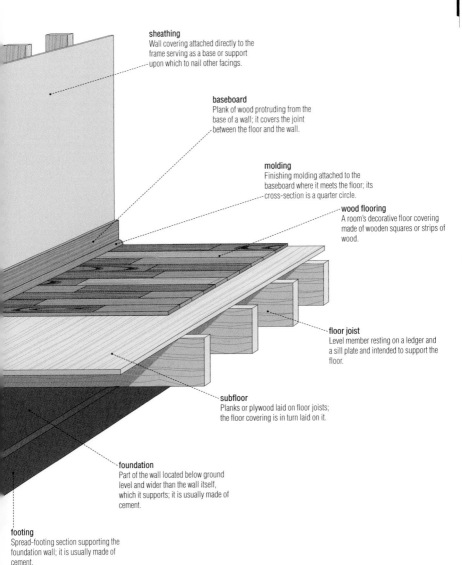

sheathing
Wall covering attached directly to the
frame serving as a base or support
upon which to nail other facings.

baseboard
Plank of wood protruding from the
base of a wall; it covers the joint
between the floor and the wall.

molding
Finishing molding attached to the
baseboard where it meets the floor; its
cross-section is a quarter circle.

wood flooring
A room's decorative floor covering
made of wooden squares or strips of
wood.

floor joist
Level member resting on a ledger and
a sill plate and intended to support the
floor.

subfloor
Planks or plywood laid on floor joists;
the floor covering is in turn laid on it.

foundation
Part of the wall located below ground
level and wider than the wall itself,
which it supports; it is usually made of
cement.

footing
Spread-footing section supporting the
foundation wall; it is usually made of
cement.

stairs

Structural component enabling movement between floors of a house or other structure.

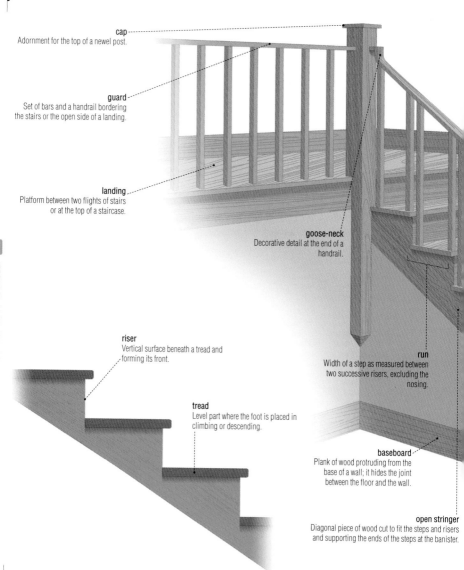

cap
Adornment for the top of a newel post.

guard
Set of bars and a handrail bordering the stairs or the open side of a landing.

landing
Platform between two flights of stairs or at the top of a staircase.

goose-neck
Decorative detail at the end of a handrail.

riser
Vertical surface beneath a tread and forming its front.

run
Width of a step as measured between two successive risers, excluding the nosing.

tread
Level part where the foot is placed in climbing or descending.

baseboard
Plank of wood protruding from the base of a wall; it hides the joint between the floor and the wall.

open stringer
Diagonal piece of wood cut to fit the steps and risers and supporting the ends of the steps at the banister.

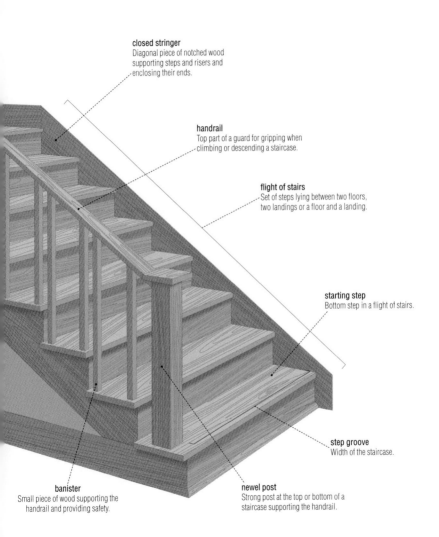

closed stringer
Diagonal piece of notched wood supporting steps and risers and enclosing their ends.

handrail
Top part of a guard for gripping when climbing or descending a staircase.

flight of stairs
Set of steps lying between two floors, two landings or a floor and a landing.

starting step
Bottom step in a flight of stairs.

step groove
Width of the staircase.

banister
Small piece of wood supporting the handrail and providing safety.

newel post
Strong post at the top or bottom of a staircase supporting the handrail.

window

Opening in a wall fitted with glass to let in light and air.

structure

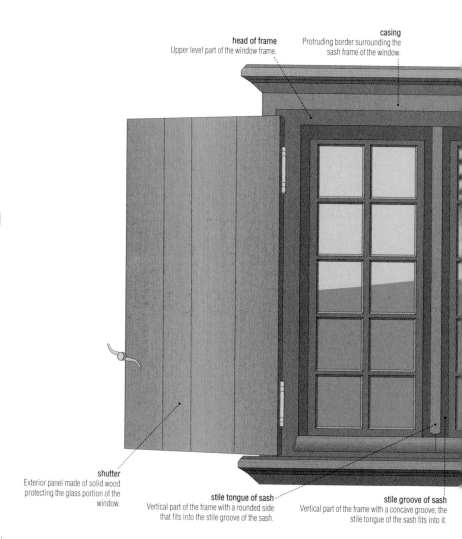

head of frame
Upper level part of the window frame.

casing
Protruding border surrounding the
sash frame of the window.

shutter
Exterior panel made of solid wood
protecting the glass portion of the
window.

stile tongue of sash
Vertical part of the frame with a rounded side
that fits into the stile groove of the sash.

stile groove of sash
Vertical part of the frame with a concave groove; the
stile tongue of the sash fits into it.

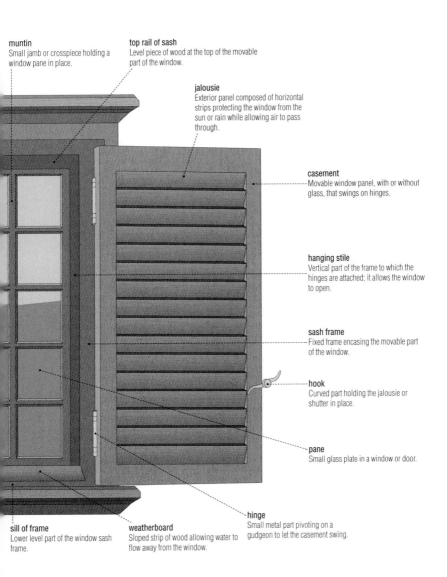

muntin
Small jamb or crosspiece holding a window pane in place.

top rail of sash
Level piece of wood at the top of the movable part of the window.

jalousie
Exterior panel composed of horizontal strips protecting the window from the sun or rain while allowing air to pass through.

casement
Movable window panel, with or without glass, that swings on hinges.

hanging stile
Vertical part of the frame to which the hinges are attached; it allows the window to open.

sash frame
Fixed frame encasing the movable part of the window.

hook
Curved part holding the jalousie or shutter in place.

pane
Small glass plate in a window or door.

sill of frame
Lower level part of the window sash frame.

weatherboard
Sloped strip of wood allowing water to flow away from the window.

hinge
Small metal part pivoting on a gudgeon to let the casement swing.

HOUSE AND DO-IT-YOURSELF

exterior door

The exterior door comprises a moving part, the leaf, plus a frame. It provides access to and egress from the house.

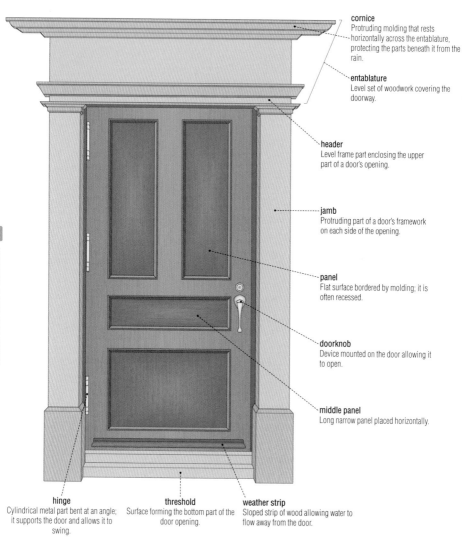

cornice
Protruding molding that rests horizontally across the entablature, protecting the parts beneath it from the rain.

entablature
Level set of woodwork covering the doorway.

header
Level frame part enclosing the upper part of a door's opening.

jamb
Protruding part of a door's framework on each side of the opening.

panel
Flat surface bordered by molding; it is often recessed.

doorknob
Device mounted on the door allowing it to open.

middle panel
Long narrow panel placed horizontally.

hinge
Cylindrical metal part bent at an angle; it supports the door and allows it to swing.

threshold
Surface forming the bottom part of the door opening.

weather strip
Sloped strip of wood allowing water to flow away from the door.

lock

Device mounted on the door allowing it to lock by using a key.

general view

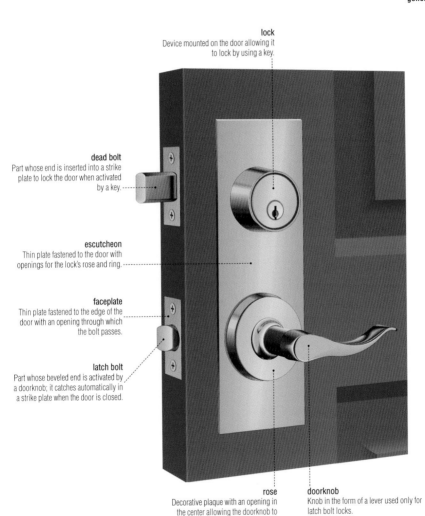

lock
Device mounted on the door allowing it to lock by using a key.

dead bolt
Part whose end is inserted into a strike plate to lock the door when activated by a key.

escutcheon
Thin plate fastened to the door with openings for the lock's rose and ring.

faceplate
Thin plate fastened to the edge of the door with an opening through which the bolt passes.

latch bolt
Part whose beveled end is activated by a doorknob; it catches automatically in a strike plate when the door is closed.

rose
Decorative plaque with an opening in the center allowing the doorknob to turn.

doorknob
Knob in the form of a lever used only for latch bolt locks.

HOUSE AND DO-IT-YOURSELF

wood firing

Creates heat by burning wood; nowadays, heating with wood is usually reserved as a backup.

fireplace
Masonry structure topped with a chimney and open in front; burning wood emits heat that is reflected from the inner hearth.

hood
Part of a fireplace located above the mantel; it hides the chimney and allows the smoke to escape to the outdoors.

lintel
Horizontal crosspiece above the hearth and supporting the mantel.

mantel shelf
Level top part of a fireplace's mantel.

mantel
Part of the fireplace protruding over the hearth.

corbel piece
Piece protruding from a jamb or wall; it supports the mantel of a fireplace.

jamb
Vertical facing making up the side of the hearth and supporting the upper parts of the fireplace.

firebrick back
Vertical facing making up the back of the hearth.

base
Pedestal protecting a room's floor from the heat produced by the fireplace.

inner hearth
Part of a fireplace where combustion takes place.

woodbox
Part of the fireplace where wood is stored.

frame
Metal piece around the edge of the fireplace opening.

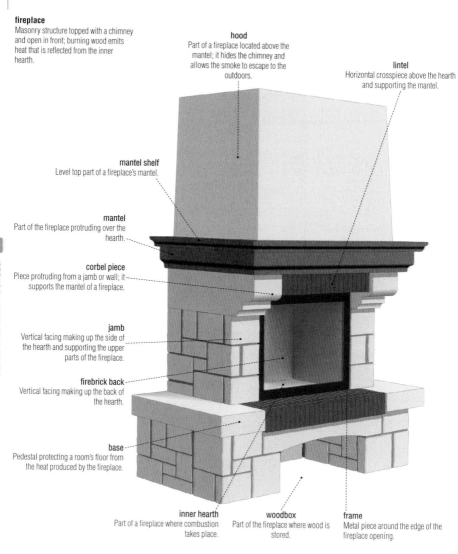

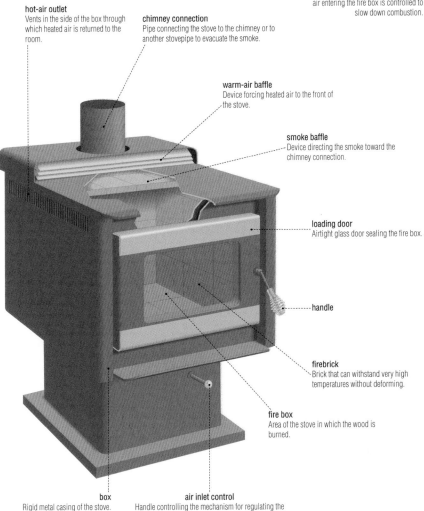

slow-burning stove
Closed heating device; the amount of air entering the fire box is controlled to slow down combustion.

hot-air outlet
Vents in the side of the box through which heated air is returned to the room.

chimney connection
Pipe connecting the stove to the chimney or to another stovepipe to evacuate the smoke.

warm-air baffle
Device forcing heated air to the front of the stove.

smoke baffle
Device directing the smoke toward the chimney connection.

loading door
Airtight glass door sealing the fire box.

handle

firebrick
Brick that can withstand very high temperatures without deforming.

fire box
Area of the stove in which the wood is burned.

box
Rigid metal casing of the stove.

air inlet control
Handle controlling the mechanism for regulating the amount of air entering the fire box.

HOUSE AND DO-IT-YOURSELF

air-conditioning appliances

These appliances help make a house comfortable by cooling, filtering and humidifying or dehumidifying the ambient air.

programmable thermostat
Electronic device for keeping a house or a room at a certain temperature; it can be programmed to follow a schedule.

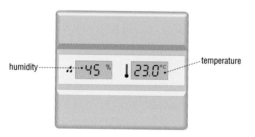

display
Screen showing digital data (time and temperature).

housing

arrow key
Button for changing the programmed time and house temperature.

choosing key
Button for confirming the selected time and temperatures programmed.

programming control
Button for regulating the thermostat according to the schedule chosen.

hygrometer
Device measuring the amount of humidity in a room's air.

humidity

temperature

room thermostat
Mechanism that, by sensing changes in temperature, can be set to automatically switch the heating or air-conditioning or off in a room or house.

cover

temperature control
Knob for selecting the desired temperature.

desired temperature
Desired temperature of the ambient air.

actual temperature
A built-in thermometer shows the current temperature of the room in which it is located.

pointer
Metal needle attached to the thermometer showing the ambient temperature.

room air conditioner
Device installed in a window for cooling and circulating the air in a room.

fan motor
Device transforming electric energy into mechanical energy to drive a device; in this case, the fan.

evaporator blower
Device drawing in warm air from the room, directing it over the cold evaporator coils and then returning it to the room.

condenser fan
Propeller-shaped fan drawing outdoor air through the vents and over the hot condenser coils to cool them.

louver
Device directing cool air into the room.

condenser coil
Tube in which the hot refrigerant dissipates the room's heat to the outdoors.

casing

control panel
Panel containing the controls that operate the air conditioner.

vent
Grate through which outdoor air is drawn inward.

grille
Grille through which the heated air is diffused in the room.

evaporator coil
Tube carrying refrigerant that absorbs the room's heat.

blower motor
Device transforming electric energy into mechanical energy to drive a device; in this case, the fan.

HOUSE AND DO-IT-YOURSELF

plumbing system

In a house, there are four plumbing systems enabling water to circulate: hot and cold water distribution, pipe ventilation and wastewater evacuation.

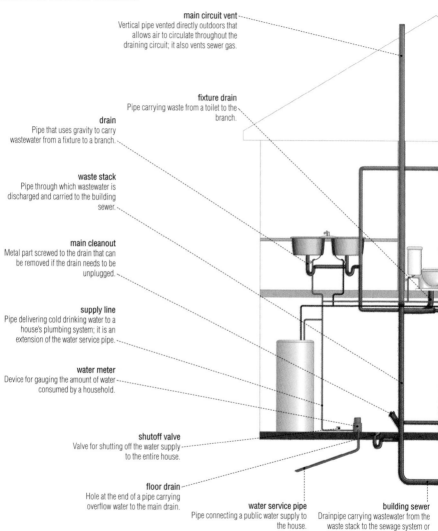

main circuit vent
Vertical pipe vented directly outdoors that allows air to circulate throughout the draining circuit; it also vents sewer gas.

fixture drain
Pipe carrying waste from a toilet to the branch.

drain
Pipe that uses gravity to carry wastewater from a fixture to a branch.

waste stack
Pipe through which wastewater is discharged and carried to the building sewer.

main cleanout
Metal part screwed to the drain that can be removed if the drain needs to be unplugged.

supply line
Pipe delivering cold drinking water to a house's plumbing system; it is an extension of the water service pipe.

water meter
Device for gauging the amount of water consumed by a household.

shutoff valve
Valve for shutting off the water supply to the entire house.

floor drain
Hole at the end of a pipe carrying overflow water to the main drain.

water service pipe
Pipe connecting a public water supply to the house.

building sewer
Drainpipe carrying wastewater from the waste stack to the sewage system or septic tank.

circuit vent
Allows air to circulate and maintains
constant pressure throughout the entire
draining circuit.

shower and tub fixture
Device for mixing hot and cold water for the bath or
shower.

overflow
Drainpipe for draining off a fixture's
overflow when the water level reaches a
certain level.

trap
U-shaped pipe beneath a fixture
containing a quantity of water to
prevent sewage gases from escaping.

branch
Pipe draining wastewater from the
fixtures to the waste stack.

hot-water riser
Vertical pipe carrying hot water to a house's
upper floors.

cold-water riser
Vertical pipe carrying cold water to a house's
upper floors.

 draining circuit
Set of interconnected pipes allowing wastewater to
drain into the building sewer.

 hot-water circuit
Set of interconnected pipes distributing hot water
from a hot-water heater.

 ventilating circuit
Set of interconnected pipes allowing air to circulate
in the circuit.

 cold-water circuit
Set of interconnected pipes distributing cold
drinking water throughout a house.

pedestal-type sump pump

Device removing water from a pit dug in the ground in order to evacuate it to a sewer or septic tank.

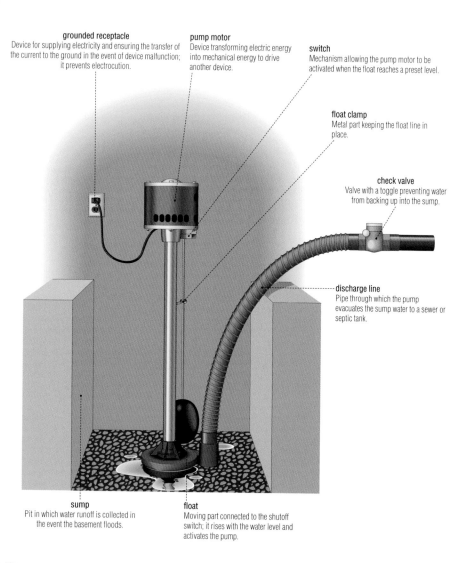

grounded receptacle
Device for supplying electricity and ensuring the transfer of the current to the ground in the event of device malfunction; it prevents electrocution.

pump motor
Device transforming electric energy into mechanical energy to drive another device.

switch
Mechanism allowing the pump motor to be activated when the float reaches a preset level.

float clamp
Metal part keeping the float line in place.

check valve
Valve with a toggle preventing water from backing up into the sump.

discharge line
Pipe through which the pump evacuates the sump water to a sewer or septic tank.

sump
Pit in which water runoff is collected in the event the basement floods.

float
Moving part connected to the shutoff switch; it rises with the water level and activates the pump.

septic tank

Underground system in which sewage is treated and dispersed.

distribution box
Device spreading water evenly through the network of drains.

tank
Wastewater settles and sewage decomposes naturally in the first compartment. Water then flows into the second compartment.

gravel
Bed of small stones absorbing smaller particles found in water to prevent them from blocking the perforated pipes; it also keeps the perforated pipes in place.

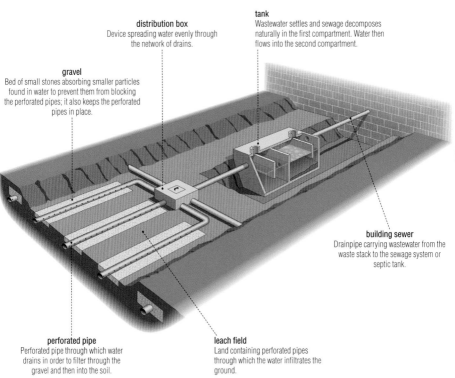

building sewer
Drainpipe carrying wastewater from the waste stack to the sewage system or septic tank.

perforated pipe
Perforated pipe through which water drains in order to filter through the gravel and then into the soil.

leach field
Land containing perforated pipes through which the water infiltrates the ground.

HOUSE AND DO-IT-YOURSELF

bathroom

Room designed for personal hygiene; it is equipped with running water and sanitary fixtures.

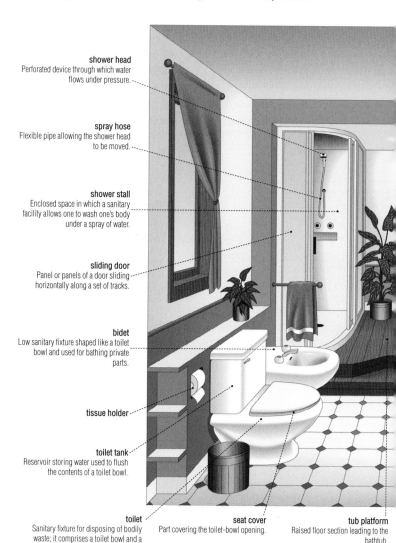

shower head
Perforated device through which water
flows under pressure.

spray hose
Flexible pipe allowing the shower head
to be moved.

shower stall
Enclosed space in which a sanitary
facility allows one to wash one's body
under a spray of water.

sliding door
Panel or panels of a door sliding
horizontally along a set of tracks.

bidet
Low sanitary fixture shaped like a toilet
bowl and used for bathing private
parts.

tissue holder

toilet tank
Reservoir storing water used to flush
the contents of a toilet bowl.

toilet
Sanitary fixture for disposing of bodily
waste; it comprises a toilet bowl and a
tank.

seat cover
Part covering the toilet-bowl opening.

tub platform
Raised floor section leading to the
bathtub.

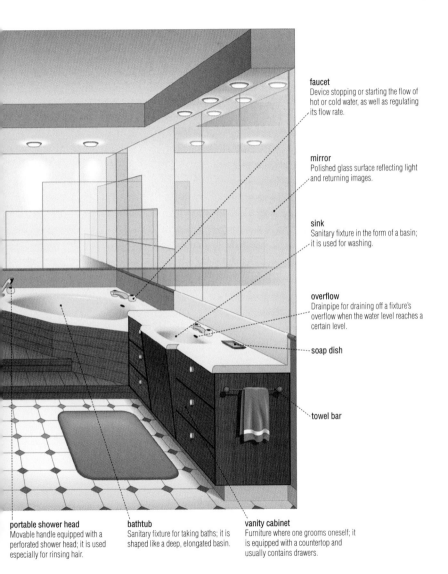

faucet
Device stopping or starting the flow of hot or cold water, as well as regulating its flow rate.

mirror
Polished glass surface reflecting light and returning images.

sink
Sanitary fixture in the form of a basin; it is used for washing.

overflow
Drainpipe for draining off a fixture's overflow when the water level reaches a certain level.

soap dish

towel bar

portable shower head
Movable handle equipped with a perforated shower head; it is used especially for rinsing hair.

bathtub
Sanitary fixture for taking baths; it is shaped like a deep, elongated basin.

vanity cabinet
Furniture where one grooms oneself; it is equipped with a countertop and usually contains drawers.

HOUSE AND DO-IT-YOURSELF

toilet

Sanitary fixture for disposing of bodily waste; it comprises a toilet bowl and a tank.

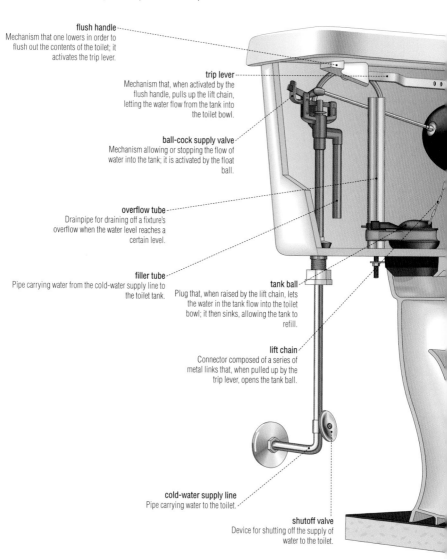

flush handle
Mechanism that one lowers in order to flush out the contents of the toilet; it activates the trip lever.

trip lever
Mechanism that, when activated by the flush handle, pulls up the lift chain, letting the water flow from the tank into the toilet bowl.

ball-cock supply valve
Mechanism allowing or stopping the flow of water into the tank; it is activated by the float ball.

overflow tube
Drainpipe for draining off a fixture's overflow when the water level reaches a certain level.

filler tube
Pipe carrying water from the cold-water supply line to the toilet tank.

tank ball
Plug that, when raised by the lift chain, lets the water in the tank flow into the toilet bowl; it then sinks, allowing the tank to refill.

lift chain
Connector composed of a series of metal links that, when pulled up by the trip lever, opens the tank ball.

cold-water supply line
Pipe carrying water to the toilet.

shutoff valve
Device for shutting off the supply of water to the toilet.

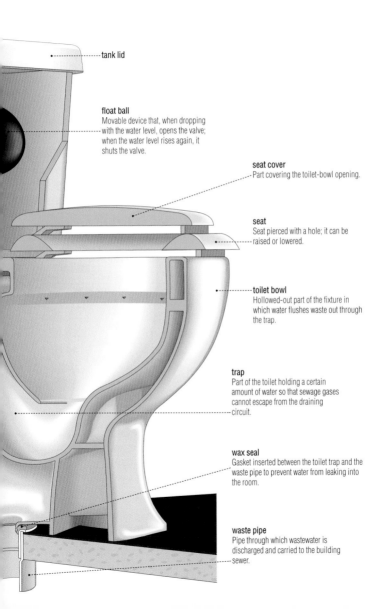

tank lid

float ball
Movable device that, when dropping with the water level, opens the valve; when the water level rises again, it shuts the valve.

seat cover
Part covering the toilet-bowl opening.

seat
Seat pierced with a hole; it can be raised or lowered.

toilet bowl
Hollowed-out part of the fixture in which water flushes waste out through the trap.

trap
Part of the toilet holding a certain amount of water so that sewage gases cannot escape from the draining circuit.

wax seal
Gasket inserted between the toilet trap and the waste pipe to prevent water from leaking into the room.

waste pipe
Pipe through which wastewater is discharged and carried to the building sewer.

examples of branching

Branching: the way in which an appliance is hooked up to a house's plumbing system.

garbage disposal sink
Appliance used in a kitchen, sometimes with two basins, that is fed by water and equipped with a drain and a garbage disposal unit.

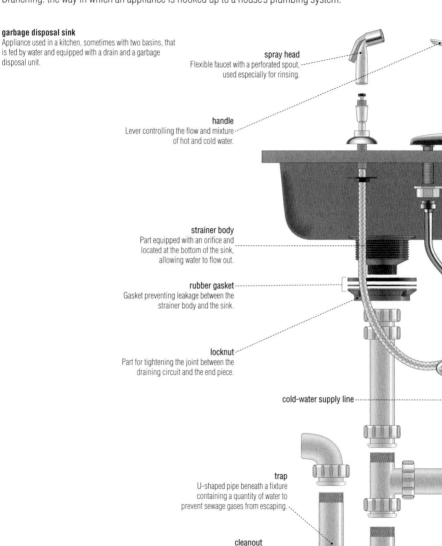

spray head
Flexible faucet with a perforated spout, used especially for rinsing.

handle
Lever controlling the flow and mixture of hot and cold water.

strainer body
Part equipped with an orifice and located at the bottom of the sink, allowing water to flow out.

rubber gasket
Gasket preventing leakage between the strainer body and the sink.

locknut
Part for tightening the joint between the draining circuit and the end piece.

cold-water supply line

trap
U-shaped pipe beneath a fixture containing a quantity of water to prevent sewage gases from escaping.

cleanout
Part screwed into the trap that can be removed in case it needs to be unblocked.

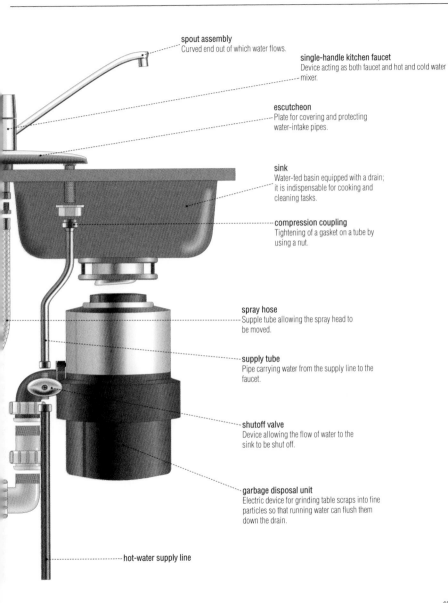

spout assembly
Curved end out of which water flows.

single-handle kitchen faucet
Device acting as both faucet and hot and cold water mixer.

escutcheon
Plate for covering and protecting water-intake pipes.

sink
Water-fed basin equipped with a drain; it is indispensable for cooking and cleaning tasks.

compression coupling
Tightening of a gasket on a tube by using a nut.

spray hose
Supple tube allowing the spray head to be moved.

supply tube
Pipe carrying water from the supply line to the faucet.

shutoff valve
Device allowing the flow of water to the sink to be shut off.

garbage disposal unit
Electric device for grinding table scraps into fine particles so that running water can flush them down the drain.

hot-water supply line

examples of branching

washer
Household appliance that washes clothes automatically.

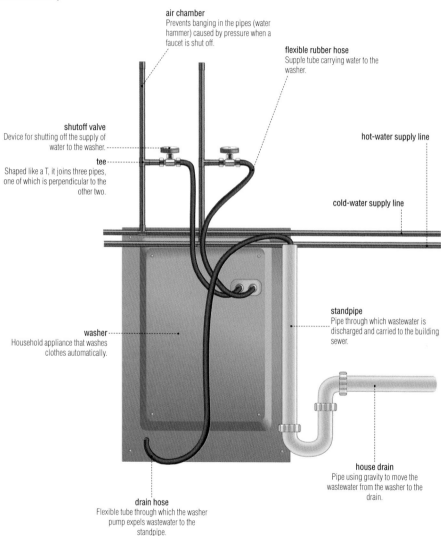

air chamber
Prevents banging in the pipes (water hammer) caused by pressure when a faucet is shut off.

flexible rubber hose
Supple tube carrying water to the washer.

shutoff valve
Device for shutting off the supply of water to the washer.

tee
Shaped like a T, it joins three pipes, one of which is perpendicular to the other two.

hot-water supply line

cold-water supply line

standpipe
Pipe through which wastewater is discharged and carried to the building sewer.

washer
Household appliance that washes clothes automatically.

house drain
Pipe using gravity to move the wastewater from the washer to the drain.

drain hose
Flexible tube through which the washer pump expels wastewater to the standpipe.

dishwasher
Appliance designed to automatically
wash and dry dishes.

air chamber
Prevents banging in the pipes (water hammer) caused by pressure when a faucet is shut off.

drain hose
Pipe collecting wastewater from the dishwasher and carrying it to the drain.

dishwasher
Appliance designed to automatically wash and dry dishes.

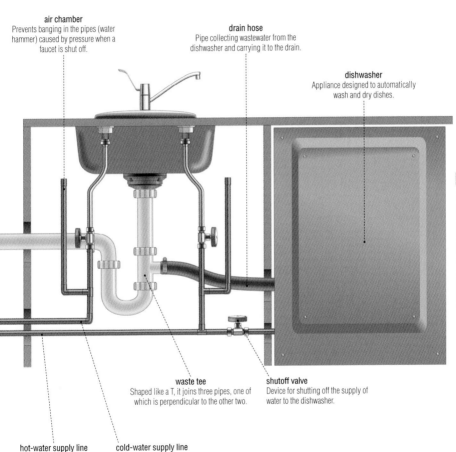

waste tee
Shaped like a T, it joins three pipes, one of which is perpendicular to the other two.

shutoff valve
Device for shutting off the supply of water to the dishwasher.

hot-water supply line

cold-water supply line

distribution panel

Set of devices forming the junction of the public electricity grid and the electric circuits of a dwelling.

double circuit breaker
Protection device for a 240-volt circuit that, in the event of overload, is released and thus cuts off electricity to the circuits.

main breaker
Mechanism controlling the supply of electricity to the hot bus bars; it allows the current to all the dwelling's circuits to be cut.

single circuit breaker
Protection device for a 120-volt circuit that, in the event of overload, is released and thus cuts off electricity to the circuits.

neutral wire
Wire having no electric charge that allows the current to return to the distribution panel and the grid.

plastic insulator
Plate made of nonconductive material preventing the hot bus bars from coming in contact with the back of the panel.

hot bus bar
Conductive part of the panel into which the breakers for each circuit are plugged.

ground/neutral bus bar
Receives the current from the neutral grounded wires of the various circuits and conducts them to the neutral service wire and the ground connection.

terminal
Part of the ground/neutral bus bar to which a neutral wire and the ground wire of a circuit are attached.

ground wire
Wire conducting the current from the ground/neutral bus bar to the ground connection in the event of a short circuit.

ground connection
Metal conductor attached to the ground wire in order to ground the entire circuit.

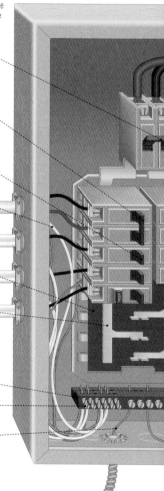

240-volt feeder cable
Cable consisting of three wires, one neutral and two live, conducting an electric current from the grid to the distribution panel.

connector
Device for screwing the electric-connection conduit to the panel box.

bonding jumper
Screw inserted into the metal box of the panel allowing it to be connected to the neutral hot bus bar.

main power cable
Live wire conducting the electric current.

ground bond
Links the bonding jumper to the neutral hot bus bar.

240-volt circuit
Composed of two lives wires, one neutral wire and one grounded wire; this allows electricity to reach devices requiring a lot of power.

120-volt circuit
Composed of one live wire, one neutral wire and one grounded wire; it allows electricity to reach a small appliance or a light.

neutral service wire
Wire having no electric charge that, via the neutral hot bus bar, returns the current from domestic circuits to the grid.

ground
Part connecting the neutral hot bus bar that allows the current from the circuits' neutral wires to be transferred to the neutral service wire.

contact devices

Examples of components that connect a device to an electric circuit.

switch
Mechanism allowing the current in an
electric circuit to be established or
interrupted.

dimmer switch
Switch for varying the brightness of a
lighting installation.

switch plate
Protective plate covering an outlet or,
in this case, a switch.

electrical box
Box housing the electric connections
in order to protect the part of the
dwelling's frame upon which it is
mounted.

Set of devices allowing light to be diffused in a dwelling.

parts of a lamp socket

cap
Component fitting onto the outer shell and covering the upper end of a lamp's socket.

socket
Device into which a lamp's base is inserted in order to connect it to the electric-supply circuit and to keep it in place.

insulating sleeve
Component protecting the outer shell from the heat.

outer shell
Decorative component covering the socket and the insulating sleeve.

tungsten-halogen lamp
Lamp that is brighter and lasts longer than a traditional incandescent lamp, but that lets off more heat.

bulb
Gas sealed in a glass envelope into which the luminous body of a lamp is inserted.

pin
Cylindrical metal part that establishes electric contact when inserted into the corresponding outlet.

bayonet base
Base fitted with two short metal pins so that it can be placed in the corresponding socket.

screw base
Base fitted with a screw pitch so it can be inserted into the corresponding socket.

lighting

incandescent lamp
Lamp in which a filament heated by an electric
current produces light rays.

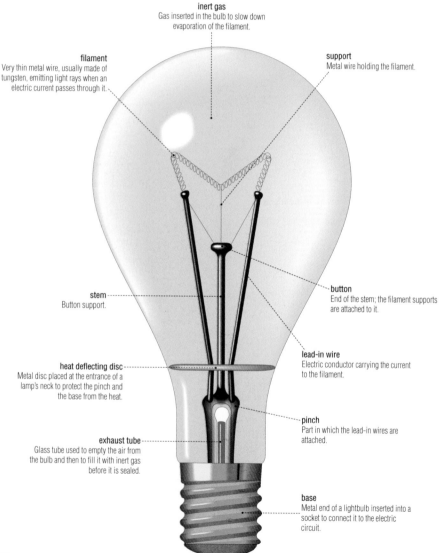

inert gas
Gas inserted in the bulb to slow down
evaporation of the filament.

support
Metal wire holding the filament.

filament
Very thin metal wire, usually made of
tungsten, emitting light rays when an
electric current passes through it.

button
End of the stem; the filament supports
are attached to it.

stem
Button support.

lead-in wire
Electric conductor carrying the current
to the filament.

heat deflecting disc
Metal disc placed at the entrance of a
lamp's neck to protect the pinch and
the base from the heat.

pinch
Part in which the lead-in wires are
attached.

exhaust tube
Glass tube used to empty the air from
the bulb and then to fill it with inert gas
before it is sealed.

base
Metal end of a lightbulb inserted into a
socket to connect it to the electric
circuit.

tungsten-halogen lamp
Lamp that is brighter and lasts longer than a
traditional incandescent lamp, but that lets off
more heat.

bulb
Gas sealed in a glass envelope into
which the luminous body of a lamp is
inserted.

filament support
Metal wire holding the filament.

tungsten filament
Very thin metal wire emitting light rays
when an electric current passes though
it.

inert gas
Gas inserted in the bulb to slow down
evaporation of the filament; iodine or
bromine are added as they combine with
the tungsten at high temperatures.

electric circuit
Lamp component allowing the electric
current to circulate through the
tungsten filament.

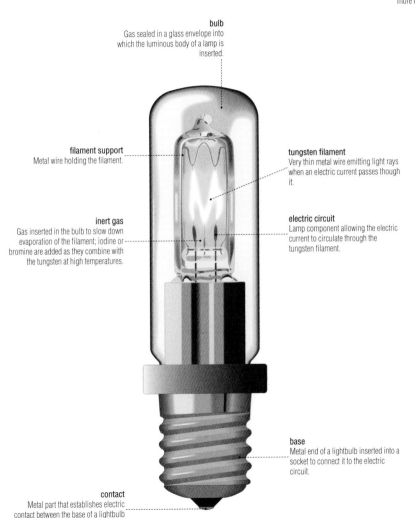

base
Metal end of a lightbulb inserted into a
socket to connect it to the electric
circuit.

contact
Metal part that establishes electric
contact between the base of a lightbulb
and the socket.

lighting

energy-saving bulb
Bulb whose electricity consumption is lower and
its life longer than an incandescent bulb.

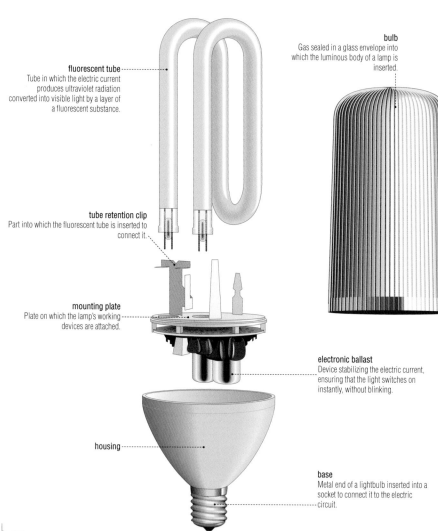

fluorescent tube
Tube in which the electric current
produces ultraviolet radiation
converted into visible light by a layer of
a fluorescent substance.

bulb
Gas sealed in a glass envelope into
which the luminous body of a lamp is
inserted.

tube retention clip
Part into which the fluorescent tube is inserted to
connect it.

mounting plate
Plate on which the lamp's working
devices are attached.

electronic ballast
Device stabilizing the electric current,
ensuring that the light switches on
instantly, without blinking.

housing

base
Metal end of a lightbulb inserted into a
socket to connect it to the electric
circuit.

HOUSE AND DO-IT-YOURSELF

fluorescent tube
Tube in which the electric current
produces ultraviolet radiation converted
into visible light by a layer of a
fluorescent substance.

lead-in wire
electric conductor carrying the current
to the filament.

exhaust tube
Glass tube used to empty the air from
the bulb and then to fill it with inert gas
before it is sealed.

electrode
A device placed at each end of the tube;
an electric discharge arcs between the
two of them.

bulb
Long glass cylinder enclosing the
components of this type of tube and
diffusing light.

phosphorescent coating
The tube's internal coating; it is
composed of phosphate particles that
convert ultraviolet rays into visible
light.

pin base
End of the tube equipped with two pins
that, when inserted into the socket,
connect the tube with the electric
circuit.

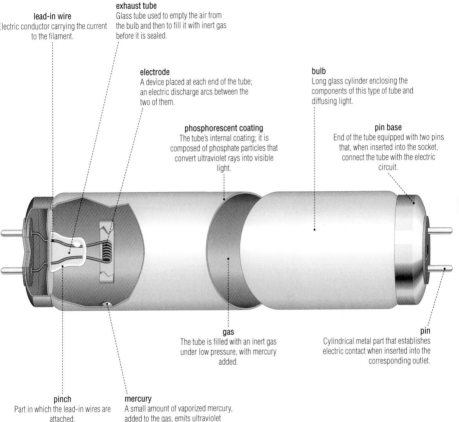

gas
The tube is filled with an inert gas
under low pressure, with mercury
added.

pin
Cylindrical metal part that establishes
electric contact when inserted into the
corresponding outlet.

pinch
Part in which the lead-in wires are
attached.

mercury
A small amount of vaporized mercury,
added to the gas, emits ultraviolet
radiation during the electric discharge.

HOUSE AND DO-IT-YOURSELF

armchair

Chair consisting of arms, a back and legs.

parts

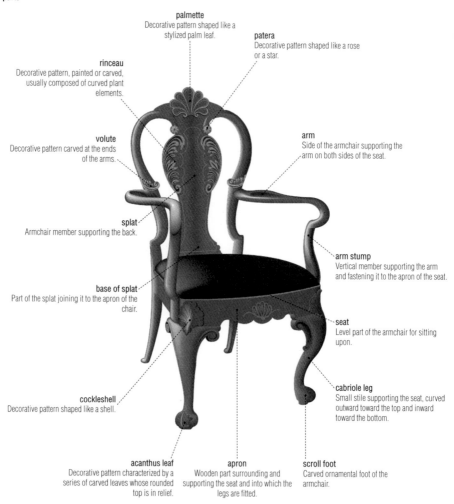

palmette
Decorative pattern shaped like a stylized palm leaf.

patera
Decorative pattern shaped like a rose or a star.

rinceau
Decorative pattern, painted or carved, usually composed of curved plant elements.

volute
Decorative pattern carved at the ends of the arms.

arm
Side of the armchair supporting the arm on both sides of the seat.

splat
Armchair member supporting the back.

arm stump
Vertical member supporting the arm and fastening it to the apron of the seat.

base of splat
Part of the splat joining it to the apron of the chair.

seat
Level part of the armchair for sitting upon.

cockleshell
Decorative pattern shaped like a shell.

cabriole leg
Small stile supporting the seat, curved outward toward the top and inward toward the bottom.

acanthus leaf
Decorative pattern characterized by a series of carved leaves whose rounded top is in relief.

apron
Wooden part surrounding and supporting the seat and into which the legs are fitted.

scroll foot
Carved ornamental foot of the armchair.

examples of armchairs

Wassily chair
Armchair with a tubular metal frame and whose back and seat are made of leather.

director's chair
Wooden armchair with a canvas back and seat that folds up in the middle.

rocking chair
Armchair with curved runners to rock on.

club chair
Large deep upholstered armchair, usually made of leather.

bergère
Upholstered armchair with a cushioned seat.

cabriolet
Wooden 18th-century armchair with a curved back and armrests that curve outward.

récamier
Long lounge chair on which one can recline,
equipped with an upholstered headrest and
back, the latter extending only a part of the
length of the chair.

méridienne
Sofa with an irregular back joining two
arms of different heights.

chesterfield
Upholstered quilted sofa whose arms
are the same height as its back.

love seat
Sofa that seats two people.

sofa
Long upholstered armchair that seats
several people.

seats

Furniture designed for sitting.

bean bag chair
Seat composed of an upholstered bag; it assumes the form of the human body.

ottoman
Low upholstered seat having neither arms nor back.

step chair
Chair whose foldaway lower part can be pulled out to form a step.

footstool
Seat with legs, having neither arms nor back, of various heights.

bar stool
Seat with legs, having neither arms nor back, high enough so that a person can sit at the level of a bar.

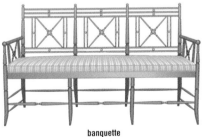

banquette
Bench with an upholstered seat.

bench
Long narrow unupholstered seat with or without a back, seating several people.

side chair

Seat consisting of a back and legs but no arms.

parts

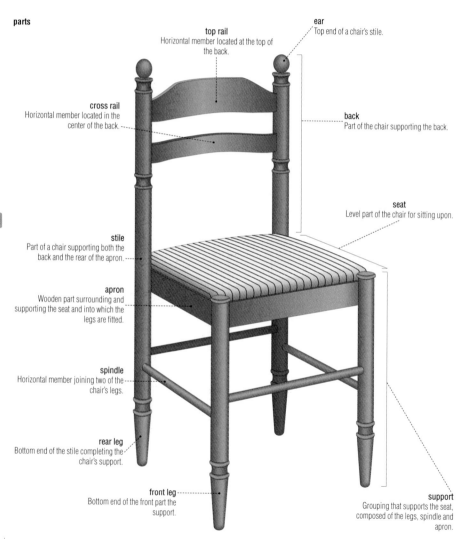

top rail
Horizontal member located at the top of the back.

ear
Top end of a chair's stile.

cross rail
Horizontal member located in the center of the back.

back
Part of the chair supporting the back.

seat
Level part of the chair for sitting upon.

stile
Part of a chair supporting both the back and the rear of the apron.

apron
Wooden part surrounding and supporting the seat and into which the legs are fitted.

spindle
Horizontal member joining two of the chair's legs.

rear leg
Bottom end of the stile completing the chair's support.

front leg
Bottom end of the front part the support.

support
Grouping that supports the seat, composed of the legs, spindle and apron.

table

Piece of furniture consisting of a level top supported by one or several legs and whose uses are numerous.

gate-leg table
Table equipped with a folding panel that can be raised to enlarge the tabletop surface.

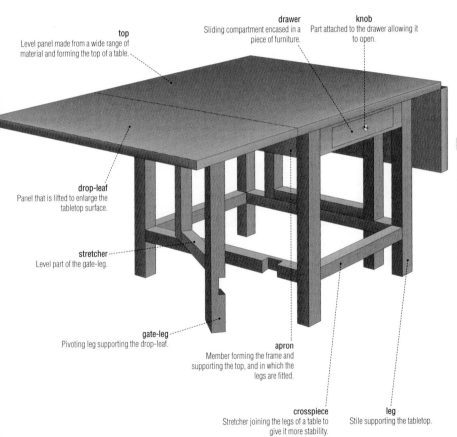

top
Level panel made from a wide range of material and forming the top of a table.

drawer
Sliding compartment encased in a piece of furniture.

knob
Part attached to the drawer allowing it to open.

drop-leaf
Panel that is lifted to enlarge the tabletop surface.

stretcher
Level part of the gate-leg.

gate-leg
Pivoting leg supporting the drop-leaf.

apron
Member forming the frame and supporting the top, and in which the legs are fitted.

crosspiece
Stretcher joining the legs of a table to give it more stability.

leg
Stile supporting the tabletop.

storage furniture

Furniture serving to archive, support or protect various objects.

armoire

Tall piece of furniture enclosed by panels and equipped with shelves to store items such as linens, clothing and supplies.

frame
Set of stiles and rails comprising an armoire's structure.

door
Each of an armoire's moving parts, acting as doors.

frieze
Ornamental molding above the cornice.

top rail
Horizontal wooden member located at the top of the frame.

hinge
Cylindrical metal part bent at an angle; it supports the door and allows it to swing.

diamond point
Decorative pattern whose embossment resembles the facets of a diamond.

rail
Flat section of the panel between two decorative relief patterns.

bottom rail
Horizontal wooden member located at the bottom of the frame.

foot
Wooden member, usually decorative, supporting the armoire.

cornice
Set of protruding moldings across the top of an armoire.

door panel
Carved or painted surface demarcated by a molding.

center post
Fixed center stile of an armoire's frame.

hanging stile
Vertical member of the frame to which the hinges are fastened.

lock
Device mounted on the door allowing it to lock by using a key.

frame stile
Wooden member making up the sides of the frame.

peg
Dowel made of wood or metal used for fastening various members.

bracket base
Lower part of the frame.

storage furniture

linen chest
Low piece of furniture shaped like a
chest and closed by a lid.

display cabinet
Glass cabinet for displaying
collectibles and knickknacks.

chiffonier
Tall narrow piece of furniture equipped
with stacked drawers for storing
accessories and clothes.

drawer
Sliding compartment encased in a
piece of furniture.

secretary
Piece of furniture for storing office
supplies and stationery; it includes a
drop panel serving as a writing table.

compartment
Compartment for storing various
objects.

fall front
Panel closing the upper part of the
secretary; it is lowered to form a
writing table.

HOUSE AND DO-IT-YOURSELF

wardrobe
Piece of furniture in which one part is
equipped with shelves and drawers for
storing clothes and the other with a rod
for hanging them.

closet
Part of an armoire equipped with a rod
for hanging clothes.

shelf
Level board on which clothes are
stored.

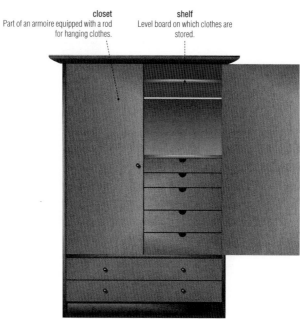

buffet
Dining room or kitchen furniture for
storing dishes, silverware and table
linens.

storage furniture

dresser
Piece of furniture for the bedroom
equipped with drawers, used for
storing clothes; it often has a mirror
mounted on top.

corner cupboard
Piece of furniture designed to be
placed in the angle formed by two
walls.

glass-fronted display cabinet
Piece of furniture consisting of a buffet
in the lower part and shelves for
displaying dishes in the upper part.

liquor cabinet
Piece of furniture for storing liquor and
the accessories used for making
drinks.

bed

Piece of furniture to stretch out on for resting or sleeping.

sofa bed
Sofa that can be converted into a bed.

futon
Cotton mattress of Japanese origin.

frame
Set of components forming the
structure of the piece of furniture.

bed

parts

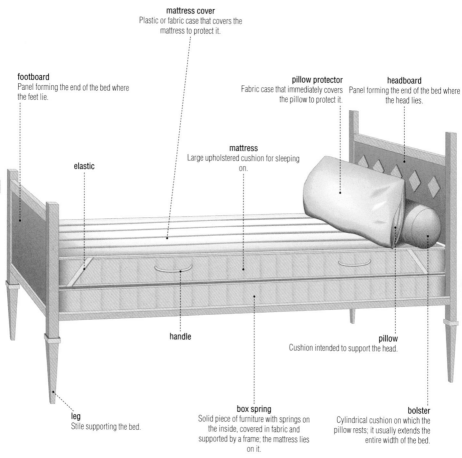

mattress cover
Plastic or fabric case that covers the
mattress to protect it.

footboard
Panel forming the end of the bed where
the feet lie.

pillow protector
Fabric case that immediately covers
the pillow to protect it.

headboard
Panel forming the end of the bed where
the head lies.

mattress
Large upholstered cushion for sleeping
on.

elastic

handle

pillow
Cushion intended to support the head.

leg
Stile supporting the bed.

box spring
Solid piece of furniture with springs on
the inside, covered in fabric and
supported by a frame; the mattress lies
on it.

bolster
Cylindrical cushion on which the
pillow rests; it usually extends the
entire width of the bed.

linen
Set of fabrics, blankets and pillows
covering a bed.

scatter cushion
Stuffed piece of fabric to lie against or
decorate a bed.

comforter
Cloth case stuffed with down, feathers or
synthetic material and often quilted; it is
used as a cover or for decorative
purposes.

neckroll
Ornamental cylindrical cushion.

sham
Decorative cloth envelope covering a
pillow that matches the bedcover.

blanket
Covering for the sheet made of various
warm fabrics; it protects against the
cold.

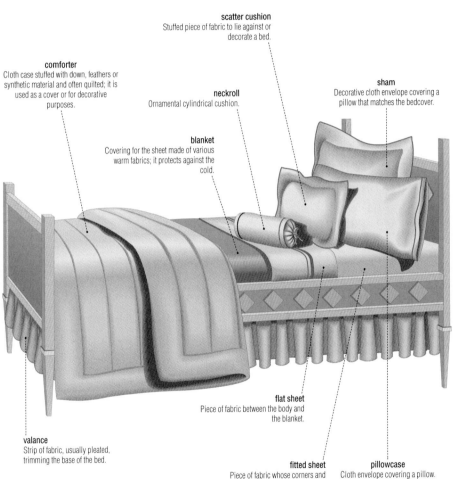

HOUSE AND DO-IT-YOURSELF

flat sheet
Piece of fabric between the body and
the blanket.

valance
Strip of fabric, usually pleated,
trimming the base of the bed.

fitted sheet
Piece of fabric whose corners and
edges are designed to tuck snugly
under the mattress.

pillowcase
Cloth envelope covering a pillow.

children's furniture

Furniture designed and adapted for young children.

crib
Deep bed for a baby surrounded by bars, one side of which can be lowered; it is equipped with a mattress whose height can be changed.

headboard
End of the bed where the head of the baby is placed.

barrier
Assembly of bars enclosing the side of the bed.

slat
Vertical part of the barrier forming the sides of the bed.

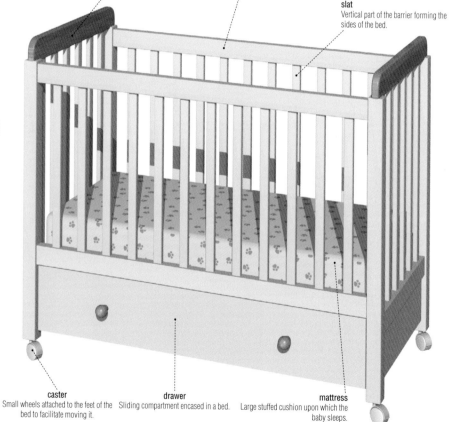

caster
Small wheels attached to the feet of the bed to facilitate moving it.

drawer
Sliding compartment encased in a bed.

mattress
Large stuffed cushion upon which the baby sleeps.

changing table
Piece of furniture equipped with storage space and a changing area.

playpen
Bed that closes up, usually used when traveling.

changing table
Detachable shelf for tending to the various needs of the baby.

top rail
Elevated part of the sides of the bed protecting the baby from falling.

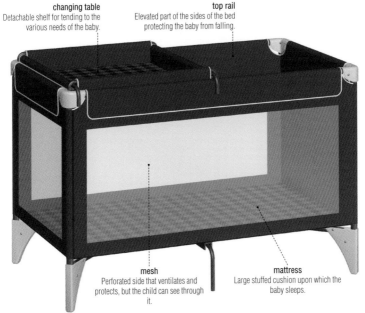

mesh
Perforated side that ventilates and protects, but the child can see through it.

mattress
Large stuffed cushion upon which the baby sleeps.

HOUSE AND DO-IT-YOURSELF

children's furniture

booster seat
Seat that, when set upon a chair, raises the child so that he or she can sit at table level.

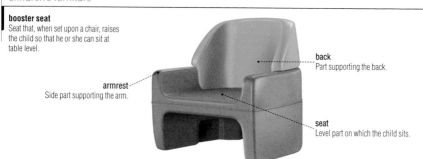

armrest
Side part supporting the arm.

back
Part supporting the back.

seat
Level part on which the child sits.

high chair
Elevated seat, closed in front by a removable tray, in which a baby sits for feeding.

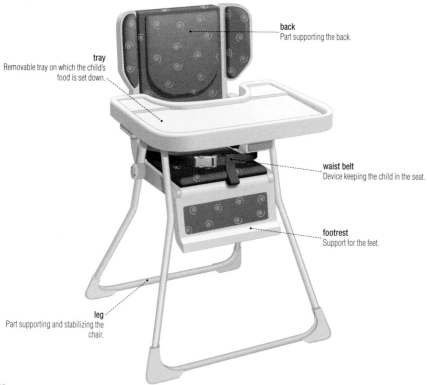

back
Part supporting the back.

tray
Removable tray on which the child's food is set down.

waist belt
Device keeping the child in the seat.

footrest
Support for the feet.

leg
Part supporting and stabilizing the chair.

window accessories

Set of elements decorating a window.

curtain
Formal drapery placed in front of a window, often composed of several layers of curtains.

overdrapery
Curtain covering another curtain.

sheer curtain
Curtain made of a light fabric that filters the light entering a room.

cornice
Strip of fabric affixed to rigid canvas or cardboard; it covers and hides the curtain rod.

draw drapery
Piece of decorative fabric sliding in front of a window to filter or block the light and provide privacy.

holdback
Part attached to the wall for hooking the tieback.

cord tieback
Plaited rope serving as a tieback.

tassel
Decorative end of a cord tieback.

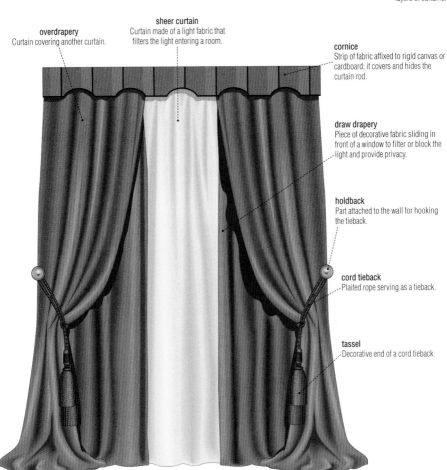

window accessories

examples of curtains

The various types of curtains can create a particular atmosphere in a room.

attached curtain
Curtain on two curtain rods; it has pleated sleeves at the top and bottom of the fabric.

loose curtain
Curtain hung from a single curtain rod and falling in soft pleats.

crisscross curtains
Curtains whose held-back sides form an overlap.

balloon curtain
Curtain that is raised like a blind and whose pleats are gathered to make them puffy.

HOUSE AND DO-IT-YOURSELF

blinds
Devices that roll or fold up, serving to filter or block light and provide privacy.

Venetian blind
Shade made of adjustable horizontal laths containing a mechanism for controlling its height and orientation.

headrail
Grooved metal rod containing the shade's mechanism and used to mount the blinds in front of a window.

drum
Cylindrical mechanism allowing the cord and laths to move.

lift cord lock
Mechanism keeping the shade at the desired height.

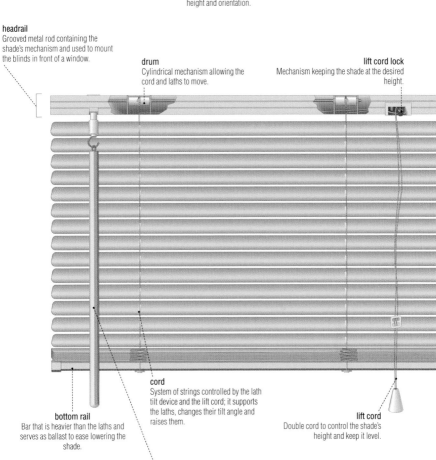

bottom rail
Bar that is heavier than the laths and serves as ballast to ease lowering the shade.

cord
System of strings controlled by the lath tilt device and the lift cord; it supports the laths, changes their tilt angle and raises them.

lift cord
Double cord to control the shade's height and keep it level.

lath tilt device
Rod used for pivoting the tilt tube.

lath
Thin flat strips made of aluminum, wood or plastic, the constituent parts of the shade.

HOUSE AND DO-IT-YOURSELF

491

window accessories

roller shade
Shade with a roller containing a spring that
causes the shade cloth to roll up.

shade cloth
Piece of vinyl or stiffened cloth
dressing a window.

roller
Tube housing the spring; the shade
cloth wraps around it.

winding mechanism
Spring mechanism allowing the shade cloth to
roll up and down.

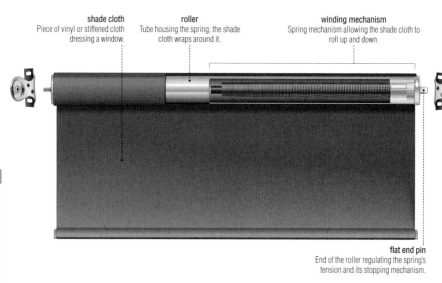

flat end pin
End of the roller regulating the spring's
tension and its stopping mechanism.

roll-up blind
Shade made of nonadjustable laths rolled
up by a system of cords and pulleys.

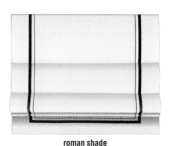

roman shade
Shade that forms layered pleats as it is
raised by means of cords sliding through
rings on the back of the cloth.

HOUSE AND DO-IT-YOURSELF

lights

Fixed or portable devices designed and used to diffuse electric light.

arm
Articulated moving bar for adjusting the position of the lamp shade.

base
Relatively heavy support for stabilizing the lamp.

halogen desk lamp
Desk lamp of greater luminous intensity and longer duration than a traditional lamp but that emits more heat.

shade
Translucent screen directing the lamp's light while decreasing its glare.

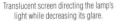

stand
Ornamental base of a lamp of various materials and shapes; it supports the socket while concealing the electric wires.

table lamp
Movable light with a short stand; it is placed on furniture.

desk lamp
Portable light equipped with an opaque shield that directs and diffuses the light onto the worktable.

floor lamp
Portable lamp having a high stand that
is placed on the floor.

clamp spotlight
Small portable spotlight with a
concentrated beam; it can be mounted
on furniture with a clamp.

bed lamp
Small reading light that can be
mounted on the back of a book or the
headboard of a bed.

adjustable lamp
Multidirectional light usually mounted on a
worktable by an adjustable clamp.

on-off switch
Button for turning the device on or off.

arm
Articulated moving bar for adjusting
the position of the lamp shade.

shade
Opaque shield directing the lamp's
light onto the work surface.

spring
Elastic metal coil for changing and
maintaining the position for the two
sections of the arm.

base
The lamp's flat-bottomed circular
support that makes it stable.

adjustable clamp
Mechanism in the form of a vise for
mounting the lamp to the edge of the
worktable.

wall fitting
Interior light mounted on a wall.

wall lantern
Exterior light mounted on a wall,
consisting of a translucent or
transparent cage containing a light
source.

swivel wall lamp
Interior light equipped with a movable articulated arm
mounted on a wall.

post lantern
Exterior light having a high stand that is
fixed to the ground; it consists of a
translucent or transparent cage containing
a light source.

track lighting
Device mounted to the ceiling to support spots and supply electricity to them.

bar frame
Part of the track fitted with two metal strips; the electric current passes through it.

contact lever
Device for attaching the transformer and plugging it into the bar frame.

transformer
Device adapting the electric current from the track to the spot's voltage.

spot
Small adjustable spotlight with a concentrated beam.

ceiling fitting
Light mounted directly on the ceiling.

hanging pendant
Light designed to be hung from the ceiling.

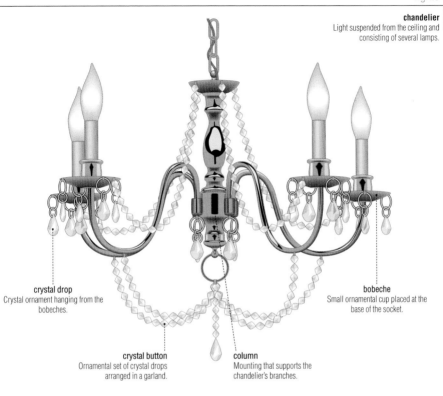

chandelier
Light suspended from the ceiling and consisting of several lamps.

crystal drop
Crystal ornament hanging from the bobeches.

bobeche
Small ornamental cup placed at the base of the socket.

crystal button
Ornamental set of crystal drops arranged in a garland.

column
Mounting that supports the chandelier's branches.

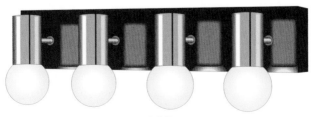

strip light
Device composed of a set of lights that are mounted on the same base.

domestic appliances

Domestic appliances operating on electricity.

steam iron
Electric appliance producing steam
and used to iron fabric.

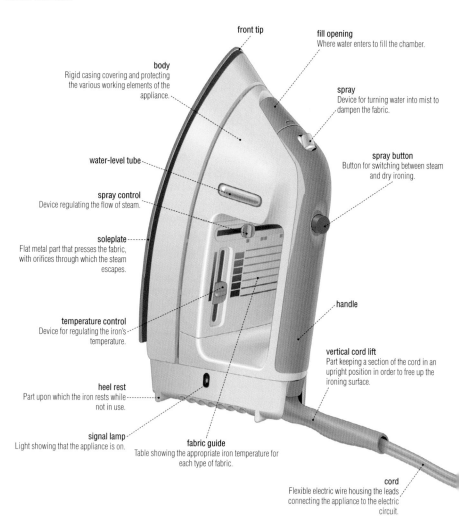

front tip

fill opening
Where water enters to fill the chamber.

body
Rigid casing covering and protecting
the various working elements of the
appliance.

spray
Device for turning water into mist to
dampen the fabric.

water-level tube

spray button
Button for switching between steam
and dry ironing.

spray control
Device regulating the flow of steam.

soleplate
Flat metal part that presses the fabric,
with orifices through which the steam
escapes.

handle

temperature control
Device for regulating the iron's
temperature.

vertical cord lift
Part keeping a section of the cord in an
upright position in order to free up the
ironing surface.

heel rest
Part upon which the iron rests while
not in use.

signal lamp
Light showing that the appliance is on.

fabric guide
Table showing the appropriate iron temperature for
each type of fabric.

cord
Flexible electric wire housing the leads
connecting the appliance to the electric
circuit.

upright vacuum cleaner
Vertical one-piece vacuum cleaner that is steered by means of a handle-grip.

on-off switch
Button for turning the device on or off.

tool storage area
Space for storing the cleaning tools.

hose
Flexible pipe to which cleaning tools are attached.

bag compartment
Space for housing the bag that collects the dust and dirt.

cleaner height adjustment knob
Mechanism for controlling brush height depending on the thickness of the rug or pile carpet to be cleaned.

brush
Rotating instrument equipped with bristles for dislodging dirt encrusted in the rug or pile carpet fibers.

tools
Small accessories that one attaches to the end of the hose to vacuum dust and dirt.

HOUSE AND DO-IT-YOURSELF

domestic appliances

cylinder vacuum cleaner
Electric appliance for vacuuming dust
and dirt; it is equipped with wheels and
a flexible hose.

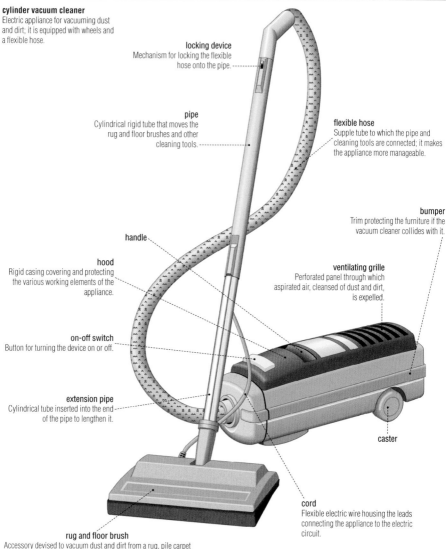

locking device
Mechanism for locking the flexible
hose onto the pipe.

pipe
Cylindrical rigid tube that moves the
rug and floor brushes and other
cleaning tools.

flexible hose
Supple tube to which the pipe and
cleaning tools are connected; it makes
the appliance more manageable.

bumper
Trim protecting the furniture if the
vacuum cleaner collides with it.

handle

hood
Rigid casing covering and protecting
the various working elements of the
appliance.

ventilating grille
Perforated panel through which
aspirated air, cleansed of dust and dirt,
is expelled.

on-off switch
Button for turning the device on or off.

extension pipe
Cylindrical tube inserted into the end
of the pipe to lengthen it.

caster

rug and floor brush
Accessory devised to vacuum dust and dirt from a rug, pile carpet
or floor.

cord
Flexible electric wire housing the leads
connecting the appliance to the electric
circuit.

HOUSE AND DO-IT-YOURSELF

cleaning tools
Small accessories that one attaches to the end of the hose to vacuum dust and dirt.

crevice tool
Accessory for vacuuming dust and dirt from hard-to-reach places.

dusting brush
Accessory for vacuuming dust from various surfaces.

floor brush
Accessory equipped with bristles to avoid scratching the floor while vacuuming.

upholstery nozzle
Accessory for vacuuming dust and dirt from fabric.

hand vacuum cleaner
Portable cordless appliance for vacuuming dust and dirt.

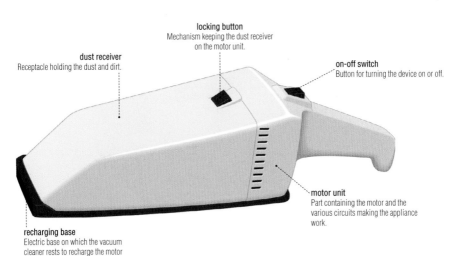

locking button
Mechanism keeping the dust receiver on the motor unit.

dust receiver
Receptacle holding the dust and dirt.

on-off switch
Button for turning the device on or off.

motor unit
Part containing the motor and the various circuits making the appliance work.

recharging base
Electric base on which the vacuum cleaner rests to recharge the motor unit's battery.

domestic appliances

gas range
Appliance for cooking food, equipped
with gas-fed burners and an oven.

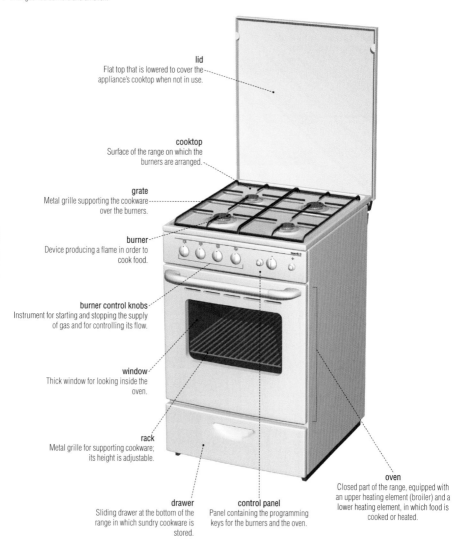

lid
Flat top that is lowered to cover the
appliance's cooktop when not in use.

cooktop
Surface of the range on which the
burners are arranged.

grate
Metal grille supporting the cookware
over the burners.

burner
Device producing a flame in order to
cook food.

burner control knobs
Instrument for starting and stopping the supply
of gas and for controlling its flow.

window
Thick window for looking inside the
oven.

rack
Metal grille for supporting cookware;
its height is adjustable.

oven
Closed part of the range, equipped with
an upper heating element (broiler) and a
lower heating element, in which food is
cooked or heated.

drawer
Sliding drawer at the bottom of the
range in which sundry cookware is
stored.

control panel
Panel containing the programming
keys for the burners and the oven.

chest freezer
Large horizontal appliance for
conserving food at a very low
temperature (0°F).

lid
Moving part hermetically closing the
freezer.

lock

cabinet
Large insulated compartment for
storing food.

basket
Removable container for storing food.

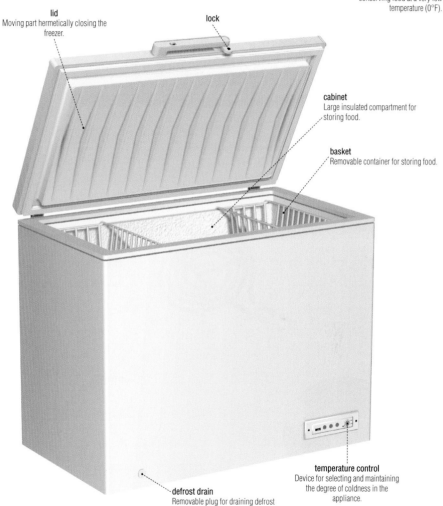

temperature control
Device for selecting and maintaining
the degree of coldness in the
appliance.

defrost drain
Removable plug for draining defrost
water.

HOUSE AND DO-IT-YOURSELF

domestic appliances

range hood
Ventilation appliance expelling or
recycling air that contains cooking
fumes and odors.

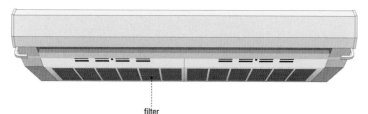

filter
Device catching the cooking grease.

surface element
Heating element on which cooking
takes place.

tubular element
Spiral-shaped electric resistor that
heats up as a current passes through it.

terminal
Metal part making electric contact.

drip bowl
Small container placed beneath the
surface element to catch cooking
spills.

trim ring
Decorative part supporting the drip
bowl and surface element.

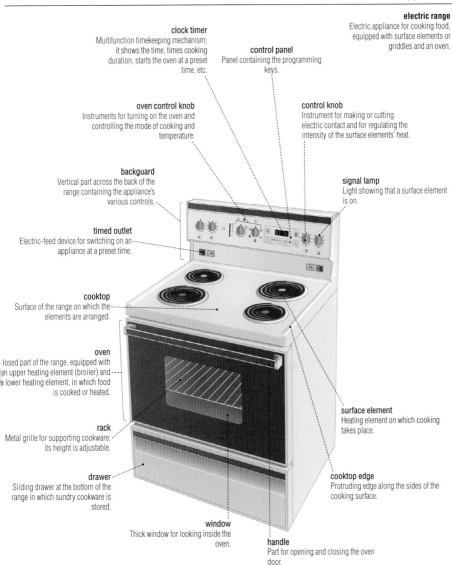

electric range
Electric appliance for cooking food, equipped with surface elements or griddles and an oven.

clock timer
Multifunction timekeeping mechanism; it shows the time, times cooking duration, starts the oven at a preset time, etc.

control panel
Panel containing the programming keys.

oven control knob
Instruments for turning on the oven and controlling the mode of cooking and temperature.

control knob
Instrument for making or cutting electric contact and for regulating the intensity of the surface elements' heat.

backguard
Vertical part across the back of the range containing the appliance's various controls.

signal lamp
Light showing that a surface element is on.

timed outlet
Electric-feed device for switching on an appliance at a preset time.

cooktop
Surface of the range on which the elements are arranged.

oven
Closed part of the range, equipped with an upper heating element (broiler) and a lower heating element, in which food is cooked or heated.

surface element
Heating element on which cooking takes place.

rack
Metal grille for supporting cookware; its height is adjustable.

drawer
Sliding drawer at the bottom of the range in which sundry cookware is stored.

cooktop edge
Protruding edge along the sides of the cooking surface.

window
Thick window for looking inside the oven.

handle
Part for opening and closing the oven door.

domestic appliances

refrigerator
Appliance with two compartments, one for keeping food cold and the other for freezing it.

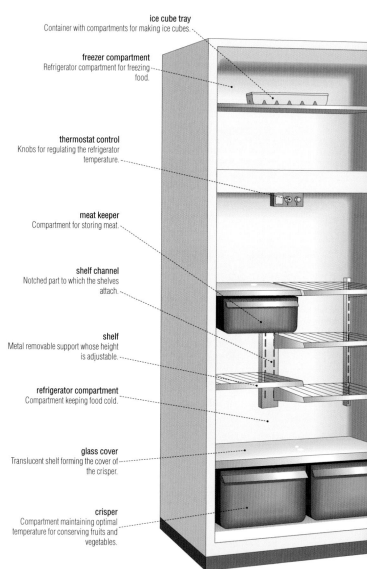

ice cube tray
Container with compartments for making ice cubes.

freezer compartment
Refrigerator compartment for freezing food.

thermostat control
Knobs for regulating the refrigerator temperature.

meat keeper
Compartment for storing meat.

shelf channel
Notched part to which the shelves attach.

shelf
Metal removable support whose height is adjustable.

refrigerator compartment
Compartment keeping food cold.

glass cover
Translucent shelf forming the cover of the crisper.

crisper
Compartment maintaining optimal temperature for conserving fruits and vegetables.

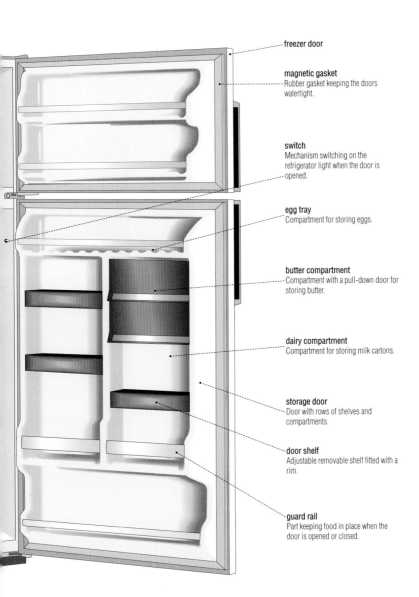

freezer door

magnetic gasket
Rubber gasket keeping the doors watertight.

switch
Mechanism switching on the refrigerator light when the door is opened.

egg tray
Compartment for storing eggs.

butter compartment
Compartment with a pull-down door for storing butter.

dairy compartment
Compartment for storing milk cartons.

storage door
Door with rows of shelves and compartments.

door shelf
Adjustable removable shelf fitted with a rim.

guard rail
Part keeping food in place when the door is opened or closed.

HOUSE AND DO-IT-YOURSELF

domestic appliances

washer
Household appliance that washes
clothes automatically.

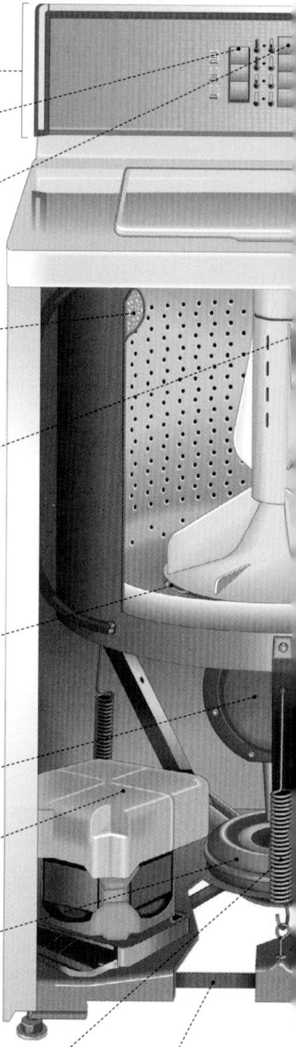

backguard
Vertical part across the back of the
washer on which the appliance's
various controls are found.

water-level selector

temperature selector

tub rim
Protrusion that reduces splashing.

agitator
Device stirring the laundry.

lint filter
Device collecting fiber residue from
fabric.

transmission
Mechanism allowing the agitator and
basket to turn at various speeds.

motor
Device transforming electric energy
into mechanical energy to drive
another device.

torque converter
Mechanism controlling and adjusting the
agitator and basket action.

spring
Metal elastic piece attached to the
suspension arm to reduce tub
vibrations.

drive belt
Device using a system of pulleys to
transfer the motor's mechanical energy
to the washer's transmission.

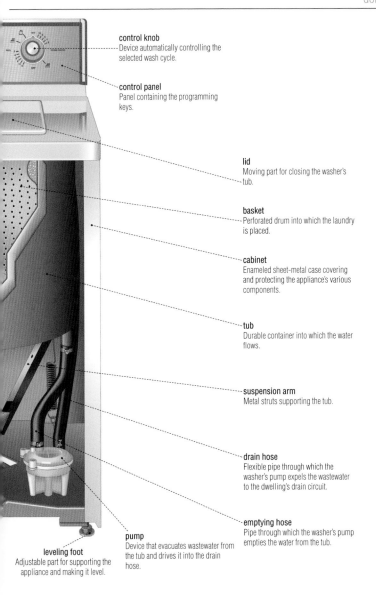

control knob
Device automatically controlling the selected wash cycle.

control panel
Panel containing the programming keys.

lid
Moving part for closing the washer's tub.

basket
Perforated drum into which the laundry is placed.

cabinet
Enameled sheet-metal case covering and protecting the appliance's various components.

tub
Durable container into which the water flows.

suspension arm
Metal struts supporting the tub.

drain hose
Flexible pipe through which the washer's pump expels the wastewater to the dwelling's drain circuit.

emptying hose
Pipe through which the washer's pump empties the water from the tub.

pump
Device that evacuates wastewater from the tub and drives it into the drain hose.

leveling foot
Adjustable part for supporting the appliance and making it level.

domestic appliances

electric dryer
Appliance for automatically drying laundry.

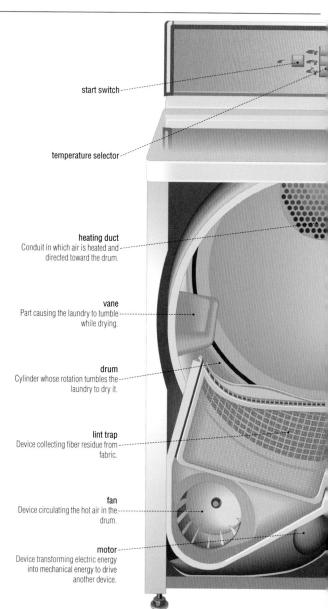

start switch

temperature selector

heating duct
Conduit in which air is heated and directed toward the drum.

vane
Part causing the laundry to tumble while drying.

drum
Cylinder whose rotation tumbles the laundry to dry it.

lint trap
Device collecting fiber residue from fabric.

fan
Device circulating the hot air in the drum.

motor
Device transforming electric energy into mechanical energy to drive another device.

HOUSE AND DO-IT-YOURSELF

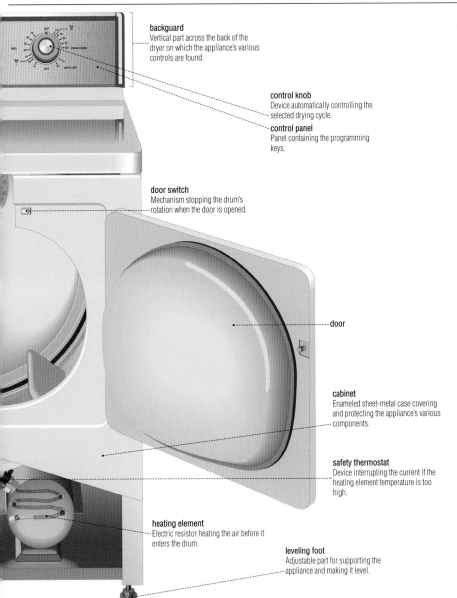

backguard
Vertical part across the back of the dryer on which the appliance's various controls are found.

control knob
Device automatically controlling the selected drying cycle.

control panel
Panel containing the programming keys.

door switch
Mechanism stopping the drum's rotation when the door is opened.

door

cabinet
Enameled sheet-metal case covering and protecting the appliance's various components.

safety thermostat
Device interrupting the current if the heating element temperature is too high.

heating element
Electric resistor heating the air before it enters the drum.

leveling foot
Adjustable part for supporting the appliance and making it level.

domestic appliances

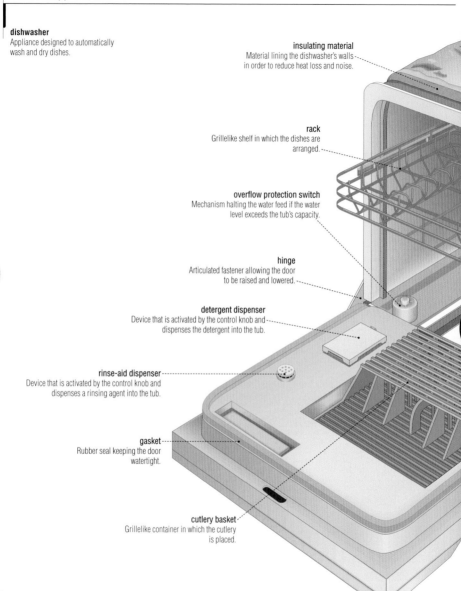

dishwasher
Appliance designed to automatically wash and dry dishes.

insulating material
Material lining the dishwasher's walls in order to reduce heat loss and noise.

rack
Grillelike shelf in which the dishes are arranged.

overflow protection switch
Mechanism halting the water feed if the water level exceeds the tub's capacity.

hinge
Articulated fastener allowing the door to be raised and lowered.

detergent dispenser
Device that is activated by the control knob and dispenses the detergent into the tub.

rinse-aid dispenser
Device that is activated by the control knob and dispenses a rinsing agent into the tub.

gasket
Rubber seal keeping the door watertight.

cutlery basket
Grillelike container in which the cutlery is placed.

HOUSE AND DO-IT-YOURSELF

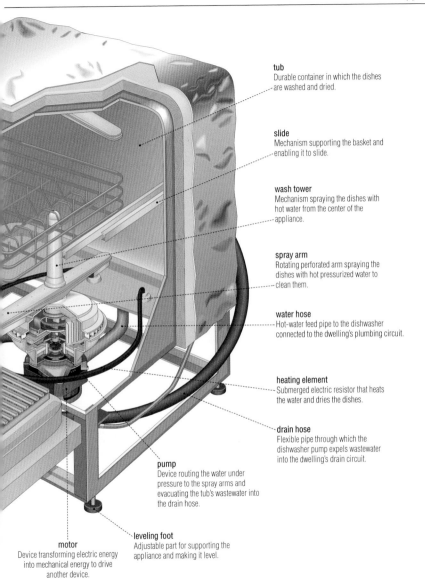

tub
Durable container in which the dishes are washed and dried.

slide
Mechanism supporting the basket and enabling it to slide.

wash tower
Mechanism spraying the dishes with hot water from the center of the appliance.

spray arm
Rotating perforated arm spraying the dishes with hot pressurized water to clean them.

water hose
Hot-water feed pipe to the dishwasher connected to the dwelling's plumbing circuit.

heating element
Submerged electric resistor that heats the water and dries the dishes.

drain hose
Flexible pipe through which the dishwasher pump expels wastewater into the dwelling's drain circuit.

pump
Device routing the water under pressure to the spray arms and evacuating the tub's wastewater into the drain hose.

motor
Device transforming electric energy into mechanical energy to drive another device.

leveling foot
Adjustable part for supporting the appliance and making it level.

carpentry: nailing tools

Carpentry: working with wood to build simple furniture or carry out construction and renovation projects.

claw hammer
Cleaved-peen hammer much used in construction, for driving nails in and pulling them out.

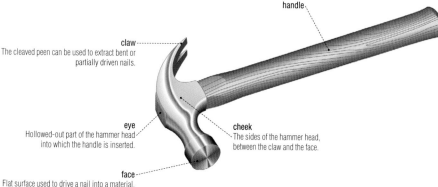

handle

claw
The cleaved peen can be used to extract bent or partially driven nails.

eye
Hollowed-out part of the hammer head into which the handle is inserted.

cheek
The sides of the hammer head, between the claw and the face.

face
Flat surface used to drive a nail into a material.

nail set
Tool used to push a nail completely into wood without damaging its surface.

carpenter's hammer
Hammer whose tapered peen is ideal for starting small nails; once they catch, the hammering can continue using the face.

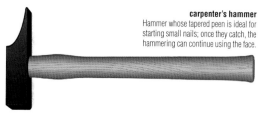

ball-peen hammer
Perfect for driving chisels and punches, it has a spherical peen often used for flattening rivets and working metals.

ball peen
Rounded part located opposite the face.

mallet
Large-headed hammer, often made of wood or rubber, used for directly striking materials or for hammering woodworking tools.

head
Striking end of a mallet.

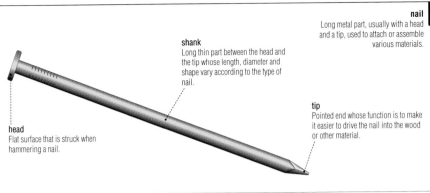

nail
Long metal part, usually with a head and a tip, used to attach or assemble various materials.

shank
Long thin part between the head and the tip whose length, diameter and shape vary according to the type of nail.

tip
Pointed end whose function is to make it easier to drive the nail into the wood or other material.

head
Flat surface that is struck when hammering a nail.

examples of nails

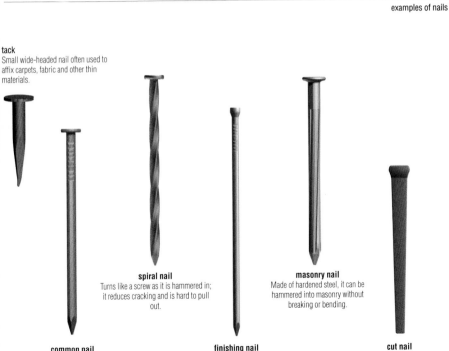

tack
Small wide-headed nail often used to affix carpets, fabric and other thin materials.

spiral nail
Turns like a screw as it is hammered in; it reduces cracking and is hard to pull out.

masonry nail
Made of hardened steel, it can be hammered into masonry without breaking or bending.

common nail
Sturdy wide-headed nail, used for general woodwork and carpentry.

finishing nail
The head, scarcely wider than the shank, can easily be hammered in and concealed; it is ideal for finishing work and moldings.

cut nail
The flat shank and head do not harm fibers; it is used especially for laying wood flooring.

carpentry: screwing tools

screwdriver
Hand tool used for tightening or loosening screws and bolts by applying a rotating motion.

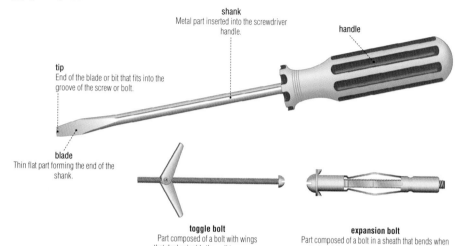

shank
Metal part inserted into the screwdriver handle.

handle

tip
End of the blade or bit that fits into the groove of the screw or bolt.

blade
Thin flat part forming the end of the shank.

toggle bolt
Part composed of a bolt with wings that deploy inside the wall to ensure a solid fastening.

expansion bolt
Part composed of a bolt in a sheath that bends when the bolt is inserted, then flattens out against the inside of the wall.

cordless screwdriver
Battery-driven screwdriver with interchangeable bits, used for tightening and loosening screws and bolts.

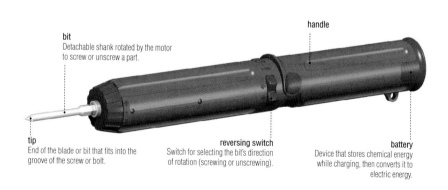

handle

bit
Detachable shank rotated by the motor to screw or unscrew a part.

tip
End of the blade or bit that fits into the groove of the screw or bolt.

reversing switch
Switch for selecting the bit's direction of rotation (screwing or unscrewing).

battery
Device that stores chemical energy while charging, then converts it to electric energy.

spiral screwdriver
Screwdriver with interchangeable bits fitted into a
mechanism for screwing or unscrewing by simply
pushing the handle.

spiral
Mechanism converting pressure
applied on the handle into the rotation
motion of the blade.

ratchet
Mechanical instrument for setting the
direction of rotation of the spiral and
the blade (screwing or unscrewing).

blade
Thin flat part forming the end of the bit.

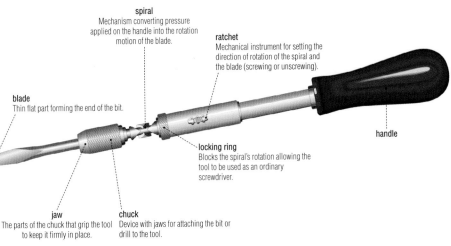

handle

locking ring
Blocks the spiral's rotation allowing the
tool to be used as an ordinary
screwdriver.

jaw
The parts of the chuck that grip the tool
to keep it firmly in place.

chuck
Device with jaws for attaching the bit or
drill to the tool.

examples of tips
Tip: end part of the blade or bit; it adapts to the screw
or bolt's groove.

square-headed tip
Tip whose end cut fits into a socket-head screw.

flat tip
Tip that fits into a screw's slot.

cross-headed tip
Tip whose crisscross end fits into a cross-headed
screw.

screw
Metal part, composed of a head and a partially or completely threaded shank, used to secure fastenings and assemblies.

head
Broadened end of the screw, whose shape and slot vary.

shank
Nonthreaded part of a screw's shank.

slot
Notch in the head into which a corresponding screwdriver tip can be inserted.

thread
Spiral protrusion on the shank's surface, for driving the screw into a solid material by turning.

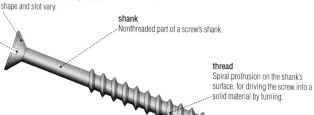

examples of heads
Head: broadened end of the screw, whose shape and slot vary.

flat head
Slotted head becoming flush with the surface of the wood when completely embedded.

one-way head
Slotted head having two opposing quarters removed so that the screw can be turned one way only, making it very difficult to unscrew.

round head
Slotted rounded head whose base is flat so that it presses against the wood or metal surface.

oval head
Slotted head topped with an ornamental spherical part that is not driven beneath the wood's surface.

Phillips
Head whose crisscross indentation keeps the screwdriver in the middle of the head, providing a very firm grip.

socket head
Head with a square socket that varies in size.

carpentry: sawing tools

hacksaw
Frame handsaw for sawing metal of varying thicknesses.

adjustable frame
Rigid metal mount keeping the blade under tension. Extendable, it can be adjusted for blades of various lengths.

grip handle

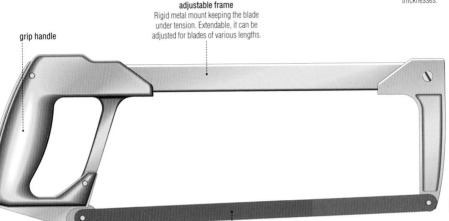

blade
It has very hard teeth; their thickness depends on the type of metal.

coping saw
Small handsaw with a frame, used for cutting out curves or delicate patterns in a piece of relatively thin wood.

frame
Rigid metal mount keeping the blade under tension to prevent it from buckling.

handle
The rotation of the handle regulates the tension of the blade on the frame.

blade
Thin, flexible and very straight, it can move at various angles to make irregular cuts.

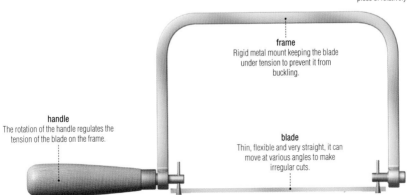

carpentry: sawing tools

compass saw
Small handsaw used mostly to cut regular or curved openings in wood and panels.

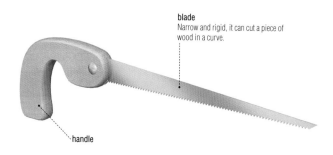

blade
Narrow and rigid, it can cut a piece of wood in a curve.

handle

handsaw
Very common manual saw, suited for straight cuts in boards or wood panels.

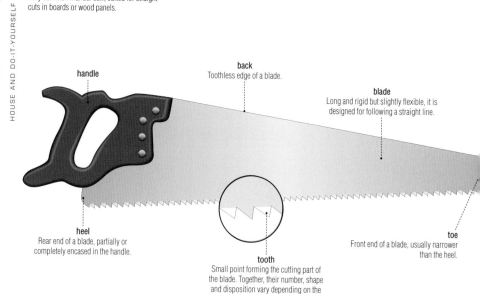

handle

back
Toothless edge of a blade.

blade
Long and rigid but slightly flexible, it is designed for following a straight line.

heel
Rear end of a blade, partially or completely encased in the handle.

tooth
Small point forming the cutting part of the blade. Together, their number, shape and disposition vary depending on the intended use.

toe
Front end of a blade, usually narrower than the heel.

hand miter saw
Device consisting of a handsaw and a guide for cutting a piece at a precise angle.

miter box
Grooved instrument for guiding the saw to make cuts at precise angles.

fence
Perpendicular plate on the surface bracing the piece to be cut.

blade
It is set in a rigid frame, which is part of a movable device that moves the blade vertically and horizontally.

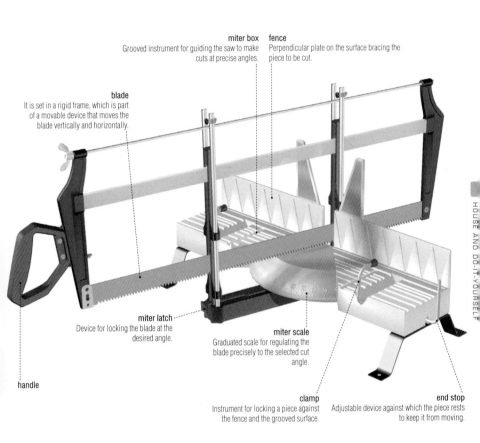

miter latch
Device for locking the blade at the desired angle.

miter scale
Graduated scale for regulating the blade precisely to the selected cut angle.

handle

clamp
Instrument for locking a piece against the fence and the grooved surface.

end stop
Adjustable device against which the piece rests to keep it from moving.

HOUSE AND DO-IT-YOURSELF

carpentry: sawing tools

circular saw
Portable electric saw with a circular blade; it is used for
making straight cuts in various materials.

height adjustment scale
Regulates the blade's height under the base plate, to control the
depth of the cut.

blade
Thin metal disk with teeth; it rotates to
cut pieces of metal or wood.

trigger switch
Connection mechanism for starting or stopping the tool
by squeezing with the finger.

handle
For optimal control of the tool, it is
advisable to place one hand on the
handle and the other on the knob
handle.

upper blade guard
Fixed sheath covering the upper part of the blade
to protect the user's hands and prevent sawdust
from escaping.

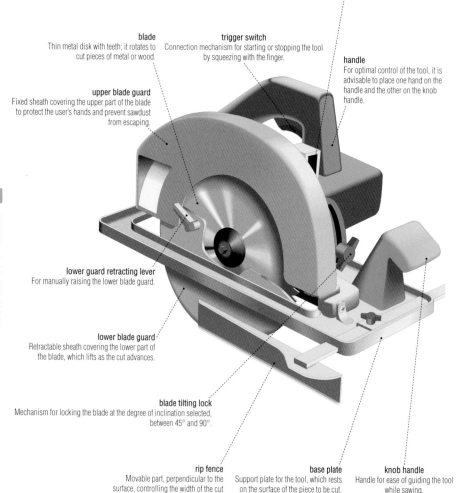

lower guard retracting lever
For manually raising the lower blade guard.

lower blade guard
Retractable sheath covering the lower part of
the blade, which lifts as the cut advances.

blade tilting lock
Mechanism for locking the blade at the degree of inclination selected,
between 45° and 90°.

rip fence
Movable part, perpendicular to the
surface, controlling the width of the cut
in the lengthwise direction.

base plate
Support plate for the tool, which rests
on the surface of the piece to be cut.

knob handle
Handle for ease of guiding the tool
while sawing.

jig saw
Electric portable saw whose blade has an up-and-down motion; it is used for making straight or curved cuts.

speed selector switch
Device for controlling the rhythm of the blade's up-and-down motion.

trigger switch
Connection mechanism for starting or stopping the tool by squeezing with the finger.

lock-on button
Device locking the switch in position to keep the saw working continuously during long or complex cuts.

orbital-action selector
Mechanism regulating the pendular motion of the blade. A slight or no pendular motion gives a better finish but takes longer.

handle

chip cover
Protective cover preventing sawdust and fragments from flying toward the user or toward the cutting line.

blade
It moves up and down but can also move from front to back, which increases the efficiency of the sawing.

base
The tool's support plate, which rests on the surface of the piece to be cut. It can be inclined to make beveled cuts.

power cord
Flexible electric wire housing the leads connecting the appliance to the electric circuit.

HOUSE AND DO-IT-YOURSELF

carpentry: drilling tools

electric drill
Portable electric tool using variable-speed rotation to pierce holes and to drive drills and bits.

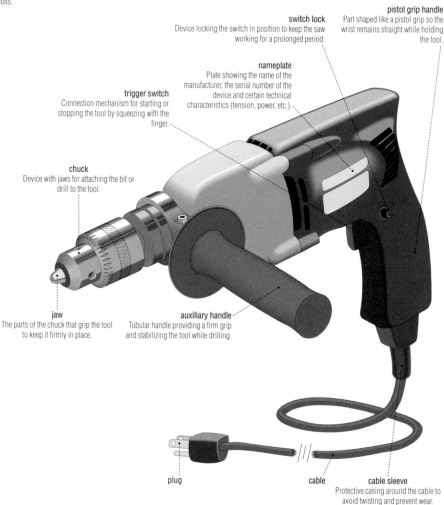

pistol grip handle
Part shaped like a pistol grip so the wrist remains straight while holding the tool.

switch lock
Device locking the switch in position to keep the saw working for a prolonged period.

nameplate
Plate showing the name of the manufacturer, the serial number of the device and certain technical characteristics (tension, power, etc.).

trigger switch
Connection mechanism for starting or stopping the tool by squeezing with the finger.

chuck
Device with jaws for attaching the bit or drill to the tool.

jaw
The parts of the chuck that grip the tool to keep it firmly in place.

auxiliary handle
Tubular handle providing a firm grip and stabilizing the tool while drilling.

plug

cable

cable sleeve
Protective casing around the cable to avoid twisting and prevent wear.

brace
Hand tool, made up of an angled crank
and a pawl and ratchet mechanism, for
drilling holes.

handle
Movable part for turning the crank.

crank
Angled shank whose rotation drives
the chuck, by the agency of a pawl and
ratchet mechanism.

cam ring
Metal cylinder covering the crank above
the pawl.

chuck
Device with jaws for attaching the bit or
drill to the tool.

pawl
Small lever for changing the chuck's
direction of rotation by reversing the
ratchet motion.

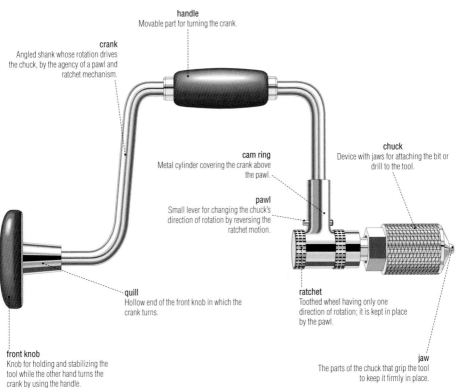

quill
Hollow end of the front knob in which the
crank turns.

ratchet
Toothed wheel having only one
direction of rotation; it is kept in place
by the pawl.

front knob
Knob for holding and stabilizing the
tool while the other hand turns the
crank by using the handle.

jaw
The parts of the chuck that grip the tool
to keep it firmly in place.

examples of bits and drills

While both are intended for drilling holes in various materials, the bit has a center point while the drill ends in a cutting-edge cone.

solid center auger bit
Bit made up of a central shank encircled by a twist; it is very durable and especially designed for making deep holes.

twist bit
Bit with a spiral drill flute; it drills straight uniform holes and is very practical for inserting dowels.

shank
Upper part of the bit, on which pressure from the chuck's jaws is exerted.

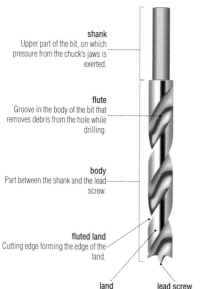

shank
Upper part of the bit, on which pressure from the chuck's jaws is exerted.

flute
Groove in the body of the bit that removes debris from the hole while drilling.

twist
Spiral protrusion around the bit's shank; it removes debris from the hole being drilled.

body
Part between the shank and the lead screw.

spur
Lip that covers the outline of the hole and removes debris, which is then pushed to the twist and disposed of.

lead screw
Threaded pointed end for centering the bit in the middle of the hole at the start of drilling.

fluted land
Cutting edge forming the edge of the land.

land
Flat surface between the flutes.

lead screw
Threaded pointed end for centering the bit in the middle of the hole at the start of drilling.

twist drill
Usually used to drill holes in metal or wood, it is the most common type of drill.

masonry drill
The carbide and tungsten tip, hard and durable, is designed to drill through material such as brick, concrete and stone.

spade bit
Bit designed for shallow holes of wide diameter; it has a long lead screw for positioning on the center of the hole.

double-twist auger bit
Bit made up of two opposing twists; it removes debris quickly as the hole is drilled.

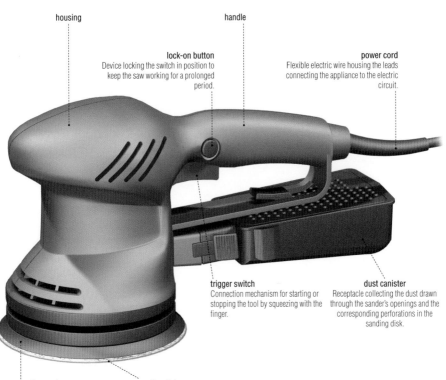

random orbit sander
Portable electric tool whose abrasive disk moves two ways (rotating and eccentric) to sand various types of surface.

housing

handle

lock-on button
Device locking the switch in position to keep the saw working for a prolonged period.

power cord
Flexible electric wire housing the leads connecting the appliance to the electric circuit.

trigger switch
Connection mechanism for starting or stopping the tool by squeezing with the finger.

dust canister
Receptacle collecting the dust drawn through the sander's openings and the corresponding perforations in the sanding disk.

sanding pad
Cushion to which the sanding disk is attached. Usually made of flexible material, it is used for sanding flat and curved surfaces.

sanding disk
Paper, usually perforated and self-adhesive, that fits the sander's sanding pad.

sanding disk
Paper, usually perforated and self-adhesive, that fits the sander's sanding pad.

HOUSE AND DO-IT-YOURSELF

router
Portable electric tool using rotating bits to
mill moldings, grooves and wood joints.

head
Flat top of the router; the tool rests on
it when not in use.

motor

depth adjustment
Device that regulates the depth of the
bit, thus controlling the depth of the
milling.

switch
Button for turning the device on or off.

cord sleeve
Protective casing around the cable to
lessen twisting and prevent wear.

guide handle
Used to hold and guide the tool.

base
Support plate for the tool, which rests
on the surface of the piece to be
worked on.

collet
Ring-shaped part for tightening or
loosening the tool holder.

tool holder
Device fitted with jaws for attaching the
bit to the router.

examples of bits

Bits: detachable tools fitted with edges or abrasive parts;
a router applies a rotating motion on them to mill a piece
of work.

rounding-over bit
Depending on the way it is positioned, it
is a bit for rounding the edge of a piece of
wood or for making a convex molding
with a shoulder.

core box bit
Bit usually used to mill grooves in
wood in the shape of semicircles.

dovetail bit
Bit for making cuts shaped like a
dove's tail, often used in joining
drawers.

cove bit
Bit used especially for concave moldings or
for cutting articulating joints for a gate-leg
table.

rabbet bit
Bit for cutting an edge at right angles,
used especially for making frames and
for various cabinetmaking joints.

chamfer bit
Bit for beveling edges at a 45° angle to
create decorative edges and joints.

HOUSE AND DO-IT-YOURSELF

carpentry: shaping tools

plane
Hand tool with a cutting blade, intended mainly for planing a wood surface or to give it a shape (e.g., beveled, chamfered).

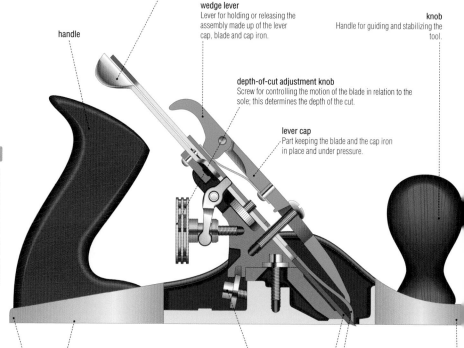

lateral-adjustment lever
Device for aligning the cutting edge of the blade with the plane of the sole.

wedge lever
Lever for holding or releasing the assembly made up of the lever cap, blade and cap iron.

knob
Handle for guiding and stabilizing the tool.

handle

depth-of-cut adjustment knob
Screw for controlling the motion of the blade in relation to the sole; this determines the depth of the cut.

lever cap
Part keeping the blade and the cap iron in place and under pressure.

sole
Support plate, which rests on the surface of the piece to be planed.

frog-adjustment screw
Screw adjusting the blade's slant and, therefore, the width of the opening (mouth) that removes the shavings.

toe
Front end of the tool.

heel
Rear end of the tool.

blade
Metal plate whose beveled edge constitutes the cutting edge of the plane.

cap iron
Metal part in apposition to the blade; it breaks off the wood shavings to facilitate their removal.

file
Hand tool made up of a metal blade
whose striated surface allows for pieces
of wood, metal or plastic to be smoothed,
altered or burnished.

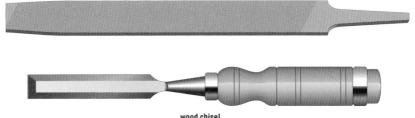

wood chisel
Hand tool with a metal blade whose
end is beveled for woodworking.

rasp
Hand tool made up of a metal blade
whose tooth-covered surface can
quickly rough out wood, metal or
plastic.

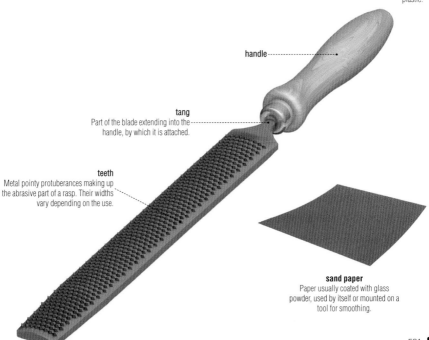

handle

tang
Part of the blade extending into the
handle, by which it is attached.

teeth
Metal pointy protuberances making up
the abrasive part of a rasp. Their widths
vary depending on the use.

sand paper
Paper usually coated with glass
powder, used by itself or mounted on a
tool for smoothing.

carpentry: gripping and tightening tools

pliers
Hand tools with two movable jaws of fixed or variable gaps, intended for gripping or clamping objects.

slip joint pliers
Pliers with curved jaws and ending in a straight part, adjustable to two widths of opening.

curved jaw
Jaw whose internal side is rounded for gripping or clamping a round object.

handle
Long part that, in concert with its twin, exerts pressure to open or close the jaws.

slip joint
Pliers' articulating axle, which slides between two positions to change the jaws' gap.

locking pliers
Used as pliers, wrench and vice, it has variable-gap jaws for gripping and clamping objects.

spring
Tight when the handles are closed to lock the pliers, it resumes its shape when unlocked and the handles return to their initial position.

toothed jaw
Striated straight or curved part that, with its twin, grasps or clamps an object.

rivet
Riveted assembly part that is the axle of articulation for the release lever.

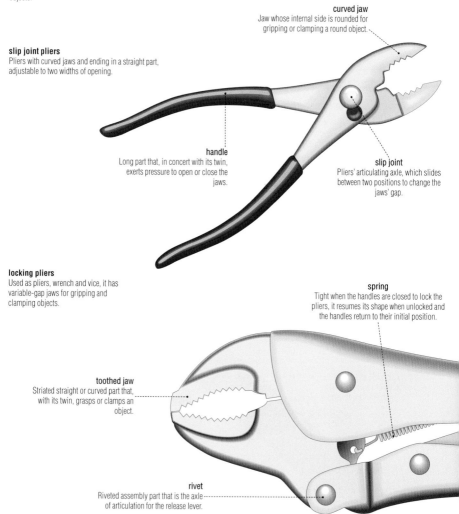

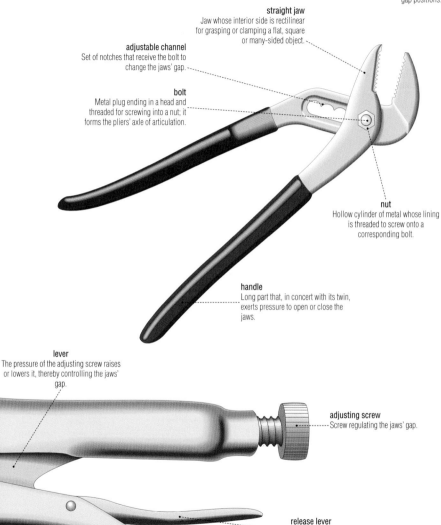

rib joint pliers
Pliers with straight jaws, adjustable to several gap positions.

straight jaw
Jaw whose interior side is rectilinear for grasping or clamping a flat, square or many-sided object.

adjustable channel
Set of notches that receive the bolt to change the jaws' gap.

bolt
Metal plug ending in a head and threaded for screwing into a nut; it forms the pliers' axle of articulation.

nut
Hollow cylinder of metal whose lining is threaded to screw onto a corresponding bolt.

handle
Long part that, in concert with its twin, exerts pressure to open or close the jaws.

lever
The pressure of the adjusting screw raises or lowers it, thereby controlling the jaws' gap.

adjusting screw
Screw regulating the jaws' gap.

release lever
Lever for unlocking the pliers and releasing the grip.

carpentry: gripping and tightening tools

wrenches

Hand tools with fixed or variable openings, used for tightening and loosening nuts and bolts, and for assembling and disassembling objects.

ratchet socket wrench

Wrench fitted with a pawl and a ratchet: the pawl sets the direction of rotation, while the ratchet lets the handle turn in the opposite direction over the socket.

socket set

Set made up of hollow cylinders of different sizes and interior profiles that fit onto a ratchet socket wrench.

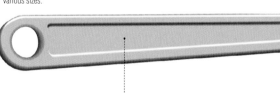

open end wrench

Wrench with two openings of different sizes, each having parallel jaws.

box end wrench

Wrench that is usually bent and has two many-sided rings of different sizes; it grips the nut more firmly than the open end wrench.

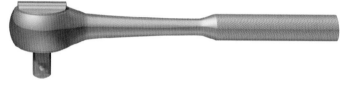

fixed jaw

Upper branch of the fork, which is an extension of the tool's handle.

crescent wrench

Wrench whose jaws' gap is adjustable for gripping nuts, bolts or plumbing fittings of various sizes.

handle

thumbscrew

Small striated wheel controlling the movable jaw's gap.

movable jaw

Lower branch of the fork, whose gap enables the tool to adjust to the size of the object to be gripped.

nuts

Metal parts with holes whose surfaces are threaded
for screwing onto the corresponding bolts.

hexagon nut
Most common nut; it has six sides for
tightening with a wrench.

acorn nut
Nut capped with a hollow dome that
covers and protects the threaded end of
the bolt.

wing nut
Nut comprised of two protruding ends
for tightening or loosening by hand.

bolts

Metal plugs ending in a head and threaded so they
can be tightly screwed into nuts to secure
fastenings and assemblies.

bolt
Metal threaded plug ending in a head;
it is tightly screwed into a nut to secure
fastenings and assemblies.

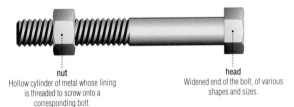

nut
Hollow cylinder of metal whose lining
is threaded to screw onto a
corresponding bolt.

head
Widened end of the bolt, of various
shapes and sizes.

shoulder bolt
Bolt whose head comprises a section of smaller
diameter for concentrating the tightening pressure.

threaded rod
Elongated part whose surface has a
spiral protrusion for screwing into a
corresponding nut.

shoulder
Cylindrical nonthreaded protrusion
used as a bracket as the bolt is being
tightened.

HOUSE AND DO-IT-YOURSELF

C-clamp
Portable tool with a C-shaped frame, used for keeping objects from moving while working on them.

adjusting screw
Threaded shank whose rotation is controlled by the handle; it moves the jaw toward or away from the piece to be clamped.

movable jaw
Smooth or striated jaw that presses an object against the fixed jaw.

fixed jaw
Smooth or striated part against which the movable jaw presses an object.

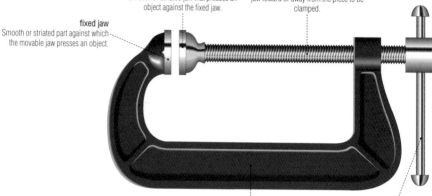

frame
Rigid metal support in the shape of a C, having the fixed jaw on one end, while the other end contains a hole for the adjusting screw.

handle
Sliding bar for tightening or loosening the adjusting screw, thereby spreading or closing the jaws.

pipe clamp
Large press comprising a metal pipe supporting a jaw and a tail stop.

handle
Sliding bar that adjusts the screw to slide the tail stop's jaw up or down the pipe.

clamping screw
Threaded shank whose rotation, controlled by the clamping lever, causes the jaw to slide along the pipe to or from the object to be clamped.

tail stop
Movable jaw whose motion along the pipe quickly adjusts the tool to the length of the object to be clamped.

jaw
Movable part for pressing more objects against the tail stop.

pipe
Hollow cylinder of varying length, along which the jaw and the tail stop slide.

locking lever
Handle that fixes the tail stop at the desired position on the pipe.

vise
Press with two jaws; it is attached to a worktable and used for clamping objects.

movable jaw
Smooth or striated jaw that presses an object against the fixed jaw.

fixed jaw
Smooth or striated part against which the movable jaw presses an object.

handle
Sliding bar for tightening or loosening the adjusting screw, thereby spreading or closing the jaws.

adjusting screw
Threaded shank whose rotation is controlled by the handle; it moves the jaw toward or away from the piece to be clamped.

swivel base
Rotating surface surmounting the fixed base, which allows the vise to turn 360°.

swivel lock
Sliding bar clamping down the swivel base by locking it into the desired position.

fixed base
The tool's supporting block, usually bolted onto a work bench.

bolt
Threaded metal plug with a head that is tightly screwed into a nut to secure the vise to a work bench.

carpentry: measuring and marking tools

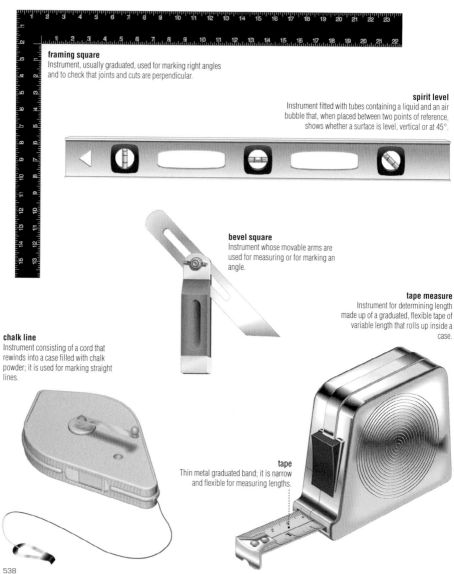

framing square
Instrument, usually graduated, used for marking right angles and to check that joints and cuts are perpendicular.

spirit level
Instrument fitted with tubes containing a liquid and an air bubble that, when placed between two points of reference, shows whether a surface is level, vertical or at 45°.

bevel square
Instrument whose movable arms are used for measuring or for marking an angle.

tape measure
Instrument for determining length made up of a graduated, flexible tape of variable length that rolls up inside a case.

chalk line
Instrument consisting of a cord that rewinds into a case filled with chalk powder; it is used for marking straight lines.

tape
Thin metal graduated band; it is narrow and flexible for measuring lengths.

HOUSE AND DO-IT-YOURSELF

tool belt
Band worn around the waist, fitted with pockets and accessories for holding tools and instruments needed close at hand.

belt

pocket

hammer loop
Metal bracket for holding the head of a hammer.

tool box
Rigid container, fitted with a cover and a tray, for storing and carrying tools.

handle

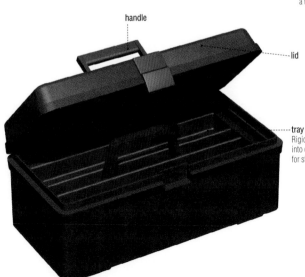

lid

tray
Rigid detachable container, divided into compartments and usually used for storing hardware or small tools.

plumbing tools

The purpose of plumbing is to install, maintain and repair a dwelling's pipes and sanitary fixtures.

Teflon tape
Flexible waterproof ribbon for covering threaded pipe joints to prevent leakage.

basin wrench
Wrench whose jaws are perpendicular to a telescoping handle, and pivot to open at variable positions; it is used for working in cramped spaces.

pipe wrench
Wrench with notched jaws and adjustable opening for firmly gripping nuts, couplings and thick-walled pipes.

plumber's snake
Metal semirigid auger whose end is usually fitted with a hook or corkscrew; it is used for unblocking pipes.

plunger
Rubber funnel-shaped instrument, attached to the end of a handle, for unblocking toilets, sinks and other drains.

The purpose of masonry is to build and repair structures or to cover walls with brick, stone or concrete blocks.

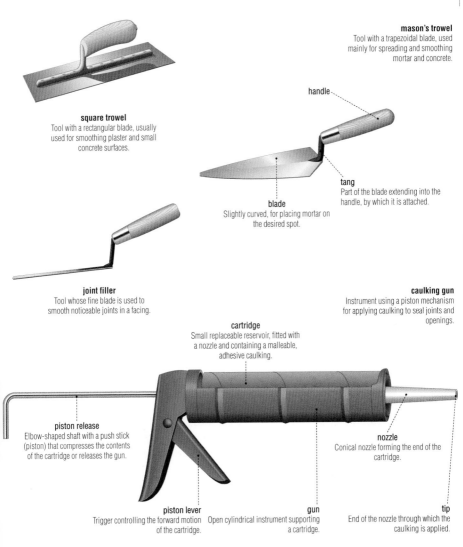

mason's trowel
Tool with a trapezoidal blade, used mainly for spreading and smoothing mortar and concrete.

square trowel
Tool with a rectangular blade, usually used for smoothing plaster and small concrete surfaces.

handle

blade
Slightly curved, for placing mortar on the desired spot.

tang
Part of the blade extending into the handle, by which it is attached.

joint filler
Tool whose fine blade is used to smooth noticeable joints in a facing.

caulking gun
Instrument using a piston mechanism for applying caulking to seal joints and openings.

cartridge
Small replaceable reservoir, fitted with a nozzle and containing a malleable, adhesive caulking.

piston release
Elbow-shaped shaft with a push stick (piston) that compresses the contents of the cartridge or releases the gun.

nozzle
Conical nozzle forming the end of the cartridge.

piston lever
Trigger controlling the forward motion of the cartridge.

gun
Open cylindrical instrument supporting a cartridge.

tip
End of the nozzle through which the caulking is applied.

HOUSE AND DO-IT-YOURSELF

electricity tools

The purpose of the electrical trade is to install, maintain and repair electrical wiring and devices in a place or building.

neon tester
Instrument used for detecting the presence of an electric current in low-voltage appliances, devices and circuits.

multipurpose tool
Pliers fitted with straight jaws, used especially for gripping, cutting and stripping electric wires.

lineman's pliers
Pliers fitted with straight jaws that provide a powerful grip; they also include a wire cutter and jaws for pulling fish wire.

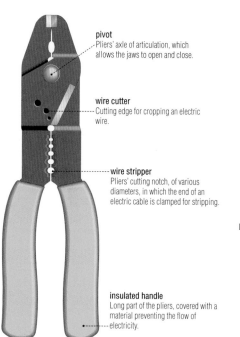

pivot
Pliers' axle of articulation, which allows the jaws to open and close.

wire cutter
Cutting edge for cropping an electric wire.

wire stripper
Pliers' cutting notch, of various diameters, in which the end of an electric cable is clamped for stripping.

insulated handle
Long part of the pliers, covered with a material preventing the flow of electricity.

jaw
Straight striated part that, with its twin, opens and closes to grip, twist or cut an electric cable, wire or other object.

wire cutter
Part fitted with two cutting edges for cropping an electric wire.

pivot
Pliers' axle of articulation, which allows the jaws to open and close.

insulated handle
Long part of the pliers, covered with a material preventing the flow of electricity.

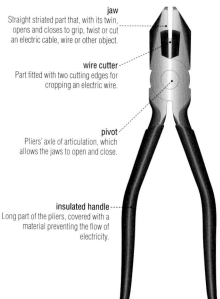

receptacle analyzer
Instrument for detecting any faults in the receptacle, such as grounding problems and crossed or unconnected wires.

voltage tester
Screwdriver used for detecting an electric current in appliances, devices and low-voltage circuits.

---- insulated blade

insulated handle
Part for gripping the tool, made from a material that prevents an electric current from passing through it.

neon lamp
Small tube that lights up when the blade is in contact with a live conductor.

drop light
Portable electric lamp protected by a guard and fitted with a long cord allowing it to be moved.

hook ----

reflector
Metal half sphere concentrating and directing the light from a lightbulb.

bulb
Glass envelope filled with gas, in which a luminous body is inserted.

guard ----
Metal mesh protecting the lightbulb while the drop light is being handled.

convenience outlet
Device connected to an electric circuit; it transmits the current to an electrical appliance when its plug is inserted into the outlet.

handle ----

cord
Flexible electric wire housing the leads connecting the appliance to the electric circuit.

HOUSE AND DO-IT-YOURSELF

headgear

Item of attire used to cover, protect or adorn the head.

unisex headgear
Headgear worn by members of both sexes.

stocking cap
Woolen headgear made from a cylindrical piece that is folded over for double thickness, sewn at one end and decorated with a pompom.

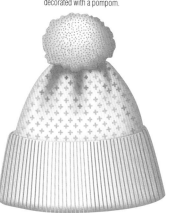

beret
Soft brimless headgear with a round flat crown that sometimes puffs out; it fits on the head by means of a simple hemmed rim or a narrow headband.

balaclava
Woolen cap covering the head and neck and with an opening for the face.

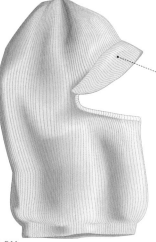

peak
Part that juts out over the eyes to protect them.

felt hat
Soft hat with a dented crown that is adorned with a wide ribbon; it is made from a single piece and has a brim of uniform width.

gob hat
Headgear made of soft light material that is worn over the brow and fits snugly on the head; the brim can be worn down to shade the face.

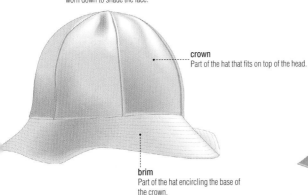

crown
Part of the hat that fits on top of the head.

brim
Part of the hat encircling the base of the crown.

southwester
Waterproof headgear with a narrow brim that widens over the nape of the neck to protect it from inclement weather.

toque
Brimless headgear made of fabric or fur, with a cylindrical crown and a flat top that fits snugly on the head.

turban
Headgear made of a long strip of fabric, wound around so that it covers the entire head but leaves the forehead uncovered.

pillbox hat
Small low, round or oval toque worn perched on top of the head or pulled down.

cartwheel hat
Headgear in fashion from the early 20th century, made of straw or light fibers with a large soft brim of uniform width.

cloche
Hat of the 1920s and '30s with a cylindrical crown and a narrow brim.

men's headgear

felt hat
Soft hat with a dented crown that is adorned with a wide ribbon; it is made from a single piece and has a brim of uniform width.

binding
Strip of fabric running along the edge of the hat.

crown
Part of the hat that fits on top of the head.

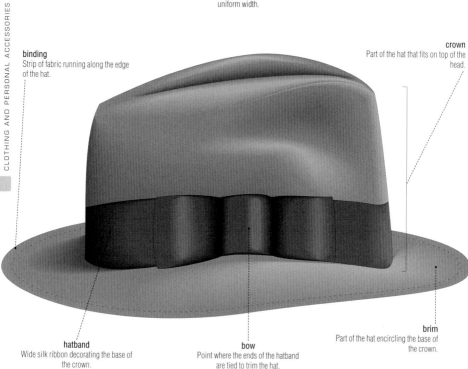

hatband
Wide silk ribbon decorating the base of the crown.

bow
Point where the ends of the hatband are tied to trim the hat.

brim
Part of the hat encircling the base of the crown.

boater
Stiff straw headgear with a flat brim of uniform width and an oval crown circled with a ribbon; it was worn at the end of the 19th century.

skullcap
Small round cap covering only the top of the head.

derby
Headgear primarily for men that appeared at the end of the 19th century; it is made of stiff felt with a circular rounded crown and an upturned narrow brim.

garrison cap
Elongated brimless headgear with a soft flexible crown; it is worn over the brow and takes the shape of the head.

top hat
Stiff silk headgear with a high cylindrical crown circled with a ribbon and a narrow brim that is turned up at the sides; it was worn toward the end of the 18th century.

shapka
Fur hat that is native to Poland; it has ear flaps that can be turned up and tied on top of the head.

cap
Brimless, somewhat soft headgear that appeared at the end of the 19th century; it has a peak and a flat crown.

hunting cap
Thick soft cap with a peak and ear flaps, which give protection against the cold.

ear flap
Flap that covers the nape of the neck and the ears to keep them warm; it can be turned up and held in place on top of the head.

panama
Soft headgear from the end of the 19th and the early 20th century; it is made from woven jipijapa leaves and has a dented crown circled with a ribbon.

peak
Part that juts out over the eyes to protect them.

shoes

Items of attire that protect and support the foot, covering the ankle and leg to varying degrees.

unisex shoes
Shoes worn by members of both sexes.

mule
Flat light, usually indoor shoe; it has a vamp only, leaving the heel bare.

tennis shoe
Flat canvas shoe with a flexible nonskid sole and a reinforced toe; the sole and toe are both made of rubber.

espadrille
Canvas shoe characterized by a woven rope sole; it is held on the foot by a lace tied around the ankle.

moccasin
Flat, very soft slip-on casual shoe with ridged seams; it is characterized by an apron sewn onto the vamp, which molds to the instep.

loafer
Dressy moccasin with a flat heel.

sandal
Shoe with a flat sole that is held on the
foot by thin straps and sometimes a
toe-ring.

thong
Sandal that is attached to the foot with
nothing more than a Y-shaped strap,
which passes between the first two
toes.

clog
Toeless mule with a thick, generally
wooden sole; it is held on the foot by a
thick strap.

sandal
Flat light sport shoe with a cutout vamp that
turns into a tongue; a bar passes through
the tongue and fastens at the side with a
buckle.

hiking boot
Sturdy walking shoe with a thick nonskid
sole; it is supported at the ankle and
instep by laces threaded through hooks.

shoes

women's shoes

sandal
Light shoe leaving especially the heel uncovered; it often consists only of a sole held on the foot by variously configured straps.

ballerina
Light supple unlined shoe that is tightened by a thin lace and sometimes has a small heel; it leaves the instep uncovered to the base of the toes.

pump
Plain delicate lightweight shoe that leaves the instep uncovered; it has a heel, a thin sole and no fastening system.

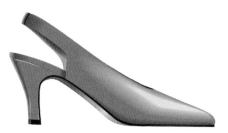

sling back shoe
Pump with a rear bar; it can be open at the toe.

one-bar shoe
Heeled shoe characterized by a bar crossing the instep and fastened to the quarter by a buckle or button.

T-strap shoe
Heeled shoe derived from the one-bar shoe; the vamp turns into a strap that extends over the instep and ends in a bar.

casual shoe
Comfortable town shoe that is suited to walking; it usually has laces and a sturdy heel.

boot
Shoe that comes up to at least the calf.

thigh-boot
Boot that comes up to the thigh, covering most of it.

ankle boot
Tight-fitting laced or buttoned shoe that comes up over the ankle; it was worn at the turn of the 20th century.

men's shoes

parts of a shoe

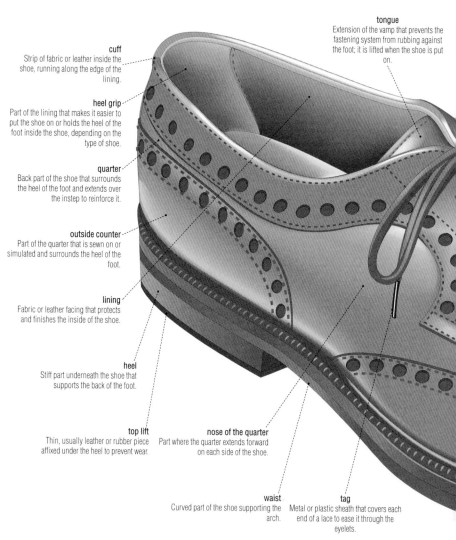

tongue
Extension of the vamp that prevents the fastening system from rubbing against the foot; it is lifted when the shoe is put on.

cuff
Strip of fabric or leather inside the shoe, running along the edge of the lining.

heel grip
Part of the lining that makes it easier to put the shoe on or holds the heel of the foot inside the shoe, depending on the type of shoe.

quarter
Back part of the shoe that surrounds the heel of the foot and extends over the instep to reinforce it.

outside counter
Part of the quarter that is sewn on or simulated and surrounds the heel of the foot.

lining
Fabric or leather facing that protects and finishes the inside of the shoe.

heel
Stiff part underneath the shoe that supports the back of the foot.

top lift
Thin, usually leather or rubber piece affixed under the heel to prevent wear.

nose of the quarter
Part where the quarter extends forward on each side of the shoe.

waist
Curved part of the shoe supporting the arch.

tag
Metal or plastic sheath that covers each end of a lace to ease it through the eyelets.

eyelet tab
Piece sewn on to the nose of the
quarter to reinforce the shoe; the laces
pass through it.

eyelet
Small metal-rimmed hole through
which the lace passes.

shoelace
Narrow cord of fabric or leather, flat or
round, that is threaded through eyelets
or hooks to tighten the shoe.

vamp
Part of the shoe that covers the front of
the foot.

stitch
Visible stitching that both embellishes
and reinforces the shoe.

punch hole
Each of the small holes made in the
shoe to form a decorative pattern.

perforated toe cap
Part of the shoe that covers the toes,
with perforations forming a more or
less conventional decorative pattern.

welt
Thin strip used to join the bottom of the
shoe to the part that goes around the
foot.

outsole
Sturdy piece of rubber or leather that
forms the bottom of the shoe and is in
contact with the ground.

oxford shoe
Shoe where the top of the nose of the quarter is
attached to the vamp, so that only the upper part of
the lacing system opens for the foot to slip in.

blucher oxford
Shoe where the noses of the quarter
can be spread far apart to make the
shoe easier to put on.

chukka
Ankle-high shoe made of light unlined
suede or leather and fastened with
laces with two or three sets of eyelets.

bootee
Shoe often lined with fur, that covers
the ankle.

heavy duty boot
Sturdy shoe, with a thick nonskid sole,
that comes up to the ankle and is tied
with laces.

rubber
Overshoe made of relatively thin
rubber that protects the shoe from mud
and water.

shoeshine kit
Box or case used to store various shoe care products.

shoe polisher
Electric appliance with interchangeable brushes, used to polish or shine shoes.

chamois leather
Soft velvety hide used to shine leather shoes.

insole
Removable object placed inside the shoe to improve its fit, absorb sweat from the foot or keep it dry.

case

shoebrush
Bunches of bristles, horsehair or synthetic fibers attached to a usually wooden handle and used to clean shoes.

shoe polish
Wax-based mixture, packaged in tins, that is applied to leather to make it shine.

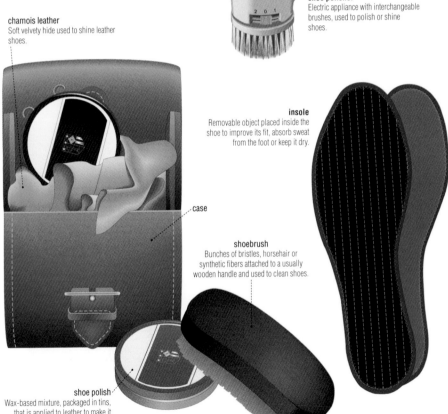

gloves

Items of attire covering the hand to at least the wrist and having finger separations.

women's gloves

gauntlet
Glove to which a somewhat flared cuff is attached at the wrist; it is made of various, often decorative kinds of material.

short glove
Glove covering only the hand or extending slightly over the wrist.

evening glove
Glove where the gauntlet extends over the elbow.

mitt
Often dressy glove, either long or of medium length; it fits tightly along the arm and covers only the first finger joints.

gauntlet
Relatively long part of a glove that extends from the base of the thumb to the top of the glove.

wrist-length glove
Plain unembellished glove with a flared gauntlet covering the wrist.

men's gloves

back of a glove

palm of a glove

fourchette
Narrow strip of leather sewn between the fingers to form their sides.

glove finger
Part of the glove that covers each of the fingers.

palm
Part of the glove that covers the hollow of the hand.

thumb
Part of a glove or a mitten covering the thumb.

seam
Set of stitches joining two pieces of the glove.

stitching
Ribbed seam or embroidery; there are generally three lines of stitching on the back of the glove aligned with points between the fingers.

snap fastener
Fastening mechanism made of a socket disk and a ball disk that snap shut when pressed together.

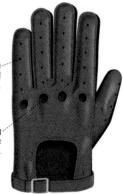

perforation
Each of the small holes in the back of the fingers.

opening
Holes made in the glove over the knuckles.

mitten
Covering with a separation only for the thumb, providing better protection against the cold while allowing the wearer to grasp objects.

driving glove
Short soft, usually leather glove with perforations; it has a vent and other openings that allow the hand to move freely.

men's clothing

double-breasted jacket
Jacket where the front panels overlap when closed; it has a vertical double line of buttons.

collar
Piece sewn onto a garment that finishes or adorns the neck.

lining
Soft fabric cut from the same pattern as the garment inside which it is sewn; it gives body to the garment, embellishes it, hides its seams and makes it warmer.

peaked lapel
Lapel forming a very small angle where it meets the collar.

breast welt pocket
Small decorative pocket to the left of a jacket's lapel where the pocket handkerchief is placed.

flap
Piece of fabric or other material that hangs from the top of a pocket opening to hide it.

sleeve
Part of the garment covering the arm; it can be of various shapes and lengths.

patch pocket
Pocket of various shapes and sizes, made of a piece of material sewn onto the garment's outer surface.

outside ticket pocket
Small pocket placed at waist level above the jacket's right pocket or sometimes inside the lining on the left side.

side back vent
Vertical opening with overlapping edges on each side of the back of a jacket, giving it fullness.

single-breasted jacket
Jacket that is neither close-fitting nor flared.

lining
Soft fabric cut from the same pattern as the garment inside which it is sewn; it gives body to the garment, embellishes it, hides its seams and makes it warmer.

notch
Angle formed where the collar and the lapel meet.

pocket handkerchief
Small delicate handkerchief that adorns the upper pocket of a jacket.

lapel
Part of a garment turned down over the chest, extending the collar.

front
Part of the jacket covering the front of the torso.

flap pocket
Pocket cut into the garment with a flap that can be tucked inside the pocket or worn outside.

back
Part of the jacket covering the back of the torso.

sleeve
Part of the garment covering the arm; it can be of various shapes and lengths.

center back vent
Vertical opening with overlapping edges at the bottom of a jacket; it extends the center seam at the back, giving the jacket fullness.

men's clothing

shirt
Garment covering the torso with a collar, a yoke at the back, shirttails and buttons down the front.

yoke
Variably shaped piece of fabric at the top of the garment, in front, in back or both; it begins at the shoulders or the waist, depending on the garment.

collar
Piece sewn onto a garment that finishes or adorns the neck.

set-in sleeve
Sleeve cut separately from the garment and sewn to the armhole.

collar point
Somewhat pointed tip of the collar.

breast pocket
Pocket of various styles usually on the side of the garment at chest height.

front
Part of the shirt covering the front of the torso.

button
Small, often round object that is sewn onto a garment and used to fasten or adorn it.

pointed tab end
Narrow strip of fabric ending in a point and adorning the sleeve slit.

cuff
Strip of fabric sewn onto the end of the sleeve tightening it and covering the wrist.

buttoned placket
Narrow strip of fabric along the opening of a garment containing the buttonholes.

shirttail
Extension of the bottom of the garment; it can be left hanging out or tucked into the pants.

buttondown collar
Collar whose points are buttoned to the shirtfront.

spread collar
Collar whose points are spread far apart.

collar stay
Small plastic or metal strip inside the collar point that prevents it from curling.

men's clothing

CLOTHING AND PERSONAL ACCESSORIES

necktie
Long narrow strip of fabric placed under the shirt collar and knotted; the front apron, usually wider than the rear one, makes the shirt more attractive.

rear apron
Narrower apron that is threaded through the loop to keep it behind the front apron.

neck end
Part of the necktie that goes around the neck, under the collar.

front apron
Wider apron that makes the shirtfront more attractive.

slip-stitched seam
Seam running the length of the necktie, in the middle of the reverse side.

loop
Flat ring behind the front apron that the rear apron passes through to hold it in place.

lining
Fabric sewn inside the tie to give it body.

ascot tie
Wide necktie with pleats that narrow the part that goes around the neck; it is knotted loosely and worn inside the open collar of a shirt.

bow tie
Short necktie consisting of a knot at the center and a wing on each side of it.

pants
Garment for the lower body; it extends from the waist or the hips to the ankles, covering each leg separately.

waistband
Strip of fabric sewn at the waist of pants forming a hem and holding them in place.

waistband extension
Strip of fabric that extends the waistband and is used to fasten it.

knife pleat
Pleat created by a vertical fold pointing in one direction and of constant width.

belt loop
Thin vertical strip of material sewn at the waist of pants; a belt passes through it to hold the pants in place.

fly
Vertical opening at the middle front of the pants; it closes with buttons or a zipper and is usually covered by the folded edge of the opening.

front top pocket
Front pants pocket that is often curved or diagonal; the opening is cut into the garment or is hidden inside a seam.

crease
Visible mark that remains where the fold has been ironed in.

back pocket
Pocket of various kinds in the back of the pants.

cuff
Folded end of the pant leg.

men's clothing

suspenders
Narrow straps of adjustable length that are often elasticized; they cross in the back, go over the shoulders and fasten to the pants to keep them in place.

elastic webbing
Narrow strip of stretchable sturdy material.

adjustment slide
Flat ring attached to the elastic strap; it can be moved up or down to adjust the length.

suspender clip
Fastening system made up of two hinged tabs; it can replace the leather end on suspenders.

leather end
Usually leather strip used to button the elastic strap to the pants.

button loop
Small slit in a garment through which a button is pushed.

belt
Strap made of various materials often with a buckle; it is worn around the waist to adjust the fit of a garment, hold it in place or adorn it.

tongue
Metal tip that pivots on the buckle's axis and fits into a hole, buckling the belt.

tip
End of the belt that passes through the buckle.

top stitching
Stitching used to embellish the belt.

punch hole
Perforation in the belt through which the tongue passes.

panel
Smooth side of a piece of leather.

buckle
Fastener made up of a ring that secures the two ends of a belt.

belt loop
Flat ring next to the buckle usually made of the same material as the belt; one end of the belt passes through it.

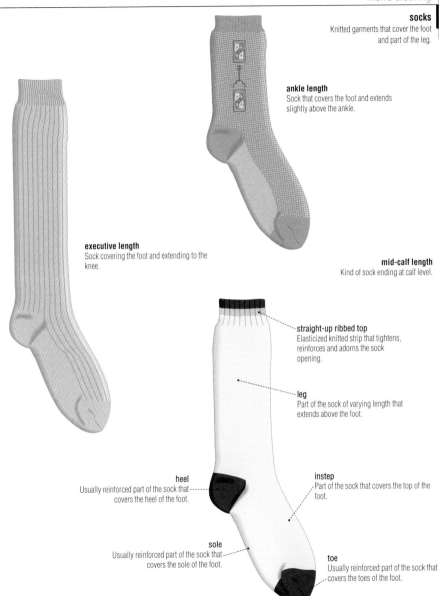

socks
Knitted garments that cover the foot and part of the leg.

ankle length
Sock that covers the foot and extends slightly above the ankle.

executive length
Sock covering the foot and extending to the knee.

mid-calf length
Kind of sock ending at calf level.

straight-up ribbed top
Elasticized knitted strip that tightens, reinforces and adorns the sock opening.

leg
Part of the sock of varying length that extends above the foot.

heel
Usually reinforced part of the sock that covers the heel of the foot.

instep
Part of the sock that covers the top of the foot.

sole
Usually reinforced part of the sock that covers the sole of the foot.

toe
Usually reinforced part of the sock that covers the toes of the foot.

men's clothing

underwear
Garments worn next to the skin and
under other garments.

athletic shirt
Sleeveless tight-fitting undergarment
with a very wide neck and armholes.

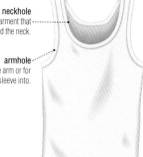

neckhole
Somewhat low part of the garment that
goes around the neck.

armhole
Opening in a garment for the arm or for
fitting a sleeve into.

union suit
Warm undergarment that buttons up the front
and combines a long-sleeved undershirt and
long drawers.

drawers
Undergarment covering the legs; it has
a waistband and is gathered at the
ankles with fine ribbing.

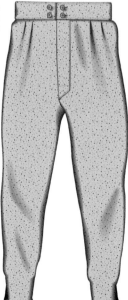

briefs
Short legless undergarment with
elastic at the waist and thighs and a fly.

waistband
Strip of elasticized material fitting
snugly over the hips to hold the
garment in place.

fly
Opening in the front of the briefs.

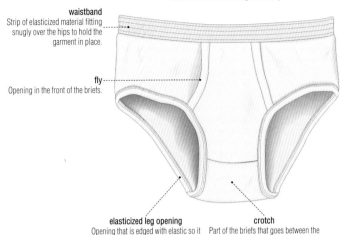

elasticized leg opening
Opening that is edged with elastic so it
fits snugly around the thigh.

crotch
Part of the briefs that goes between the
legs.

bikini briefs
Snug-fitting briefs, low-cut on the hips
and high-cut on the thighs.

boxer shorts
Undergarment covering the tops of the
thighs and held in place by an
elasticized waistband.

men's clothing

coats

Outerwear that is fastened in front; coats are worn over other garments to protect against the cold and inclement weather.

raincoat
Coat, sometimes with a hood, that keeps the rain off because of the kind of material used to make it or because it has been waterproofed.

collar
Piece sewn onto a garment that finishes or adorns the neck.

raglan sleeve
Sleeve extending over the shoulder and attached front and back with a slanted seam running from under the armhole to the neck.

notched lapel
Lapel forming an angle where it meets the collar.

tab
Narrow strip of fabric attached horizontally to the sleeve end to embellish it.

broad welt side pocket
Angled pocket; the outer edge of the opening has a wide welt.

buttonhole
Small slit in a garment through which a button is pushed.

side panel
Extension of the coat that is left hanging loose.

overcoat
Coat ending below the knee and made of heavy fabric, fur or leather.

notched lapel
Lapel forming an angle where it meets the collar.

breast pocket
Pocket of various styles usually on the side of the garment at chest height.

flap pocket
Pocket whose opening is covered by a piece of fabric hanging from the top of it.

breast dart
Pleat that is narrower at the bottom than at the top; it is sewn into the reverse side of the fabric to reduce fullness around the waist.

three-quarter coat
Coat ending above the knee and made of quality fabric, fur or leather, with double-breasted buttoning and outside pockets.

men's clothing

trench coat
Raincoat characterized by double-breasted buttoning, a belt, gun flaps, a collar with lapels, large pockets and tabs on the sleeves and shoulders.

epaulet
Decorative tab attached to the shoulder and sometimes buttoned down; it is inspired by the military uniform.

two-way collar
Collar designed to be worn in various ways.

raglan sleeve
Sleeve extending over the shoulder and attached front and back with a slanted seam running from under the armhole to the neck.

gun flap
Loose front and back yoke used as a decorative element and as protection against wind and rain.

sleeve strap loop
Thin strip of material attached vertically to the sleeve; the sleeve strap threads through it to hold it in place.

double-breasted buttoning
Fastening system made up of two parallel rows of buttons.

belt
Strap made of various materials often with a frame; it is worn around the waist to adjust the fit of a garment, hold it in place or adorn it.

sleeve strap
Narrow strip of fabric that is sewn horizontally at the bottom of the sleeve to make it less full.

belt loop
Flat ring next to the frame usually made of the same material as the belt; one end of the belt passes through it.

broad welt side pocket
Angled pocket; the outer edge of the opening has a wide welt.

frame
Fastener made up of a ring that secures the two ends of a belt.

parka
Sporty waterproof coat that is often padded or fleece-lined; it has big pockets, a front zipper and sometimes a hood.

snap-fastening tab
Strip of material that borders the front opening of a garment, closing with a row of snap fasteners.

zipper
Closure made up of two lengths of tape edged with teeth that interlock by means of a slide.

jacket
Full jacket ending at the waist, where it is gathered so it puffs out; it is often made of leather or waterproof material and has cuffed sleeves.

sheepskin jacket
Three-quarter coat that crosses over in front and has a belt and patch flap pockets; it is usually made of waterproof fabric, leather or suede with a lining and a wide collar made of sheepskin.

hand-warmer pocket
Pocket in the front of the garment above the waist where the hand can be tucked to protect it against the cold and to rest the arm.

elastic waistband
Strip of elasticized fabric that fits snugly around the waist to hold the garment in place.

snap fastener
Fastening mechanism made of a socket disk and a ball disk that snap shut when pressed together.

men's clothing

hood
Headgear attached at the garment's neck that can be pulled over the head as protection against cold, rain and snow.

duffle coat
Hooded casual coat ending at mid-thigh and made of heavy woolen fabric; it is characterized by a yoke and frog closures.

yoke
Variably shaped piece of fabric at the top of the garment, in front, in back or both; it begins at the shoulders or the waist, depending on the garment.

frog
Ornamental loops of braided fabric used to fasten a garment; one serves as the buttonhole and the toggle of the other one passes through it.

patch pocket
Pocket of various shapes and sizes, made of a piece of material sewn onto the garment's outer surface.

toggle fastening
Wooden button in the shape of a small log.

windbreaker
Jacket ending below the waist and made of leather or waterproof material.

drawstring
Thin string that is threaded inside the waistband and adjusts the windbreaker around the hips.

waistband
Hem at the bottom of a garment that finishes it and encases the drawstring, which adjusts the garment around the hips.

coats
Outerwear that is fastened in front and extends at
least the hips; coats are worn over other garments
as protection against cold and inclement weather.

suit
Outfit made up of a skirt or pants and a
long-sleeved jacket made from the
same high-quality fabric.

jacket
Garment with sleeves that extends to the
hips; it is fastened in front with single- or
double-breasted buttoning and
sometimes has a belt.

cape
Very full coat of variable length that covers
the body and arms; it has no sleeves or
armholes and sometimes has a hood and
slits for the arms.

arm slit
Lateral slit through which the arm can
be slipped to give it some freedom of
movement.

skirt
Garment held in place by an inner
waistband or a belt that goes around
the waist; the length of the garment
varies.

pea jacket
Long jacket made of heavy fabric and
characterized by double-breasted
buttoning, a tailored collar and hand-
warmer pockets.

tailored collar
Collar whose fold covers the back of
the neck; its lapels form a V where they
cross on the chest.

hand-warmer pocket
Pocket in the front of the garment
above the waist where the hand can be
tucked to protect it against the cold and
to rest the arm.

mock pocket
Decoration (placket, flap or welt) that
simulates a pocket.

raglan
Somewhat full coat characterized by
raglan sleeves and broad welt side
pockets.

raglan sleeve
Sleeve extending over the shoulder
and attached front and back with a
slanted seam running from under the
armhole to the neck.

fly front closing
Fastening covered by a placket and
consisting of a row of buttons, which
are held in place by buttonholes.

broad welt side pocket
Angled pocket; the outer edge of the
opening has a wide welt.

overcoat
Long-sleeved article of outerwear
made of heavy fabric; it extends to the
calf and closes in front with various
fastening systems.

top coat
Coat fitted at the waist and flared at the
bottom.

car coat
Coat loosely based on a man's three-quarter coat but changing more often to reflect the current style; it is shorter than the garment it covers and together they can make an outfit.

pelerine
Coat with a short pelerine.

pelerine
Cape covering the shoulders and chest.

seam pocket
Pocket where the opening is in a side seam of the garment.

poncho
Cape made from a rectangular piece of material with a hole in the middle for the head to go through.

jacket
Garment with sleeves that extends to the hips; it is fastened in front with single- or double-breasted buttoning and sometimes has a belt.

women's clothing

examples of dresses

Dress: garment made up of a bodice with or without sleeves or a collar and extending into a skirt of variable length.

sheath dress
Unbelted, very tight form-fitting dress.

princess dress
Unbelted dress with a fitted bodice and a full or straight skirt whose cut accentuates the figure.

coat dress
Dress cut like a coat; it fastens all the way up the front and might be lined.

polo dress
Dress whose bodice imitates the knit shirt.

house dress
Simply styled dress made of light comfortable fabric; it usually has front buttons, a belt and patch pockets.

shirtwaist dress
Dress with a bodice that resembles a man's shirt; it usually has a belt and buttons all the way up the front.

wraparound dress
Dress that is open from top to bottom; it is fastened by folding one side over the other and holding them in place with a belt.

tunic dress
Two-piece dress made up of a quite long straight skirt and a straight bodice that hangs down over the skirt, sometimes to the knees.

jumper
Sleeveless dress with a very low-cut neckline and armholes; it is worn over a blouse or a sweater.

drop waist dress
Dress with its waist at hip level.

trapeze dress
Unbelted dress with an increasingly flared skirt that hangs from a tight bodice.

sundress
Very low-cut dress with slim straps, which leave the back and shoulders uncovered.

women's clothing

examples of skirts

Skirt: garment held in place by an inner waistband or a belt that
goes around the waist; the length of the garment varies.

kilt
Pleated wraparound skirt made of tartan; a
usually narrow panel crosses over in front
and fastens with a pin or a button.

gored skirt
Flared skirt made up of several panels
of fabric sewn vertically.

sarong
Beach skirt of variable length and made
from a piece of fabric wrapped around
the waist.

wraparound skirt
Skirt made up of a single panel crossing
over in front or sometimes behind and
buttoning on the side.

sheath skirt
Skirt that is narrow at the waist and fits
tightly over the hips and legs.

ruffled skirt
Skirt made up of several horizontal strips of material in superimposed layers; the free edge falls loose, creating folds.

straight skirt
Skirt that is narrow at the waist, tight-fitting over the hips and falls straight.

gather skirt
Skirt that is gathered at the waist and falls in wide folds.

yoke skirt
Skirt with a piece added on, forming the part from the waist to the hips.

culottes
Garment with a crotch that is hidden by its full folds thus resembling a skirt.

women's clothing

examples of pleats

Pleat: part of a garment folded over to form a double thickness of material.

inverted pleat

Pleat formed by two folds that meet in front and touch on the outside of the fabric, thus forming a hollow in the fabric.

kick pleat

Inverted or flat back pleat at the bottom of a straight skirt, providing greater ease of movement.

accordion pleat

Set of thin upright pleats of uniform width along the grain of the fabric.

top stitched pleat

Pleat extending from a series of ornamental stitches on the outside of the fabric.

knife pleat

Pleat created by a vertical fold pointing in one direction and of constant width.

jackets, vest and sweaters
Examples of garments covering the chest; they are worn over other garments as protection against the cold or as an accessory.

twin-set
Outfit made up of a sweater, often crew neck, and a matching cardigan or vest.

crew neck sweater
Sweater with a close-fitting rounded neck.

vest
Short garment worn over a shirt and under a jacket; it is sleeveless, buttons up the front and has a deep V-neck. The back is made out of lining material.

cardigan
Fine long-sleeved sweater ending at the hips and characterized by front buttoning, a round neck and a ribbed bottom and wrists.

spencer
Tight-fitting unbelted jacket ending at the waist; it has long sleeves and often a collar with lapels.

bolero
Small jacket, sometimes sleeveless and without collar or lapel, that is worn as an accessory only; it ends above the waist and does not fasten.

safari jacket
Lightweight long-sleeved shirt-jacket made of plain weave and having a belt and four pockets.

blazer
Often navy-blue, hip-length jacket characterized by a notched collar, long wide lapels and patch pockets.

gusset pocket
Patch pocket made fuller by an expandable bottom and sides or by an inverted or round pleat in the middle of the pocket.

women's clothing

examples of pants

Pants: garment for the lower body; they extend from the
waist or the hips to the ankles, covering each leg separately.

Bermuda shorts
Long shorts ending above the knee.

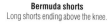

shorts
Very short pants covering only the top
of the thighs.

ski pants
Generally stretchy pants with legs that
narrow toward the ankle, ending in an
footstrap.

bell bottoms
Pants that are tight-fitting to the knee then flare out
and end at the ankle.

footstrap
Strip of elasticized fabric that goes
under the foot to keep the pants
stretched tight.

jumpsuit
Garment that closes at the front and combines pants and a sometimes sleeveless bodice.

overalls
Pants with shoulder straps and a piece that covers the chest.

knickers
Pants with full legs that are gathered below the knee or at the calf.

jeans
Pants made of durable, usually blue fabric with topstitched seams and pockets that are often reinforced by rivets.

pedal pushers
Tight-fitting pants ending at mid-calf and having a slit on the outside of the leg at the knee, which can be fastened in various ways.

women's clothing

examples of blouses

Blouses: women's garments covering the torso and worn directly over underwear; there are many different varieties made of all kinds of fabric.

shirttail
Extension of the bottom of the garment; it can be left hanging out or tucked into the pants.

classic blouse
Front-buttoning blouse with a collar and long sleeves; it is gathered at the wrists and ends at the hips.

mini shirtdress
Full shirt-blouse ending at mid-thigh and usually worn over a skirt or pants; it has a side slit and rounded shirttails.

yoke
Variably shaped piece of fabric at the top of the garment, in front, in back or both; it begins at the shoulders or the waist, depending on the garment.

gather
Small narrow pleat made by drawing thread through the fabric; it is not ironed or sewn down.

crotch piece
Part of the bikini that goes between the legs; it can sometimes be unfastened so the blouse can be put on over the head.

body shirt
Tight-fitting blouse in stretchy fabric and ending in a bikini bottom.

smock
Long unfitted blouse made of soft lightweight material; it is often buttoned in the back and is usually worn over other garments to protect them.

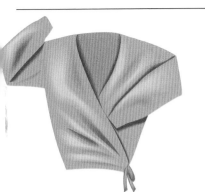

wrapover top
Blouse with two front panels that cross over one another, creating a V-neck; it has ties that fasten at the waist, back or hip.

over-blouse
Straight long-sleeved tunic that is often put on over the head; it is gathered by a belt or a tie at the waist and hangs over a skirt or pants.

middy
Straight full blouse with a sailor collar and no front opening, ending at the hips.

tunic
Straight full blouse ending below the waist.

polo shirt
Usually short-sleeved sweater that has a pointed turned-down collar; it is often fastened with a placket ending at mid-chest.

585

dog ear collar
Turned-down collar characterized by long, fairly wide points, which are rounded at the tips.

shawl collar
Wide turned-down collar with long rounded lapels that partially cross in front.

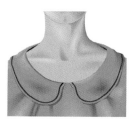

Peter Pan collar
Flat collar of uniform width with rounded tips; it is sewn onto a fairly open neck.

tailored collar
Collar whose fold covers the back of the neck; its lapels form a V where they cross on the chest.

shirt collar
Collar with rounded or tapered points that is sewn onto the neck and turned down along a fold line, which is higher in back than in front.

bow collar
Collar made of a long strip of soft fabric sewn onto a round neck; it can be tied in front in various ways.

jabot
Decoration made up of one or two pieces of fine soft pleated fabric; it is attached at the base of the neck and spreads out over the chest.

sailor collar
Collar that is square in back and has long lapels extending over the chest; it is fastened to a V-neck and, out of modesty, the plunging neckline is often concealed with a piece of fabric.

mandarin collar
Stand-up collar with rounded upper points that come together at the neck, forming a V.

collaret
Piece of delicate, pleated or gathered fabric that adorns the neck of a dress; its shape has varied greatly from one period to another.

bertha collar
Collar made of a strip of fabric of variable width and attached to the edge of a neckline or round neck.

turtleneck
High-necked collar that is folded over; it is usually snug around the neck and does not fasten.

polo collar
Turned-down pointed collar fastened with a buttoned placket, which ends at mid-chest.

cowl neck
Turtleneck that is large enough to be draped over the head, making a kind of hood that frames the face.

stand-up collar
Collar made of a narrow strip of fabric that sticks up from a round neck; its edges meet in front but do not fasten.

women's clothing

underwear

Garments worn next to the skin and
under other garments.

camisole

Short undergarment with an open neck
and shoulder straps; the part covering
the chest can be shaped like a bra.

corselette

Support undergarment combining a
girdle and a bra.

teddy

Garment combining a camisole and briefs.

body suit

Garment combining a bodice and
briefs in a single garment.

panty corselette
Undergarment combining a girdle, a bra and briefs.

princess seaming
Decorative seam running from the shoulder or the armhole to the garment's hem, accentuating the figure.

foundation slip
Undergarment with wide nonadjustable shoulder straps, worn under a see-through dress.

slip
Undergarment with narrow adjustable shoulder straps; the part covering the chest is usually shaped like a bra.

half-slip
Undergarment made up of a lightweight skirt and an elasticized waist, substituting for lining.

wasp-waisted corset
Small corset made up of a bra and garter belt, slimming the figure.

strapless bra
Bra without shoulder straps and with a midriff band that extends to the waist; the cups are preshaped and have underwires and steels.

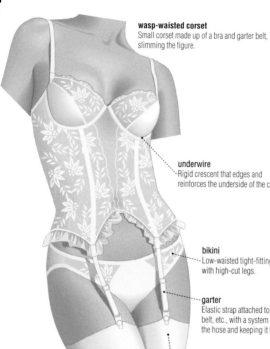

underwire
Rigid crescent that edges and reinforces the underside of the cups.

steel
Narrow flexible strip of metal or plastic inserted into a garment to keep it stiff.

bikini
Low-waisted tight-fitting undergarment with high-cut legs.

garter
Elastic strap attached to a girdle, garter belt, etc., with a system for fastening the hose and keeping it taut.

hose
Relatively light knitted women's garment covering the foot and the leg up to the thigh.

push-up bra
Bra with cups that leave the upper chest bare and with shoulder straps that sit on the outer edge of the shoulder.

décolleté bra
Very low-cut bra with cups that extend upward toward the shoulder straps.

bra
Undergarment made up of cups, shoulder straps and a midriff band, designed to support the chest.

shoulder strap
Narrow strip of fabric that is often adjustable; it goes over the shoulder to connect a garment's front and back.

cup
Main part of the bra that covers and supports the breasts.

girdle
Elasticized undergarment with a stomach panel; it is designed to shape the waist and hips.

midriff band
Strip of stretchable fabric connecting the cups; it varies in width and fastens with hooks.

briefs
Undergarment that extends fairly low over the hips and is held in place by an elasticized waist.

panel
Foundation piece that flattens the stomach.

garter belt
Narrow belt with garters that fastens around the hips.

panty girdle
Girdle usually made up of briefs, with or without legs, and removable garters.

corset
Sturdy undergarment with steels and often garters; it is designed to shape the waist and hips.

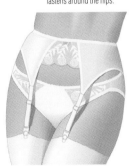

women's clothing

hose

Garments of various stretchy fabrics used to cover the foot and leg; each pair of hose has a different name, depending on its length.

anklet
Sock that covers the foot and extends slightly above the ankle.

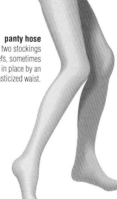

short sock
Light short sock covering only the foot and the ankle.

sock
Sock covering the leg to just below the knee.

net stocking
Stocking made of stretchable mesh.

knee-high sock
Sock covering the foot and extending to the knee.

panty hose
Garment made up of two stockings joined by a pair of briefs, sometimes reinforced and held in place by an elasticized waist.

stocking
Relatively light knitted women's garment covering the foot and the leg up to the thigh.

thigh-high stocking
Stocking ending a little above the knee.

Garments worn by children from birth to about three years of age.

bathing wrap
Absorbent piece of fabric with a hood at one corner; it is wrapped around a baby when it comes out of the bath.

hood
Part of the garment that is pulled over the head.

decorative braid
Narrow thick closely woven piece of fabric that edges or adorns a garment.

false tuck
Strip of material designed to hide a garment's seam or decorate its edge.

bib
Absorbent piece of fabric tied around a child's neck to protect its clothes from food and saliva.

ruffled rumba pants
Undergarment with an elasticized waist that extends to the top of the thighs; it is large enough to be worn over a diaper.

ruching
One of several narrow decorative strips of light fabric, gathered and sewn onto a garment.

nylon rumba tights
Long drawers with feet; they are made of stretchy or knitted fabric and have ruching at the back.

jumpsuit
Low-cut one-piece sleeveless garment with legs and feet.

bunting bag
Hooded coat with a front zipper; it is sewn closed at the bottom and sometimes has no armholes.

shirt
Long-sleeved baby shirt used as an under- or overgarment, depending on its weight; its characteristic lap shoulders allow the shirt's neck to expand when it is being put on.

newborn children's clothing

high-back overalls

Pants extended by a front piece covering the chest and another covering the back, connected with shoulder straps.

adjustable strap
Strip of adjustable fabric that goes over the shoulder to connect a garment's front and back.

bib
Upper part of the overalls, covering the chest from the waist up.

patch pocket
Pocket of various shapes and sizes, made of a piece of material sewn onto the garment's outer surface.

top stitching
Stitches on the right side of the fabric used to embellish and reinforce the garment.

fly
Vertical opening at the middle front of the pants; it closes with buttons or a zipper and is usually covered by the folded edge of the opening.

inside-leg snap-fastening
Part along the inner leg of the garment, where snap fasteners make it easier to put the pants on.

diaper
Absorbent article of clothing used as briefs for babies.

disposable diaper
Throwaway piece of fabric with a waterproof outer layer and usually elasticized leg holes, which allow the child to move freely.

Velcro® closure
Fastening system made up of two strips with surfaces that grip on contact.

waterproof pants
Part of the diaper gathered around the top of the thighs.

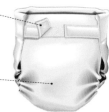

sleepers
Infant nightwear that fastens all the way up the front with snap fasteners.

raglan sleeve
Sleeve extending over the shoulder and attached front and back with a slanted seam running from under the armhole to the neck.

snap-fastening front
A line of snap fasteners on the front of a garment.

blanket sleepers
One-piece long-sleeved nightwear for babies that has legs and feet, a long front zipper and a rear panel, which opens at the waist.

ribbing
Tight elastic knitted strip around the sleeve or the bottom of a garment for tightening, reinforcing and adorning them.

inside-leg snap-fastening
Part along the inner leg of the garment, where snap fasteners make it easier to put the pants on.

grow sleepers
Newborn sleepwear shaped like a bag or with feet; the garment can be lengthened in various ways: here, with snap fasteners at the waist.

crew neck
Rounded neck fitting close to the wearer's neck.

screen print
Pattern printed or sewn on the garment to decorate it.

zipper
Closure made up of two lengths of tape edged with teeth that interlock by means of a slide.

snap-fastening waist
Each of the snap fasteners sewn around the waist so the garment's length can be adjusted.

vinyl grip sole
Outsole whose material or textured surface prevents the foot from slipping.

foot
Part of the garment covering the foot.

sweaters

Garments covering the torso and manufactured by hand or by machine from fabric with varying tightness of weave.

V-neck cardigan
Woolen sweater ending at the hips and characterized by front buttons, a V-neck and ribbing at the bottom and wrists.

hanger loop
Small strap attached to the inside of a garment at the neck and used to hang it.

V-neck
Plunging part of the garment encircling the neck and forming a V over the chest.

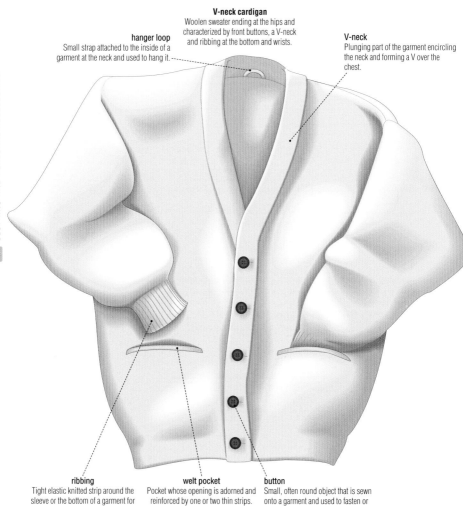

ribbing
Tight elastic knitted strip around the sleeve or the bottom of a garment for tightening, reinforcing and adorning them.

welt pocket
Pocket whose opening is adorned and reinforced by one or two thin strips.

button
Small, often round object that is sewn onto a garment and used to fasten or adorn it.

sweater vest
Sleeveless sweater usually with a wide neck and armholes, intended for wearing over another garment.

buttoned placket
Narrow strip of fabric edging the opening of a knit shirt and containing several buttonholes.

knit shirt
Usually short-sleeved sweater that has a pointed turned-down collar; it is often fastened with a placket ending at mid-chest.

turtleneck
Sweater with a high close-fitting neck made of ribbing that is folded down; it usually has no fastener.

crew neck sweater
Sweater with a close-fitting rounded neck.

cardigan
Fine long-sleeved sweater ending at the hips and characterized by front buttoning, a round neck and a ribbed bottom and wrists.

CLOTHING AND PERSONAL ACCESSORIES

sportswear

Clothing and accessories designed for sports, dancing or acrobatics.

running shoe
Light but sturdy canvas and rubber or leather
shoe worn for sports or leisure.

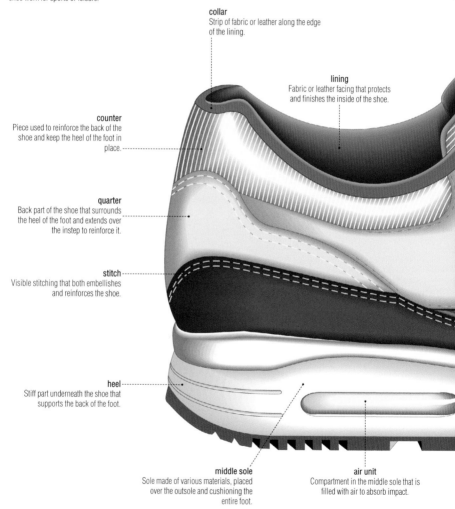

collar
Strip of fabric or leather along the edge
of the lining.

lining
Fabric or leather facing that protects
and finishes the inside of the shoe.

counter
Piece used to reinforce the back of the
shoe and keep the heel of the foot in
place.

quarter
Back part of the shoe that surrounds
the heel of the foot and extends over
the instep to reinforce it.

stitch
Visible stitching that both embellishes
and reinforces the shoe.

heel
Stiff part underneath the shoe that
supports the back of the foot.

middle sole
Sole made of various materials, placed
over the outsole and cushioning the
entire foot.

air unit
Compartment in the middle sole that is
filled with air to absorb impact.

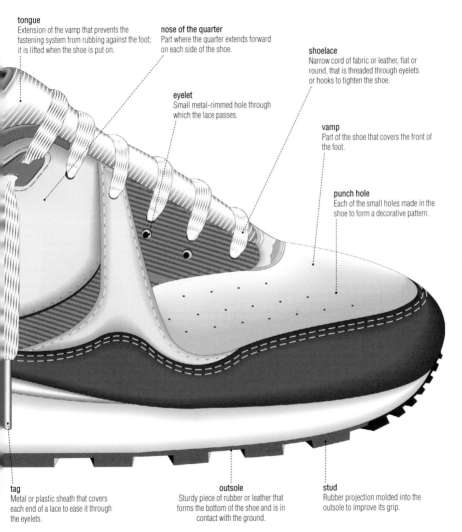

tongue
Extension of the vamp that prevents the fastening system from rubbing against the foot; it is lifted when the shoe is put on.

nose of the quarter
Part where the quarter extends forward on each side of the shoe.

shoelace
Narrow cord of fabric or leather, flat or round, that is threaded through eyelets or hooks to tighten the shoe.

eyelet
Small metal-rimmed hole through which the lace passes.

vamp
Part of the shoe that covers the front of the foot.

punch hole
Each of the small holes made in the shoe to form a decorative pattern.

tag
Metal or plastic sheath that covers each end of a lace to ease it through the eyelets.

outsole
Sturdy piece of rubber or leather that forms the bottom of the shoe and is in contact with the ground.

stud
Rubber projection molded into the outsole to improve its grip.

exercise wear
Clothing appropriate for sports, dancing or acrobatics.

swimming trunks
Low-waisted briefs with very high-cut legs; they are usually stretchy and tight-fitting and are worn by men for swimming.

swimsuit
Women's swimming garment that is tight-fitting and usually stretchy; it can be in one piece or consist of briefs and a bikini top.

leg-warmer
Knitted tube-shaped covering that extends from the ankle to the knee or mid-thigh and keeps the muscles warm.

leotard
Tight-fitting stretch knit garment combining a bodice and briefs.

footless tights
Tight-fitting stretch knit pants that end at the ankle and usually have an elasticized waist.

anorak
Waterproof sports jacket with long
sleeves, a drawstring hood and waist
and gathered wrists.

pants
Garment for the lower body; they
extend from the waist or the hips to the
ankles, covering each leg separately.

tank top
Short, fairly tight low-cut shirt without
sleeves or a collar.

boxer shorts
Briefs covering the top of the thighs;
they are gathered by an elasticized
waist and have an inner bikini bottom.

jewelry

Finely crafted articles of adornment that are valued for their materials (gold, silver, gemstones) and workmanship.

earrings
Article of jewelry worn on the earlobe.

screw earrings
Earrings attached to the earlobe by a small screw behind the ear.

clip earrings
Earrings attached to the earlobe by a spring clip.

pierced earrings
Earrings with a post that passes through the pierced earlobe and is capped with a clasp.

drop earrings
Earrings where the ornamental part hangs down from the ear and varies in shape and length.

hoop earrings
Hoop-shaped earrings with a post that passes through the pierced earlobe and fits into the other end of the ring.

necklaces

Article of jewelry worn around the neck that consists of a band of gold or silver, a circle of set or unset precious stones or pearls strung together.

pendant
Article of jewelry hung from a chain or a necklace.

locket
Usually round or oval pendant that opens to receive a memento of a loved one.

velvet-band choker
Choker consisting of a ribbon to which an ornament is attached.

rope
Necklace that is over 3 ft long and can be looped several times around the neck and knotted over the chest.

opera-length necklace
Necklace that is approximately 30 in long and falls over the chest.

choker
Necklace that sometimes consists of many rows and is worn at the base of the neck.

bib necklace
Ncklace consisting of three or more rows.

matinee-length necklace
Necklace that is approximately 20 in long and falls above the chest.

jewelry

semiprecious stones

Next to precious stones, these stones are the ones whose beauty and durability make them most suitable for jewelry.

amethyst
Stone whose color ranges from pale mauve to deepest purple.

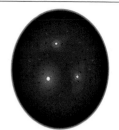

lapis lazuli
Opaque, dark blue stone that is usually speckled; the glittering flecks are proof of its authenticity.

tourmaline
Usually multicolored stone with a rich array of colors from red to pink and green and on to blue.

aquamarine
Stone whose color ranges from whitish-pale blue to a deep blue-aqua color.

topaz
Stone with a wide range of colors, including yellowish-orange (the most common), green (the rarest), pink (the most sought-after), blue, brown and colorless.

opal
Soft opaque stone that is milky-white or quite dark and gives off rainbowlike reflections.

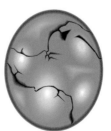

turquoise
Opaque, light blue stone with tinges of green; it often contains brown, gray or black veins.

garnet
Stone whose color ranges from green to yellow to dark red.

precious stones
The value of these four gemstones is based
on their rarity, brilliance and durability.

diamond
The hardest stone is colorless
although there are also blue, yellow
and pink varieties; it is the most
renowned precious stone.

ruby
The rarest of all precious stones is
extremely hard; its color varies from a
bright pinkish-red to a purplish red, which
is the most sought-after color.

sapphire
This stone can be blue, pink, orange,
yellow, green, purple or even colorless;
the most sought-after color is
purplish-blue.

emerald
Stone whose color varies from
greenish-yellow to greenish-blue; an
emerald's value is based more on its
color than on its purity.

rings

Article of jewelry worn on the finger; it
might have symbolic significance.

parts of a ring

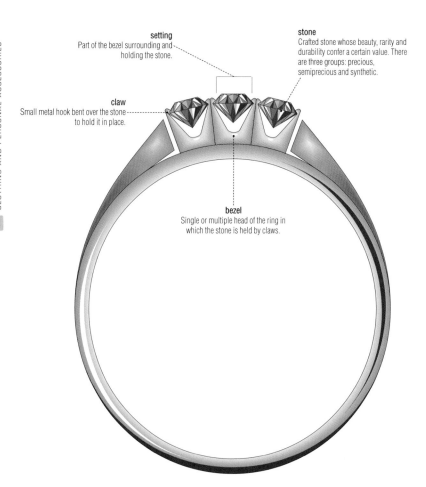

setting
Part of the bezel surrounding and
holding the stone.

stone
Crafted stone whose beauty, rarity and
durability confer a certain value. There
are three groups: precious,
semiprecious and synthetic.

claw
Small metal hook bent over the stone
to hold it in place.

bezel
Single or multiple head of the ring in
which the stone is held by claws.

class ring
Ring worn by a graduate that is
engraved with the school crest and the
student's class year.

signet ring
Ring with a large flat top that is
decorated with initials or coats of arms.

band ring
Ring of uniform width with no bezel.

wedding ring
Ring that is usually a circle of precious metal
or two intertwined circles; it is worn by a
married person on the left ring finger.

engagement ring
Ring that is often decorated with a
stone and is worn by an engaged
woman on her left ring finger.

solitaire ring
Ring decorated with a single jem that is
usually brilliant cut.

charms
Small pieces of costume jewelry attached to a chain or a bracelet.

nameplate
Charm shaped like a small plaque that is usually engraved with a name.

horseshoe
Charm shaped like a horseshoe that is said to bring good luck.

horn
Charm shaped like a horn.

bracelets
Flexible article of jewelry worn on the wrist, the arm or sometimes the ankle.

bangle
Ring-shaped rigid bracelet that slips on over the hand.

identification bracelet
Charm bracelet with a plate that is usually engraved with a first name.

charm bracelet
Bracelet that is made of flattened links and fitted with a clasp.

pins

Article of jewelry used to fasten and adorn a garment.

stickpin
Article of jewelry consisting of a pointed stem and a decorative head; it is usually worn on women's coat lapels.

brooch
Article of jewelry usually worn by women that consists of a pin with a decorative clasp; it is used to fasten a shawl or collar or adorn a bodice.

tie bar
Pincer-shaped article of jewelry clipped halfway up a tie to keep it attached to the shirt.

collar bar
Article of jewelry consisting of a rod with two capped pins; it is used to hold shirt collar points in place.

tiepin
Article of jewelry consisting of a short pointed stem with a head; it is used to hold the two tie aprons together.

nail care

The means of making the hands and especially the nails more beautiful.

manicure set
Range of instruments used for nail care.

cuticle pusher
Spatula-shaped instrument used to push back the strip of skin edging the base of the nail.

cuticle trimmer
Blade with a concave end that follows the shape of the nail; it is used to trim the strip of skin edging the base of the nail (cuticle).

nail shaper
Beveled blade that is also used to trim the skin edging the nail base.

nail file
Ridged metal blade used to file down and smooth nails.

nail scissors
Scissors with short flat, slightly curved edges that are used to trim fingernails and toenails.

eyebrow tweezers
Delicate pincers used to pluck out hairs.

case
Usually rigid-sided case that is shaped to fit the articles it is designed to hold.

zipper
Closure made up of two lengths of tape edged with teeth that interlock by means of a slide.

cuticle scissors
Scissors used to trim cuticles; the thin, flat or curved blades are designed to reach the corners of the nails.

cuticle nippers
Pincers with short convex jaws that are used to trim cuticles.

strap
Strip of leather or sometimes elasticized material keeping the instruments in place.

nail polish
Product applied to the nails that dries to become a clear or colored coating protecting and adorning the nails.

safety scissors
Scissors used to trim nails that are safer to use because of their rounded tips.

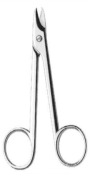

toenail scissors
Scissors with long shanks that are used to trim toenails.

nail clippers
Small pincers with curved jaws and often a file that are used to trim nails.

lever
Rod attached to a fulcrum that brings the jaws together when it is pressed down.

nail buffer
Curved instrument used to smooth and polish the surface of the nails.

nail cleaner
Fine-tipped beveled blade used to clean the nail's outer edge.

chamois leather
Soft velvety hide used to polish nails.

jaw
Cutting edges of the nail clippers.

folding nail file
Ridged metal blade used to file down and smooth nails.

nail whitener pencil
Pencil that is run under the outer edge of the nail to make it white.

emery boards
Cardboard file with a coarse-grained side used to file down the nail and a finer-grained side to smooth it.

makeup

Range of beauty products designed to accentuate the facial features and conceal their imperfections.

facial makeup
Range of beauty products designed to improve the appearance of facial skin.

compact
Small flat case housing a container with pressed powder, a powder puff and a mirror.

pressed powder
Creamy compact powder used to touch up skin tone during the day; it usually comes in a compact.

loose powder brush
Big round-tipped brush with soft flexible bristles; it is used to pick up and apply loose powder.

fan brush
Very flat, very thin brush used to brush away excess loose powder.

synthetic sponge
Sponge used to spread foundation evenly over the skin.

powder puff
Small round, often cotton pad used to apply loose or pressed powder.

blusher brush
Slender round-tipped brush with soft flexible bristles; it is smaller than the loose powder brush and is used to pick up and apply powder blusher.

powder blusher
Powdered product applied to the cheekbones and cheeks to accentuate facial lines and emphasize skin tone.

liquid foundation
Liquid product applied to the face and neck to even out skin tone.

loose powder
Very fine powder that evens out skin tone, controls oily shine, sets foundation and acts as a base for blusher.

makeup

eye makeup
Range of beauty products designed to accentuate the eyes and conceal their imperfections.

eyelash curler
Clamp that closes over the lashes to curl them thus making the eyes look bigger.

sponge-tipped applicator
Brush with a sponge at the tip that is used to apply and blend eyeshadow.

mascara brush
Small brush used to apply mascara to the lashes.

cake mascara
Creamy compact product applied to the lashes with a brush to lengthen or thicken them or change their color.

eyeshadow
Product that comes mainly in pressed powder form and is applied to the eyelids to give them color.

eyebrow pencil
Sharp pencil used to enhance eyebrows or change their shape.

brow brush and lash comb
The brush is used to smooth the brows and the comb to separate the lashes after mascara has been applied.

liquid eyeliner
Dark liquid product applied at the base of the lashes with a fine-tipped brush to accentuate the eyes.

liquid mascara
Liquid product applied to the lashes with a brush to lengthen or thicken them or change their color.

CLOTHING AND PERSONAL ACCESSORIES

lip makeup
Range of beauty products designed to redraw the lipline and accentuate the lips.

lipbrush
Very delicate brush with short stiff bristles; it is used to draw the lipline and apply lipstick inside that line.

lipstick
Waxy product that comes in stick or pencil form and is applied to the lips to give them color.

lipliner
Pencil used to redraw and enhance the lipline.

hygiene

Means and objects used to ensure cleanliness and health.

tissues
Small, disposable pieces of paper used for blowing or wiping the nose.

toilet paper
Thin soft sanitary absorbent paper, usually in a roll, for bathroom use.

hairdressing

Care and styling of the hair using numerous appliances and accessories.

hairbrushes

Instruments made up of fibers of varying stiffness embedded in a backing; they are used to detangle and style hair.

flat-back brush
Brush with bristles set in a soft rubber backing that is used to detangle wet hair.

quill brush
Brush with round-tipped bristles set in a concave backing that massages the scalp; it is used for detangling and arranging hair.

round brush
Brush with bristles that completely encircle the backing so that hair can be given a soft wave.

vent brush
Brush with very widely spaced bristles set in a perforated backing; it is used during blow-drying to detangle hair and style it for a natural look.

hairdressing

combs

Devices with teeth of varying width and closeness that
are used to detangle and style the hair.

pitchfork comb
Comb combining a teaser comb and an
Afro pick.

tail comb
Comb with small, closely spaced teeth
that is used to arrange the hair.

barber comb
Comb with large, widely spaced teeth for
detangling the hair on one side and small,
closely spaced teeth used to arrange the hair
on the other side.

Afro pick
Comb with long, widely spaced teeth
used for detangling and tidying tightly
curled hair without undoing the curls.

teaser comb
Comb whose head has teeth of three
different lengths; it is used to brush up
the hair to give it more body.

rake comb
Comb with broad, widely spaced teeth
for detangling hair without damaging
it.

hair roller
Instrument around which a lock of hair is wrapped to make it curl.

hair roller pin
Pin stuck through the roller to hold the lock of wrapped hair in place.

roller
Cylinder whose length depends on the length of the lock of rolled hair and whose diameter depends on the desired curl size.

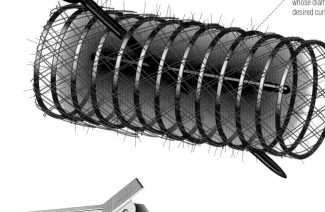

hair clip
Metal pin with elongated jaws that is used during styling to separate out sections of hair not being worked on.

bobby pin
Bent filament with tightly closed arms; it is used to secure a section of hair by holding it firmly in place.

wave clip
Plastic pin with interlocking teeth used to secure a lock of hair.

hairpin
Bent filament with spread arms that is used to loosely secure a section of hair such as a chignon.

barrette
Bobby pin with a clasp; it is used as adornment or to secure a lock of hair or the whole head of hair.

hairdressing

curling iron
Electric appliance used to curl hair.

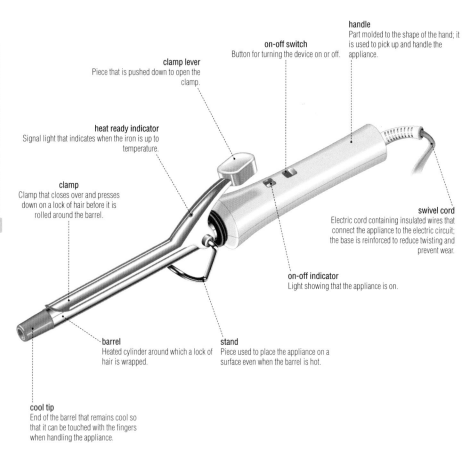

handle
Part molded to the shape of the hand; it is used to pick up and handle the appliance.

on-off switch
Button for turning the device on or off.

clamp lever
Piece that is pushed down to open the clamp.

heat ready indicator
Signal light that indicates when the iron is up to temperature.

clamp
Clamp that closes over and presses down on a lock of hair before it is rolled around the barrel.

swivel cord
Electric cord containing insulated wires that connect the appliance to the electric circuit; the base is reinforced to reduce twisting and prevent wear.

on-off indicator
Light showing that the appliance is on.

barrel
Heated cylinder around which a lock of hair is wrapped.

stand
Piece used to place the appliance on a surface even when the barrel is hot.

cool tip
End of the barrel that remains cool so that it can be touched with the fingers when handling the appliance.

hair dryer
Electric appliance that blows hot air to dry hair.

fan housing
Part of the appliance's frame that houses the motor and the fan that blows hot air.

barrel
Part housing the hair dryer's heating element.

air-inlet grille
Grating through which air is drawn in; it prevents hair and other matter from entering the appliance's housing.

air-outlet grille
Grating through which the hot air is blown; it prevents any contact with the heating element inside.

on-off switch
Button for turning the device on or off.

heat selector switch
Device regulating air temperature.

speed selector switch
Device that regulates fan speed and hence the power of the airflow.

handle
Part used to pick up and handle the appliance.

air concentrator
Piece that fits over the end of the appliance to concentrate the flow of hot air over the hair.

power supply cord
Flexible electric wire housing the leads connecting the appliance to the electric circuit.

hang-up ring
Ring for hanging the hair dryer on a hook when it is not in use.

body care

Range of methods promoting physical hygiene and beauty.

CLOTHING AND PERSONAL ACCESSORIES

stopper
Device inserted into the neck of the bottle or screwed onto it to close the bottle.

bottle
Small bottle that is often made of glass.

eau de parfum
Scented concoction added to a water/alcohol mix; it is more concentrated and lingers longer than eau de toilette.

bubble bath
Product that is poured into the bath under the faucet water; it produces large amounts of foam and scents and colors the bathwater.

deodorant
Product applied to the armpits that eliminates or reduces perspiration odors.

eau de toilette
Scented concoction that is more diluted with a water/alcohol mix than eau de parfum.

haircolor
Product applied to the hair to color it.

toilet soap
Fragrant fat-based product that is used for washing the body.

hair conditioner
Product applied to the hair after shampooing to strengthen it, improve its appearance and make styling easier.

shampoo
Product used to wash the hair and the scalp.

washcloth
Bath mitt usually made of terry cloth; it fits over the
hand and is used for washing all or part of the body.

bath towel
Usually terry cloth article of bath linen used for drying
parts of the body after bathing.

natural sponge
Particularly soft, flexible absorbent
material that comes from the dried
skeleton of marine animals and is used
for bathing.

washcloth
Small square towel that is usually made of terry
cloth and is used for washing the face.

massage glove
Rough glove used for rubbing the body to exfoliate the
skin and stimulate the circulation.

loofah
Particularly soft, flexible absorbent
material that comes from dried plant
matter and is used for bathing.

bath sheet
Large bath towel used for drying the body after a shower or bath.

bath brush
Brush with relatively soft, flexible
bristles that is used for scrubbing the
body during baths or showers.

back brush
Bath brush with a handle long enough
to scrub all of the back.

shaving

Range of appliances and accessories used to cut the beard close to the skin.

CLOTHING AND PERSONAL ACCESSORIES

electric razor
Razor with power-activated blades.

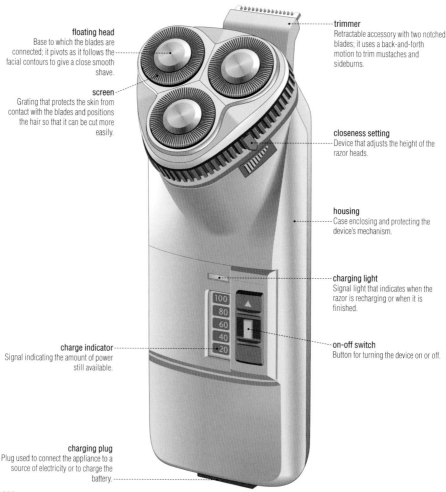

floating head
Base to which the blades are connected; it pivots as it follows the facial contours to give a close smooth shave.

screen
Grating that protects the skin from contact with the blades and positions the hair so that it can be cut more easily.

trimmer
Retractable accessory with two notched blades; it uses a back-and-forth motion to trim mustaches and sideburns.

closeness setting
Device that adjusts the height of the razor heads.

housing
Case enclosing and protecting the device's mechanism.

charging light
Signal light that indicates when the razor is recharging or when it is finished.

charge indicator
Signal indicating the amount of power still available.

on-off switch
Button for turning the device on or off.

charging plug
Plug used to connect the appliance to a source of electricity or to charge the battery.

cleaning brush
Brush used for cleaning the blades and inside the heads.

plug adapter
Electric accessory adapting a plug to an outlet of a different configuration.

shaving foam
Product applied to the beard before shaving to soften the hairs and help the blade glide more smoothly.

power cord
Flexible electric wire housing the leads connecting the appliance to the electric circuit.

shaving brush
Brush with long firm bristles that is used to apply a thin coat of shaving lather to the face.

bristle
Part of the shaving brush made of hog's hair or, more rarely, badger hair.

after shave
Lotion applied to the face after shaving to soothe and scent the skin.

shaving mug
Container in which the shaving lather is made before it is applied to the beard.

shaving

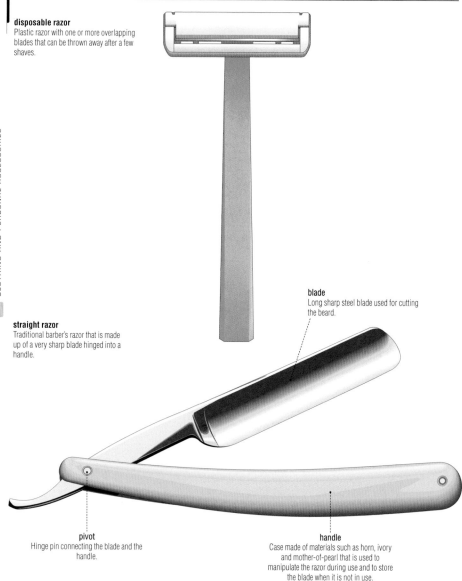

disposable razor
Plastic razor with one or more overlapping blades that can be thrown away after a few shaves.

straight razor
Traditional barber's razor that is made up of a very sharp blade hinged into a handle.

blade
Long sharp steel blade used for cutting the beard.

pivot
Hinge pin connecting the blade and the handle.

handle
Case made of materials such as horn, ivory and mother-of-pearl that is used to manipulate the razor during use and to store the blade when it is not in use.

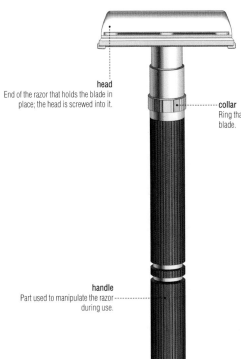

double-edged razor
Manual metal razor; it has a double-edged blade that can be replaced as needed.

head
End of the razor that holds the blade in place; the head is screwed into it.

collar
Ring that adjusts the angle of the blade.

handle
Part used to manipulate the razor during use.

CLOTHING AND PERSONAL ACCESSORIES

blade injector
Small metal box containing spare blades.

double-edged blade
Disposable blade with two cutting edges doubling the blade's useful life.

dental care

Procedures to care for the mouth and especially the teeth that include brushing, flossing and using mouthwash.

toothbrush
Instrument that uses a back-and-forth motion to clean teeth.

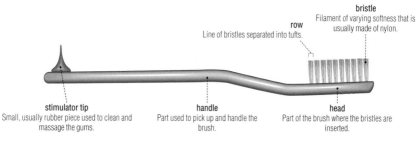

row
Line of bristles separated into tufts.

bristle
Filament of varying softness that is usually made of nylon.

stimulator tip
Small, usually rubber piece used to clean and massage the gums.

handle
Part used to pick up and handle the brush.

head
Part of the brush where the bristles are inserted.

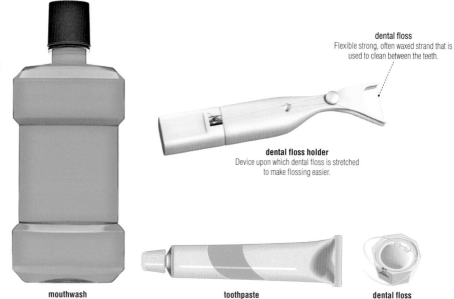

dental floss
Flexible strong, often waxed strand that is used to clean between the teeth.

dental floss holder
Device upon which dental floss is stretched to make flossing easier.

mouthwash
Liquid used to gargle, rinse the mouth and freshen the breath.

toothpaste
Paste or gel used to clean teeth and gums by brushing it over the teeth and making it foam.

dental floss
Flexible strong, often waxed strand that is used to clean between the teeth.

oral hygiene center
Electric appliance consisting of a toothbrush and an oral irrigator.

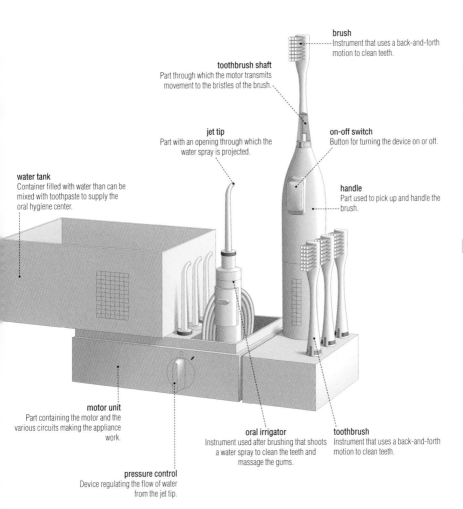

brush
Instrument that uses a back-and-forth motion to clean teeth.

toothbrush shaft
Part through which the motor transmits movement to the bristles of the brush.

jet tip
Part with an opening through which the water spray is projected.

on-off switch
Button for turning the device on or off.

water tank
Container filled with water than can be mixed with toothpaste to supply the oral hygiene center.

handle
Part used to pick up and handle the brush.

motor unit
Part containing the motor and the various circuits making the appliance work.

oral irrigator
Instrument used after brushing that shoots a water spray to clean the teeth and massage the gums.

toothbrush
Instrument that uses a back-and-forth motion to clean teeth.

pressure control
Device regulating the flow of water from the jet tip.

eyeglasses

Lenses set in frames that are placed in front of the eyes to correct vision or to protect the eyes from the Sun's brilliant rays.

eyeglasses parts

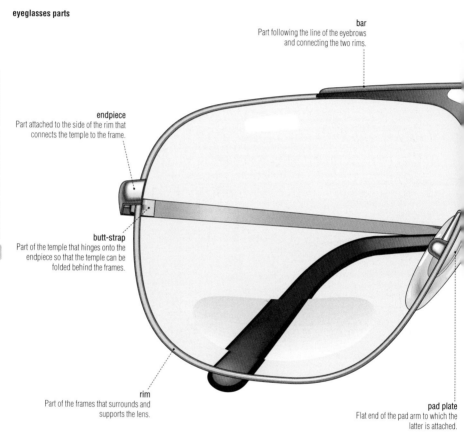

bar
Part following the line of the eyebrows and connecting the two rims.

endpiece
Part attached to the side of the rim that connects the temple to the frame.

butt-strap
Part of the temple that hinges onto the endpiece so that the temple can be folded behind the frames.

rim
Part of the frames that surrounds and supports the lens.

pad plate
Flat end of the pad arm to which the latter is attached.

glass lens
Transparent lens with optical characteristics designed for the needs of a specific person and shaped to fit a specific frame.

bridge
Part of the frames that connects the two lens rims and rests on the nose.

temple
Hinged stem connected to the side of the rim; the end of it bends behind the ear to hold the lenses in place in front of the eyes.

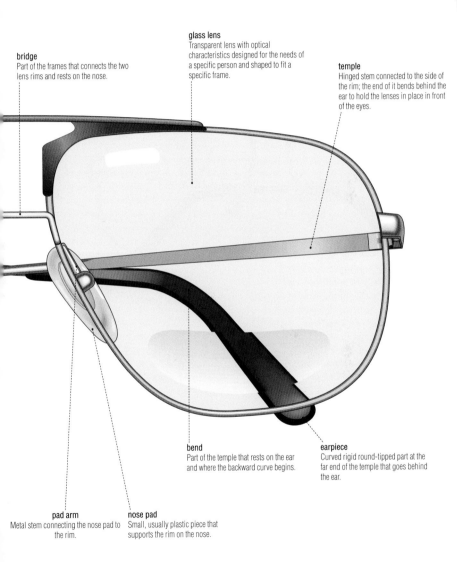

bend
Part of the temple that rests on the ear and where the backward curve begins.

earpiece
Curved rigid round-tipped part at the far end of the temple that goes behind the ear.

pad arm
Metal stem connecting the nose pad to the rim.

nose pad
Small, usually plastic piece that supports the rim on the nose.

eyeglasses

frames
Mounting that supports the lenses and holds them in place in front of the eyes.

distance
Upper part of a bifocal lens that corrects nearsightedness.

bifocal len
Glasses with two parts: one to corre farsightedness and the other fc nearsightednes

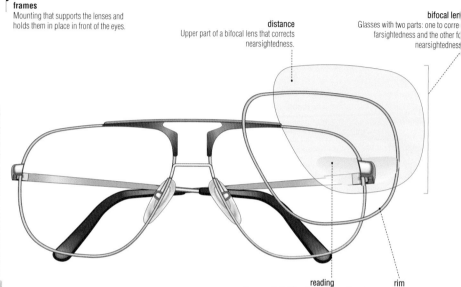

reading
Lower part of a bifocal lens that corrects farsightedness.

rim
Part of the frames that surrounds and supports the lens.

examples of eyeglasses
The shape of glasses varies depending on the period and their use (e.g., correcting far- or nearsightedness, protecting the eye, magnifying).

pince-nez
Glasses whose frame has a spring bridge that grips the nose.

lorgnette
Glasses held in front of the eyes by a handle attached to the side of one rim.

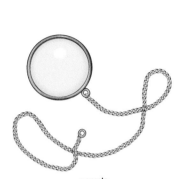

monocle
Single lens held in place under the ridge of the eyebrow.

scissors-glasses
Lorgnette whose lenses fold back over one another and can be slipped into the handle, which also acts as a case.

opera glasses
Optical magnifying instrument held in front of the eyes; it is used for looking at relatively close objects such as at the theater.

half-glasses
Glasses with half lenses to correct farsightedness; the empty space above them is used to see distances.

sunglasses
Glasses with lenses that filter the sun's glare to protect the eyes.

contact lenses

Transparent visual aid placed over the cornea to correct defective vision.

disposable contact lens
Soft lens that lasts from one to 30 days.

soft contact lens
Very thin lens that molds perfectly to the shape of the eye and lasts from one to two years.

hard contact lens
Thicker than the soft contact lens, this lens lasts from two to 10 years.

left side
Place where the lens worn in the left eye is kept.

right side
Place where the lens worn in the right eye is kept.

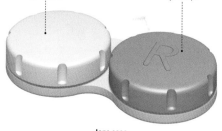

lens case
Container in which the lenses are kept bathed in a multipurpose solution.

multipurpose solution
Product that cleans, rinses, disinfects and conserves the lenses.

lubricant eye drops
Product applied in drops to the eyes to moisten them; the lens does not have to be removed.

Personal articles made of leather or fake leather.

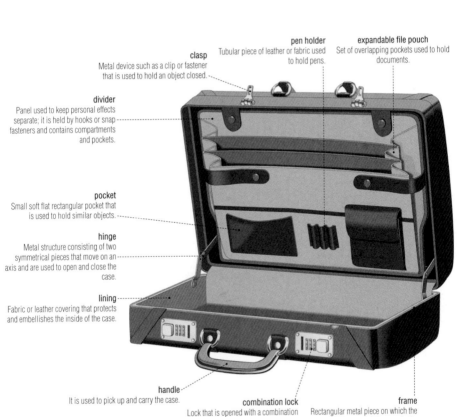

attaché case
Small plain case with rigid sides that is used to carry documents.

pen holder
Tubular piece of leather or fabric used to hold pens.

expandable file pouch
Set of overlapping pockets used to hold documents.

clasp
Metal device such as a clip or fastener that is used to hold an object closed.

divider
Panel used to keep personal effects separate; it is held by hooks or snap fasteners and contains compartments and pockets.

pocket
Small soft flat rectangular pocket that is used to hold similar objects.

hinge
Metal structure consisting of two symmetrical pieces that move on an axis and are used to open and close the case.

lining
Fabric or leather covering that protects and embellishes the inside of the case.

handle
It is used to pick up and carry the case.

combination lock
Lock that is opened with a combination of numbers.

frame
Rectangular metal piece on which the shell is mounted; it supports the hinges, locks and handle.

CLOTHING AND PERSONAL ACCESSORIES

leather goods

bottom-fold portfolio
Briefcase with a handle; its sides expand to accommodate more documents or books.

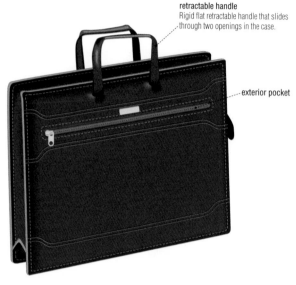

retractable handle
Rigid flat retractable handle that slides through two openings in the case.

exterior pocket

briefcase
Rectangular bag with compartments that is used to carry items such as documents, files and books.

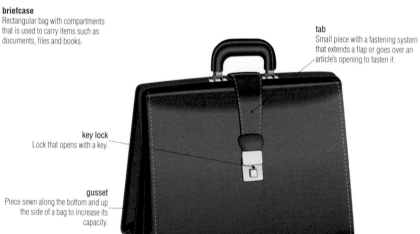

tab
Small piece with a fastening system that extends a flap or goes over an article's opening to fasten it.

key lock
Lock that opens with a key.

gusset
Piece sewn along the bottom and up the side of a bag to increase its capacity.

checkbook/secretary clutch
Article with compartments of various sizes that is intended to hold identity papers, cards, banknotes, change, a pen and a checkbook.

trimming
Metal piece used to reinforce the edge or the corner of certain articles.

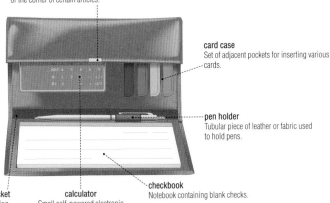

card case
Set of adjacent pockets for inserting various cards.

pen holder
Tubular piece of leather or fabric used to hold pens.

hidden pocket
Pocket with a hidden opening.

calculator
Small self-powered electronic instrument used to automatically make numerical calculations.

checkbook
Notebook containing blank checks.

card case
Article used to hold, organize and protect identity papers and other cards while making them easily visible.

bill compartment
Flat compartment between the back and the inside of a wallet or a card case where banknotes are kept.

windows
Transparent compartments that hold photographs or identity cards.

tab
Small piece with a fastening system that extends a flap or goes over an article's opening to fasten it.

slot
Narrow elongated opening into which a card is inserted with a part of it projecting so it can be easily recognized.

ID window
A window behind which an identity cards is inserted to protect it and make its front side visible.

leather goods

purse
Small soft-sided bag with a zipper or
clasp that is used to store change and
sometimes banknotes.

billfold
Case with a number of dividers that is
folded in half and used only for
banknotes.

coin purse
Small case of various sizes that is
designed to hold change and is usually
carried in a pocket.

checkbook case
Case that protects a checkbook from
handling and rubbing against the
inside of a pocket or bag.

underarm portfolio
Slim briefcase with only one
compartment.

wallet
Article with compartments of various sizes that is designed to hold identity papers, cards, banknotes and change.

passport case
Case usually separated into several compartments; one of them is shaped to hold and protect a passport.

key case
Case accommodating a number of keys that is designed to protect a bag or garment from contact with them.

writing case
Article for holding correspondence materials such as paper and a pen; it has a rigid surface for writing.

eyeglasses case
Holder with relatively rigid sides that is shaped to fit glasses and used to carry and protect them.

handbags

Relatively soft and light accessory that contains a pocket and is carried in the hand, under the arm or over the shoulder; it is used to carry various objects.

satchel bag
Sturdy bag with a handle and sometimes shoulder straps; it combines a handbag with a briefcase.

handle
It is used to pick up and carry the bag.

flap
Piece sometimes equipped with a fastening system that goes over the opening of an object to close it.

clasp
Metal device such as a clip or fastener that is used to hold an object closed.

lock
Mechanism for an owner to secure an article using a key or a combination.

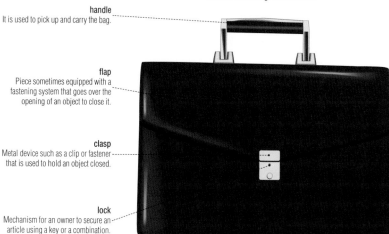

carrier bag
Large sturdy bag with handles that is used to carry groceries.

shopping bag
Large carrier bag.

box bag
Rigid-sided bag with one or two
handles.

hobo bag
Bag whose bottom consists of a strip that comes
up each side as far as the opening and then forms
a point where the shoulder strap is attached.

drawstring bag
Soft cylindrical bag with only one
compartment that closes with a drawstring
and has a shoulder strap.

drawstring bag
Soft-sided cylindrical flat-bottomed
bag with a single compartment that
might have handles or a shoulder
strap.

eyelet
Small metal-rimmed hole through
which the drawstring passes.

drawstring
Narrow leather or fabric cord that is flat
or round; it is threaded through the
eyelets and used to close the bag.

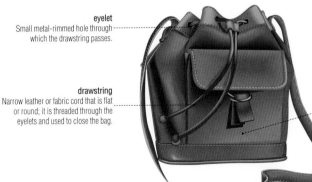

front pocket

CLOTHING AND PERSONAL ACCESSORIES

tote bag
Fairly large bag having neither divider
nor pocket but with a shoulder strap; it
is practical, simple and sturdy.

muff
Small light flat bag with a cord that
hangs from the wrist; it is used for
carrying very small objects.

gusset
Piece sewn along the bottom and up
the side of a bag to increase its
capacity.

duffel bag
Cylindrical bag usually with a zipper
along its entire length; it has two
symmetrical handles or a shoulder strap.

accordion bag
Bag that has soft adjacent pockets with
gussets and often zippers; the whole bag
is closed with a flap.

men's bag
Small plain, usually rectangular bag
for men with a handle and sometimes a
shoulder strap.

sea bag
Large, usually leather-bottomed
drawstring bag with a shoulder strap
attached down the side.

shoulder bag
Bag with an adjustable shoulder strap
and a flap or zipper closure.

buckle
Fastener made up of a ring that secures
the two ends of a shoulder strap.

shoulder strap
Long belt often with a buckle to adjust
it; it is used to carry the bag over the
shoulder or diagonally across the
chest.

luggage

Articles such as suitcases, boxes and bags that are used to store and protect items packed for a trip.

CLOTHING AND PERSONAL ACCESSORIES

tote bag
Light travel bag with soft sides and
only one compartment.

carry-on bag
Travel bag that can be carried into an
airplane cabin because its dimensions
do not exceed the limits set by carriers.

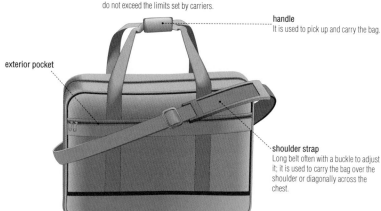

handle
It is used to pick up and carry the bag.

exterior pocket

shoulder strap
Long belt often with a buckle to adjust
it; it is used to carry the bag over the
shoulder or diagonally across the
chest.

Pullman case
Large rectangular piece of hand luggage that is often equipped with wheels to facilitate transport.

frame
Rectangular metal piece on which the shell is mounted; it supports the hinges, locks and handle.

handle
It is used to pick up and carry the suitcase.

pull strap
Leash attached to the suitcase that is placed over the wrist to pull the suitcase along on its wheels.

identification tag
Small transparent case attached to a suitcase; a label with the owner's name and address is inserted inside it.

wheel
Small castor attached to a suitcase so that it can be rolled rather than carried.

trim
Parts made of various materials designed to reinforce the bottom of the suitcase.

painting and drawing

Arts that use graphics and color to represent or suggest visible or imagined concepts on a surface.

equipment

Materials, instruments and accessories used to create a drawing or painting.

watercolor/gouache tube
Tube containing watercolor or gouache in paste form.

watercolor/gouache cakes
Small watercolor or gouache disks inserted into cells to prevent the colors from mixing.

dry pastel
Mixture of pigment powder agglutinated using a gum-based binder, then shaped into sticks and dried.

wax crayons
Sticks composed of pigment molded with wax.

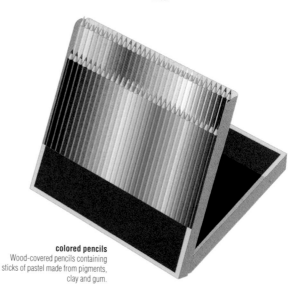

oil pastel
Mixture of pigments, wax and sometimes oily substances in stick form.

colored pencils
Wood-covered pencils containing sticks of pastel made from pigments, clay and gum.

oil/acrylic paint
Oil-based or acrylic pigment that comes in a tube; the artist uses oil or essences to dilute it and prepare it for application.

ink
Liquid preparation, black or colored, used to write or draw.

marker
Bevel-tipped color felt pen of variable size.

felt tip pen
Pen whose felt tip is permeated with ink; it comes in a variety of colors.

fan brush
Brush used to achieve color gradations by blending colors that have already been applied to a canvas.

charcoal
Stick of charcoal used for sketching; it erases easily.

brush
Natural or synthetic bristles attached to a handle, used for spreading paint, varnish or stain on a base.

palette knife
Instrument with a trowel-shaped blade used to mix colors and to spread them on and remove them from the canvas.

reservoir-nib pen
Drawing instrument with a curved tip containing a small amount of ink.

spatula
Instrument with a flat flexible blade used to mix colors, spread them on a canvas or scrape down the palette.

flat brush
Brush made from natural or synthetic bristles affixed to a handle and used mostly for oil painting on large surfaces.

sumi-e brush
Brush made from natural bristles affixed to a bamboo handle and used for drawing with India ink.

movie set

Sets, materials and personnel needed to shoot a movie or a television program.

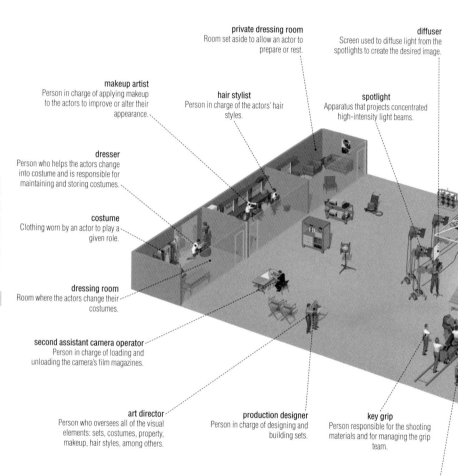

private dressing room
Room set aside to allow an actor to prepare or rest.

diffuser
Screen used to diffuse light from the spotlights to create the desired image.

makeup artist
Person in charge of applying makeup to the actors to improve or alter their appearance.

hair stylist
Person in charge of the actors' hair styles.

spotlight
Apparatus that projects concentrated high-intensity light beams.

dresser
Person who helps the actors change into costume and is responsible for maintaining and storing costumes.

costume
Clothing worn by an actor to play a given role.

dressing room
Room where the actors change their costumes.

second assistant camera operator
Person in charge of loading and unloading the camera's film magazines.

art director
Person who oversees all of the visual elements: sets, costumes, property, makeup, hair styles, among others.

production designer
Person in charge of designing and building sets.

key grip
Person responsible for the shooting materials and for managing the grip team.

director's control monitors
Display screen for checking the quality of the film frame.

director of photography
Person responsible for the technical and artistic quality of the image.

actress
Female actor performing a role.

set
Collective term for the elements that reproduce the setting where the action takes place.

gaffer
Person responsible for lighting and for managing the team of electricians.

lighting grid
Grid used to hold the spotlights.

set dresser
Person in charge of arranging set elements.

property man
Person responsible for locating and maintaining property.

boom operator
Person who handles the boom, installs the stationary microphones and supplies the sound film.

sound engineer
Person responsible for capturing and recording sound and for managing the team of boom operators.

stills photographer
Person who takes photographs during the shooting; these may be used for reference purposes from one shot to the next or as promotional material.

continuity person
Person who records all the technical and artistic details during shooting to ensure continuity.

director
Person in charge of the technical and artistic direction while a movie or a television program is being shot.

producer
Person in charge of the financing and administration of a film or television program.

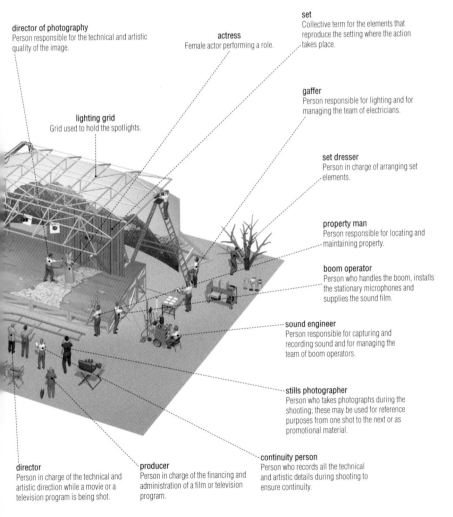

theater

Establishment built to present plays, shows, dance performances, concerts and so forth.

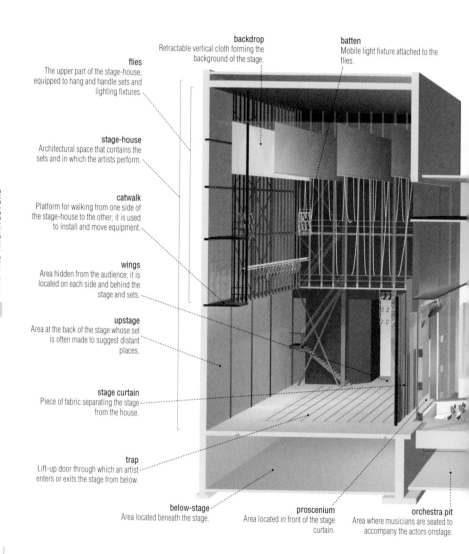

backdrop
Retractable vertical cloth forming the background of the stage.

batten
Mobile light fixture attached to the flies.

flies
The upper part of the stage-house, equipped to hang and handle sets and lighting fixtures.

stage-house
Architectural space that contains the sets and in which the artists perform.

catwalk
Platform for walking from one side of the stage-house to the other; it is used to install and move equipment.

wings
Area hidden from the audience; it is located on each side and behind the stage and sets.

upstage
Area at the back of the stage whose set is often made to suggest distant places.

stage curtain
Piece of fabric separating the stage from the house.

trap
Lift-up door through which an artist enters or exits the stage from below.

below-stage
Area located beneath the stage.

proscenium
Area located in front of the stage curtain.

orchestra pit
Area where musicians are seated to accompany the actors onstage.

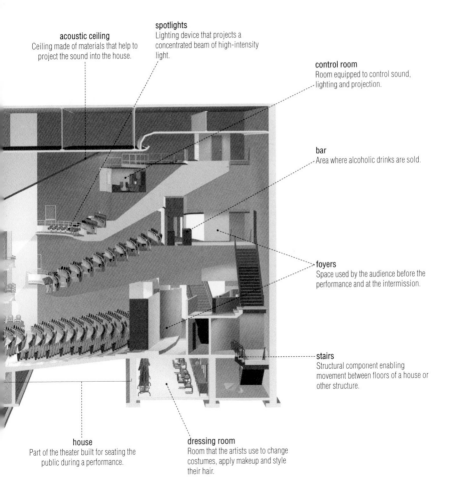

acoustic ceiling
Ceiling made of materials that help to project the sound into the house.

spotlights
Lighting device that projects a concentrated beam of high-intensity light.

control room
Room equipped to control sound, lighting and projection.

bar
Area where alcoholic drinks are sold.

foyers
Space used by the audience before the performance and at the intermission.

stairs
Structural component enabling movement between floors of a house or other structure.

house
Part of the theater built for seating the public during a performance.

dressing room
Room that the artists use to change costumes, apply makeup and style their hair.

photography

Process that captures an image on a light-sensitive surface by admitting light through a shutter.

single-lens reflex (SLR) camera: front view
Still camera with an interchangeable lens that can be used for both viewing and shooting, hence the term "reflex".

accessory shoe
Device for attaching an accessory to the camera (usually an external flash).

exposure adjustment knob
Knob that can deliberately underexpose or overexpose a film when the camera is in automatic exposure mode.

film advance mode
Control button used to advance the film in the camera body (frame by frame or continuously).

command control dial
Dial used to adjust the various parameters of a mode.

exposure mode
Button for choosing an automatic, semiautomatic or manual setting to control the amount of light that comes in contact with the film.

multiple exposure mode
Control button that blocks the film from advancing to create multiple exposures (several images superimposed on the same frame).

film speed
Control button that sets the film's sensitivity to light as expressed by the ISO or ASA number; the higher the number, the more sensitive the film.

depth-of-field preview button
Button that closes the diaphragm so that the relative clarity of various depths can be seen through the viewfinder.

camera body
Rigid sturdy box that contains the camera's mechanism and shields the film from light.

focus mode selector
Button that allows the user to choose between an automatic or manual focus to ensure a clear image.

shutter release button
Button that controls the exposure through control of the focal plane shutter opening.

objective lens
Optical system made up of a set of lenses fixed on a mount; it allows a clear image to be produced on film.

single-lens reflex (SLR) camera: camera back

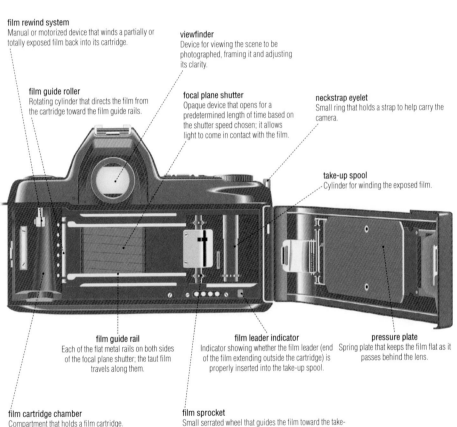

film rewind system
Manual or motorized device that winds a partially or totally exposed film back into its cartridge.

viewfinder
Device for viewing the scene to be photographed, framing it and adjusting its clarity.

film guide roller
Rotating cylinder that directs the film from the cartridge toward the film guide rails.

focal plane shutter
Opaque device that opens for a predetermined length of time based on the shutter speed chosen; it allows light to come in contact with the film.

neckstrap eyelet
Small ring that holds a strap to help carry the camera.

take-up spool
Cylinder for winding the exposed film.

film guide rail
Each of the flat metal rails on both sides of the focal plane shutter; the taut film travels along them.

film leader indicator
Indicator showing whether the film leader (end of the film extending outside the cartridge) is properly inserted into the take-up spool.

pressure plate
Spring plate that keeps the film flat as it passes behind the lens.

film cartridge chamber
Compartment that holds a film cartridge.

film sprocket
Small serrated wheel that guides the film toward the take-up spool.

photography

digital reflex camera: control panel

ARTS AND ARCHITECTURE

sensitivity
Value describing the sensor's sensitivity to light, generally expressed as an ISO index.

metering mode
Method of measuring the intensity of the light hitting and reflected by a subject in order to determine the exposure required.

aperture
Number indicating the aperture of the diaphragm, measured as an f-stop number (the higher the f-stop number, the smaller the aperture).

shutter speed
Number indicating the interval of time during which the sensor should be exposed to light, generally measured in fractions of a second.

frames remaining/timer
Display of the number of frames remaining or the time before the taking of a photograph set with the timer.

white balance
Correction of colors to compensate for ambient light (daylight, fluorescent or tungsten lighting, etc.)

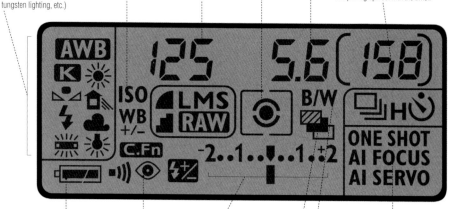

battery level
Indicator that displays the level of energy in the batteries that supply power to the camera.

exposure correction
Number representing the modification made to the exposure data when the user wishes to deliberately underexpose or overexpose the subject.

autofocus
Automatic focusing function that ensures a sharp image.

red-eye reduction
Mechanism that reduces the red-eye effect by producing a small flash before the main flash goes off.

bracketing
Procedure consisting of photographing a single subject several times while varying the exposure index or the white balance.

black-and-white
Function enabling an image to be recorded using only white, black, and shades of gray.

digital reflex camera: camera back
Reflex camera that contains a sensor and a
microprocessor rather than film; they record and store
images in digital form on a memory card.

liquid crystal display
Screen that uses light reflected off
liquid crystals to display alphanumeric
data or images.

viewfinder
Device for viewing the scene to be
photographed, framing it and adjusting
its clarity.

compact memory card
Removable rigid card; it is a storage
medium for photographs taken with a
digital camera.

power switch
Button for turning the device on or off.

image review button
Button that displays recorded images.

erase button
Button that erases a recorded image from
memory.

four-way selector
Button for selecting from the various
menus or scrolling through the
recorded images.

video and digital terminals
Devices for attaching a camera to a television or
a computer.

ARTS AND ARCHITECTURE

ARTS AND ARCHITECTURE

cross section of a reflex camera
A slanted mirror allows the user to view and shoot at the same time; the mirror flips up when the shutter release button is pressed.

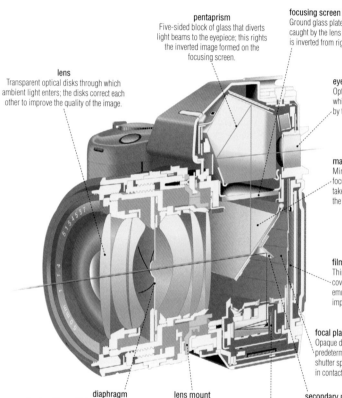

pentaprism
Five-sided block of glass that diverts light beams to the eyepiece; this rights the inverted image formed on the focusing screen.

focusing screen
Ground glass plate on which the image caught by the lens is formed; at this point, it is inverted from right to left.

lens
Transparent optical disks through which ambient light enters; the disks correct each other to improve the quality of the image.

eyepiece
Optical disk or system of disks through which the eye sees the image produced by the lens.

main reflex mirror
Mirror that redirects light toward the focusing screen; when the photo is taken, it retracts so that light reaches the film.

film
Thin flexible transparent band that is covered with a light-sensitive emulsion, which allows images to be imprinted.

focal plane shutter
Opaque device that opens for a predetermined length of time based on the shutter speed chosen; it allows light to come in contact with the film.

diaphragm
Device with a variable opening that controls the amount of light entering the camera.

lens mount
Device used to attach a lens to a camera.

secondary mirror
Mirror that directs part of the light entering the lens through the center of the main reflex mirror and toward the light sensor.

light sensor
Sensor that measures the light intensity; it is used to determine the correct exposure (shutter speed and diaphragm opening).

films

Thin, flexible, transparent media covered with light-sensitive materials that enable images to be imprinted in a film camera.

film pack
Small rigid box containing a certain number of sheet films, which are dispensed successively as the camera operates; they are used in Polaroid® cameras.

sheet film
Semirigid film made to fit specific applications; it is usually loaded into a view camera.

cartridge film
Small lightproof container that holds a roll of film with a number of exposures, which is loaded into a camera.

roll film
Band of film with a number of exposures; it is rolled on a spool and used in midsize cameras.

ARTS AND ARCHITECTURE

memory cards
Rigid cards used as a storage medium to record photographs taken with a digital camera.

xD-Picture card
Very-small-format flash memory card, designed in 2002.

compact flash card
Rigid card used as a storage medium to record photos taken with digital cameras.

Secure Digital card
Small-format flash memory card that includes a copyright-protection mechanism. It was developed in 2000.

Memory Stick
Flash memory card in a rectangular-shape case. It was developed in 2000.

photography

still cameras

Cameras whose principal components are a lightproof chamber and an optical system, which causes an image to be imprinted on a light-sensitive surface.

compact camera
Small, easy-to-use camera.

disposable camera
Small lightweight easy-to-use camera containing a film; it is designed to be used only once.

ultracompact camera
Very small camera, usually completely automatic.

single-lens reflex (SLR) camera
Camera whose interchangeable lens is used to both view and shoot through a slanted mirror that flips up (reflex).

underwater camera
Camera composed of a watertight pressure-resistant body; it is used mainly for underwater photography.

Polaroid® camera
Camera that develops photos instantly. After a photo is taken, the exposed film is ejected from the camera and develops automatically in a few minutes.

medium format SLR (6 x 6)
Midsize camera with interchangeable lenses; it produces 6 cm x 6 cm images on a roll of film.

twin-lens reflex camera
Camera whose upper lens uses a mirror to view while its lower lens is used to shoot.

view camera
Large camera composed of two telescopic blocks connected to an expansible bellows, which allows the perspective and focus to be checked and adjusted as needed.

ARTS AND ARCHITECTURE

traditional musical instruments

Collective term for the instruments, current or ancient, that characterize a culture, era or style of music.

accordion
Wind instrument composed of keyboards and a manual bellows used to cause the reeds to vibrate and produce sound.

harmonica
Instrument composed of small tubes with free reeds recessed in a frame, which the player causes to vibrate by exhaling and inhaling.

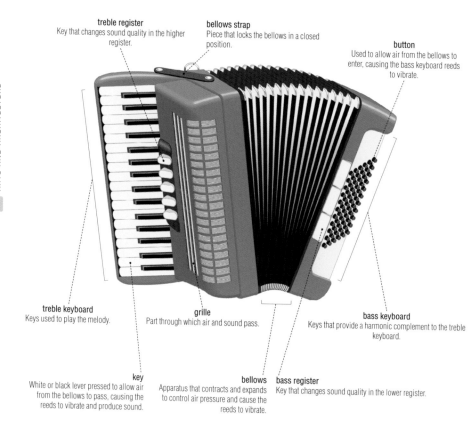

treble register
Key that changes sound quality in the higher register.

bellows strap
Piece that locks the bellows in a closed position.

button
Used to allow air from the bellows to enter, causing the bass keyboard reeds to vibrate.

treble keyboard
Keys used to play the melody.

grille
Part through which air and sound pass.

bass keyboard
Keys that provide a harmonic complement to the treble keyboard.

key
White or black lever pressed to allow air from the bellows to pass, causing the reeds to vibrate and produce sound.

bellows
Apparatus that contracts and expands to control air pressure and cause the reeds to vibrate.

bass register
Key that changes sound quality in the lower register.

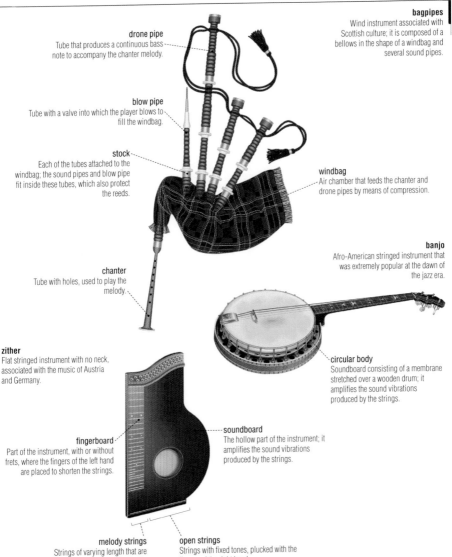

bagpipes
Wind instrument associated with Scottish culture; it is composed of a bellows in the shape of a windbag and several sound pipes.

drone pipe
Tube that produces a continuous bass note to accompany the chanter melody.

blow pipe
Tube with a valve into which the player blows to fill the windbag.

stock
Each of the tubes attached to the windbag; the sound pipes and blow pipe fit inside these tubes, which also protect the reeds.

windbag
Air chamber that feeds the chanter and drone pipes by means of compression.

banjo
Afro-American stringed instrument that was extremely popular at the dawn of the jazz era.

chanter
Tube with holes, used to play the melody.

zither
Flat stringed instrument with no neck, associated with the music of Austria and Germany.

circular body
Soundboard consisting of a membrane stretched over a wooden drum; it amplifies the sound vibrations produced by the strings.

fingerboard
Part of the instrument, with or without frets, where the fingers of the left hand are placed to shorten the strings.

soundboard
The hollow part of the instrument; it amplifies the sound vibrations produced by the strings.

melody strings
Strings of varying length that are plucked with a pick attached to the right thumb to create the melody.

open strings
Strings with fixed tones, plucked with the fingers of the right hand.

ARTS AND ARCHITECTURE

symphony orchestra

Group composed of numerous musicians under the direction of a conductor; it includes various categories of instruments, depending on the work to be performed.

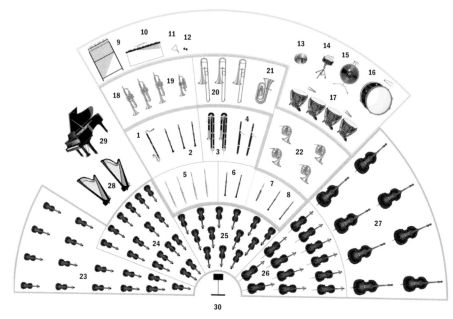

woodwind family
Group of wind instruments originally made from wood.

bass clarinet
1 Clarinet with a curved tube; its range is one octave lower than the ordinary clarinet.

clarinets
2 Single-reed instruments whose cylindrical tube contains holes (some closed by keys) and ends in a flared bell.

contrabassoons
3 Double-reed wind instruments consisting of several tubes; their range is one octave lower than the bassoon.

bassoons
4 Double-reed instruments consisting of a curved conical wooden tube; the double-reed is inserted into a curved mouthpiece.

flutes
5 Instruments with a side mouthpiece and a tube containing holes, some of which are closed by keys.

oboes
6 Double-reed instruments consisting of a conical tube with holes (some closed by keys) and a slightly flared bell.

piccolo
7 Small transverse flute whose range is an octave higher than the regular transverse flute.

English horns
8 Alto oboes with a pear-shaped bell.

percussion instruments
Group of instruments that are struck directly with the hands or with sticks, mallets, etc. to produce a sound.

tubular bells
9 Series of metal tubes arranged vertically in order of size; small hammers are used to strike the tops of the tubes.

xylophone
10 Instrument consisting of wooden bars placed on top of resonators arranged in chromatic order in two rows; the bars are struck with mallets.

triangle
11 Instrument composed of a metal bar bent to form a triangle open at one end; the triangle is struck with a metal rod.

castanets
12 Instrument composed of two shell-shaped pieces of wood held in one hand and struck together using the fingers.

cymbals
13 Instrument consisting of two metal disks that are struck together.

snare drum
14 Flat drum consisting of two membranes; stretched across the lower head are snares that produce a rattling sound.

gong
15 Instrument consisting of a large metal disk with a raised central portion that is struck using a mallet.

bass drum
16 Large drum set on a vertical frame and struck using a pedal-controlled wooden mallet.

timpani
17 Instruments consisting of a parabolic copper basin covered with a stretched batter head that is struck with a mallet.

brass family
Group of wind instruments made from metal and played with cup-shaped mouthpieces.

trumpets
18 Valved instruments consisting of a curved cylindrical tube and a flared bell.

cornet
19 Valved instrument consisting of a curved conical tube and a flared bell.

trombones
20 Instruments consisting of a curved tube with a slide that is lengthened to produce notes varying in pitch by semitones.

tuba
21 Valved instrument whose tonal range is the lowest in the brass family; it consists of a coiled conical tube and an upturned bell.

French horns
22 Valved instruments consisting of a coiled conical tube and a flared bell.

violin family
Group of stringed instruments played with a bow.

first violins
23 The violins that play the melody.

second violins
24 The violins that support the first violins.

violas
25 Four-stringed instruments similar to a violin but played a fifth lower.

cellos
26 Four-stringed instruments placed between the legs when played; they are about twice the size of a violin and their range is one octave lower than the viola.

double basses
27 Four- or five-stringed instruments played upright; the largest of the violin family, they also have the lowest range.

harps
28 Plucked stringed instruments consisting of strings of unequal length attached to a triangular frame.

piano
29 Piano whose mechanism is horizontal, allowing the pianist to better control the sound; it varies in size from 8 to 9 ft.

conductor's podium
30 Small dais that the conductor stands on to direct the musicians as they play.

ARTS AND ARCHITECTURE

stringed instruments

Instruments whose sound, amplified by a sound box, is produced by the vibration of plucked or bowed strings stretched along a neck.

violin
Four-stringed instrument that the musician plays with a bow and holds between the shoulder and the chin.

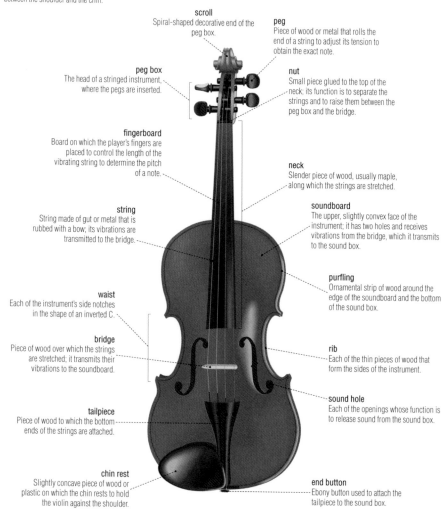

scroll
Spiral-shaped decorative end of the peg box.

peg
Piece of wood or metal that rolls the end of a string to adjust its tension to obtain the exact note.

peg box
The head of a stringed instrument, where the pegs are inserted.

nut
Small piece glued to the top of the neck; its function is to separate the strings and to raise them between the peg box and the bridge.

fingerboard
Board on which the player's fingers are placed to control the length of the vibrating string to determine the pitch of a note.

neck
Slender piece of wood, usually maple, along which the strings are stretched.

string
String made of gut or metal that is rubbed with a bow; its vibrations are transmitted to the bridge.

soundboard
The upper, slightly convex face of the instrument; it has two holes and receives vibrations from the bridge, which it transmits to the sound box.

purfling
Ornamental strip of wood around the edge of the soundboard and the bottom of the sound box.

waist
Each of the instrument's side notches in the shape of an inverted C.

bridge
Piece of wood over which the strings are stretched; it transmits their vibrations to the soundboard.

rib
Each of the thin pieces of wood that form the sides of the instrument.

sound hole
Each of the openings whose function is to release sound from the sound box.

tailpiece
Piece of wood to which the bottom ends of the strings are attached.

chin rest
Slightly concave piece of wood or plastic on which the chin rests to hold the violin against the shoulder.

end button
Ebony button used to attach the tailpiece to the sound box.

bow
A wooden stick with horsehair stretched from end to end; by means of friction, it makes the strings of an instrument vibrate.

violin family
Group of stringed instruments played with a bow.

head
The upper end of the bow.

point
Part that secures the horsehair to the upper end of the bow.

stick
Thin flexible rod curved along a third of its length and along which hair is stretched.

hair
Part of the bow consisting of horsehair that is rubbed across the strings to make them vibrate.

handle
Part held when the bow is used.

heel
The lower end of the bow.

frog
Sliding part that secures the hair to the lower end of the bow; the frog is moved to adjust the tension of the hair.

screw
Threaded piece that moves the frog.

viola
Four-stringed instrument slightly larger than the violin; its range is a fifth lower than the violin.

violin
Four-stringed instrument that the musician plays with a bow and holds between the shoulder and the chin.

cello
Four-stringed instrument held between the legs when played; it is about twice the size of the violin and its range is an octave lower than the viola.

double bass
Four- or five-stringed instrument, played upright; the largest member of the violin family, it also has the lowest range.

ARTS AND ARCHITECTURE

stringed instruments

harp
Plucked stringed instrument consisting
of strings of various lengths attached
to a triangular frame.

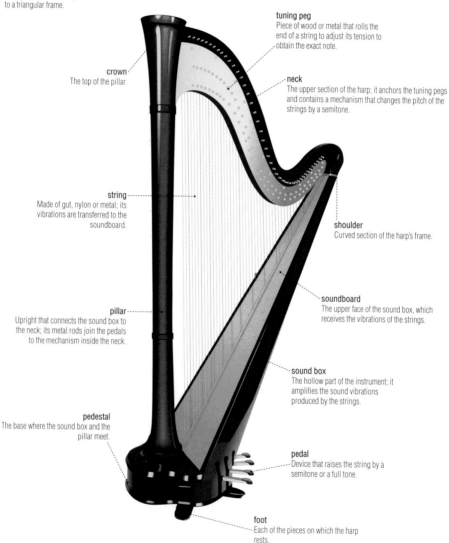

tuning peg
Piece of wood or metal that rolls the
end of a string to adjust its tension to
obtain the exact note.

crown
The top of the pillar.

neck
The upper section of the harp; it anchors the tuning pegs
and contains a mechanism that changes the pitch of the
strings by a semitone.

string
Made of gut, nylon or metal; its
vibrations are transferred to the
soundboard.

shoulder
Curved section of the harp's frame.

soundboard
The upper face of the sound box, which
receives the vibrations of the strings.

pillar
Upright that connects the sound box to
the neck; its metal rods join the pedals
to the mechanism inside the neck.

sound box
The hollow part of the instrument; it
amplifies the sound vibrations
produced by the strings.

pedestal
The base where the sound box and the
pillar meet.

pedal
Device that raises the string by a
semitone or a full tone.

foot
Each of the pieces on which the harp
rests.

ARTS AND ARCHITECTURE

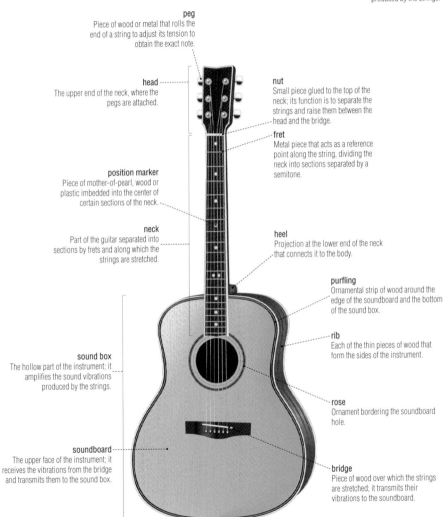

acoustic guitar
Plucked stringed instrument whose
hollow body amplifies the vibrations
produced by the strings.

peg
Piece of wood or metal that rolls the
end of a string to adjust its tension to
obtain the exact note.

head
The upper end of the neck, where the
pegs are attached.

nut
Small piece glued to the top of the
neck; its function is to separate the
strings and raise them between the
head and the bridge.

fret
Metal piece that acts as a reference
point along the string, dividing the
neck into sections separated by a
semitone.

position marker
Piece of mother-of-pearl, wood or
plastic imbedded into the center of
certain sections of the neck.

neck
Part of the guitar separated into
sections by frets and along which the
strings are stretched.

heel
Projection at the lower end of the neck
that connects it to the body.

purfling
Ornamental strip of wood around the
edge of the soundboard and the bottom
of the sound box.

rib
Each of the thin pieces of wood that
form the sides of the instrument.

sound box
The hollow part of the instrument; it
amplifies the sound vibrations
produced by the strings.

rose
Ornament bordering the soundboard
hole.

soundboard
The upper face of the instrument; it
receives the vibrations from the bridge
and transmits them to the sound box.

bridge
Piece of wood over which the strings
are stretched; it transmits their
vibrations to the soundboard.

ARTS AND ARCHITECTURE

stringed instruments

electric guitar
Guitar with microphones that convert
string vibrations into electric signals,
which are then amplified and converted
into sound.

tuning peg
Device that adjusts the tension of the
strings.

head
The upper end of the neck where the
tuning pegs are attached.

nut
Small piece glued to the top of the
neck; its function is to separate the
strings and raise them between the
head and the bridge.

fret
Metal piece that acts as a reference
point along the string, dividing the
neck into sections separated by a
semitone.

fingerboard
Board on which the player's fingers are
placed to control the length of the
vibrating string to determine the pitch
of a note.

neck
Part of the guitar separated into
sections by frets and along which the
strings are stretched.

bass pickup
Device that converts low-frequency string
vibrations into electric signals.

position marker
Piece of mother-of-pearl, wood or
plastic imbedded into the center of
certain sections of the neck.

midrange pickup
Device that converts middle-frequency string
vibrations into electric signals.

vibrato arm
Device that raises and lowers the
bridge to adjust string tension and
thereby alter the pitch of the notes.

treble pickup
Device that converts high-frequency string
vibrations into electric signals.

volume control
Button that controls the loudness of the
instrument.

tone control
Button that adjusts the frequency of the
electric signals in order to control the
tone of the guitar.

bridge assembly
Assembly consisting of the bridge, the
tailpiece and the vibrato arm.

body
Hollow nonresonant part of the
instrument where the guitar's electrical
components are housed.

output jack
Plug for the cable that transmits the
electric signals to the amplifier.

bass guitar
Guitar whose tonal range is lower than that of the electric guitar; it usually has four strings.

tuning peg
Device that adjusts the tension of the strings.

head
The upper end of the neck where the tuning pegs are attached.

nut
Small piece glued to the top of the neck; its function is to separate the strings and raise them between the head and the bridge.

fingerboard
Board on which the player's fingers are placed to control the length of the vibrating string to determine the pitch of a note.

fret
Metal piece that acts as a reference point along the string, dividing the neck into sections separated by a semitone.

neck
Part of the guitar separated into sections by frets and along which the strings are stretched.

position marker
Piece of mother-of-pearl, wood or plastic imbedded into the center of certain sections of the neck.

strap system

bass tone control
Button that adjusts the frequency of the electric signals produced by the bass microphone.

treble tone control
Button that adjusts the frequency of the electric signals produced by the treble microphone.

pickups
Device that converts the vibrations of the strings into electric signals.

bridge
Piece over which the lower ends of the strings stretch; it also attaches them to the body.

balancer
Button that lets the player choose between one or both microphones.

volume control
Button that controls the loudness of the instrument.

body
Hollow nonresonant part of the instrument where the guitar's electrical components are housed.

ARTS AND ARCHITECTURE

keyboard instruments

Instruments with a series of keys that are pressed to strike or pluck strings and thereby produce sound.

upright piano
A stringed instrument whose strings are
struck by hammers controlled by the keys
on a keyboard; its soundboard and strings
are arranged vertically.

pressure bar
Metal bar under which the strings
pass, marking the top of the section of
vibrating strings.

muffler felt
Strip of felt that comes between the strings
and the hammer heads when the muffler
pedal is pressed; it lowers the volume of
sound.

strings
Metal wires stretched between two
fixed points; the hammers strike them,
causing them to vibrate and produce
sound.

treble bridge
Piece of wood over which the strings in
the treble range are stretched; it
transmits their vibrations to the
soundboard.

bass bridge
Piece of wood over which the bass
strings are stretched; it transmits their
vibrations to the soundboard.

pedal rod
Piece of wood that connects the pedal
to the mechanism.

soft pedal
In the upright piano, it brings the hammers closer
to the strings to reduce their impact; in a grand
piano, it limits the hammer impact to a section of
the string.

muffler pedal
In an upright piano, it lowers the muffler felt; in a grand piano, it prolongs the notes
(sostenuto pedal).

damper pedal
Pedal that increases the duration of string resonance by
keeping the dampers raised.

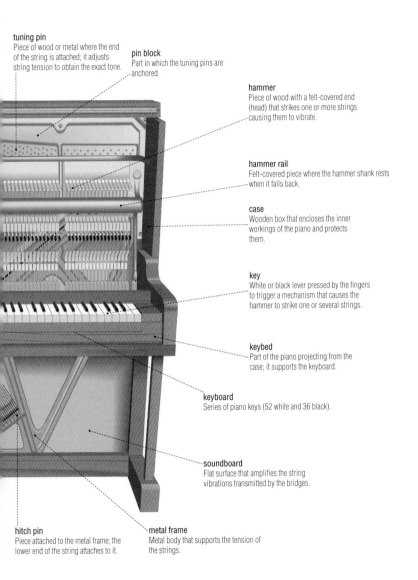

tuning pin
Piece of wood or metal where the end of the string is attached; it adjusts string tension to obtain the exact tone.

pin block
Part in which the tuning pins are anchored.

hammer
Piece of wood with a felt-covered end (head) that strikes one or more strings causing them to vibrate.

hammer rail
Felt-covered piece where the hammer shank rests when it falls back.

case
Wooden box that encloses the inner workings of the piano and protects them.

key
White or black lever pressed by the fingers to trigger a mechanism that causes the hammer to strike one or several strings.

keybed
Part of the piano projecting from the case; it supports the keyboard.

keyboard
Series of piano keys (52 white and 36 black).

soundboard
Flat surface that amplifies the string vibrations transmitted by the bridges.

hitch pin
Piece attached to the metal frame; the lower end of the string attaches to it.

metal frame
Metal body that supports the tension of the strings.

ARTS AND ARCHITECTURE

keyboard instruments

upright piano action
Combination of elements whereby energy applied to
a key is transferred to the hammer, which in turn
causes the strings to vibrate.

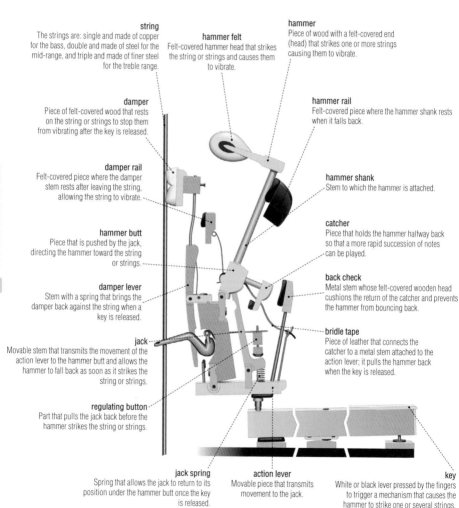

string
The strings are: single and made of copper
for the bass, double and made of steel for the
mid-range, and triple and made of finer steel
for the treble range.

hammer felt
Felt-covered hammer head that strikes
the string or strings and causes them
to vibrate.

hammer
Piece of wood with a felt-covered end
(head) that strikes one or more strings
causing them to vibrate.

damper
Piece of felt-covered wood that rests
on the string or strings to stop them
from vibrating after the key is released.

hammer rail
Felt-covered piece where the hammer shank rests
when it falls back.

damper rail
Felt-covered piece where the damper
stem rests after leaving the string,
allowing the string to vibrate.

hammer shank
Stem to which the hammer is attached.

hammer butt
Piece that is pushed by the jack,
directing the hammer toward the string
or strings.

catcher
Piece that holds the hammer halfway back
so that a more rapid succession of notes
can be played.

damper lever
Stem with a spring that brings the
damper back against the string when a
key is released.

back check
Metal stem whose felt-covered wooden head
cushions the return of the catcher and prevents
the hammer from bouncing back.

jack
Movable stem that transmits the movement of the
action lever to the hammer butt and allows the
hammer to fall back as soon as it strikes the
string or strings.

bridle tape
Piece of leather that connects the
catcher to a metal stem attached to the
action lever; it pulls the hammer back
when the key is released.

regulating button
Part that pulls the jack back before the
hammer strikes the string or strings.

jack spring
Spring that allows the jack to return to its
position under the hammer butt once the key
is released.

action lever
Movable piece that transmits
movement to the jack.

key
White or black lever pressed by the fingers
to trigger a mechanism that causes the
hammer to strike one or several strings.

examples of keyboard instruments

concert grand
Piano whose mechanism is horizontal,
allowing the pianist to better control the
sound; it varies in size from 8 to 9 ft.

baby grand
Grand piano measuring around 5.5 ft.

ARTS AND ARCHITECTURE

boudoir grand
Grand piano measuring from 6 to 7 ft.

harpsichord
Plucked string instrument consisting
of one or several keyboards.

wind instruments

Collective term for instruments that produce sound by blowing, which causes the air column inside the tube to vibrate; a reed or the lips are used to play them.

saxophone
Single-reed instrument consisting of a conical copper tube with a flared bell and holes closed by keys.

mouthpiece
Beveled mouthpiece similar to that of the clarinet; the reed attaches to its flat surface and the player blows into it.

reed
Part used to produce sound; it consists of a tongue that vibrates against the edge of the instrument's mouthpiece.

crook key
Key that opens and closes the instrument's smallest hole, located on the crook.

ligature
Part that attaches the reed to the flat surface of the mouthpiece.

crook
Curved part connecting the mouthpiece to the body.

octave mechanism
Part that increases the pitch of the notes by an octave.

double reed
Part of the mouthpiece used to produce sound; it consists of two tongues that vibrate against each other.

single reed
Part used to produce sound on a woodwind instrument; it consists of a tongue that vibrates against the edge of the mouthpiece.

key lever
Part that controls a key plate.

bell
Flared end of the instrument.

bell brace
Ring that connects the bell of the instrument to the body.

key
Mechanism composed of a lever and a plate; it opens and closes the holes when notes are played.

key guard
Metal part that protects the keys from impact.

body
Conical tube located between the crook and the breech and containing most of the keys.

thumb rest
Part on which the thumb is placed to support the instrument.

key finger button
Piece of mother-of-pearl that moves the key plate.

breech
Curved part connecting the bell to the body.

breech guard
Metal part that protects the keys on the breech from impact.

ARTS AND ARCHITECTURE

ARTS AND ARCHITECTURE

piccolo
Small transverse flute whose range is
an octave higher than the regular
transverse flute.

clarinet
Single-reed instrument consisting of a
cylindrical tube with holes (some
closed by keys) and a flared bell.

transverse flute
Instrument consisting of a metal or
wooden tube with holes (some closed
by keys) and a side mouthpiece; it is
held horizontally.

bassoon
Instrument with a double reed that fits
into a curved mouthpiece; it consists
of two parallel wooden tubes joined at
the base.

oboe
Double-reed instrument consisting of a
conical tube with holes (some closed
by keys) and a slightly flared bell.

English horn
Alto oboe with a pear-shaped bell.

tuba
Valved instrument whose tonal range is the lowest in the brass family; it consists of a coiled conical tube and an upturned bell.

saxhorn
Valved instrument whose range is a fifth lower than the cornet; it consists of a curved conical tube and a large bell.

French horn
Valved instrument consisting of a coiled conical tube and a flared bell.

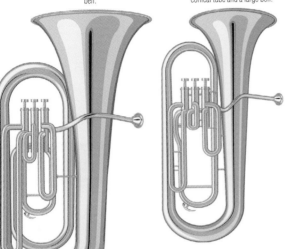

trombone
Instrument with a curved tube and a slide that is lengthened to produce notes varying in pitch by semitones; its register is lower than that of the trumpet.

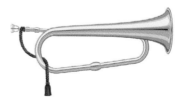

cornet
Valved instrument consisting of a curved conical tube and a flared bell.

bugle
Instrument with a conical tube and no valves or keys; it is used mainly for military calls.

wind instruments

trumpet
Valved instrument consisting of a
coiled cylindrical tube and a flared bell.

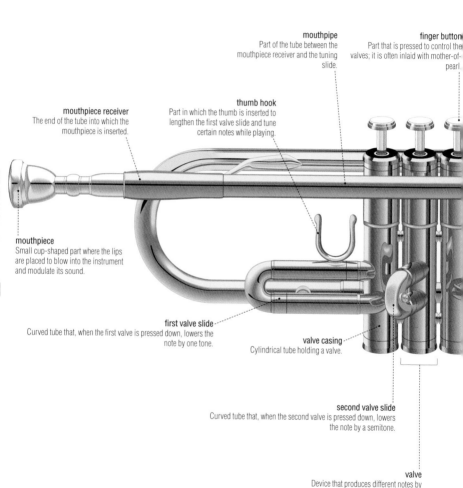

mouthpipe
Part of the tube between the
mouthpiece receiver and the tuning
slide.

finger button
Part that is pressed to control the
valves; it is often inlaid with mother-of-
pearl.

mouthpiece receiver
The end of the tube into which the
mouthpiece is inserted.

thumb hook
Part in which the thumb is inserted to
lengthen the first valve slide and tune
certain notes while playing.

mouthpiece
Small cup-shaped part where the lips
are placed to blow into the instrument
and modulate its sound.

first valve slide
Curved tube that, when the first valve is pressed down, lowers the
note by one tone.

valve casing
Cylindrical tube holding a valve.

second valve slide
Curved tube that, when the second valve is pressed down, lowers
the note by a semitone.

valve
Device that produces different notes by
lengthening the air column inside the
tube and releasing the slides.

ARTS AND ARCHITECTURE

little finger hook
Part used to support the little finger of
the right hand.

ring
Part that lengthens the third valve
slide to tune certain notes while
playing.

bell
Flared end of the instrument.

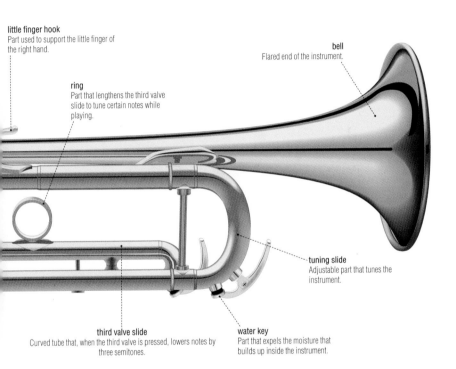

tuning slide
Adjustable part that tunes the
instrument.

third valve slide
Curved tube that, when the third valve is pressed, lowers notes by
three semitones.

water key
Part that expels the moisture that
builds up inside the instrument.

mute
Device that is inserted into the bell to
muffle the sound.

percussion instruments

Group of instruments that are struck directly with the hands or with sticks, mallets, etc. to produce a sound.

drums
All the percussion instruments played
by a single musician, the drummer.

cymbal
Instrument consisting of a metal disk
mounted on a stand; it is struck with a
mallet, a drumstick or a wire brush.

tom-tom
Instrument consisting of two single-
membrane drums struck with a mallet
or a drumstick.

high-hat cymbal
Instrument consisting of two cymbals;
the movable superior cymbal,
controlled by a pedal, is used to strike
the inferior cymbal.

batter head
Stretched membrane on a snare drum
that is struck with a drumstick or a wire
brush.

snare drum
Flat drum consisting of two membranes;
stretched across the lower membrane are
snares that produce a rattling sound.

bass drum
Large drum set on a vertical frame and
struck using a pedal-controlled
wooden mallet.

tenor drum
Drum that makes a muted sound; it is
struck with a mallet or a drumstick.

tension screw
Part that adjusts the tension of the
membrane.

mallet
Metal rod whose end (made of felt,
cork, skin, etc.) is used to strike the
membrane of the bass drum.

pedal
Device that controls the mallet used to
strike the membrane.

spur
Retractable metal rod attached to the
bottom of a bass drum to stabilize it.

kettledrum
Instrument consisting of a parabolic copper basin covered with a stretched membrane that is struck with mallets.

shell
Parabolic copper basin that functions as a sound box.

batter head
Membrane that is struck with a mallet.

tie rod
Metal part connected to the tension rod; by adjusting the tension of the batter head, it changes the drum's pitch.

metal counterhoop
Metal hoop that stretches the membrane over the shell to control the tone of the instrument.

tuning gauge
Part used to adjust the pitch of a note and obtain precise tuning of the instrument.

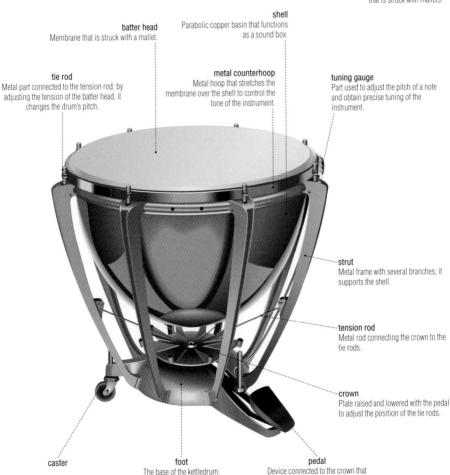

strut
Metal frame with several branches; it supports the shell.

tension rod
Metal rod connecting the crown to the tie rods.

crown
Plate raised and lowered with the pedal to adjust the position of the tie rods.

caster

foot
The base of the kettledrum.

pedal
Device connected to the crown that adjusts the tension of the membrane to change the tuning of the instrument.

ARTS AND ARCHITECTURE

percussion instruments

snare drum
Flat drum consisting of two membranes; stretched across the lower membrane are snares that produce a rattling sound.

lug
Part that secures the metal hoops that stretch the membranes.

tension rod
Device that brings the snare closer to or farther from the snare head.

snare strainer
Knob that adjusts snare tension and tone.

snare head
Soundboard over which the snare is stretched.

snare
Metal snares that vibrate on the snare head when the batter head is struck, producing a rattling sound.

tambourine
Instrument consisting of a wooden hoop covered with a membrane and fitted with jingles; it can be struck, brushed or shaken.

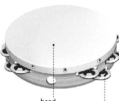

head
Membrane struck with the palm or the thumb.

jingle
Small cymbals that knock together when the tambourine is shaken.

bongos
Instrument consisting of two small connected drums; they are usually struck with the hands.

sticks
Sticks of wood with olive-shaped heads used to strike a percussion instrument.

mallets
Metal or wooden rods whose end (made of felt, skin, rubber, etc.) is used to strike an instrument.

wire brush
Instrument consisting of extremely fine steel wires that are brushed across a cymbal or the batter head on a snare drum.

sleigh bells
Set of hollow metal pieces with a free-moving steel ball inside; they are tied to a ribbon and used as accompaniment.

set of bells
Series of small bells attached to a ribbon and used as accompaniment.

castanets
Instrument composed of two shell-shaped pieces of wood held in one hand and struck together using the fingers.

gong
Instrument consisting of a large metal disk with a raised central portion that is struck using a mallet.

triangle
Instrument composed of a metal bar bent to form a triangle open at one end; the triangle is struck with a metal rod.

metal rod
Steel rod used to strike the triangle.

sistrum
Instrument consisting of a frame with crossbars and attached metal disks that knock together when the instrument is shaken.

tubular bells
Series of metal tubes arranged vertically in order of size; small hammers are used to strike the tops of the tubes.

xylophone
Instrument consisting of wooden bars placed on top of resonators arranged in chromatic order in two rows; the bars are struck with mallets.

cymbals
Instrument consisting of two metal disks that are struck together.

bar
Wooden slats that the player strikes with mallets.

frame

resonator
Metal tube whose function is to amplify sound.

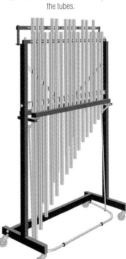

Greek temple

Building that, in antiquity, was dedicated to a divinity and featured a statue of that divinity.

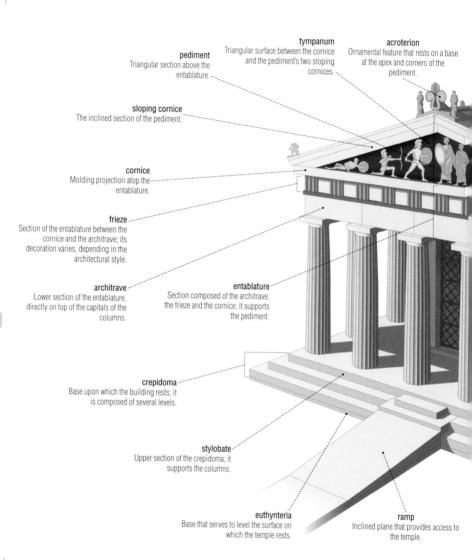

pediment
Triangular section above the entablature.

tympanum
Triangular surface between the cornice and the pediment's two sloping cornices.

acroterion
Ornamental feature that rests on a base at the apex and corners of the pediment.

sloping cornice
The inclined section of the pediment.

cornice
Molding projection atop the entablature.

frieze
Section of the entablature between the cornice and the architrave; its decoration varies, depending in the architectural style.

architrave
Lower section of the entablature, directly on top of the capitals of the columns.

entablature
Section composed of the architrave, the frieze and the cornice; it supports the pediment.

crepidoma
Base upon which the building rests; it is composed of several levels.

stylobate
Upper section of the crepidoma; it supports the columns.

euthynteria
Base that serves to level the surface on which the temple rests.

ramp
Inclined plane that provides access to the temple.

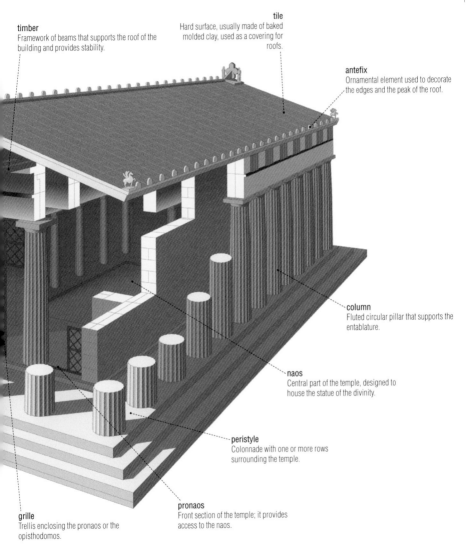

timber
Framework of beams that supports the roof of the building and provides stability.

tile
Hard surface, usually made of baked molded clay, used as a covering for roofs.

antefix
Ornamental element used to decorate the edges and the peak of the roof.

column
Fluted circular pillar that supports the entablature.

naos
Central part of the temple, designed to house the statue of the divinity.

peristyle
Colonnade with one or more rows surrounding the temple.

grille
Trellis enclosing the pronaos or the opisthodomos.

pronaos
Front section of the temple; it provides access to the naos.

ARTS AND ARCHITECTURE

pyramid

Construction with a square base and four triangular faces; it served as a tomb for the pharaohs of ancient Egypt, represented here by the pyramid of Cheops.

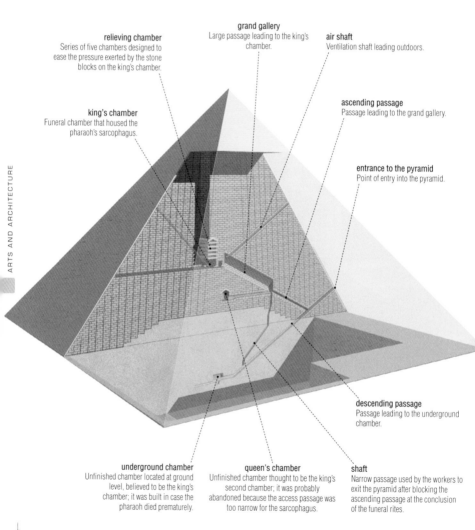

grand gallery
Large passage leading to the king's chamber.

relieving chamber
Series of five chambers designed to ease the pressure exerted by the stone blocks on the king's chamber.

air shaft
Ventilation shaft leading outdoors.

king's chamber
Funeral chamber that housed the pharaoh's sarcophagus.

ascending passage
Passage leading to the grand gallery.

entrance to the pyramid
Point of entry into the pyramid.

descending passage
Passage leading to the underground chamber.

underground chamber
Unfinished chamber located at ground level, believed to be the king's chamber; it was built in case the pharaoh died prematurely.

queen's chamber
Unfinished chamber thought to be the king's second chamber; it was probably abandoned because the access passage was too narrow for the sarcophagus.

shaft
Narrow passage used by the workers to exit the pyramid after blocking the ascending passage at the conclusion of the funeral rites.

architectural styles

The architectural styles, or orders, of ancient Greece are distinguished by rules of proportion that govern a building's columns, entablature and pediment.

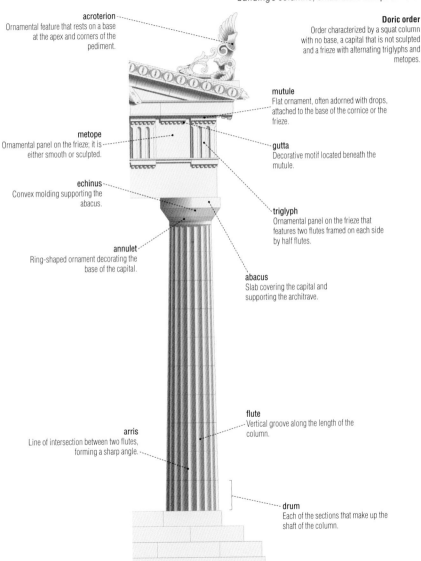

acroterion
Ornamental feature that rests on a base at the apex and corners of the pediment.

Doric order
Order characterized by a squat column with no base, a capital that is not sculpted and a frieze with alternating triglyphs and metopes.

mutule
Flat ornament, often adorned with drops, attached to the base of the cornice or the frieze.

metope
Ornamental panel on the frieze; it is either smooth or sculpted.

gutta
Decorative motif located beneath the mutule.

echinus
Convex molding supporting the abacus.

triglyph
Ornamental panel on the frieze that features two flutes framed on each side by half flutes.

annulet
Ring-shaped ornament decorating the base of the capital.

abacus
Slab covering the capital and supporting the architrave.

flute
Vertical groove along the length of the column.

arris
Line of intersection between two flutes, forming a sharp angle.

drum
Each of the sections that make up the shaft of the column.

architectural styles

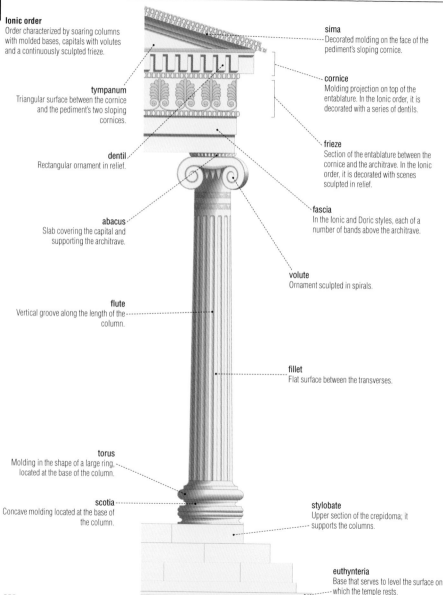

Ionic order
Order characterized by soaring columns with molded bases, capitals with volutes and a continuously sculpted frieze.

sima
Decorated molding on the face of the pediment's sloping cornice.

tympanum
Triangular surface between the cornice and the pediment's two sloping cornices.

cornice
Molding projection on top of the entablature. In the Ionic order, it is decorated with a series of dentils.

frieze
Section of the entablature between the cornice and the architrave. In the Ionic order, it is decorated with scenes sculpted in relief.

dentil
Rectangular ornament in relief.

fascia
In the Ionic and Doric styles, each of a number of bands above the architrave.

abacus
Slab covering the capital and supporting the architrave.

volute
Ornament sculpted in spirals.

flute
Vertical groove along the length of the column.

fillet
Flat surface between the transverses.

torus
Molding in the shape of a large ring, located at the base of the column.

scotia
Concave molding located at the base of the column.

stylobate
Upper section of the crepidoma; it supports the columns.

euthynteria
Base that serves to level the surface on which the temple rests.

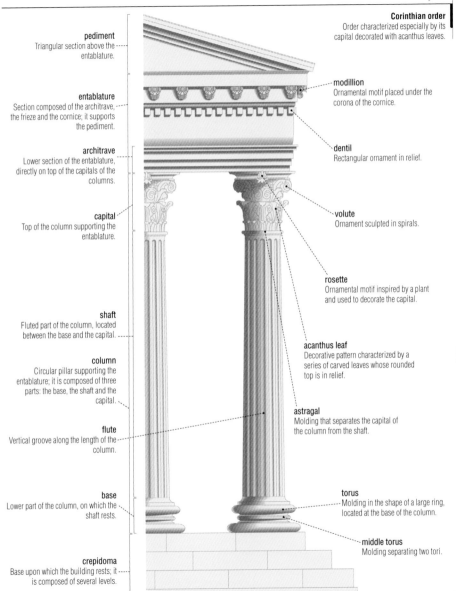

pediment
Triangular section above the entablature.

entablature
Section composed of the architrave, the frieze and the cornice; it supports the pediment.

architrave
Lower section of the entablature, directly on top of the capitals of the columns.

capital
Top of the column supporting the entablature.

shaft
Fluted part of the column, located between the base and the capital.

column
Circular pillar supporting the entablature; it is composed of three parts: the base, the shaft and the capital.

flute
Vertical groove along the length of the column.

base
Lower part of the column, on which the shaft rests.

crepidoma
Base upon which the building rests; it is composed of several levels.

Corinthian order
Order characterized especially by its capital decorated with acanthus leaves.

modillion
Ornamental motif placed under the corona of the cornice.

dentil
Rectangular ornament in relief.

volute
Ornament sculpted in spirals.

rosette
Ornamental motif inspired by a plant and used to decorate the capital.

acanthus leaf
Decorative pattern characterized by a series of carved leaves whose rounded top is in relief.

astragal
Molding that separates the capital of the column from the shaft.

torus
Molding in the shape of a large ring, located at the base of the column.

middle torus
Molding separating two tori.

ARTS AND ARCHITECTURE

Roman house

For wealthy Romans, family life unfolded in spacious luxurious houses whose rooms were arranged around open-air spaces.

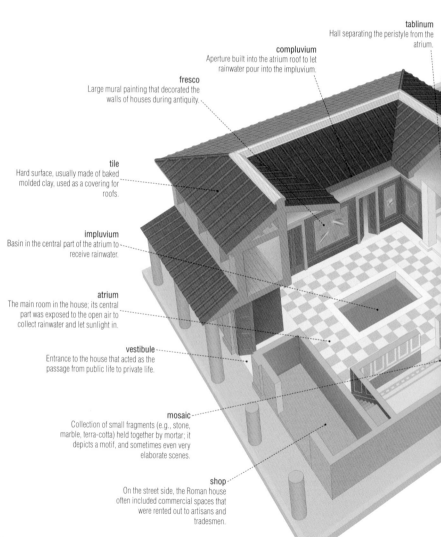

tablinum
Hall separating the peristyle from the atrium.

compluvium
Aperture built into the atrium roof to let rainwater pour into the impluvium.

fresco
Large mural painting that decorated the walls of houses during antiquity.

tile
Hard surface, usually made of baked molded clay, used as a covering for roofs.

impluvium
Basin in the central part of the atrium to receive rainwater.

atrium
The main room in the house; its central part was exposed to the open air to collect rainwater and let sunlight in.

vestibule
Entrance to the house that acted as the passage from public life to private life.

mosaic
Collection of small fragments (e.g., stone, marble, terra-cotta) held together by mortar; it depicts a motif, and sometimes even very elaborate scenes.

shop
On the street side, the Roman house often included commercial spaces that were rented out to artisans and tradesmen.

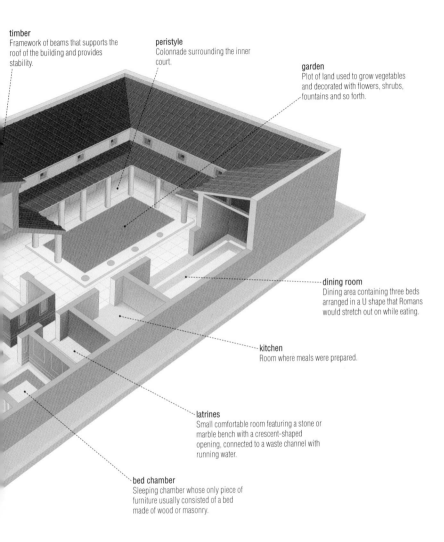

timber
Framework of beams that supports the roof of the building and provides stability.

peristyle
Colonnade surrounding the inner court.

garden
Plot of land used to grow vegetables and decorated with flowers, shrubs, fountains and so forth.

dining room
Dining area containing three beds arranged in a U shape that Romans would stretch out on while eating.

kitchen
Room where meals were prepared.

latrines
Small comfortable room featuring a stone or marble bench with a crescent-shaped opening, connected to a waste channel with running water.

bed chamber
Sleeping chamber whose only piece of furniture usually consisted of a bed made of wood or masonry.

Roman amphitheater

Oval or round building composed of an arena surrounded by tiers; it was used mainly to stage gladiator fights.

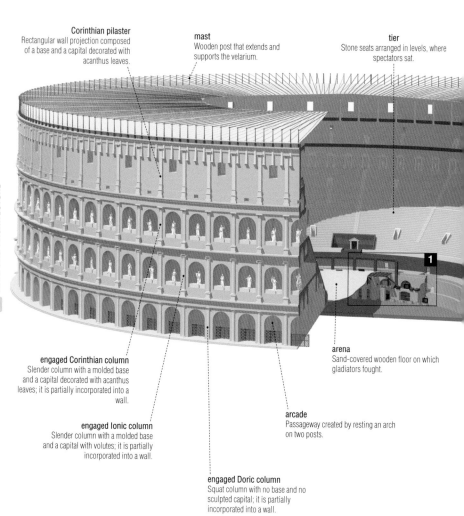

Corinthian pilaster
Rectangular wall projection composed of a base and a capital decorated with acanthus leaves.

mast
Wooden post that extends and supports the velarium.

tier
Stone seats arranged in levels, where spectators sat.

engaged Corinthian column
Slender column with a molded base and a capital decorated with acanthus leaves; it is partially incorporated into a wall.

engaged Ionic column
Slender column with a molded base and a capital with volutes; it is partially incorporated into a wall.

engaged Doric column
Squat column with no base and no sculpted capital; it is partially incorporated into a wall.

arena
Sand-covered wooden floor on which gladiators fought.

arcade
Passageway created by resting an arch on two posts.

velarium
Awning suspended over the tiers to protect spectators from the Sun and the rain.

barrel vault
Arched masonry construction resting on posts.

underground
Area located beneath the arena, designed for easy access for prisoners, gladiators and animals.

elevator
Device that used a counterweight system to raise the animals to arena level.

cage
Barred cell used to lock up and transport animals.

trapdoor
Lift-up door through which gladiators and animals entered the arena.

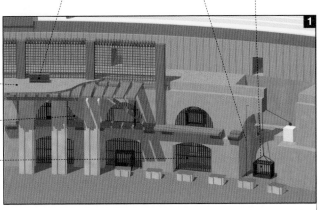

arena
Sand-covered wooden floor on which gladiators fought.

ramp
Sloping passage used to reach another level.

cell
Barred room in which prisoners condemned to take part in the games were held.

castle

Fortified residence of a feudal lord, designed to protect against assailants.

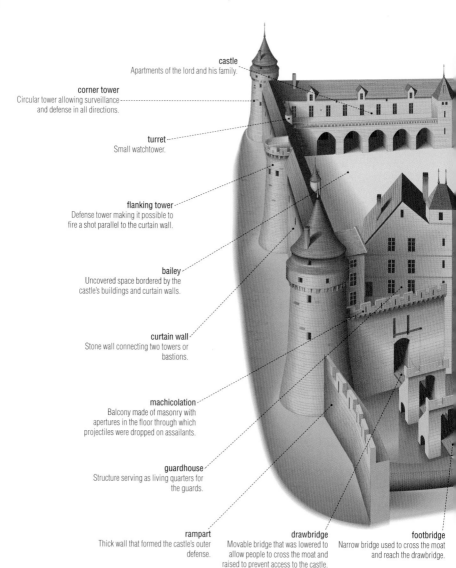

castle
Apartments of the lord and his family.

corner tower
Circular tower allowing surveillance
and defense in all directions.

turret
Small watchtower.

flanking tower
Defense tower making it possible to
fire a shot parallel to the curtain wall.

bailey
Uncovered space bordered by the
castle's buildings and curtain walls.

curtain wall
Stone wall connecting two towers or
bastions.

machicolation
Balcony made of masonry with
apertures in the floor through which
projectiles were dropped on assailants.

guardhouse
Structure serving as living quarters for
the guards.

rampart
Thick wall that formed the castle's outer
defense.

drawbridge
Movable bridge that was lowered to
allow people to cross the moat and
raised to prevent access to the castle.

footbridge
Narrow bridge used to cross the moat
and reach the drawbridge.

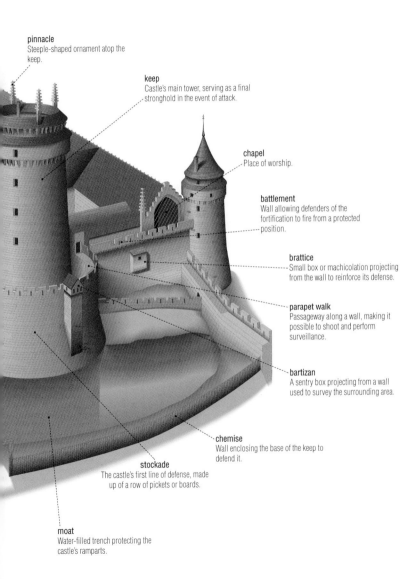

pinnacle
Steeple-shaped ornament atop the keep.

keep
Castle's main tower, serving as a final stronghold in the event of attack.

chapel
Place of worship.

battlement
Wall allowing defenders of the fortification to fire from a protected position.

brattice
Small box or machicolation projecting from the wall to reinforce its defense.

parapet walk
Passageway along a wall, making it possible to shoot and perform surveillance.

bartizan
A sentry box projecting from a wall used to survey the surrounding area.

chemise
Wall enclosing the base of the keep to defend it.

stockade
The castle's first line of defense, made up of a row of pickets or boards.

moat
Water-filled trench protecting the castle's ramparts.

ARTS AND ARCHITECTURE

cathedral

The main church of a diocese, the site of the bishop's see.

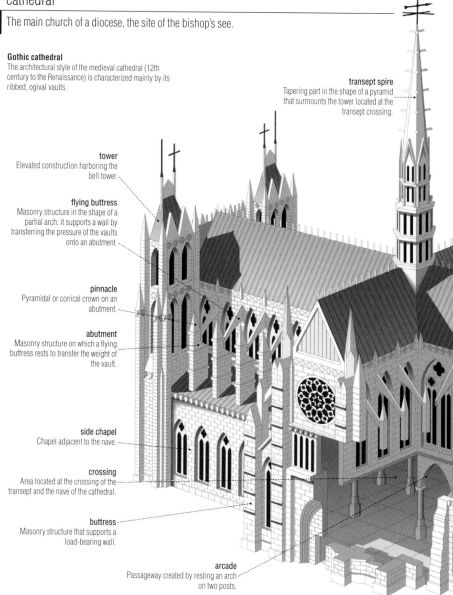

Gothic cathedral
The architectural style of the medieval cathedral (12th century to the Renaissance) is characterized mainly by its ribbed, ogival vaults.

transept spire
Tapering part in the shape of a pyramid that surmounts the tower located at the transept crossing.

tower
Elevated construction harboring the bell tower.

flying buttress
Masonry structure in the shape of a partial arch; it supports a wall by transferring the pressure of the vaults onto an abutment.

pinnacle
Pyramidal or conical crown on an abutment.

abutment
Masonry structure on which a flying buttress rests to transfer the weight of the vault.

side chapel
Chapel adjacent to the nave.

crossing
Area located at the crossing of the transept and the nave of the cathedral.

buttress
Masonry structure that supports a load-bearing wall.

arcade
Passageway created by resting an arch on two posts.

vault
The vault of a Gothic cathedral rests on a series of arches that cross at the summit of the nave and are supported by lateral pillars.

keystone
Wedge-shaped stone above the nave where the arches meet; it supports the arches and stabilizes the overall structure.

lierne
Rib connecting the top of the tierceron to the keystone.

traverse arch
Arch that supports the vault and is perpendicular to the axis of the nave.

tierceron
Rib connected to a lierne but not to the keystone.

diagonal buttress
Arch connecting two of the vault's corners through the keystone; it is also called an ogive.

formeret
Arch that supports the vault and is parallel to the axis of the nave.

Lady chapel
Chapel located beyond the walls at the back of the cathedral, in the axis of the nave.

pillar
Column designed to support a masonry structure.

choir
Area just beyond the transept where the clergy stand during the liturgy.

apsidiole
Small lateral chapel arranged in a semicircle behind the choir surrounding the apse.

newspaper

Usually daily publication whose main purpose is to report and comment on the latest news of society, politics, the arts, sports and other areas of interest.

front page
First page of the newspaper.

nameplate
Title of the newspaper presented in a specific graphic style.

heading
Upper portion of the front page; it usually features the nameplate, the volume number and the date.

banner
Large headline appearing immediately below the heading and running across multiple columns.

article
Stand-alone text forming a whole; it usually presents information, explanation or commentary.

front picture

caption
Short explanatory text accompanying a photograph, image or illustration.

kicker
Short text appearing above the headline that puts the article in context or highlights certain key points.

headline
Word or group of words in large print that introduces an article.

deck
Short block of text under the headline that completes it.

index
Brief summary of the contents of a newspaper, usually in the form of a table of contents.

subhead
Secondary title that separates and introduces the various parts of an article.

section
All the pages of a newspaper that are devoted to one subject such as the arts, the economy, sports, tourism or finance.

literary supplement
Separate publication dealing with books and authors that is inserted into a newspaper on a regular basis or from time to time.

tabloid
Publication whose format is about half the size of a regular newspaper and contains news in a condensed form.

magazine
A section of the newspaper that resembles a magazine; it is usually abundantly illustrated and deals with subjects for a mass audience.

color supplement
Separate publication that is inserted into a newspaper regularly or from time to time; it is printed in color and often on glossy paper.

newspaper

COMMUNICATIONS AND OFFICE AUTOMATION

cartoon
Humorous or satirical drawing; it is usually accompanied by a caption and comments on a news event.

editorial
In-depth article that reflects the collective viewpoint of a newspaper's editorial board.

lead
Short text at the beginning of an article that introduces it or summarizes its contents.

letters to the editor
Part of the newspaper where readers' opinions on topics of general interest are published.

rule
Line of varying thickness used to separate columns, articles and different graphic elements.

Op-Ed article
Article appearing next to or on the page opposite to the editorial and expressing an individual's point of view.

column
The vertical sections of a page; they are separated by white space or a rule.

advertisement
Message paid for by an advertiser to inform readers about a business, product or service.

A2   INTERNATIONAL SUNDAY, NOVEMBER 25, 2002

Editorial

Ullamcorper suscipit lobortis

Lorem ipsum dolor sit amet, consectetuer adipiscing elit, sed diam nonummy nibh euismod tincidunt ut laoreet dolore magna aliquam erat volutpat.

Luc Roberge

Lorem ipsum dolor sit amet, consectetuer adipiscing elit, sed diam nonummy nibh euismod tincidunt ut laoreet dolore magna aliquam erat volutpat. Ut wisi enim ad minim veniam, quis nostrud exerci ta...

Aliquam

Dolor in hendrerit in vulputate

Ut wisi enim ad minim veniam

Paul-Émile Tremblay
Notaire
La Malbaie

Andrew Eastman
Professeur
Strasbourg

Consequat

Serge D'Amico commodo consequa

Marie-Nicole Cimon

Euismod

masthead
Space that usually contains information about the newspaper such as its address, main contributors and subscription information.

column
Regularly published article that presents the comments of one author (reporter or personality) on a chosen subject.

News

Nonummy

Dolor in hendrerit in vulputate

news items
Accounts of various events with no central unifying theme such as accidents, natural disasters and crimes.

shorts
Short untitled informative texts.

Wisi enim ad minim

television program schedule

Le Titanic sed diam nonummy

Theo Diamantis

restaurant review
Article in which a reporter gives a personal evaluation of a restaurant.

photo credit line
Mandatory mention of the individual holding the rights to the photograph used to illustrate an article or a publication.

Lobortis

Commodo

classified advertisements
Short ads that are placed by individuals and grouped into categories according to the goods or services offered or sought.

obituaries
Listing of death notices and anniversaries of deaths, cards of thanks and remembrances.

broadcast satellite communication

Transmission of television signals (pictures and sound) to the general public by means of radio waves relayed by satellite.

satellite
Space vehicle placed in geostationary orbit at an altitude of 22,000 mi to transmit sound and visual signals in the form of radio waves.

relay station
Facility receiving and amplifying signals from a transmitting tower and relaying them to another receiver.

Hertzian wave transmission
Hertzian waves, also called radio waves, are low-frequency electromagnetic waves; the full spectrum of radio waves is divided into bands for specific uses such as radio and TV. Each band is in turn divided into channels.

home antenna
Small receiving antenna used by a subscriber to capture radio waves emitted by a transmitting tower or relay station.

transmitting tower
Facility used to transmit radio waves to a receiver so that television programs can be broadcast locally.

cable distributor
Company specializing in the transmission of television signals to customers through a cable network.

distribution by aerial cable network
Signals can be relayed to the customer through a network of suspended cables.

national broadcasting network
All the public installations that produce and broadcast television or radio programs on a given frequency band.

mobile unit
Vehicle equipped with a transmitter that broadcasts live or recorded news
reports or programs from locations outside a television studio.

transceiving parabolic antenna
Device with a saucer-shaped reflector that emits and
receives radio waves.

private broadcasting network
All the private installations that produce and
broadcast television or radio programs on a
given frequency band.

local station
Television station that is usually part of
a national or private network.

direct home reception
Radio waves are emitted by a satellite and
captured directly by the subscriber's parabolic
antenna.

telecommunications by satellite

Transmission of data such as images, sound and computer data using radio waves relayed by satellites.

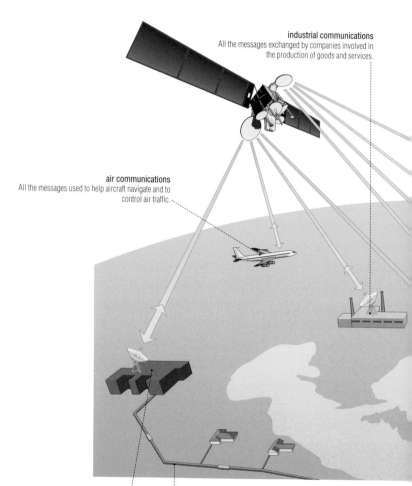

industrial communications
All the messages exchanged by companies involved in
the production of goods and services.

air communications
All the messages used to help aircraft navigate and to
control air traffic.

telephone network
All the installations allowing the exchange of data
or voice messages, sounds or images between two
or more customers.

distribution by underground cable network
Signals can be relayed through a network of
underground cables.

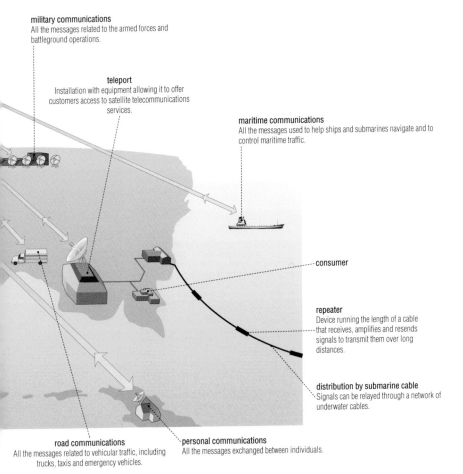

military communications
All the messages related to the armed forces and
battleground operations.

teleport
Installation with equipment allowing it to offer
customers access to satellite telecommunications
services.

maritime communications
All the messages used to help ships and submarines navigate and to
control maritime traffic.

consumer

repeater
Device running the length of a cable
that receives, amplifies and resends
signals to transmit them over long
distances.

distribution by submarine cable
Signals can be relayed through a network of
underwater cables.

road communications
All the messages related to vehicular traffic, including
trucks, taxis and emergency vehicles.

personal communications
All the messages exchanged between individuals.

television

The first long-distance transmission of black and white pictures took place in the 1920s; color television was introduced in 1951.

studio and control rooms

A television studio is made up of a set and three control rooms housing a variety of facilities for controlling broadcasting and recording.

studio floor
Room designed for recording television program sounds and images; it might be soundproof or not.

lighting/camera control area
Room equipped to control camera shots and lighting.

audio control room
Room with the control and monitoring equipment required for sound recording.

production control room
Area equipped to select and compose pictures to be broadcast or recorded; it is also used to coordinate activities in other control rooms and the studio.

lighting board operator
Person responsible for making lighting changes during production.

lighting technician
Person responsible for drawing up lighting plans and supervising the installation and operation of the spotlights.

camera control technician
Person responsible for camera operations and the quality of the pictures.

technical producer
Person responsible for all technical elements of a production, including sound and picture quality.

video switcher technician
Person responsible for switching from one camera to the other as requested by the producer.

producer
Person in charge of the technical and artistic direction while a movie or a television program is being shot.

production adviser
Production associate who is responsible mainly for overseeing the proper flow of a program.

audio technician
Person responsible for sound recording.

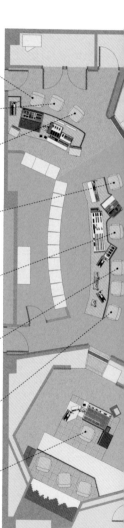

lighting grid access
Area providing access to the catwalk above the lighting grid.

auxiliary facilities room
Room in which various technical and administrative activities are carried out.

connection box
Panel containing all the jacks that connect control room equipment such as cameras, microphones and intercoms.

additional production personnel
Team of assistants and consultants involved in producing a television program.

camera
Filming device whose optical system separates light into the three primary colors and converts it into electronic signals for broadcast.

microphone boom
Arm from which a microphone is suspended and positioned above the performers' heads and thus off-camera.

equipment rack
Cabinet used to store control room technical equipment.

COMMUNICATIONS AND OFFICE AUTOMATION

television

camera
Filming device whose optical system separates
light into the three primary colors and converts it
into electronic signals for broadcast.

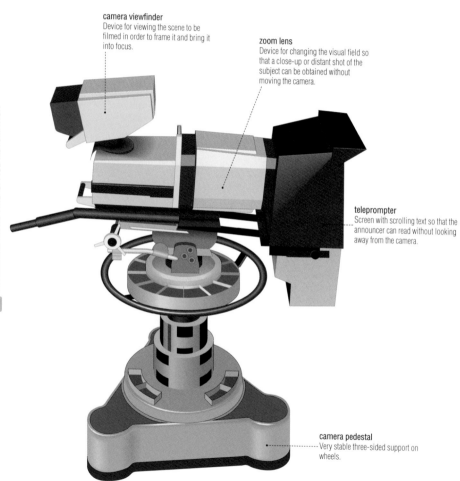

camera viewfinder
Device for viewing the scene to be
filmed in order to frame it and bring it
into focus.

zoom lens
Device for changing the visual field so
that a close-up or distant shot of the
subject can be obtained without
moving the camera.

teleprompter
Screen with scrolling text so that the
announcer can read without looking
away from the camera.

camera pedestal
Very stable three-sided support on
wheels.

liquid crystal display (LCD) television
Television set with a flat, thin screen that reproduces
images by reflecting light onto liquid crystals.

plasma television
Television set with a flat, thin screen that reproduces
images using light emitted by a mixture of gases.

cathod ray tube (CRT) television
Receiving device that generates the sound and
picture elements of programs broadcast by a
television station or recorded on cassette or
disc.

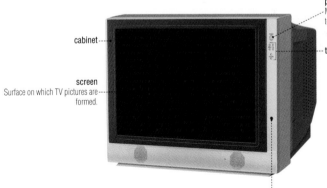

cabinet

power button
Mechanical connection that turns the
television on or off.

tuning controls

screen
Surface on which TV pictures are
formed.

remote control sensor
Device that receives infrared signals emitted by a
remote control so that certain functions can be
operated from a distance.

television

videocassette
Rigid case containing a magnetic tape
on which sounds and images can be
recorded.

reel
Cylindrical part used to wind and unwind
the magnetic tape.

recording tape
Flexible tape whose surface is covered with a
magnetic substance; it is used as a recording
medium.

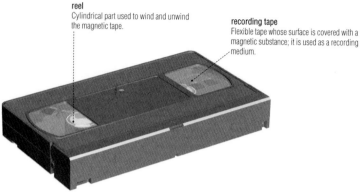

videocassette recorder (VCR)
Device for playing back or recording
audio and video signals on the
magnetic tape of a videocassette.

cassette compartment
Space designed to receive a videocassette.

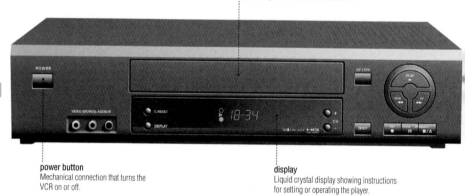

power button
Mechanical connection that turns the
VCR on or off.

display
Liquid crystal display showing instructions
for setting or operating the player.

digital versatile disc (DVD)
Digital recording medium available in various formats, including video, audio and multimedia; it has greater storage capacity than a compact disc.

DVD recorder
Device that uses a laser beam to record and play back data recorded on a DVD video.

power button
Mechanical connection that turns the player on or off.

record button
Button that starts recording of a program.

stop button
Button that stops playback or recording.

channel select
Numbered keys used to select the desired channel directly.

disc compartment control
Button used to open or close the disc tray.

play button
Button that starts playback of a disc.

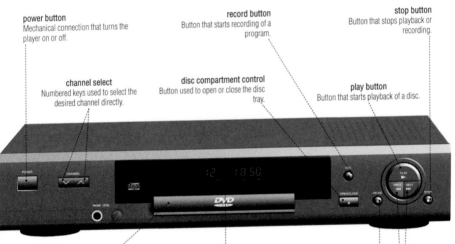

disc tray
Part in which a disc is inserted to be played back.

display
Liquid crystal display showing instructions for setting or operating the player.

pause/still button
Key that stops a tape momentarily during playback to produce a still image on the screen.

track search/fast operation buttons
Keys used to move to the next or previous scene, or to reverse or fast-forward the playback of a disc.

remote control
Device for operating from a distance
some functions of a television set, VCR
or DVD player.

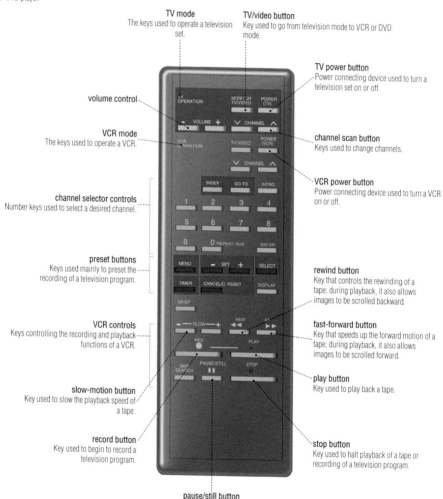

TV mode
The keys used to operate a television
set.

TV/video button
Key used to go from television mode to VCR or DVD
mode.

TV power button
Power connecting device used to turn a
television set on or off.

volume control

VCR mode
The keys used to operate a VCR.

channel scan button
Keys used to change channels.

VCR power button
Power connecting device used to turn a VCR
on or off.

channel selector controls
Number keys used to select a desired channel.

preset buttons
Keys used mainly to preset the
recording of a television program.

rewind button
Key that controls the rewinding of a
tape; during playback, it also allows
images to be scrolled backward.

VCR controls
Keys controlling the recording and playback
functions of a VCR.

fast-forward button
Key that speeds up the forward motion of a
tape; during playback, it also allows
images to be scrolled forward.

play button
Key used to play back a tape.

slow-motion button
Key used to slow the playback speed of
a tape.

record button
Key used to begin to record a
television program.

stop button
Key used to halt playback of a tape or
recording of a television program.

pause/still button
Key that stops a tape momentarily during
playback to produce a still image on the screen.

compact videocassette adapter
Case allowing a compact videocassette to be viewed
using a standard VCR.

cassette compartment
Space designed to receive a
videocassette.

miniDV cassette
Digital videocassette onto which
images and sounds are recorded.

hard disk drive camcorder
Portable video camera that records
sounds and images in digital format on
an internal hard disk.

DVD camcorder
Portable video camera that records
sounds and images in digital format
directly on a digital versatile disc
(DVD).

television

mini-DV camcorder: front view
Portable video camera that records sounds and
images in digital format on a miniDV cassette.

photoshot button
Button used to record a still image on a
memory card.

electronic viewfinder
Small video monitor for viewing the
scene to be filmed in order to frame it
and bring it into focus.

zoom button
Button used to adjust the zoom to
obtain a distant or close-up view of the
subject being filmed.

recording mode
Button used to select a recording
medium (cassette or memory card).

zoom lens
Lens for changing the visual field so that
a close-up or distant shot of the subject
can be obtained without moving the
camcorder.

terminal cover
Cover that protects the camcorder's input
and output jacks (microphone, audio-
video, DV).

lamp
Device that produces a light beam used
to light the subject being filmed.

microphone
Device that converts electric pulses
into broadcast or recorded sounds.

shoulder strap
Adjustable strap for carrying the
camcorder over the shoulder or across
the chest.

power/functions switch
Button used to turn the camcorder on or off and to
select the operating mode including camera,
playback and battery recharge.

mini-DV camcorder: rear view

focus button
Button used to focus the image automatically or manually.

nightshot button
Button for activating the mode that allows filming in the dark.

backlighting button
Button used to improve contrast on the LCD screen in order to improve its readability.

recording start/stop button
Button used to start and stop the recording of pictures and sounds.

videotape operation controls
Buttons that control viewing of recorded images; they include playback, stop, pause, fast-forward and rewind.

eyepiece
Optical disk or system of disks through which the eye sees the image produced by the lens.

widescreen/data code button
Button used to start recording in widescreen format or to insert various data (date, time, etc.) onto the filmed image.

speaker
Integrated device used to generate sound.

card slot
Covered slot in which a memory card is inserted to record still images taken with the camcorder.

rechargeable battery pack
Device that stores chemical energy while charging, then converts it to electric energy.

liquid crystal display
Screen that uses light reflected off liquid crystals to display alphanumeric data or images.

menu button
Button used to display menus for changing settings and accessing the camcorder's options.

sound reproducing system

System for reproducing sound that consists mainly of a tuner, playback equipment, an amplifier and loudspeakers.

system components

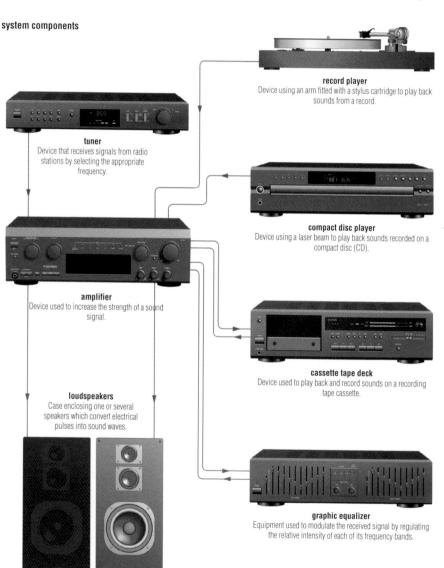

record player
Device using an arm fitted with a stylus cartridge to play back sounds from a record.

tuner
Device that receives signals from radio stations by selecting the appropriate frequency.

compact disc player
Device using a laser beam to play back sounds recorded on a compact disc (CD).

amplifier
Device used to increase the strength of a sound signal.

cassette tape deck
Device used to play back and record sounds on a recording tape cassette.

loudspeakers
Case enclosing one or several speakers which convert electrical pulses into sound waves.

graphic equalizer
Equipment used to modulate the received signal by regulating the relative intensity of each of its frequency bands.

tuner
Device that receives signals from radio stations by selecting the appropriate frequency.

tuning mode
Button for choosing between automatic (scanning) or manual selection of stations.

mode selector
Button used to select the sound reproduction mode (monophonic or stereophonic).

band selector
Button used to select an AM or FM band.

tuning control
Button used to select a broadcast frequency.

preset tuning button
Button used to tune into a station held in memory.

digital frequency display
Liquid crystal display showing the broadcast frequency of a tuned station.

active tracking
Button used to browse the full frequency band to locate and select a station.

graphic equalizer
Equipment used to modulate the received signal by regulating the relative intensity of each of its frequency bands.

frequency bands
All the frequencies contained in a sound signal.

power button
Mechanical connection that turns the graphic equalizer on or off.

frequency setting slide control
Sliding part used to tone down or amplify the sound signal associated with a given frequency band.

sound reproducing system

ampli-tuner: front view
Device combining the functions of a tuner (receiving radio signals)
and an amplifier (increasing the strength of a sound signal).

input lights
Small indicator lights showing the selected
input.

volume control

power button
Mechanical connection that turns the
ampli-tuner on or off.

treble tone control
Button used to adjust the relative level of
high-frequency sounds.

input selector
Button that selects the source of signals in
the device including tuner, cassette deck,
CD or DVD player.

band select button
Button used to select an AM or FM band.

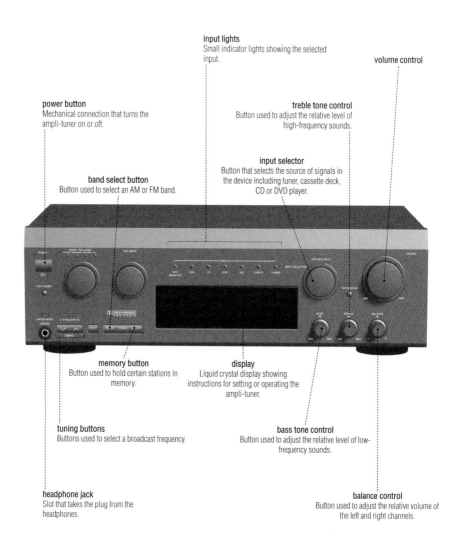

memory button
Button used to hold certain stations in
memory.

display
Liquid crystal display showing
instructions for setting or operating the
ampli-tuner.

tuning buttons
Buttons used to select a broadcast frequency.

bass tone control
Button used to adjust the relative level of low-
frequency sounds.

headphone jack
Slot that takes the plug from the
headphones.

balance control
Button used to adjust the relative volume of
the left and right channels.

power cord
Flexible electric wire housing the leads connecting the appliance to the electric circuit.

cooling fan
Fan that circulates air to cool the internal components of the ampli-tuner.

switched outlet
Device that provides electricity to the equipment connected to it when the ampli-tuner is on.

antenna terminals
Jacks that connect the AM and FM receiving antennas to the ampli-tuner.

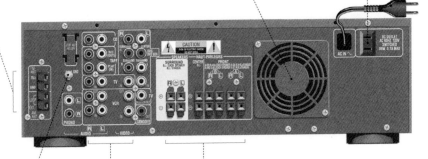

ground terminal
Device that grounds the electric current to prevent electrocution due to faulty equipment.

loudspeaker terminals
Jacks that connect the loudspeakers to the ampli-tuner.

input/output audio/video jacks
Coupling jacks that transfer audio and video signals between the ampli-tuner and the various playback and recording devices.

sound reproducing system

cassette
Rigid case containing a recording tape on
which sounds can be recorded.

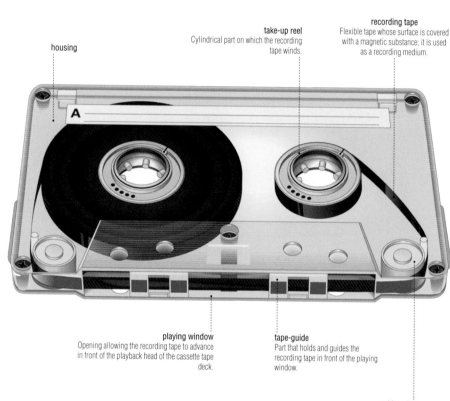

housing

take-up reel
Cylindrical part on which the recording
tape winds.

recording tape
Flexible tape whose surface is covered
with a magnetic substance; it is used
as a recording medium.

playing window
Opening allowing the recording tape to advance
in front of the playback head of the cassette tape
deck.

tape-guide
Part that holds and guides the
recording tape in front of the playing
window.

guide roller
Spool that guides the recording tape.

cassette tape deck
Device used to play back and record sounds on a recording tape cassette.

counter reset button
Key used to reset a tape counter to zero.

tape counter
Device showing the length of a recorded segment on a tape.

peak level meter
Device showing the intensity of the sound signals being played back or recorded.

eject button
Key activating the mechanism to eject a cassette from the cassette holder.

tape selector
The buttons used to indicate clearly the type of recording tape (normal, chrome or metal).

cassette holder
Compartment receiving the cassette for playback.

pause button
Key used to temporarily stop the playback or recording of a tape.

rewind button
Control key used to rewind a tape.

record button
Key used to activate the sound recording mechanism on a tape.

play button
Key used to play back a tape.

fast-forward button
Control key used to fast-forward a tape.

stop button
Key used to interrupt the playback, recording, rewinding or fast-forwarding of a tape.

COMMUNICATIONS AND OFFICE AUTOMATION

sound reproducing system

record
Usually vinyl, circular medium on
which sounds are recorded.

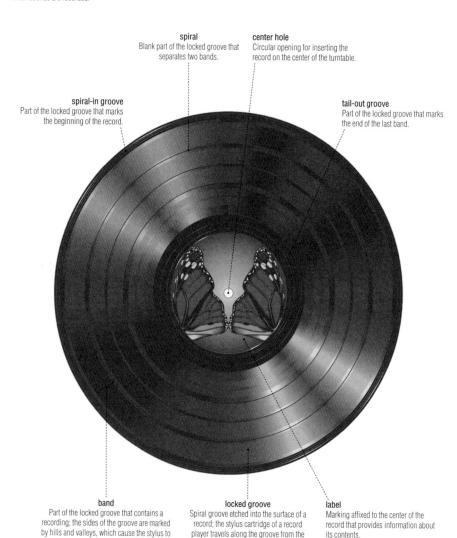

spiral
Blank part of the locked groove that
separates two bands.

center hole
Circular opening for inserting the
record on the center of the turntable.

spiral-in groove
Part of the locked groove that marks
the beginning of the record.

tail-out groove
Part of the locked groove that marks
the end of the last band.

band
Part of the locked groove that contains a
recording; the sides of the groove are marked
by hills and valleys, which cause the stylus to
vibrate.

locked groove
Spiral groove etched into the surface of a
record; the stylus cartridge of a record
player travels along the groove from the
outside in.

label
Marking affixed to the center of the
record that provides information about
its contents.

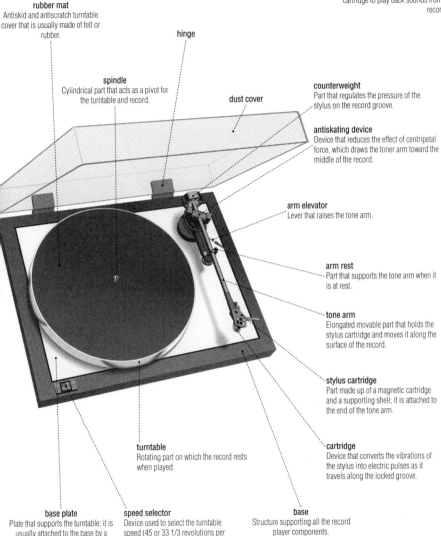

record player
Device using an arm fitted with a stylus cartridge to play back sounds from a record.

rubber mat
Antiskid and antiscratch turntable cover that is usually made of felt or rubber.

hinge

spindle
Cylindrical part that acts as a pivot for the turntable and record.

dust cover

counterweight
Part that regulates the pressure of the stylus on the record groove.

antiskating device
Device that reduces the effect of centripetal force, which draws the toner arm toward the middle of the record.

arm elevator
Lever that raises the tone arm.

arm rest
Part that supports the tone arm when it is at rest.

tone arm
Elongated movable part that holds the stylus cartridge and moves it along the surface of the record.

stylus cartridge
Part made up of a magnetic cartridge and a supporting shell; it is attached to the end of the tone arm.

cartridge
Device that converts the vibrations of the stylus into electric pulses as it travels along the locked groove.

turntable
Rotating part on which the record rests when played.

base plate
Plate that supports the turntable; it is usually attached to the base by a springy suspension.

speed selector
Device used to select the turntable speed (45 or 33 1/3 revolutions per minute).

base
Structure supporting all the record player components.

COMMUNICATIONS AND OFFICE AUTOMATION

sound reproducing system

compact disc
Digital recording medium with multiple formats (including video and audio) and variable storage capacity.

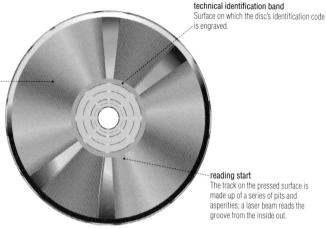

technical identification band
Surface on which the disc's identification code is engraved.

pressed area
Surface that contains the recording; it is coded on a spiral groove pressed into the disc.

reading start
The track on the pressed surface is made up of a series of pits and asperities; a laser beam reads the groove from the inside out.

compact disc reading
During playback of a compact disc, a sensor analyzes laser beam variations reflected by the disc's surface to re-create the original sound signal.

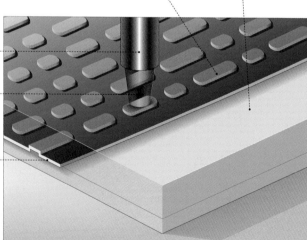

asperity
Each of the small protuberances of varying length that encode data on the disc's surface.

resin surface
Transparent film that covers and protects the aluminum layer.

objective lens
Optical system made up of a set of lenses attached to a mount; it focuses the laser beam onto the section to be played.

laser beam
Highly concentrated light beam that scans the surface of a disc; the pits and asperities determine how the light beam is reflected.

aluminum layer
The surface of the disc is covered with a thin layer of aluminum, which reflects the laser beam toward the sensor.

compact disc player
Device using a laser beam to play back sounds
recorded on a compact disc (CD).

stop button
Button used to stop playback of a disc.

track search/fast operation buttons
Buttons used to skip to the next or previous
track or to accelerate playback forward or
backward.

play button
Button used to start playback of a disc.

display
LCD screen displaying device settings
or operations executed.

direct disc access buttons
Buttons used to play back one of the
discs inserted in the player.

shuffle play
Button used to play back tracks in
random order chosen by the device.

power button
Mechanical connection that turns the
player on or off.

repeat button
Button allowing repeated playback of one
or several tracks.

pause button
Button used to stop playback of a disc
temporarily.

disc compartment
Compartment that contains the tray into
which discs are inserted for playback.

disc compartment control
Button that opens and closes the disc tray.

headphone jack
Socket for a headphone plug.

disc skip
Button used to skip to the next disc.

mini stereo sound system

Sound reproduction system with miniaturized components (including ampli-tuner, speakers and reader).

compact disc recorder
Equipment used to record sounds by laser etching onto a recordable compact disc.

compact disc player
Device using a laser beam to play back sounds recorded on a compact disc (CD).

ampli-tuner
Device combining the functions of a tuner (receiving radio signals) and an amplifier (increasing the strength of a sound signal).

loudspeaker
Case enclosing one or several speakers, which convert electric pulses into sound waves by means of an amplifier.

dual cassette deck
Equipment with two slots for cassettes; it is used to play back and record sounds on a recording tape cassette.

portable sound systems

Small self-contained sound reproduction equipment that can be carried easily from one place to another.

telescoping antenna
FM receiving antenna made up of
sections that extend upward.

handle

portable radio
Equipment used to receive signals
transmitted by radio stations.

frequency display
Device showing the broadcast
frequency of a tuned station.

tuning control
Button used to select a broadcast
frequency.

treble tone control
Button used to adjust the relative level of
high-frequency sounds.

bass tone control
Button used to adjust the relative level of low-
frequency sounds.

volume control
Button that controls the loudness of the
radio.

portable sound systems

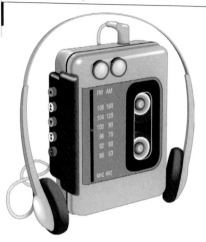

personal radio cassette player
Portable cassette player that also contains a tuner.

clock radio
Portable radio with a built-in alarm clock
whose wake-up mechanism is a buzzer or a
radio station setting.

portable compact disc player
Portable CD player.

display
Liquid crystal display showing
instructions for setting or operating the
player.

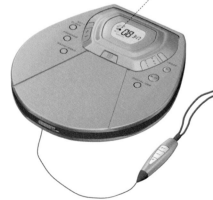

earphones
Small speakers placed directly over the
ears to listen to sounds from the
player.

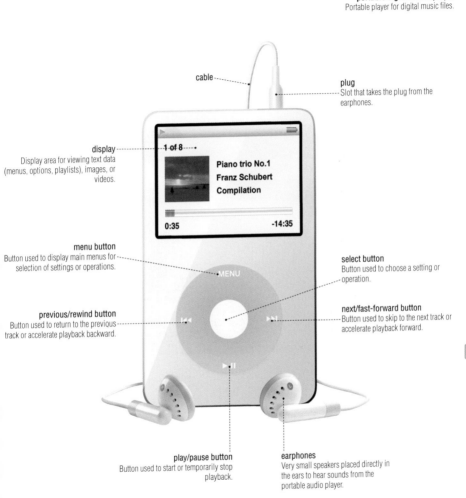

portable digital audio player
Portable player for digital music files.

cable

plug
Slot that takes the plug from the earphones.

display
Display area for viewing text data (menus, options, playlists), images, or videos.

1 of 8

Piano trio No.1
Franz Schubert
Compilation

0:35   -14:35

menu button
Button used to display main menus for selection of settings or operations.

MENU

select button
Button used to choose a setting or operation.

previous/rewind button
Button used to return to the previous track or accelerate playback backward.

next/fast-forward button
Button used to skip to the next track or accelerate playback forward.

play/pause button
Button used to start or temporarily stop playback.

earphones
Very small speakers placed directly in the ears to hear sounds from the portable audio player.

portable sound systems

satellite radio receiver
Device that receives signals from radio stations broadcast to a large territory via satellite.

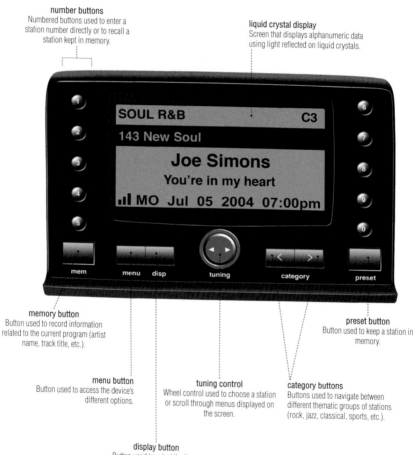

number buttons
Numbered buttons used to enter a station number directly or to recall a station kept in memory.

liquid crystal display
Screen that displays alphanumeric data using light reflected on liquid crystals.

SOUL R&B   C3
143 New Soul
Joe Simons
You're in my heart
ıl MO Jul 05 2004 07:00pm

mem   menu disp   tuning   category   preset

memory button
Button used to record information related to the current program (artist name, track title, etc.).

preset button
Button used to keep a station in memory.

menu button
Button used to access the device's different options.

tuning control
Wheel control used to choose a station or scroll through menus displayed on the screen.

category buttons
Buttons used to navigate between different thematic groups of stations (rock, jazz, classical, sports, etc.).

display button
Button used to select the items displayed on the screen (artist name, track title, duration, etc.).

wireless communication

Transmission of voice or alphanumeric messages by radio waves; it uses small devices that are equipped with a transmitting or receiving antenna.

walkie-talkie
Portable two-way radio used to relay the human voice over short distances.

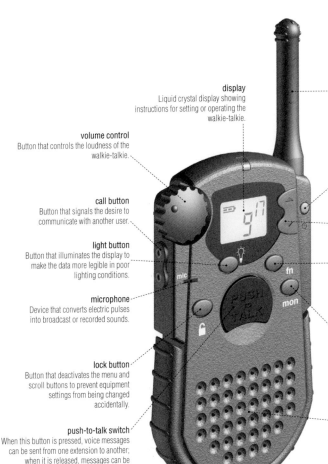

display
Liquid crystal display showing instructions for setting or operating the walkie-talkie.

antenna
Device that emits and receives radio waves.

volume control
Button that controls the loudness of the walkie-talkie.

power button
Mechanical switching device that turns the walkie-talkie on or off.

call button
Button that signals the desire to communicate with another user.

scroll button
Button that adjusts the speaker volume and changes equipment settings.

light button
Button that illuminates the display to make the data more legible in poor lighting conditions.

menu button
Button that displays the menus so that settings and operations can be selected.

microphone
Device that converts electric pulses into broadcast or recorded sounds.

monitor button
Button used to check if a broadcast or receiving channel is free before transmitting.

lock button
Button that deactivates the menu and scroll buttons to prevent equipment settings from being changed accidentally.

speaker
Integrated device used to generate sound.

push-to-talk switch
When this button is pressed, voice messages can be sent from one extension to another; when it is released, messages can be received.

wireless communication

numeric pager
Portable device that receives digital
messages (usually the telephone
number of the caller).

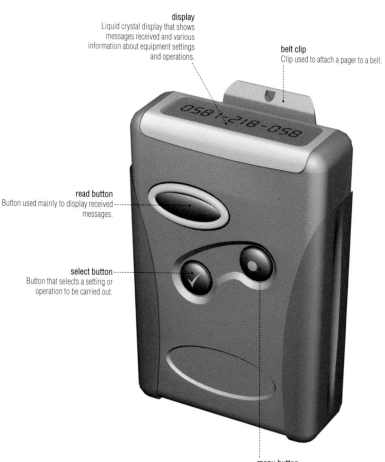

display
Liquid crystal display that shows
messages received and various
information about equipment settings
and operations.

belt clip
Clip used to attach a pager to a belt.

read button
Button used mainly to display received
messages.

select button
Button that selects a setting or
operation to be carried out.

menu button
Button that displays the menus so that
settings and operations can be
selected.

CB radio
Two-way radio often installed in a vehicle;
it transmits the human voice over reserved
frequencies on a public band.

push-to-talk switch
When this button is pressed, voice
messages can be sent from one CB unit to
another; when it is released, messages
can be received.

microphone
Device that converts electric pulses
into broadcast or recorded sounds.

cord

display
Liquid crystal display that shows the
channel in use.

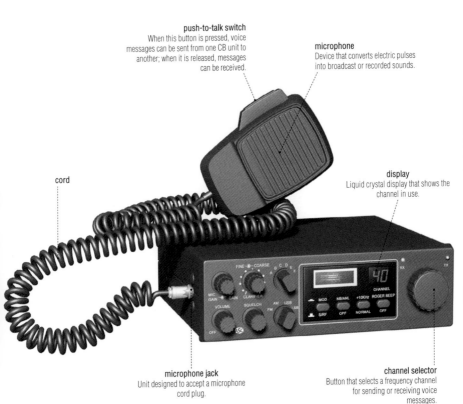

microphone jack
Unit designed to accept a microphone
cord plug.

channel selector
Button that selects a frequency channel
for sending or receiving voice
messages.

communication by telephone

Transmission of data, voice, audio or video messages between parties linked by a telephone network.

portable cellular telephone
Small telephone that transmits voice or text messages via radio waves.

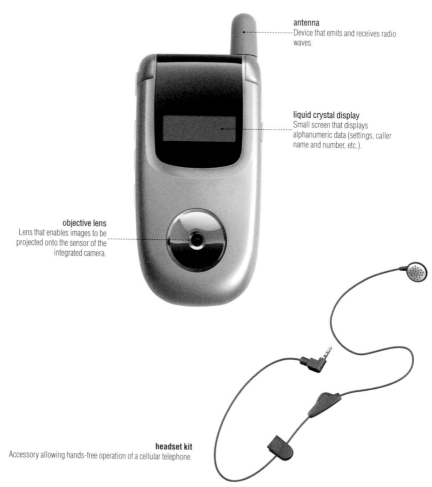

antenna
Device that emits and receives radio waves.

liquid crystal display
Small screen that displays alphanumeric data (settings, caller name and number, etc.).

objective lens
Lens that enables images to be projected onto the sensor of the integrated camera.

headset kit
Accessory allowing hands-free operation of a cellular telephone.

receiver
Small voice reproduction speaker that is placed over the ear.

liquid crystal display
Screen that displays images or alphanumeric data (settings and options, text messages, numbers dialed, address book, etc.).

MENU

EXIT   SELECT

menu key
Button providing direct access to the phone's main menu.

navigation key
Button used mainly to scroll through the phone's menus and directories.

soft key
Button used for a user-defined function.

camera key
Button providing access to the functions of the phone's integrated camera.

end/power key
Button used to end a phone call and to turn the phone's power on or off.

talk key
Button used to make or answer a call.

alphanumeric keypad
Keys corresponding to letters, numbers and symbols that are used to dial a number, compose a message or access functions.

microphone
Device that converts electric pulses into broadcast or recorded sounds.

communication by telephone

telephone set
Device allowing the human voice to be
transmitted over a distance by means
of a network of telephone lines.

handset
Movable part of the telephone made up
of the receiver and the transmitter.

receiver volume control

transmitter
Device that converts electric pulses
into broadcast or recorded sounds.

handset cord

push buttons
Keys corresponding to letters, numbers
and symbols that are used to dial a
number or access functions.

telephone index
List of frequently used names and
telephone numbers.

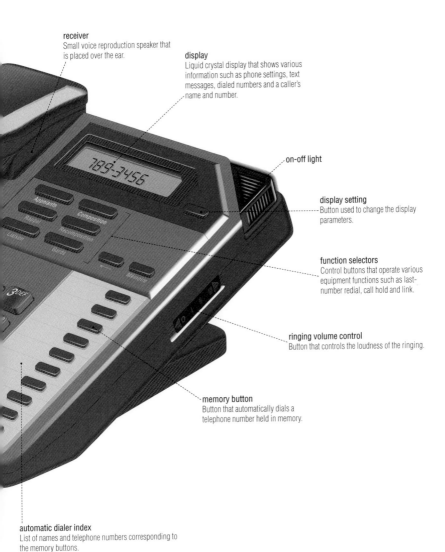

receiver
Small voice reproduction speaker that is placed over the ear.

display
Liquid crystal display that shows various information such as phone settings, text messages, dialed numbers and a caller's name and number.

on-off light

display setting
Button used to change the display parameters.

function selectors
Control buttons that operate various equipment functions such as last-number redial, call hold and link.

ringing volume control
Button that controls the loudness of the ringing.

memory button
Button that automatically dials a telephone number held in memory.

automatic dialer index
List of names and telephone numbers corresponding to the memory buttons.

communication by telephone

COMMUNICATIONS AND OFFICE AUTOMATION

pay phone
Telephone located in public places; it functions when coins or payment cards are inserted into the phone box.

coin slot
Slot for inserting coins into a telephone to pay for a call.

display
Liquid crystal display that shows a variety of information such as dialed number and prepaid card balance.

volume control
Button that controls the loudness of the phone.

next call
Button used to make another telephone call without hanging up the handset.

language display button

push button
Key corresponding to letters, numbers and symbols that are used to dial a number or access functions.

handset
Movable part of the telephone made up of the receiver and the transmitter.

card reader
Device used to read a payment card (credit card, calling card or prepaid card).

armored cord

coin return bucket
Small chamber for retrieving coins.

push-button telephone
Device with alphanumeric keys to dial a number or access functions; it has gradually replaced the dial phone.

smartphone
Device integrating the communication functions of a portable cell phone and the management functions of a personal digital assistant.

display
Liquid crystal display screen on which graphics or text data are displayed.

function keys
Keys used to execute operations (making a phone call, sending an e-mail) or access applications (notepad, address book, agenda).

keypad
Group of keys corresponding to letters, numbers, or symbols, used to generate characters or execute functions.

cordless telephone
Device featuring a handset with an antenna that is linked by radio waves to a base.

call director telephone
Device that redirects calls within an organization's internal telephone network.

communication by telephone

facsimile (fax) machine
Equipment used to send written documents over a telephone network.

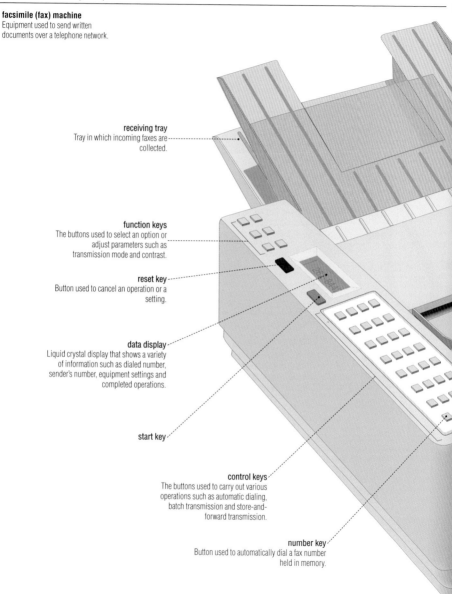

receiving tray
Tray in which incoming faxes are collected.

function keys
The buttons used to select an option or adjust parameters such as transmission mode and contrast.

reset key
Button used to cancel an operation or a setting.

data display
Liquid crystal display that shows a variety of information such as dialed number, sender's number, equipment settings and completed operations.

start key

control keys
The buttons used to carry out various operations such as automatic dialing, batch transmission and store-and-forward transmission.

number key
Button used to automatically dial a fax number held in memory.

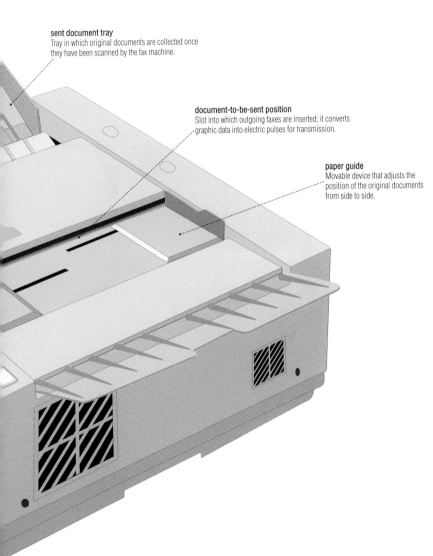

sent document tray
Tray in which original documents are collected once
they have been scanned by the fax machine.

document-to-be-sent position
Slot into which outgoing faxes are inserted; it converts
graphic data into electric pulses for transmission.

paper guide
Movable device that adjusts the
position of the original documents
from side to side.

office furniture

All the furniture in an office; it is intended mainly for filing, storage and carrying out work tasks.

work furniture
Furniture designed to facilitate office work, from writing to working at a computer or typewriter.

computer table
Table designed to hold a computer monitor and keyboard.

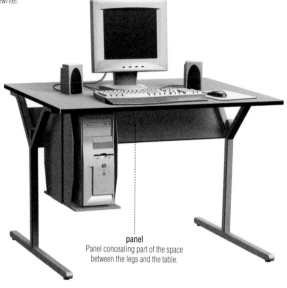

panel
Panel concealing part of the space between the legs and the table.

printer table
Table designed to hold a printer and its accessories.

desk mat
Accessory on which paper is placed for writing; it protects the desktop.

shelf
Horizontal space on which various accessories can be stored (extra paper, for example).

swivel-tilter armchair
Armchair designed to swivel horizontally around an axis and to tilt forward and back.

typist's chair
Padded chair on casters; the back can be tilted and adjusted for height.

executive desk
Desk with a large desktop work space and two built-in file drawers.

secretarial desk
Desk with two desktops meeting at right angles and one or two built-in file drawers.

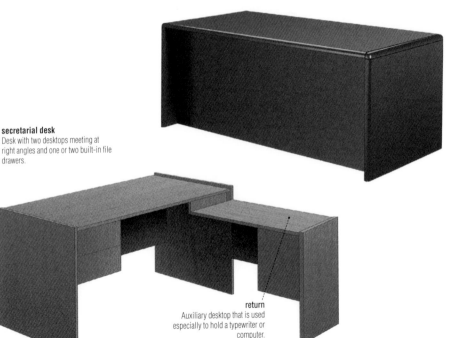

return
Auxiliary desktop that is used especially to hold a typewriter or computer.

filing furniture

Piece of furniture used to file documents by category or
in a given order.

mobile filing unit
Small piece of furniture on casters; it is
used to hold hanging files.

mobile drawer unit
Small piece of furniture on casters or legs; it
contains drawers and is usually placed under
a desk or table.

lateral filing cabinet
Compartmentalized piece of furniture with flipper
doors; it is used to hold hanging files.

photocopier
Equipment fitted with a photographic
device, which reproduces written texts
and images.

document handler
Device in which one or several sheets of
paper are placed to be photocopied.

cover
Movable part covering the glass plate
on which original documents are
placed to be photocopied.

control panel
Panel housing the photocopier's
operating buttons.

feeder output tray
Device used to collect unsorted photocopies.

bypass feeder
Device used to photocopy multiple
pages of a document consecutively.

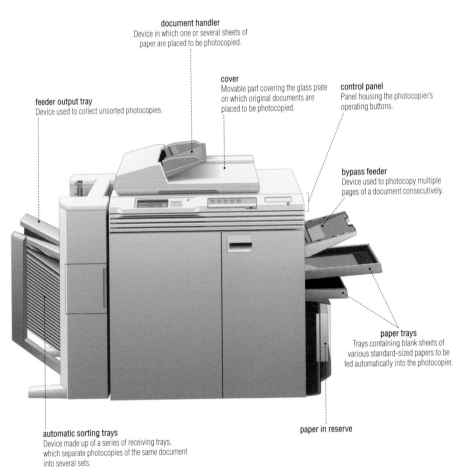

paper trays
Trays containing blank sheets of
various standard-sized papers to be
fed automatically into the photocopier.

automatic sorting trays
Device made up of a series of receiving trays,
which separate photocopies of the same document
into several sets.

paper in reserve

personal computer

Compact data processor consisting of a central processing unit that is connected to a monitor, a keyboard and various other peripherals.

tower case: front view
Tower case: rectangular enclosure that is taller than it is wide; it houses the operating components and peripherals of a personal computer.

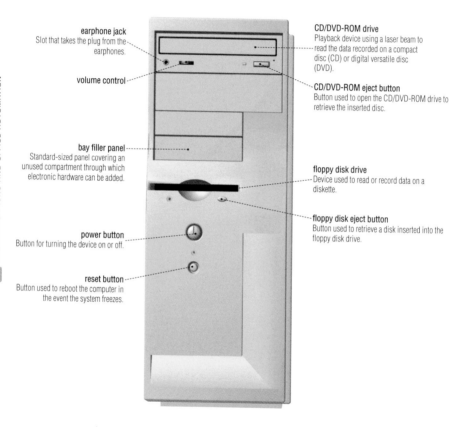

earphone jack
Slot that takes the plug from the earphones.

volume control

bay filler panel
Standard-sized panel covering an unused compartment through which electronic hardware can be added.

power button
Button for turning the device on or off.

reset button
Button used to reboot the computer in the event the system freezes.

CD/DVD-ROM drive
Playback device using a laser beam to read the data recorded on a compact disc (CD) or digital versatile disc (DVD).

CD/DVD-ROM eject button
Button used to open the CD/DVD-ROM drive to retrieve the inserted disc.

floppy disk drive
Device used to read or record data on a diskette.

floppy disk eject button
Button used to retrieve a disk inserted into the floppy disk drive.

tower case: back view

power cable plug
Device with metal prongs that connects the
computer by power cable to an electric
circuit.

mouse port
Round connector that links the
computer to the mouse.

power supply fan
Device blowing air to cool the internal
components of the power supply unit.

keyboard port
Round connector that links the
computer to the keyboard.

case fan
Device blowing air to cool the internal
components of the tower case.

USB port
Connector used to link several USB
standard peripherals simultaneously; it is
faster than serial and parallel ports.

network port
Connector that attaches the computer
to a network.

video port
Connector used to attach the computer
monitor to the video board; the latter is
inserted in the tower case and controls the
display of texts and graphics.

parallel port
Connector used mainly to attach the
computer to a printer; it is faster than a
serial port as it exchanges data in eight-bit
groups.

serial port
Connector used to attach a computer to
various peripherals such as an external
modem; it is slower than a parallel port as it
exchanges only one bit at a time.

game/MIDI port
Connector that attaches the computer to a
game device (e.g., a joystick) or a digital
musical instrument.

audio jack
Connection device that attaches the computer
to a variety of sound recording and
reproduction equipment such as a
microphone and loudspeakers.

internal modem port
Connector used to attach the internal
modem (a two-way digital signal
changing device) to a telephone line.

COMMUNICATIONS AND OFFICE AUTOMATION

personal computer

tower case: interior view

motherboard
Main circuit board that houses the components essential to the computer's operations, including the processor, chipset and connectors.

CD/DVD-ROM drive
Playback device using a laser beam to read the data recorded on a compact disc (CD) or digital versatile disc (DVD).

battery
Electric energy reserve used to power computer functions, which are still active when the computer is turned off.

random access memory (RAM) module
Module containing RAM chips, which temporarily store programs and data while they are being used or processed.

random access memory (RAM) connector
Device accepting a RAM module.

floppy disk drive
Device used to read or record data on a diskette.

secondary hard disk drive
Device used to play and record data on a secondary hard disk that complements the primary hard disk.

speaker
Integrated device used to generate sound.

primary hard disk drive
Device that reads and records data on the primary hard disk; it is the main storage medium for programs and data.

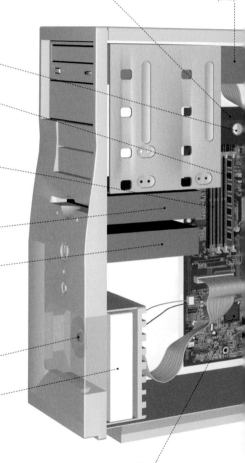

chipset
The integrated circuits (chips) welded to the motherboard, which coordinates the exchange of data between the computer's various components.

COMMUNICATIONS AND OFFICE AUTOMATION

bus
The wires and circuits allowing transmission of data, in the form of electric signals, between the computer's components.

power supply unit
Device that converts the power system's alternating current (AC) into direct current (DC) to supply power to the personal computer's internal components.

heat sink
Metal piece that disperses the heat generated by the processor's circuits.

processor
Central processing unit (CPU) that reads and executes programmed instructions.

AGP expansion connector
Socket accepting a video board designed according to AGP standards; it is extremely fast and provides high-quality 3-D displays.

filler plate
Plate covering an unused expansion connector.

PCI expansion connector
Socket accepting a PCI expansion card; it provides a higher transmission speed than an ISA conductor.

PCI expansion card
Circuit board designed according to PCI standards that is used to add functions to the computer; it can act as a video board, network interface board or soundboard.

ISA expansion connector
Socket accepting an expansion card designed according to ISA standards (usually a modem card or sound card).

power cable
Flexible electric cable that contains the conductors used to attach the power supply unit to the electric circuit.

input devices

Electronic devices used to transmit data and commands to a computer.

keyboard and pictograms

The keyboard contains a group of keys that correspond to characters and functions; the latter are represented by pictograms.

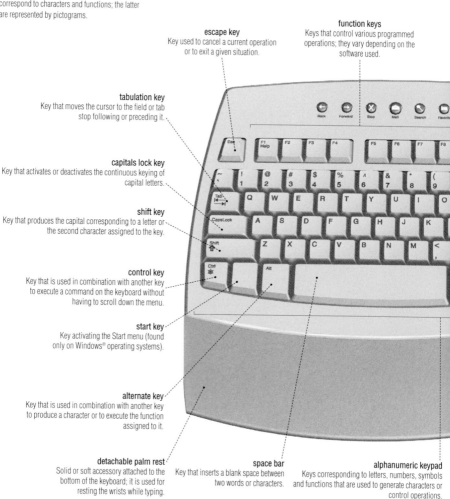

escape key
Key used to cancel a current operation or to exit a given situation.

function keys
Keys that control various programmed operations; they vary depending on the software used.

tabulation key
Key that moves the cursor to the field or tab stop following or preceding it.

capitals lock key
Key that activates or deactivates the continuous keying of capital letters.

shift key
Key that produces the capital corresponding to a letter or the second character assigned to the key.

control key
Key that is used in combination with another key to execute a command on the keyboard without having to scroll down the menu.

start key
Key activating the Start menu (found only on Windows® operating systems).

alternate key
Key that is used in combination with another key to produce a character or to execute the function assigned to it.

detachable palm rest
Solid or soft accessory attached to the bottom of the keyboard; it is used for resting the wrists while typing.

space bar
Key that inserts a blank space between two words or characters.

alphanumeric keypad
Keys corresponding to letters, numbers, symbols and functions that are used to generate characters or control operations.

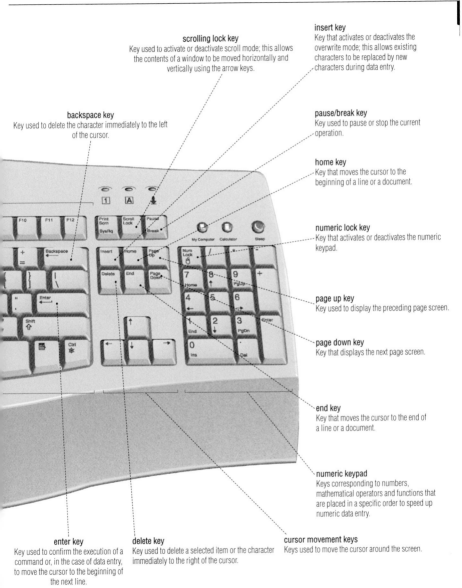

scrolling lock key
Key used to activate or deactivate scroll mode; this allows the contents of a window to be moved horizontally and vertically using the arrow keys.

insert key
Key that activates or deactivates the overwrite mode; this allows existing characters to be replaced by new characters during data entry.

backspace key
Key used to delete the character immediately to the left of the cursor.

pause/break key
Key used to pause or stop the current operation.

home key
Key that moves the cursor to the beginning of a line or a document.

numeric lock key
Key that activates or deactivates the numeric keypad.

page up key
Key used to display the preceding page screen.

page down key
Key that displays the next page screen.

end key
Key that moves the cursor to the end of a line or a document.

numeric keypad
Keys corresponding to numbers, mathematical operators and functions that are placed in a specific order to speed up numeric data entry.

enter key
Key used to confirm the execution of a command or, in the case of data entry, to move the cursor to the beginning of the next line.

delete key
Key used to delete a selected item or the character immediately to the right of the cursor.

cursor movement keys
Keys used to move the cursor around the screen.

input devices

wheel mouse
Mechanical or optical mouse that
contains a scroll wheel.

scroll wheel
Thumb wheel used to scroll down the
contents of a window without using the
scroll bar.

cable
Flexible cable containing the
conductors by which the mouse is
attached to the computer.

control button
Button that transmits various
commands to the computer.

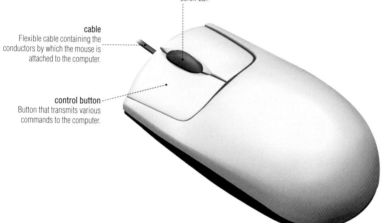

cordless mouse
Mechanical or optical mouse
connected to the computer by infrared
or radio signals.

mechanical mouse
Mouse whose case contains a movable rubber ball underneath to direct the movements of the pointer on the screen.

roller
Device that detects the ball's movements and transmit them to the computer.

cable
Flexible cable containing the conductors by which the mouse is attached to the computer.

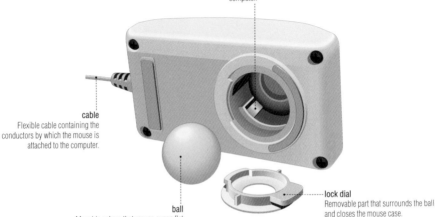

lock dial
Removable part that surrounds the ball and closes the mouse case.

ball
Movable sphere that moves over a flat surface (usually a mouse pad) to make the pointer move on the screen.

optical mouse
Mouse in which the ball is replaced by an optical system (light-emitting diode and sensor); it has no movable parts.

optical sensor
Device that measures the mouse's movements by analyzing the light rays (emitted by a diode) reflected from its support surface.

COMMUNICATIONS AND OFFICE AUTOMATION

input devices

microphone
Device that converts electric pulses
into broadcast or recorded sounds.

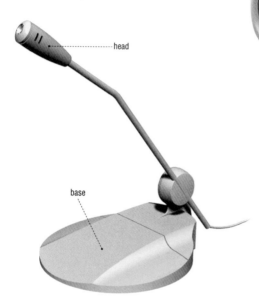

head

base

trackball
Device with a movable sphere on the
upper part of its case; it directs the
movements of the pointer on the
screen.

bar code reader
Device that uses an optical scanning
process to decode information
contained in bar codes.

mouse pad
Smooth antiskid surface over which the
mouse moves.

joystick
Device used in video games to direct the
movements of an object or character and to
transmit various commands.

hat switch
Multidirectional button that mainly
changes the view displayed on the
screen.

twist handle
Command lever that rotates around a
vertical axis to change the view or
make an object or character turn.

trigger
Device used mostly in combat games
to fire a projectile.

programmable buttons
Buttons that transmit various preset
commands to the computer.

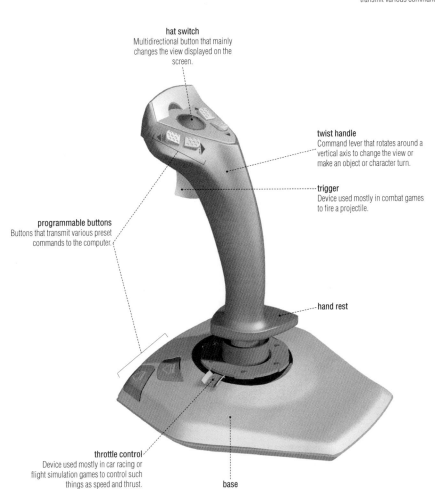

hand rest

throttle control
Device used mostly in car racing or
flight simulation games to control such
things as speed and thrust.

base

COMMUNICATIONS AND OFFICE AUTOMATION

input devices

Webcam
Miniature digital camera used to transmit video images in real time or for videoconferencing over the Internet.

cable
Flexible cable containing the conductors used to connect the Webcam to the computer.

microphone
Device that converts electric pulses into broadcast or recorded sounds.

lens
Optical system made up of a set of lenses fixed on a mount; it is used to transmit a filmed scene to a sensor.

base

COMMUNICATIONS AND OFFICE AUTOMATION

digital camcorder
Portable video camera in which the recording tape is replaced by a processor, which records and stores sounds and images in digital format.

digital camera
Camera that contains a sensor and a microprocessor rather than film; it records and stores images in digital form, which can then be viewed on a screen.

CD/ROM player
Equipment that uses a laser beam to read data
recorded on a compact disc.

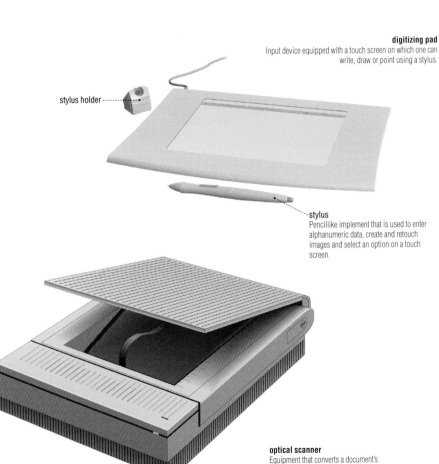

digitizing pad
Input device equipped with a touch screen on which one can
write, draw or point using a stylus.

stylus holder

stylus
Pencillike implement that is used to enter
alphanumeric data, create and retouch
images and select an option on a touch
screen.

optical scanner
Equipment that converts a document's
graphics or texts into digital data.

COMMUNICATIONS AND OFFICE AUTOMATION

755

output devices

Electronic devices used to view or print the results of data processing done on a computer.

flat screen monitor
Thin screen that usually has a liquid crystal display or plasma display surface.

video monitor
Device with a cathode ray surface that displays computer-generated graphics and texts visually.

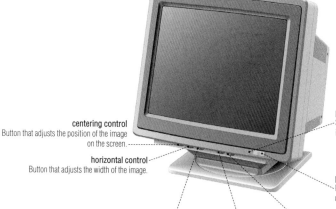

centering control
Button that adjusts the position of the image on the screen.

horizontal control
Button that adjusts the width of the image.

vertical control
Button that adjusts the height of the image.

contrast control
Button that adjusts the black and white part of an image.

power indicator
Signal light indicating that the screen is on.

power switch
Mechanical device that turns the monitor on or off.

brightness control
Button that increases or decreases the contrast between the light and dark parts of an image.

projector
Device that projects electronic images on a screen from sources such as computers, DVD players, camcorders and VCRs.

power switch
Mechanical connection that turns the projector on or off.

connector panel
The jacks used to connect the projector to various video equipment such as DVD players, camcorders and VCRs.

control panel
Panel housing the projector's operating buttons.

computer connector
Connector that links the projector to a computer.

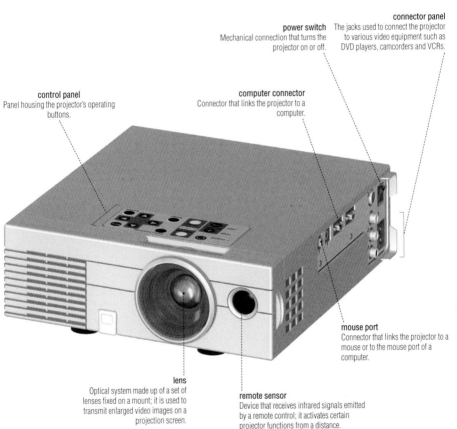

mouse port
Connector that links the projector to a mouse or to the mouse port of a computer.

lens
Optical system made up of a set of lenses fixed on a mount; it is used to transmit enlarged video images on a projection screen.

remote sensor
Device that receives infrared signals emitted by a remote control; it activates certain projector functions from a distance.

COMMUNICATIONS AND OFFICE AUTOMATION

output devices

inkjet printer

Printer with a movable printhead that sprays tiny droplets of ink onto paper to produce characters or images.

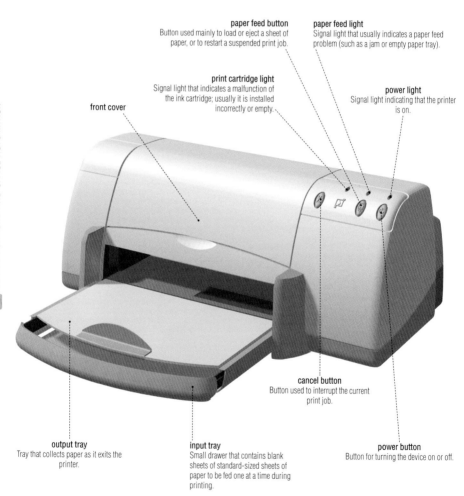

paper feed button
Button used mainly to load or eject a sheet of paper, or to restart a suspended print job.

paper feed light
Signal light that usually indicates a paper feed problem (such as a jam or empty paper tray).

print cartridge light
Signal light that indicates a malfunction of the ink cartridge; usually it is installed incorrectly or empty.

power light
Signal light indicating that the printer is on.

front cover

cancel button
Button used to interrupt the current print job.

output tray
Tray that collects paper as it exits the printer.

input tray
Small drawer that contains blank sheets of standard-sized sheets of paper to be fed one at a time during printing.

power button
Button for turning the device on or off.

toner cartridge
Removable container filled with fine particles of dry ink; it is designed for a laser printer.

output tray
Tray that collects paper as it exits the printer.

laser printer
Printer in which powdered ink in a cartridge is projected onto a rotating cylinder by laser beam and then fixed onto the paper using heated rollers.

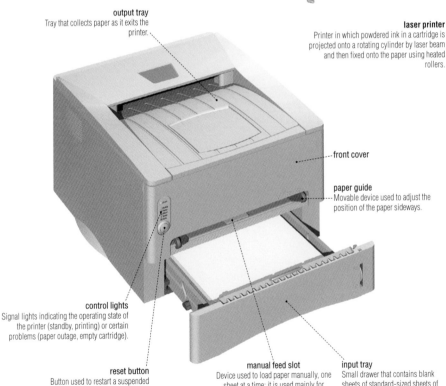

front cover

paper guide
Movable device used to adjust the position of the paper sideways.

control lights
Signal lights indicating the operating state of the printer (standby, printing) or certain problems (paper outage, empty cartridge).

reset button
Button used to restart a suspended print job.

manual feed slot
Device used to load paper manually, one sheet at a time; it is used mainly for special or odd-sized paper.

input tray
Small drawer that contains blank sheets of standard-sized sheets of paper to be fed one at a time during printing.

data storage devices

Electronic devices used to record or save data on a magnetic or optical medium.

hard disk drive
Device integrated into the computer that reads and
writes data on the hard disk inside the case.

disk
Rigid magnetic medium that is
mounted on a central axis; its surface
is divided into tracks and sectors on
which data are written.

disk motor
Device that converts the electric energy
powering it into mechanical energy so that
disks can rotate at several thousand
revolutions per minute.

actuator arm motor
Device that converts the electric energy powering
it into mechanical energy to move the actuator
arm according to the computer's instructions.

read/write head
Device used to extract stored data from a disk
or to write new data on a disk.

actuator arm
Movable arm bearing the read/write
head; it moves the head across the
surface of the disk.

memory card reader
Independent device, linked to a
computer via a cable or a USB
connector, that reads and records data
on a memory card.

removable hard disk drive
Stand-alone device that is connected by cable to a
computer; it is used to read and write data on a removable
hard disk.

removable hard disk
Case that contains a set of hard
magnetic disks for insertion into a
removable hard disk drive.

disk eject button
Button used to retrieve a removable hard disk
inserted in the drive.

COMMUNICATIONS AND OFFICE AUTOMATION

761

data storage devices

external floppy disk drive
Stand-alone device that is linked by
cable to a computer; it is used to read
and write data on a diskette.

USB flash drive
Small removable case containing a flash memory,
which enables the user to transfer, transport, and
store data.

USB connector
Connector that links the flash drive to a
computer's USB port.

diskette
Rigid case that contains a small flexible
magnetic disk on which data can be written,
erased and rewritten several times.

access window
Opening in the case where a disk passes
in front of the read/write head of a floppy
disk drive.

shutter
Sliding part that covers the read slot when the
diskette is not in use.

jacket

protect tab
Sliding part that covers the write protection
notch; it protects the diskette against any
accidental changes to its contents.

cassette
Rigid case that contains a recording tape on
which data can be recorded.

cassette drive
Device used to read and record data on a cassette recording tape.

DVD burner
Device used to record data on a writable or rewritable compact
disc by means of laser engraving.

disc tray
Part in which a disc is inserted to be
played back.

rewritable DVD disc
Digital recording medium on which data can
be engraved and erased several times.

Internet

Global network consisting of thousands of public and private networks of varying sizes; it is linked by a set of standard communications protocols.

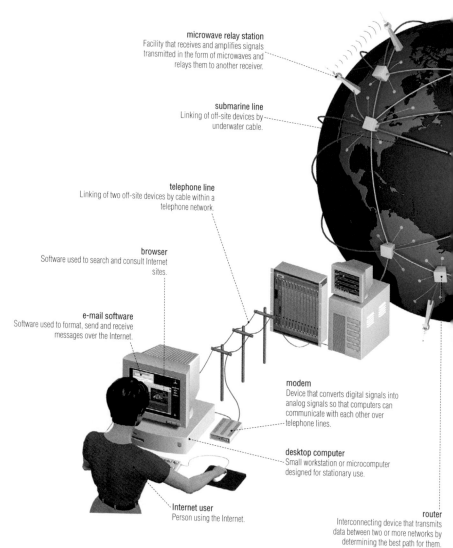

microwave relay station
Facility that receives and amplifies signals transmitted in the form of microwaves and relays them to another receiver.

submarine line
Linking of off-site devices by underwater cable.

telephone line
Linking of two off-site devices by cable within a telephone network.

browser
Software used to search and consult Internet sites.

e-mail software
Software used to format, send and receive messages over the Internet.

modem
Device that converts digital signals into analog signals so that computers can communicate with each other over telephone lines.

desktop computer
Small workstation or microcomputer designed for stationary use.

Internet user
Person using the Internet.

router
Interconnecting device that transmits data between two or more networks by determining the best path for them.

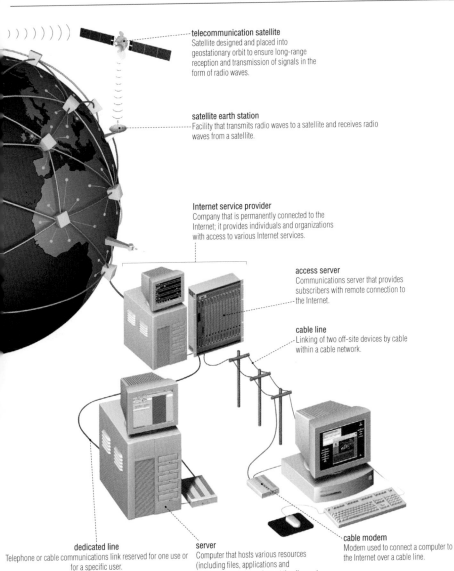

telecommunication satellite
Satellite designed and placed into
geostationary orbit to ensure long-range
reception and transmission of signals in the
form of radio waves.

satellite earth station
Facility that transmits radio waves to a satellite and receives radio
waves from a satellite.

Internet service provider
Company that is permanently connected to the
Internet; it provides individuals and organizations
with access to various Internet services.

access server
Communications server that provides
subscribers with remote connection to
the Internet.

cable line
Linking of two off-site devices by cable
within a cable network.

dedicated line
Telephone or cable communications link reserved for one use or
for a specific user.

server
Computer that hosts various resources
(including files, applications and
databases) and places them at the disposal
of all the devices connected to the network.

cable modem
Modem used to connect a computer to
the Internet over a cable line.

Internet uses

A number of user types use Internet tools and resources to communicate, find information and entertainment, make purchases and manage funds.

government organization
The Internet has made it easy for government departments and agencies to communicate with other organizations and with the citizens they serve.

cultural organization
The Internet allows the public to learn about programs offered by cultural organizations in a city or region.

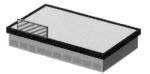

home user
Anyone can access the Internet from home through an Internet service provider (ISP).

educational institution
The Internet provides teachers, researchers and students with countless opportunities to research and exchange information.

enterprise
The Internet facilitates exchanges between employees within the same company and between the company and its customers and suppliers.

commercial concern
A company that specializes in product marketing can use the Internet to contact suppliers and customers.

industry
The Internet allows a manufacturer to communicate with its suppliers, customers and regulatory bodies.

health organization
The Internet fosters exchanges between researchers, health professionals and patients.

chat room
Activity allowing two or more Internet users to converse in writing in real time.

e-commerce
Sale or promotion of products and services over the Internet.

podcasting
Service for automatic downloading of audio or video documents to a digital portable audio player to be listened to later.

e-mail
Service by which messages are exchanged between users of a computer network.

newsgroup
Service enabling a group of people to discuss various subjects live or on a time-delay basis.

database
Group of data related to the same topic that is arranged in order and available for direct consultation by several users.

information spreading
Transmission of information about an organization, an event, a product or a topic, usually by creating or updating a Web site.

search
Locating information on a given topic in the hope of finding something useful; it is usually done with the help of a search engine.

online game
Video game accessible over the Internet; users can play solo or with multiple players at a distance.

blog
Web site in the form of a personal journal in which a person shares opinions or impressions in notes or short articles.

business transactions
Operations involving financing and funds management (e.g., arranging a loan or transferring funds) over the Internet.

laptop computer

Small stand-alone microcomputer with a screen and integrated keyboard; it is powered by an internal battery.

laptop computer: front view

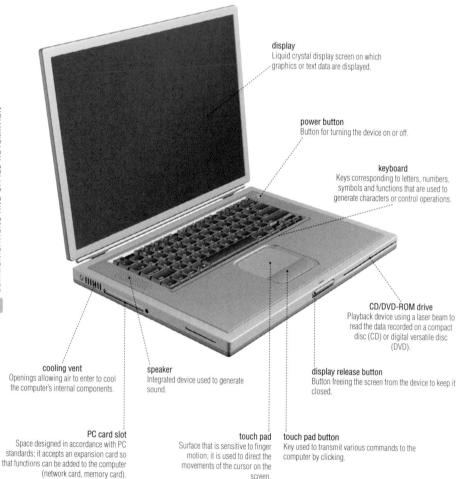

display
Liquid crystal display screen on which graphics or text data are displayed.

power button
Button for turning the device on or off.

keyboard
Keys corresponding to letters, numbers, symbols and functions that are used to generate characters or control operations.

CD/DVD-ROM drive
Playback device using a laser beam to read the data recorded on a compact disc (CD) or digital versatile disc (DVD).

cooling vent
Openings allowing air to enter to cool the computer's internal components.

speaker
Integrated device used to generate sound.

display release button
Button freeing the screen from the device to keep it closed.

PC card slot
Space designed in accordance with PC standards; it accepts an expansion card so that functions can be added to the computer (network card, memory card).

touch pad
Surface that is sensitive to finger motion; it is used to direct the movements of the cursor on the screen.

touch pad button
Key used to transmit various commands to the computer by clicking.

laptop computer: rear view

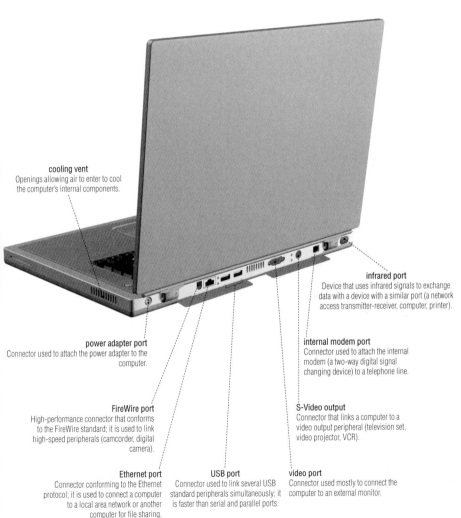

COMMUNICATIONS AND OFFICE AUTOMATION

cooling vent
Openings allowing air to enter to cool
the computer's internal components.

infrared port
Device that uses infrared signals to exchange
data with a device with a similar port (a network
access transmitter-receiver, computer, printer).

power adapter port
Connector used to attach the power adapter to the
computer.

internal modem port
Connector used to attach the internal
modem (a two-way digital signal
changing device) to a telephone line.

FireWire port
High-performance connector that conforms
to the FireWire standard; it is used to link
high-speed peripherals (camcorder, digital
camera).

S-Video output
Connector that links a computer to a
video output peripheral (television set,
video projector, VCR).

Ethernet port
Connector conforming to the Ethernet
protocol; it is used to connect a computer
to a local area network or another
computer for file sharing.

USB port
Connector used to link several USB
standard peripherals simultaneously; it
is faster than serial and parallel ports.

video port
Connector used mostly to connect the
computer to an external monitor.

handheld computer

Small portable computer with a miniature operating system; it is used mostly for personal management tasks (agenda, address book).

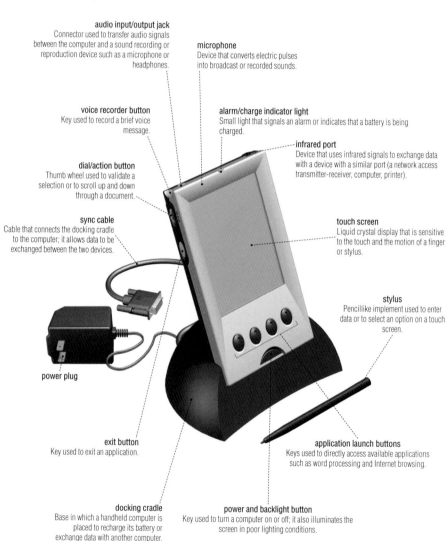

audio input/output jack
Connector used to transfer audio signals between the computer and a sound recording or reproduction device such as a microphone or headphones.

microphone
Device that converts electric pulses into broadcast or recorded sounds.

voice recorder button
Key used to record a brief voice message.

alarm/charge indicator light
Small light that signals an alarm or indicates that a battery is being charged.

infrared port
Device that uses infrared signals to exchange data with a device with a similar port (a network access transmitter-receiver, computer, printer).

dial/action button
Thumb wheel used to validate a selection or to scroll up and down through a document.

sync cable
Cable that connects the docking cradle to the computer; it allows data to be exchanged between the two devices.

touch screen
Liquid crystal display that is sensitive to the touch and the motion of a finger or stylus.

stylus
Pencillike implement used to enter data or to select an option on a touch screen.

power plug

exit button
Key used to exit an application.

application launch buttons
Keys used to directly access available applications such as word processing and Internet browsing.

docking cradle
Base in which a handheld computer is placed to recharge its battery or exchange data with another computer.

power and backlight button
Key used to turn a computer on or off; it also illuminates the screen in poor lighting conditions.

Equipment, instruments and accessories needed to carry out office tasks.

pocket calculator
Small self-powered electronic
instrument used to automatically make
numerical calculations.

divide key
Key used to calculate the quotient of
two numbers.

clear-entry key
Key used to erase the last number entered.

wallet

solar cell
Device that converts sunlight into
electric current to power a pocket
calculator.

display
Liquid crystal display that shows the
last number entered or the result of
operations carried out.

clear key
Key used to return the pocket
calculator to zero.

multiply key
Key used to calculate the product of
two numbers.

number key
Key used to enter a number.

square root key
Key used to derive the square root of a
number; this is the number that is
multiplied by itself to give the basic
number.

subtract key
Key used to calculate the difference
between two numbers.

change sign key
Key used to change the plus or minus sign
of the displayed number.

decimal key
Key used to insert a decimal symbol to
separate the whole and fraction parts of a
number.

equals key
Key used to display the results of
operations carried out.

percent key
Key used to obtain the decimal form of
a displayed number by dividing it by
100; it is used mainly to calculate
percentages.

add key
Key used to add two numbers.

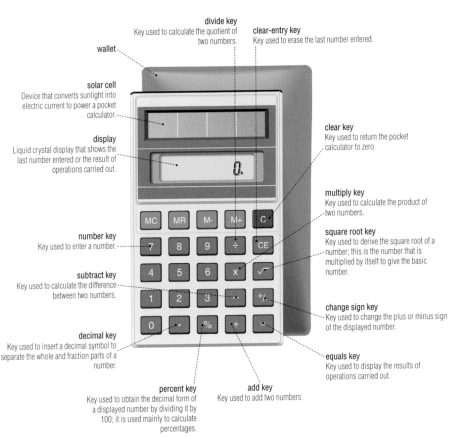

COMMUNICATIONS AND OFFICE AUTOMATION

stationery

scientific calculator
Calculator designed to execute mathematical operations
specific to science and technology.

access to the second level of operations
Key used to select a second function controlled by a
key.

result line
Part of the screen that shows the
solution to the problem.

entries line
Part of the screen that shows the
problem to be solved.

cursor movement keys
Keys used to move the cursor around the screen.

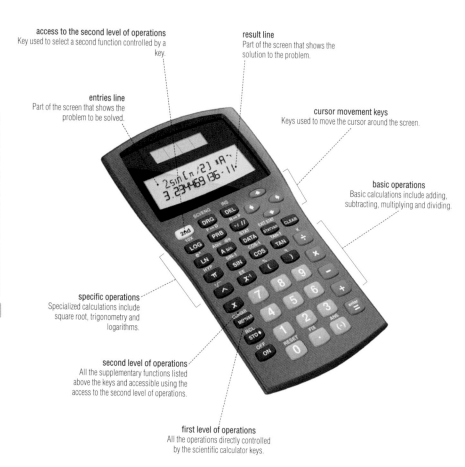

basic operations
Basic calculations include adding,
subtracting, multiplying and dividing.

specific operations
Specialized calculations include
square root, trigonometry and
logarithms.

second level of operations
All the supplementary functions listed
above the keys and accessible using the
access to the second level of operations.

first level of operations
All the operations directly controlled
by the scientific calculator keys.

printing calculator
Office calculator with an integrated printer; it is used mainly in business and administration.

multiple use key
Key that facilitates certain financial calculations (margin, selling price, costs).

non-add/subtotal
Key used to print numbers other than calculations (codes, dates) or to obtain the results of an operations subset.

printer
Device that makes a hard copy of data transmitted by the calculator.

add/equals key
Key used to display the results of operations carried out; on some calculators, it can also be used to do repeated calculations.

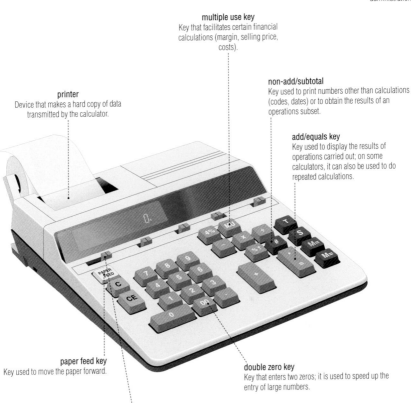

paper feed key
Key used to move the paper forward.

double zero key
Key that enters two zeros; it is used to speed up the entry of large numbers.

number of decimals
Device used to adjust the number of decimals making up the fraction of a number.

for time management

personal digital assistant
Small pocket computer that stores in memory and manages a variety of information such as addresses, telephone numbers and appointments.

display
Liquid crystal display screen on which graphics or text data are displayed.

alphabetical keypad
Keys corresponding to letters, symbols and functions used to generate characters or control operations.

numeric keypad
Keys corresponding to numbers, mathematical operators and functions that are placed in a specific order to speed up numeric data entry.

time clock
Device used to print the arrival and departure times
of employees on time cards.

display
Liquid crystal display showing a
variety of information (including date,
hour and settings).

time card
Card on which an employee's arrival and
departure times are listed so that worked
time can be precisely calculated.

self-stick note
Small piece of paper with a sticky strip
on the back for temporary attachment
to a surface.

COMMUNICATIONS AND OFFICE AUTOMATION

stationery

tear-off calendar
Pad of tear-off sheets printed with the day and date; it is used to jot down appointments and things to do.

calendar pad
Sheets of paper printed with the day and date and on a ring base; it is used to jot down appointments and things to do.

appointment book
Notebook that is printed with the day and date; it is used to jot down appointments and things to do.

memo pad
Set of tear-off sheets of paper used mainly for taking notes.

for correspondence

postage meter
Machine used to print a postage meter
stamp on an envelope or label in lieu
of using a postage stamp.

postmarking module
Unit housing the machine's control buttons; it
is used to set the prepaid postage meter with
the correct amount of postage.

feed deck
Device on which envelopes are placed
to be stamped with a postage meter.

letter opener
Small knife used to open envelopes
and cut sheets of paper.

base

finger tip
Rubber sheath to cover the finger; it is used
mainly to turn pages more easily or to sort
papers or banknotes more quickly.

stationery

COMMUNICATIONS AND OFFICE AUTOMATION

rotary file
Device with a set of files that rotate on
a spindle for easy consultation.

moistener
Device used to moisten postage
stamps and labels.

letter scale
Scale used to weigh a letter or parcel.

desk tray
Container that usually has several
compartments; it is used to handle
incoming and outgoing mail.

padded envelope
Envelope that is lined with bubble wrap
to protect the contents from humidity
and impact damage.

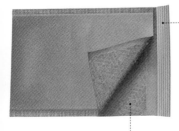

self-sealing flap
Flap coated with an adhesive
substance; it seals an envelope on
contact.

telephone index
Book in which frequently used names,
addresses and telephone numbers are
written and stored in alphabetical
order.

air bubbles
Small air pockets that form a protective
cushion around the contents of an
envelope.

signature book
Register made up of sheets of blotting
paper; documents that require a
manager's signature are placed in it.

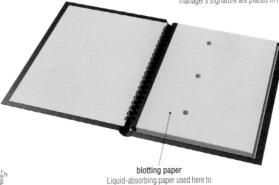

blotting paper
Liquid-absorbing paper used here to
remove excess ink from newly signed
documents.

steno book
Spiral-bound sheets of lined paper;
these books were originally used by
stenographers to take dictation.

stamp rack
Rack used to hold such items as
rubber stamps for dating and
numbering.

stamp pad
Ink-saturated pad on which a rubber
stamp is moistened prior to stamping.

numbering machine
Device consisting of movable strips
embossed with a series of digits; it is
used to print numbers.

rubber stamp
Device consisting of an embossed
rubber strip that is inked to print a
stamp on an object or document.

dater
Device consisting of movable strips
embossed with a series of digits and
letters; it is used to print the date.

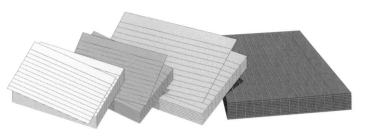

index cards
Heavyweight sheets of paper of varying sizes that are used to record information on a given topic.

label maker
Device used to print characters on a self-adhesive strip.

self-adhesive labels
Small pieces of paper used to identify objects; they are coated on one side with an adhesive that sticks without wetting.

tab
Piece of metal or plastic that is attached to a file guide, folder or file so they can be quickly retrieved.

window tab
Tab with an opening to hold an identification label.

dividers
Heavyweight sheets of paper with side
tabs; they are used to separate groups
of pages inside a binder.

clamp binder
Binder fitted with a spring clip; it is used to hold and
file sheets of paper.

spring binder
Binder in which sheets of paper are held in
place by the pressure of springs.

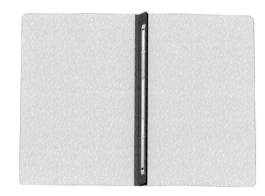

fastener binder
Binder with a flexible rod fitted with
two sliding rings; it is used to hold and
file punched sheets of paper.

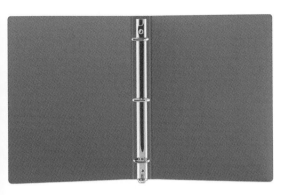

ring binder
Hardcover binder fitted with rings; it is used
to hold and file punched sheets of paper.

spiral binder
Notebook made up of a set of punched sheets
of paper bound together with a spiral wire of
metal or plastic.

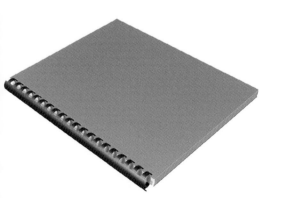

comb binding
Notebook made up of a set of punched
sheets of paper that are bound together with
a toothed plastic strip.

post binder
Binder with two rods that fit into a
hinge; it is used to hold and file
punched sheets of paper.

document folder
Folder with pockets used to hold information documents; they are often handed out to meeting participants or journalists.

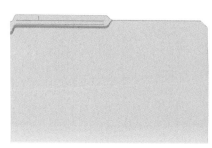

folder
Rigid cardboard that is folded in half; documents on the same topic are placed in it.

file guides
Heavyweight sheets of paper with a tab at the top; they are used to separate groups of documents or folders in a filing cabinet drawer.

hanging file
Folder fitted with metal hangers that is hung in a filing cabinet drawer.

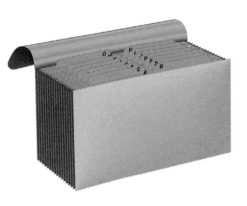

expanding file
Usually expandable file with compartments; it is used to store documents by subject.

paper punch
Device used to punch holes in sheets of paper.

filing box
Small open cardboard box that is mainly used to hold magazines, catalogs and brochures.

clipboard
Rigid board fitted with a spring clip under which sheets of paper are placed mainly to take notes.

archboard
Rigid board fitted with two arched metal clips on which punched sheets are placed.

index card cabinet
Small file drawer designed to hold and
store index cards in a set order.

index card drawer
Small built-in drawer designed for
storage and filing of index cards.

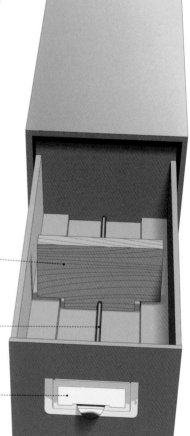

compressor
Movable panel that holds index cards
in an upright position.

metal rail
Cylindrical rod along which the
compressor moves.

label holder
Part with an opening to hold an
identification label.

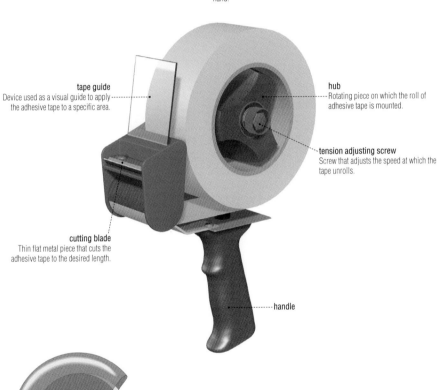

box sealing tape dispenser
Device that is used to unroll, apply and cut a roll of adhesive tape using one hand.

tape guide
Device used as a visual guide to apply the adhesive tape to a specific area.

hub
Rotating piece on which the roll of adhesive tape is mounted.

tension adjusting screw
Screw that adjusts the speed at which the tape unrolls.

cutting blade
Thin flat metal piece that cuts the adhesive tape to the desired length.

handle

tape dispenser
Holder that eases the unrolling and cutting of a roll of adhesive tape.

COMMUNICATIONS AND OFFICE AUTOMATION

eraser holder
Tube containing an eraser that is advanced by using a pushbutton.

stick holder
Pencil with an eraser at one end.

clip
Device with two articulated arms that are pressed together to hold such items as sheets of paper and index cards.

eraser
Small block of rubber used to erase pencil marks and some types of ink.

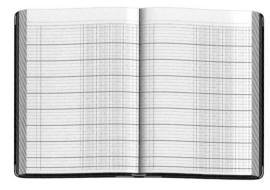

account book
Book with columns in which the financial data of an organization (such as sales, purchases, receipts and expenditures) are recorded.

paper clips
Small clips made from a piece of bent metal wire; they are used to hold a few sheets of paper or index cards.

thumb tacks
Small tacks with short pointy ends; they are easily pushed in with the finger and are used to attach sheets of paper, cardboard or posters to a surface.

paper fasteners
Small clips made of two bars, which spread open to hold sheets of paper or cardboard.

paper clip holder
Small box containing paper clips, which are released one by one through a magnetic opening.

magnet
Material that produces a magnetic field; it attracts paper clips to the top and holds them in place around the opening.

bill-file
Holder fitted with a pointy rod on which notes and bills are stacked.

stationery

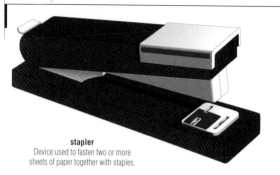

stapler
Device used to fasten two or more
sheets of paper together with staples.

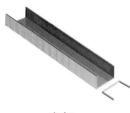

staples
Pieces of metal wire for loading in a
stapler; they are used to fasten sheets
of paper together.

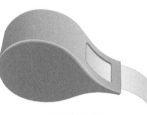

correction paper
Adhesive tape that covers up printed or
written characters so that corrections
can be made.

staple remover
Device used to remove staples from
sheets of paper.

correction fluid
Liquid that covers up printed or written
characters so that corrections can be
made.

pencil sharpener
Portable device used to sharpen
pencils by rotating them in a cone-
shaped chamber fitted with a blade.

pencil sharpener
Office device with a rotating blade that
is controlled by a crank; it is used to
sharpen pencils.

overhead projector
Device that projects the enlarged image of
a document printed on a transparency on a
screen located behind the user.

projection head
Movable part that contains the lens and
mirror; a focusing ring changes its position to
give a clear image on the screen.

mirror
Polished glass surface that directs
light from the lens toward the
projection screen.

optical lens
Transparent optical disk that captures
the light from the optical stage and
makes it converge toward the mirror.

optical stage
Glass plate that is lit by an internal
light; the document to be projected is
placed on it.

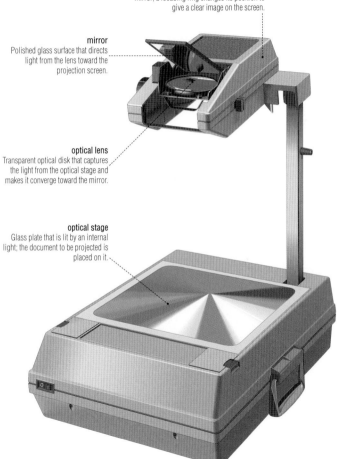

COMMUNICATIONS AND OFFICE AUTOMATION

road system

Network of thoroughfares providing for the flow of traffic.

cross section of a road
Road: thoroughfare connecting two geographical
points, usually urban centers.

surface course
Roadway's driving surface; it is
smooth, impermeable and provides a
good grip for vehicles.

roadway
Surface upon which vehicles drive.

solid line
Line demarcating the edge of the
roadway or, when in the center of the
roadway, indicating that passing is
prohibited.

shoulder
Area between the roadway and the
ditch, providing the roadway lateral
support; it is also a place for
emergency stops.

base
Series of layers above the embankment
reducing stress exerted by the traffic and
preventing the bed from deforming.

bed
Composed of the embankment and the
earth foundation; the base rests on it.

earth foundation
Part of the ground that was not
excavated during the road's
construction.

broken line
Line demarcating the two lanes of the
roadway and showing that passing is
permitted.

TRANSPORTATION

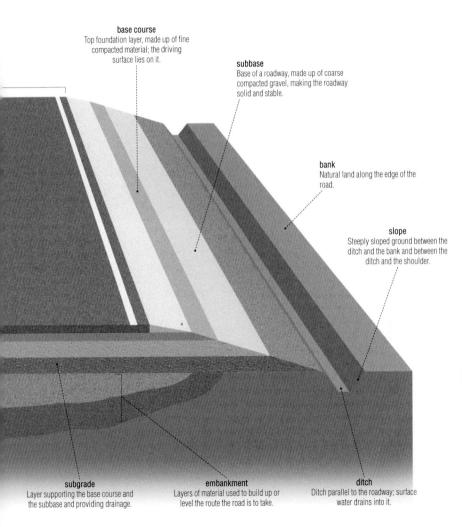

base course
Top foundation layer, made up of fine compacted material; the driving surface lies on it.

subbase
Base of a roadway, made up of coarse compacted gravel, making the roadway solid and stable.

bank
Natural land along the edge of the road.

slope
Steeply sloped ground between the ditch and the bank and between the ditch and the shoulder.

subgrade
Layer supporting the base course and the subbase and providing drainage.

embankment
Layers of material used to build up or level the route the road is to take.

ditch
Ditch parallel to the roadway; surface water drains into it.

TRANSPORTATION

road system

cloverleaf
Interchange with four branches where the inside loops are for turning left and the direct links for turning right.

loop
Wide circular curve for moving from one highway to another in order to change direction.

broken line
Line demarcating the two lanes of the roadway and showing that passing is permitted.

traffic lanes
Parts of the roadway demarcated by lines, each accommodating a single line of vehicles.

freeway
Large thoroughfare with separate one-way lanes and no crossing streets; reserved for high-speed traffic.

acceleration lane
Temporary lane where vehicles entering the freeway gain speed in order to safely merge into the traffic lane.

passing lane
Far left traffic lane where faster-moving vehicles pass other traffic.

traffic lane
Part of the roadway demarcated by lines, each accommodating a single line of vehicles.

deceleration lane
Temporary lane where vehicles slow down after leaving the traffic lanes.

slower traffic
Far right traffic lane for slower-moving vehicles.

ramp
Connecting lane between two highways or between a road and a highway for changing direction.

TRANSPORTATION

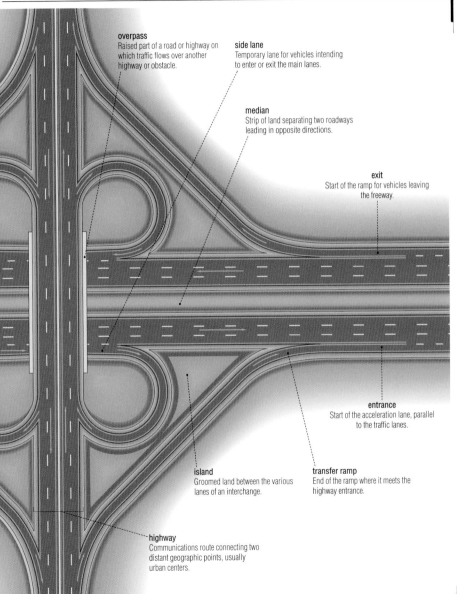

overpass
Raised part of a road or highway on which traffic flows over another highway or obstacle.

side lane
Temporary lane for vehicles intending to enter or exit the main lanes.

median
Strip of land separating two roadways leading in opposite directions.

exit
Start of the ramp for vehicles leaving the freeway.

entrance
Start of the acceleration lane, parallel to the traffic lanes.

island
Groomed land between the various lanes of an interchange.

transfer ramp
End of the ramp where it meets the highway entrance.

highway
Communications route connecting two distant geographic points, usually urban centers.

TRANSPORTATION

examples of interchanges

Interchange: structure linking roads or freeways so they do not intersect.

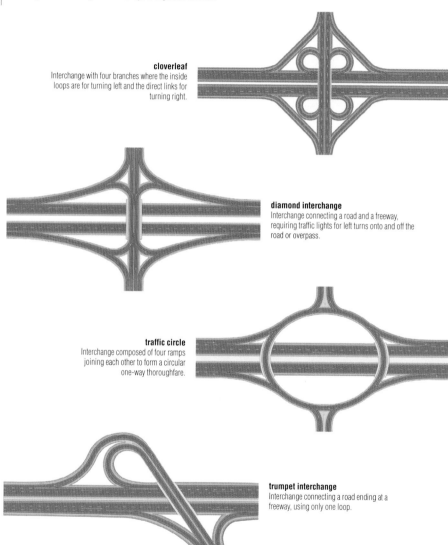

cloverleaf
Interchange with four branches where the inside loops are for turning left and the direct links for turning right.

diamond interchange
Interchange connecting a road and a freeway, requiring traffic lights for left turns onto and off the road or overpass.

traffic circle
Interchange composed of four ramps joining each other to form a circular one-way thoroughfare.

trumpet interchange
Interchange connecting a road ending at a freeway, using only one loop.

fixed bridges

Structures enabling traffic to clear an obstacle, such as a river, gorge or highway.

beam bridge
Bridge whose deck is composed of one or several beams, which are supported by piers across the open space.

abutment
A pier's point of support on firm ground.

overpass
Raised part of a road or highway on which traffic flows over another highway or obstacle.

continuous beam
Extended load-bearing part supported by abutments and piers.

parapet
Chest-high barrier on each side of the deck, preventing people and vehicles from falling off.

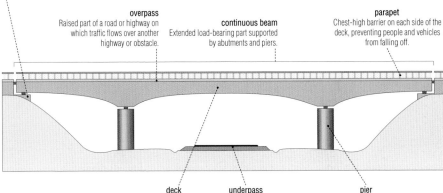

deck
Set of components making up the structure that carries the bridge's traffic lanes.

underpass
Lowered part of a thoroughfare, enabling traffic to flow under another roadway or obstacle.

pier
Sturdy load-bearing component placed at intervals to support the bridge's beams.

cantilever bridge
Bridge whose two main spans extend toward each other and support a short suspended span, which bears less load.

cantilever span
Span with a complex framework on each side of a central pillar; one end of the span rests on the ground and the other supports a suspended span.

suspended span
Short center span resting on the ends of the two cantilever spans.

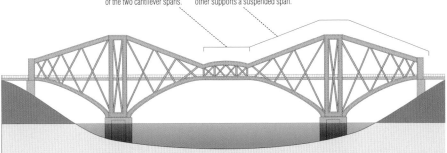

fixed bridges

arch bridge
Bridge whose deck is supported by
suspenders attached to an arch, which
exerts diagonal thrust against the
lateral supports.

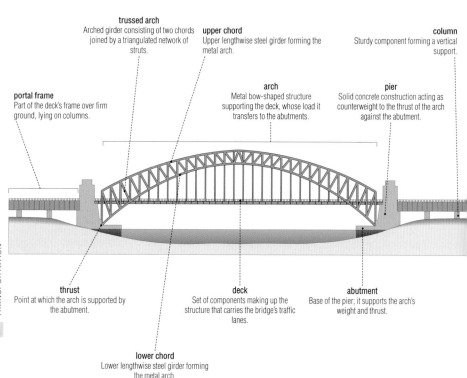

trussed arch
Arched girder consisting of two chords
joined by a triangulated network of
struts.

upper chord
Upper lengthwise steel girder forming the
metal arch.

column
Sturdy component forming a vertical
support.

portal frame
Part of the deck's frame over firm
ground, lying on columns.

arch
Metal bow-shaped structure
supporting the deck, whose load it
transfers to the abutments.

pier
Solid concrete construction acting as
counterweight to the thrust of the arch
against the abutment.

thrust
Point at which the arch is supported by
the abutment.

deck
Set of components making up the
structure that carries the bridge's traffic
lanes.

abutment
Base of the pier; it supports the arch's
weight and thrust.

lower chord
Lower lengthwise steel girder forming
the metal arch.

TRANSPORTATION

suspension bridge
Bridge whose long deck is suspended from
load-bearing cables, which are supported by
the towers and anchored in the ground at
both ends of the bridge.

suspender
Cable or metal rod connecting the
suspension cable to the deck,
supporting it.

approach ramp
Lane for accessing the bridge.

deck
Set of components making up the
structure that carries the bridge's traffic
lanes.

suspension cable
Very strong, flexible component made
of steel wires; it bears the weight of the
deck.

tower
Elevated structure made of metal or
reinforced concrete; it supports the
cables.

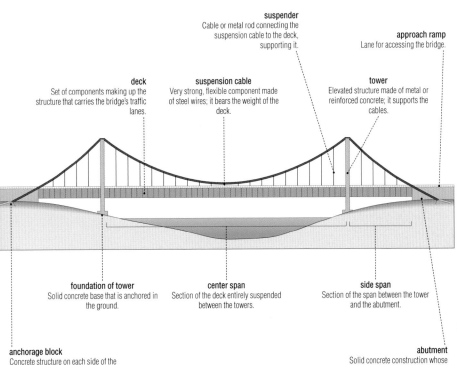

foundation of tower
Solid concrete base that is anchored in
the ground.

center span
Section of the deck entirely suspended
between the towers.

side span
Section of the span between the tower
and the abutment.

anchorage block
Concrete structure on each side of the
abutment; it is buried deep in the ground and
the end of the suspension cable is attached to it.

abutment
Solid concrete construction whose
mass counterbalances the weight of
the suspended roadway.

TRANSPORTATION

movable bridges

Bridges whose decks move to free up the transportation channel they cross, or that are built temporarily while awaiting a permanent structure.

swing bridge
Bridge whose deck pivots around a vertical axle.

turntable
Moving mechanical structure on a pier enabling the deck to pivot.

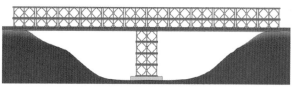

Bailey bridge
Steel bridge, often temporary, whose standardized truss components make it easy to assemble quickly.

floating bridge
Bridge whose deck rests on pontoons that can be taken apart to open the bridge.

manrope
Chest-high barrier on each side of the deck, preventing people and vehicles from falling off.

pontoon
Floating caisson filled with air and supporting the deck.

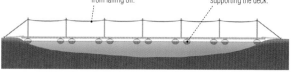

trolley
Part of the bridge moved by a motor; it glides along rails installed under the deck.

transporter bridge
Bridge with a very high deck from which a moving platform is suspended to transport pedestrians and vehicles.

platform
Cabin suspended from the trolley by cables; it moves from one shore to the other.

double-leaf bascule bridge
Bridge whose deck is composed of two spans joining each other at the middle of the bridge and pivoting around a vertical axle at each abutment.

single-leaf bascule bridge
Bridge whose deck is raised by means of a counterweight mechanism.

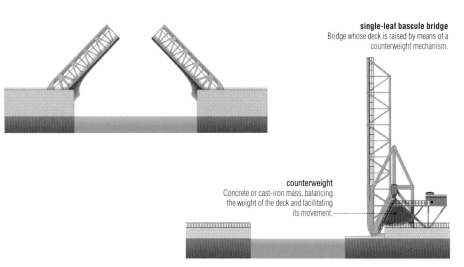

counterweight
Concrete or cast-iron mass, balancing the weight of the deck and facilitating its movement.

guiding tower
Pylon equipped with pulleys and cables for hoisting the deck.

lift bridge
Bridge whose deck is raised by a system of cables.

lift span
Deck suspended at each end by cables hoisting it up along the guiding towers.

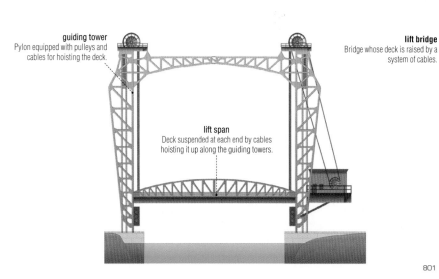

TRANSPORTATION

automobile

Motor vehicle comprising four wheels, developed for transporting a small number of people and small loads.

examples of bodies

Styles vary from manufacturer to manufacturer and from year to year but there is little variation in the basic model.

micro compact car
Very small automobile comprising two seats and integrated cargo area, designed to be driven and parked in large cities.

sports car
Automobile with an aerodynamic look comprising two doors, a small trunk separate from the passenger compartment and, sometimes, narrow rear seats.

two-door sedan
Automobile comprising two doors, a trunk separate from the passenger compartment and four places.

hatchback
Automobile comprising two doors and a lift gate, folding front seats granting access to the rear seats, and a cargo area integrated with the passenger compartment.

four-door sedan
Automobile comprising four doors and a trunk separate from the passenger compartment.

convertible
Automobile comprising two or four doors and a soft or hard retractable roof.

station wagon
Automobile comprising four doors, a large cargo area integrated with the passenger compartment and folding rear seats for enlarging the cargo area.

minivan
Automobile comprising three rows of seats; the last row can be folded down to enlarge the cargo area.

sport-utility vehicle
Automobile designed to be driven on any kind of roadway or on rugged terrain.

pickup truck
Automobile comprising only one row of seats and an uncovered bed closed off by a gate.

limousine
Spacious deluxe sedan comprising four or more doors; the passenger area is separated from the chauffeur's.

TRANSPORTATION

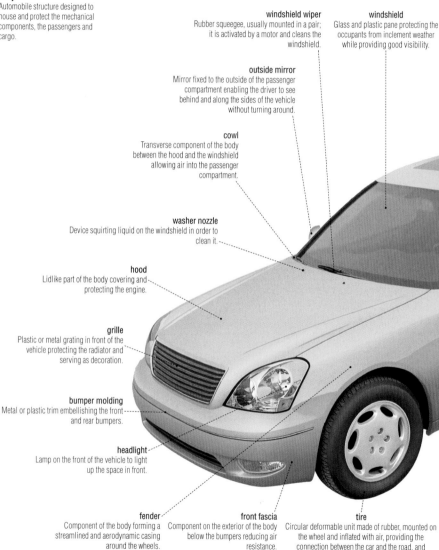

body
Automobile structure designed to house and protect the mechanical components, the passengers and cargo.

windshield wiper
Rubber squeegee, usually mounted in a pair; it is activated by a motor and cleans the windshield.

windshield
Glass and plastic pane protecting the occupants from inclement weather while providing good visibility.

outside mirror
Mirror fixed to the outside of the passenger compartment enabling the driver to see behind and along the sides of the vehicle without turning around.

cowl
Transverse component of the body between the hood and the windshield allowing air into the passenger compartment.

washer nozzle
Device squirting liquid on the windshield in order to clean it.

hood
Lidlike part of the body covering and protecting the engine.

grille
Plastic or metal grating in front of the vehicle protecting the radiator and serving as decoration.

bumper molding
Metal or plastic trim embellishing the front and rear bumpers.

headlight
Lamp on the front of the vehicle to light up the space in front.

fender
Component of the body forming a streamlined and aerodynamic casing around the wheels.

front fascia
Component on the exterior of the body below the bumpers reducing air resistance.

tire
Circular deformable unit made of rubber, mounted on the wheel and inflated with air, providing the connection between the car and the road, and absorbing the unevenness of the road.

sliding sunroof
Moving part in the roof that opens up over the front seats to let air into the passenger compartment.

roof
Exterior component with a slightly curving surface forming the vehicle's covering.

antenna
Device receiving radio waves broadcast by a station.

center post
Vertical safety pillar between the two doors connecting the upper part of the body to the lower part.

drip molding
Small open canal capturing rainwater from the roof and carrying it to the rear, where it drips off.

trunk
Enclosed space at the rear of the vehicle, or sometimes at the front, designed to hold and transport cargo that is not too large.

quarter window
Small window among the series of windows on the side of the body.

fuel door
Flap concealing the fuel-tank opening, which is plugged by a cap.

mud flap
Piece of rubber or plastic attached behind the rear wheels to repel projectiles.

window
Side window that can be lowered, protecting against inclement weather while providing good visibility.

wheel cover
Decorative metal or plastic part concealing the wheel hub.

door
Moving panel with a handle, attached to the body by hinges or a sliding system, providing access to the passenger compartment.

door lock
Mechanism housed in the door to lock it; it is manipulated with a key or button.

body side molding
Metal or plastic part attached along the doors to protect them against light impact.

door handle
Device for activating the door's opening mechanism.

automobile

dashboard
Component in the passenger compartment
comprising the instrument panel, the manual
controls, storage and other accessories.

wiper switch
Electric mechanism for switching on the windshield
wipers, controlling their speed and activating the
windshield washer fluid.

cruise control
Mechanism enabling the driver to maintain a cruising
speed for the vehicle.

ignition switch
Switch activated by a contact key
allowing a current from the battery to
flow to the starter.

headlight/turn signal
Lever having several positions that control the turn signals and the low and
high beams.

horn
Device emitting a loud sound that the
driver can use to attract the attention of
a pedestrian or other user of the road.

steering wheel
Circular instrument used by the driver
for steering the guide wheels.

clutch pedal
Pedal pushed to change gears.

brake pedal
Lever that the driver presses with the
foot to activate the brake system.

gas pedal
Unit controlled by the foot to increase,
maintain or decrease the vehicle's
speed.

TRANSPORTATION

rearview mirror
Mirror mounted on the windshield, positioned by the driver so that the vehicles following behind can be seen in it.

vanity mirror
Small mirror on the inside of the sun visor.

sun visor
Movable panel that the passenger can lower over the upper part of the windshield or of the side window to prevent being blinded by the Sun.

on-board computer
Computer integrated into the vehicle; it provides information about the vehicle's main components and helps the driver with tasks related to driving.

vent
Opening, usually covered by an adjustable grille, allowing warm or cold air into the passenger compartment.

glove compartment
Small storage space fitted with a locking door.

climate control
Mechanism operating the heating or air-conditioning system and controlling its intensity.

audio system
Sound-reproduction device comprising a tuner and a cassette or CD player.

gearshift lever
Control for the gearbox that is manually activated by the driver to change gears.

parking brake lever
Lever connected to the rear-wheel brakes that the driver activates manually to stop the vehicle, or in case of emergency.

center console
Component located between the front seats and containing certain accessories and control devices, especially the parking brake and gearshift levers.

TRANSPORTATION

tire

Circular deformable unit made of rubber, mounted on the wheel and inflated with air, providing the connection between the car and the road, and absorbing the unevenness of the road.

examples of tires

Depending on the intended conditions and uses, tire construction (e.g., type of rubber, tread design, width) varies widely.

performance tire
Wide tire that withstands particularly high temperatures and offers superior performance in holding the road and handling turns.

all-season tire
Tire designed for driving on roads that are dry, wet or slightly snow-covered.

winter tire
Tire characterized by ridges providing a good grip on snow- and ice-covered roads.

touring tire
Tire designed for driving on dry or wet roads, but not recommended for snow or ice.

studded tire
Tire whose tread is fitted with metal studs, which provide a good grip on icy roads.

TRANSPORTATION

wheel
Circular unit turning around an axle; it supports the weight of the vehicle and transmits the thrust, steering and braking actions.

rim
Metal circle constituting the wheel's circumference and on which the tire is mounted.

rim flange
Edge of the rim providing lateral support to the tire bead so that it adheres solidly to it.

technical specifications
Alphanumeric code molded onto the side of the tire, showing its characteristics.

disk
A part of the rim that is fixed at its center on the wheel's axle.

tread design
Raised part of the tire tread that improves traction for various usage conditions.

bead
Part of the tire that encloses a rigid steel wire that keeps the tire on the rim and makes it watertight.

rubbing strip
Round protrusion of the rubber wall, protecting it from side impact and wear.

rubber wall
Part of the tire located between the tread and the bead.

TRANSPORTATION

types of engines

Engines: machines that convert the combustion of an air/fuel mixture into mechanical energy.

gasoline engine
Engine in which a mixture of air and gasoline is compressed and ignited to produce an explosion whose energy is converted into mechanical energy.

camshaft
Axle driven by a belt, a chain or gears connected to the crankshaft, controlling the opening and closing of the valves.

inlet valve
Part that opens to let the air/fuel mixture into the cylinder.

valve spring
Spring that brings the valve back into the closed position.

combustion chamber
Part of the cylinder in which the pressurized air/fuel mixture is ignited and burned.

timing belt
Strap connecting the crankshaft to the camshaft.

piston skirt
Side surface of a piston guiding it along the inside of the cylinder.

connecting rod
Articulated shank powered by the gas explosion; it transmits the thrust from the piston to the crankshaft.

alternator
Current generator driven by the engine, which recharges the battery to supply the electric system.

cooling fan
Mechanism with blades blowing air across the radiator in order to cool the liquid it contains.

pulley
Part attached to a shaft, whose rotational movement it transmits by means of a belt.

crankshaft
Shaft consisting of a series of cranks, which convert the alternate rectilinear motion of the piston/connecting-rod assembly into a continuous circular motion.

fan belt
Rubberized bands mounted on a pulley and linked to the engine, driving the fan and the alternator.

oil drain plug
Plug closing the hole at the bottom of the oil pan through which used oil is evacuated.

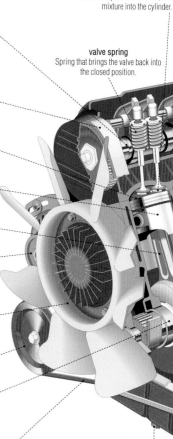

fuel injector
Device pulverizing the fuel in the combustion chamber.

intake manifold
Passages through which the air/fuel mixture enters the cylinder.

distributor cap
Unit supplying the electric current necessary for producing sparks that ignite the fuel in the engine.

vacuum diaphragm
Device connected to the distributor cap specifying the precise moment ignition must be produced relative to the engine's rotation speed.

cylinder head cover
Part of the engine covering the cylinder heads, where the fuel is burned.

spark plug
Electric device whose two electrodes produce the spark necessary to ignite the air/fuel mixture in the cylinder.

exhaust valve
Part that opens to allow the burned gases to escape.

exhaust manifold
Set of pipes at the exit of the cylinders, capturing the combustion gases to conduct them to the exhaust pipe.

flywheel
Disk connected to the crankshaft, which uses the kinetic energy produced at combustion to regulate the crankshaft rotation during the rest of the cycle.

engine block
Main engine casing, which encloses the cylinders.

oil pan
Container closing the bottom of the engine block; it is the reservoir for the oil that lubricates the engine's moving parts.

air conditioner compressor
Component of the air-conditioning system circulating coolant, which cools the air in the passenger compartment when it is hot outside.

piston
Metal moving part in the cylinder and attached to the connecting rod; it compresses the air/fuel mixture, then receives the thrust from the burned gases.

campers

Motorized or towed vehicle fitted out as a dwelling.

tent trailer
Caravan with a collapsible section that is opened up when at rest and folded up again before moving, to lessen wind resistance.

roof
Rigid part enclosing the top of the body and protecting the sections when they are folded up.

canopy
Canvas awning supported by a framework; it protects an outdoor space from the rain and sun.

window
Flexible canvas opening, letting in air and light, supported by a framework when it is opened out.

bunk
Area for sleeping, supported by a frame when it opened out.

body
Rigid metal frame comprising the body of the caravan.

stabilizer jack
Retractable support placed under the caravan to keep it steady when parked.

spare tire
Supplementary wheel for replacing a wheel whose tire is punctured.

screen door
Door fitted with a wire cloth that lets air and light pass through while protecting against mosquitoes.

motor home
Van whose passenger compartment is fitted out as a dwelling.

luggage rack
Support mounted on the roof; baggage is stowed on it using straps.

air conditioner
Device cooling and ventilating the caravan's interior air when it is hot outside.

ladder
Device composed of steps and stiles, for accessing the vehicle's roof.

bus

Motorized vehicle for city or intercity transportation of passengers who are standing or seated.

double-decker bus
Bus equipped with two superimposed compartments, connected by stairs.

upper deck
Upper floor of the bus.

route sign
Screen usually on the front, rear and right side of the vehicle, displaying the number of the bus's route.

school bus
Motorized vehicle for transporting schoolchildren and equipped with specialized safety devices.

outside mirror
Mirror fixed to the outside of the passenger compartment enabling the driver to see behind and along the sides of the vehicle without turning around.

blind spot mirror
Exterior convex mirror providing a wider field of vision than a conventional mirror.

blinking lights
Flashing red lights at the front and rear of the bus that the driver activates at each stop to signal other vehicles to stop.

crossing arm
Pivoting rod deployed at each stop so that the schoolchildren stay in the driver's field of vision while passing in front of the bus.

crossover mirror
Convex mirror allowing the driver to see the front of the bus.

TRANSPORTATION

city bus
Motorized vehicle for city transportation of passengers who are standing or seated.

air intake
Opening in the roof, fitted with a cover, for letting fresh air into the bus.

route sign
Screen usually on the front, rear and right side of the vehicle, displaying the number of the bus's route.

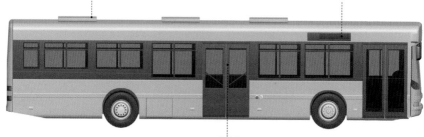

two-leaf door
Wide door divided into two movable parts, which double back to each side to allow several people to pass through at once.

coach
Motorized vehicle for intercity transportation of seated passengers over medium and long distances.

engine air intake
Opening through which outside air enters the vehicle's engine.

entrance door

engine compartment
Housing for the engine under the vehicle's chassis, accessible by a door.

baggage compartment
Large compartment beneath the vehicle's floor, fitted with side doors, in which passengers' baggage is deposited.

van
Motorized vehicle for transporting about 10 passengers, sometimes equipped with a lift for wheelchairs.

West Coast mirror
Mirror fixed to the outside of the passenger compartment enabling the driver to see behind and along the sides of the vehicle without turning around.

lift door

handrail
Support rail equipped with a belt restraining the wheelchair when the platform is being raised and lowered.

platform
Horizontal part moving up and down for the wheelchair; it rests on the ground in the lower position and forms the doorsill in the upper position.

entrance door

blind spot mirror
Exterior convex mirror providing a wider field of vision than a conventional mirror.

wheelchair lift
Electric lifting device deployed so that a person in a wheelchair can be raised into and lowered from a minibus.

articulated bus
Bus with two aligned compartments, connected by an articulated joint.

rear rigid section

articulated joint
Part connecting the rigid sections by a waterproof bellows and a turning platform shared by the two sections.

front rigid section

TRANSPORTATION

trucking

Transportation of cargo by truck.

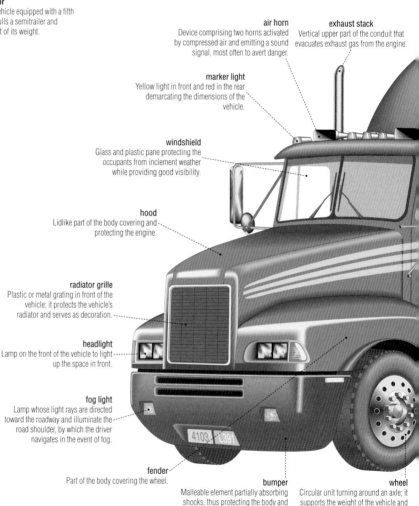

truck tractor
Motorized vehicle equipped with a fifth wheel that pulls a semitrailer and supports part of its weight.

air horn
Device comprising two horns activated by compressed air and emitting a sound signal, most often to avert danger.

exhaust stack
Vertical upper part of the conduit that evacuates exhaust gas from the engine.

marker light
Yellow light in front and red in the rear demarcating the dimensions of the vehicle.

windshield
Glass and plastic pane protecting the occupants from inclement weather while providing good visibility.

hood
Lidlike part of the body covering and protecting the engine.

radiator grille
Plastic or metal grating in front of the vehicle; it protects the vehicle's radiator and serves as decoration.

headlight
Lamp on the front of the vehicle to light up the space in front.

fog light
Lamp whose light rays are directed toward the roadway and illuminate the road shoulder, by which the driver navigates in the event of fog.

fender
Part of the body covering the wheel.

bumper
Malleable element partially absorbing shocks, thus protecting the body and the engine parts from damage.

wheel
Circular unit turning around an axle; it supports the weight of the vehicle and transmits the thrust, steering and braking actions.

wind deflector
Aerodynamic device mounted on the tractor's roof to reduce the semitrailer's wind resistance.

West Coast mirror
Mirror fixed to the outside of the passenger compartment enabling the driver to see behind and along the sides of the vehicle without turning around.

sleeper-cab
Part behind the cab fitted out with a bed or bunk beds and storage space.

grab handle
Vertical handle placed at shoulder height near the door, for gripping while climbing up to or down from the cab.

storage compartment
Compartment for storing bulky objects, usually accessible from the inside and outside of the cab.

fifth wheel
Coupling device enabling the tractor to be connected to the semitrailer and supporting its front portion.

tire
Circular deformable unit made of rubber, mounted on the wheel and inflated with air, providing the connection between the truck tractor and the road, and absorbing the unevenness of the road.

mud flap
Piece of rubber or plastic attached behind the rear wheels to repel projectiles.

step
Tread or set of treads built into the body for climbing up to or down from the cab.

fuel tank
Reservoir containing the diesel fuel that makes the vehicle self-sufficient.

filler cap
Part screwed into the fuel filler neck to close it.

trucking

refrigerated semitrailer
Semitrailer equipped with a
refrigeration unit and an insulated
compartment for transporting
perishable goods.

frontwall

refrigeration unit
Device using compression to lower the
temperature inside the semitrailer to a
predetermined level.

mud flap
Piece of rubber or plastic attached
behind the rear wheels to repel
projectiles.

marker light
Yellow light in front and red in the rear
demarcating the dimensions of the
vehicle.

vent door
Grille through which the air cools the
refrigerant.

sidewall

partlow chart
Device monitoring the temperature in the
semitrailer.

kingpin
Axle of attachment housed in the tractor's
fifth wheel; it allows the semitrailer and the
tractor to articulate.

reflector
Device reflecting light back toward its
source so that other drivers can see the
semitrailer.

landing gear
Telescopic support keeping the
semitrailer level when uncoupled.

battery box
Compartment containing the battery
supplying the electric energy required
to operate the refrigeration unit.

side rail
Thick piece along the length of the
chassis frame, reinforcing it.

sand shoe
Part attached to the foot of the landing
gear to increase stability.

electrical connection
Electric wire connecting the
semitrailer's lighting and signaling
system with that of the tractor.

auxiliary tank
Reservoir containing the fuel used to
operate the refrigeration unit.

landing gear crank
Bent lever activating the elevating cylinder to
deploy the landing gear.

TRANSPORTATION

flatbed semitrailer
Semitrailer composed of a platform
around which detachable side panels can
be placed.

stake pocket
Support placed on the side edges of
the deck, holding in place a belt hook
or a post for attaching the side panels.

turn signal
Device emitting an intermittent light, signaling a
change of the vehicle's direction or a temporary
hazard to other vehicles.

bulkhead
Panel fixed to the front of the deck to
prevent cargo from moving forward.

deck
Floor of the semitrailer serving as the
loading plane for the cargo.

taillight
Lamp turning on automatically when the
front lights are lit, making the vehicle
visible for up to 150 meters.

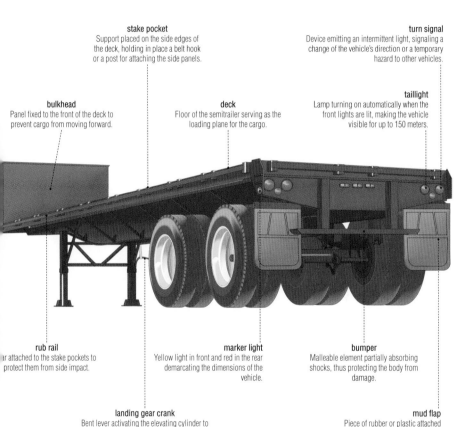

rub rail
ar attached to the stake pockets to
protect them from side impact.

marker light
Yellow light in front and red in the rear
demarcating the dimensions of the
vehicle.

bumper
Malleable element partially absorbing
shocks, thus protecting the body from
damage.

landing gear crank
Bent lever activating the elevating cylinder to
deploy the landing gear.

mud flap
Piece of rubber or plastic attached
behind the rear wheels to repel
projectiles.

TRANSPORTATION

examples of semitrailers

Semitrailers: trailers whose front portion is equipped with a
kingpin for coupling them to a tractor.

tandem tractor trailer

Set of vehicles comprising a tractor, a semitrailer and a
trailer.

semitrailer
Trailer whose front part is equipped
with a kingpin for coupling it to the
tractor.

truck trailer
Motorless vehicle for transporting
cargo and connected by a coupling bar
to the vehicle towing it.

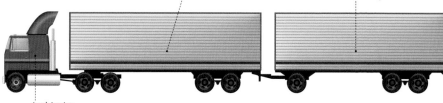

truck tractor
Motorized vehicle equipped with a fifth
wheel that pulls a semitrailer and
supports part of its weight.

tank trailer
Semitrailer for transporting bulk
products in liquid, powder or gas form.

container semitrailer
Semitrailer comprising only a chassis;
containers of standard sizes are loaded on it
to transport cargo.

tank body
Closed tank divided into several
compartments of various sizes.

twist lock
Locking mechanism housed in each
bottom corner of the container to
secure it to the semitrailer.

double drop lowbed semitrailer
Semitrailer for transporting heavy machinery.

automobile transport semitrailer
Semitrailer equipped with several sloped platforms
for transporting vehicles.

dump body
Open or closed container; when raised
by the elevation cylinder, it discharges
its bulk material.

dump semitrailer
Semitrailer equipped with a dump
body for transporting in bulk.

chip van
Semitrailer designed to transport wood in chip
form.

van body semitrailer
Semitrailer comprising a closed box,
rigid or made of thick fabric (tarpaulin
and sliding curtains).

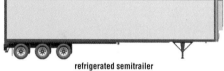

refrigerated semitrailer
Semitrailer equipped with a
refrigeration unit and an insulated
compartment for transporting
perishable goods.

possum-belly body semitrailer
Semitrailer designed to transport livestock; it comprises several
perforated compartments.

log semitrailer
Semitrailer with folding side posts for transporting tree
trunks.

TRANSPORTATION

examples of trucks
Trucks: motorized vehicles for transporting cargo
and providing maintenance and safety.

tow truck
Truck for towing vehicles that have
broken down.

hook
Part that is detached from the towing device
while the vehicle's front wheels are placed in
position, then reattached to raise it.

boom
Thick sturdy metal beam, which the
elevating cylinder raises.

cable

winch
Mechanism with a steel cable rolled
around a spool, for pulling and raising
heavy loads, such as a vehicle that has
broken down.

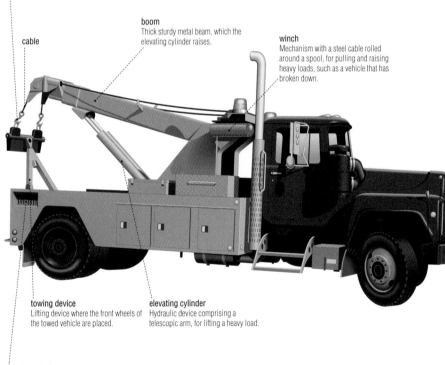

towing device
Lifting device where the front wheels of
the towed vehicle are placed.

elevating cylinder
Hydraulic device comprising a
telescopic arm, for lifting a heavy load.

winch controls
Control mechanisms for the electric
motor, which powers the spool's
rotation.

box van
Truck whose box is rigid and closed.

dump body
Open or closed container; when raised by the elevation cylinder it discharges its bulk material.

dump truck
Truck equipped with a dump body; it is used for bulk transport.

septic truck
Truck equipped with a tank, a pump and a long pipe, for emptying septic tanks and other pipes.

TRANSPORTATION

trucking

street sweeper
Vehicle for cleaning city streets, equipped with a collection body, rotating brushes, a vacuum cleaner and a watering device.

collection body
Container for the trash swept up by the central brush.

central brush
Rotating brush that cleans the width of the roadway.

lateral brush
Rotating brush that cleans the edge of the roadway.

watering tube
Pipe supplying water to the brush as it cleans the roadway.

detachable body truck
Truck for transporting containers, which it loads and unloads using a mechanical arm.

snowblower
Vehicle with a mechanism that draws up snow from the road and projects it some distance or into a dump truck.

projection device
Adjustable funnel through which the snow is expelled in a chosen direction.

worm
Mechanism grinding hardened snow before a screw forces it into the projection device.

loading hopper
Large reservoir that takes the trash bags and then feeds them to the packer body.

packer body
Bin equipped with a hydraulic system that compresses household trash.

trash truck
Dump truck for collecting household trash.

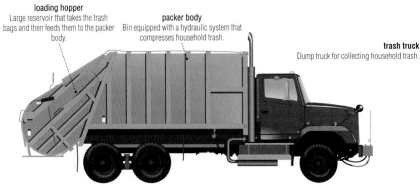

tank body
Closed tank divided into several compartments of various sizes.

tank truck
Truck for transporting bulk products in liquid, powder or gas form.

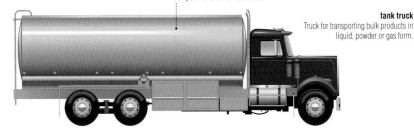

cement mixer
Truck equipped with a rotating tub, for transporting fresh cement, which it pours out down a chute.

TRANSPORTATION

motorcycle

Two-wheeled motorized vehicle whose engine cylinder is larger than 125 cubic centimeters.

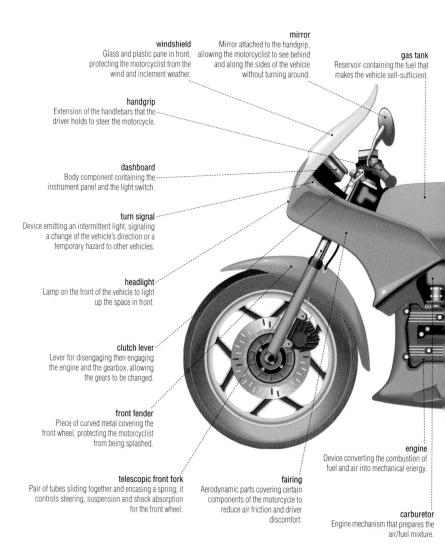

mirror
Mirror attached to the handgrip,
allowing the motorcyclist to see behind
and along the sides of the vehicle
without turning around.

windshield
Glass and plastic pane in front,
protecting the motorcyclist from the
wind and inclement weather.

gas tank
Reservoir containing the fuel that
makes the vehicle self-sufficient.

handgrip
Extension of the handlebars that the
driver holds to steer the motorcycle.

dashboard
Body component containing the
instrument panel and the light switch.

turn signal
Device emitting an intermittent light, signaling
a change of the vehicle's direction or a
temporary hazard to other vehicles.

headlight
Lamp on the front of the vehicle to light
up the space in front.

clutch lever
Lever for disengaging then engaging
the engine and the gearbox, allowing
the gears to be changed.

front fender
Piece of curved metal covering the
front wheel, protecting the motorcyclist
from being splashed.

engine
Device converting the combustion of
fuel and air into mechanical energy.

telescopic front fork
Pair of tubes sliding together and encasing a spring; it
controls steering, suspension and shock absorption
for the front wheel.

fairing
Aerodynamic parts covering certain
components of the motorcycle to
reduce air friction and driver
discomfort.

carburetor
Engine mechanism that prepares the
air/fuel mixture.

TRANSPORTATION

frame
Set of hollow metal tubes welded together, forming the motorcycle's framework.

pillion footrest
Metal rods, one on each side of the motorcycle frame, for resting the passenger's feet on.

dual seat
Usually leather seat allowing the driver to sit in front and the passenger to sit behind.

rear shock absorber
Cylindrical mechanism attached to the rear wheel and coupled with a spring; it absorbs shocks caused by unevenness in the road.

turn signal
Device emitting an intermittent light, signaling a change of the vehicle's direction or a temporary hazard to other vehicles.

taillight
Lamp that lights up automatically when the front lights are lit and emits a brighter light when the driver applies the brakes.

brake caliper
Viselike part comprising a piston, which straddles the brake disc and supports the brake pads.

exhaust pipe
Compartmentalized chamber in which the escaping gases expand, thus reducing the noise from the engine.

rim
Metal circle constituting the wheel's circumference and on which the tire is mounted.

disc brake
Braking mechanism comprising a disc attached to the wheel, whose rotation is slowed down when the brake pads exert friction on it.

front footrest
Metal rods, one on each side of the motorcycle frame, for resting the driver's feet on.

main stand
Fold-down support comprising two rods; it keeps the motorcycle upright with one of its wheels off the ground.

gearshift lever
Pedal located under the motorcyclist's left foot, for changing the ratio between the motor's speed of rotation and that of the wheels.

TRANSPORTATION

motorcycle

protective helmet
Rigid headgear covering the head to
protect it in the event of accident.

bubble
Exterior surface made of durable
materials (thermoplastic or composite
materials) that absorb shocks.

visor
Transparent swing-away part,
protecting the eyes while providing
good visibility.

air inlet
Opening in the bubble allowing air to
circulate in the helmet and preventing
fog from forming on the visor.

chin protector
Part of the bubble protecting the
motorcyclist's chin.

visor hinge
Articulated fastener for raising and
lowering the visor.

motorcycle dashboard
Body component containing the instrument panel and the
ignition switch.

high beam warning indicator
Light showing that the high beam is lit.

tachometer
Dial showing the engine's rotation
speed in revolutions per minute.

speedometer
Dial showing the speed at which the
vehicle is moving, in kilometers or
miles per hour.

oil pressure warning indicator
Light showing that the oil pressure in the engine's
lubrication system is below the minimum necessary.

neutral indicator
Light showing that none of the gears is engaged; that is,
the engine's rotation is not being transmitted to the
wheels.

ignition switch
Switch activated by a contact key
allowing a current from the battery to
flow to the starter.

turn signal indicator
Intermittent light, often accompanied by a
sound, showing that a turn signal is in use.

TRANSPORTATION

motorcycle

examples of motorcycles

off-road motorcycle
Motorcycle designed for traveling over rough terrain, with features such as a raised engine, extended suspension, elevated muffler and tires with studs.

seat
Usually leather seat where the driver sits.

telescopic front fork
Pair of sliding tubes enclosing a spring; it controls steering, suspension and shock absorption on the front wheel.

knobby tread tire
Tire whose tread is fitted with blocks of rubber, providing better traction on rough terrain.

windshield
Glass and plastic pane in front, protecting the motorcyclist from the wind and inclement weather.

touring motorcycle
Motorcycle providing comfort for the driver and the passenger, with features such as wide fairing, extended handgrips and footrests for stretching the legs.

antenna
Device receiving radio waves broadcast by a station.

backrest
Part supporting the back.

top box
Usually rigid and waterproof compartment, behind the passenger seat, for stowing light objects.

passenger seat
Usually leather, individual seat with a back; it is higher than the driver seat, for the passenger to sit.

saddlebag
Usually rigid and waterproof luggage, attached to each side of the passenger seat.

driver seat
Usually leather, individual seat, sometimes equipped with a back, for the driver to sit.

TRANSPORTATION

motorcycle

motor scooter
Motorized vehicle with two small wheels, embellished with fairing, characterized by an open frame and a flat floor.

mirror
Mirror attached to the handgrip, allowing the motorcyclist to see behind and along the sides of the vehicle without turning around.

seat
Usually leather seat where the driver sits.

apron
Aerodynamic component in sheet metal or plastic, trimming the steering column and protecting the driver from the wind and inclement weather.

luggage rack
Support at the rear of the vehicle, for attaching a trunk or for lashing down luggage using straps.

floorboard
Wide flat surface for resting the feet on.

moped
Vehicle designed like a bicycle, but equipped with an engine whose cylinder is no larger than 50 cubic centimeters.

carrier
Support at the rear of the vehicle, for attaching a trunk or for lashing down luggage using straps.

kickstand
Fold-down support on the right side of the moped to keep it almost upright when at rest.

4 X 4 all-terrain vehicle

Four-wheeled all-terrain vehicle (ATV) for traversing most kinds of terrain, equipped with a motorcycle engine.

rear fender
Piece of curved metal covering the rear wheel, for protecting the motorcyclist from being splashed.

rear cargo rack
Support at the rear of the vehicle, for attaching a trunk or for lashing down luggage using straps.

gas tank
Reservoir containing the fuel that makes the vehicle self-sufficient.

handgrip
Extension of the handlebars used for steering the ATV.

bumper
Malleable component partly absorbing impact in the event of a front-on collision.

seat
Usually leather seat where the driver sits.

gearshift lever
Pedal located under the driver's foot, for changing the ratio between the motor's speed of rotation and that of the wheels.

muffler
Compartmentalized chamber in which the escaping gases expand, thus reducing the noise from the engine.

front shock absorber
Cylindrical mechanism attached to the front wheel and coupled with a spring; it absorbs shocks caused by unevenness in the road.

bicycle

Frame vehicle steered by the front wheel and propelled by the rear wheel, which in turn is driven, via a chain, by a pedal mechanism.

parts of a bicycle

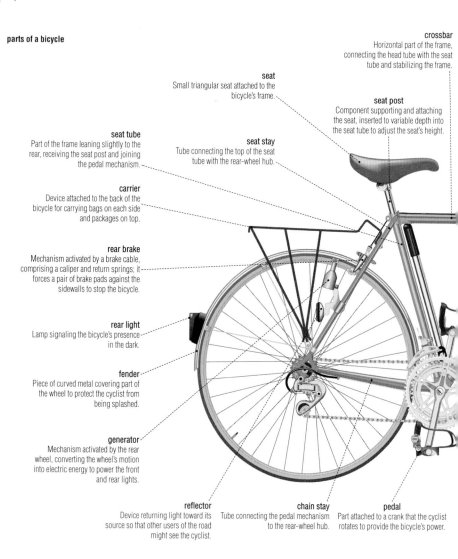

crossbar
Horizontal part of the frame, connecting the head tube with the seat tube and stabilizing the frame.

seat
Small triangular seat attached to the bicycle's frame.

seat post
Component supporting and attaching the seat, inserted to variable depth into the seat tube to adjust the seat's height.

seat tube
Part of the frame leaning slightly to the rear, receiving the seat post and joining the pedal mechanism.

seat stay
Tube connecting the top of the seat tube with the rear-wheel hub.

carrier
Device attached to the back of the bicycle for carrying bags on each side and packages on top.

rear brake
Mechanism activated by a brake cable, comprising a caliper and return springs; it forces a pair of brake pads against the sidewalls to stop the bicycle.

rear light
Lamp signaling the bicycle's presence in the dark.

fender
Piece of curved metal covering part of the wheel to protect the cyclist from being splashed.

generator
Mechanism activated by the rear wheel, converting the wheel's motion into electric energy to power the front and rear lights.

reflector
Device returning light toward its source so that other users of the road might see the cyclist.

chain stay
Tube connecting the pedal mechanism to the rear-wheel hub.

pedal
Part attached to a crank that the cyclist rotates to provide the bicycle's power.

head tube
Tube using ball bearings to transmit the steering movement to the fork.

brake cable
Sheathed steel cable transmitting the pressure exerted on the brake lever to the brake.

stem
Part whose height is adjustable; it is inserted into the head tube and supports the handlebars.

handlebars
Device made up of two handles connected by a tube, for steering the bicycle.

brake lever
Lever attached to the handlebars for activating the brake caliper via a cable.

front brake
Mechanism activated by a brake cable, comprising a caliper and return springs; it forces a pair of brake pads against the sidewalls to slow down the front wheel.

headlight
Lamp illuminating the ground a few yards in front of the bicycle.

fork
Two tubes connected to the head tube and attached to each end of the front-wheel hub.

hub
Central part of the wheel from which spokes radiate. Inside the hub are ball bearings enabling it to rotate around its axle.

rim
Metal circle constituting the wheel's circumference and on which the tire is mounted.

spoke
Thin metal spindle connecting the hub to the rim.

water bottle clip
Support attached to the down tube or the seat tube for carrying the water bottle.

down tube
Part of the frame connecting the head tube to the pedal mechanism; it is the longest and thickest tube in the frame and gives it its rigidity.

tire valve
Small clack valve sealing the inflation opening of the inner tube; it allows air to enter but prevents it from escaping.

examples of bicycles

BMX bike
Strong small bicycle, for acrobatics
and competitions on bumpy tracks.

Dutch bicycle
City bicycle designed for comfort and in such a
way that the cyclist sits upright; its features
include a built-in chain guard and a drop-down
fender.

city bicycle
Bicycle designed for comfort and
safety while taking short trips on city
streets.

mountain bike
Bicycle with large wheels with treads with
studs, a strong frame, numerous gears and
powerful brakes, for navigating all kinds of
terrain.

TRANSPORTATION

road bicycle
Bicycle with narrow tires, lightweight frame and handlebars that position the cyclist for optimum aerodynamics, designed for road racing.

touring bicycle
Intermediate bicycle between a road bicycle and a city bicycle, designed for traveling long distances in comfort.

child's tricycle
Very stable three-wheeled vehicle with pedals driving either the front wheel or the rear wheels, for the use of young children.

tandem bicycle
Bicycle with two places; both cyclists pedal simultaneously but only the person in front steers.

TRANSPORTATION

railroad station

Covered building for the public where trains and passengers arrive and depart.

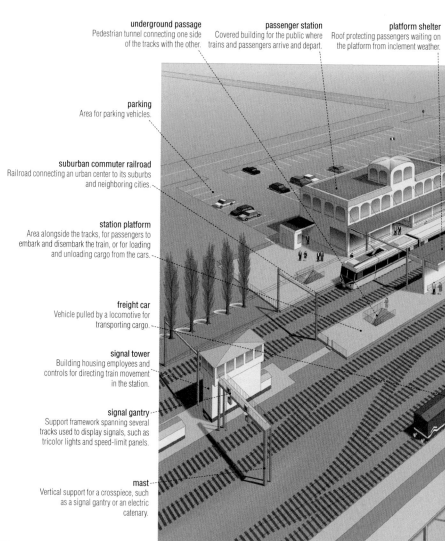

underground passage
Pedestrian tunnel connecting one side of the tracks with the other.

passenger station
Covered building for the public where trains and passengers arrive and depart.

platform shelter
Roof protecting passengers waiting on the platform from inclement weather.

parking
Area for parking vehicles.

suburban commuter railroad
Railroad connecting an urban center to its suburbs and neighboring cities.

station platform
Area alongside the tracks, for passengers to embark and disembark the train, or for loading and unloading cargo from the cars.

freight car
Vehicle pulled by a locomotive for transporting cargo.

signal tower
Building housing employees and controls for directing train movement in the station.

signal gantry
Support framework spanning several tracks used to display signals, such as tricolor lights and speed-limit panels.

mast
Vertical support for a crosspiece, such as a signal gantry or an electric catenary.

commuter train
Local train running frequently each day between an urban center and its suburbs or neighboring cities.

footbridge
Elevated walkway for passengers to cross over a set of tracks.

semaphore
Light for relaying information such as the speed of trains and the distance between them.

main line
Tracks for trains traveling long distances.

grade crossing
Intersection of a railroad and a road, with or without warning lights.

bumper
Buffer placed at the end of a track stopping the train from running off the end of the track.

siding
Side track not used for railroad traffic but for shunting, marshaling or loading and unloading.

diesel shop
Building for maintaining and refueling diesel locomotives.

freight station
Set of railroad installations and buildings required for transporting cargo.

switch
A pair of movable track rails (switch rails) for guiding the train from one track to another.

scissors crossing
Track enabling a train to change tracks.

high-speed train

High-speed passenger train (between 135 and 190 mph) powered by electricity, with a power car at each end and a limited number of cars in between.

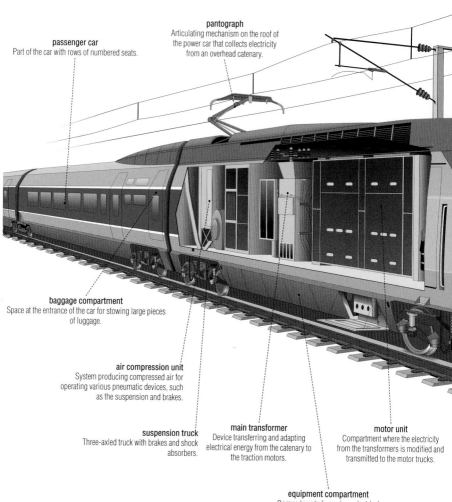

pantograph
Articulating mechanism on the roof of the power car that collects electricity from an overhead catenary.

passenger car
Part of the car with rows of numbered seats.

baggage compartment
Space at the entrance of the car for stowing large pieces of luggage.

air compression unit
System producing compressed air for operating various pneumatic devices, such as the suspension and brakes.

suspension truck
Three-axled truck with brakes and shock absorbers.

main transformer
Device transferring and adapting electrical energy from the catenary to the traction motors.

motor unit
Compartment where the electricity from the transformers is modified and transmitted to the motor trucks.

equipment compartment
Compartments for various electrical equipment.

TRANSPORTATION

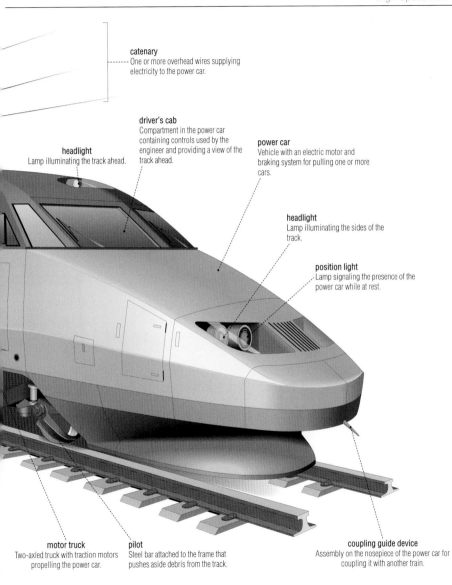

catenary
One or more overhead wires supplying electricity to the power car.

driver's cab
Compartment in the power car containing controls used by the engineer and providing a view of the track ahead.

headlight
Lamp illuminating the track ahead.

power car
Vehicle with an electric motor and braking system for pulling one or more cars.

headlight
Lamp illuminating the sides of the track.

position light
Lamp signaling the presence of the power car while at rest.

motor truck
Two-axled truck with traction motors propelling the power car.

pilot
Steel bar attached to the frame that pushes aside debris from the track.

coupling guide device
Assembly on the nosepiece of the power car for coupling it with another train.

diesel-electric locomotive

Vehicle with a diesel engine turning a generator that in turn powers the electric traction motors.

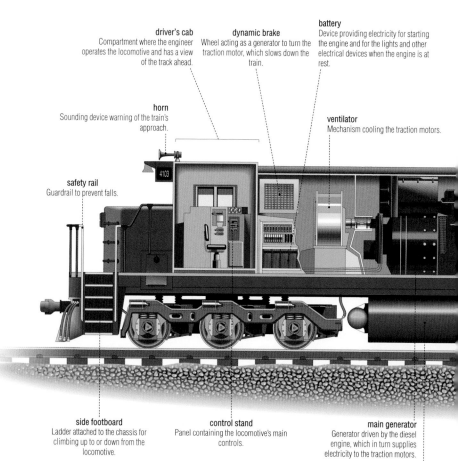

driver's cab
Compartment where the engineer operates the locomotive and has a view of the track ahead.

dynamic brake
Wheel acting as a generator to turn the traction motor, which slows down the train.

battery
Device providing electricity for starting the engine and for the lights and other electrical devices when the engine is at rest.

horn
Sounding device warning of the train's approach.

ventilator
Mechanism cooling the traction motors.

safety rail
Guardrail to prevent falls.

side footboard
Ladder attached to the chassis for climbing up to or down from the locomotive.

control stand
Panel containing the locomotive's main controls.

main generator
Generator driven by the diesel engine, which in turn supplies electricity to the traction motors.

fuel tank
Reservoir containing the diesel fuel that makes the vehicle self-sufficient.

air compressor
Device supplying the compressed air that operates various pneumatic equipment, especially the brakes.

water tank
Reservoir for the cooling water.

ventilating fan
Bladed mechanism blowing air through the radiators to cool the coolant inside them.

diesel engine
Combustion engine in which the compressed air becomes sufficiently hot to ignite the injected fuel.

radiator
Vessel in which the coolant, which circulates around the engine, is cooled by means of flowing air.

air filter
Device removing dust from the air entering the engine.

headlight
Lamp illuminating the track.

lubricating system
Device circulating oil throughout the engine to reduce friction between its moving parts.

compressed air reservoir
Storage chamber for the compressed air.

pilot
Steel bar attached to the frame that pushes aside debris from the track.

sandbox
Container for the sand that is strewn on the track in front of the wheels to provide friction.

coupler head
Device on each end of a locomotive or car for attaching it to another locomotive or car.

TRANSPORTATION

car

Vehicle pulled by a locomotive for transporting cargo.

box car
Car covered with a waterproof casing and having sliding side doors, for transporting cargo that must be protected from the weather and theft.

corner cap
Metal part reinforcing and protecting the edges of the car.

horizontal end handhold
Crossbar for holding onto when moving from one side of the car to the other while coupling.

hand brake wheel
Wheel for manually activating the brake.

end ladder
Ladder for climbing up and down the car to carry out certain tasks, such as uncoupling the cars and setting the hand brake.

hand brake gear housing
Part covering a chain transmitting the wheel's turning movement to the hand brake winding lever.

sliding channel
Groove guiding and supporting the door as it slides open and shut.

hand brake winding lever
Vertical metal shaft, with one end connected by a chain to the hand brake wheel and the wheel house, for setting the hand brake.

side ladder
Ladder on the side of the car for accessing the end ladder.

telescoping uncoupling rod
Rod ending in a bent handle for uncoupling the cars.

sill step
U-shaped support situated under the car's frame for reaching the ladder.

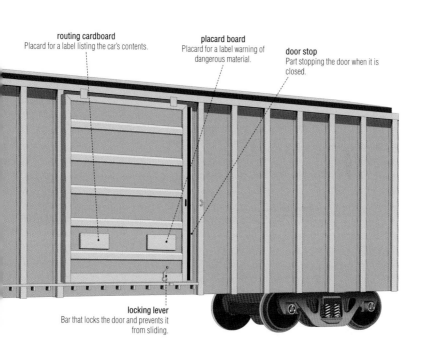

routing cardboard
Placard for a label listing the car's contents.

placard board
Placard for a label warning of dangerous material.

door stop
Part stopping the door when it is closed.

locking lever
Bar that locks the door and prevents it from sliding.

automatic coupler
Device on each end of a locomotive or car for attaching it to another locomotive or car.

coupler knuckle pin
Part around which the coupler knuckle pivots to open and uncouple.

coupler knuckle
Articulated component that interlocks with the corresponding part on another car or locomotive.

TRANSPORTATION

examples of freight cars

The shape of the cars varies depending on the type of cargo being transported.

gondola car
Open-top car for carrying heavy bulk material, such as scrap metal and construction material.

flat car
Car with a simple wooden deck for carrying large objects, such as pipes, logs and heavy machinery.

hopper ore car
Usually open-top hopper car of limited capacity for carrying minerals.

bulkhead flat car
Flat car with sturdy plates at each end for carrying loose cargo (usually logs).

depressed-center flat car
Car with two extra trucks and a lowered deck for carrying heavy equipment.

wood chip car
Open-top gondola car with a large compartment for carrying wood chips.

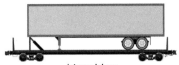

intermodal car
Flat car for carrying semitrailers.

hard top gondola
Gondola with of a retractable metal roof for carrying bulk cargo.

hopper car
Car for carrying bulk cargo; it has dump doors on the bottom for unloading the cargo.

tank car
Car with a sealed reservoir for carrying liquids and gases.

refrigerator car
Closed-box insulated car with a
refrigeration unit for carrying
perishable foodstuffs.

caboose
Car that is usually at the end of the train; it houses
personnel, provisions and tools.

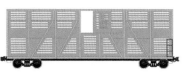

livestock car
Car with slatted sides for carrying livestock; it
sometimes has two decks.

box car
Car covered with a waterproof casing and
having sliding side doors, for
transporting cargo that must be protected
from the weather and theft.

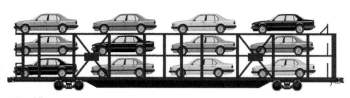

automobile car
Multilevel car for carrying vehicles, which are strapped
down.

container car
Flat car for carrying standard-size shipping boxes.

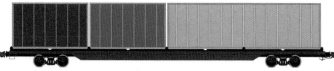

TRANSPORTATION

subway

Electrified urban railroad built mainly underground for transporting passengers at frequent intervals.

subway station
Structure and facilities that provide passengers access to the subway.

exterior sign
Sign placed outside the entrance to the subway that makes it visible from afar.

station entrance
Small structure built on a public thoroughfare that provides access to the subway station.

exit turnstile
Device that allows one user at a time to exit.

escalator
Installation that consists of articulated steps on a continuously turning chain; it allows movement between two levels of a building.

mezzanine
Intermediate level that is accessible by stairs and serves as a landing between the station entrance and the platforms.

ticket collecting booth
Kiosk protected by glass where an agent sells tickets and passes, and controls who enters and exits.

entrance turnstile
Automatic device that allows a user to enter after swiping a pass or inserting a ticket or transfer.

stairs
Structural component that enables movement between levels.

line map
Chart that shows a train's route and the stations it serves.

tunnel
Underground passageway through which the subway train travels between stations.

advertising panel
Space rented by a business to place a poster promoting products or services.

subway train
Set of cars that is pulled by a motor car and carries passengers.

track
Course that consists of parallel electrified rails on which trains roll.

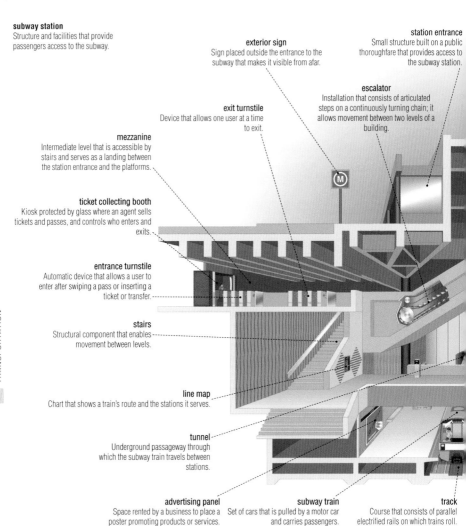

transfer dispensing machine
Device that dispenses tickets entitling the user to
subsequently board another means of transportation
linked with the subway system, such as a bus, streetcar
or train.

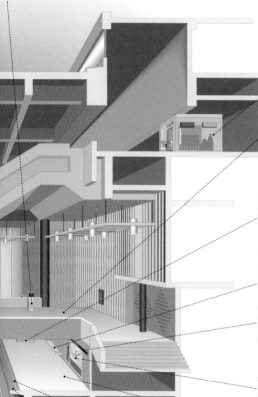

kiosk
Small store in the halls or the entrance
of the station that sells newspapers and
refreshments.

footbridge
Bridge that spans the tracks and
provides access to both platforms.

directional sign
Sign that indicates the terminus of the
train arriving at that platform.

bench
Long narrow unupholstered seat with
or without a back, seating several
people.

station name
Sign on the platform wall that shows
the name of the station so that
passengers in the train can see it.

subway map
Map that shows the entire subway system; each
subway line is illustrated in a different color.

platform
Area adjacent to the tracks where
passengers board and exit trains; it is
at the same level as the floor of the
trains.

platform edge
Zone along the edge of the platform,
usually demarcated by a safety line.

safety line
Visible or textured line warning passengers
of the margin of safety.

passenger car
Vehicle that rolls along subway tracks
and transports passengers.

ventilator
Grille that circulates fresh air
throughout the car.

side door
Sliding door that opens onto the
station platforms for passengers to
enter and exit.

light
Fixtures for illuminating the interior of
the car.

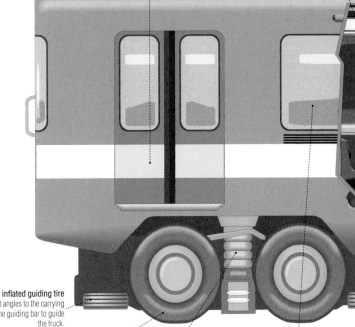

inflated guiding tire
Tire mounted at right angles to the carrying
tire; it rolls against the guiding bar to guide
the truck.

inflated carrying tire
Nitrogen-filled tire that supports and conveys
the car.

suspension
Assembly that dissipates the vibrations
occurring as the wheels roll along the
tracks.

window
Opening containing thick glass that
does not open.

advertising sign
Poster on a space rented by a business that promotes products or services.

side handrail
Handle on the wall next to the door for passengers to hold onto while the train is in motion.

emergency brake
Device that stops the train; it is available to users in case of emergency.

communication set
Loudspeaker phone used for talking to the train driver.

subway map
Map that shows the entire subway system; each subway line is illustrated in a different color.

handrail
Floor-to-ceiling pole in the middle of the aisle for passengers to hold onto while the train is in motion.

single seat
Seat for one passenger.

double seat
Bench with space for two passengers.

heating grille
Grating through which warm air is forced to heat the car interior.

subway train
Set of cars that is pulled by a motor car and carries passengers.

motor car
Vehicle with an electric motor and braking system for pulling one or more cars.

trailer car
Freewheeling car pulled by a motor car.

motor car
Vehicle with an electric motor and braking system for pulling one or more cars.

harbor

Site for refueling and repairing ships, loading and unloading cargo and embarking and disembarking passengers.

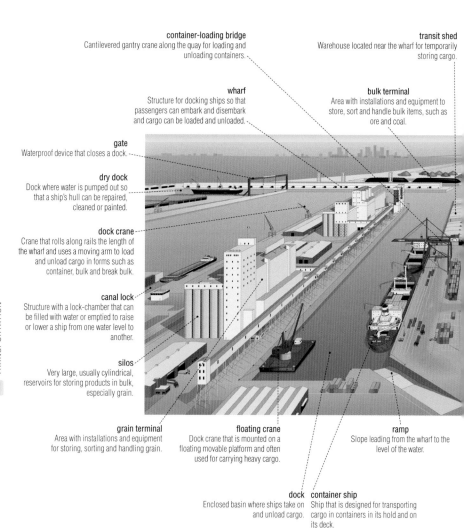

container-loading bridge
Cantilevered gantry crane along the quay for loading and unloading containers.

transit shed
Warehouse located near the wharf for temporarily storing cargo.

wharf
Structure for docking ships so that passengers can embark and disembark and cargo can be loaded and unloaded.

bulk terminal
Area with installations and equipment to store, sort and handle bulk items, such as ore and coal.

gate
Waterproof device that closes a dock.

dry dock
Dock where water is pumped out so that a ship's hull can be repaired, cleaned or painted.

dock crane
Crane that rolls along rails the length of the wharf and uses a moving arm to load and unload cargo in forms such as container, bulk and break bulk.

canal lock
Structure with a lock-chamber that can be filled with water or emptied to raise or lower a ship from one water level to another.

silos
Very large, usually cylindrical, reservoirs for storing products in bulk, especially grain.

grain terminal
Area with installations and equipment for storing, sorting and handling grain.

floating crane
Dock crane that is mounted on a floating movable platform and often used for carrying heavy cargo.

ramp
Slope leading from the wharf to the level of the water.

dock
Enclosed basin where ships take on and unload cargo.

container ship
Ship that is designed for transporting cargo in containers in its hold and on its deck.

TRANSPORTATION

lighthouse
Tower with a powerful lamp at the top
for guiding ships.

passenger terminal
Structures and facilities where
passengers embark and disembark
ships.

cold shed
Insulated refrigerated structure for
storing perishable foodstuffs.

ferryboat
Shuttle boat for carrying vehicles with
their cargo and passengers.

oil terminal
Area with installations and equipment
to store petroleum products and load
them into tankers.

tanker
Ship with large reservoirs for
transporting liquid petroleum
products.

office building
Structure where personnel who
administer the port work.

customs house
Structure where inspection and legal
operations related to imported and
exported cargo are carried out.

road transport
Transportation of cargo by truck on
public roads.

container terminal
Area with installations and equipment
to store, sort and handle containers.

terminal railway
Railroad tracks leading onto a wharf for
transshipping containers from a ship to a
car or vice versa.

parking lot
Area for parking vehicles.

bridge
Structure consisting of a girder and
posts that rolls along tracks moving
containers.

TRANSPORTATION

four-masted bark

Sailboat with four masts and square sails except for the jiggermast, which carries a gaff sail.

masting and rigging
Masting: masts, yards, ropes and other movable sailing equipment that support and manipulate the rigging.

mizzenmast
One of the principal masts of the ship; it is located aft of the mainmast between the ship's center of gravity and its rudder.

jiggermast
Mast located aft on the four-masted bark.

mainmast
One of the principal parts of the ship; it is located closest to the center of gravity.

foremast
Mast nearest the prow of the boat.

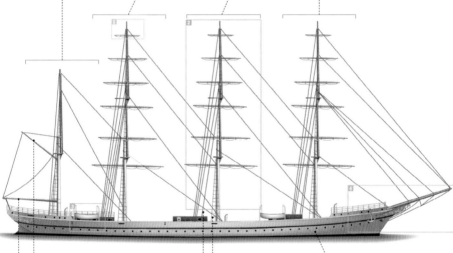

gaff
Diagonal yard aft of a mast and supporting the top part of a gaff sail.

shroud
Heavy taut rope between a mast and the side of the ship; it secures and supports the mast on the sides.

side
Longitudinal surface of the ship.

gaff sail boom
Horizontal yard articulating on a mast; it keeps the bottom edge of a sail taut.

backstay
Long taut rope between the mast and the deck; it secures and supports the mast athwartships and aft.

pole
Tapered top end of a mast.

yard
Long pole that is supported by the mast and holds up the edge of a sail.

fore-royal mast
Mast above the fore-topgallant mast that carries a royal sail.

footrope
Rope hanging along the entire length of a yard that is used by sailors to trim the sails.

fore-topgallant mast
Mast above the fore-topmast that carries a topgallant sail.

masthead
Topmost section of a mast that is sometimes doubled with the lower section of the mast supporting it; the stays and shrouds are attached to it.

fore-topmast
Mast that is immediately above a lower mast and carries a topsail.

lifeboat
Boat for transporting passengers and crew in the event of shipwreck.

top
Platform at the top of the lower mast from which the upper rigging can be manipulated.

davit
Skid hanging over the edge of the ship that supports a boat and is used to lower and raise it.

lower mast
Bottom section of a mast that is solid and thick so it can support the upper sections.

stem
Main timber reinforcing the prow.

stay
Taut rope between a mast and another point on the masting; it secures and supports the mast fore of it.

bobstay
Rope counterbalancing the tension caused by the stays and the staysail-stays on the bowsprit.

bowsprit
Mast extending before the stem; additional jibs can be attached to it.

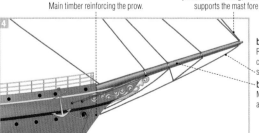

four-masted bark

sails
A sailboat's sails that are rigged on the bowsprit, the foremast, the main masts, the jiggermast and between these masts.

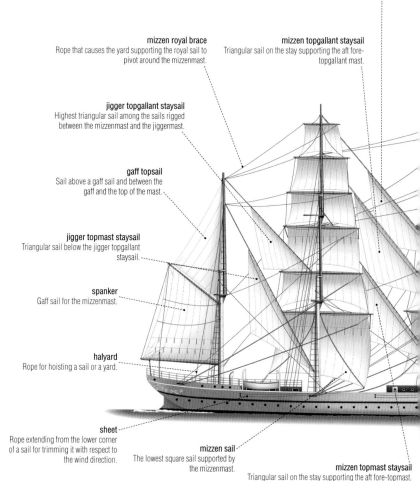

mizzen royal staysail
Triangular sail rigged on the stay supporting the aft fore-royal mast.

mizzen royal brace
Rope that causes the yard supporting the royal sail to pivot around the mizzenmast.

mizzen topgallant staysail
Triangular sail on the stay supporting the aft fore-topgallant mast.

jigger topgallant staysail
Highest triangular sail among the sails rigged between the mizzenmast and the jiggermast.

gaff topsail
Sail above a gaff sail and between the gaff and the top of the mast.

jigger topmast staysail
Triangular sail below the jigger topgallant staysail.

spanker
Gaff sail for the mizzenmast.

halyard
Rope for hoisting a sail or a yard.

sheet
Rope extending from the lower corner of a sail for trimming it with respect to the wind direction.

mizzen sail
The lowest square sail supported by the mizzenmast.

mizzen topmast staysail
Triangular sail on the stay supporting the aft fore-topmast.

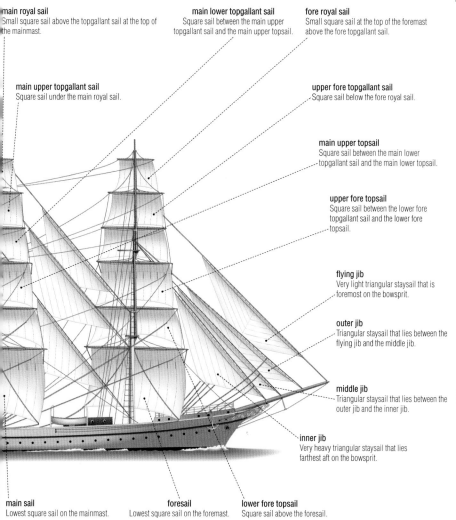

main royal sail
Small square sail above the topgallant sail at the top of the mainmast.

main lower topgallant sail
Square sail between the main upper topgallant sail and the main upper topsail.

fore royal sail
Small square sail at the top of the foremast above the fore topgallant sail.

main upper topgallant sail
Square sail under the main royal sail.

upper fore topgallant sail
Square sail below the fore royal sail.

main upper topsail
Square sail between the main lower topgallant sail and the main lower topsail.

upper fore topsail
Square sail between the lower fore topgallant sail and the lower fore topsail.

flying jib
Very light triangular staysail that is foremost on the bowsprit.

outer jib
Triangular staysail that lies between the flying jib and the middle jib.

middle jib
Triangular staysail that lies between the outer jib and the inner jib.

inner jib
Very heavy triangular staysail that lies farthest aft on the bowsprit.

main sail
Lowest square sail on the mainmast.

foresail
Lowest square sail on the foremast.

lower fore topsail
Square sail above the foresail.

TRANSPORTATION

examples of boats and ships

Boats and ships: floating structures for underwater exploration and transporting passengers and cargo across water.

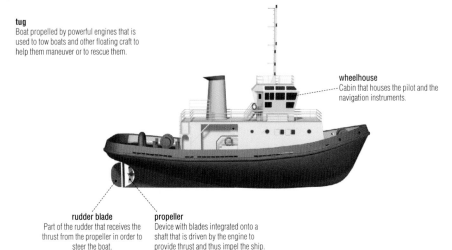

tug
Boat propelled by powerful engines that is used to tow boats and other floating craft to help them maneuver or to rescue them.

wheelhouse
Cabin that houses the pilot and the navigation instruments.

rudder blade
Part of the rudder that receives the thrust from the propeller in order to steer the boat.

propeller
Device with blades integrated onto a shaft that is driven by the engine to provide thrust and thus impel the ship.

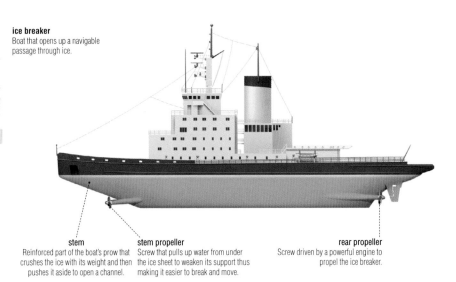

ice breaker
Boat that opens up a navigable passage through ice.

stem
Reinforced part of the boat's prow that crushes the ice with its weight and then pushes it aside to open a channel.

stem propeller
Screw that pulls up water from under the ice sheet to weaken its support thus making it easier to break and move.

rear propeller
Screw driven by a powerful engine to propel the ice breaker.

hydrofoil boat
Fast boat with foils, which lift and
support the hull above water when
cruising speed is reached.

radar
Detection device that emits radio waves and
receives their echo; it is used to avoid
collisions and to navigate when visibility is
reduced.

radio antenna
Metal conductor that emits and
receives radio waves for
communications.

passenger cabin
Compartment where the passengers sit
during the trip.

compass bridge
Covered glassed-in platform from
which officers and crew navigate the
vessel.

life buoy
ing made of buoyant material that is
thrown to anyone who has fallen
overboard to help them float.

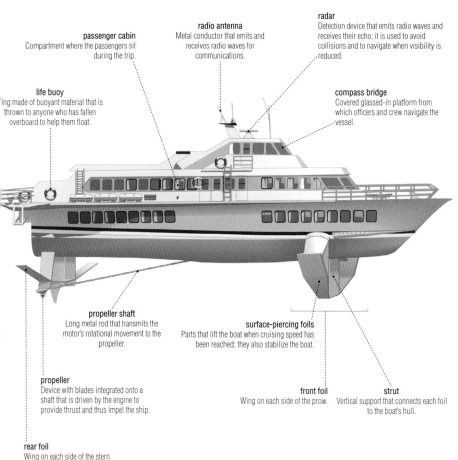

propeller shaft
Long metal rod that transmits the
motor's rotational movement to the
propeller.

surface-piercing foils
Parts that lift the boat when cruising speed has
been reached; they also stabilize the boat.

propeller
Device with blades integrated onto a
shaft that is driven by the engine to
provide thrust and thus impel the ship.

front foil
Wing on each side of the prow.

strut
Vertical support that connects each foil
to the boat's hull.

rear foil
Wing on each side of the stern.

examples of boats and ships

container ship
Ship that is designed for transporting cargo in its hold and on its deck.

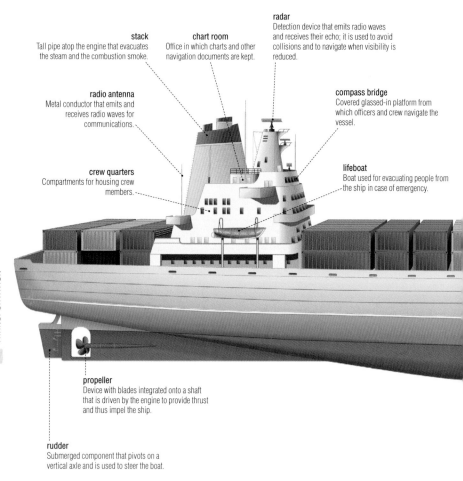

stack
Tall pipe atop the engine that evacuates the steam and the combustion smoke.

chart room
Office in which charts and other navigation documents are kept.

radar
Detection device that emits radio waves and receives their echo; it is used to avoid collisions and to navigate when visibility is reduced.

radio antenna
Metal conductor that emits and receives radio waves for communications.

compass bridge
Covered glassed-in platform from which officers and crew navigate the vessel.

crew quarters
Compartments for housing crew members.

lifeboat
Boat used for evacuating people from the ship in case of emergency.

propeller
Device with blades integrated onto a shaft that is driven by the engine to provide thrust and thus impel the ship.

rudder
Submerged component that pivots on a vertical axle and is used to steer the boat.

TRANSPORTATION

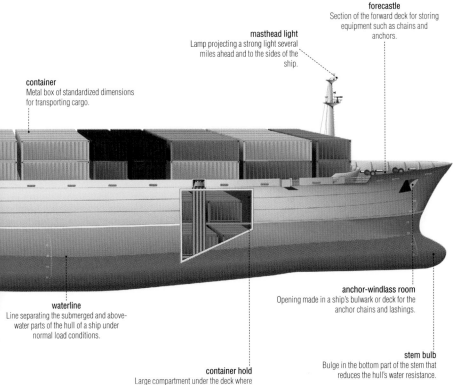

forecastle
Section of the forward deck for storing equipment such as chains and anchors.

masthead light
Lamp projecting a strong light several miles ahead and to the sides of the ship.

container
Metal box of standardized dimensions for transporting cargo.

waterline
Line separating the submerged and above-water parts of the hull of a ship under normal load conditions.

anchor-windlass room
Opening made in a ship's bulwark or deck for the anchor chains and lashings.

container hold
Large compartment under the deck where containers are stowed.

stem bulb
Bulge in the bottom part of the stem that reduces the hull's water resistance.

TRANSPORTATION

examples of boats and ships

hovercraft
Propeller vehicle that moves above water
(or land) by gliding on a cushion of air it
creates by blowing downward.

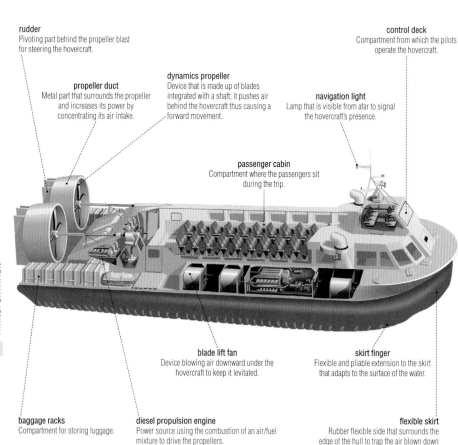

rudder
Pivoting part behind the propeller blast
for steering the hovercraft.

control deck
Compartment from which the pilots
operate the hovercraft.

propeller duct
Metal part that surrounds the propeller
and increases its power by
concentrating its air intake.

dynamics propeller
Device that is made up of blades
integrated with a shaft; it pushes air
behind the hovercraft thus causing a
forward movement.

navigation light
Lamp that is visible from afar to signal
the hovercraft's presence.

passenger cabin
Compartment where the passengers sit
during the trip.

blade lift fan
Device blowing air downward under the
hovercraft to keep it levitated.

skirt finger
Flexible and pliable extension to the skirt
that adapts to the surface of the water.

baggage racks
Compartment for storing luggage.

diesel propulsion engine
Power source using the combustion of an air/fuel
mixture to drive the propellers.

flexible skirt
Rubber flexible side that surrounds the
edge of the hull to trap the air blown down
by the lift fan; this increases pressure,
which in turn causes lift.

TRANSPORTATION

ferry boat
Shuttle boat for carrying vehicles with
their cargo and passengers.

telecommunication antenna
Multipurpose antenna that receives and
transmits various signals such as video,
telephone and digital.

radio antenna
Metal conductor that emits and
receives radio waves for
communications.

restaurant
Compartment where meals are
prepared and eaten.

radar
Detection device that emits radio waves
and receives their echo; it is used to avoid
collisions and to navigate when visibility
is reduced.

bow loading door
Door for loading vehicles; another is located
aft for unloading cars.

heating/air-conditioning equipment
Machinery that regulates the cabin's temperature
and humidity.

compass bridge
Covered glassed-in platform from which
officers and crew navigate the vessel.

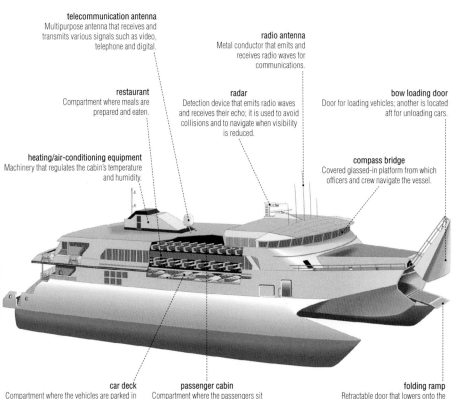

car deck
Compartment where the vehicles are parked in
such a way as to keep the ferry balanced.

passenger cabin
Compartment where the passengers sit
during the trip.

folding ramp
Retractable door that lowers onto the
quay to load and unload vehicles.

TRANSPORTATION

examples of boats and ships

tanker
Ship with large reservoirs for transporting liquid petroleum products.

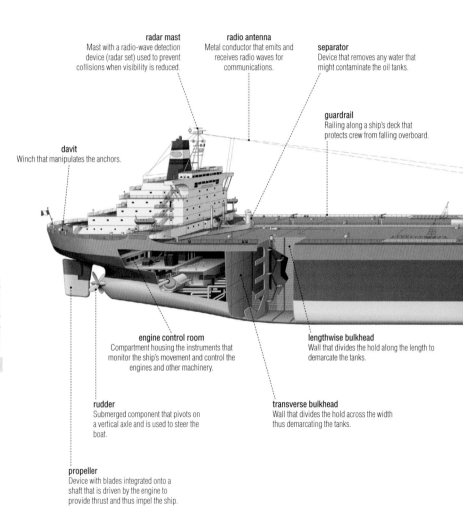

radar mast
Mast with a radio-wave detection device (radar set) used to prevent collisions when visibility is reduced.

radio antenna
Metal conductor that emits and receives radio waves for communications.

separator
Device that removes any water that might contaminate the oil tanks.

guardrail
Railing along a ship's deck that protects crew from falling overboard.

davit
Winch that manipulates the anchors.

engine control room
Compartment housing the instruments that monitor the ship's movement and control the engines and other machinery.

lengthwise bulkhead
Wall that divides the hold along the length to demarcate the tanks.

rudder
Submerged component that pivots on a vertical axle and is used to steer the boat.

transverse bulkhead
Wall that divides the hold across the width thus demarcating the tanks.

propeller
Device with blades integrated onto a shaft that is driven by the engine to provide thrust and thus impel the ship.

TRANSPORTATION

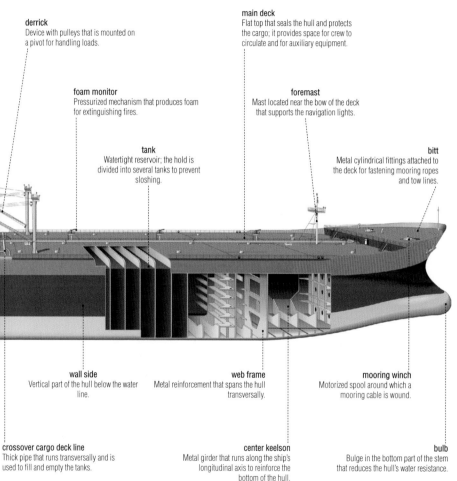

derrick
Device with pulleys that is mounted on a pivot for handling loads.

main deck
Flat top that seals the hull and protects the cargo; it provides space for crew to circulate and for auxiliary equipment.

foam monitor
Pressurized mechanism that produces foam for extinguishing fires.

foremast
Mast located near the bow of the deck that supports the navigation lights.

tank
Watertight reservoir; the hold is divided into several tanks to prevent sloshing.

bitt
Metal cylindrical fittings attached to the deck for fastening mooring ropes and tow lines.

wall side
Vertical part of the hull below the water line.

web frame
Metal reinforcement that spans the hull transversally.

mooring winch
Motorized spool around which a mooring cable is wound.

crossover cargo deck line
Thick pipe that runs transversally and is used to fill and empty the tanks.

center keelson
Metal girder that runs along the ship's longitudinal axis to reinforce the bottom of the hull.

bulb
Bulge in the bottom part of the stem that reduces the hull's water resistance.

TRANSPORTATION

examples of boats and ships

passenger liner
Large cruise ship, fitted like a luxury
hotel and with diverse recreation
facilities for passengers.

hall
Room fitted with armchairs for
passengers to meet.

funnel
Long vertical pipe above the machinery
evacuating exhaust gases from the engines,
with filters for absorbing carbon particles.

promenade deck
Open deck for strolling that is
sometimes glassed in.

lounge
Area with a counter and tables where
alcoholic drinks are sold.

stern
Rear end of a ship.

playing area
Fenced-in area for playing ball sports.

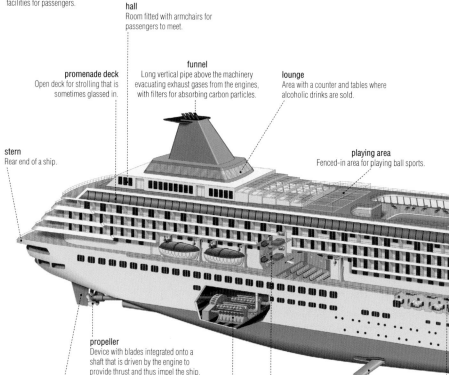

propeller
Device with blades integrated onto a
shaft that is driven by the engine to
provide thrust and thus impel the ship.

rudder
Submerged component that pivots on
a vertical axle and is used to steer the
boat.

engine room
Room housing the engines, turbines
and related machinery that propel the
ship.

stabilizer fin
Small pivoting winglike flaps on each
side of the hull to reduce the rolling
motion.

cabin
Room that accommodates one or
several passengers.

dining room
Hall for eating meals.

telecommunication antenna
Multipurpose antenna that receives and transmits various signals such as video, telephone and digital.

radio antenna
Metal conductor that emits and receives radio waves for communications.

sundeck
Usually the highest and sunniest deck with a pool and lounge chairs.

radar
Detection device that emits radio waves and receives their echo; it is used to avoid collisions and to navigate when visibility is reduced.

open-air terrace
Outdoor platform that is formed from the roof of the deck below and is protected by a guardrail.

compass bridge
Covered glassed-in platform from which officers and crew navigate the vessel.

port hand
Left side of the ship when looking forward.

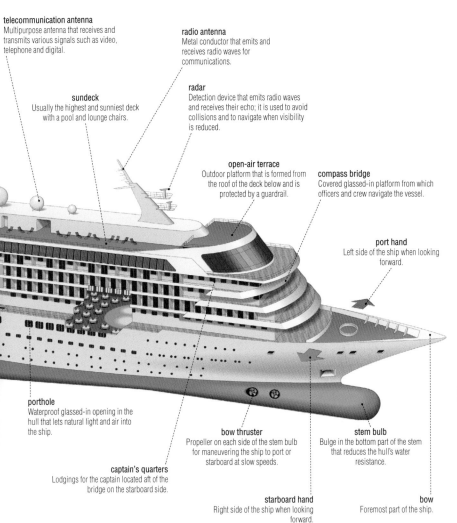

porthole
Waterproof glassed-in opening in the hull that lets natural light and air into the ship.

bow thruster
Propeller on each side of the stem bulb for maneuvering the ship to port or starboard at slow speeds.

stem bulb
Bulge in the bottom part of the stem that reduces the hull's water resistance.

captain's quarters
Lodgings for the captain located aft of the bridge on the starboard side.

starboard hand
Right side of the ship when looking forward.

bow
Foremost part of the ship.

TRANSPORTATION

airport

Location that contains all the technical and commercial facilities needed to support air traffic.

high-speed exit taxiway
Lane linking the landing runway with a taxiway that is used by aircraft after landing to free up the runway.

control tower cab
Glassed-in office where the air traffic controllers coordinate aircraft movement such as takeoff, landing and flight.

control tower
Structure supporting the control tower cab, which provides a wide view of the runways and terminals.

by-pass taxiway
Branch for right turns.

taxiway
Lane used by aircraft for entering and exiting the apron.

service road
Lane reserved for airport service vehicles.

taxiway
Lane used by aircraft for entering or exiting a takeoff or landing runway.

maintenance hangar
Structure where aircraft are maintained and repaired.

parking area
Area where aircraft park between flights for maintenance or overhaul.

access road
Part of the network of roads serving the airport.

passenger terminal
Structure through which passengers pass before or after their flight to pick up or leave their baggage and to go through customs.

telescopic corridor
Mobile corridor connecting the passenger loading area with the aircraft.

radial passenger loading area
Pavilion for passengers to reach aircraft that is linked by an underground corridor or by vehicles with the main terminal.

maneuvering area
Area crossed by an aircraft to enter or exit a parking spot.

apron
Lane used by aircraft for entering or exiting the maneuvering area.

taxiway line
Yellow line painted on the ground that shows aircraft the route to follow on the apron or the maneuvering area.

service area
Area around an aircraft that is reserved for service vehicles and ground crew attending to arriving or departing aircraft.

boarding walkway
Underground corridor linking the main terminal with a radial passenger loading area.

TRANSPORTATION

long-range jet

Aircraft that transports passengers and cargo traveling long distances at high altitudes (between 30,000 and 40,000 ft).

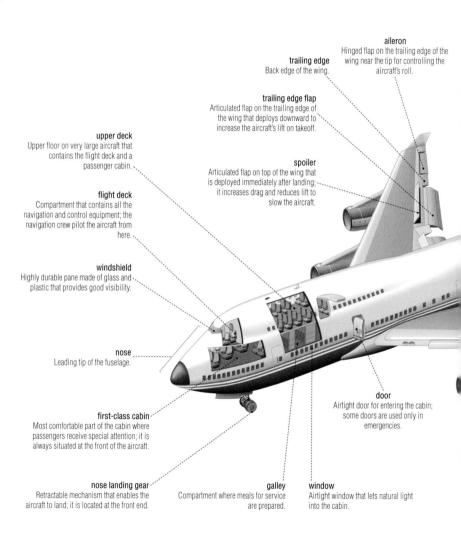

aileron
Hinged flap on the trailing edge of the wing near the tip for controlling the aircraft's roll.

trailing edge
Back edge of the wing.

trailing edge flap
Articulated flap on the trailing edge of the wing that deploys downward to increase the aircraft's lift on takeoff.

upper deck
Upper floor on very large aircraft that contains the flight deck and a passenger cabin.

spoiler
Articulated flap on top of the wing that is deployed immediately after landing; it increases drag and reduces lift to slow the aircraft.

flight deck
Compartment that contains all the navigation and control equipment; the navigation crew pilot the aircraft from here.

windshield
Highly durable pane made of glass and plastic that provides good visibility.

nose
Leading tip of the fuselage.

door
Airtight door for entering the cabin; some doors are used only in emergencies.

first-class cabin
Most comfortable part of the cabin where passengers receive special attention; it is always situated at the front of the aircraft.

nose landing gear
Retractable mechanism that enables the aircraft to land; it is located at the front end.

galley
Compartment where meals for service are prepared.

window
Airtight window that lets natural light into the cabin.

rudder

fin Articulated flap at the rear of the fin that
Fixed vertical part of the tail assembly steers the aircraft and corrects any yaw **tail**
that keeps the aircraft stable. that might occur. Rear part of the fuselage.

tail assembly
Moving and fixed surfaces that are
located at the tail of the aircraft for
steering and stabilizing it.

horizontal stabilizer
Wing made up of the fixed horizontal tail assembly; it
stabilizes the aircraft horizontally.

elevator
Articulated flap that is attached to the
trailing edge of the horizontal stabilizer; it
is used to change altitude and correct any
pitch that may occur.

passenger cabin
Compartment in which most of the
passengers travel and receive basic services;
it is also called economy class.

fuselage
Aircraft body that is divided into several
compartments and whose aerodynamic
form reduces air friction; it is supported by
the wings in flight.

freight hold
Compartment where baggage and
cargo are stored.

wing
Horizontal surface on which
aerodynamic forces are exerted to keep
the aircraft in the air.

winglet
Protruding surface at the wingtip that
enhances aerodynamics.

turbojet engine
Jet-propulsion turbine producing hot
gases that are expelled at high speed to
provide the thrust necessary to propel
the aircraft.

leading edge
Front edge of the wing.

navigation light
Light signaling the direction in which the
aircraft is flying: red on the left wing
(port), green on the right wing (starboard)
and white on the tail.

TRANSPORTATION

examples of airplanes

Ever since the first airplane, Éole, in 1890, the shape of aircraft has evolved constantly as new aerodynamic discoveries were made and engine power increased.

float seaplane
Airplane designed to take off from and land on water.

three-blade propeller
Propulsion device with three blades that are arranged around an axle and driven by a motor.

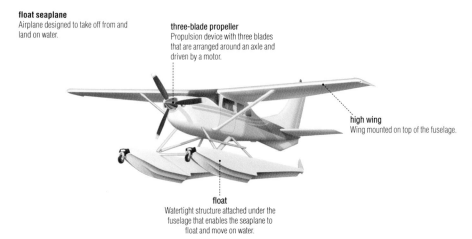

high wing
Wing mounted on top of the fuselage.

float
Watertight structure attached under the fuselage that enables the seaplane to float and move on water.

light aircraft
Airplane that usually has a single engine and cruises between 90 and 150 mph; it is used for recreation and traveling short distances.

high frequency antenna cable
Wire enabling radio communication for the aircraft.

wing strut
Rigid or flexible component that braces an airplane's wing and connects the wing to the fuselage or connects the two wings on a biplane.

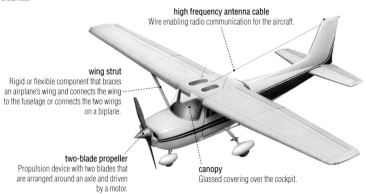

two-blade propeller
Propulsion device with two blades that are arranged around an axle and driven by a motor.

canopy
Glassed covering over the cockpit.

biplane
Airplane with two superimposed and parallel sets of wings.

upper wing

wings
Surfaces upon which aerodynamic forces are exerted to cause the airplane to fly.

lower wing

amphibious fire-fighting aircraft
Airplane with large water tanks; it is used to fight forest fires.

three-blade propeller
Propulsion device with three blades that are arranged around an axle and driven by a motor.

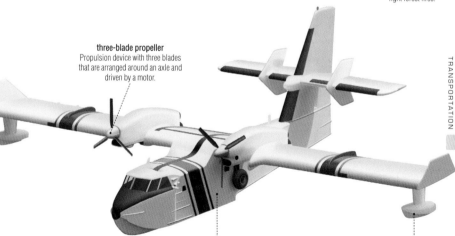

TRANSPORTATION

water-tank area
Area with a hatch that scoops up water from the surface of a body of water to fill its tanks so that it can dump the water in flight.

float
Watertight structure that prevents the airplane from tipping when it fills its tanks.

examples of airplanes

business aircraft
Airplane with a limited number of seats; it is usually used by heads of corporations for business trips.

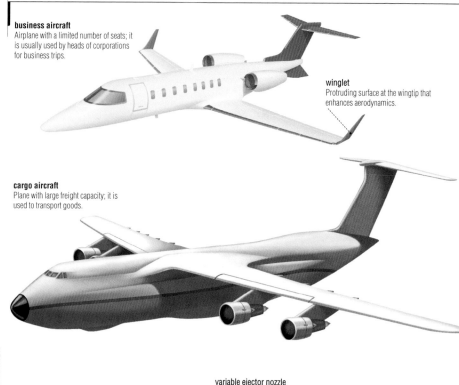

winglet
Protruding surface at the wingtip that enhances aerodynamics.

cargo aircraft
Plane with large freight capacity; it is used to transport goods.

TRANSPORTATION

supersonic jetliner
Passenger aircraft whose cruising speed (1500 mph) is faster than the speed of sound (761 mph). The Concorde was the best known commercial aircraft of this type.

variable ejector nozzle
Duct whose mouth widens as the plane climbs, thus enabling the engines to increase output.

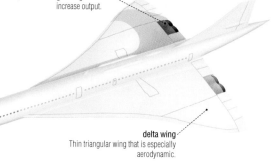

droop nose
Articulated nose that is lowered on takeoff and landing to provide the pilot with better visibility.

delta wing
Thin triangular wing that is especially aerodynamic.

vertical take-off and landing aircraft
Airplane that can move vertically in order to take off from and land on short runways; it is usually used in combat.

swiveling nozzle
Duct that can be pointed downward to increase the engine's vertical thrust during vertical landing and takeoff.

radar-absorbent material
Material that absorbs radar waves before they strike any metal part of the aircraft in order to muffle the sound of the echo.

stealth aircraft
Aircraft that cannot be detected by radar because of the radar-absorbing facets covering its fuselage.

facet
Flat surface with a protruding edge that disperses any radar waves hitting it and makes them undetectable.

radar aircraft
Surveillance aircraft for locating and identifying aircraft in flight.

rotodome
Domelike rotating structure that houses radar antennae.

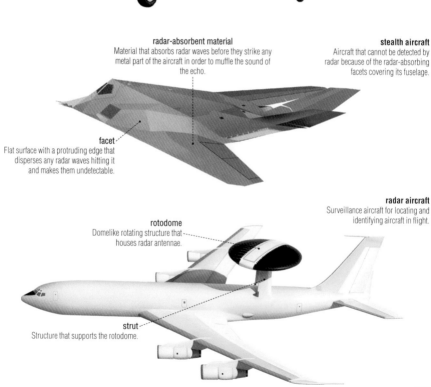

strut
Structure that supports the rotodome.

helicopter

Aircraft whose lift agent is a rotor on a vertical axle.

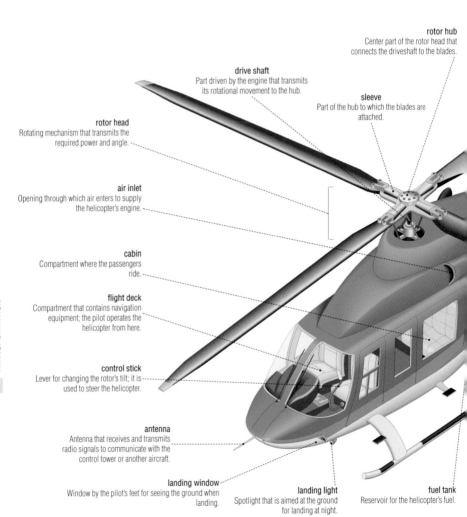

rotor hub
Center part of the rotor head that connects the driveshaft to the blades.

drive shaft
Part driven by the engine that transmits its rotational movement to the hub.

sleeve
Part of the hub to which the blades are attached.

rotor head
Rotating mechanism that transmits the required power and angle.

air inlet
Opening through which air enters to supply the helicopter's engine.

cabin
Compartment where the passengers ride.

flight deck
Compartment that contains navigation equipment; the pilot operates the helicopter from here.

control stick
Lever for changing the rotor's tilt; it is used to steer the helicopter.

antenna
Antenna that receives and transmits radio signals to communicate with the control tower or another aircraft.

landing window
Window by the pilot's feet for seeing the ground when landing.

landing light
Spotlight that is aimed at the ground for landing at night.

fuel tank
Reservoir for the helicopter's fuel.

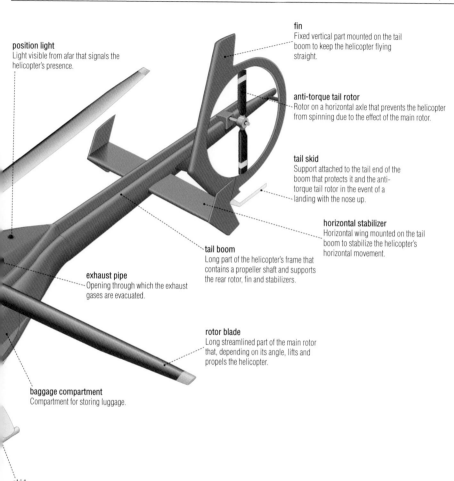

fin
Fixed vertical part mounted on the tail boom to keep the helicopter flying straight.

position light
Light visible from afar that signals the helicopter's presence.

anti-torque tail rotor
Rotor on a horizontal axle that prevents the helicopter from spinning due to the effect of the main rotor.

tail skid
Support attached to the tail end of the boom that protects it and the anti-torque tail rotor in the event of a landing with the nose up.

horizontal stabilizer
Horizontal wing mounted on the tail boom to stabilize the helicopter's horizontal movement.

tail boom
Long part of the helicopter's frame that contains a propeller shaft and supports the rear rotor, fin and stabilizers.

exhaust pipe
Opening through which the exhaust gases are evacuated.

rotor blade
Long streamlined part of the main rotor that, depending on its angle, lifts and propels the helicopter.

baggage compartment
Compartment for storing luggage.

skid
Tube on which the helicopter lands and rests.

matter

Any substance that has mass, is composed of atoms and occupies space.

atom
Fundamental unit of matter having unique chemical properties; it is composed of a nucleus and an electron cloud. One atom is distinguished from another by the number of protons in its nucleus.

nucleus
Central part of the atom whose electric charge is positive; it is composed of protons and neutrons, around which electrons revolve.

neutron
Constituent particle of an atom's nucleus whose electric charge is neutral; it is composed of one u quark and two d quarks.

proton
Constituent particle of an atom's nucleus whose electric charge is positive; it is composed of two u quarks and one d quark.

proton
Constituent particle of an atom's nucleus whose electric charge is positive; it is composed of two u quarks and one d quark.

electron
Particle having a negative electric charge that moves around the nucleus of the atom.

molecule
Matter composed of atoms that constitutes the smallest unit of a pure body that can exist in a free state (e.g., water and carbon dioxide).

atoms
All matter in the universe is composed of approximately 100 types of atoms.

neutron
Constituent particle of an atom's nucleus whose electric charge is neutral; it is composed of one u quark and two d quarks.

d quark
The d quark (down) is one of six types of quarks (constituent particles of protons and neutrons) having a negative electric charge.

u quark
The u quark (up) is one of six types of quarks (constituent particles of the protons and neutrons) having a positive electric charge.

chemical bond
Force that unites two atoms through the sharing of a common electron (covalent bond) or the transfer of electrons (ionic bond) to form a molecule.

states of matter
Matter exists in three fundamental states (solid, liquid and gaseous), which depend on the temperature and pressure to which the matter is subjected.

condensation
Change of a substance from a gaseous state to a liquid state; it results from cooling.

sublimation
Change of a substance from a solid state directly to a gaseous state without passing through the liquid state; it results from heating.

gas
Malleable and expandable matter whose only definable property is mass; its atoms are fully mobile with respect to each other.

evaporation
Change of a substance from a liquid state to a gaseous state; it results from heating.

crystallization
Change of a substance from an amorphous state to a crystallized state; it results from cooling, which causes the atoms to become ordered.

supercooling
The process of cooling a liquid below the point at which it normally freezes (solidifies); its atoms become unstable.

amorphous solid
Body that resembles a congealed liquid whose atoms are not ordered.

condensation
Change of a substance from a gaseous state to a liquid state; it results from cooling.

liquid
Matter having a definite mass and volume but no shape; its atoms are relatively mobile in relation to each other.

solid
Rigid body possessing mass, volume and a definite form; its atoms are linked to each other and are almost completely at rest.

freezing
Change of a substance from a liquid state to a solid state; it results from cooling.

melting
Change of a substance from a solid state to a liquid state; it results from heating.

matter

nuclear fission
Process by which the atoms' nuclei become
fragmented (e.g., in a nuclear reactor);
neutrons are released and energy is produced
in the form of heat.

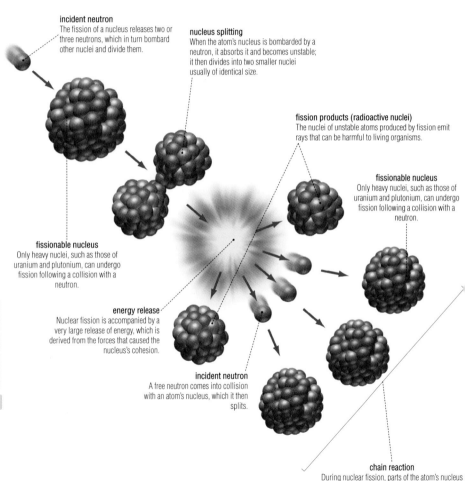

incident neutron
The fission of a nucleus releases two or
three neutrons, which in turn bombard
other nuclei and divide them.

nucleus splitting
When the atom's nucleus is bombarded by a
neutron, it absorbs it and becomes unstable;
it then divides into two smaller nuclei
usually of identical size.

fission products (radioactive nuclei)
The nuclei of unstable atoms produced by fission emit
rays that can be harmful to living organisms.

fissionable nucleus
Only heavy nuclei, such as those of
uranium and plutonium, can undergo
fission following a collision with a
neutron.

fissionable nucleus
Only heavy nuclei, such as those of
uranium and plutonium, can undergo
fission following a collision with a
neutron.

energy release
Nuclear fission is accompanied by a
very large release of energy, which is
derived from the forces that caused the
nucleus's cohesion.

incident neutron
A free neutron comes into collision
with an atom's nucleus, which it then
splits.

chain reaction
During nuclear fission, parts of the atom's nucleus
that have been broken off by collision with the
neutron will in turn bombard other nuclei to
produce more fission.

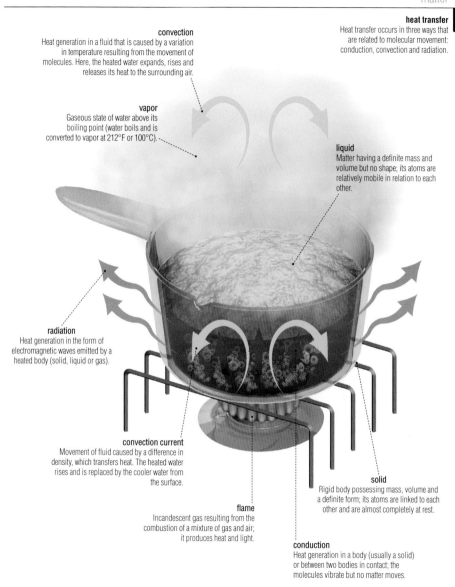

heat transfer
Heat transfer occurs in three ways that are related to molecular movement: conduction, convection and radiation.

convection
Heat generation in a fluid that is caused by a variation in temperature resulting from the movement of molecules. Here, the heated water expands, rises and releases its heat to the surrounding air.

vapor
Gaseous state of water above its boiling point (water boils and is converted to vapor at 212°F or 100°C).

liquid
Matter having a definite mass and volume but no shape; its atoms are relatively mobile in relation to each other.

radiation
Heat generation in the form of electromagnetic waves emitted by a heated body (solid, liquid or gas).

convection current
Movement of fluid caused by a difference in density, which transfers heat. The heated water rises and is replaced by the cooler water from the surface.

flame
Incandescent gas resulting from the combustion of a mixture of gas and air; it produces heat and light.

solid
Rigid body possessing mass, volume and a definite form; its atoms are linked to each other and are almost completely at rest.

conduction
Heat generation in a body (usually a solid) or between two bodies in contact; the molecules vibrate but no matter moves.

SCIENCE AND ENERGY

chemistry symbols

Symbols that simplify the writing of the elements, formulas and chemical reactions.

negative charge
Symbol that indicates a surplus of electrons in an atom, which means the atom has a negative electric charge. The chlorine atom, for example, forms a negative ion that is denoted as Cl⁻.

positive charge
Symbol that indicates a loss of electrons in an atom, which means the atom has a positive electric charge. The sodium atom, for example, forms a positive ion that is denoted as Na+.

reversible reaction
Chemical reaction that can occur in both directions; the products obtained (direct reaction) react between them to change back into the original reactants (inverse reaction).

reaction direction
A chemical reaction corresponds to the conversion of reactants in products and is obtained by the loss of one of the reactants. The arrow indicates the direction in which this irreversible reaction occurs.

lever

System consisting of a bar pivoting on a fulcrum to lift a load. The amount of effort required is related to the position of the pivot and the length of the bar.

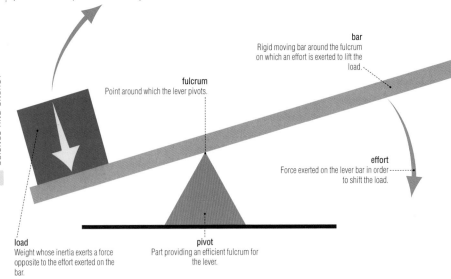

bar
Rigid moving bar around the fulcrum on which an effort is exerted to lift the load.

fulcrum
Point around which the lever pivots.

effort
Force exerted on the lever bar in order to shift the load.

load
Weight whose inertia exerts a force opposite to the effort exerted on the bar.

pivot
Part providing an efficient fulcrum for the lever.

gearing systems

Mechanisms consisting of toothed parts that mesh to transmit the rotational motion of the shafts they are a part of.

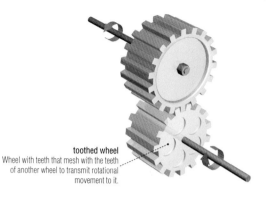

rack and pinion gear
Gearing system converting a rotational movement into a horizontal movement (and vice versa); it is often used in the steering systems of automobiles.

toothed wheel
Wheel with teeth that mesh with the teeth of another wheel to transmit rotational movement to it.

spur gear
Most common gearing system linking two parallel shafts that changes the speed and force of a rotation; it is used especially in automobile transmissions.

shaft
Cylindrical part that transfers the rotational movement of one part to another.

gear tooth
Protrusion on the gear wheel; the teeth of one wheel enter the gaps of another wheel to form a gearing system.

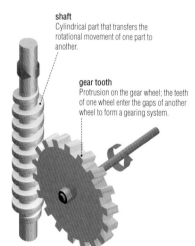

worm gear
One-way gearing system (only the screw can drive the wheel) for slowing down the speed of rotation between two perpendicular axles; it is used especially in the automobile industry (Torsen differential).

bevel gear
Gearing system linking two shafts at right angles that changes the direction of rotation; it is used especially in car jacks.

double pulley system

System consisting of two pulleys with a rope running around them to lift a load. Using two or more pulleys reduces the amount of effort needed.

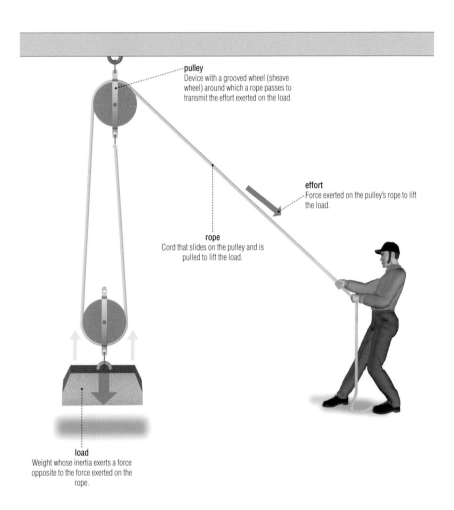

pulley
Device with a grooved wheel (sheave wheel) around which a rope passes to transmit the effort exerted on the load.

effort
Force exerted on the pulley's rope to lift the load.

rope
Cord that slides on the pulley and is pulled to lift the load.

load
Weight whose inertia exerts a force opposite to the force exerted on the rope.

parallel electrical circuit

It is divided into independent branches, through which the current flows with partial intensity (in a series circuit, all the elements receive the same intensity).

cells
Devices that transform chemical energy into electric energy in order to power electric devices (here, a lightbulb).

battery
Device composed of one or more interrelated cells; each one accumulates a reserve of electricity whose purpose is to supply electricity to the circuit.

negative terminal
Polarity element of the battery from which the current flows through the circuit.

positive terminal
Polarity element of the battery toward which the current flows through the circuit.

direction of electron flow
Electrons move from the negative terminal toward the positive terminal; this is opposite to the conventional direction of the current, which flows from the positive toward the negative.

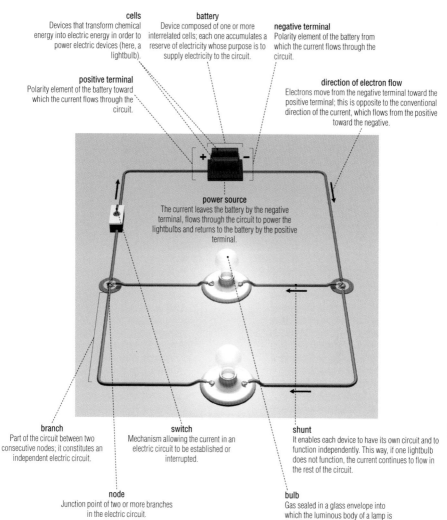

power source
The current leaves the battery by the negative terminal, flows through the circuit to power the lightbulbs and returns to the battery by the positive terminal.

branch
Part of the circuit between two consecutive nodes; it constitutes an independent electric circuit.

switch
Mechanism allowing the current in an electric circuit to be established or interrupted.

shunt
It enables each device to have its own circuit and to function independently. This way, if one lightbulb does not function, the current continues to flow in the rest of the circuit.

node
Junction point of two or more branches in the electric circuit.

bulb
Gas sealed in a glass envelope into which the luminous body of a lamp is inserted.

dry cells

Devices that transform chemical energy into electric energy (direct current); they usually cannot be recharged and the electrolyte is fixed in place.

carbon-zinc cell
Battery that produces 1.5 V (also called Leclanché); its use is very widespread (pocket calculators, portable radios, alarm clocks).

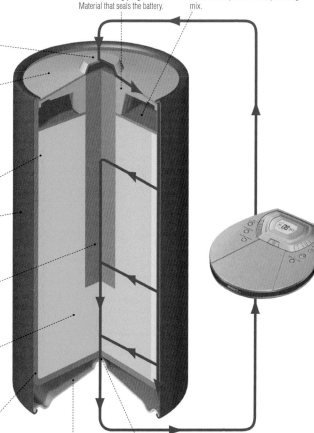

sealing plug
Material that seals the battery.

washer
Disk that compresses the depolarizing mix.

positive terminal
Polarity element of the battery from which the current flows.

top cap
Upper metal cover; the positive terminal is located at its center.

electrolytic separator
Porous paper combined with a chemical paste (ammonium chloride) that separates the two electrodes; this allows electrons to pass, thus conducting electricity.

jacket
Battery's protective plastic casing.

carbon rod (cathode)
Carbon rod set in the depolarizing mix; it constitutes the battery's negative electrode (cathode) collecting the electrons returning from the circuit.

depolarizing mix
Mixture of carbon and manganese dioxide that augments conductivity by acting as a barrier to polarization.

zinc can (anode)
Zinc receptacle that constitutes the battery's positive electrode (anode).

bottom cap
Lower metal cover; the negative terminal is located at its center.

negative terminal
Polarity element of the battery toward which the current flows.

alkaline manganese-zinc cell
High-performance battery that produces 1.5 V and has a longer life span than the carbon-zinc cell; it is used in devices such as flashlights, portable CD players and camera flash units.

sealing material
Material (nylon) that seals the battery.

zinc-electrolyte mix (anode)
Substance that is made up of zinc and electrolyte (potassium hydroxide); it constitutes the positive electrode (anode).

electron collector
Zinc rod that is connected to the bottom cap; it collects the electrons from the anode that are attracted to the cathode.

steel casing
Covering that protects the battery.

separator
Porous paper combined with a chemical paste (potassium hydroxide) that separates the two electrodes; this allows electrons to pass, thus conducting electricity.

manganese mix (cathode)
Substance made up of manganese dioxide and carbon; it constitutes the negative electrode (cathode).

sealing plug
Material that seals the battery.

bottom cap
Lower metal cover; the negative terminal is located at its center.

direction of electron flow
When a chemical reaction occurs, the electrons move from the negative terminal toward the positive terminal, thus creating an electric current.

SCIENCE AND ENERGY

electronics

The scientific study of the behavior of the electron and its applications, such as computers, medicine and automation.

printed circuit board
Usually plastic insulated card with holes containing electronic components; the circuit is printed on its surface.

ceramic capacitor
Component with two conductive plates (silver, copper) separated by an insulator (ceramic); it stores weak electric charge.

plastic film capacitor
Commonly used component with two conductive plates (aluminum, tin) separated by an insulator (plastic); it stores electric charge.

electrolytic capacitors
Polarized components with two conductive components (aluminum, tantalum) separated by an insulator (electrolyte); they store strong electric charge.

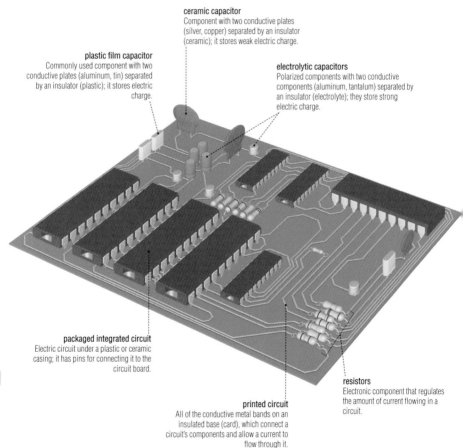

packaged integrated circuit
Electric circuit under a plastic or ceramic casing; it has pins for connecting it to the circuit board.

printed circuit
All of the conductive metal bands on an insulated base (card), which connect a circuit's components and allow a current to flow through it.

resistors
Electronic component that regulates the amount of current flowing in a circuit.

packaged integrated circuit
Integrated circuits are used especially in microprocessors, stereo equipment, calculators, watches and electronic games.

integrated circuit
Miniature electronic circuit made up of a large number of components (such as transistors and capacitors); it is created on a semiconducting wafer usually made of silicon.

lid
Cover that protects the integrated circuit in its package.

wire
Conductive element that connects the circuit components to a connection pin.

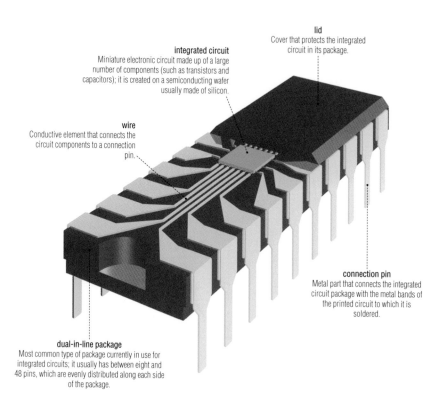

connection pin
Metal part that connects the integrated circuit package with the metal bands of the printed circuit to which it is soldered.

dual-in-line package
Most common type of package currently in use for integrated circuits; it usually has between eight and 48 pins, which are evenly distributed along each side of the package.

SCIENCE AND ENERGY

magnetism

Action exerted by magnets and magnetic fields and phenomena. Magnetism can be characterized by the forces of attraction and repulsion between two masses.

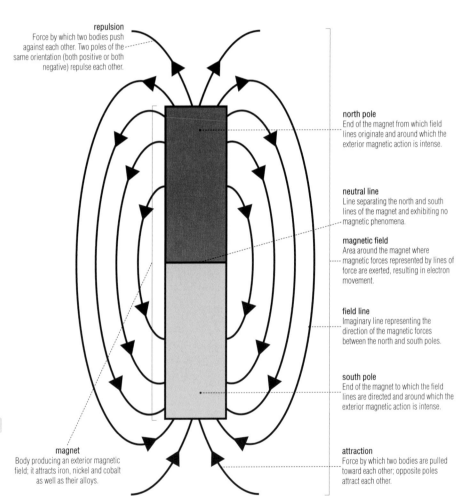

repulsion
Force by which two bodies push against each other. Two poles of the same orientation (both positive or both negative) repulse each other.

north pole
End of the magnet from which field lines originate and around which the exterior magnetic action is intense.

neutral line
Line separating the north and south lines of the magnet and exhibiting no magnetic phenomena.

magnetic field
Area around the magnet where magnetic forces represented by lines of force are exerted, resulting in electron movement.

field line
Imaginary line representing the direction of the magnetic forces between the north and south poles.

south pole
End of the magnet to which the field lines are directed and around which the exterior magnetic action is intense.

magnet
Body producing an exterior magnetic field; it attracts iron, nickel and cobalt as well as their alloys.

attraction
Force by which two bodies are pulled toward each other; opposite poles attract each other.

wave

Oscillation caused by a disturbance; as it propagates through a medium (mechanical waves) or a vacuum (electromagnetic waves), it carries energy.

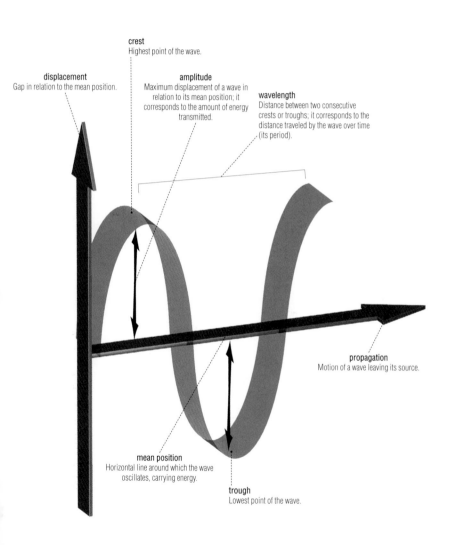

crest
Highest point of the wave.

displacement
Gap in relation to the mean position.

amplitude
Maximum displacement of a wave in relation to its mean position; it corresponds to the amount of energy transmitted.

wavelength
Distance between two consecutive crests or troughs; it corresponds to the distance traveled by the wave over time (its period).

propagation
Motion of a wave leaving its source.

mean position
Horizontal line around which the wave oscillates, carrying energy.

trough
Lowest point of the wave.

electromagnetic spectrum

Electromagnetic waves that are classified in ascending order of energy (frequency); they propagate at the speed of light (300,000 km/s).

radio waves
Very long electromagnetic waves (about 1 meter) having low frequency; they are used to transmit information (television, radio).

ultraviolet radiation
Electromagnetic waves used especially to tan skin and in microscopy, medicine and lighting (fluorescent tubes).

infrared radiation
Electromagnetic waves emitted by warm objects; their many uses include heating, medicine, aerial photography and weaponry.

gamma rays
Electromagnetic waves of very high frequency that are emitted by radioactive bodies; they are the most radiant and harmful rays and are used especially in treating cancer.

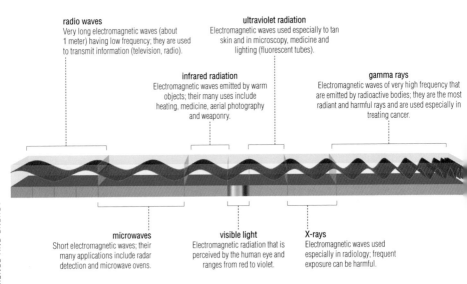

microwaves
Short electromagnetic waves; their many applications include radar detection and microwave ovens.

visible light
Electromagnetic radiation that is perceived by the human eye and ranges from red to violet.

X-rays
Electromagnetic waves used especially in radiology; frequent exposure can be harmful.

color synthesis

Technique of generating color by combining light rays or subtracting them to obtain a colored image.

additive color synthesis
The superimposition of primary colors (blue, green and red) is used especially in electronic screens (television, computer, video) to obtain intermediate tints.

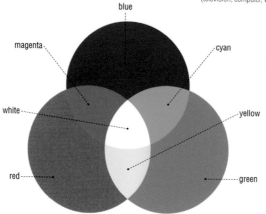

subtractive color synthesis
The absorption of certain light rays (blue, green, red) by colored filters (yellow, magenta, cyan) is used in industries such as photography, film production and printing to obtain intermediate tints.

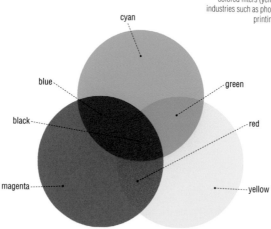

SCIENCE AND ENERGY

vision

Ability to perceive shapes, distances, motion and colors; it is related to light rays and varies depending on the degree of sensitivity of the eye.

normal vision
The image of an object is formed on the retina after passing through the lens, which, depending on the distance of the object, expands or contracts to give a sharp image.

retina
Inner membrane at the back of the eye covered in light-sensitive nerve cells (photoreceptors); these transform light into an electrical impulse that is carried to the optic nerve.

cornea
Transparent fibrous membrane extending the sclera and whose curved shape makes light rays converge toward the inside of the eye.

object
Light rays emanating from an object pass through the eye's various media to form an inverted image on the retina.

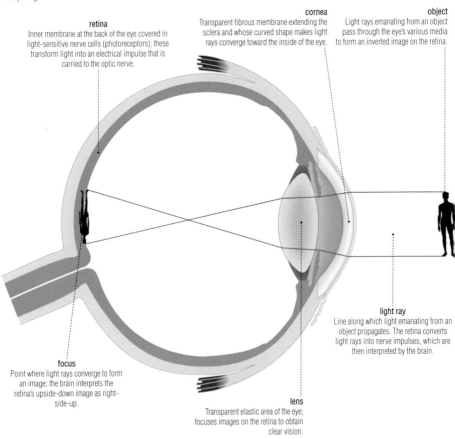

focus
Point where light rays converge to form an image; the brain interprets the retina's upside-down image as right-side-up.

light ray
Line along which light emanating from an object propagates. The retina converts light rays into nerve impulses, which are then interpreted by the brain.

lens
Transparent elastic area of the eye; focuses images on the retina to obtain clear vision.

vision defects

Images do not form on the retina, thus resulting in blurry vision; such defects are corrected by eyeglasses, contact lenses or even surgery.

focus
Point where light rays converge to form an image; the brain interprets the retina's upside-down image as right-side-up.

myopia
The image of a distant object is formed in front of the retina due to a defect in the light rays' convergence. This makes distant objects hard to see.

concave lens
Corrects myopia by causing light rays emanating from an object to diverge and project an image onto the focus of the retina.

focus
Point where light rays converge to form an image; the brain interprets the retina's upside-down image as right-side-up.

hyperopia
The image of an object is formed behind the retina due to a defect in the light rays' convergence as they pass through the lens. This makes near objects hard to see.

convex lens
Corrects hyperopia by causing light rays emanating from an object to converge and project an image onto the focus of the retina.

focus
Point where light rays converge to form an image; the brain interprets the retina's upside-down image as right-side-up.

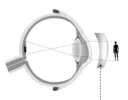

astigmatism
Usually caused by a curvature of the cornea, it is manifested by blurred vision when viewing both near and far objects, depending on various axes.

toric lens
Has various powers depending on the rays' axes of convergence; it is used to offset the visual distortion caused by the cornea.

lenses

Transparent pieces of material (usually glass) that cause light rays to converge or diverge to form a sharp image (eyeglasses, microscopes, telescopes, cameras).

converging lenses
Thicker in the center than on the edges; they cause parallel light rays emanating from an object to converge onto the same point.

positive meniscus
Lens where the concave side (curving inward) is less pronounced than the convex side (bulging outward).

biconvex lens
Lens with both faces bulging outward.

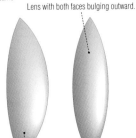

convex lens
Lens with one side bulging outward; the greater the bulge, the more the light rays converge.

plano-convex lens
Lens with one flat side and one convex side (bulging outward).

diverging lenses
Thicker on the edges than in the center; they cause parallel light rays emanating from an object to diverge.

plano-concave lens
Lens with one flat side and one concave side (curving inward).

concave lens
Lens with one side curving inward; the greater the curvature, the more the light rays diverge.

biconcave lens
Lens with both sides curving inward.

negative meniscus
Lens where the concave side (curving inward) is more pronounced than the convex side (bulging outward).

pulsed ruby laser

Device that produces a thin and very intense colored light beam; its various applications include fiber optics, manufacturing and surgery.

fully reflecting mirror
Reflects all the light energy toward the partially reflecting mirror. The reflection between the mirrors intensifies the light to form a highly concentrated beam.

reflecting cylinder
Laser's metal casing whose inside is polished so that it reflects the light toward the ruby cylinder.

cooling cylinder
Casing in which water generally circulates to cool the ruby cylinder, which becomes very hot as it produces the beam.

photon
Energy particle that emits the ruby-chromium atoms as they are excited by flashes in the tube.

ruby cylinder
Ruby bar (crystallized alumina) that contains chromium atoms. It has mirrors at each end, which form the amplification medium to produce the laser beam.

laser beam
Straight and powerful monochrome light beam that is emitted by the device.

partially reflecting mirror
Its partial transparency allows light beams to escape.

flash tube
Lamp that acts as an energy source by emitting a flash of white light, which excites the ruby atoms and causes them to emit photons.

prism binoculars

Optical instrument made up of two identical telescopes, one for each eye; it magnifies both near and distant objects.

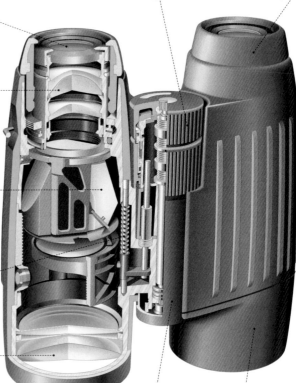

central focusing wheel
Focusing ring for both the objective lenses; it is used to manually adjust the sharpness of the image.

focusing ring
Ring on each eyepiece for manually correcting for the difference between the user's eyes.

eyepiece
Optical disk or system of disks through which the eye sees the image produced by the lens.

lens system
Optical system made up of a set of lenses through which light passes to transmit a magnified image of an object to the eye.

Porro prism
Dual-prism system (blocks of glass at right angles) found in most binoculars; it diverts the light rays toward the eyepiece to correct the inverted image formed in the objective lens.

hinge
Mechanism for adjusting the distance between the eyepieces to the user's eyes.

objective lens
Lens that captures the light from the observed object and causes it to converge to form a magnified inverted image.

bridge
Part of the frame joining the two telescopes.

body
Cylindrical body of the binoculars that houses the optical system and through which the light rays pass.

magnifying glass and microscopes

Optical instruments used to magnify the image of a near object; they range in strength from low (magnifying glass) to strong (microscope).

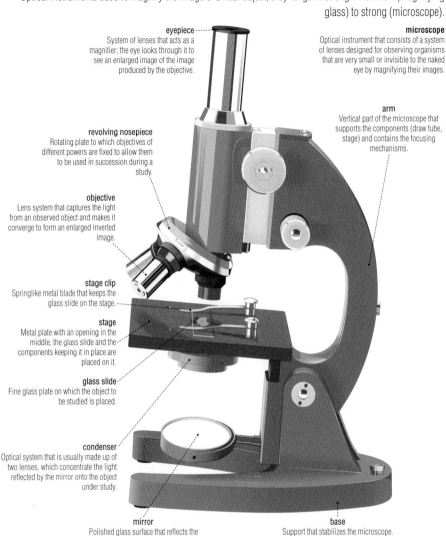

eyepiece
System of lenses that acts as a magnifier; the eye looks through it to see an enlarged image of the image produced by the objective.

microscope
Optical instrument that consists of a system of lenses designed for observing organisms that are very small or invisible to the naked eye by magnifying their images.

arm
Vertical part of the microscope that supports the components (draw tube, stage) and contains the focusing mechanisms.

revolving nosepiece
Rotating plate to which objectives of different powers are fixed to allow them to be used in succession during a study.

objective
Lens system that captures the light from an observed object and makes it converge to form an enlarged inverted image.

stage clip
Springlike metal blade that keeps the glass slide on the stage.

stage
Metal plate with an opening in the middle; the glass slide and the components keeping it in place are placed on it.

glass slide
Fine glass plate on which the object to be studied is placed.

condenser
Optical system that is usually made up of two lenses, which concentrate the light reflected by the mirror onto the object under study.

mirror
Polished glass surface that reflects the surrounding light onto the object under study to illuminate it.

base
Support that stabilizes the microscope.

SCIENCE AND ENERGY

magnifying glass and microscopes

magnifying glass
Converging lens that magnifies the image of an object.

convex lens
Lens with one side bulging outward; the greater the bulge, the more the light rays converge.

handle

telescopic sight

Optical instrument mounted on a rifle or a measuring device to increase accuracy.

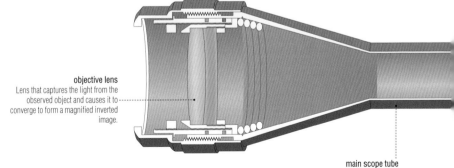

objective lens
Lens that captures the light from the observed object and causes it to converge to form a magnified inverted image.

main scope tube
Cylindrical body of the telescopic sight that houses the optical system and through which the light travels.

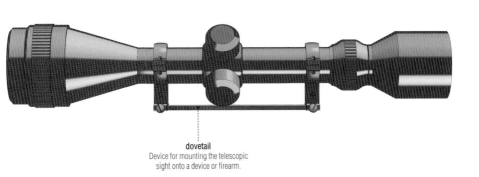

dovetail
Device for mounting the telescopic
sight onto a device or firearm.

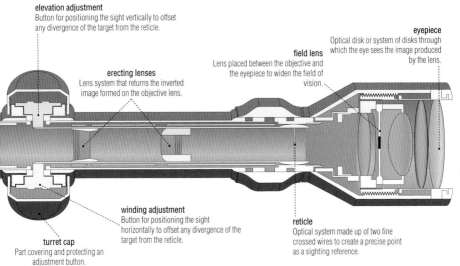

elevation adjustment
Button for positioning the sight vertically to offset
any divergence of the target from the reticle.

erecting lenses
Lens system that returns the inverted
image formed on the objective lens.

field lens
Lens placed between the objective and
the eyepiece to widen the field of
vision.

eyepiece
Optical disk or system of disks through
which the eye sees the image produced
by the lens.

winding adjustment
Button for positioning the sight
horizontally to offset any divergence of the
target from the reticle.

reticle
Optical system made up of two fine
crossed wires to create a precise point
as a sighting reference.

turret cap
Part covering and protecting an
adjustment button.

SCIENCE AND ENERGY

measure of temperature

Temperature: physical quantity corresponding to the level of heat or cold, which is measured by means of a thermometer.

thermometer
Instrument for measuring temperature by means of a substance (usually a liquid or a gas) contained in a graduated tube.

Fahrenheit scale
Temperature scale that is used in some English-speaking countries, on which the freezing point of water is at 32 and the boiling point at 212.

F degrees
Symbol representing a unit of measurement on the Fahrenheit scale (Fahrenheit degree).

alcohol column
Quantity of alcohol that is contained in the glass tube; its height varies with the temperature.

Celsius scale
Temperature scale that is based on a graduation from 0 (freezing point of water) to 100 (boiling point of water); it was formerly called the centigrade scale.

C degrees
Symbol representing a unit of measurement on the Celsius scale (Celsius degree).

alcohol bulb
Glass reservoir containing colored alcohol (methanol, ethanol) that expands and rises in the capillary bore as the temperature rises.

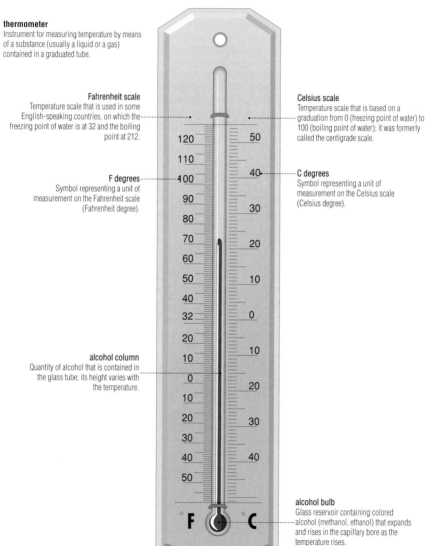

clinical thermometer
More precise than the alcohol thermometer, it is used to take the temperature of the human body; it is graduated from 94°F to 108°F.

expansion chamber
Space that is taken up by the gas in the capillary bore; it is pushed back as the mercury rises into it.

capillary tube
End of the glass tube in which the mercury rises or falls with the temperature; the mercury thermometer tube is filled with gas.

scale
Divisions of equal length (degrees) marked on the thermometer that constitute the units of measurement.

stem
Glass tube containing the capillary bore.

column of mercury
Quantity of mercury that is contained in the capillary bore; its height varies with the temperature.

constriction
Narrowing that prevents the mercury from spontaneously dropping into the bulb as the temperature lowers (the thermometer must be shaken to make it go down).

mercury bulb
Glass reservoir containing mercury (a liquid metal) that expands and rises in the capillary tube as the temperature rises.

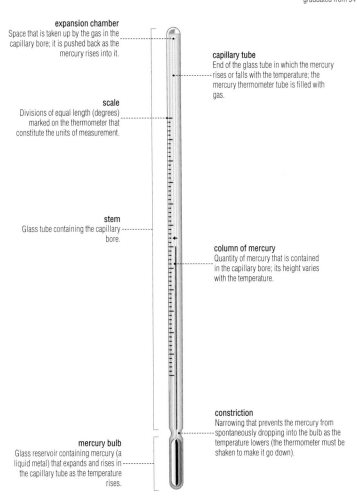

measure of temperature

digital thermometer
Thermometer that indicates the
temperature in digits on a liquid crystal
display screen.

bimetallic thermometer
Thermometer that uses the difference in expansion of two
metals (usually iron and brass) to measure temperatures
between 30°C or 86°F and 300°C or 375F°; it is used
especially in industry.

pointer
Metal needle connected to the shaft
that indicates the temperature on the
dial.

dial
Graduated face with a pointer in front
to indicate the temperature.

shaft
Rod that transmits the bimetallic helix's
rotational motion to the pointer as a
result of warping caused by heat.

bimetallic helix
Band made by welding together two
metals with different coefficients of
expansion; it curves as the temperature
changes.

case
Outer covering that encloses and
protects the device's mechanism.

Time: physical quantity corresponding to a phenomenon or an event that is measured with devices such as watches and stopwatches.

stopwatch
Instrument that precisely measures time in minutes, seconds and fractions of seconds.

start button
Knob that is pushed to start the stopwatch and measure the duration of a phenomenon or event.

ring
Round part for holding or hanging the stopwatch.

minute hand
Metal needle that indicates minutes on a dial graduated from 0 to 30 minutes.

stop button
Knob that is pushed to stop the hands, which then display the precise amount of elapsed time.

reset button
Button that is pushed to return the stopwatch's hands to 0.

second hand
Metal needle that indicates the 60 equal divisions (seconds) of a minute by moving in small jumps.

case
Outer covering that encloses and protects the device's mechanism.

1/10 second hand
Metal needle that indicates the 10 equal divisions of a second on the dial.

SCIENCE AND ENERGY

measure of time

mechanical watch
Set of geared wheels that reduce the force transmitted by a spiral spring to cause the watch's hands to rotate.

fourth wheel
Wheel that transmits energy to the third wheel.

jewel
Very hard stone (formerly a ruby, today a rock crystal) that resists wear; the rotation axle of a wheel rests on it.

third wheel
Wheel that receives energy from the fourth wheel and drives the center wheel.

escape wheel
Last wheel of the gear train with special teeth that causes the watch to operate regularly and continuously; it controls the movement of the other wheels.

winder
Part that rewinds the mechanism, consisting of a series of wheels.

hairspring
Flat spiral spring that causes the wheels of a watch to move over a certain period of time.

click
Small lever that is engaged between the ratchet-wheel teeth and prevents it from rotating counter to its normal direction.

center wheel
Wheel that is connected to the hands and causes them to rotate on the dial.

ratchet wheel
Toothed wheel having only one direction of rotation; it is kept in place by the click.

gnomon
Part aligned with the Earth's axis; its shadow indicates the time as it moves over the sundial.

sundial
Vertical or horizontal face with divisions that correspond to the hours of the day, which are indicated by the shadow of a gnomon cast by the Sun.

shadow
Dark area that results when the gnomon blocks the sunlight and indicates the time in accordance with the position of the Sun.

dial
Face marked with numbers over which shadows are cast by the gnomon to indicate the approximate time of day.

analog watch
The time is displayed by hands, which move around the dial.

digital watch
The time is read from letters and numbers that appear on a clear background.

dial
Graduated face over which the hands move to indicate the time.

strap
Leather, fabric, plastic or metal bracelet with a clasp; it is used to hold a watch on the wrist.

liquid crystal display
Crystal that darkens when submitted to electrical current and displays the shapes of letters and numbers.

crown
Knob with sprockets that is connected to the winder; it is used to manually wind the watch and set its time.

measure of weight

Mass: physical quantity that characterizes an amount of matter (mass) that is measured by means of a scale.

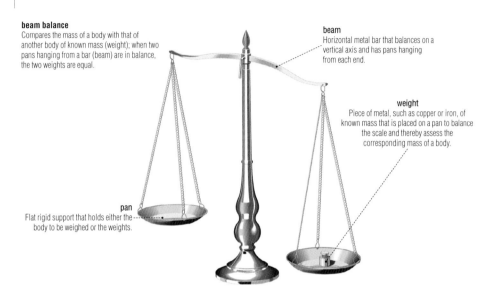

beam balance
Compares the mass of a body with that of another body of known mass (weight); when two pans hanging from a bar (beam) are in balance, the two weights are equal.

beam
Horizontal metal bar that balances on a vertical axis and has pans hanging from each end.

weight
Piece of metal, such as copper or iron, of known mass that is placed on a pan to balance the scale and thereby assess the corresponding mass of a body.

pan
Flat rigid support that holds either the body to be weighed or the weights.

Roberval's balance
Commonly used scale that operates on the same principle as the beam balance; the pans are stabilized by a shank and rest on the beam.

dial
Graduated surface with a pointer in front that indicates the point of equilibrium for the two pans.

pointer
Metal needle that indicates the point of equilibrium on the dial when the beam is level.

weight
Piece of metal, such as copper or iron, of known mass that is placed on a pan to balance the scale and thereby assess the corresponding mass of a body.

pan
Flat rigid support that holds either the body to be weighed or the weights.

base
Support that provides stability to the scale.

beam
Horizontal metal bar that balances on a vertical axis and supports a pan on each end.

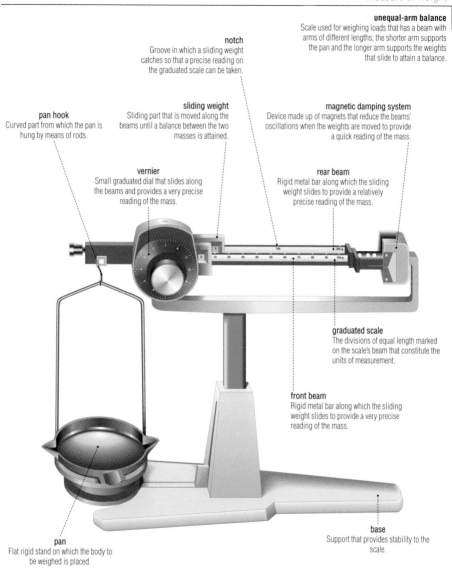

unequal-arm balance
Scale used for weighing loads that has a beam with arms of different lengths; the shorter arm supports the pan and the longer arm supports the weights that slide to attain a balance.

notch
Groove in which a sliding weight catches so that a precise reading on the graduated scale can be taken.

sliding weight
Sliding part that is moved along the beams until a balance between the two masses is attained.

magnetic damping system
Device made up of magnets that reduce the beams' oscillations when the weights are moved to provide a quick reading of the mass.

pan hook
Curved part from which the pan is hung by means of rods.

vernier
Small graduated dial that slides along the beams and provides a very precise reading of the mass.

rear beam
Rigid metal bar along which the sliding weight slides to provide a relatively precise reading of the mass.

graduated scale
The divisions of equal length marked on the scale's beam that constitute the units of measurement.

front beam
Rigid metal bar along which the sliding weight slides to provide a very precise reading of the mass.

pan
Flat rigid stand on which the body to be weighed is placed.

base
Support that provides stability to the scale.

measure of weight

electronic scale
Commercial scale that weighs and
calculates the price of a quantity of
merchandise and displays these
elements.

weight
Liquid crystal display that shows the
weight of the item.

unit price
Liquid crystal display that shows the unit
price of an item.

platform
Flat rigid surface on which the items to
be weighed are placed.

display
Each of the three liquid crystal displays
that show various numeric information
(e.g., weight, unit price and total price).

numeric keyboard
Set of keys with numbers and symbols
that are used especially to enter the
unit prices or codes of items.

total
Liquid crystal display that shows the
price of each weighed article and, at
the end of the transaction, the total
price of all purchases.

function keys
Set of keys that perform various
operations (e.g., data entry,
calculations and printing receipts).

POIDS/WEIGHT kg

PRIX/PRICE/kg $

TOTAL $

product code
Key with a number that corresponds to
the code assigned to a product.

printout
Paper on which various data are
printed (e.g., the weight, quantity and
price of the items weighed).

analytical balance
Used especially in the laboratory for taking very precise weight measurements.

glass case
Glass box that protects the pan from air currents and dust that might cause a false reading of the weight.

door access
Sliding doors that provide easy access to the inside of the glass case.

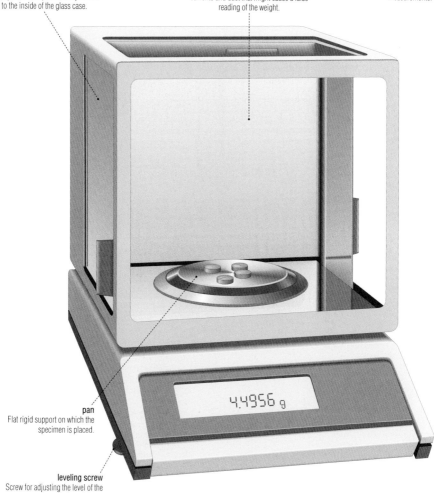

4.4956 g

pan
Flat rigid support on which the specimen is placed.

leveling screw
Screw for adjusting the level of the balance's base.

SCIENCE AND ENERGY

measure of weight

spring balance
Scale made up of a hook attached to a spring that stretches in proportion to the weight of the object being weighed.

ring
Round part for holding or hanging the spring balance.

pointer
Pointer connected to the spring that moves along a graduated scale to indicate the weight of the body being weighed.

graduated scale
The divisions of equal length that are marked on the spring balance and constitute the units of measurement.

hook
Curved part on which the body to be weighed is hung.

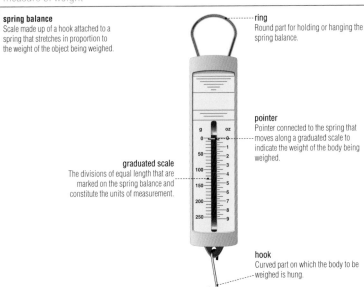

digital display
Liquid crystal display that indicates the weight in numbers.

bathroom scale
Scale used for weighing a person; it has a spring mechanism that compresses in proportion to the weight.

weighing platform
Flat base that a person stands upon to be weighed.

measure of length

Length: the longer dimension of an object as opposed to its width.

ruler
Instrument for measuring length.

scale
The divisions of equal length that are marked on the ruler and constitute the units of measurement.

measure of distance

Distance: interval separating two points in space.

pedometer
Device that counts the number of steps taken by a walker or runner to measure the distance traveled.

reset button
Key used to reset the counter to 0.

distance traveled
Number of steps taken by the walker or runner converted into miles.

clip
Metal fastener for attaching the pedometer to a belt or article of clothing.

step setting
Button for adjusting the average length of a step in the walk or run.

case
Outer covering that encloses and protects the device's mechanism.

SCIENCE AND ENERGY

international system of units

Decimal system established by the 11th General Conference on Weights and Measures (GCWM) in 1960 and used by many countries.

measurement of electric potential difference

V
volt
Difference in potential between two points of a conductor carrying a constant current of 1 ampere when the power between these points is 1 watt.

measurement of frequency

Hz
hertz
Frequency of a periodic phenomenon whose period is 1 second.

measurement of electric charge

C
coulomb
Amount of electricity carried in 1 second by a current of 1 ampere.

measurement of energy

J
joule
Amount of energy released by the force of 1 newton acting through a distance of 1 meter.

measurement of power

W
watt
Energy transfer of 1 joule during 1 second.

measurement of force

N
newton
Force required to impart an acceleration of 1 m/s^2 to a body having a mass of 1 kg.

measurement of electric resistance

ohm
Electrical resistance between two points of a conductor carrying a current of 1 ampere when the difference in potential between them is 1 volt.

measurement of electric current

A
ampere
Constant current of 1 joule per second in a conductor.

measurement of length

meter
Distance traveled by light in a vacuum
in 1/299,792,458 of a second.

measurement of mass

kg

kilogram
Mass of a platinum prototype that was
accepted as the international reference in
1889; it is stored at the International Bureau of
Weights and Measures.

measurement of Celsius temperature

degree Celsius
Division into 100 parts of the difference
between the freezing point of water (0°C) and
its boiling point (100°C) at standard
atmospheric pressure.

measurement of thermodynamic temperature

K

kelvin
Zero Kelvin is equal to minus
273.16°C.

measurement of pressure

pascal
Uniform pressure exerted on a flat
surface of 1 m² with a force of
1 newton.

measurement of amount of substance

mol

mole
Quantity of matter equal to the number
of atoms in 0.012 kg of carbon 12.

measurement of radioactivity

becquerel
Radioactivity of a substance in which
one atom disintegrates per second.

measurement of luminous intensity

cd

candela
Unit of light intensity equivalent to a
radiant intensity of 1/683 watts per
steradian (solid angle).

SCIENCE AND ENERGY

mathematics

The science that uses deductive reasoning to study the properties of abstract entities such as numbers, space and functions and the relations between them.

minus/negative
Sign denoting that a number is to be subtracted from another; the result is a difference.

plus/positive
Sign denoting that a number is to be added to another; the result is a sum.

multiplied by
Sign denoting that a number is to be multiplied by another; the result is a product.

divided by
Sign denoting a number (dividend) is to be divided by another (divisor); the result is a quotient.

equals
Sign denoting the result of an operation.

is not equal to
Sign denoting that the result of an operation is not close to the same value as the one on the right.

is approximately equal to
Sign denoting that the result of an operation is close to the same value as the one on the right.

is equivalent to
Sign denoting that the value on the left is the same magnitude as the one on the right.

is identical with
Binary sign denoting that the result of the operation noted on the left has the same value as the operation noted on the right.

is not identical with
Binary sign denoting that the result of the operation noted on the left does not have the same value as the operation noted on the right.

empty set
Sign denoting that a set contains no elements.

union of two sets
Binary sign denoting that a set is composed of the sum of the elements of two sets.

intersection of two sets
Binary sign denoting that two sets M and N have elements in common.

is included in/is a subset of
Binary sign denoting that a set A on the left is part of the set B on the right.

plus or minus
Sign denoting that the positive and
negative values of the number that
follows bracket a range of values.

is less than or equal to
Sign denoting that the result of an
operation is equal to or of smaller
magnitude than the number that
follows.

is greater than
Sign denoting that the value on the left
is of greater magnitude than the
number that follows.

is greater than or equal to
Sign denoting that the result of an
operation is equal to or of greater
magnitude than the number that
follows.

is less than
Sign denoting that the value on the left
is of smaller magnitude than the
number that follows.

percent
Sign denoting that the number
preceding it is a fraction of 100.

is an element of
Binary sign denoting that the element
on the left is included in the set on the
right.

is not an element of
Binary sign denoting that the element
on the left is not included in the set on
the right.

sum
Sign indicating that several values are
to be added together (their sum).

square root of
Sign denoting that, when a number is
multiplied by itself, the result is the
number that appears below the bar.

fraction
Sign denoting that the number on the
left of the slash (numerator) is one part
of the number on the right of the slash
(denominator).

infinity
Symbol denoting that a value has no
upper limit.

integral
Result of the integral calculation used
especially to determine an area and to
resolve a differential equation.

factorial
Product of all positive whole numbers
less than and equal to a given number.
For example, the factorial of 4 is: 4! =
1x2x3x4 = 24.

mathematics

Roman numerals
Uppercase letters that represented numbers in ancient Rome; they are still seen today in uses such as clock and watch dials and pagination.

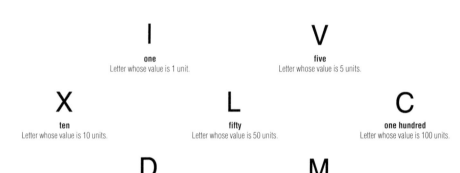

I

one
Letter whose value is 1 unit.

V

five
Letter whose value is 5 units.

X

ten
Letter whose value is 10 units.

L

fifty
Letter whose value is 50 units.

C

one hundred
Letter whose value is 100 units.

D

five hundred
Letter whose value is 500 units.

M

one thousand
Letter whose value is 1,000 units.

biology

The scientific study of living organisms (humans, animals and plants) from the point of view of their structure and how they function and reproduce.

male
Symbol denoting that a being has male reproductive organs.

female
Symbol denoting that a being has female reproductive organs.

blood factor positive
Individuals are Rh positive when their red blood cells carry an Rh molecule (antigen); the Rh factor is positive in about 85% of the population.

blood factor negative
Individuals not carrying the Rh molecule (antigen) are Rh negative; the Rh factor plays an important role in pregnancy (the parents' factors must be compatible).

death
Symbol placed before a date denoting a person's year of death.

birth
Symbol placed before a date denoting a person's year of birth.

geometry

Mathematical discipline that studies the relations between points, straight lines, curves, surfaces and volumes.

degree
Symbol placed in superscript after a number to denote the opening of an angle or the length of an arc, or in front of an uppercase letter to identify a scale of measurement.

minute
Symbol placed in superscript after a number that denotes degrees in sixtieths of a measure.

second
Symbol placed in superscript after a number that denotes degrees in sixtieths of a minute.

pi
Constant that represents the ratio of a circle's circumference to its diameter; its value is approximately 3.1416.

perpendicular
Symbol denoting that a straight line meets another at a right angle.

is parallel to
Symbol denoting that two straight lines remain at a constant distance from one another.

is not parallel to
Symbol denoting that two straight lines do not remain at a constant distance from one other.

right angle
Angle formed by two lines or two perpendicular planes that measures 90°.

obtuse angle
Angle between 90° and 180°.

acute angle
Angle that is smaller than a right angle (less than 90°).

geometrical shapes

Drawings that represent various geometric forms such as straight lines, circles and polygons.

examples of angles
Angle: figure formed by two intersecting lines or planes; it is measured in degrees.

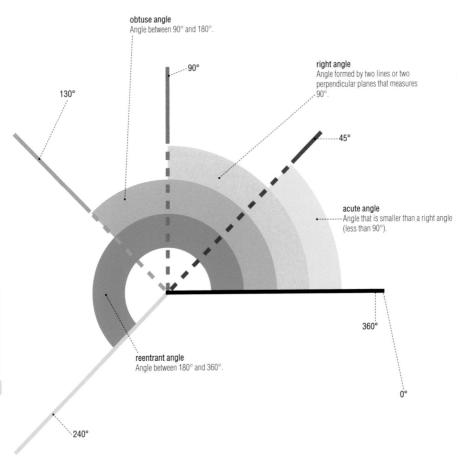

obtuse angle
Angle between 90° and 180°.

90°

130°

right angle
Angle formed by two lines or two perpendicular planes that measures 90°.

45°

acute angle
Angle that is smaller than a right angle (less than 90°).

reentrant angle
Angle between 180° and 360°.

360°

0°

240°

plane surfaces
Set of points on a plane that describes
an area of space.

parts of a circle
Circle: closed plane curve; all its
points are the same distance from a
fixed point (center).

center
Point located at the same distance from
every point on the circle's
circumference.

radius
Line that joins a point on a circle's
circumference to its center; it is one
half of the diameter.

arc
Section of a circle between two points
on the circle.

quadrant
Quarter of a circle's circumference; it
corresponds to an arc of 90°.

sector
Surface bounded by two radii and an
arc of a circle.

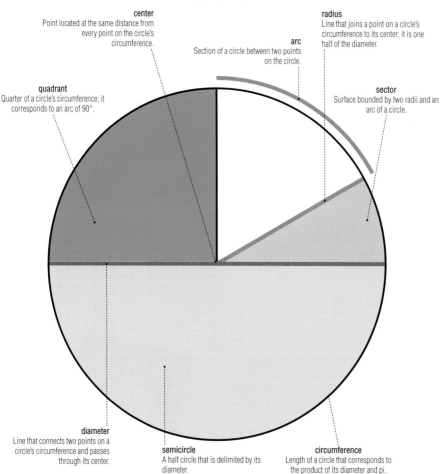

diameter
Line that connects two points on a
circle's circumference and passes
through its center.

semicircle
A half circle that is delimited by its
diameter.

circumference
Length of a circle that corresponds to
the product of its diameter and pi.

geometrical shapes

polygons

Geometric plane figures with several sides and a number of equal angles.

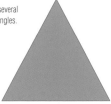

triangle
Three-sided polygon; triangles are scalene (no side is equal to any other) isosceles (two sides equal) or equilateral (all sides equal).

square
Equilateral rectangle with four right angles.

rectangle
Quadrilateral whose opposite sides are equal in length; the sides meet at right angles.

rhombus
Equilateral parallelogram.

trapezoid
Quadrilateral with two sides (bases) that are parallel. It is isosceles when it has two sides that are equal and not parallel, and rectangle when two of its sides form a right angle.

parallelogram
Trapezoid whose opposite sides are parallel and of equal length; the sides do not meet at right angles.

quadrilateral
Any plane figure with four sides and four angles.

regular pentagon
Polygon with five (penta = five) sides and equal angles.

regular hexagon
Polygon with six (hexa = six) sides and equal angles.

regular heptagon
Polygon with seven (hepta = seven) sides and equal angles.

regular octagon
Polygon with eight (octo = eight) sides and equal angles.

regular nonagon
Polygon with nine (nona = nine) sides and equal angles.

regular decagon
Polygon with 10 (deca = ten) sides and equal angles.

regular hendecagon
Polygon with 11 (hendeca = eleven) sides and equal angles.

regular dodecagon
Polygon with 12 (dodeca = twelve) sides and equal angles.

SCIENCE AND ENERGY

geometrical shapes

solids
Geometric shapes in three dimensions
that are delimited by surfaces.

torus
Volume or solid generated by the
rotation of a circle at an equal distance
from its center of rotation.

helix
Volume or solid of spiral shape that
turns at a constant angle.

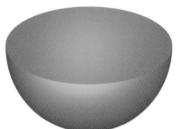

hemisphere
Half sphere cut along its diameter.

sphere
Volume with all the points on its
surface the same distance from its
center; the solid thus delimited is a
round ball.

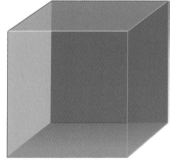

cube
Volume or solid with six square sides
of equal area and six equal edges; it
has eight vertices.

cone
Volume or solid generated by the
rotation of a straight line (generatrix)
along a circular line (directrix) from a
fixed point (vertex).

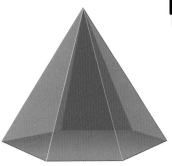

pyramid
Volume or solid generated by straight
lines (edges) connecting the angles of a
polygon (base) to the vertex and whose
sides form triangles.

cylinder
Volume or solid generated by the
rotation of a straight line (generatrix)
moving along a curved line (directrix).

parallelepiped
Volume or solid with six sides
(parallelograms) that are parallel in
pairs.

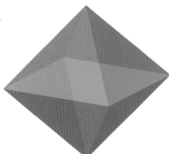

regular octahedron
Volume or solid with eight triangular
sides of equal area; it has six vertices
and 12 edges.

SCIENCE AND ENERGY

production of electricity from geothermal energy

Hot water contained in the ground near a volcano, geyser or thermal source is piped to the surface by drilling to extract steam and produce electricity.

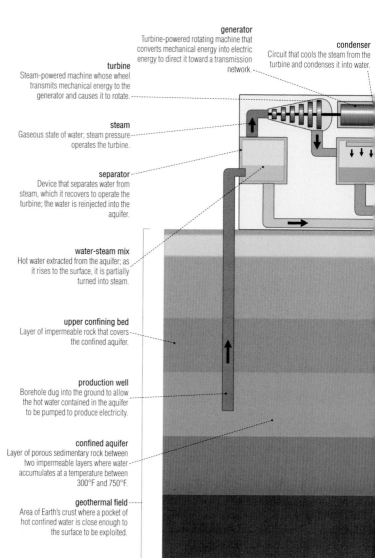

generator
Turbine-powered rotating machine that converts mechanical energy into electric energy to direct it toward a transmission network.

condenser
Circuit that cools the steam from the turbine and condenses it into water.

turbine
Steam-powered machine whose wheel transmits mechanical energy to the generator and causes it to rotate.

steam
Gaseous state of water; steam pressure operates the turbine.

separator
Device that separates water from steam, which it recovers to operate the turbine; the water is reinjected into the aquifer.

water-steam mix
Hot water extracted from the aquifer; as it rises to the surface, it is partially turned into steam.

upper confining bed
Layer of impermeable rock that covers the confined aquifer.

production well
Borehole dug into the ground to allow the hot water contained in the aquifer to be pumped to produce electricity.

confined aquifer
Layer of porous sedimentary rock between two impermeable layers where water accumulates at a temperature between 300°F and 750°F.

geothermal field
Area of Earth's crust where a pocket of hot confined water is close enough to the surface to be exploited.

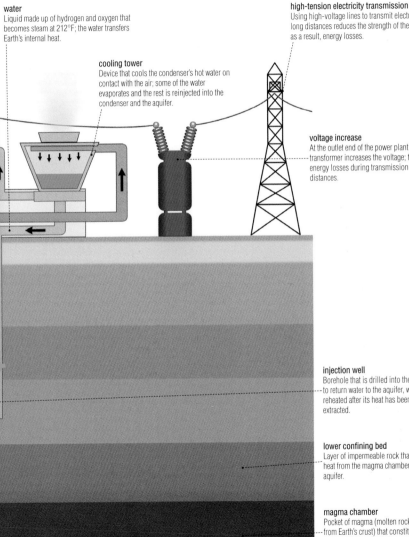

water
Liquid made up of hydrogen and oxygen that becomes steam at 212°F; the water transfers Earth's internal heat.

high-tension electricity transmission
Using high-voltage lines to transmit electricity over long distances reduces the strength of the current and, as a result, energy losses.

cooling tower
Device that cools the condenser's hot water on contact with the air; some of the water evaporates and the rest is reinjected into the condenser and the aquifer.

voltage increase
At the outlet end of the power plant, the transformer increases the voltage; this reduces energy losses during transmission over long distances.

injection well
Borehole that is drilled into the ground to return water to the aquifer, where it is reheated after its heat has been extracted.

lower confining bed
Layer of impermeable rock that transmits heat from the magma chamber to the aquifer.

magma chamber
Pocket of magma (molten rock emerging from Earth's crust) that constitutes a heat source; it transmits its thermal energy to water.

thermal energy

Energy that is produced by turning water into steam through the burning of fuel (e.g., petroleum and coal) or through nuclear reaction.

production of electricity from thermal energy
The heat that is given off by burning combustible fuels in the thermal power plant converts water into steam; the steam turns a turbo-alternator unit to produce electricity.

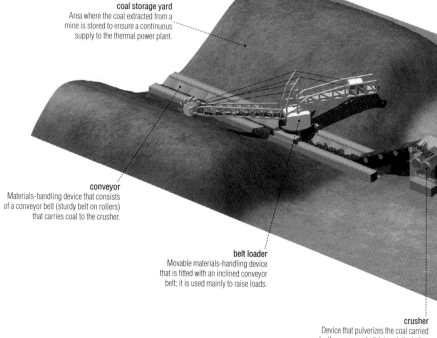

coal storage yard
Area where the coal extracted from a mine is stored to ensure a continuous supply to the thermal power plant.

conveyor
Materials-handling device that consists of a conveyor belt (sturdy belt on rollers) that carries coal to the crusher.

belt loader
Movable materials-handling device that is fitted with an inclined conveyor belt; it is used mainly to raise loads.

crusher
Device that pulverizes the coal carried by the conveyor belt into relatively fine fragments.

pulverizer
Device that pulverizes coal into a very fine powder so that it burns more easily in the steam generator.

steam generator
Device that uses the heat produced from burning coal to convert water into steam; the steam powers the turbo-alternator unit.

stack
Pipe through which gases produced by burning coal are discharged; these gases are first partially cleaned to reduce pollution.

voltage increase
At the outlet end of the power plant, the transformer increases the voltage; this reduces energy losses during transmission over long distances.

high-tension electricity transmission
Using high-voltage lines to transmit electricity over long distances reduces the strength of the current and, as a result, energy losses.

voltage decrease
The transformer reduces the voltage in order to increase the strength of the current; this allows a greater number of consumers to be served.

cooling tower
Device that cools the heated water in the condenser through contact with the air; a small amount of water evaporates and the rest is reinjected into the condenser.

transmission to consumers
Electricity is carried to areas of consumption over low-voltage distribution lines.

coal-fired thermal power plant
Plant that produces electricity from thermal energy by burning coal.

condenser
Circuit that cools the steam from the turbine and condenses it into water, which is reintroduced into the steam generator.

turbo-alternator unit
Device with a turbine that transmits the water's mechanical energy to the alternator's rotor to make it turn to produce electricity.

coal mine

The underground or open-pit facilities that are set up around a coal deposit in order to extract it.

underground mine
Property in which excavations are carried out to extract deeply embedded (between 30 and 11,500 ft) coal for industrial mining.

headframe
Opening at the top of the shaft that connects the aboveground facilities (including ventilation fans and hoists) to the underground areas being mined.

vertical shaft
Shaft that is dug perpendicular to the surface; it serves various levels and is used mainly to transport personnel, equipment and ore.

elevator
Power lift fitted with a cab that transports coal or miners between the various levels.

pillar
Mass of ore that is left unmined at regular intervals in an excavation (chamber); it provides stability for the upper layers.

room
Cavity that remains after the ore is extracted; pillars support its roof.

chute
Vertical or inclined passageway through which ore, equipment, personnel and air move from one level of the mine to the other.

cross cut
Horizontal passageway that cuts through the ore bed perpendicularly; it provides communication between the passageways and helps to ventilate the mine.

manway
Passageway allowing workers to move around in the mine.

drift
Passageway dug horizontally along the grade line of the ore seam; it can also be dug into the ore vertically.

winze
Vertical or inclined passageway that connects two levels; it is dug downward from inside the mine and not from the surface.

face
Opening that is dug laterally into the rock as coal is extracted.

winding tower
Building that houses the shaft's hoisting equipment (including motors and hoisting cables); it provides communication between the surface and the mine galleries.

winding shaft
Shaft that is dug vertically into the ground; coal is removed from the mine through it using hoisting machinery.

level
The horizontal passageways that branch off from the shaft at the same depth; they are usually at regular intervals.

top road
Horizontal passageway that serves the highest level of a panel.

deck
Extraction layer between two levels; mining is usually done in stages and in descending order.

skip
Elevator consisting of a skip bucket that is activated by a hoist; it is used to bring coal and people to the surface.

ore pass
Inclined route that takes coal to a lower level; coal that falls on the mine floor is usually crushed before being brought to the surface.

panel
Unit of rock that is being mined; it is contained between vertical and horizontal planes and is demarcated by various passageways.

bottom road
Horizontal passageway that serves the base of a panel.

landing
Landing located around a shaft on each level; coal is collected here before being moved to the surface.

sump
Bottom of the shaft in which water runoff accumulates inside the mine before being pumped to the surface.

oil

Flammable, relatively viscous oily liquid that is used as an energy source; it is made up of various hydrocarbons resulting from the decomposition of plant life over millions of year.

drilling rig
All the drilling machinery and devices that are used to excavate and extract oil from the ground.

derrick
Metal structure erected over an oil well; tools for drilling through rock are raised and lowered through it.

swivel
Piece attached to the lifting hook and the kelly; it is used to introduce mud into the drill pipe to cool and lubricate the bit.

drilling drawworks
Device that consists of a cylinder on which hoisting cables are wound; it is used to lower the drill pipes and bit into the well and to lift them out.

mud injection hose
Flexible hose that introduces the drilling mud into the swivel.

substructure
Metal infrastructure that supports the derrick, engines and auxiliary equipment.

vibrating mudscreen
Perforated vibrating tray that is used to filter mud as it exits the well to remove debris and recycle the mud.

drill pipe
Hollow steel rods that are joined together according to the depth of the excavation; their rotation activates the bit.

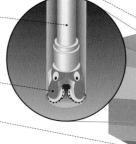

bit
Rotating drill bit with toothed steel or diamond wheels; it bores into rock to break it up and drill a hole.

oil
Flammable, relatively viscous oily liquid that is used as an energy source; it is made up of various hydrocarbons resulting from the decomposition of plant life over millions of year.

gas
Mixture of gaseous hydrocarbons (mainly methane) that are found in underground deposits, which sometimes also contain crude oil; it is used mainly as a fuel.

rotary system
Drilling device in which a kelly is attached to a rotary table; with the help of powerful motors, it transmits the rotative movement to the kellys.

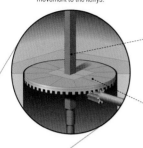

kelly
Special square rod that is screwed to the top of the drill pipes and driven by the rotary table.

rotary table
Circular table that is moved by powerful motors; it transmits its rotative movement to the drill pipes by means of the kelly.

engine
Device converting the combustion of fuel and air into mechanical energy.

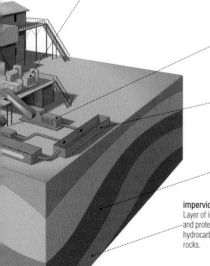

mud pump
Device that circulates the mud in the drilling rig.

mud pit
Basin that contains mud (a mixture of water, clay and chemical products) used mainly to cool and lubricate the bit and to remove debris.

anticline
Geologic stratum that results from the convex folding of rock formations; large pools of oil often accumulate in it.

impervious rock
Layer of impermeable rock that covers and protects the oil deposit; it prevents hydrocarbons from migrating into other rocks.

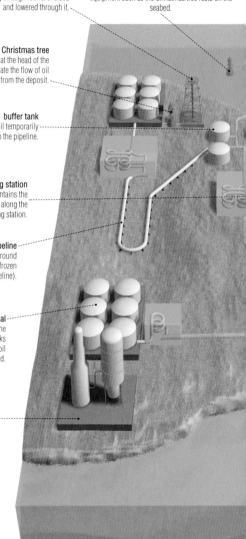

crude-oil pipeline
Continuous underground, aboveground or underwater oil pipeline that can be thousands of miles long (the Trans-Siberian pipeline is 3,800 mi long).

derrick
Metal structure erected over an oil well; tools for drilling through rock are raised and lowered through it.

offshore well
Hole dug in the sea floor to extract oil deposits; equipment such as the Christmas tree rests on the seabed.

Christmas tree
Group of devices at the head of the producing well that regulate the flow of oil being extracted from the deposit.

buffer tank
Large container that stores crude oil temporarily before it is pumped back into the pipeline.

central pumping station
Powerful pumping station that maintains the pressure required to move the oil along the pipeline to the next pumping station.

aboveground pipeline
Oil pipeline that rests on aboveground supports to protect it from frozen ground (e.g., the Alaska pipeline).

terminal
Facility located at the end of the pipeline that includes equipment such as tanks and pumps; it receives the crude oil before it is refined.

refinery
Plant in which crude oil is refined (separated and scrubbed) to obtain a broad range of finished products (including motor fuel and oils).

production platform
Facility used to extract underwater oil deposits; the separation and treatment of hydrocarbons are mainly done here.

submarine pipeline
Pipeline installed on the seabed that carries oil extracted from an underwater deposit to shore.

pumping station
Installation located at regular intervals along the pipeline that is fitted with motorized pumps; it ensures that the oil flows inside the pipeline.

tank farm
All the facilities (such as tanks and pumps) that store large quantities of crude oil to be sent later to the refinery.

pipeline
The steel piping that carries oil from one treatment facility to another.

intermediate booster station
Booster station that reinforces the action of the central station and maintains the flow of oil in the pipeline network.

hydroelectric complex

The reservoir structures and installations that use water power to produce electricity.

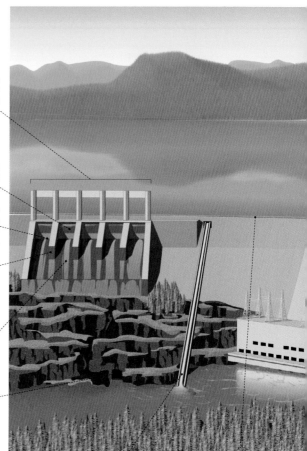

spillway
Channel that discharges excess water from the reservoir during flooding to avoid submerging the dam.

spillway gate
Movable vertical panel; it is opened to allow the reservoir's overflow to pass through.

crest of spillway
Cement crest over which the reservoir's overflow discharges when the spillway gates are opened.

training wall
Wall that separates the spillway chutes; it is used to direct the water flow.

spillway chute
Inclined surface along which discharged water flows out.

diversion tunnel
Underground conduit that diverts water during construction.

log chute
Structure that allows floating wood to travel from upstream to downstream of the dam.

top of dam
Upper part of the dam; it rises above the water level of the reservoir by several yards.

SCIENCE AND ENERGY

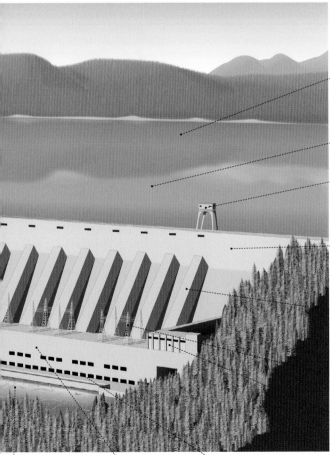

reservoir
Basin formed by the construction of a dam; it holds back a very large volume of water so that the flow rate can be controlled.

headbay
Part of the reservoir immediately in front of the dam where the current originates.

gantry crane
Hoisting device in the form of a bridge; it moves along rails.

dam
Barrier built across a watercourse in order to build up a supply of water for use as an energy source.

penstock
Channel that carries water under pressure to the power plant's turbines.

bushing
Device that allows the conductor to pass through the wall of the transformer and separates it from the latter.

control room
Area that contains the various control and monitoring devices required for the production of electricity.

afterbay
Area of the watercourse where water is discharged after passing through the turbines.

power plant
Plant that uses an energy source, here water, and converts it into electricity.

machine hall
Area that houses the generator units used to produce electricity.

hydroelectric complex

cross section of a hydroelectric power plant
Hydroelectric power plant: plant that produces electricity
from energy generated by flowing water.

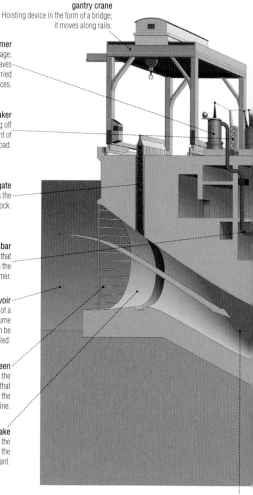

gantry crane
Hoisting device in the form of a bridge;
it moves along rails.

transformer
Device used to alter the electric voltage;
voltage is increased as the current leaves
the power plant so that it can be carried
over long distances.

circuit breaker
Mechanism automatically cutting off
the power supply in the event of
overload.

gate
Movable vertical panel that controls the
volume of water in the penstock.

busbar
Large aluminum conductor that
transmits electric current from the
alternator to the transformer.

reservoir
Basin formed by the construction of a
dam; it holds back a very large volume
of water so that the flow rate can be
controlled.

screen
Assembly of bars placed in front of the
water intake to hold back anything that
could hinder the operation of the
turbine.

water intake
Structure that directs water from the
headbay to the penstock to power the
plant.

penstock
Channel that carries water under
pressure to the power plant's turbines.

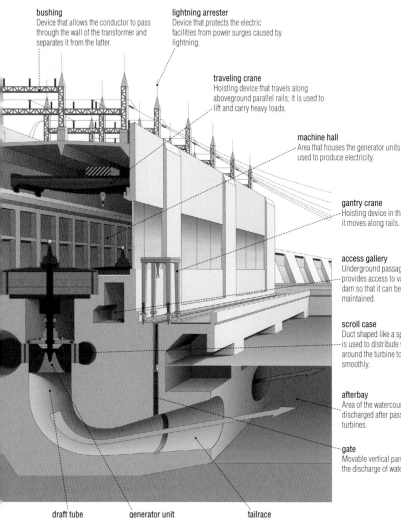

bushing
Device that allows the conductor to pass through the wall of the transformer and separates it from the latter.

lightning arrester
Device that protects the electric facilities from power surges caused by lightning.

traveling crane
Hoisting device that travels along aboveground parallel rails; it is used to lift and carry heavy loads.

machine hall
Area that houses the generator units used to produce electricity.

gantry crane
Hoisting device in the form of a bridge; it moves along rails.

access gallery
Underground passageway that provides access to various parts of the dam so that it can be inspected and maintained.

scroll case
Duct shaped like a spiral staircase that is used to distribute water uniformly around the turbine to make it turn smoothly.

afterbay
Area of the watercourse where water is discharged after passing through the turbines.

gate
Movable vertical panel that controls the discharge of water to the tailrace.

draft tube
Conduit at the base of the turbine that increases the runner's output by reducing the pressure of the water as it exits.

generator unit
Device with a turbine that transmits the water's mechanical energy to the generator's rotor to make it turn to produce electricity.

tailrace
Channel that discharges water toward the afterbay in order to return it to the watercourse.

electricity transmission

Electricity is carried by overhead and underground lines; due to high cost, underground lines are used mainly in cities.

overhead connection
The equipment and overhead conductors that connect a subscriber's electric system to the public distribution network.

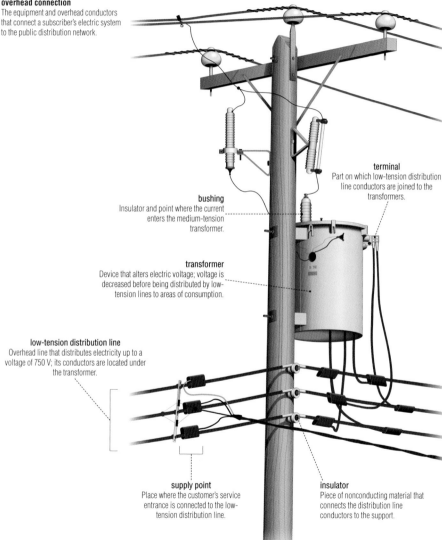

terminal
Part on which low-tension distribution line conductors are joined to the transformers.

bushing
Insulator and point where the current enters the medium-tension transformer.

transformer
Device that alters electric voltage; voltage is decreased before being distributed by low-tension lines to areas of consumption.

low-tension distribution line
Overhead line that distributes electricity up to a voltage of 750 V; its conductors are located under the transformer.

supply point
Place where the customer's service entrance is connected to the low-tension distribution line.

insulator
Piece of nonconducting material that connects the distribution line conductors to the support.

medium-tension distribution line
Overhead line that distributes electricity at a voltage
between 750 and 50,000 V; its conductors are
located at the top of electricity poles.

brace
Slanted part that connects the pole to
the crossarm to hold it in place
horizontally.

hot line connector
Linking piece with a bolt, which is tightened to
bring together two conductors to establish an
electric connection between them.

insulator
Piece of nonconducting material that
connects the distribution line
conductors to the support.

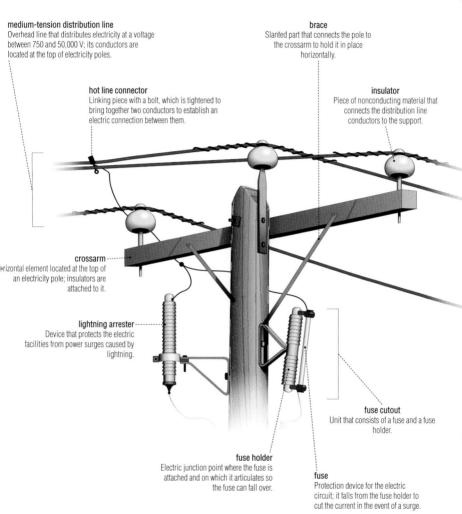

crossarm
Horizontal element located at the top of
an electricity pole; insulators are
attached to it.

lightning arrester
Device that protects the electric
facilities from power surges caused by
lightning.

fuse cutout
Unit that consists of a fuse and a fuse
holder.

fuse holder
Electric junction point where the fuse is
attached and on which it articulates so
the fuse can fall over.

fuse
Protection device for the electric
circuit; it falls from the fuse holder to
cut the current in the event of a surge.

SCIENCE AND ENERGY

production of electricity from nuclear energy

A nuclear fission chain reaction is started and controlled inside the reactor to produce electricity.

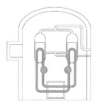

coolant
Liquid or gas (including heavy water and carbon dioxide) that circulates inside the reactor; it harnesses and transports the heat released during fission of the fuel.

containment building
Concrete building used to collect the radioactive steam from the reactor in the event of an accident.

dousing water tank
Vat that contains water to cool the radioactive steam in the reactor in the event of an accident; this prevents a rise in pressure.

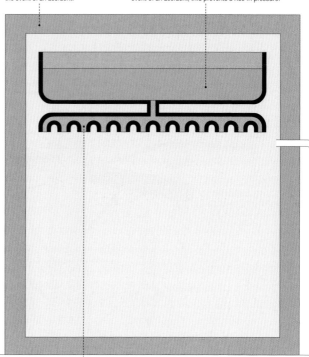

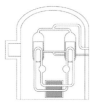

moderator
Substance (ordinary water, heavy water, graphite) that slows the fast-moving neutrons emitted during fission to increase the probability of new collisions.

sprinklers
Devices that release water to condense radioactive steam.

fuel
Matter placed in the core of the reactor that contains heavy atoms (uranium, plutonium); energy is extracted from it by fission.

SCIENCE AND ENERGY

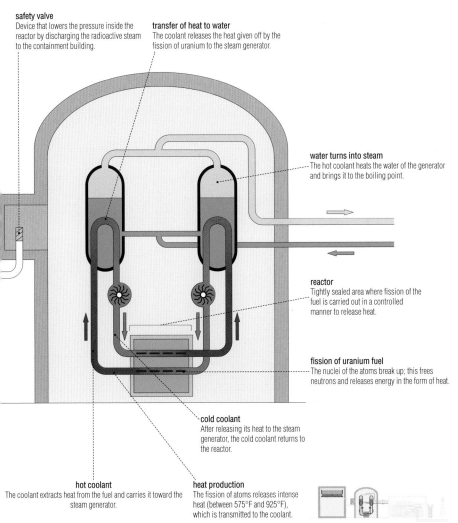

safety valve
Device that lowers the pressure inside the reactor by discharging the radioactive steam to the containment building.

transfer of heat to water
The coolant releases the heat given off by the fission of uranium to the steam generator.

water turns into steam
The hot coolant heats the water of the generator and brings it to the boiling point.

reactor
Tightly sealed area where fission of the fuel is carried out in a controlled manner to release heat.

fission of uranium fuel
The nuclei of the atoms break up; this frees neutrons and releases energy in the form of heat.

cold coolant
After releasing its heat to the steam generator, the cold coolant returns to the reactor.

hot coolant
The coolant extracts heat from the fuel and carries it toward the steam generator.

heat production
The fission of atoms releases intense heat (between 575°F and 925°F), which is transmitted to the coolant.

turbine shaft turns generator
The rotational movement of the turbine is transmitted to the generator's rotor.

steam pressure drives turbine
Steam from the steam generator turns the turbine runner, which is connected to the generator.

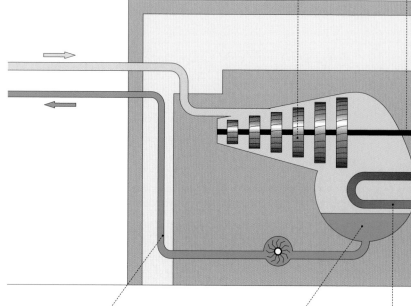

water is pumped back into the steam generator
After passing through the turbine, water produced by the condensation of the steam returns to the steam generator.

condensation of steam into water
At the turbine outlet, the steam cools and condenses into water.

water cools the used steam
Cooling of the steam from the turbine is done with river or lake water.

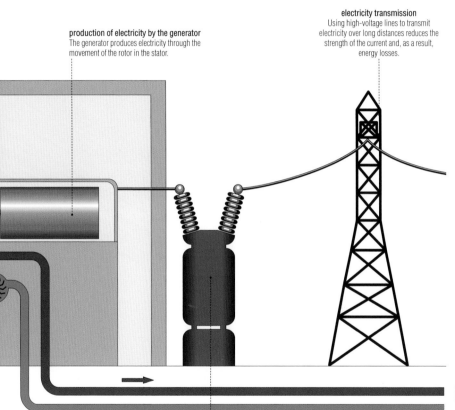

electricity transmission
Using high-voltage lines to transmit electricity over long distances reduces the strength of the current and, as a result, energy losses.

production of electricity by the generator
The generator produces electricity through the movement of the rotor in the stator.

voltage increase
At the outlet end of the power plant, the transformer increases the voltage; this reduces energy losses during transmission over long distances.

SCIENCE AND ENERGY

fuel bundle

Fuel pencils that are grouped in parallel for introduction into the reactor.

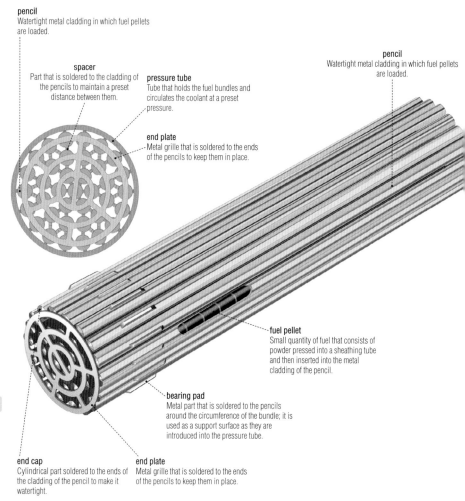

pencil
Watertight metal cladding in which fuel pellets are loaded.

spacer
Part that is soldered to the cladding of the pencils to maintain a preset distance between them.

pressure tube
Tube that holds the fuel bundles and circulates the coolant at a preset pressure.

end plate
Metal grille that is soldered to the ends of the pencils to keep them in place.

pencil
Watertight metal cladding in which fuel pellets are loaded.

fuel pellet
Small quantity of fuel that consists of powder pressed into a sheathing tube and then inserted into the metal cladding of the pencil.

bearing pad
Metal part that is soldered to the pencils around the circumference of the bundle; it is used as a support surface as they are introduced into the pressure tube.

end cap
Cylindrical part soldered to the ends of the cladding of the pencil to make it watertight.

end plate
Metal grille that is soldered to the ends of the pencils to keep them in place.

nuclear reactor

Tightly sealed area where fission of the fuel is carried out in a controlled manner to release heat.

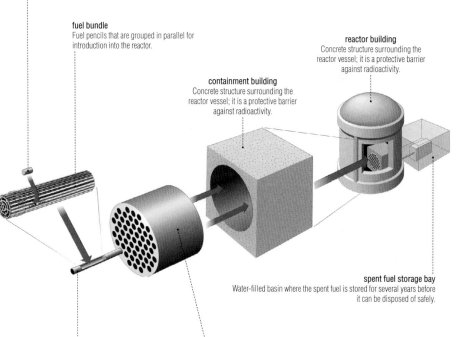

fuel pellet
Small quantity of fuel that consists of powder pressed into a sheathing tube and then inserted into the metal cladding of the pencil.

fuel bundle
Fuel pencils that are grouped in parallel for introduction into the reactor.

reactor building
Concrete structure surrounding the reactor vessel; it is a protective barrier against radioactivity.

containment building
Concrete structure surrounding the reactor vessel; it is a protective barrier against radioactivity.

spent fuel storage bay
Water-filled basin where the spent fuel is stored for several years before it can be disposed of safely.

pressure tube
Tube that holds the fuel bundles and circulates the coolant at a preset pressure.

reactor vessel
The core of the nuclear reactor consists of tubular spaces where fission is produced and the coolant and moderator circulate.

SCIENCE AND ENERGY

945

solar cell

Device used to convert solar energy directly into electric energy (photovoltaic effect).

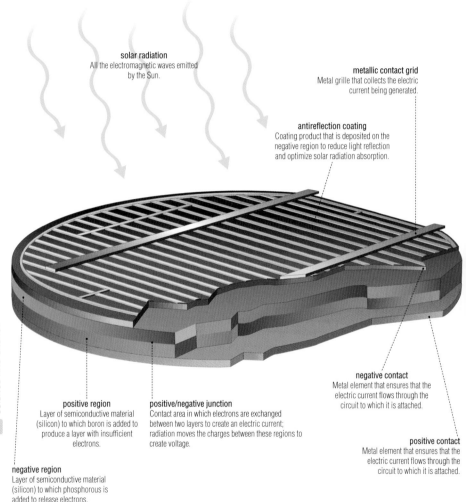

solar radiation
All the electromagnetic waves emitted by the Sun.

metallic contact grid
Metal grille that collects the electric current being generated.

antireflection coating
Coating product that is deposited on the negative region to reduce light reflection and optimize solar radiation absorption.

positive region
Layer of semiconductive material (silicon) to which boron is added to produce a layer with insufficient electrons.

positive/negative junction
Contact area in which electrons are exchanged between two layers to create an electric current; radiation moves the charges between these regions to create voltage.

negative contact
Metal element that ensures that the electric current flows through the circuit to which it is attached.

positive contact
Metal element that ensures that the electric current flows through the circuit to which it is attached.

negative region
Layer of semiconductive material (silicon) to which phosphorous is added to release electrons.

flat-plate solar collector

Device that collects solar radiation and heats a coolant, which in turn will be used in residential settings to heat water or the home.

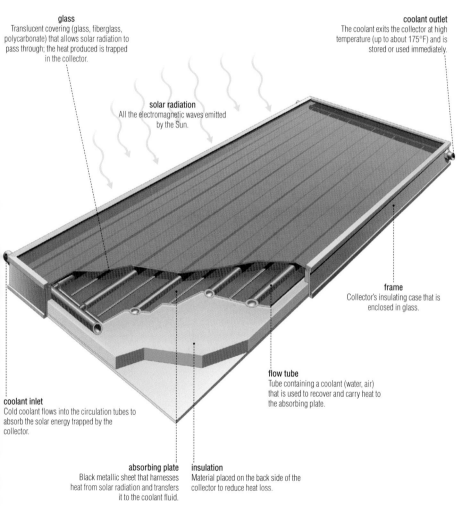

glass
Translucent covering (glass, fiberglass, polycarbonate) that allows solar radiation to pass through; the heat produced is trapped in the collector.

coolant outlet
The coolant exits the collector at high temperature (up to about 175°F) and is stored or used immediately.

solar radiation
All the electromagnetic waves emitted by the Sun.

frame
Collector's insulating case that is enclosed in glass.

flow tube
Tube containing a coolant (water, air) that is used to recover and carry heat to the absorbing plate.

coolant inlet
Cold coolant flows into the circulation tubes to absorb the solar energy trapped by the collector.

absorbing plate
Black metallic sheet that harnesses heat from solar radiation and transfers it to the coolant fluid.

insulation
Material placed on the back side of the collector to reduce heat loss.

windmill

Machine that converts wind energy into mechanical energy; it was used in the past to mill grain and pump water.

tower mill
The tower mill appeared later than the post mill; it consists of a usually circular, stationary body and a roof that rotates with the help of a fantail.

cap
Movable upper part of the tower that contains the rotor; it turns to position the sails facing the wind.

windshaft
Cylindrical part on which the sails turn; it transmits the movement of the rotor to the windmill machinery.

stock
Wooden arm to which the sail frame is attached.

frame
All the sailbars forming the outline of the sail.

fantail
Orientation device that is attached to the cap, allowing it to rotate to keep the sails in the direction of the wind.

sailbar
Elongated piece of wood that forms a sail.

sail cloth
Cloth attached to a sail that collects wind energy; a large sail cloth is used for weak winds and a small sail cloth for strong winds.

sail
Wooden structure that is attached to the stock; the force of the wind turns it to drive the rotor.

tower
Structure that supports the cap; it houses all the machinery for milling grain.

hemlath
Thick wooden sailbar on the side of the frame that keeps the narrower sailbars inside the sail.

floor
Level for accessing the inside of the mill; grain is usually stored at its base.

gallery
Passageway used to move around the mill floor.

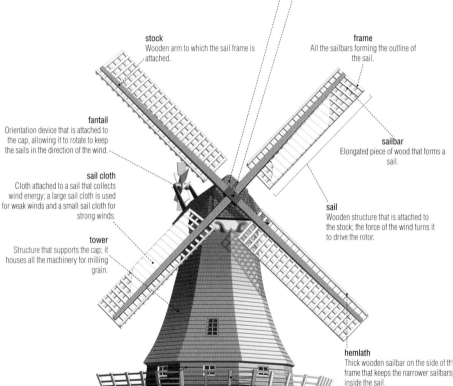

Wind turbine: machine that harnesses energy from the wind and converts it into mechanical energy to activate the alternator.

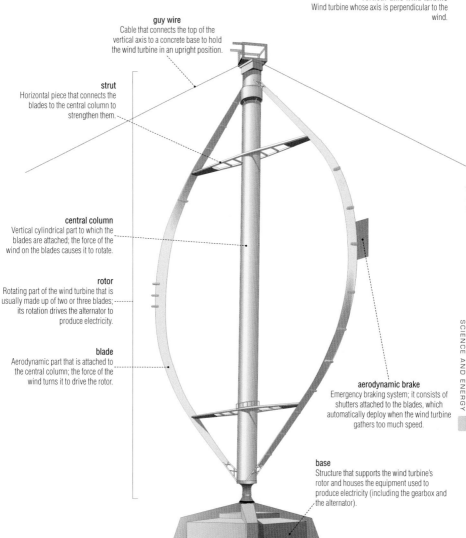

vertical-axis wind turbine
Wind turbine whose axis is perpendicular to the wind.

guy wire
Cable that connects the top of the vertical axis to a concrete base to hold the wind turbine in an upright position.

strut
Horizontal piece that connects the blades to the central column to strengthen them.

central column
Vertical cylindrical part to which the blades are attached; the force of the wind on the blades causes it to rotate.

rotor
Rotating part of the wind turbine that is usually made up of two or three blades; its rotation drives the alternator to produce electricity.

blade
Aerodynamic part that is attached to the central column; the force of the wind turns it to drive the rotor.

aerodynamic brake
Emergency braking system; it consists of shutters attached to the blades, which automatically deploy when the wind turbine gathers too much speed.

base
Structure that supports the wind turbine's rotor and houses the equipment used to produce electricity (including the gearbox and the alternator).

SCIENCE AND ENERGY

949

wind turbines and electricity production

horizontal-axis wind turbine
The most common type of wind turbine; its axis
positions itself in the direction of the wind.

blade
Aerodynamic part that is attached to
the hub; the force of the wind causes it
to rotate to drive the rotor.

nacelle
Metal structure that encloses and protects the
main mechanical elements of the wind turbine
(including the gearbox and the alternator).

hub
Part of the rotor to which the blades are
attached; it turns the low-speed shaft.

tower
Tower that reaches 260 ft in height; it
supports the nacelle and rotor and
houses the electric cables.

SCIENCE AND ENERGY

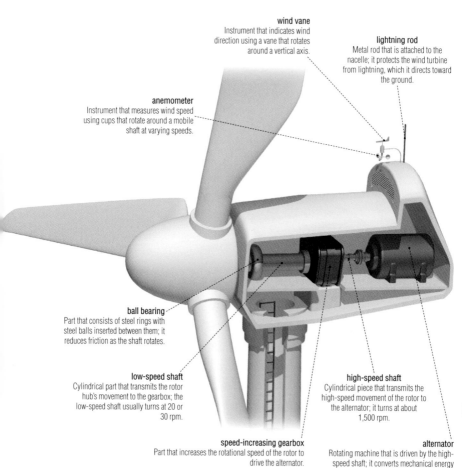

wind vane
Instrument that indicates wind direction using a vane that rotates around a vertical axis.

lightning rod
Metal rod that is attached to the nacelle; it protects the wind turbine from lightning, which it directs toward the ground.

anemometer
Instrument that measures wind speed using cups that rotate around a mobile shaft at varying speeds.

ball bearing
Part that consists of steel rings with steel balls inserted between them; it reduces friction as the shaft rotates.

low-speed shaft
Cylindrical part that transmits the rotor hub's movement to the gearbox; the low-speed shaft usually turns at 20 or 30 rpm.

high-speed shaft
Cylindrical piece that transmits the high-speed movement of the rotor to the alternator; it turns at about 1,500 rpm.

speed-increasing gearbox
Part that increases the rotational speed of the rotor to drive the alternator.

alternator
Rotating machine that is driven by the high-speed shaft; it converts mechanical energy into electric energy and then directs it to the transmission network.

SCIENCE AND ENERGY

arena

Field designed for participating in track and field and for staging competitions; it is often surrounded by grandstands for seating spectators.

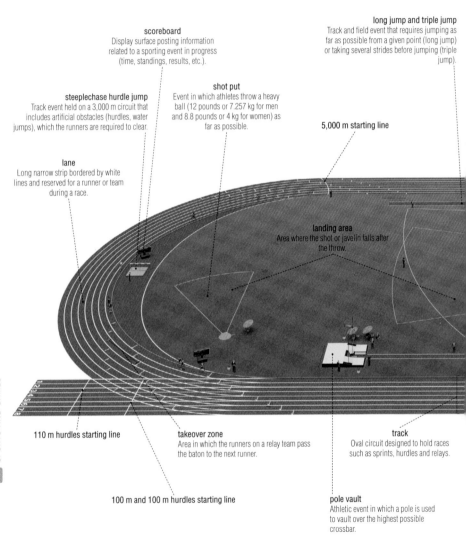

scoreboard
Display surface posting information related to a sporting event in progress (time, standings, results, etc.).

long jump and triple jump
Track and field event that requires jumping as far as possible from a given point (long jump) or taking several strides before jumping (triple jump).

shot put
Event in which athletes throw a heavy ball (12 pounds or 7.257 kg for men and 8.8 pounds or 4 kg for women) as far as possible.

steeplechase hurdle jump
Track event held on a 3,000 m circuit that includes artificial obstacles (hurdles, water jumps), which the runners are required to clear.

5,000 m starting line

lane
Long narrow strip bordered by white lines and reserved for a runner or team during a race.

landing area
Area where the shot or javelin falls after the throw.

110 m hurdles starting line

takeover zone
Area in which the runners on a relay team pass the baton to the next runner.

track
Oval circuit designed to hold races such as sprints, hurdles and relays.

100 m and 100 m hurdles starting line

pole vault
Athletic event in which a pole is used to vault over the highest possible crossbar.

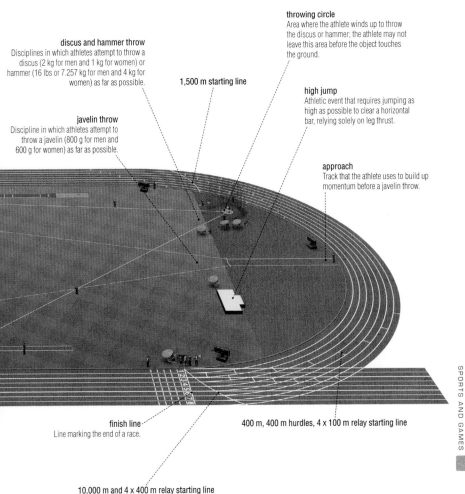

throwing circle
Area where the athlete winds up to throw the discus or hammer; the athlete may not leave this area before the object touches the ground.

discus and hammer throw
Disciplines in which athletes attempt to throw a discus (2 kg for men and 1 kg for women) or hammer (16 lbs or 7.257 kg for men and 4 kg for women) as far as possible.

1,500 m starting line

high jump
Athletic event that requires jumping as high as possible to clear a horizontal bar, relying solely on leg thrust.

javelin throw
Discipline in which athletes attempt to throw a javelin (800 g for men and 600 g for women) as far as possible.

approach
Track that the athlete uses to build up momentum before a javelin throw.

finish line
Line marking the end of a race.

400 m, 400 m hurdles, 4 x 100 m relay starting line

10,000 m and 4 x 400 m relay starting line

SPORTS AND GAMES

soccer

Sport with two opposing teams of 11 players who attempt to score in the opponent's goal by kicking or knocking the ball in with any part of the body except the arms and hands.

playing field
Rectangular surface covered with natural or synthetic grass on which a soccer match is played; a game has two 45-minute halves.

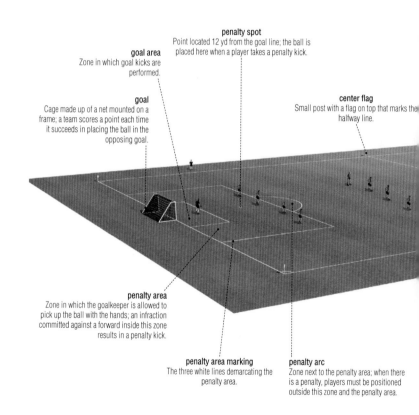

penalty spot
Point located 12 yd from the goal line; the ball is placed here when a player takes a penalty kick.

goal area
Zone in which goal kicks are performed.

goal
Cage made up of a net mounted on a frame; a team scores a point each time it succeeds in placing the ball in the opposing goal.

center flag
Small post with a flag on top that marks the halfway line.

penalty area
Zone in which the goalkeeper is allowed to pick up the ball with the hands; an infraction committed against a forward inside this zone results in a penalty kick.

penalty area marking
The three white lines demarcating the penalty area.

penalty arc
Zone next to the penalty area; when there is a penalty, players must be positioned outside this zone and the penalty area.

SPORTS AND GAMES

referee
Official responsible for applying the rules; this individual keeps time, signals penalties, issues warnings (yellow card) and ejects players (red card).

corner flag
Small post with a flag on top; it marks the intersection of the goal line and the touch line.

center spot
Point in the middle of the halfway line where the ball is placed before a kickoff at the start of a half or after a goal has been scored.

corner arc
Zone where the ball is placed when there is a corner kick, which is awarded when a defender puts the ball behind the goal line.

linesman
Official who signals offsides and penalties not seen by the referee or when the ball is out of play.

center circle
Circle drawn at midfield; during kickoffs, only the players on the team with ball possession are allowed into this circle.

halfway line
Line dividing the field into two zones, one for each team; the teams switch zones at halftime.

touch line
Line along the sides of the playing field; when the ball crosses this line, it is put back into play at the same place.

substitute's bench
Area reserved for coaches, technical staff and substitute players; a team cannot make more than three substitutions per game.

soccer

soccer player
A soccer player is allowed to touch the ball with any part of the body except the arms and hands.

team shirt
Flexible garment covering the upper body; it features the team emblem and the player's name and number.

shorts
Very short pants covering only the top of the thighs.

shin guard
Piece of equipment made up of a hard plastic molding; it protects the soccer player's legs.

sock
Garment worn over the foot and up to the knee; it completely covers the shin guard.

soccer ball
Inflated ball made of leather or synthetic material; its circumference varies between 27 and 27.5 in.

soccer shoe
Shoe made of leather, soft rubber or plastic; studs are attached to its sole to provide good traction.

goalkeeper's gloves
Gloves that cover and protect the goalkeeper's hands and wrists and improve the grip on the ball.

interchangeable studs
Removable studs attached to the sole; they vary in size and can be changed to adapt to the state of the field.

baseball

Sport with two opposing teams of nine players who attempt to score points by hitting a ball with a bat and running from one base to the next until they reach home plate; a game lasts nine innings, during which teams alternate from offense (at bat) to defense (in the field).

bat
Piece of wood that the batter uses to hit the ball; its maximum length is 42 inches.

crest
Symbol representing the brand of the bat or its manufacturer.

knob
Circular piece on the end of the handle; it prevents the hand from slipping off the bat.

handle
The narrowest part of the bat that the player grasps; it is sometimes covered with antislip material.

hitting area
The widest part of the bat and the part that strikes the ball; it must not exceed 2.75 inches in diameter.

fielder's glove
Piece of leather covering the hand and wrist and varying in size and shape, depending on the player's position; it is used to catch the ball.

web
Part of the glove between the thumb and the index finger; it forms a small pocket in which the ball is caught.

baseball
Hard ball with a circumference of 9 inches; its outer layer is made of two white pieces of leather sewn together.

strap
The intersecting leather straps that make up the web.

thumb
Part of the glove covering the thumb.

finger
Part of the glove that covers each of the fingers.

heel
The bottom part of the glove.

palm
Part of the glove that covers the hollow of the hand.

lace
Narrow cord passed through the eyelets to join or tighten the parts of the glove.

SPORTS AND GAMES

baseball

field
Surface on which a baseball game is played; it is in the shape of a quarter circle and is covered with dirt and natural or synthetic grass.

third base
Cushion attached to the ground that the player tries to reach after touching second base; if the player reaches home plate without being retired, one point is scored.

foul line
Two straight lines bordering the playing field; they run from home plate to the outfield fence.

dugout
Partially closed area for the coaches, manager, substitute players and the team at bat.

coach's box
Each of two areas reserved for base coaches who use signals to communicate strategy to runners and batters.

infield
Playing surface inside the perimeter marked by the three bases and home plate; it includes a dirt area bordering the outfield.

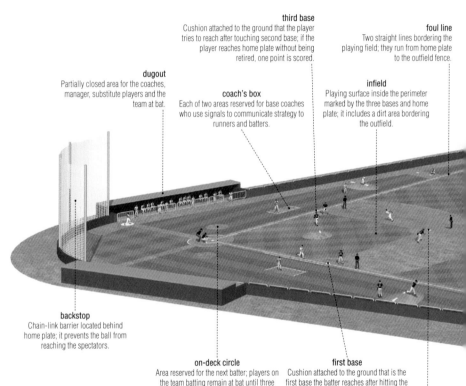

backstop
Chain-link barrier located behind home plate; it prevents the ball from reaching the spectators.

on-deck circle
Area reserved for the next batter; players on the team batting remain at bat until three outs have been recorded.

first base
Cushion attached to the ground that is the first base the batter reaches after hitting the ball; the player may stop there or move on to other bases.

second base
Cushion attached to the ground that the player tries to reach after touching first base, after the ball has been hit.

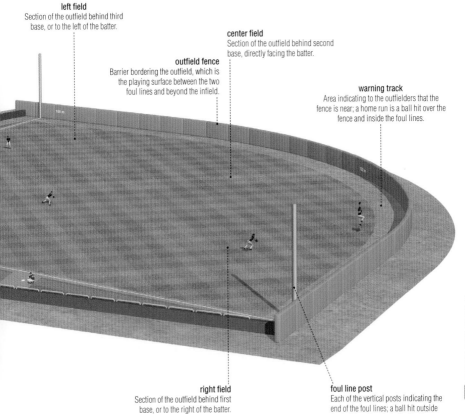

left field
Section of the outfield behind third base, or to the left of the batter.

center field
Section of the outfield behind second base, directly facing the batter.

outfield fence
Barrier bordering the outfield, which is the playing surface between the two foul lines and beyond the infield.

warning track
Area indicating to the outfielders that the fence is near; a home run is a ball hit over the fence and inside the foul lines.

right field
Section of the outfield behind first base, or to the right of the batter.

foul line post
Each of the vertical posts indicating the end of the foul lines; a ball hit outside the foul lines is called a foul ball.

football

Sport with two opposing teams of 11 players who attempt to score points by moving the ball into the end zone or kicking it between the goalposts.

playing field
Rectangular surface (53.3 x 120 yards) covered with natural or synthetic grass on which a football game is played; a game consists of four 15-minute quarters.

football
Inflatable oval leather ball that is smaller than a rugby ball; it has laces that provide a grip on the ball.

inbounds line
The broken lines marking off yards; the lines and inbounds lines mark the line of scrimmage when play resumes.

goal line
Line marking the start of the end zone.

fifty-yard line
Line dividing the field into two zones, one for each team; it is 50 yards from the goal lines.

end zone
Zone in which a touchdown (six points) is scored when a player crosses it in possession of the ball.

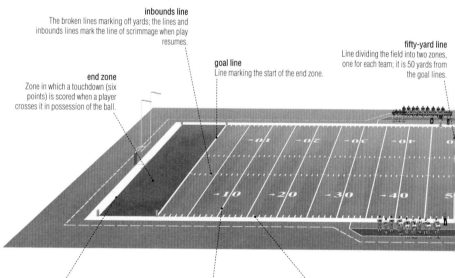

end line
Line marking the far extremity of the end zone; the white area behind the goal is not part of the playing field.

yard line
The solid lines at five-yard intervals that mark the distance from the goal line; at the start of a game, the ball is kicked off from the thirty-yard line.

sideline
Line demarcating the sides of the playing field; the play is whistled dead when the ball or a player in possession of the ball crosses it.

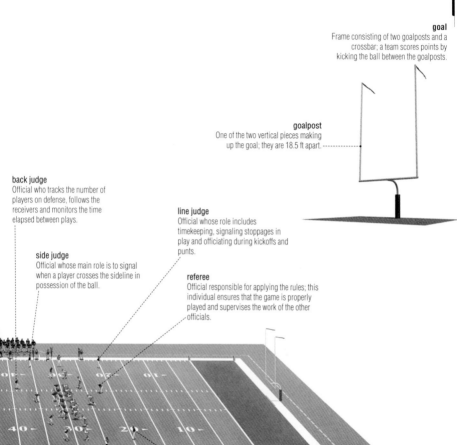

goal
Frame consisting of two goalposts and a crossbar; a team scores points by kicking the ball between the goalposts.

goalpost
One of the two vertical pieces making up the goal; they are 18.5 ft apart.

back judge
Official who tracks the number of players on defense, follows the receivers and monitors the time elapsed between plays.

line judge
Official whose role includes timekeeping, signaling stoppages in play and officiating during kickoffs and punts.

side judge
Official whose main role is to signal when a player crosses the sideline in possession of the ball.

referee
Official responsible for applying the rules; this individual ensures that the game is properly played and supervises the work of the other officials.

players' bench
Area for substitute players and coaches; a team's players are divided into three units: offense, defense and special teams.

umpire
Official in charge of checking player equipment and signaling infractions near the line of scrimmage.

head linesman
Official who signals stoppages in play and indicates exactly where to position the ball after it leaves the field of play.

SPORTS AND GAMES

basketball

Sport with two opposing teams of five players who score points by throwing a ball into the opposing team's basket.

court
Hard rectangular surface (50 ft x 94 ft) on which a basketball game is played.

scorer
Official who records points and fouls committed by the players.

timekeeper
Official who keeps time; this individual stops the clock when play stops and starts it again when play resumes.

clock operator
Official who keeps track of a team's possession time.

semicircle
Semicircular zone where the player takes position to make a free throw, which is worth one point.

referee
Official who assists the first referee and also stays at the perimeter of the court so as not to interfere with the players.

referee
Official responsible for applying the rules; this individual does tip-offs and signals fouls.

restricting circle
Circle around the center circle; players not taking part in the tip-off must be outside this circle.

center line
Line dividing the court into two halves, one for each team.

sideline
Line along the sides of the court; when the ball crosses this line, it is put back into play at the same place.

center circle
Circle at center court used for tip-offs at the start of a half and after a goal; a tip-off is when two players jump for the ball and try to push it toward their teammates.

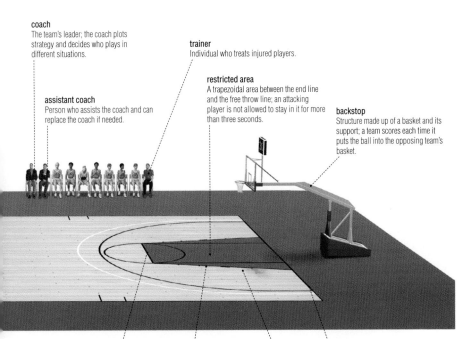

coach
The team's leader; the coach plots strategy and decides who plays in different situations.

trainer
Individual who treats injured players.

restricted area
A trapezoidal area between the end line and the free throw line; an attacking player is not allowed to stay in it for more than three seconds.

assistant coach
Person who assists the coach and can replace the coach if needed.

backstop
Structure made up of a basket and its support; a team scores each time it puts the ball into the opposing team's basket.

free throw line
Line parallel to the end line; the shooter stands behind it for a free throw (throw awarded after a foul).

second space
Space along the restricted area near the free throw line; one of the shooter's teammates is in this space when there is a free throw.

end line
Line marking the ends of the court; when the ball crosses this line, one team puts it back into play at the same place.

first space
Space along the restricted area near the end line; one of the opposing players is in this space when there is a free throw.

volleyball

Sport with two opposing teams of six players who try to ground the ball in the opposing zone by hitting it over the net with their hands.

court
Hard rectangular surface (30 ft x 60 ft) on which a volleyball game is played; the first team to win three sets wins the game.

umpire
Official who signals net faults or faults committed on the attack line and advises the referee when required.

left attacker
Position to the left of the attack zone; this player's main role is making attack hits to score points.

left back
Position on the left side of the back zone; this player's main role is making digs on short balls.

white tape
Strip of tape with a cable passing through it; it is attached to posts to suspend the net.

players' bench
Area for substitute players and coaches; a team can have 12 players, six of whom are on the court during play.

scorer
Official who fills in the score sheet, calls stoppages in play and supervises player rotations.

center back
Position in the back zone; this player's main role is to recover long balls and blocked balls.

right back
Position on the right side of the back zone; this player's main role is making digs on short balls.

center attacker
Position that covers the center of the attack zone; this player's main role is to counter the opponent's attacks.

attack line
Line 10 ft from the net; the backs must make attack hits from behind this line.

right attacker
Position to the right of the attack zone; this player's main role is making attack hits to score points.

antenna
Flexible rods at each end of the net; they mark off the net area and the ball must stay inside them to remain in play.

end line
Line demarcating the ends of the court; the right back takes position behind this line to deliver a serve.

referee
Official responsible for applying the rules; this individual follows the game from a raised platform set up at one end of the net.

libero
Position specialized in receiving serves; this player only plays back while other teammates change positions during the course of a game.

back zone
Area between the attack line and the end line; it is usually occupied by the backs.

free zone
Area at least 6.5 ft wide surrounding the court.

linesman
One of four officials who use a red flag to signal a dead ball, service faults, contact with the antennas, etc.

sideline
Line that demarcates the sides of the play area; a rally ends when the ball falls outside the sideline.

post
Upright used to stretch the net using white tape; the top of the net is just over 2 m above floor level.

attack zone
Area between the net and the attack line; it is usually occupied by the attackers.

vertical side band
Vertical strip of white canvas at the ends of the net.

net
Loosely stitched divider stretched across the middle of the court; players must hit the ball over it.

volleyball
Inflated ball covered with soft leather and with a circumference of about 26 in; it must always be hit and cannot be held or thrown.

table tennis

Sport with two or four opposing players with paddles; they hit a ball onto opposite sides of a net dividing a table in half.

table
Rectangular wooden table (9 ft x 5 ft) that is 2.5 ft above the ground; it is divided in half by a net.

net
Loosely stitched divider across the middle of the table; players must hit the ball over it.

white tape
Strip of material with a cord passing through it; the cord is attached to the net supports to suspend the net.

sideline
Line marking the sides of the playing surface.

upper edge
Line marking the upper edges of the tabletop.

mesh
The tiny squares make up the net; they are formed of interlaced threads.

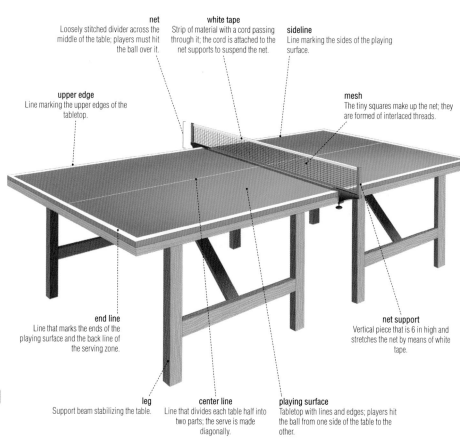

end line
Line that marks the ends of the playing surface and the back line of the serving zone.

net support
Vertical piece that is 6 in high and stretches the net by means of white tape.

leg
Support beam stabilizing the table.

center line
Line that divides each table half into two parts; the serve is made diagonally.

playing surface
Tabletop with lines and edges; players hit the ball from one side of the table to the other.

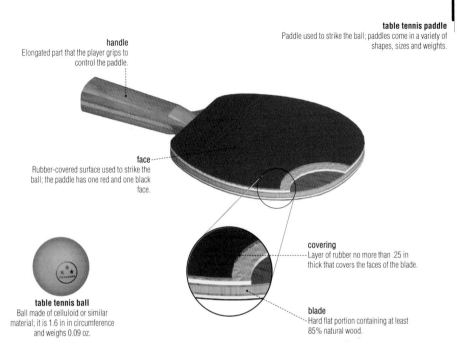

table tennis paddle
Paddle used to strike the ball; paddles come in a variety of shapes, sizes and weights.

handle
Elongated part that the player grips to control the paddle.

face
Rubber-covered surface used to strike the ball; the paddle has one red and one black face.

covering
Layer of rubber no more than .25 in thick that covers the faces of the blade.

table tennis ball
Ball made of celluloid or similar material; it is 1.6 in circumference and weighs 0.09 oz.

blade
Hard flat portion containing at least 85% natural wood.

types of grips
There are two principal paddle grips.

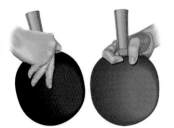

penholder grip
Grip that is suited to offensive play although it weakens the backhand: the table tennis player uses only one paddle face.

shake-hands grip
The most common grip; both paddle faces can be used and the player can hit forehand and backhand.

badminton

Sport with two or four opposing players that is similar to tennis; players use rackets to hit a shuttlecock onto opposite sides of a net that divides a court in half.

court
Synthetic or hardwood surface that is designed to provide good traction; badminton is usually played indoors.

service judge
Official who monitors the execution of the serve (player position, arrival of the shuttlecock in the appropriate zone, etc.).

linesman
One of 10 officials who ensure that the shuttlecock remains inside the lines of play and inform the umpire when a fault is committed.

center line
Line dividing each court half into two sides; the center line separates the left and right service zones.

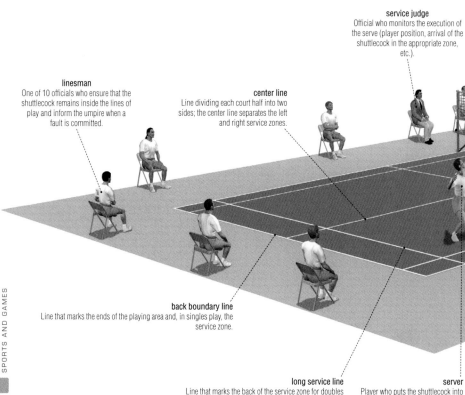

back boundary line
Line that marks the ends of the playing area and, in singles play, the service zone.

long service line
Line that marks the back of the service zone for doubles matches.

server
Player who puts the shuttlecock into play; the server and receiver stand diagonally opposite each other.

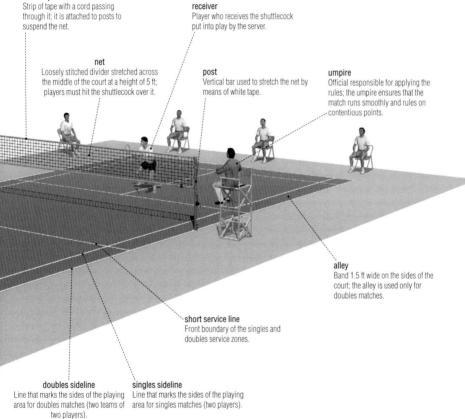

white tape
Strip of tape with a cord passing through it; it is attached to posts to suspend the net.

receiver
Player who receives the shuttlecock put into play by the server.

net
Loosely stitched divider stretched across the middle of the court at a height of 5 ft; players must hit the shuttlecock over it.

post
Vertical bar used to stretch the net by means of white tape.

umpire
Official responsible for applying the rules; the umpire ensures that the match runs smoothly and rules on contentious points.

alley
Band 1.5 ft wide on the sides of the court; the alley is used only for doubles matches.

short service line
Front boundary of the singles and doubles service zones.

doubles sideline
Line that marks the sides of the playing area for doubles matches (two teams of two players).

singles sideline
Line that marks the sides of the playing area for singles matches (two players).

badminton

badminton racket

The racket used to strike the shuttlecock is lighter (about 3 oz) and narrower than a tennis racket; its head is about 9 in long and 11 in wide.

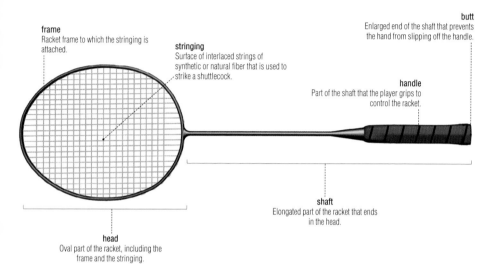

frame
Racket frame to which the stringing is attached.

stringing
Surface of interlaced strings of synthetic or natural fiber that is used to strike a shuttlecock.

butt
Enlarged end of the shaft that prevents the hand from slipping off the handle.

handle
Part of the shaft that the player grips to control the racket.

head
Oval part of the racket, including the frame and the stringing.

shaft
Elongated part of the racket that ends in the head.

feathered shuttlecock
Small piece of cork with 14 to 16 feathers; it is used in competitions.

feather crown
Feathers or synthetic materials attached to the shuttlecock tip to stabilize it and make it aerodynamic.

cork tip
The rounded base of the shuttlecock; it can also be made of synthetic materials.

synthetic shuttlecock
Small plastic cone that is sturdier than the feathered shuttlecock and is usually used for training; it weighs about 0.2 oz, the same as the feathered shuttlecock.

tennis

Sport with two or four opposing players with rackets who hit a ball onto opposite sides of a net dividing a court in half.

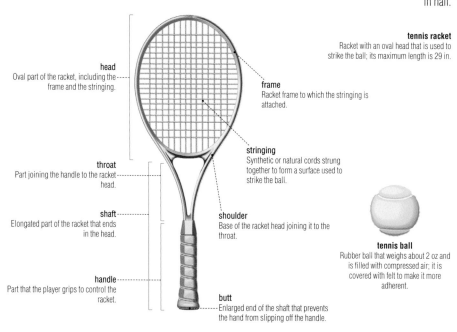

tennis racket
Racket with an oval head that is used to strike the ball; its maximum length is 29 in.

head
Oval part of the racket, including the frame and the stringing.

frame
Racket frame to which the stringing is attached.

stringing
Synthetic or natural cords strung together to form a surface used to strike the ball.

throat
Part joining the handle to the racket head.

shaft
Elongated part of the racket that ends in the head.

shoulder
Base of the racket head joining it to the throat.

handle
Part that the player grips to control the racket.

butt
Enlarged end of the shaft that prevents the hand from slipping off the handle.

tennis ball
Rubber ball that weighs about 2 oz and is filled with compressed air; it is covered with felt to make it more adherent.

playing surfaces
Tennis is played on various indoor and outdoor surfaces; playing strategies are adapted to the court surface.

grass
Extremely fast playing surface that favors a serve-and-volley game; grass surfaces are increasingly rare due to high maintenance costs.

hard surface (cement)
Surface given to fast bounces; hard surfaces quickly wear out shoes and balls.

clay
Slow and comfortable surface given to long rallies; clay courts require regular but low-cost maintenance.

synthetic surface
Soft elastic surface that offers excellent bounce and reduces the risk of injury.

tennis

court
Rectangular surface (78 ft x 27 ft for singles, 78 ft x 36 ft for doubles) designed for playing tennis; it is divided in half by a net.

pole
Vertical pole that stretches the net by means of a net band, keeping it 3.5 ft above the court.

umpire
Official responsible for applying the rules; the umpire ensures that the match runs smoothly and rules on contentious points.

ball boy
Person who retrieves balls from the court after each rally in a tournament.

service judge
Official who signals service line faults and informs the umpire when the server commits a fault.

service line
Line on each side of the net and parallel to it at a distance of 21 ft; it marks the back boundary of the service courts.

doubles sideline
Line that marks the sides of the playing area for doubles matches (two teams of two players).

center line judge
Official who signals center line service faults and informs the umpire when the server commits a fault.

alley
Band that is 4.5 ft wide on the sides of the court; the alley is used only for doubles matches.

linesman
One of the officials who ensure that the ball remains inside the lines of play and inform the umpire when a player commits a fault.

center mark
Broken line marking the middle of the baseline; players use the center mark to take position for serving or receiving.

receiver
Player who returns the ball put into play by the server.

foot fault judge
Official responsible for signaling foot faults, which occur when the server steps on the baseline.

server
Player who puts the ball into play; the server and receiver must stand in diagonally opposite zones.

center strap
Strip of fabric connected to the ground in the center of the net; it keeps the net at regulation height (3 ft).

right service court
Zone in which the serve must bounce; it is diagonally opposite the server.

left service court
Zone in which the serve must bounce; it is diagonally opposite the server.

baseline
Line marking the end of the court; the server stands behind the baseline.

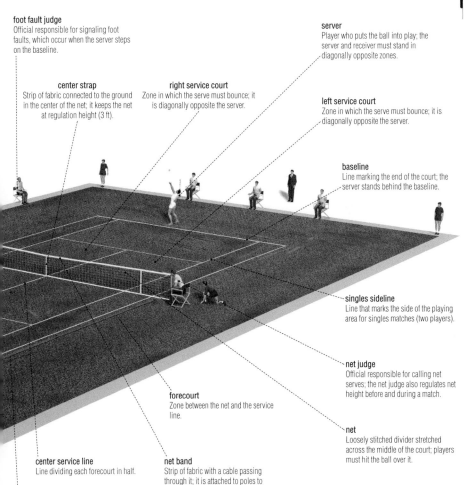

singles sideline
Line that marks the side of the playing area for singles matches (two players).

net judge
Official responsible for calling net serves; the net judge also regulates net height before and during a match.

forecourt
Zone between the net and the service line.

net
Loosely stitched divider stretched across the middle of the court; players must hit the ball over it.

center service line
Line dividing each forecourt in half.

net band
Strip of fabric with a cable passing through it; it is attached to poles to suspend the net.

backcourt
Zone between the service line and the baseline.

SPORTS AND GAMES

gymnastics

Sports discipline practiced on the ground with apparatuses such as rings, bars and beams.

event platform
Platform that contains the necessary material and apparatuses to hold gymnastics competitions.

overall standings scoreboard
Board on which the performances and the gymnasts' marks are posted.

pommel horse
Men's gymnastics apparatus with two handles (pommels), around which the gymnast maneuvers.

line judge
Official who ensures that the gymnasts on the floor stay within the floor exercise area.

uneven parallel bars
Women's gymnastics apparatus made up of two horizontal bars of different heights for performing various acrobatic exercises.

balance beam
Women's gymnastics apparatus made up of a long horizontal bar, on which the gymnast performs static and dynamic balance exercises.

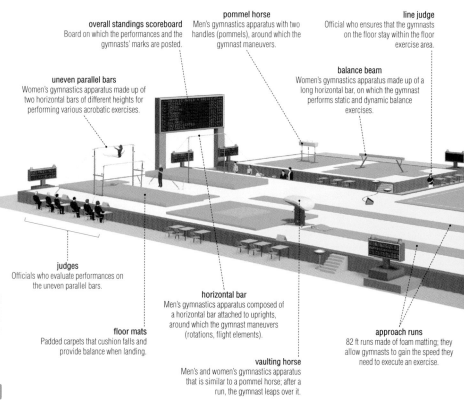

judges
Officials who evaluate performances on the uneven parallel bars.

floor mats
Padded carpets that cushion falls and provide balance when landing.

horizontal bar
Men's gymnastics apparatus composed of a horizontal bar attached to uprights, around which the gymnast maneuvers (rotations, flight elements).

vaulting horse
Men's and women's gymnastics apparatus that is similar to a pommel horse; after a run, the gymnast leaps over it.

approach runs
82 ft runs made of foam matting; they allow gymnasts to gain the speed they need to execute an exercise.

floor exercise area
40 ft² pad on which the gymnast performs
exercises on the floor.

rings
Men's gymnastics apparatus made up of two
rings that hang from cables, which are fixed to
a frame; they are used especially for power
elements and fast swing exercises.

current event scoreboard
Judges grade exercises performed by the
gymnasts based on execution, technique and
artistic value.

parallel bars
Men's gymnastics apparatus made up of
two horizontal bars set at the same
height; they are for performing various
acrobatic exercises.

judges
Officials who evaluate floor exercises.

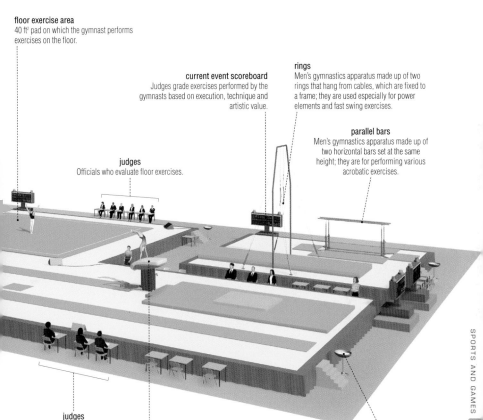

judges
Officials who evaluate the
performances on the vaulting horse
(women).

vaulting horse
Men's and women's gymnastics apparatus
that is similar to a pommel horse; after a
run, the gymnast supports the body on it
with both hands to make a jump.

magnesium powder
White magnesium-based powder that
absorbs sweat from the gymnasts'
hands; this provides a surer grip on the
apparatuses.

SPORTS AND GAMES

975

swimming

Sport consisting of swimming a defined distance (which varies depending on the four recognized stroke categories) as quickly as possible.

competitive course
The events, for singles and teams, take place in a pool that is 25 m or 50 m (Olympic-sized pool) long.

referee
Official who enforces the rules and oversees the progress of the competition; the referee ratifies the judges' decisions and resolves any disputes that may arise.

stroke judge
Each of the four officials checking the acceptability of the swimmers' movements, depending on the stroke category.

finish wall
Wall that the swimmer must touch to end a race; it is also the wall for turning around during events longer than 100 m in an Olympic-sized pool.

starter
Official who gives the start signal; false starts lead to the disqualification of the swimmer in error.

false start rope
Rope that is 50 ft from the wall; it is dropped into the water in the event of a false start to inform the swimmers that they must resume their starting positions.

placing judge
Official who confirms the times registered by the electronic timer after checking with the timekeepers.

lane timekeeper
Official who manually registers the finish time of the competitor swimming in an assigned lane.

starting block
Metal elevated structure from which the swimmer dives into the pool to start a race.

chief timekeeper
Official who collects the times registered by the lane timekeepers; these data are used in the event the electronic timer fails.

backstroke turn indicator
Rope with pennants that is strung 16 ft from the finish and turning walls; backstroke swimmers use it to judge distance.

sidewall
Wall forming the side of the pool; there is at least 20 in between the side wall and the outside lane ropes.

turning wall
Wall that the swimmer must touch before turning around; during the turn, the athlete pushes from the wall with the feet.

turning judges
Officials checking the validity of the turns; in the 800 m and 1500 m events, they inform the swimmers of how many lengths they have left to do.

lane
The strips, numbered from 1 to 8, that are reserved for swimmers during a race; swimmers must stay in the same lane throughout the event.

lane rope
Cord with floaters along it that delimits the eight lanes of the pool; it is designed to reduce turbulence on the surface of the water.

bottom line
Continuous line on the bottom of the pool in the center of each lane; it is a visual guide for the swimmer.

automatic electronic timer
Apparatus for automatically registering the swimmer's finish time; it is activated at the start and stops when the swimmer comes into contact with the wall.

swimming pool
Pool where swimming competitions take place; the water in it is maintained at a constant temperature (around 78°F) and depth.

swimming

types of strokes

Four basic categories are recognized by the International Amateur Swimming Federation (FINA): the breaststroke, the butterfly, the backstroke and freestyle (the crawl).

front crawl stroke

Stroke performed on the stomach in which the arms alternate in moving toward the front; it is very fast and is usually used in freestyle races.

breaststroke

Stroke characterized by a series of simultaneous arm movements (toward the front, toward the outside and toward the rear) that are synchronized with the beating of the legs.

turning wall

Wall that the swimmer must touch before turning around; during the turn, the athlete pushes from the wall with the feet.

butterfly stroke

Stroke on the stomach in which the two arms are thrust simultaneously toward the front and then brought backward.

backstroke

Stroke characterized by an alternating rotation of the arms toward the back; the outstretched legs make an alternating beating movement at the same time.

SPORTS AND GAMES

diving

Sport consisting of executing simple to complex dives into the water from a platform or a springboard.

diving installations
Equipment (such as springboards, platforms and tower) for diving; during a competition, the divers execute several dives and the points they earn are cumulative.

diving tower
Fixed structure supporting several platforms of various heights; at the Olympic Games, only the 10 m platform is used.

10 m platform

judges
Individuals who evaluate the performances; seven judges (nine for synchronized diving) award a mark out of 10 based on technique and poise.

5 m platform
Platform: fixed rigid board with a skidproof surface from which dives are performed.

7.5 m platform

speaker
Official who presents the competitors, the dives executed (and their degree of difficulty) and the final marks.

3 m springboard
Springboard: structure with a flexible board and a skidproof surface from which dives are performed.

3 m platform

referee
Official in charge of enforcing the rules, giving the starting signal and marking the major errors committed during a dive.

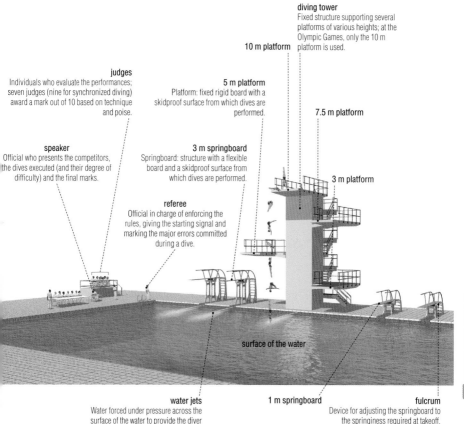

surface of the water

water jets
Water forced under pressure across the surface of the water to provide the diver points of reference during a dive.

1 m springboard

fulcrum
Device for adjusting the springboard to the springiness required at takeoff.

SPORTS AND GAMES

sailing

Sport navigation practiced on a sailboat. There are several classes of sailboats and various types of competitions such as regattas and transoceanic races.

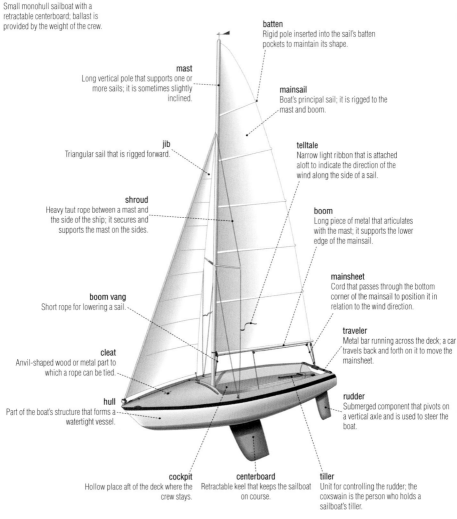

sailboat
Small monohull sailboat with a retractable centerboard; ballast is provided by the weight of the crew.

batten
Rigid pole inserted into the sail's batten pockets to maintain its shape.

mast
Long vertical pole that supports one or more sails; it is sometimes slightly inclined.

mainsail
Boat's principal sail; it is rigged to the mast and boom.

jib
Triangular sail that is rigged forward.

telltale
Narrow light ribbon that is attached aloft to indicate the direction of the wind along the side of a sail.

shroud
Heavy taut rope between a mast and the side of the ship; it secures and supports the mast on the sides.

boom
Long piece of metal that articulates with the mast; it supports the lower edge of the mainsail.

mainsheet
Cord that passes through the bottom corner of the mainsail to position it in relation to the wind direction.

boom vang
Short rope for lowering a sail.

traveler
Metal bar running across the deck; a car travels back and forth on it to move the mainsheet.

cleat
Anvil-shaped wood or metal part to which a rope can be tied.

hull
Part of the boat's structure that forms a watertight vessel.

rudder
Submerged component that pivots on a vertical axle and is used to steer the boat.

cockpit
Hollow place aft of the deck where the crew stays.

centerboard
Retractable keel that keeps the sailboat on course.

tiller
Unit for controlling the rudder; the coxswain is the person who holds a sailboat's tiller.

sailboard

Floating board with a sail; it is used in windsurfing, a sport consisting of gliding on water.

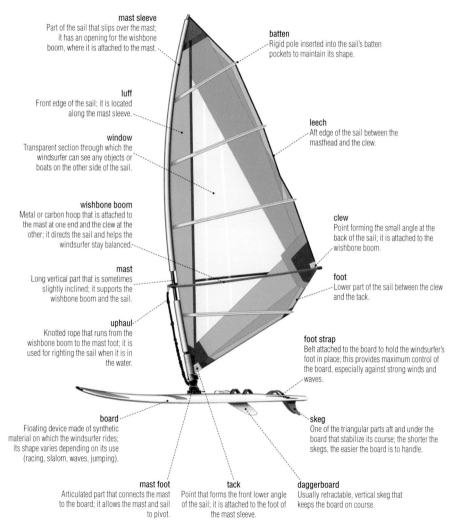

mast sleeve
Part of the sail that slips over the mast; it has an opening for the wishbone boom, where it is attached to the mast.

batten
Rigid pole inserted into the sail's batten pockets to maintain its shape.

luff
Front edge of the sail; it is located along the mast sleeve.

leech
Aft edge of the sail between the masthead and the clew.

window
Transparent section through which the windsurfer can see any objects or boats on the other side of the sail.

wishbone boom
Metal or carbon hoop that is attached to the mast at one end and the clew at the other; it directs the sail and helps the windsurfer stay balanced.

clew
Point forming the small angle at the back of the sail; it is attached to the wishbone boom.

mast
Long vertical part that is sometimes slightly inclined; it supports the wishbone boom and the sail.

foot
Lower part of the sail between the clew and the tack.

uphaul
Knotted rope that runs from the wishbone boom to the mast foot; it is used for righting the sail when it is in the water.

foot strap
Belt attached to the board to hold the windsurfer's foot in place; this provides maximum control of the board, especially against strong winds and waves.

board
Floating device made of synthetic material on which the windsurfer rides; its shape varies depending on its use (racing, slalom, waves, jumping).

skeg
One of the triangular parts aft and under the board that stabilize its course; the shorter the skegs, the easier the board is to handle.

mast foot
Articulated part that connects the mast to the board; it allows the mast and sail to pivot.

tack
Point that forms the front lower angle of the sail; it is attached to the foot of the mast sleeve.

daggerboard
Usually retractable, vertical skeg that keeps the board on course.

SPORTS AND GAMES

canoe-kayak: whitewater

Sport of traveling in a canoe or kayak in water ranging from calm to turbulent in a river or man-made course.

canoe
Closed boat that is somewhat wider than a kayak and seats one or two people; it is propelled with a single-bladed paddle in a kneeling position.

single-bladed paddle
Instrument made up of a flat oar blade attached to a handle for propelling and steering a canoe.

kayak
Long narrow closed boat with a round hull that provides stability and maneuverability; it is propelled with a double-bladed paddle in a seated position.

spray skirt
Flexible waterproof part that is attached around the opening; it fits snugly around the kayaker's waist to prevent water from entering the boat.

double-bladed paddle
Instrument with two curved oar blades that are attached to a handle; it propels and steers the kayak by paddling on alternating sides of the boat.

scuba diving

Sport consisting of descending underwater and swimming around; it can be done holding one's breath or with scuba gear.

scuba diver
Person who practices scuba diving; the diver wears diving gear and carries equipment that makes it possible to stay underwater for as long as the air supply lasts.

mask
Watertight part that is made up of glass surrounded by a rubber skirt; it covers the nose and eyes and provides good visibility underwater.

hood
Synthetic rubber cap that covers the head and neck to protect them against the cold.

snorkel
Rigid or flexible tube that enables the diver to breathe from just under the surface without lifting the head out of the water; it provides a comfortable and efficient position for swimming.

harness
Piece of equipment with straps and suspenders; the diver uses it to carry one or more cylinders of compressed air on the back.

regulator first stage
Apparatus attached to the cylinder valve that lowers the air pressure coming from the cylinder to an intermediate value (medium pressure).

regulator second stage
Apparatus that changes the pressure of the air coming from the regulator first stage to the pressure of the ambient air; the diver breathes this air in through a mouthpiece.

air hose
Flexible tube that connects the regulator first stage to the emergency regulator.

inflator
Apparatus that inflates the buoyancy compensator; it often includes a mechanical system attached to the regulator as well as a mouthpiece for inflating it manually.

buoyancy compensator
Float device whose volume of air can be increased or decreased at will to stabilize the diver underwater; it can be used to return to the surface and to keep afloat without effort.

weight belt
Fabric sash worn around the waist; it contains a variable number of weights to compensate for the diver's natural flotation.

compressed-air cylinder
Device containing air of diminished volume due to pressure; it stores air that can be used by the diver to move underwater.

information console
Ergonomic box that houses various measuring devices, which are useful to the diver.

diving glove
Piece of synthetic rubber that covers the hand and wrist to protect them from the cold and from being hurt by underwater objects, plants and animals.

emergency regulator
Regulator second stage that is connected by a hose to the regulator first stage; it is used to supply air to a diver in difficulty.

wet suit
Insulating outfit made out of synthetic rubber; a small amount of water is usually allowed to seep in and assume the diver's body temperature.

boot
Synthetic rubber boot that protects the foot and ankle from the cold and from being rubbed by the fin.

fin
Rubber or plastic flipper that is attached to the foot and improves the diver's propulsion in the water.

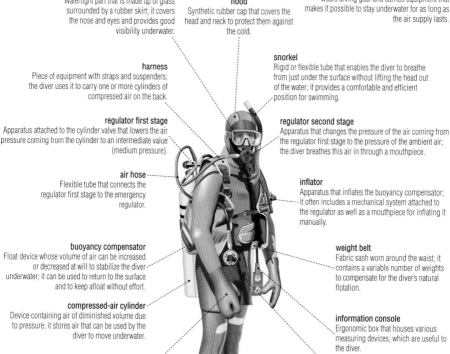

SPORTS AND GAMES

boxing

Sport in which two opponents wearing gloves fight each other with their fists (English boxing) or with their fists and feet (French boxing) following a code of rules.

ring
Square podium that is surrounded by stretched ropes and measures from 18 to 22 ft on the inside of the ropes; the boxing bout takes place on it.

referee
Official who enforces the rules and directs the fight in the ring; after the bout, this individual collects and checks the judges' scores.

corner pad
Padded layer covering the posts to prevent injuries.

boxer
Athlete who practices boxing; boxers are classified into weight categories.

ring post
Pole located at the four corners of the ring that supports and stretches the ropes.

trainer
Person who supervises the boxer's training and is present during contests to coach the boxer on strategy.

second
Person who assists a boxer and ministers to him between rounds.

corner stool
Corner seat on which the boxer sits during breaks.

physician
Person who treats the boxers in the event of injury; a doctor's presence is mandatory and this individual may end a fight in the event of serious injury.

canvas
Covering for breaking falls that is made of flexible material and is about .5 in thick; a canvas is stretched on it.

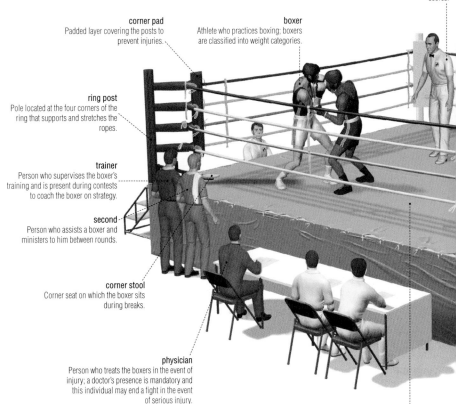

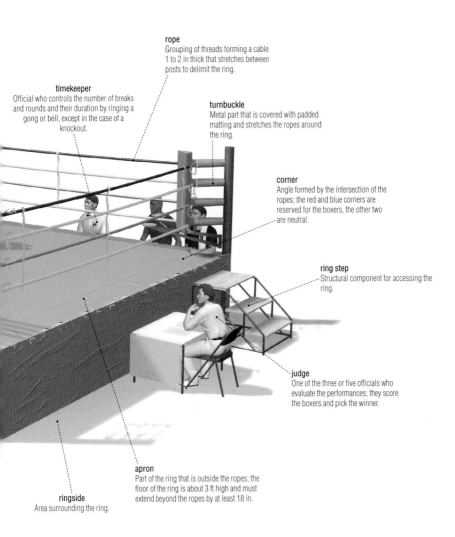

rope
Grouping of threads forming a cable 1 to 2 in thick that stretches between posts to delimit the ring.

timekeeper
Official who controls the number of breaks and rounds and their duration by ringing a gong or bell, except in the case of a knockout.

turnbuckle
Metal part that is covered with padded matting and stretches the ropes around the ring.

corner
Angle formed by the intersection of the ropes; the red and blue corners are reserved for the boxers, the other two are neutral.

ring step
Structural component for accessing the ring.

judge
One of the three or five officials who evaluate the performances; they score the boxers and pick the winner.

apron
Part of the ring that is outside the ropes; the floor of the ring is about 3 ft high and must extend beyond the ropes by at least 18 in.

ringside
Area surrounding the ring.

boxing

boxer
Athlete who practices boxing; boxers are classified into weight categories.

headgear
Rigid piece of equipment that protects the head especially during training and in Olympic boxing.

glove
Padded covering for the hand and wrist to dampen the impact of punching.

boxing trunks
Shorts coming down to mid-thigh.

punching bag
Leather or canvas bag that is filled with sand and weighs about 65 lb; the boxer trains by hitting it powerfully.

speed ball
Inflated leather bag that the boxer hits when training; it helps develop speed and punching coordination.

mouthpiece
Protective device for the boxer's teeth that is placed between the cheeks and teeth during a fight.

lace
Narrow cord that passes through the glove's eyelets to tighten it around the hand and wrist.

boxing gloves
The gloves are provided by the organizers before the bout.

bandage
Band of soft fabric (gauze) that is wrapped around the hand underneath the glove; it protects the hand against fractures and supports the wrist.

protective cup
Molded plastic equipment that protects an athlete's genitals.

wrestling

Sport in which two opponents fight bare-handed and seek to pin each other to the floor using various holds.

wrestler
Athlete who practices wrestling; wrestlers are classified into weight categories.

singlet
Tight-fitting one-piece outfit.

wrestling shoe
Flexible leather boot that covers the ankle; it has no heel and no metal parts.

wrestling area
Mat with an area of 40 ft² for a wrestling match; a bout has two 3-minute periods with a break of 30 seconds.

referee
Official in charge of enforcing the rules who directs the fight on the mat and wears red and blue sleeves to indicate points.

protection area
Area that is 5 ft wide and surrounds the passivity zone; it provides safety if the wrestler is thrown out of the wrestling area.

judge
Official who assigns the points for the technical action as instructed by the referee or the mat chairperson and registers them on the scoreboard.

mat chairperson
Official who coordinates the work of the referee and the judge; in the event of disagreement, he settles it. He may also interrupt the bout.

passivity zone
Red band that is 3.2 ft wide; it delimits and is part of the wrestling surface (30 ft in diameter).

wrestler
Athlete who practices wrestling; wrestlers are classified into weight categories.

central wrestling area
Circle inside the passivity zone that is 23 ft in diameter; the bout takes place within it.

SPORTS AND GAMES

987

judo

Sport of Japanese origin that is practiced with bare hands and consists of unbalancing the opponent with holds; Judo means "the gentle way".

mat
Surface that measures 46 ft x 52 ft and is used for practicing judo; it is made up of smaller mat squares (tatamis).

medical team
Physicians tend to the judokas in the event of injury; their presence is mandatory and they may end a bout in the event of serious injury.

contestant
One of two athletes (here, judokas) who confront each other in a bout; contestants are classified into weight categories.

scorers and timekeepers
The scorers show the results on the scoreboards and the timekeepers monitor the time during the bout.

scoreboard
Board that displays various data about the contest taking place (such as points and penalties); there are two scoreboards, one manual and one electronic, in each contest area.

safety area
Surface that is 10 ft wide and surrounds the danger area; it provides safety if the contestant if thrown out of the contest area.

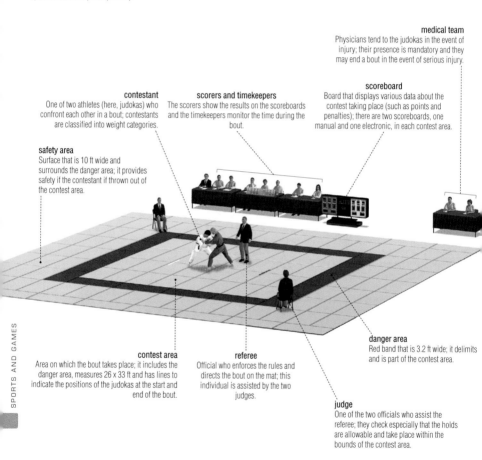

contest area
Area on which the bout takes place; it includes the danger area, measures 26 x 33 ft and has lines to indicate the positions of the judokas at the start and end of the bout.

referee
Official who enforces the rules and directs the bout on the mat; this individual is assisted by the two judges.

danger area
Red band that is 3.2 ft wide; it delimits and is part of the contest area.

judge
One of the two officials who assist the referee; they check especially that the holds are allowable and take place within the bounds of the contest area.

examples of holds and throws

There are more than 40 holds in judo: floor grips (strangles, locks, holdings) and standing throws (shoulders, arms, hips, legs).

stomach throw
The assailant pulls the opponent forward and puts a foot on the his stomach, causing the opponent to be thrown over the assailant's shoulder.

sweeping hip throw
The assailant pushes the opponent's leg, causing the opponent's torso to rotate and flip over the assailant's hip.

holding
The assailant uses pressure on the shoulders to pin the opponent to the floor.

major outer reaping throw
Using the right leg, the assailant sweeps up the opponent's left leg from behind, causing the opponent to fall backward.

naked strangle
From behind, the assailant's arm puts pressure on the opponent's neck, constricting breathing or cutting off the flow of blood and oxygen to the brain.

major inner reaping throw
Using the right leg, the assailant sweeps up the opponent's right leg from the front, causing the opponent to fall backward.

arm lock
To force submission, the assailant exerts pressure on the opponent's elbow joint against its natural bending direction.

one-arm shoulder throw
Placing the forearms under the opponent's armpits, the assailant lifts the opponent over his back, propelling the opponent forward.

karate

Self-defense sport of Japanese origin that is practiced with bare hands; the blows, which are usually given with the hands and the feet, must stop before reaching the opponent's body.

karateka
Athlete who practices karate; some, but not all, organizations classify karatekas by weight.

karate-gi
Clothing worn when practicing karate; it includes a jacket and pants that are usually made of cotton.

obi
Long wide belt that is tied around the waist to close the jacket; its color indicates the contestant's level.

competition area
Surface for practicing karate; bouts last a maximum of three minutes.

referee
Official who enforces the rules, directs the bout on the mat, awards the points and gives out warnings and penalties.

arbitration committee
Group of upper-level officials who especially supervise the bout as it unfolds and check that the referee and the judges perform their duties correctly.

corner judge
One of the four officials who assist the referee, give their opinions especially about the referee's decisions and judge the actions of the karatekas.

scorekeeper
Official who tracks the karatekas' points and penalties.

karateka
Athlete who practices karate; some, but not all, organizations classify karatekas by weight.

timekeeper
Official who monitors the duration of the bout.

aikido

Defensive sport of Japanese origin that consists of neutralizing an armed or unarmed opponent by means of dodging, throwing and holding, using bare hands.

jo
Wooden stick about 4.2 ft long; it is used mainly for training.

aikidoka
Athlete who practices aikido; it requires good coordination, well-developed reflexes, suppleness and keen concentration.

bokken
Wooden saber about 3.2 ft long that is used for training; the jo and the bokken help develop the concepts of distance and position.

aikidogi
Clothing worn for practicing aikido; for beginners, it consists of a white jacket made of sturdy cloth and white pants.

obi
Long wide belt that is tied around the waist to close the jacket; its color indicates the aikidoka's level.

hakama
Long skirt for hiding foot movement.

kung fu

One of several types of sport of Chinese origin practiced with or without weapons; it is similar to karate but requires more legwork.

kung fu practitioner
Athlete who practices kung fu; contestants must be quick, precise and supple, and possess keen concentration.

traditional jacket
Closed by buttons and with a stand-up collar, it is most often black, but may also be red, yellow or white, which are the traditional colors in China.

sash
Belt whose color usually indicates the contestant's level; the colors vary from one style to another and according to the school and level.

weightlifting

Sport that consists of lifting the heaviest load possible (barbell) over the head using two types of lifts (clean and jerk; snatch).

barbell
Gym equipment made up of cast-iron disks of various weights attached in equal weights to each end of a long bar, which is lifted with two hands.

sleeveless jersey
Tight top that covers the torso while leaving the shoulders free; a T-shirt may be worn under the jersey.

wristband
Band of fabric that is 4 in wide or less and is worn around the wrist to support it when lifting.

weightlifting belt
Girdle that is 5 in wide or less and supports the dorsal and abdominal muscles during lifting.

knee wrap
Band of fabric 1 ft wide or less that is worn around the knee to support it when lifting.

trunks
Tight shorts that end above the knees.

strap
Adjustable band for tightening the shoe around the foot.

weightlifting shoe
Shoe with an antiskid sole and raised heel that stabilizes the foot during lifting.

clean and jerk
Type of lift that is executed in two stages; the bar is first raised to shoulder level (clean) and then quickly raised over the head (jerk), using the leg muscles.

snatch
Type of lift that is more difficult than the clean and jerk; it consists of raising the load over the head as high as possible in a continuous quick movement.

fitness equipment

Material and apparatuses for carrying out exercises aimed at maintaining the physique and increasing muscular strength, flexibility and endurance.

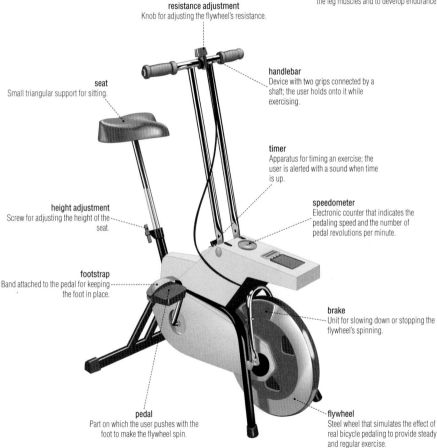

stationary bicycle
Bicycle attached to a base for training in a room or apartment; it is used mainly to work the leg muscles and to develop endurance.

resistance adjustment
Knob for adjusting the flywheel's resistance.

handlebar
Device with two grips connected by a shaft; the user holds onto it while exercising.

seat
Small triangular support for sitting.

timer
Apparatus for timing an exercise; the user is alerted with a sound when time is up.

height adjustment
Screw for adjusting the height of the seat.

speedometer
Electronic counter that indicates the pedaling speed and the number of pedal revolutions per minute.

footstrap
Band attached to the pedal for keeping the foot in place.

brake
Unit for slowing down or stopping the flywheel's spinning.

pedal
Part on which the user pushes with the foot to make the flywheel spin.

flywheel
Steel wheel that simulates the effect of real bicycle pedaling to provide steady and regular exercise.

SPORTS AND GAMES

fitness equipment

weight machine
Apparatus for carrying out various
exercises that consist of lifting or pushing
loads to strengthen muscles.

cable
Steel wire that connects the weights to
the machine's apparatuses.

lateral bar
Sitting on the bench, the user pulls the
bar down to chest level using both
arms; this strengthens the back
muscles.

pectoral deck
Apparatus with two handles that the user
brings together with the arms until they
touch; this develops the chest muscles.

press bar
Lying on the back, the user pulls the
bar downward with the arms; this
strengthens the chest muscles.

bench
Padded seat that is long and narrow;
the user lies or sits on it to perform
weight-training exercises.

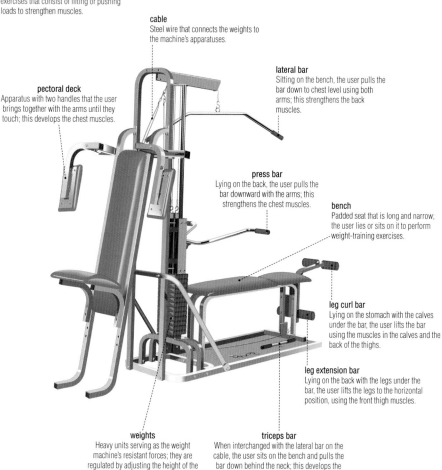

leg curl bar
Lying on the stomach with the calves
under the bar, the user lifts the bar
using the muscles in the calves and the
back of the thighs.

leg extension bar
Lying on the back with the legs under the
bar, the user lifts the legs to the horizontal
position, using the front thigh muscles.

weights
Heavy units serving as the weight
machine's resistant forces; they are
regulated by adjusting the height of the
weights to be lifted.

triceps bar
When interchanged with the lateral bar on the
cable, the user sits on the bench and pulls the
bar down behind the neck; this develops the
triceps (arm muscles).

ankle/wrist weight
Wide flexible band of preset mass that is worn around the wrist or ankle to increase resistance during exercise.

dumbbell
Gym equipment that consists of two equal weights attached to each end of a short bar, which is lifted with one hand to develop mainly the arm muscles.

stair climber
Apparatus that simulates the movement of climbing stairs; it is designed mainly to develop cardiorespiratory capacity and strengthen the leg muscles.

bar
Metal shaft that connects two weights; the athlete grips it to manipulate the weights.

weight
Round metal mass of various weights and sizes that is attached to each end of the bar.

jump rope
Cord with handles that is repeatedly swung over the head then jumped over; the athlete jumps once per cycle to strengthen mainly the leg and buttock muscles.

rowing machine
Apparatus that simulates the movement of rowing; it is designed mainly to develop cardiorespiratory capacity and strengthen a number of muscles in the body.

oar
Lever connected to the hydraulic resistance; it operates the rowing machine.

sliding seat
Part on which the user sits; it slides back and forth on rails to increase the amplitude and efficiency of the oars.

hydraulic resistance
Device with a hydraulic pump (silent system simulating water resistance); it constitutes the force exerted against the oars.

foot support
Part with a strap for the foot.

push-up stand
Handle gripped by the user to raise the body from a horizontal position on the floor (push-ups).

SPORTS AND GAMES

billiards

Games that are played on a special table; they use a cue to hit a cue ball either against two balls or to drive another into a pocket.

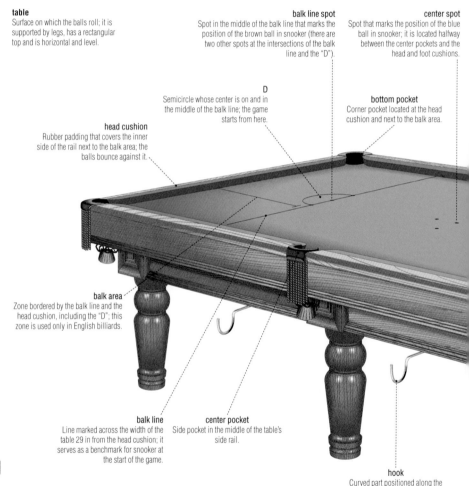

table
Surface on which the balls roll; it is supported by legs, has a rectangular top and is horizontal and level.

balk line spot
Spot in the middle of the balk line that marks the position of the brown ball in snooker (there are two other spots at the intersections of the balk line and the "D").

center spot
Spot that marks the position of the blue ball in snooker; it is located halfway between the center pockets and the head and foot cushions.

D
Semicircle whose center is on and in the middle of the balk line; the game starts from here.

bottom pocket
Corner pocket located at the head cushion and next to the balk area.

head cushion
Rubber padding that covers the inner side of the rail next to the balk area; the balls bounce against it.

balk area
Zone bordered by the balk line and the head cushion, including the "D"; this zone is used only in English billiards.

balk line
Line marked across the width of the table 29 in from the head cushion; it serves as a benchmark for snooker at the start of the game.

center pocket
Side pocket in the middle of the table's side rail.

hook
Curved part positioned along the tables that holds the cues and the rack.

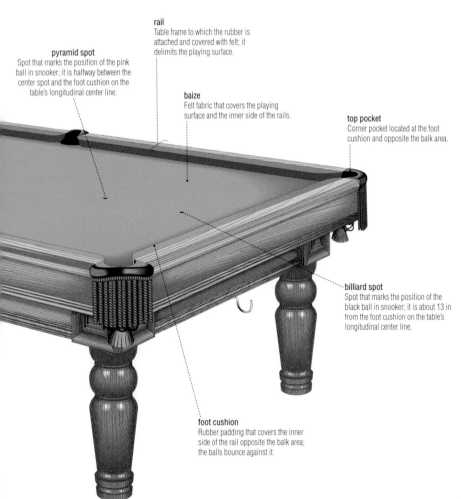

rail
Table frame to which the rubber is attached and covered with felt; it delimits the playing surface.

pyramid spot
Spot that marks the position of the pink ball in snooker; it is halfway between the center spot and the foot cushion on the table's longitudinal center line.

baize
Felt fabric that covers the playing surface and the inner side of the rails.

top pocket
Corner pocket located at the foot cushion and opposite the balk area.

billiard spot
Spot that marks the position of the black ball in snooker; it is about 13 in from the foot cushion on the table's longitudinal center line.

foot cushion
Rubber padding that covers the inner side of the rail opposite the balk area; the balls bounce against it.

SPORTS AND GAMES

billiards

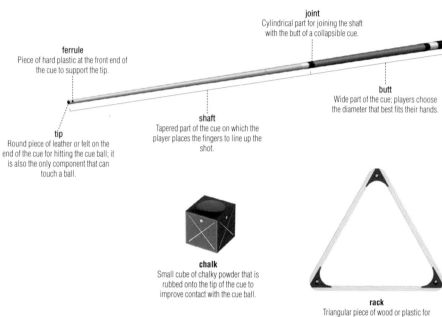

billiard cue
Long wooden stick that the player holds to hit the cue ball; the player chooses the cue's diameter, length and weight (no more than 25 oz).

joint
Cylindrical part for joining the shaft with the butt of a collapsible cue.

ferrule
Piece of hard plastic at the front end of the cue to support the tip.

butt
Wide part of the cue; players choose the diameter that best fits their hands.

shaft
Tapered part of the cue on which the player places the fingers to line up the shot.

tip
Round piece of leather or felt on the end of the cue for hitting the cue ball; it is also the only component that can touch a ball.

chalk
Small cube of chalky powder that is rubbed onto the tip of the cue to improve contact with the cue ball.

rack
Triangular piece of wood or plastic for lining up the balls on the table at the start of a game.

bridge
Stick with a toothed head for shooting with the cue when the cue ball is out of the player's reach.

endpiece
Piece of toothed metal to support and guide the cue.

notch
Space between the teeth on which the cue's shaft is placed.

shaft
Long part of the bridge; the endpiece is attached to it.

archery

Sport that consists of using a bow to shoot an arrow as close as possible to the middle of a target set a fixed distance away.

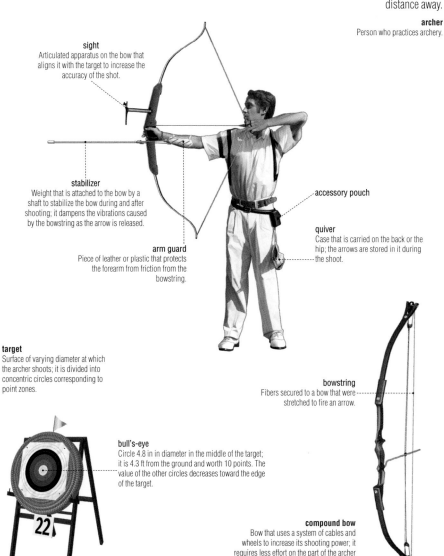

archer
Person who practices archery.

sight
Articulated apparatus on the bow that aligns it with the target to increase the accuracy of the shot.

stabilizer
Weight that is attached to the bow by a shaft to stabilize the bow during and after shooting; it dampens the vibrations caused by the bowstring as the arrow is released.

arm guard
Piece of leather or plastic that protects the forearm from friction from the bowstring.

accessory pouch

quiver
Case that is carried on the back or the hip; the arrows are stored in it during the shoot.

target
Surface of varying diameter at which the archer shoots; it is divided into concentric circles corresponding to point zones.

bowstring
Fibers secured to a bow that were stretched to fire an arrow.

bull's-eye
Circle 4.8 in in diameter in the middle of the target; it is 4.3 ft from the ground and worth 10 points. The value of the other circles decreases toward the edge of the target.

compound bow
Bow that uses a system of cables and wheels to increase its shooting power; it requires less effort on the part of the archer when aiming.

22

golf

Sport whose objective is to complete a set course by hitting a ball with a club; the player who uses the least number of strokes is the winner.

par 5 hole
The player tries to reach the green in three strokes and then make two putts to sink the ball in the hole; an eagle is a hole made in two strokes under par.

teeing ground
Grassy surface mown very short from which the player tees off; teeing grounds are arranged at various distances from the hole as a function of the players' skill.

green
Grass surface mown very short surrounding each of the course's holes; the golfer uses a putter to roll the ball into the hole.

water hazard
If the golfer hits a ball into this obstacle, it must be played where it is; if it is unplayable, a new ball is put into play and counted as a penalty stroke.

fairway
Mown part of the course between the teeing ground for the hole and its green.

natural environment
Part of the course that is left in its original state; it can consist of trees, bushes and undergrowth.

sand bunker
Section of the fairway of varying size that is filled with sand; if the ball becomes stuck here, the player uses a sand wedge to hit it out.

rough
Part of the course on the edge of the fairways where the grass grows freely.

hole
Cavity dug out of the green; the player must roll the ball into it to complete a hole.

removable flag pole
Long rod with a flag that is planted in a hole to mark the hole's location so that it can be seen from far away.

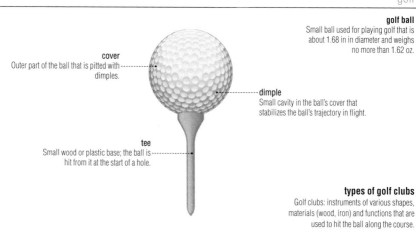

golf ball
Small ball used for playing golf that is about 1.68 in in diameter and weighs no more than 1.62 oz.

cover
Outer part of the ball that is pitted with dimples.

dimple
Small cavity in the ball's cover that stabilizes the ball's trajectory in flight.

tee
Small wood or plastic base; the ball is hit from it at the start of a hole.

types of golf clubs
Golf clubs: instruments of various shapes, materials (wood, iron) and functions that are used to hit the ball along the course.

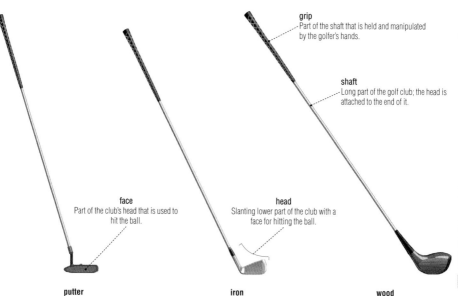

grip
Part of the shaft that is held and manipulated by the golfer's hands.

shaft
Long part of the golf club; the head is attached to the end of it.

face
Part of the club's head that is used to hit the ball.

head
Slanting lower part of the club with a face for hitting the ball.

putter
Club whose head has a vertical face for putting on the green.

iron
Club with a metal head and a shaft that is shorter than the wood's; it is used for medium- and short-distance strokes.

wood
Club with a long shaft that is used for long distances, especially at tee-off; originally made of wood, most of these clubs are now made of metal.

SPORTS AND GAMES

golf bag
Sack for transporting golf clubs and accessories; a player can use no more than 14 different clubs during a competition.

golf shoes
Leather shoes with cleats attached to the soles.

shoulder strap
Large belt that distributes the weight of the golf bag on the shoulder.

head cover
Part that covers and protects the head of a golf club while it is not being used.

pocket
Small exterior storage compartment that contains various accessories (such as balls, gloves and tees).

golf glove
Item that covers the hand to provide a better grip on the club; it is worn on one hand only (on the left hand for a right-handed person).

bag well
Rack at the back of the golf cart in which golfers carry their equipment over the golf course.

golf cart
Two-wheeled rack that is pulled by a handle to transport the golf bag along the course.

electric golf cart
Small motorized vehicle that is used by golfers to move from one hole to another along the golf course.

SPORTS AND GAMES

BMX

Sport that consists of performing freestyle acrobatics using a small, one-speed bicycle.

helmet
Hard piece of equipment designed to protect the head.

handlebars
Grips with a system of rings that pivot around an axle; this enables the handlebars to turn 360°.

glove
Leather item that reduces vibration and protects the hand against impact.

single chain wheel
Wheel with teeth that is connected to the sprocket by a chain enabling the wheel to turn; the wheel has only one chain wheel as there is only one gear.

foot pegs
Supports attached to the hub; the athlete stands on them to perform certain freestyle acrobatics.

single sprocket
Wheel with teeth that is connected to the chain wheel by a chain enabling the wheel to turn; the bicycle has only one sprocket as there is only one gear.

half-pipe
Wooden U-shaped track that is set up for performing various acrobatic stunts (such as jumps and slides).

road racing

Sport that consists of racing a bicycle on a road for one day or in stages.

road cycling competition
Event that consists of riding a bicycle a given distance on a road as quickly as possible.

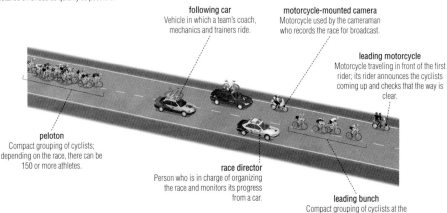

following car
Vehicle in which a team's coach, mechanics and trainers ride.

motorcycle-mounted camera
Motorcycle used by the cameraman who records the race for broadcast.

leading motorcycle
Motorcycle traveling in front of the first rider; its rider announces the cyclists coming up and checks that the way is clear.

peloton
Compact grouping of cyclists; depending on the race, there can be 150 or more athletes.

race director
Person who is in charge of organizing the race and monitors its progress from a car.

leading bunch
Compact grouping of cyclists at the front of the race.

road-racing bicycle and cyclist
Road-racing bicycle: bicycle that is designed for speed; it has narrow tires, a lightweight frame and handlebars conducive to an aerodynamic position for the cyclist.

jersey
Stretchy tight clothing that covers the top of the athlete's body.

helmet
Hard piece of equipment designed to protect the head.

shorts
Tight clothing that covers the athlete's thighs to prevent them from rubbing against the seat.

glove
Leather item that reduces vibration and protects the hand against impact.

frame
Bicycle structure made of aluminum or carbon fiber; it is rigid, lightweight and very sturdy.

wheel
Disk that turns around an axle at its center and enables the bicycle to move; its weight and shape influence the bike's performance.

shoe
Shoe with notches in the sole that fit into a corresponding part on the pedal to keep the foot secure on the pedal.

derailleur
Mechanism for changing the rear gears by lifting the chain from one gear wheel to another; it allows the cyclist to adapt to road conditions.

track cycling

Sport that consists of riding a bicycle on a closed track; the two types of track cycling events are speed and endurance.

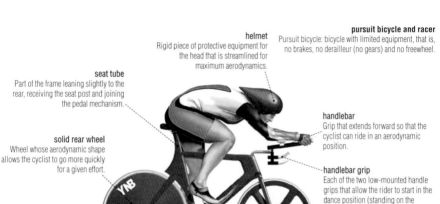

helmet
Rigid piece of protective equipment for the head that is streamlined for maximum aerodynamics.

pursuit bicycle and racer
Pursuit bicycle: bicycle with limited equipment, that is, no brakes, no derailleur (no gears) and no freewheel.

seat tube
Part of the frame leaning slightly to the rear, receiving the seat post and joining the pedal mechanism.

handlebar
Grip that extends forward so that the cyclist can ride in an aerodynamic position.

solid rear wheel
Wheel whose aerodynamic shape allows the cyclist to go more quickly for a given effort.

handlebar grip
Each of the two low-mounted handle grips that allow the rider to start in the dance position (standing on the pedals).

track
Inclined oval course that is 250 m long (short track) or 333.33 m or 400 m long (long tracks) and whose width varies from 7 to 9 m.

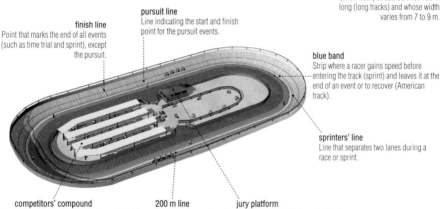

finish line
Point that marks the end of all events (such as time trial and sprint), except the pursuit.

pursuit line
Line indicating the start and finish point for the pursuit events.

blue band
Strip where a racer gains speed before entering the track (sprint) and leaves it at the end of an event or to recover (American track).

sprinters' line
Line that separates two lanes during a race or sprint.

competitors' compound
Rest and assistance area for athletes between races where the coaches, mechanics and trainers stand by.

200 m line
Point from which the racers are timed in the sprint event.

jury platform
Place where the 10 judges stand by to monitor the progress of the race and give the results.

SPORTS AND GAMES

mountain biking

Sport that consists of performing acrobatic exercises or racing offtrack (on a rough or steep course) on a bicycle.

cross-country bicycle and cyclist
Cross-country bicycle: relatively small, sturdy bicycle designed for performing acrobatics and competing in competitions on rough terrain.

goggles
Eyewear with plastic lenses fitted in a frame with arms; it protects the eyes from flying mud, stones and insects.

back suspension
Device that dampens vibrations from the wheels; this increases the bicycle's stability and its grip on the trail.

front fork
Fork whose air/oil or elastomer suspension provides a controlled ride over rough terrain.

clipless pedal
Pedal with a safety system so that the foot can be attached or detached quickly.

downhill bicycle and cyclist
Downhill bicycle: small, very sturdy bicycle for racing on rough ground with steep hills and strewn with obstacles.

protective goggles
One-piece watertight eyewear that protects the eyes from flying mud, stones and insects.

chin strap
Part of the helmet that protects the cyclist's chin.

pedal with wide platform
Wide pedal providing good footing.

raised handlebar
Grip whose elevated position makes the bicycle easier to steer when going downhill.

hydraulic disc brake
Brake with jaws that squeeze a disc to slow down the wheel; the braking power is produced by hydraulic pressure.

car racing

Speed event in which competitors driving race cars must make a predetermined number of laps around a track.

formula 1 car
Single-seater for racing on a closed circuit that can reach speeds of 225 mph; formula 1 is very popular in Europe.

camera
Exposure apparatus for following a driver's vehicle during an event; each car is equipped with at least one camera.

radio antenna
Device that emits and receives radio waves for communications between the driver and the team during the event.

wing
Part using air pressure to increase the load on the rear and front wheels to improve the tires' grip on the track.

cockpit
Part of the body where the driver sits that houses the equipment necessary for driving the car.

Pitot tube
Measuring device for calculating the actual speed of the car by taking into account the influence of the wind.

side fairings
Malleable structure that absorbs the impact from a collision; the side fairings house especially radiators and electronic components.

steering wheel
Unit enabling the driver to steer the turning wheels; a veritable dashboard, it is equipped with several controls such as the clutch and gear shifter.

roll structure
Structure composed of metal loops to protect the driver if the car rolls over.

wet-weather tire
Molded tire used on a wet track to evacuate a large quantity of water. At 185 mph, it evacuates more than 6.5 gallons of water per second.

dry-weather tire
Grooved tire providing a good grip on a dry track.

motorcycling

Competitions involving motorcycles whose engine cylinder size is larger than 125 cubic centimeters.

supercross circuit
Sometimes covered, man-made track that is composed of earth or a mixture of sand and clay; it is strewn with obstacles and bumps for jumps.

obstacles
Elements, such as bumps, spines and bridges, that the racers must clear during an event.

multiple jumps
Series of several bumps that the racer clears in a single jump, as opposed to clearing each jump separately.

start area
The starting line must be wide enough to accommodate the racers lined up abreast; each one needs a breadth of 3.3 ft.

triple jump
Obstacle made up of three bumps in a row that the racer must clear in one jump; the motorcycle must land on the far incline of the third bump.

bump
Rounded protrusion on the circuit that constitutes an obstacle for the racers.

spine
High bump enabling the racers to perform spectacular jumps.

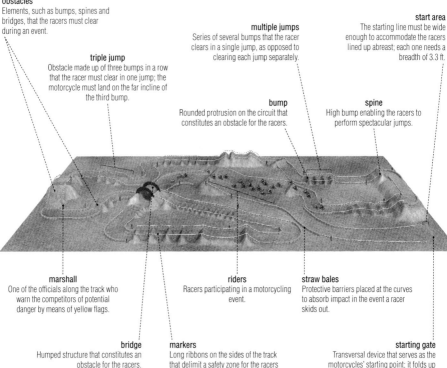

marshall
One of the officials along the track who warn the competitors of potential danger by means of yellow flags.

riders
Racers participating in a motorcycling event.

straw bales
Protective barriers placed at the curves to absorb impact in the event a racer skids out.

bridge
Humped structure that constitutes an obstacle for the racers.

markers
Long ribbons on the sides of the track that delimit a safety zone for the racers and spectators.

starting gate
Transversal device that serves as the motorcycles' starting point; it folds up or down so that the racers can push off.

motocross and supercross motorcycle
Slim lightweight motorcycle for racing on a closed rough circuit
with uneven ground, bumps and hillocks.

glove
Item that covers the hand and wrist in
order to protect them; it is made of
synthetic material and is padded inside
and out.

helmet
Hard piece of equipment designed to
protect the head.

protective suit
Clothing consisting of a top and pants that
protect the driver in the event of a fall;
protection (such as for the elbows, knees
and back) is optional.

protective goggles
Equipment that protects the eyes; it is
covered with several layers of plastic,
which the driver peels off when they
become dirty.

pants
Garment for the lower body; it extends
from the waist or the hips to the ankles,
covering each leg separately.

hand protector
Rigid part in front of the handlebar to
protect the hand in the event of impact.

number plate
Rectangular plate on the front and
sides of the motorcycle; it carries a
number to identify the driver.

fork
Sliding tube that encloses a spring; it
forms the steering, suspension and
shock-absorbing mechanisms of the
front wheel.

nubby tire
Tire whose tread is fitted with blocks of
rubber, providing better traction on
rough terrain.

boot
High leather boot protecting the
ankles.

protective plate
Metal part under the motorcycle that
protects it from shocks and prevents it
from striking obstacles.

ice hockey

Sport that is played on an ice rink with two opposing teams of six players; goals are scored by using a stick to put a puck in the opposing net.

rink
Ice surface on which a hockey game is played; a game consists of three 20-minute periods with two 15-minute intermissions.

goal line
Red line that the puck must cross for a goal to be scored; the red line also marks the icing line.

left defense
Position to the left of the center and behind the wing; this player tries to prevent the opponent from approaching the goal.

glass protector
Reinforced glass panel that is mounted on top of the boards to protect spectators from high shots and players' sticks.

linesman
One of two officials who signal offsides and icings; they do most of the face-offs and also signal infractions to the referee.

rink corner
The four rounded corners of the rink where body checks are often thrown.

players' bench
Bench used by the coaches and by inactive players; each team has about 20 players but only six are on the ice at the same time.

goal judge
Off-ice official who is positioned at the end of the rink behind the goal; the goal judge turns on a red light when the puck crosses the goal line.

goalkeeper
Player whose role is to prevent the puck from entering the goal; the goalkeeper usually plays the entire game.

face-off spot
Each of the spots where a referee or linesman drops the puck to put it in play.

blue line
Two lines that divide the rink into three equal parts; an offside is called when a player crosses the opposing blue line before the puck.

boards
Wooden or fiberglass boards that surround the rink and delimit the playing area.

face-off circle
Circle around each of the five face-off spots; two players line up on each side of this spot for a face-off while the other players remain outside the circle.

right defense
Position to the right of the center and behind the wing; this player tries to prevent the opponent from approaching the goal.

left wing
Offensive position to the left of the center; this player's role is to score goals and to check the opposing left wing.

referee
Official who is responsible for applying the rules; the referee, who wears a red armband, officiates and drops the puck for face-offs at the start of a period.

goal crease
Semicircle reserved for the goalkeeper; the referee disallows a goal if a player interferes with the goalkeeper inside the goal crease.

goal
Cage formed of netting mounted on a metal frame; a team scores a goal each time it lodges the puck inside the opposing goal.

coach
The team's leader; the coach plots strategy and decides who plays in different situations.

neutral zone
Area between the two blue lines where player changes are made and where various offensive and defensive strategies are initiated.

goal lights
The red light signals a goal while the green light, which is connected to the official time clock, signals a stoppage in play or the end of a period.

penalty bench
Bench reserved for penalized players; penalties vary between two and 10 minutes, depending on the seriousness of the infraction.

right wing
Offensive position to the right of the center; this player's role is to score goals and to check the opposing right wing.

center line
Line that divides the rink into two zones, one for each team; teams change zones after each period.

officials' bench
Bench reserved for some of the off-ice officials (timekeeper and penalty keeper, scorer, announcer).

center face-off circle
Circle in the middle of the rink; face-offs are held in the center circle at the start of a period and after a goal.

center
Player who usually takes the face-offs; a key player on a team, the center plays an offensive and a defensive role.

curling

Sport with two opposing teams of four players who slide stones over an ice surface in the direction of a target.

sheet
Ice surface on which a match is played; when an end is complete, the next end starts from the opposite end of the sheet.

lateral line
Band or line that delimits the sides of the sheet; a stone that strikes the lateral line is removed from play.

vice-skip
Player who assists the skip in devising playing tactics; the vice-skip usually throws third in an end.

umpire
Official who is responsible for applying the rules; in particular, the umpire rules on the correctness of throws and determines the distance between the stones and the tee.

second
Second player to throw stones in an end.

skip
Player who leads the team and determines strategy; the skip is usually the last to throw in an end.

lead
First player to throw stones in an end.

outer circle
Circle forming the outer limit of the house.

back line
Line at the back of the house that marks the boundary of the playing area; a stone that crosses this line is removed from play.

sheet
Surface of the ice; it is watered regularly with fine droplets to reduce friction between the ice and the stone.

hog line
Line at the front of the house that marks the boundary of the playing area; the stones must be released before this line and must cross the opposite hog line to remain in play.

hack
Rubber foothold at each end of the sheet that the thrower uses to push off.

tee line
Line across the center of the house; behind this line, players are allowed to brush in front of an opponent's stone in an effort to make it overshoot the house.

curler
Curling player who throws two stones in each of the 10 ends that make up a match.

tee
Circle forming the center of the house; once all the stones are thrown, the team with the stone closest to the tee wins the end.

inner circle
Circle surrounding the tee.

speed skating

Race on ice between individuals or teams held on a long or short track.

short track
Four to six skaters who race against one another; the skater who finishes with the fastest time wins the race.

finish judges
Officials who determine the order in which the skaters finish.

track
Oval 120 yd long on a standard rink; unlike the long track, there are no reserved lanes.

start judge
Official who gives the start signal and indicates false starts; a competitor is disqualified for making two consecutive false starts.

protective mat
Padding that covers the boards to cushion the impact when a skater falls.

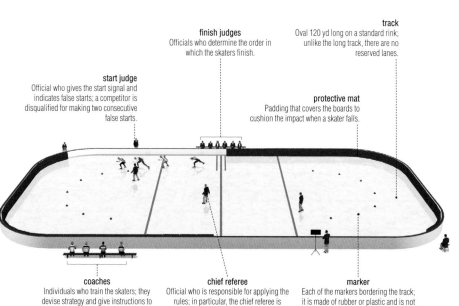

coaches
Individuals who train the skaters; they devise strategy and give instructions to the skaters throughout the race.

chief referee
Official who is responsible for applying the rules; in particular, the chief referee is authorized to disqualify a competitor who commits a fault.

marker
Each of the markers bordering the track; it is made of rubber or plastic and is not affixed to the ice to avoid damaging it.

speed skating

long track
Two competitors occupy specific lanes;
they take off simultaneously and skate
against a clock on an oval track 400 m
long.

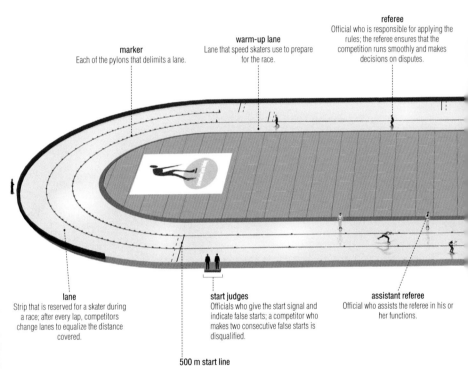

marker
Each of the pylons that delimits a lane.

warm-up lane
Lane that speed skaters use to prepare
for the race.

referee
Official who is responsible for applying the
rules; the referee ensures that the
competition runs smoothly and makes
decisions on disputes.

lane
Strip that is reserved for a skater during
a race; after every lap, competitors
change lanes to equalize the distance
covered.

start judges
Officials who give the start signal and
indicate false starts; a competitor who
makes two consecutive false starts is
disqualified.

assistant referee
Official who assists the referee in his or
her functions.

500 m start line

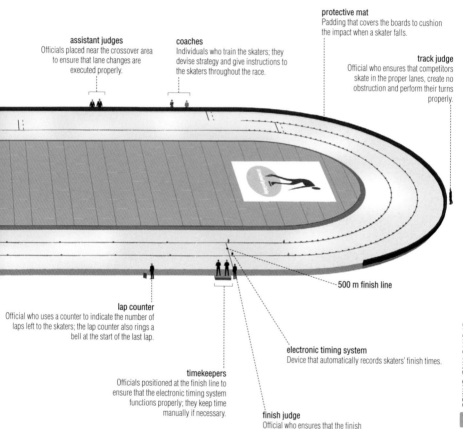

assistant judges
Officials placed near the crossover area to ensure that lane changes are executed properly.

coaches
Individuals who train the skaters; they devise strategy and give instructions to the skaters throughout the race.

protective mat
Padding that covers the boards to cushion the impact when a skater falls.

track judge
Official who ensures that competitors skate in the proper lanes, create no obstruction and perform their turns properly.

500 m finish line

lap counter
Official who uses a counter to indicate the number of laps left to the skaters; the lap counter also rings a bell at the start of the last lap.

electronic timing system
Device that automatically records skaters' finish times.

timekeepers
Officials positioned at the finish line to ensure that the electronic timing system functions properly; they keep time manually if necessary.

finish judge
Official who ensures that the finish conforms to regulations.

speed skating

skater: short track

Because of the high risk of falling and the close proximity of competitors, short-track speed skaters wear protection on vulnerable parts of the body.

helmet
Hard piece of equipment designed to protect the head.

glove
Covering for the hand and wrist that reduces the risk of injury, especially on turns where the skater places a hand on the ice.

knee pad
Piece of equipment made of hard molded plastic that protects the knee.

throat protector
Nylon neck guard that is worn under the racing suit to protect the skater's neck and throat.

shin guard
Piece of equipment that consists of hard molded plastic to protect the skater's legs.

skater: long track
The long-track speed skater wears an aerodynamic racing suit with a hood and an armband; competitors on inside and outside lanes wear different colors.

hood
Headgear attached to the neck of the racing suit; it is pulled over the head before a race to improve aerodynamics.

racing suit
Skintight one-piece garment that reduces air resistance; short-track speed skaters wear a similar racing suit but one without a hood.

short track skate
Skate with a blade that is curved in the direction of the turn and offset to the left for better cornering at high speed.

clapskate
Long-track skate with a blade that detaches from the heel; it provides longer contact with the ice to improve thrust.

SPORTS AND GAMES

figure skating

Sport that consists of executing jumps, spins and figures while skating to music; it includes singles skating, pairs skating and ice dancing.

figure skate
Reinforced boot with a blade that makes it possible to glide over the ice; figure skating is hard on the ankles so the skate provides maximum ankle support.

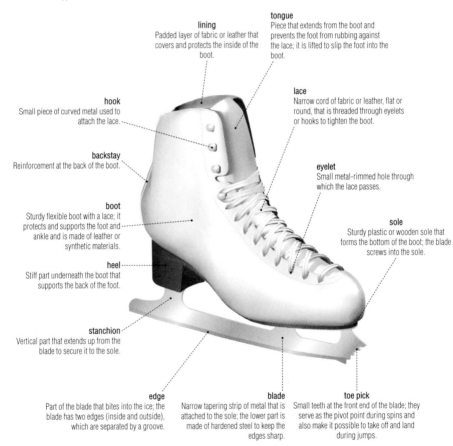

lining
Padded layer of fabric or leather that covers and protects the inside of the boot.

tongue
Piece that extends from the boot and prevents the foot from rubbing against the lace; it is lifted to slip the foot into the boot.

hook
Small piece of curved metal used to attach the lace.

lace
Narrow cord of fabric or leather, flat or round, that is threaded through eyelets or hooks to tighten the boot.

backstay
Reinforcement at the back of the boot.

eyelet
Small metal-rimmed hole through which the lace passes.

boot
Sturdy flexible boot with a lace; it protects and supports the foot and ankle and is made of leather or synthetic materials.

sole
Sturdy plastic or wooden sole that forms the bottom of the boot; the blade screws into the sole.

heel
Stiff part underneath the boot that supports the back of the foot.

stanchion
Vertical part that extends up from the blade to secure it to the sole.

edge
Part of the blade that bites into the ice; the blade has two edges (inside and outside), which are separated by a groove.

blade
Narrow tapering strip of metal that is attached to the sole; the lower part is made of hardened steel to keep the edges sharp.

toe pick
Small teeth at the front end of the blade; they serve as the pivot point during spins and also make it possible to take off and land during jumps.

rink
Ice surface on which skaters execute their programs; program duration varies depending on the event (between 2 min. 40 sec. and 4 min. 30 sec.).

assistant referee
Individual who assists the referee and is authorized to replace him or her if necessary.

referee
Official who is responsible for the eligibility of officials, skaters and the judging panel and the allowability of controversial decisions.

technical delegates
Official who ensures that technical installations are in compliance with the standards of the International Skating Union (ISU).

judges
Officials who are responsible for evaluating performances; during international competitions, nine judges are chosen at random from the nations represented.

timekeeper
Person who monitors the length of performances to ensure that skaters respect the allotted time.

pair
Team formed of a man and a woman; like singles skaters, pairs take part in two events: the technical program and the free program.

technical controller
Official who supervises the work of the technical specialist. He or she can immediately correct any error observed.

coaches
Individuals who oversee the training and preparation of skaters for competitions; coaches provide final advice prior to performances.

technical specialist
Official who identifies the technical elements performed by the skater and their level of difficulty. The information is then transmitted to the judges.

dance blade
Blade whose heel is shorter and whose toe picks are less pronounced to facilitate the execution of complex movements and to prevent the toe picks from catching.

free skating blade
Blade with toe picks that facilitate the execution of jumps and spins; its curvature is more pronounced than that of the dance blade.

SPORTS AND GAMES

snowboarding

Sport that consists of sliding over a snow-covered surface on a board fitted with foot bindings; the snowboard is steered by bending the knees.

snowboarder
Athlete who practices snowboarding; the snowboarder usually specializes in one particular discipline.

helmet
Rigid piece of equipment that is designed to protect the head; helmets are mandatory for racing.

goggles
Equipment that protects the eyes against the sun and the elements; the filtered lenses optimize depth perception.

coveralls
Skintight one-piece garment that reduces air resistance.

glove
Covering for the hand and wrist that protects them against the cold and snow in the event of a fall.

shin guard
Piece of equipment made of hard molded plastic that protects the snowboarder's legs.

snowboard
Board with foot bindings that is designed for sliding over snow-covered surfaces.

flexible boot
Flexible boot that is designed for freestyle
and all-terrain snowboarding; it allows the
snowboarder to perform a broad range of
movements and figures.

hard boot
Boot used for alpine events; it provides
firm support and makes it possible to
immediately transfer body movement
to the board.

freestyle snowboard
Wide flexible snowboard used for figures;
the nose and tail are identical so that the
snowboarder can take off and land in both
directions.

soft binding
Binding used with flexible boots; the soft
binding has straps to secure the foot and
padded ankle supports.

alpine snowboard
Long narrow rigid snowboard that is
designed to reach high speeds.

plate binding
Binding used with hard boots; it has a
metal toeplate that keeps the boot firmly
in place to provide maximum stability.

nose
Front end of the snowboard; its slightly
upturned curve cuts through the snow
and helps to avoid catching an edge.

tail
Back end of the snowboard; unlike the
tail of the freestyle snowboard, the
alpine snowboard tail is not designed
for going backward.

edge
Metal edge along the sole of the
snowboard; the edge digs into the
snow and makes turning possible.

SPORTS AND GAMES

alpine skiing

Sport that consists of racing on alpine skis down a snow-covered slope with a medium or steep drop.

ski
Long board with foot bindings that is designed for gliding over a snow-covered surface; it is usually made of wood or composite fibers.

safety binding
Device that attaches the boot to the ski; it features an automatic release system that frees the boot when too much pressure is exerted on it.

shovel
Front end of the ski; its upward curve cuts through snow and helps to avoid catching an edge.

tip
Rounded end of the shovel.

tail
Back end of the ski.

edge
Metal edge that runs along the bottom of the ski; it bites into the snow and makes turning possible.

ski boot
Rigid boot made of plastic or composite materials; the front and back of the ski boot attach to the ski.

inner boot
Often removable padded lining designed to keep the feet warm and to provide comfort.

tongue
Piece that extends from the inner boot and protects the foot from rubbing against the binding system; it is raised to slip the foot into the inner boot.

upper
Reinforcement at the back of the boot.

upper strap
Strap that is attached to the upper to tighten the upper cuff.

buckle
Clip made up of a metal ring that fits into an adjusting catch to tighten the ski boot.

adjusting catch
Groove in which the buckle latches; each adjusting catch corresponds to a different tightness.

hinge
Piece connecting the upper and lower shells.

sole
Sturdy piece that forms the bottom of the ski boot; it has molds at the heel and toe that fit into the binding.

alpine skier
Athlete who practices alpine skiing; alpine skiers often specialize in one or more of four events.

helmet
Rigid piece of equipment that is designed to protect the head; helmets are mandatory for racing.

ski goggles
Equipment that protects the eyes against the sun and the elements; the filtered lenses optimize depth perception.

ski suit
Skintight one-piece garment that reduces air resistance; various protective devices can be added, depending on the event.

basket
Circular piece attached to the bottom of the ski pole; it prevents the pole from sinking too deeply into the snow.

ski glove
Covering for the hand and wrist that protects them against the cold and bad weather; padded but flexible, it provides a solid grip on the handle.

ski pole
Metal or composite fiber rod with a handle and a basket; the ski pole is used for maintaining balance and for turning.

groove
Indentation along the bottom that improves glide and stability on straightaways.

handle

ski boot
Rigid boot made of plastic or composite materials; the front and back of the ski boot attach to the ski.

wrist strap
Strap that is attached to the handle and worn around the wrist to prevent the skier from losing a pole when sticking it into the ground.

bottom
Carefully polished piece that forms the bottom of the ski; a wax suited to snow conditions is applied to the bottom to obtain the best possible glide.

ski
Long board with foot bindings that is designed for gliding over a snow-covered surface; it is usually made of wood or composite fibers.

ski resort

Resort area with the facilities required for skiing and snowboarding; it also lodges skiers and snowboarders.

intermediate slope
Relatively steep slope geared to intermediate skiers and snowboarders who know the basics of their sport.

gondola
Mechanical lift made up of a series of closed cabins that are suspended from a single cable; skis and snowboards are hung outside the cabin.

chair lift
Mechanical lift that is suspended from a single cable; it is made up of a series of seats for two to eight skiers or snowboarders who wear their equipment while going up and down.

easy slope
Wide gentle and well-cleared slope for skiing and snowboarding beginners.

summit
Highest point on the mountain; it marks the starting point of most alpine ski trails.

ski area
Network of trails that makes up a ski resort; they can be built on one or more slopes, on one mountain or on adjacent mountains.

expert slope
Extremely difficult slope geared to expert skiers and snowboarders; these slopes are usually very steep and include moguls and tight turns.

difficult slope
Steep slope geared to experienced skiers and snowboarders.

alpine ski trail
Slope groomed for alpine skiing or snowboarding; a sign indicates the level of difficulty by means of a pictogram.

lodging
The businesses, buildings and dwellings that make it possible to enjoy a relatively long-term stay at a ski resort.

patrol and first aid station
Building reserved for the ski patrol; it houses equipment for administering first aid to injured or sick skiers.

main lodge
Building that brings together various services such as restaurants, bars, boutiques and day care.

cross-country skiing

Sport that consists of skiing over snow-covered surfaces on gently sloping terrain using a variety of techniques (skating step, diagonal step).

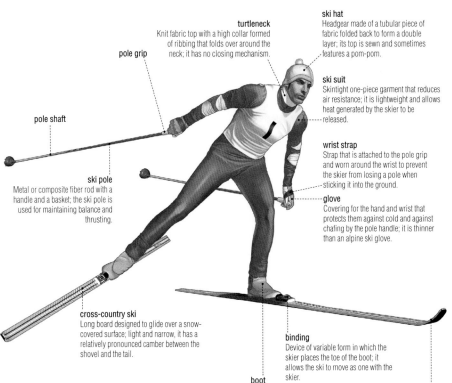

cross-country skier
Athlete who practices cross-country skiing; this athlete takes part in various individual (classic, freestyle, pursuit, sprint) and team (relay) events.

ski hat
Headgear made of a tubular piece of fabric folded back to form a double layer; its top is sewn and sometimes features a pom-pom.

turtleneck
Knit fabric top with a high collar formed of ribbing that folds over around the neck; it has no closing mechanism.

pole grip

ski suit
Skintight one-piece garment that reduces air resistance; it is lightweight and allows heat generated by the skier to be released.

pole shaft

wrist strap
Strap that is attached to the pole grip and worn around the wrist to prevent the skier from losing a pole when sticking it into the ground.

ski pole
Metal or composite fiber rod with a handle and a basket; the ski pole is used for maintaining balance and thrusting.

glove
Covering for the hand and wrist that protects them against cold and against chafing by the pole handle; it is thinner than an alpine ski glove.

cross-country ski
Long board designed to glide over a snow-covered surface; light and narrow, it has a relatively pronounced camber between the shovel and the tail.

binding
Device of variable form in which the skier places the toe of the boot; it allows the ski to move as one with the skier.

boot
Lightweight flexible boot that provides good ankle mobility; the skating step requires a more rigid boot than the traditional boot.

shovel
Front end of the ski; its upward curve cuts through snow and helps to avoid catching an edge.

SPORTS AND GAMES

1025

snowshoes

Wide soles that come in a variety of shapes and are fitted to boots; snowshoes are used to walk on snow without sinking.

elliptical snowshoe
Snowshoe with rounded ends and no tail; it is made of synthetic materials and is easy to maneuver in wooded areas.

deck
Piece of synthetic fabric that is attached to the frame; it bears the snowshoer's weight and prevents sinking into the snow.

crampon system
Metal points that are placed under the harness to improve traction on hard snow and ice.

aluminum frame
The frame of the snowshoe varies in length and width, depending on the expected use; lightweight and sturdy, the frame allows the snowshoer to glide over the snow.

Michigan snowshoe
Wooden snowshoe with a long tail; it is especially suited to walking in a straight line in open areas.

tip
Rounded, slightly raised front end of the snowshoe.

body
Central part of the snowshoe that supports the snowshoer's foot.

frame
The outline of the snowshoe is traditionally made of wood.

toe hole
Opening that allows the foot to move forward; this provides a natural walking motion and improves traction.

tail
The elongated part at the back of the snowshoe; it acts as a rudder to facilitate walking in a straight line.

master cord
Part of the lacing that supports the harness and on which the foot pivots when walking.

front crossbar
Crossbar in front of the harness that strengthens the frame; the lacing is attached to it.

lacing
The interlaced leather straps that are stretched across the frame; it bears the snowshoer's weight and prevents sinking into the snow.

back crossbar
Crossbar behind the harness that strengthens the frame; the lacing is attached to it.

harness
Device that attaches the boot to the snowshoe but allows the foot to pivot freely.

in-line skating

Range of activities that use skates fitted with small wheels: hockey, sprints, acrobatics on ramps or specially designed tracks, etc.

in-line skate
Reinforced boot with four wheels placed in a straight line; it is used to move around on a hard, relatively smooth surface.

inner boot
Cushioned, often removable lining that is designed for greater comfort inside the boot.

upper shell
Part of the boot that covers the lower part of the leg; it is usually hinged at the ankle.

adjusting buckle
Clip made up of a metal ring that fits into an adjusting catch to tighten the boot.

boot
Ankle boot that protects the foot and ankle; depending on the intended use, it can be soft, semisoft or hard (shell).

heel stop
Rubber pad at the back of the skate that enables the skater to slow down or stop.

wheel
Round object that turns on an axis so the skate can move backward or forward.

axle
Wheel's rotational axis that connects it to the frame.

truck
Device that connects the wheels to the boot.

skateboarding

Sport that involves descents, turns and tricks on a specially designed or improvised surface; the skateboarder uses a board mounted on small wheels.

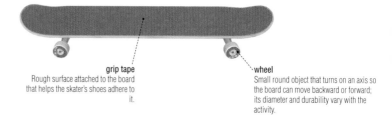

grip tape
Rough surface attached to the board that helps the skater's shoes adhere to it.

wheel
Small round object that turns on an axis so the board can move backward or forward; its diameter and durability vary with the activity.

ramp
Wooden U-shaped track that is set up for performing various acrobatic stunts (such as jumps and slides).

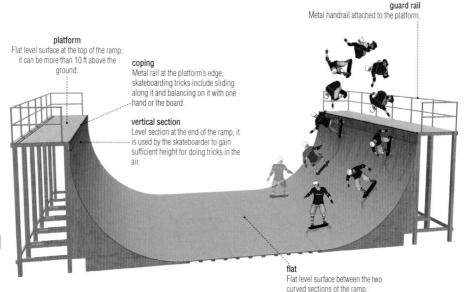

guard rail
Metal handrail attached to the platform.

platform
Flat level surface at the top of the ramp; it can be more than 10 ft above the ground.

coping
Metal rail at the platform's edge; skateboarding tricks include sliding along it and balancing on it with one hand or the board.

vertical section
Level section at the end of the ramp; it is used by the skateboarder to gain sufficient height for doing tricks in the air.

flat
Flat level surface between the two curved sections of the ramp.

skateboard
Wooden, usually concave board mounted on four small wheels; it is guided by body movements.

tail
Rear end of the board.

nose
Front end of the board.

truck
Device that connects the wheels to the board; it enables the wheels to change direction.

skateboarder
Athlete who skateboards; because of the risk of injury from falling, the athlete usually wears several pieces of protective equipment.

knee pad
Piece of equipment made of hard molded plastic that protects the knee.

elbow pad
Piece of equipment with a hard outer shell that is used to protect the elbow.

helmet
Hard piece of equipment designed to protect the head.

coping
Metal rail at the platform's edge; skateboarding tricks include sliding along it and balancing on it with one hand or the board.

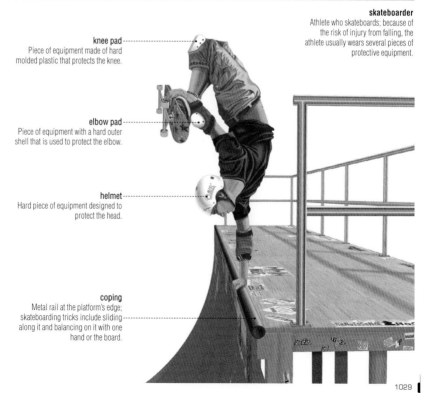

camping

Tourist activity that consists of sleeping in a portable shelter such as a tent or trailer and traveling with equipment designed for outdoor living.

examples of tents

Tents: portable waterproof soft-sided shelters that are stretched taut over a frame and temporarily pitched outdoors.

two-person tent
Tent that can accommodate two people.

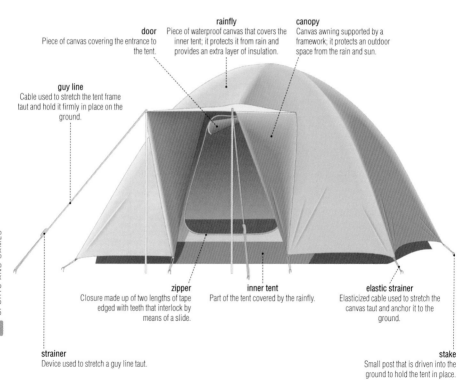

door
Piece of canvas covering the entrance to the tent.

rainfly
Piece of waterproof canvas that covers the inner tent; it protects it from rain and provides an extra layer of insulation.

canopy
Canvas awning supported by a framework; it protects an outdoor space from the rain and sun.

guy line
Cable used to stretch the tent frame taut and hold it firmly in place on the ground.

zipper
Closure made up of two lengths of tape edged with teeth that interlock by means of a slide.

inner tent
Part of the tent covered by the rainfly.

elastic strainer
Elasticized cable used to stretch the canvas taut and anchor it to the ground.

strainer
Device used to stretch a guy line taut.

stake
Small post that is driven into the ground to hold the tent in place.

wagon tent
Spacious tent with sufficient interior capacity to accommodate a number of people or group activities.

pop-up tent
Round tent with a framework that deploys automatically.

pup tent
Tent where the canvas is stretched taut on both sides of a summit rod, which is supported by two poles.

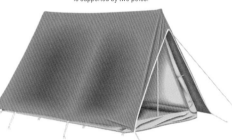

one-person tent
Small low-roofed tent with enough room to accommodate one person.

dome tent
Semicircular tent that, once pitched, can be moved without being taken down.

wall tent
Very spacious, rectangular tent that often has a number of interior dividers; it accommodates a number of people.

camping

examples of sleeping bags

Sleeping bags: insulated fabric coverings that close with a
zipper and are used to stay warm when sleeping outdoors.

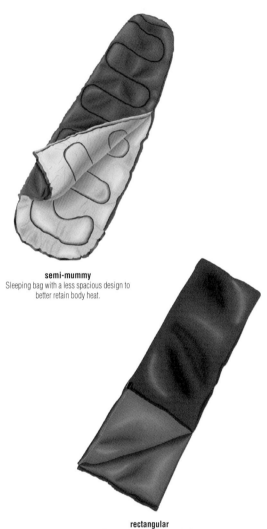

semi-mummy
Sleeping bag with a less spacious design to
better retain body heat.

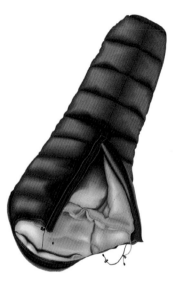

mummy
Sleeping bag shaped like the body; it has a
part that covers the head and neck with an
opening for the face.

rectangular
Rectangular sleeping bag that is
spacious enough to give the body
room to move.

inflator
Device used to inflate air mattresses.

bed and mattress
Accessories that a person lies down on
to sleep or rest.

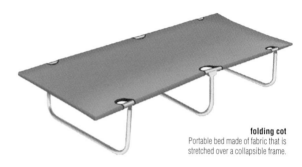

inflator-deflator
Device used to inflate and deflate air mattresses.

folding cot
Portable bed made of fabric that is
stretched over a collapsible frame.

self-inflating mattress
Rubber, plastic or nylon bag that inflates with air
by itself, without the need of an inflator.

air mattress
Rubber or plastic bag that is filled with
air; it usually has a pillow.

foam pad
Long thin cushion made of soft
material.

propane or butane accessories
Complete range of portable appliances that run on liquid or gas fuel and are used to light, cook or heat.

lantern
Safe portable light source that can be used both inside and outside a tent.

globe
Translucent or transparent heat-resistant covering that protects the light source and diffuses its light.

burner frame
Aluminum housing protecting the burner.

pressure regulator
Device that controls the pressure of the vaporized fuel and adjusts the light's brightness.

pump
Device that increases the air pressure inside the tank so the fuel vaporizes.

leakproof cap
Stopper for the fuel refill opening; it is threaded to prevent leakage.

single-burner camp stove
Single-burner appliance used to cook and reheat food.

tank
Canister containing the liquid fuel and air that supply the burner.

double-burner camp stove
Two-burner appliance used to cook and reheat food.

burner
Combustion device for an air-gas mixture.

wire support
Metal grill used as a base to support cooking utensils.

control valve
Device that switches the fuel intake on and off and adjusts its volume of flow.

tank
Canister containing the pressurized fuel that supplies the burners.

SPORTS AND GAMES

camping equipment
Range of accessories used when camping to store
food, cut wood, etc.

ruler
Instrument for measuring length.

Swiss Army knife
Multipurpose knife with a large assortment of
blades and instruments.

scissors
Instrument with two movable
overlapping shanks having sharp
inside edges; they are used for
trimming and cutting.

fish scaler
Jagged blade used to scale fish.

file
Ridged metal blade used to smooth
pieces of wood or plastic.

cross-tip screwdriver
Screwdriver whose tip has two crossed
ridges that fit into the head of a cross-head
screw.

magnifier
Converging lens that magnifies the
image of an object.

pen blade
Small thin piece of metal with a sharp
edge used as a secondary knife for
more delicate tasks.

can opener
Tool used to open cans by cutting
along the inside edge of the lid.

bottle opener
Instrument used to remove caps from
bottles.

screwdriver
Hand tool used for tightening or
loosening screws and bolts by
applying a rotating motion.

screwdriver
Hand tool used for tightening or
loosening screws and bolts by
applying a rotating motion.

nail nick
Part where the fingernail is inserted; it
is used to deploy the tool.

awl
Pointed instrument used to make
holes.

large blade
Long thin solid piece of metal with a
sharp edge that is the main knife.

corkscrew
Device shaped like a spiral; it is used
to draw the cork out of a bottle of wine.

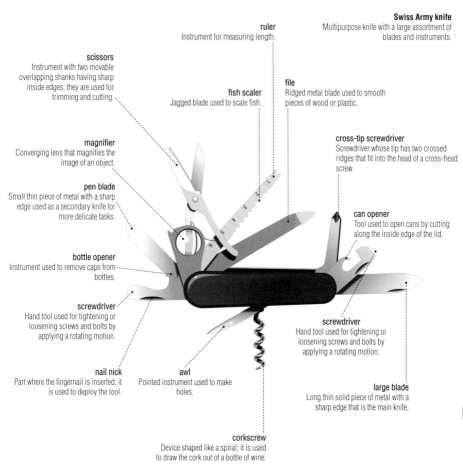

SPORTS AND GAMES

camping

backpack
Travel or hiking bag that is worn on the back and is used to transport clothing, camping equipment, etc.

top flap
Piece of fabric that folds over the opening of the backpack.

shoulder strap
Fabric band of variable length that goes over the shoulder so the bag can be carried on the back.

tightening buckle
Device used to adjust the length of the strap.

side compression strap
Fabric band that reduces the size of the bag and keeps the contents in place.

front compression strap
Fabric band connected to the top flap strap and used to fasten the backpack.

waist belt
Fabric strap that fits snugly around the hips and buckles there; it is designed to distribute the bag's weight.

strap loop
Buckle through which the strap passes.

vacuum bottle
Container with a vacuum between the inner and insulated outer walls; it is designed to maintain its contents at a desired temperature.

cooler
Thermally insulated chest that is used to keep food cold with ice cubes or blocks of ice.

bottle
Container used to hold liquids or semisolid foods.

stopper
Part used to close the neck of the bottle.

cup
Cap used as a container to consume liquid or semisolid foods.

water carrier
Container with a spigot that is used to store drinking water when camping.

magnetic compass
Instrument for finding directions; it has a graduated compass card and a magnetic needle that points toward magnetic north.

sighting mirror
Polished glass surface that reflects the image of the compass card and confirms the direction of travel.

sight
Device used to select a landmark in the direction a person chooses to walk.

sighting line
Line running parallel to the baselines; it is used to indicate the direction of travel.

magnetic needle
Pointer with a red magnetized part that points to Earth's magnetic north pole.

cover
Compartment that contains the mirror and protects the compass card when it is folded over the base plate.

edge
Compass card marks where the needle's red dot comes to rest when the compass is aligned with magnetic north.

pivot
Point around which the magnetic needle moves.

scale
Graduated line used to judge the distance to be traveled on a topographic map, in conjunction with the map's scale.

compass meridian line
Line that, when matched with the meridian line on a map, can be used to determine the direction of travel in degrees.

compass card
Rotating device that is graduated in degrees and marked with the four cardinal points; it is used to indicate the direction of travel with respect to true north.

baseline
Line marked on the base plate that is placed on top of a topographic map; it shows the direction of the place toward which the person wishes to travel.

graduated dial
Each of the equal intervals marked on the dial that indicate the angle in degrees of the points on the compass card.

base plate
Transparent surface that supports the compass card and has markings and scales.

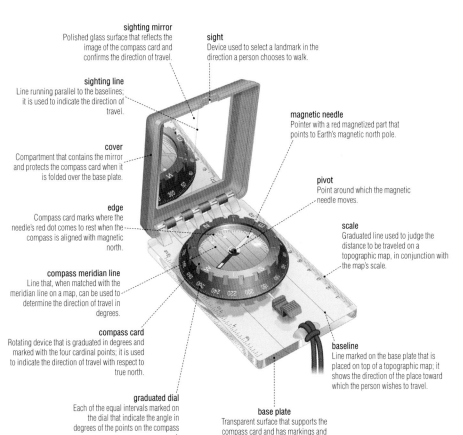

SPORTS AND GAMES

fishing

Outdoor leisure activity consisting of trying to catch fish with a fishing rod.

flyfishing
Fishing method that consists of delicately placing an artificial fly on or in the water; it simulates a real insect landing to attract fish.

fly rod
Thin sturdy stick that is flexible enough to cast a hook disguised as a winged insect (artificial fly) far over the water.

butt cap
Usually metal covering over the end of the rod to protect the rod from contact with the ground.

butt section
Sturdiest section of a rod; it holds the handgrip and the reel.

keeper ring
Circle where the fishhook hitches on to keep the fly line running along the length of the rod when it is not being used.

male ferrule
Metal tubing that fits into the female ferrule to join the two sections of the rod (butt section and tip section).

screw locking nut
Ring used to hold the reel in place on the reel seat.

handgrip
Part used to pick up and handle the rod.

guide
One of the metal parts through which the fly line runs; they are used to guide it.

reel seat
Device that attaches the reel to the rod.

tip section
Thinner and more flexible section of a rod.

tip-ring
Circle at the end of a flyfishing rod's tip.

female ferrule
Metal tubing into which the male ferrule fits to join the two sections of the rod (butt section and tip section).

artificial fly
Arrangement of thread and feathers attached to a fishhook that imitates a winged insect; it can be cast over the water (dry fly) or into the water (wet fly).

casting
Fishing that consists of letting a hook drop and sink into the water and reeling it back in to simulate the movement of a small fish.

spinning rod
Stick whose length and sturdiness varies with the kind of fishing being done; it is used to cast a hook carried along by a weight, sinker or spinner far over the water.

screw locking nut
Ring used to hold the reel in place on the reel seat.

reel seat
Device that attaches the reel to the rod.

male ferrule
Metal tubing that fits into the female ferrule to join the two sections of the rod (butt section and tip section).

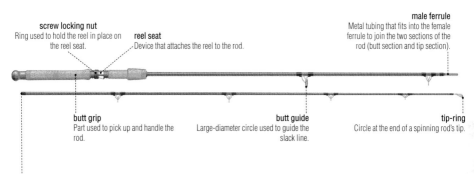

butt grip
Part used to pick up and handle the rod.

butt guide
Large-diameter circle used to guide the slack line.

tip-ring
Circle at the end of a spinning rod's tip.

female ferrule
Metal tubing into which the male ferrule fits to join the two sections of the rod (butt section and tip section).

fishhook
Metal hook of variable size attached to the end of float tackle and baited with a natural or artificial lure intended to catch a fish.

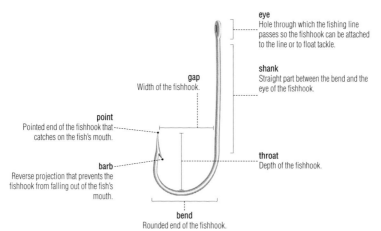

eye
Hole through which the fishing line passes so the fishhook can be attached to the line or to float tackle.

gap
Width of the fishhook.

shank
Straight part between the bend and the eye of the fishhook.

point
Pointed end of the fishhook that catches on the fish's mouth.

throat
Depth of the fishhook.

barb
Reverse projection that prevents the fishhook from falling out of the fish's mouth.

bend
Rounded end of the fishhook.

SPORTS AND GAMES

fishing

clothing and accessories

fishing vest
Sleeveless jacket with many pockets for carrying small objects (license, sinkers, etc.).

tackle box
Compartmentalized box used to store and carry bait and fishing equipment.

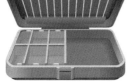

waders
Thigh-high rubber boots used to fish in shallow water.

creel
Basket used to store and carry the catch.

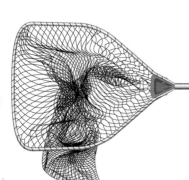

landing net
Net attached to a frame at the end of a handle; it is used to take a fish out of the water.

Outdoor activity that consists of lying in wait for or pursuing game in order to kill it.

rifle (rifled bore)
Portable firearm that shoots a single bullet: the grooved inside of the barrel imparts a spinning motion to the bullet that increases the accuracy of its trajectory.

shotgun (smooth-bore)
Portable firearm where the inside of the barrel has no grooves; it can shoot a number of lead, copper or nickel pellets at a time.

decoy
Plastic or wooden lure used to attract wild ducks.

snare
Trap consisting of a steel cable ending in a slipknot; it is used to capture small game by the neck and strangle them.

leghold trap
Apparatus meant to capture an animal by the paw.

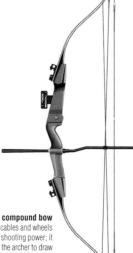

compound bow
Bow with a system of cables and wheels that increases its shooting power; it requires less effort for the archer to draw back the bowstring.

SPORTS AND GAMES

cards

Rectangular pieces of cardboard used to play various games; they have figures, signs and numbers on one side and are divided into four suits.

symbols

The colors, figures and signs on a deck of cards.

diamond
Red suit in a deck of cards that is shaped like a lozenge; this suit has the second-highest value.

spade
Black suit in a deck of cards that is shaped like a spearhead; this suit has the lowest value.

heart
Red suit in a deck of cards that is shaped like a heart; this suit has the highest value.

club
Black suit in a deck of cards that is shaped like a cloverleaf; this suit has the third-highest value.

ace
Card with a single sign that usually has the highest value in the suit.

queen
Figure depicting a queen that usually has the third-highest value in the suit.

joker
Card depicting a court jester; in most games, its value is the cardholder's choice.

king
Figure depicting a king that usually has the second-highest value in the suit.

jack
Figure depicting an equerry that usually has the fourth-highest value in the suit.

high card
When none of the five cards in the hand can be combined with any other, the highest-ranked card is played.

two pairs
Contains two pairs.

flush
Contains five nonconsecutive cards of the same suit.

four-of-a-kind
Contains four cards of equal value.

one pair
Contains two cards of equal value.

three-of-a-kind
Contains three cards of equal value.

straight flush
Contains five consecutive cards of the same suit.

standard poker hands

A poker hand consists of five cards whose combination confers a relative value on which the player bets; they have an ascending order of value.

straight
Contains five consecutive cards of different suits.

full house
Contains a three-of-a-kind and a pair.

royal flush
Contains five consecutive cards of the same suit, from the 10 to the ace.

SPORTS AND GAMES

dice and dominoes

Cubes (dice) or pieces divided into two ends (dominoes) with numbers indicated by pips or figures.

dominoes
Game that consists of setting up pieces in sequence according to their value, with adjoining pieces being identical.

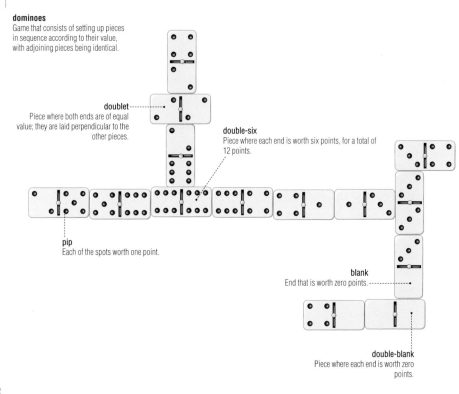

doublet
Piece where both ends are of equal value; they are laid perpendicular to the other pieces.

double-six
Piece where each end is worth six points, for a total of 12 points.

pip
Each of the spots worth one point.

blank
End that is worth zero points.

double-blank
Piece where each end is worth zero points.

ordinary die
Small cube marked on each side with one to six pips; it is used in various games (backgammon, Monopoly®, Yahtzee®, etc.).

poker die
Small cube marked on each side with card symbols; it is used to play poker dice, a game similar to poker, which is played with five dice.

SPORTS AND GAMES

board games

Complete range of games that use a playing surface on which game pieces (tokens, dice, counters, etc.) are placed.

backgammon
Game of strategy in which two players move checkers around a board; players try to collect and bear them off while preventing the opponent's checkers from moving.

outer table
Area with 12 points that the checkers must move across to reach the inner table; opponents move in opposite directions.

inner table
Table that a player's checkers must enter before they can be borne off; the player who first bears off all his or her checkers wins the game.

dice cup
Container used to shake and throw the dice.

die
One of the two small cubes marked on each side with one to six pips; the checker moves the same number of points as the number rolled.

red
Red checkers that belong to one player.

doubling die
Die used to increase the game's stakes.

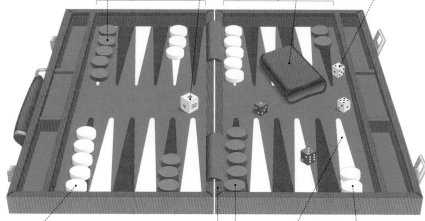

white
White checkers that belong to one player.

bar
Line that divides the board's inner and outer tables; the checkers hit by the opposing player are placed on it.

point
Each of the spaces on which the checkers are placed.

checkers
Each of the counters used to play; the checkers are moved from one point to the next based on the number of pips shown on the dice.

runner
One of two checkers belonging to a player placed at the start of the game on the opponent's inner table; it must leave that position before any other checkers of the same color can be moved.

SPORTS AND GAMES

chess
Game where two players move pieces around a board in order to "checkmate" the opponent (i.e., attack the king in such a manner that no escape is possible).

chessboard
Board divided into 64 black and white squares; the corner square on each player's left must be black.

queen's side
Each of the pieces in columns a to d on the board.

king's side
Each of the pieces in columns e to h on the board.

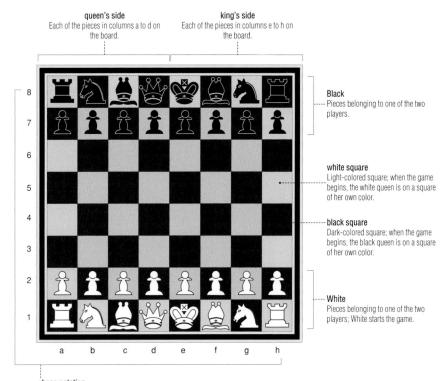

Black
Pieces belonging to one of the two players.

white square
Light-colored square; when the game begins, the white queen is on a square of her own color.

black square
Dark-colored square; when the game begins, the black queen is on a square of her own color.

White
Pieces belonging to one of the two players; White starts the game.

chess notation
Means of using letters and numbers to identify the chessboard squares; it is used to situate pieces, transcribe games, follow moves, etc.

types of movements
Each piece moves in a specific way:
diagonally, vertically, horizontally or in
a square.

diagonal movement
Forward or backward movement along
an oblique line.

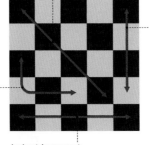
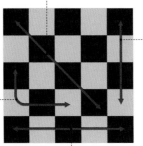

vertical movement
Moving forward or backward along a
column.

square movement
Moving one square forward or backward and
then two squares laterally, or two squares
forward or backward and then one square
laterally.

horizontal movement
Moving to the right or left along a row.

chess pieces
At the beginning of the game, each player has
16 pieces with different moves and value: a
king, a queen, two rooks, two bishops, two
knights and eight pawns.

pawn
Piece that can advance one square at a
time except at the beginning of the game,
when it can advance one or two squares; it
captures opposing pieces diagonally.

rook
Piece that can move backward or
forward horizontally or vertically for as
many squares as the player chooses.

bishop
Piece that can move backward or
forward diagonally for as many
squares as the player chooses.

knight
Piece that can move at right angles
(square movement); the knight is the
only piece that can jump over any other
piece.

king
The most important piece in the game;
it can move backward or forward in all
directions one square at a time.

queen
The most powerful attack piece; it can
move backward or forward in all
directions for as many squares as the
player chooses.

SPORTS AND GAMES

video entertainment system

Group of units (game console and visual display) that allows a person to control the action in a game displayed on a screen by means of a controller.

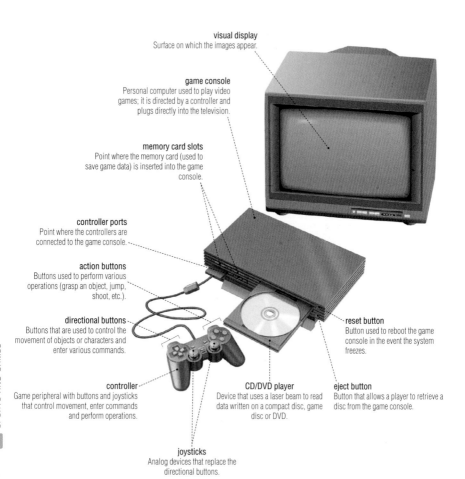

visual display
Surface on which the images appear.

game console
Personal computer used to play video games; it is directed by a controller and plugs directly into the television.

memory card slots
Point where the memory card (used to save game data) is inserted into the game console.

controller ports
Point where the controllers are connected to the game console.

action buttons
Buttons used to perform various operations (grasp an object, jump, shoot, etc.).

directional buttons
Buttons that are used to control the movement of objects or characters and enter various commands.

controller
Game peripheral with buttons and joysticks that control movement, enter commands and perform operations.

reset button
Button used to reboot the game console in the event the system freezes.

CD/DVD player
Device that uses a laser beam to read data written on a compact disc, game disc or DVD.

eject button
Button that allows a player to retrieve a disc from the game console.

joysticks
Analog devices that replace the directional buttons.

0° 918
1/10 second hand 903
1,500 m starting line 953
1 astronomical unit 3
10,000 m relay starting line 953
100 m hurdles starting line 952
100 m starting line 952
110 m hurdles starting line 952
120-volt circuit 465
130° 918
200 m line 1005
240-volt circuit 465
240-volt feeder cable 465
240° 918
35 mm still camera 20
360° 918
4 x 400 m relay starting line 953
45° 918
50 astronomical units 2
500 m finish line 1015
500 m start line 1014
5,000 m starting line 952
90° 918

A

abacus 685, 686
abalone 368
abdomen 165, 166, 174, 178, 197, 244, 248
abdominal aorta 270, 280
abdominal cavity 292, 296
abducens nerve 290
aboveground pipeline 932
abruptly pinnate 101
absorbed solar radiation 78
absorbing plate 947
absorption by clouds 78
absorption by Earth surface 78
absorption of water and mineral salts 98
abutment 694, 797, 798, 799
abyssal hill 55
abyssal plain 55
acanthus leaf 472, 687
acceleration lane 794
accelerator control 155
access gallery 937
access road 867
access server 765
access to the second level of operations 772
access window 762
accessory nerve 290
accessory pouch 999
accessory shoe 650
accordion 658
accordion bag 640
accordion pleat 580

account book 788
accuracy sports 996
ace 1042
achene 116, 120
acid rain 82, 83
acid snow 83
acorn nut 535
acorn squash 329
acoustic ceiling 649
acoustic guitar 665
acoustic meatus 301, 302
acromion 257
acroterion 682, 685
action buttons 1048
action lever 670
action of wind 76
active tracking 715
actress 647
actual temperature 450
actuator arm 760
actuator arm motor 760
acute angle 917, 918
Adam's apple 245
add key 771
add/equals key 773
additional production personnel 705
additive color synthesis 891
adductor longus 252
adductor magnus 254
adhesive disk 187
adipose tissue 291, 299
adjustable channel 533
adjustable clamp 494
adjustable frame 519
adjustable lamp 494
adjustable strap 594
adjustable thermostat 420
adjusting buckle 1027
adjusting catch 1022
adjusting screw 533, 536, 537
adjustment slide 564
adventitious roots 92
advertisement 698
advertising panel 846
advertising sign 849
adzuki bean 335
aerial cable network 700
aerocyst 90
aerodynamic brake 949
affluent 50
Africa 29
African Plate 41
Afro pick 616
aft shroud 18
after shave 623
afterbay 935, 937
afterfeather 199
agar-agar 314
agitator 508
AGP expansion connector 747
aikido 991
aikidogi 991

aikidoka 991
aileron 868
air bubbles 779
air chamber 462, 463
air communications 702
air compression unit 838
air compressor 841
air concentrator 619
air conditioner 812
air conditioner compressor 811
air conditioning equipment 861
air conditioning system 80
air filter 155, 841
air horn 816
air hose 983
air inlet 828, 874
air inlet control 449
air intake 814
air mattress 1033
air motor 760
air shaft 684
air transport 866
air unit 598
air-conditioning appliances 450
air-inlet grille 619
air-outlet grille 619
airliner 62
airport 866
ala 305
alarm/charge indicator light 770
albatross 206
alcohol bulb 900
alcohol column 900
alfalfa 332
alga 90
alga, structure 90
algae, examples 91
alkaline manganese-zinc cell 885
alkekengi 339
all-season tire 808
all-terrain vehicle 831
alley 969, 972
alligator 195
alluvial deposits 51
almond 111, 340
alphabetical keypad 774
alphanumeric keypad 733, 748
alpine ski trail 1024
alpine skier 1023
alpine skiing 1022
alpine snowboard 1021
Alsace glass 380
alternate key 748
alternator 810, 951
altocumulus 66
altostratus 66
alula 198
aluminum frame 1026
aluminum layer 722

alveolar bone 267
American bacon 363
American corn bread 355
American football, playing field 960
amethyst 604
amoeba 160
amorphous solid 877
amount of substance, measurement 913
ampere 912
amphibians 184
amphibians, examples 187
amphibious fire-fighting aircraft 871
amphitheater, Roman 690
ampli-tuner 716, 717, 724
amplifier 714
amplitude 889
ampulla of fallopian tube 294
anal fin 181, 183
analog watch 905
analytical balance 909
anatomy 252
anatomy of a sponge 162
anatomy of a turtle 192
anatomy of a venomous snake 188
anchor point 175
anchor-windlass room 859
anchorage block 799
anchovy 372
anconeus 254
andouillette 365
anemometer 951
angles, examples 918
animal cell 158
anise 350
ankle 244, 248
ankle boot 551
ankle length 565
ankle/wrist weight 995
anklet 592
annular eclipse 7
annulet 685
anode 884, 885
anorak 601
ant 169
Antarctic Circle 30, 32
Antarctic Plate 41
Antarctica 28
antefix 683
antelope 218
antenna 18, 164, 167, 179, 729, 732, 805, 829, 874, 965
antenna terminals 717
antennule 171
anterior horn 285
anterior nasal spine 262
anterior notch 301
anterior tibial artery 270
anterior tibialis 252

anterior view 244, 248, 252, 256
anther 105
anti-torque tail rotor 875
anticline 931
antihelix 301
antireflection coating 946
antiskating device 721
antitragus 301
antivibration handle 155
anus 192, 278, 293, 297
aorta 272, 277
aorta, arch 270, 273
aortic valve 273
aperture 652
aperture door 18
apex 267, 308
apical foramen 267
apocrine sweat gland 298
apothecium 86
apple 346
apple corer 405
apple, section 119
application launch buttons 770
appointment book 776
approach 953
approach ramp 799
approach runs 974
apricot 337
apron 472, 476, 477, 830, 867, 985
apsidiole 695
aquamarine 604
aquatic bird 202
arachnids 164
arachnids, examples 173
arachnoid 285
arame 314
arbitration committee 990
arbor 139
arc 919
arcade 690, 694
arch 798
arch bridge 798
arch of aorta 270, 273
arch of foot artery 270
archboard 785
archer 999
archery 999
archipelago 35
architectural styles 685
architecture 684
architrave 682, 687
Arctic 28
Arctic Circle 30, 32
Arctic Ocean 29
arena 690, 691, 952
areola 291
Ariane IV 27
Ariel 5
arm 149, 163, 238, 246, 250, 472, 493, 494, 897
arm elevator 721

UNIVERSE AND EARTH > 2-83;   PLANTS AND GARDENING > 84-157;   ANIMAL KINGDOM > 158-243;   THE HUMAN BEING > 244-311;   FOOD AND KITCHEN > 312-429;
HOUSE AND DO-IT-YOURSELF > 430-543;   CLOTHING AND PERSONAL ACCESSORIES > 544-643;   ARTS AND ARCHITECTURE > 644-695;   COMMUNICATIONS AND
OFFICE AUTOMATION > 696-791;   TRANSPORTATION > 792-875;   SCIENCE AND ENERGY > 876-951;   SPORTS AND GAMES > 952-1048

arm guard 999
arm lock 989
arm rest 721
arm slit 573
arm stump 472
armchair 472
armchairs, examples 473
armhole 566
armoire 478
armored cord 736
armpit 244, 248
armrest 488
arrector pili muscle 298
arris 685
arrow key 450
art director 646
arteries 270
artichoke 326
article 696
articulated bus 815
articulated joint 815
artificial fly 1038
artificial satellite 62
arugula 325
ascending aorta 269
ascending colon 279
ascending passage 684
ascot tie 562
ash layer 43
Asia 29
Asian pear 349
asparagus 319
asperity 722
ass 218
assistant camera operator 646
assistant coach 963
assistant judges 1015
assistant referee 1014, 1019
asteroid belt 3
asthenosphere 38
astigmatism 893
astragal 687
astronomical observatory 16
astronomical observatory, cross section 16
astronomical unit 3
athletic shirt 566
Atlantic cod 376
Atlantic Ocean 28
Atlantic salmon 377
atlas 264
atlas moth 172
atmosphere 83
atoll 58
atom 876
atoms 876
atrium 688
attaché case 633
attached curtain 490
attack line 964
attack zone 965
attitude control thrusters 24
attraction 888
audio control room 704
audio input/output jack 770
audio jack 745
audio system 807
audio technician 704
auditory meatus, external 263
auditory ossicles 303
auger bit, solid center 526

auricle, ear 301
aurora 62
Australia 29
Australian-Indian Plate 41
autofocus 652
automatic coupler 843
automatic dialer index 735
automatic drip coffee maker 423
automatic electronic timer 977
automatic sorting trays 743
automobile 802
automobile car 845
automobile transport semitrailer 821
autumn 63
autumn squash 329
autumnal equinox 63
auxiliary facilities room 705
auxiliary handle 524
auxiliary tank 818
avocado 327
awl 1035
axe 151
axillary artery 270
axillary bud 96
axillary nerve 283
axillary vein 271
axis 264
axle 1027
axon 288, 307
axon hillock 289

B

baboon 236
baby grand 671
back 196, 216, 225, 246, 250, 386, 388, 390, 392, 476, 488, 520, 559
back boundary line 968
back brush 621
back check 670
back crossbar 1026
back judge 961
back line 1012
back of a glove 557
back pocket 563
back ribs 366
back suspension 1006
back zone 965
backcourt 973
backdrop 648
backgammon 1045
backguard 505, 508, 511
backlighting button 713
backpack 1036
backrest 829
backspace key 749
backstay 852, 1018
backstop 958, 963
backstroke 978
backstroke turn indicator 977
bacon 363
bactrian camel 221
badger 220
badminton 968
badminton racket 970
bag compartment 499
bag well 1002
bagel 352

baggage compartment 814, 838, 875
baggage racks 860
bagpipes 659
baguette 352
bailey 692
Bailey bridge 800
baize 997
baking sheet 402
baking utensils 401
balaclava 544
balance beam 974
balance control 716
balancer 667
balcony 435
balcony window 435
balk area 996
balk line 996
balk line spot 996
ball 751
ball bearing 951
ball boy 972
ball peen 514
ball-cock supply valve 458
ball-peen hammer 514
ballerina shoe 550
balloon curtain 490
bamboo shoot 320
banana 347
band 720
band ring 607
band select button 716
band selector 715
bandage 986
bangle 608
banister 443
banjo 659
bank 793
banner 696
banquette 475
bar 628, 649, 681, 880, 995, 1045
bar code reader 752
bar frame 496
bar nose 154
bar stool 475
barb 199, 1039
barbell 992
barber comb 616
barley 123
barley: spike 123
barred spiral galaxy 13
barrel 618, 619
barrel vault 691
barrette 617
barrier 486
barrier beach 58
bartizan 693
basaltic layer 36
base 99, 420, 428, 448, 468, 469, 470, 493, 494, 523, 528, 687, 721, 752, 753, 754, 777, 792, 897, 906, 907, 949
base cabinet 378
base course 793
base of splat 472
base plate 522, 721, 1037
baseball 957
baseboard 441, 442
baseline 973, 1037
basement 432

basement window 431
basic operations 772
basil 350
basilic vein 271
basin wrench 540
basket 418, 423, 509, 1023
basketball 962
bass 374
bass bridge 668
bass clarinet 660
bass drum 661, 678
bass guitar 667
bass keyboard 658
bass pickup 666
bass register 658
bass tone control 667, 716, 725
bassoon 674
bassoons 660
baster 406
bat 242, 957
bat, morphology 242
bath brush 621
bath sheet 621
bath towel 621
bathing wrap 593
bathroom 434, 435, 456
bathroom scale 910
bathroom skylight 433
bathtub 434, 457
batten 648, 980, 981
batter head 678, 679
battery 516, 746, 840, 883
battery box 818
battery level 652
battlement 693
bay 8, 35
bay filler panel 744
bayonet base 467
beach 56
bead 809
beaker 398
beam 906
beam balance 906
beam bridge 797
bean bag chair 475
beans 332, 335
bearing pad 944
beater 413, 414
beater ejector 413, 414
beaters 415
beaver 213
becquerel 913
bed 483, 792, 1033
bed chamber 689
bed lamp 494
bedrock 97
bedroom 434
beech 131
beechnut 341
beef cubes 366
beef, cuts 366
beer mug 381
beet 331
beetle 169, 170
begonia 107
Belgian endive 325
bell 673, 677
bell bottoms 582
bell brace 673
bellows 658
bellows strap 658

bells 681
belly 216
belly scale 188
below-stage 648
belt 539, 564, 570
belt clip 730
belt loader 926
belt loop 563, 564, 570
beluga whale 235
bench 475, 847, 994
bend 629, 1039
beret 544
bergamot 342
bergère 473
bergschrund 46
Bering Sea 29
Bermuda shorts 582
berries 338
berry fruit 114
bertha collar 587
bevel gear 881
bevel square 538
bezel 606
bib 593, 594
bib necklace 603
biceps of arm 252
biceps of thigh 254
biconcave lens 894
biconvex lens 894
bicycle 832
bicycle, parts 832
bicycles, examples 834
bidet 456
bifocal lens 630
bikini 590
bikini briefs 567
bilberry 338
bill 197
bill compartment 635
bill-file 789
billfold 636
billhook 153
billiard cue 998
billiard spot 997
billiards 996
bills, examples 202
bimetallic helix 902
bimetallic thermometer 902
binding 546, 1025
biology 916
biplane 871
birch 130
bird 196
bird of prey 202
bird's nest fern 913
bird, morphology 196
bird, skeleton 200
birds 196
birds, examples 203
birth 916
bishop 1047
bison 221
bit 516, 930
bits 526
bits, examples 529
bitt 863
bitter melon 328
Black 1046
black 891
black bean 336
black bear 232
black currant 338

UNIVERSE AND EARTH > 2-83; PLANTS AND GARDENING > 84-157; ANIMAL KINGDOM > 158-243; THE HUMAN BEING > 244-311; FOOD AND KITCHEN > 312-429; HOUSE AND DO-IT-YOURSELF > 430-543; CLOTHING AND PERSONAL ACCESSORIES > 544-643; ARTS AND ARCHITECTURE > 644-695; COMMUNICATIONS AND OFFICE AUTOMATION > 696-791; TRANSPORTATION > 792-875; SCIENCE AND ENERGY > 876-951; SPORTS AND GAMES > 952-1048

black gram 336
black pollock 376
black radish 330
black rye bread 352
black salsify 331
black square 1046
black-and-white 652
black-eyed pea 334
blackberry 339
bladder 192
blade 92, 100, 390, 392,
  417, 427, 516, 517, 519,
  520, 521, 522, 523, 530,
  541, 624, 949, 950, 967,
  1018
blade injector 625
blade lift fan 860
blade tilting lock 522
blank 1044
blanket 485
blanket sleepers 595
blazer 581
blender 412
blending 412
blending attachment 416
blind spot mirror 813, 815
blinds 491
blinking lights 813
blog 767
blood circulation 269
blood circulation, schema
  269
blood factor negative 916
blood factor positive 916
blood sausage 365
blood vessel 298
blood vessels 243
blotting paper 779
blouses, examples 584
blow pipe 659
blower motor 451
blucher oxford 554
blue 891
blue band 1005
blue line 1010
blue mussel 369
blue-veined cheeses 361
blueberry 338
bluefish 375
blusher brush 612
BMX 1003
BMX bike 834
boa 193
board 981
board games 1045
boarding walkway 867
boards 1010
boater 547
boats 856
bobby pin 617
bobeche 497
bobstay 853
bodies, examples 802
body 308, 428, 498, 526,
  666, 667, 673, 804, 812,
  896, 1026
body care 620
body flap 25
body of fornix 287
body of nail 300
body shirt 584
body side molding 805

body suit 588
body temperature control unit
  21
bok choy 324
bokken 991
bole 128
bolero 581
bolster 390, 392, 484
bolt 533, 535, 537
bolts 535
bonding jumper 465
bongos 680
boning knife 393
bony fish 182
bony fishes 372
boom 822, 980
boom operator 647
boom vang 980
booster parachute 26
booster seat 488
boot 551, 983, 1009, 1018,
  1025, 1027
bootee 554
borage 351
bordeaux glass 380
border 430
boreal forest 137
bottle 620, 1036
bottle opener 395, 1035
bottom 1023
bottom cap 884, 885
bottom line 977
bottom pocket 996
bottom rail 478, 491
bottom road 929
bottom-fold portfolio 634
boudoir grand 671
bow 546, 663, 865
bow collar 586
bow loading door 861
bow thruster 865
bow tie 562
bow-winged grasshopper 171
bowl 388, 417, 429
bowl with serving spout 416
Bowman's gland 307
bowsprit 853
bowstring 999
box 449
box bag 639
box car 842, 845
box end wrench 534
box sealing tape dispenser
  787
box spring 484
box van 823
boxer 984, 986
boxer shorts 567, 601
boxing 984
boxing gloves 986
boxing trunks 986
bra 590, 591
brace 438, 525, 939
bracelets 608
brachial artery 270
brachial plexus 282
brachialis 252
brachioradialis 252
bracket base 479
bracketing 652
bract 120
brain 286

brains 362
brake 993
brake cable 833
brake caliper 827
brake lever 833
brake pedal 806
branch 129, 321, 453, 883
branches 129
branching, examples 460
brandy snifter 380
brass family 661
brattice 693
Brazil nut 341
bread 352
bread and butter plate 383
bread guide 421
bread knife 393
breaker 53
breast 197, 244, 248, 291
breast dart 569
breast pocket 560, 569
breast welt pocket 558
breaststroke 978
breech 673
breech guard 673
brick wall 440
bridge 629, 662, 665, 667,
  851, 896, 998, 1008
bridge assembly 666
bridges 800
bridging 438
bridle tape 670
Brie 358
briefcase 634
briefs 567, 591
brightness control 756
brim 545, 546
bristle 623, 626
broad beans 332
broad ligament of uterus 294
broad welt side pocket 568,
  570, 574
broadcast satellite
  communication 700
broadleaved trees, examples
  130
broccoli 326
broccoli rabe 326
broken line 792, 794
brooch 609
brook 50
brook trout 376
brow brush and lash comb
  613
brown alga 91
browser 764
brush 122, 499, 627, 645
Brussels sprouts 323
bubble 828
bubble bath 620
buckle 564, 641, 1022
buckwheat 126
buckwheat: raceme 126
bud 99
buffalo 220
buffer tank 932
buffet 481
bugle 675
building sewer 452, 455
bulb 320, 467, 469, 470,
  471, 543, 863, 883
bulb dibble 140

bulb vegetables 315
bulb, section 99
bulbet 99
bulbocavernous muscle 297
bulge 12
bulk terminal 850
bulkhead 819
bulkhead flat car 844
bull's-eye 999
bullfinch 211
bumblebee 170
bump 1008
bumper 500, 816, 819, 831,
  837
bumper molding 804
bundle 319
bunk 812
bunting bag 593
buoyancy compensator 983
burdock 331
burgundy glass 380
burner 408, 1034
burner frame 1034
burner ring 407
burying beetle 170
bus 747, 813
busbar 936
bush 138
bush-cricket 171
bushing 935, 937, 938
business aircraft 872
business transactions 767
butane accessories 1034
butt 970, 971, 998
butt cap 1038
butt grip 1039
butt guide 1039
butt section 1038
butt-strap 628
butte 61
butter curler 394
butter dish 383
butter knife 391
buttercup 108
butterfly 164
butterfly stroke 978
butterfly, hind leg 165
butterfly, morphology 164
butterhead lettuce 322
buttock 246, 250, 293, 297
button 468, 560, 596, 658
button loop 564
buttondown collar 561
buttoned placket 560, 597
buttonhole 568
buttress 694
by-pass taxiway 866
bypass feeder 743

C
C degrees 900
C-clamp 536
cabbage 323
cabin 864, 874
cabinet 378, 509, 511, 707
cable 524, 727, 750, 751,
  754, 822, 994
cable distributor 700
cable line 765
cable modem 765
cable sleeve 524

caboose 845
cabriole leg 472
cabriolet 473
cage 691
caiman 195
cake mascara 613
cake pan 403
calamus 199
calcaneus 260
calcar 243
calcareous sponge 162
calculator 635
calculator, pocket 771
calculator, printing 773
calendar pad 776
calf 219, 246, 250
call button 729
call director telephone 737
Callisto 4
calyx 105, 116
cam ring 525
camcorder, digital 754
camel 221
Camembert 358
camera 656, 705, 706, 1007
camera body 650
camera control technician
  704
camera key 733
camera pedestal 706
camera viewfinder 706
camera, digital 754
camisole 588
camp stove 1034
campers 812
camping 1030
camping equipment 1035
camshaft 810
can opener 395, 428, 1035
Canadian bacon 363
canal lock 850
canary melon 345
cancel button 758
candela 913
candy thermometer 399
canine 268
cannelloni 357
cannon 216
canoe 982
canoe-kayak 982
canopy 812, 870, 1030
cantaloupe 344
cantilever bridge 797
cantilever span 797
canvas 984
cap 94, 412, 442, 467, 547,
  948
cap iron 530
capacitor 886
cape 34, 573
capillary blood vessel 299
capillary tube 901
capital 687
capitals lock key 748
capitate 258
capped column 73
capsule 88
capsule, section 121
captain's quarters 865
caption 696
car 842

car coat 575
car deck 861
car racing 1007
carafe 423
carambola 349
carapace 179, 191
carbon dioxide absorption 98
carbon rod 884
carbon-zinc cell 884
carburetor 826
card case 635
card reader 736
card slot 713
cardigan 581, 597
cardinal 211
cardoon 321
cards 1042
cargo aircraft 872
cargo bay 24
cargo bay door 25
Caribbean Plate 40
caribou 220
carina 181
carnation 106
carnivorous mammals 223
carnivorous mammals, examples 228
carp 374
carpal pad 223
carpenter's hammer 514
carpentry material 539
carpentry: drilling tools 524
carpentry: nailing tools 514
carpentry: sawing tools 519
carpentry: screwing tools 516
carpentry: shaping tools 527
carpus 201, 258
carrier 830, 832
carrier bag 638
carrot 330
carry-on bag 642
cartilaginous fish 180
cartilaginous fishes 371
cartography 30
cartoon 698
cartridge 541, 721
cartridge film 655
cartwheel hat 545
carving fork 394
carving knife 393
casaba melon 344
case 555, 610, 669, 902, 903, 911
case fan 745
casement 445
cashew 340
casing 157, 444, 451
cassava 317
Cassegrain focus 16
cassette 718, 763
cassette compartment 708, 711
cassette drive 763
cassette holder 719
cassette tape deck 714
castanets 661, 681
caster 486, 500, 679
casting 1039
castle 692
casual shoe 551
cat 226

cat's head 226
cat, morphology 227
catcher 670
category buttons 728
catenary 839
cathedral 694
cathedral ceiling 435
cathedral roof 433
cathod ray tube television 707
cathode 884, 885
catwalk 648
caudal fin 181, 183
cauliflower 326
caulking gun 541
cave 48, 56
cavernous body 296
CB radio 871
cedar of Lebanon 134
ceiling fitting 496
ceiling joist 439
celeriac 331
celery 321
celery cabbage 324
celestial bodies 2
celestial coordinate system 19
celestial equator 19
celestial meridian 19
celestial sphere 19
celiac trunk 269, 280
cell 165, 691
cell body 289
cell membrane 84, 159
cell wall 84
cello 663
cellos 661
cells 883
cellular telephone, portable 732
Celsius 913
Celsius scale 900
Celsius temperature, measurement 913
celtuce 322
cement 971
cement mixer 825
cementum 267
center 919, 1011
center attacker 964
center back 964
center back vent 559
center circle 955, 962
center console 807
center face-off circle 1011
center field 959
center flag 954
center hole 720
center keelson 863
center line 962, 966, 968, 1011
center line judge 972
center mark 972
center pocket 996

center post 479, 805
center service line 973
center span 799
center spot 955, 996
center strap 973
center wheel 904
centerboard 980
centering control 756
Central America 28
central brush 824
central column 949
central disk 163
central focusing wheel 896
central incisor 268
central nervous system 284
central pumping station 932
central wrestling area 987
centrifuge module 23
centriole 158
cephalic vein 271
cephalothorax 174, 178
ceramic capacitor 886
cereal products 352
cereals 122
cerebellum 284, 286
cerebrum 284, 286
Ceres 4
cervical vertebra 264, 265
cervix of uterus 293
chain brake 154
chain of dunes 59
chain of neurons 288
chain reaction 878
chain stay 832
chainsaw 154
chainsaw chain 154
chair lift 1024
chalk 998
chalk line 538
chameleon 194
chamfer bit 529
chamois leather 555, 611
champagne flute 381
chandelier 497
change sign key 771
changing table 487
channel scan button 710
channel select 709
channel selector 731
channel selector controls 710
chanter 659
chanterelle 313
chapati bread 353
chapel 693
charcoal 645
chard 319
charge indicator 622
charging light 622
charging plug 622
charlotte mold 403
charm bracelet 608
charms 608
Charon 5
chart room 858
chat room 767
chayote 329
check valve 454
checkbook 635
checkbook case 636
checkbook/secretary clutch 635

checkers 1045
cheek 217, 224, 249, 514
cheese grater, rotary 397
cheese knife 391
cheeses, blue-veined 361
cheeses, fresh 359
cheeses, goat's-milk 359
cheeses, soft 358
cheetah 231
chemical bond 876
chemise 693
chemistry 876
chemistry symbols 880
cherimoya 349
cherry 337
chervil 351
chess 1046
chess notation 1046
chess pieces 1047
chessboard 1046
chest 217
chesterfield 474
chestnut 341
Chèvre cheese 359
chick 209
chick peas 333
chief referee 1013
chief timekeeper 976
chiffonier 480
child's tricycle 835
children's furniture 486
chimney 431
chimney connection 449
chimpanzee 237
chin 197, 245
chin protector 828
chin rest 662
chin strap 1006
chinois 400
chip cover 523
chip van 821
chipmunk 212
chipolata sausage 365
chipset 746
chive 316
chloroplast 84
choanocyte 162
choir 695
choker 603
choosing key 450
chorizo 364
Christmas tree 932
chromatin 158
chromosphere 6
chuck 517, 524, 525
chukka 554
chute 928
cicada 171
cilium 159, 161
circle, parts 919
circular body 659
circular saw 522
circumference 919
circumvallate papilla 308, 309
cirque 8
cirque, glacial 46
cirrocumulus 67
cirrostratus 66

cirrus 67
citron 343
citrus fruit 112
citrus fruits 342
citrus juicer 396, 416
city bicycle 834
city bus 814
clam 369
clamp 521, 618
clamp binder 782
clamp lever 618
clamp spotlight 494
clamping screw 536
clapskate 1017
clarinet 674
clarinets 660
clasp 633, 638
classic blouse 584
classified advertisements 699
clavicle 201, 256
claw 165, 179, 190, 197, 223, 240, 242, 514, 606
claw hammer 514
clay 971
clean and jerk 992
cleaner height adjustment knob 499
cleaning brush 623
cleaning tools 501
cleanout 460
clear key 771
clear-entry key 771
cleat 980
cleaver 393
clew 981
click 904
cliff 8, 44, 56
climate control 807
climates of the world 64
climbing plant 139
clinical thermometer 901
clip 788, 911
clip earrings 602
clipboard 785
clipless pedal 1006
clitoris 292
cloaca 192
cloche 545
clock operator 962
clock radio 726
clock timer 419, 505
clog 549
closed stringer 443
closeness setting 622
closet 437, 481
clothing and accessories 1040
cloud 74
cloud of volcanic ash 42
clouds 66
clouds of vertical development 67
cloudwater 82
cloverleaf 794, 796
club 1042
club chair 473
clump of flowers 139
clutch lever 145, 826
clutch pedal 806
coach 814, 963, 1011

UNIVERSE AND EARTH > 2-83; PLANTS AND GARDENING > 84-157; ANIMAL KINGDOM > 158-243; THE HUMAN BEING > 244-311; FOOD AND KITCHEN > 312-429; HOUSE AND DO-IT-YOURSELF > 430-543; CLOTHING AND PERSONAL ACCESSORIES > 544-643; ARTS AND ARCHITECTURE > 644-695; COMMUNICATIONS AND OFFICE AUTOMATION > 696-791; TRANSPORTATION > 792-875; SCIENCE AND ENERGY > 876-951; SPORTS AND GAMES > 952-1048

coach's box 958
coaches 1013, 1015, 1019
coal mine 928
coal storage yard 926
coal-fired thermal power plant 927
coastal features 56
coat dress 576
coats 568, 573
cob 125
cobra 193
coccyx 256, 264
cochlea 303
cochlear nerve 303
cockatoo 211
cockchafer 171
cockle 369
cockleshell 472
cockpit 980, 1007
cockroach 170
cocktail glass 381
coconut 341
Cocos Plate 40
coffee maker 423
coffee makers 423
coffee mill 427
coffee mug 382
coffee spoon 389
coin purse 636
coin return bucket 736
coin slot 736
cola nut 340
colander 400
cold air 73
cold coolant 941
cold shed 851
cold temperate climates 65
cold-water circuit 453
cold-water riser 453
cold-water supply line 458, 460, 462, 463
collar 96, 558, 560, 568, 598, 625
collar bar 609
collar point 560
collar stay 561
collards 323
collaret 587
collateral 289
collection body 824
collet 528
colon 192
color supplement 697
color synthesis 891
color television camera 21
colored pencils 644
column 48, 73, 497, 683, 687, 698, 699, 798
column of mercury 901
coma 10
comb binding 783
combat sports 984
combination lock 633
combs 616
combustion chamber 810
comet 10
comforter 485
command control dial 650
commercial concern 766
commissure of lips of mouth 304

common carotid artery 270
common coastal features 56
common extensor of fingers 254
common frog 187
common hair cap moss 89
common iliac artery 270, 280
common nail 515
common periwinkle 369
common peroneal nerve 282
common plaice 377
common polypody 93
common toad 187
communication by telephone 732
communication set 849
communication tunnel 24
communications volume controls 20
commuter train 837
compact 612
compact camera 656
compact disc 722
compact disc player 714, 724
compact disc player, portable 726
compact disc reading 722
compact disc recorder 724
compact flash card 655
compact memory card 653
compact videocassette adapter 711
compartment 480
compass 1037
compass bridge 857, 858, 861, 865
compass card 1037
compass meridian line 1037
compass saw 520
competition area 990
competitive course 976
competitors' compound 1005
complex dune 59
compluvium 688
compound bow 999, 1041
compound eye 164, 167
compound leaves 101
compressed air reservoir 841
compressed-air cylinder 983
compression coupling 461
compressor 786
computer 744
computer connector 757
computer table 740
concave lens 893, 894
concert grand 671
concha 301
conchiglie 356
condensation 76, 877
condensation of steam into water 942
condenser 897, 924, 927
condenser coil 451
condenser fan 451
condor 208
conduction 879
conductor's podium 661
cone 923
configuration of the continents 28
confined aquifer 924

confluent 50
conic projection 33
conifer 133
conifer, structure 133
conifers, examples 134
connecting rod 810
connection box 705
connection pin 887
connective tissue 299
connector 465
connector panel 757
constriction 901
consumer 703
contact 469
contact devices 466
contact lenses 632
contact lever 496
container 412, 859
container car 845
container hold 859
container semitrailer 820
container ship 850, 858
container terminal 851
container-loading bridge 850
containment building 940, 945
contest area 988
contestant 988
continent 54
continental crust 38
continental margin 54
continental rise 54
continental shelf 54
continental slope 54
continents, configuration 28
continuity person 647
continuous beam 797
contour feather 199
contrabassoons 660
contractile vacuole 160, 161
contrast control 756
control button 750
control deck 860
control key 748
control keys 738
control knob 505, 509, 511
control lights 759
control panel 419, 451, 502, 505, 509, 511, 743, 757
control room 649, 935
control rooms, television 704
control stand 840
control stick 874
control tower 866
control tower cab 866
control valve 1034
controller 1048
controller ports 1048
convection 879
convection current 879
convection zone 6
convective cell 69
convenience outlet 543
convergent plate boundaries 41
converging lenses 894
convertible 802
convex lens 893, 894, 898
conveyor 926
cook's knife 393
cooked ham 363

cookie cutters 401
cooking 418
cooking plate 420
cooking surface 420, 421
cooking utensils 407
cooktop 378, 502
cooktop edge 505
cool tip 618
coolant 940
coolant inlet 947
coolant outlet 947
cooler 1036
cooling cylinder 895
cooling fan 717, 810
cooling tower 925, 927
cooling vent 768, 769
coping 1028, 1029
coping saw 519
coracoid 200
coral snake 194
corbel piece 448
cord 156, 491, 498, 500, 543, 731
cord sleeve 528
cord tieback 489
cordate 102
cordless mouse 750
cordless screwdriver 516
cordless telephone 737
core 6, 119
core box bit 529
coriander 351
Corinthian column 690
Corinthian order 687
Corinthian pilaster 690
cork tip 970
corkscrew 395, 1035
corn 124
corn bread 355
corn salad 325
corn: cob 125
cornea 892
corner 985
corner arc 955
corner cap 842
corner cupboard 482
corner flag 955
corner judge 990
corner pad 984
corner stool 984
corner stud 439
corner tower 692
cornet 661, 675
cornice 431, 446, 479, 489, 682, 686
corolla 105
corona 6
corona radiata 295
coronal suture 263
coronet 216
corpus callosum 286
correction fluid 790
correction paper 790
correspondence 777
corselette 588
corset 591
costal shield 191
costume 646
cottage cheese 359

coulomb 912
Coulommiers 358
counter 598
counter reset button 719
countertop 378
counterweight 721, 801
coupler head 841
coupler knuckle 843
coupler knuckle pin 843
coupling guide device 839
court 962, 964, 968, 972
couscous kettle 410
cove bit 529
cover 427, 450, 743, 1001, 1037
coveralls 1020
covering 967
cow 219
cowl 804
cowl neck 587
Cowper's gland 297
coxa 165
crab 370
crab spider 173
cracked bread 354
cracked rye bread 354
crampon system 1026
cranberry 339
cranial nerves 283, 290
crank 397, 525
crankshaft 810
crater 8, 43
crater ray 8
crayfish 370
cream cheese 359
creamer 382
crease 563
creel 1040
crepidoma 682, 687
crescent wrench 534
crescentic dune 59
crest 45, 52, 889, 957
crest of spillway 934
crevasse 46
crevice tool 501
crew neck 595
crew neck sweater 581, 597
crew quarters 858
crew return vehicle 23
crib 486
crisscross curtains 490
crocodile 195
crocus 108
croissant 352
crook 672
crook key 672
crookneck squash 329
crosne 317
cross cut 928
cross rail 476
cross section of a hydroelectric power plant 936
cross section of a molar 266
cross section of a reflex camera 654
cross section of a road 792
cross section of an astronomical observatory 16
cross-country bicycle 1006

UNIVERSE AND EARTH > 2-83; PLANTS AND GARDENING > 84-157; ANIMAL KINGDOM > 158-243; THE HUMAN BEING > 244-311; FOOD AND KITCHEN > 312-429; HOUSE AND DO-IT-YOURSELF > 430-543; CLOTHING AND PERSONAL ACCESSORIES > 544-643; ARTS AND ARCHITECTURE > 644-695; COMMUNICATIONS AND OFFICE AUTOMATION > 696-791; TRANSPORTATION > 792-875; SCIENCE AND ENERGY > 876-951; SPORTS AND GAMES > 952-1048

1053

INDEX

cross-country cyclist 1004, 1006
cross-country ski 1025
cross-country skier 1025
cross-country skiing 1025
cross-headed tip 517
cross-tip screwdriver 1035
crossarm 939
crossbar 832
crossing 694
crossing arm 813
crossover cargo deck line 863
crossover mirror 813
crosspiece 477
crotch 567
crotch piece 584
Crottin de Chavignol 359
croup 216
crown 128, 133, 266, 545, 546, 664, 679, 905
CRT television 707
crude-oil pipeline 932
cruise control 806
crus of helix 301
crusher 926
crustaceans 178, 370
crustose lichen 87
crystal button 497
crystal drop 497
crystallization 877
cube 922
cuboid 260
cucumber 328
cuff 552, 560, 563
culottes 579
cultivated mushroom 313
cultural organization 766
cumulonimbus 67
cumulus 67
cuneiform, 1st 261
cuneiform, 2nd 260
cup 382, 591, 1036
cupped Pacific oyster 369
cupule 120
curled endive 325
curled kale 323
curler 1012
curling 1012
curling iron 618
currant 338
currant tomato 327
current event scoreboard 975
cursor movement keys 749, 772
curtain 489
curtain wall 692
curtains, examples 490
curved jaw 532
customs house 851
cut nail 515
cuticle nippers 610
cuticle pusher 610
cuticle scissors 610
cuticle trimmer 610
cutlery basket 512
cuts of beef 366
cuts of pork 367
cutter link 154
cutting 417
cutting blade 412, 428, 787
cutting board 394

cutting edge 390, 392
cutting tools 151
cuttlefish 368
cyan 891
cycling 1003
cyclone 68
cylinder 923
cylinder head cover 811
cylinder vacuum cleaner 500
cylindrical projection 33
cymbal 678
cymbals 661, 681
cytopharynx 161
cytoplasm 84, 159, 161, 295
cytoproct 161
cytostome 161

D

D 996
d quark 876
daffodil 108
daggerboard 981
daikon 330
dairy products 358
daisy 109
dam 935
damper 670
damper lever 670
damper pedal 668
damper rail 670
dance blade 1019
dandelion 109, 324
danger area 988
Danish Blue 361
Danish rye bread 354
dashboard 806, 826
data display 738
data storage devices 760
database 767
date 337
dater 780
davit 853, 862
dead bolt 447
deadly poisonous mushroom 95
death 916
debris 70
decagon 921
decanter 381
deceleration lane 794
decimal key 771
deck 696, 797, 798, 799, 819, 929, 1026
declination 19
décolleté bra 590
decorative braid 593
decoy 1041
dedicated line 765
deep fryer 418
deep peroneal nerve 282
deep-sea floor 36
deferent duct 297
deflector 150, 157
degree 917
degree Celsius 913
delete key 749
delicatessen 363
delicious lactarius 312
delta 51, 58
delta II 27
delta distributary 51

delta wing 872
deltoid 253
demitasse 382
dendrite 289
dental alveolus 266
dental care 626
dental floss 626
dental floss holder 626
dentil 686, 687
dentin 267
deodorant 620
deoxygenated blood 272
depolarizing mix 884
depressed-center flat car 844
depth adjustment 528
depth of focus 39
depth-of-cut adjustment knob 530
depth-of-field preview button 650
derailleur 1004
derby 547
dermis 299, 300
derrick 863, 930, 932
descending aorta 269
descending colon 279
descending passage 684
desert 59, 65, 137
desired temperature 450
desk lamp 493
desk mat 740
desk tray 778
desktop computer 764
dessert fork 387
dessert knife 391
dessert spoon 389
destroying angel 95
detachable body truck 824
detachable control 421
detachable palm rest 748
detergent dispenser 512
detrusor muscle 281
dew 75
dew pad 223
dewclaw 223
diable 411
diagonal buttress 695
diagonal movement 1047
dial 902, 905, 906
dial/action button 770
diameter 919
diamond 605, 1042
diamond interchange 796
diamond point 478
diaper 594
diaphragm 277, 654
dibble 140
dice 1044
dice cup 1045
die 1045
diesel engine 841
diesel propulsion engine 860
diesel shop 837
diesel-electric locomotive 840
difficult slope 1024
diffuser 646
diffuser pin 150
digestive system 278
digit 185, 240
digital audio player, portable 727
digital camcorder 754

digital camera 754
digital display 910
digital frequency display 715
digital nerve 283
digital pad 223
digital pulp 300
digital reflex camera 653
digital reflex camera: control panel 652
digital thermometer 902
digital versatile disc 709
digital watch 905
digitizing pad 755
digits 200
dike 42
dill 350
dimmer switch 466
dimple 1001
dinette 379, 436
dining room 437, 689, 864
dinner fork 387
dinner knife 391
dinner plate 383
dinnerware 382
Dione 5
direct disc access buttons 723
direct home reception 701
direction of electron flow 883, 885
directional buttons 1048
directional sign 847
director 647
director of photography 647
director's chair 473
director's control monitors 646
disc brake 827
disc compartment 723
disc compartment control 709, 723
disc skip 723
disc tray 709, 763
discharge line 454
discus throw 953
dish 420
dishwasher 378, 463, 512
disk 12, 760, 809
disk eject button 761
disk motor 760
diskette 12
displacement 889
display 450, 708, 709, 716, 723, 726, 727, 729, 730, 731, 735, 736, 737, 768, 771, 774, 775, 908
display button 728
display cabinet 480
display release button 768
display setting 735
disposable camera 656
disposable contact lens 632
disposable diaper 594
disposable razor 624
distal phalange 259, 261
distal phalanx 300
distance 630
distance traveled 911
distance, measure 911
distributary, delta 51
distribution box 455

distribution by aerial cable network 700
distribution by submarine cable 703
distribution by underground cable network 702
distribution panel 464
distributor cap 811
ditali 356
ditch 793
divergent plate boundaries 41
diverging lenses 894
diversion tunnel 934
divide key 771
divided by 914
divider 633
dividers 782
diving 979
diving glove 983
diving installations 979
diving tower 979
do-it-yourself 514
dock 850
dock crane 850
docking cradle 770
document folder 784
document handler 743
document-to-be-sent position 739
dodecagon 921
dog 223
dog ear collar 586
dog's forepaw 223
dog, morphology 224
dolichos beans 334
dolphin 235
dome shutter 17
dome tent 1031
domestic appliances 412, 427, 498
dominoes 1044
door 419, 478, 511, 805, 868, 1030
door access 909
door handle 805
door lock 805
door panel 479
door shelf 507
door stop 843
door switch 511
doorknob 446, 447
Doric column 690
Doric order 685
dormer window 430
dorsalis pedis artery 270
dorsum of nose 305
dorsum of tongue 308
double bass 663
double basses 661
double boiler 411
double circuit breaker 464
double drop lowbed semitrailer 820
double plate 437
double pulley system 882
double reed 672
double seat 849
double zero key 773
double-bladed paddle 982
double-blank 1044
double-breasted buttoning 570

UNIVERSE AND EARTH > 2-83; PLANTS AND GARDENING > 84-157; ANIMAL KINGDOM > 158-243; THE HUMAN BEING > 244-311; FOOD AND KITCHEN > 312-429; HOUSE AND DO-IT-YOURSELF > 430-543; CLOTHING AND PERSONAL ACCESSORIES > 544-643; ARTS AND ARCHITECTURE > 644-695; COMMUNICATIONS AND OFFICE AUTOMATION > 696-791; TRANSPORTATION > 792-875; SCIENCE AND ENERGY > 876-951; SPORTS AND GAMES > 952-1048

INDEX

double-breasted jacket 558
double-burner camp stove 1034
double-decker bus 813
double-edged blade 625
double-edged razor 625
double-leaf bascule bridge 801
double-six 1044
double-twist auger bit 526
doubles sideline 969, 972
doublet 1044
doubling die 1045
dough hook 415
Douglas, pouch 293
dousing water tank 940
dovetail 899
dovetail bit 529
down tube 833
downhill bicycle 1006
downhill cyclist 1006
downspout 430
draft tube 937
dragonfly 172
drain 452
drain hose 462, 463, 509, 513
drain tile 440
draining circuit 453
draining spoon 404
draw drapery 489
draw hoe 144
drawbridge 692
drawer 379, 477, 480, 486, 502, 505
drawers 566
drawing 644
drawing, equipment 644
drawstring 572, 639
drawstring bag 639
dredger 402
dresser 482, 646
dresses, examples 576
dressing room 646, 649
drift 928
drill pipe 930
drilling drawworks 930
drilling rig 930
drilling tools 524
drills 526
drip bowl 504
drip molding 805
drip pan 420
drip tray 425
dripping pan 409
drive belt 508
drive shaft 874
drive wheel 428
driver seat 829
driver's cab 839, 840
driveway 431
driving glove 557
drizzle 71
dromedary camel 221
drone pipe 659
droop nose 872
drop earrings 602
drop light 543
drop waist dress 577
drop-leaf 477
drum 397, 491, 510, 678, 685

drumlin 45
drums 678
drupelet 117
dry cells 884
dry climates 65
dry dock 850
dry fruits 120, 340
dry gallery 49
dry pastel 644
dry-weather tire 1007
dual cassette deck 724
dual seat 827
dual-in-line package 887
duck 210
duffel bag 640
duffle coat 572
dugout 958
dulse 314
dumbbell 995
dump body 821, 823
dump semitrailer 821
dump truck 823
dune 57, 60
dunes, examples 59
duodenum 278
dura mater 284, 285
durian 349
dust canister 527
dust cover 721
dust receiver 501
dust tail 10
dusting brush 501
Dutch bicycle 834
Dutch oven 410
DVD 709
DVD burner 763
DVD camcorder 711
DVD recorder 709
dynamic brake 840
dynamics propeller 860

E

e-commerce 767
e-mail 767
e-mail software 764
eagle 208
ear 227, 242, 245, 476
ear flap 547
ear loaf 352
ear, auricle 301
ear, structure 302
eardrum 303
earlobe 301
earphone jack 744
earphones 726, 727
earpiece 629
earrings 602
Earth 3, 4, 7, 9
Earth coordinate system 30
earth foundation 792
Earth's atmosphere, profile 62
Earth's crust 38, 39
Earth's crust, section 36
Earth's orbit 7, 9
Earth, structure 38
earthquake 39
Eastern Hemisphere 31
Eastern meridian 32
easy slope 1024

eau de parfum 620
eau de toilette 620
eccrine sweat gland 299
echinoderms 158, 163
echinus 685
eclipses, types 7, 9
ecliptic 19
ectoderm 162
edge 1018, 1021, 1022, 1037
edging 138
edible boletus 312
edible mushrooms 95
editorial 698
educational institution 766
eel 373
effluent 50
effort 880, 882
egg 168, 295
egg beater 401
egg poacher 410
egg slicer 406
egg timer 398
eggplant 328
eggs 186
ejaculatory duct 297
eject button 719, 1048
elastic 484
elastic strainer 1030
elastic waistband 571
elastic webbing 564
elasticized leg opening 567
elbow 224, 242, 246, 250
elbow pad 1029
elbows 356
electric charge, measurement 912
electric circuit 469
electric current, measurement 912
electric drill 524
electric dryer 510
electric golf cart 1002
electric grill, indoor 420
electric guitar 666
electric motor 156
electric potential difference, measurement 912
electric razor 622
electric resistance, measurement 912
electrical box 466
electrical circuit, parallel 883
electrical connection 818
electricity 464, 883
electricity tools 542
electricity transmission 938, 943
electrode 471
electrolytic capacitors 886
electrolytic separator 884
electromagnetic spectrum 890
electron 876
electron collector 885
electron flow, direction 883, 885
electronic ballast 470
electronic scale 908

electronic timing system 1015
electronic viewfinder 712
electronics 886
elephant 222
elevating cylinder 822
elevation 432
elevation adjustment 899
elevator 691, 869, 928
elevon 25
elk 220
elliptical galaxy 13
elliptical snowshoe 1026
embankment 793
emerald 605
emergency brake 849
emergency regulator 983
emery boards 611
Emmenthal 360
empty set 914
emptying hose 509
enamel 267
end button 662
end cap 944
end joist 439, 440
end key 749
end ladder 842
end line 960, 963, 965, 966
end moraine 47
end piece 295
end plate 944
end stop 521
end zone 960
end/power key 733
endocardium 272
endocarp 110, 118
endoderm 162
endoplasmic reticulum 85, 159
endpiece 628, 998
energy release 878
energy, measurement 912
energy-saving bulb 470
engaged Corinthian column 690
engaged Doric column 690
engaged Ionic column 690
engagement ring 607
engine 826, 931
engine air intake 814
engine block 811
engine compartment 814
engine control room 862
engine housing 155
engine room 864
engines, types 810
English horn 674
English horns 660
English loaf 355
enhanced greenhouse effect 80
enoki mushroom 312
entablature 446, 682, 687
enter key 749
enterprise 766
entrance 795
entrance door 814, 815
entrance to the pyramid 684
entrance turnstile 846
entries line 772

epaulet 570
epicalyx 116
epicenter 39
epicondyle 257
epidermis 299, 300
epiglottis 276, 308
epitrochlea 257
equals 914
equals key 771
Equator 19, 30, 32
equipment compartment 838
equipment rack 705
erase button 653
eraser 788
eraser holder 788
erecting lenses 899
Eris 5
escalator 846
escape key 748
escape wheel 904
escarole 322
escutcheon 447, 461
esophagus 188, 192, 277, 278
espadrille 548
espresso coffee maker 424
espresso machine 425
Ethernet port 769
Eurasia 29
Eurasian Plate 41
Europa 4
Europe 29
European experiment module 23
European robin 203
Eustachian tube 303, 307
euthynteria 682, 686
evaporation 76, 77, 877
evaporator blower 451
evaporator coil 451
evening glove 556
event platform 974
examples of airplanes 870
examples of algae 91
examples of amphibians 187
examples of angles 918
examples of arachnids 173
examples of armchairs 473
examples of bicycles 834
examples of bills 202
examples of birds 203
examples of bits 529
examples of blouses 576
examples of bodies 802
examples of branching 460
examples of broadleaved trees 130
examples of carnivorous mammals 228
examples of conifers 134
examples of curtains 490
examples of dresses 576
examples of dunes 59
examples of eyeglasses 630
examples of ferns 93
examples of flowers 106
examples of forks 387
examples of freight cars 844
examples of heads 518

UNIVERSE AND EARTH > 2-83; PLANTS AND GARDENING > 84-157; ANIMAL KINGDOM > 158-243; THE HUMAN BEING > 244-311; FOOD AND KITCHEN > 312-429;
HOUSE AND DO-IT-YOURSELF > 430-543; CLOTHING AND PERSONAL ACCESSORIES > 544-643; ARTS AND ARCHITECTURE > 644-695; COMMUNICATIONS AND
OFFICE AUTOMATION > 696-791; TRANSPORTATION > 792-875; SCIENCE AND ENERGY > 876-951; SPORTS AND GAMES > 952-1048

INDEX

1055

examples of holds and throws 989
examples of insectivorous mammals 215
examples of insects 169
examples of interchanges 796
examples of keyboard instruments 671
examples of kitchen knives 393
examples of knives 391
examples of lagomorphs 214
examples of lichens 87
examples of marine mammals 233
examples of marsupials 239
examples of mosses 89
examples of motorcycles 829
examples of nails 515
examples of pants 582
examples of pleats 580
examples of primates 236
examples of reptiles 193
examples of rodents 212
examples of semitrailers 820
examples of shorelines 58
examples of skirts 578
examples of sleeping bags 1032
examples of space launchers 27
examples of spoons 389
examples of tents 1030
examples of tips 517
examples of tires 808
examples of trucks 822
examples of ungulate mammals 218
executive desk 741
executive length 565
exercise wear 600
exhaust manifold 811
exhaust pipe 827, 875
exhaust stack 816
exhaust tube 468, 471
exhaust valve 811
exit 795
exit button 770
exit turnstile 846
exocarp 110, 112, 114, 118
exosphere 62
expandable file pouch 633
expanding file 785
expansion bolt 516
expansion chamber 901
expert slope 1024
exposure adjustment knob 650
exposure correction 652
exposure mode 650
extension pipe 500
extensor digitorum longus 252
exterior dome shell 17
exterior door 446
exterior of a house 430
exterior pocket 634, 642
exterior sign 846
external auditory meatus 263

external ear 302
external floppy disk drive 762
external fuel tank 26
external gills 186
external jugular vein 271
external nose 305
external oblique 252, 254
eye 69, 174, 177, 179, 189, 190, 227, 249, 310, 514, 1039
eye makeup 613
eye wall 69
eyeball 185
eyebrow pencil 613
eyebrow tweezers 610
eyeglasses 628
eyeglasses case 637
eyeglasses parts 628
eyeglasses, examples 630
eyelahes 226
eyelash 311
eyelash curler 613
eyelashes 226
eyelet 553, 599, 639, 1018
eyelet tab 553
eyelid 190
eyepiece 654, 713, 896, 897, 899
eyeshadow 613
eyespot 163

F

F degrees 900
fabric guide 498
face 238, 245, 514, 928, 967, 1001
face-off circle 1010
face-off spot 1010
faceplate 447
facet 873
facial makeup 612
facial nerve 290
facsimile (fax) machine 738
factorial 915
faculae 6
Fahrenheit scale 900
fairing 826
fairway 1000
falcon 208
fall front 480
fallopian tube 292
fallopian tubes 294
false start rope 976
false tuck 593
fan 510
fan belt 810
fan brush 612, 645
fan housing 619
fan motor 451
fan trellis 138
fang 174, 189
fantail 948
farmhouse bread 355
fascia 686
fast-forward button 710, 719
fastener binder 782
faucet 457
fault 39
feather crown 970

feathered shuttlecock 970
feed deck 777
feed tube 417, 429
feeder output tray 743
feijoa 349
felt hat 544, 546
felt tip pen 645
female 916
female ferrule 1038, 1039
female reproductive organs 292
femoral artery 270
femoral nerve 282
femoral vein 271
femur 165, 200, 256
fence 430, 521
fender 804, 816, 832
fennec 228
fennel 320
fern 92
fern, structure 92
ferns, examples 93
ferrule 998
ferry boat 861
ferryboat 851
fetlock 216
fetlock joint 216
fettucine 357
fibula 256, 260
fiddlehead 92
fiddlehead fern 319
field 952, 958
field lens 899
field line 888
field mouse 212
fielder's glove 957
fifth wheel 817
fifty 916
fifty-yard line 960
fig 348
figure skate 1018
figure skating 1018
filament 104, 468
filament support 469
file 531, 1035
file guides 784
filiform papilla 309
filing box 785
filing furniture 742
fill opening 498
filler cap 157, 817
filler plate 747
filler tube 458
fillet 686
filleting knife 393
film 654
film advance mode 650
film cartridge chamber 651
film guide rail 651
film guide roller 651
film leader indicator 651
film pack 655
film rewind system 651
film speed 650
film sprocket 651
films 655
filter 418, 504
filter holder 425
filum terminale 284

fin 869, 875, 983
finch 203
fine guidance system 18
finger 300, 957
finger button 676
finger tip 777
fingerboard 659, 662, 666, 667
finish judge 1015
finish judges 1013
finish line 953, 1005
finish wall 976
finishing nail 515
fir 135
fire box 449
firebrick 449
firebrick back 448
fireplace 437, 448
FireWire port 769
firing, wood 448
firn 46
first aid station 1024
first base 958
first dorsal fin 181
first floor 432, 436
first level of operations 772
first molar 268
first premolar 268
first quarter 10
first space 963
first valve slide 676
first violins 661
first-class cabin 868
fish fork 387
fish knife 391
fish platter 384
fish poacher 407
fish scaler 1035
fishes 180
fishes, bony 372
fishes, cartilaginous 371
fishhook 1039
fishing 1038
fishing vest 1040
fission of uranium fuel 941
fission products 878
fissionable nucleus 878
fitness equipment 993
fitted sheet 485
five 916
five hundred 916
fixed base 537
fixed bridges 797
fixed jaw 534, 536, 537
fixture drain 452
fjords 58
flageolet 336
flame 879
flamingo 207
flank 196
flanking tower 692
flap 558, 638
flap pocket 559, 569
flare 6
flash tube 895
flat 1028
flat brush 645
flat car 844
flat end pin 492

flat head 518
flat mirror 16
flat oyster 369
flat screen monitor 756
flat sheet 485
flat tip 517
flat-back brush 615
flat-plate solar collector 947
flatbed semitrailer 819
flea 169
flesh 111, 115, 116, 119
fleshy fruit 112, 114
fleshy leaf 99
flews 224
flexible boot 1021
flexible hose 500
flexible rubber hose 462
flexible skirt 860
flies 648
flight deck 24, 868, 874
flight of stairs 443
float 454, 870, 871
float ball 459
float clamp 454
float seaplane 870
floating bridge 800
floating crane 850
floating head 622
floodplain 51
floor 948
floor brush 501
floor drain 452
floor exercise area 975
floor joist 439, 441
floor lamp 494
floor mats 974
floorboard 830
floppy disk drive 744, 746
floppy disk eject button 744
flow tube 947
flower 96, 104
flower bed 138, 431
flower bud 96
flower, structure 104
flowers, examples 106
fluorescent tube 470, 471
flush 1043
flush handle 458
flute 526, 685, 686, 687
fluted land 526
flutes 660
fly 169, 563, 567, 594
fly agaric 95
fly front closing 574
fly rod 1038
flyfishing 1038
flying buttress 694
flying jib 855
flying mammal 242
flywheel 811, 993
foam 53
foam monitor 863
foam pad 1033
focal plane shutter 651, 654
focus 39, 892, 893
focus button 713
focus mode selector 650
focusing ring 896
focusing screen 654

UNIVERSE AND EARTH > 2-83; PLANTS AND GARDENING > 84-157; ANIMAL KINGDOM > 158-243; THE HUMAN BEING > 244-311; FOOD AND KITCHEN > 312-429; HOUSE AND DO-IT-YOURSELF > 430-543; CLOTHING AND PERSONAL ACCESSORIES > 544-643; ARTS AND ARCHITECTURE > 644-695; COMMUNICATIONS AND OFFICE AUTOMATION > 696-791; TRANSPORTATION > 792-875; SCIENCE AND ENERGY > 876-951; SPORTS AND GAMES > 952-1048

INDEX

fog 75
fog light 816
foie gras 363
folder 784
folding cot 1033
folding nail file 611
folding ramp 861
foliage 128, 133
foliate papilla 309
foliose lichen 87
follicle 120
follicle, section 120
following car 1004
fondue fork 387
fondue pot 408
fondue set 408
food mill 396
food processor 417
food vacuole 160, 161
foot 238, 240, 242, 247, 251, 260, 478, 595, 664, 679, 981
foot cushion 997
foot fault judge 973
foot pegs 1003
foot strap 981
foot support 995
football 960
football, American 960
footboard 484
footbridge 692, 837, 847
footing 439, 441
footless tights 600
footrest 488
footrope 853
footstool 379, 475
footstrap 582, 993
for filing 781
for measuring 398
for opening 395
for time management 774
foramen cecum 308
force, measurement 912
fore royal sail 855
fore-royal mast 853
fore-topgallant mast 853
fore-topmast 853
forearm 224, 246, 250
forecastle 859
forecourt 973
forehead 245
foreleg 164, 167
forelimb 185, 186, 240
forelock 217
foremast 852, 863
foresail 855
foreskin 296
forest 44
forewing 165
fork 386, 833, 1009
forked tongue 189
forks, examples 387
formeret 695
forming food vacuole 161
formula 1 car 1007
forward/reverse 145
fossil fuel 80, 82
foul line 959
foul line post 959

foundation 439, 441
foundation of tower 799
foundation slip 589
foundations 440
four blade beater 415
four-door sedan 802
four-masted bark 852
four-of-a-kind 1043
four-way selector 653
fourchette 557
fourth wheel 904
fox 228
foyers 649
fraction 915
frame 145, 438, 448, 478, 483, 519, 536, 570, 633, 643, 681, 827, 947, 948, 970, 971, 1004, 1026
frame stile 479
frames 630
frames remaining/timer 652
framing square 538
frankfurter 365
free margin 300
free skating blade 1019
free throw line 963
free zone 965
freestyle snowboard 1021
freeway 794
freezer 379
freezer bucket 427
freezer door 507
freezing 877
freezing rain 72
freight car 836
freight cars, examples 844
freight hold 869
freight station 837
French bread 352
French horn 675
French horns 661
frequency bands 715
frequency display 725
frequency setting slide control 715
frequency, measurement 912
fresco 688
fresh cheeses 359
fret 665, 666, 667
frieze 478, 682, 686
frog 184, 572, 663
frog, life cycle 186
frog, morphology 184
frog-adjustment screw 530
frond 92
front 559, 560
front apron 562
front beam 907
front brake 833
front compression strap 1036
front cover 758, 759
front crawl stroke 978
front crossbar 1026
front door 437
front fascia 804
front fender 826
front foil 857
front footrest 827
front fork 1006

front knob 525
front leg 476
front page 696
front picture 696
front pocket 639
front rigid section 815
front shock absorber 831
front tip 498
front top pocket 563
frontal bone 262
frontal sinus 306
frontalis 253
frontwall 818
frost 75
fruit vegetables 327
fruits 110, 337
fruits, tropical 347
fruticose lichen 87
fry basket 400
frying pan 411
fuel 940
fuel bundle 944, 945
fuel door 805
fuel injector 811
fuel pellet 944, 945
fuel tank 155, 817, 840, 874
fulcrum 880, 979
full house 1043
full moon 11
fully reflecting mirror 895
fumarole 42
function keys 737, 738, 748, 908
function selectors 735
fungiform papilla 309
funiculus 114
funnel 400, 864
funnel cloud 70
fur 227, 238, 241
furcula 201
furniture beetle 169
furrow 309
fuse 939
fuse cutout 939
fuse holder 939
fuselage 869
fusilli 356
futon 483

G

gable stud 438
gaff 852
gaff sail boom 852
gaff topsail 854
gaffer 647
Gai-lohn 326
galaxy 12
galaxy, classification 13
gallbladder 278
gallery 948
galley 868
game console 1048
game port 745
games 1042
gamma rays 890
Ganymede 4
gap 1039
garage 430
garbage disposal sink 460

garbage disposal unit 461
garden 689
garden cress 325
garden hose 146
garden line 140
garden path 430
garden sorrel 325
garden spider 173
garden, pleasure 138
gardening 138
garlic 316
garlic press 396
garnet 604
garrison cap 547
garter 590
garter belt 591
garter snake 193
gas 471, 877, 930
gas pedal 806
gas tank 826, 831
gasket 512
gaskin 216
gasoline engine 810
gastrocnemius 252
gate 850, 936, 937
gate-leg 477
gate-leg table 477
gather 584
gather skirt 579
gauntlet 556
gear tooth 881
gearing systems 881
gearshift lever 807, 827, 831
general view 447
generator 832, 924
generator unit 937
Genoa salami 364
geography 28
geology 36
geometrical shapes 918
geometry 917
geothermal and fossil energy 924
geothermal energy 924
geothermal field 924
germ 122
German rye bread 354
German salami 364
geyser 42
gherkin 328
gibbon 237
gill 94
gill slits 180
ginkgo nut 340
giraffe 222
girder 438
girdle 591
glacial cirque 46
glacier 46, 50
glacier tongue 46
glans penis 296
glass 947
glass case 909
glass cover 506
glass lens 629
glass protector 1010
glass slide 897
glass-fronted display cabinet 482
glassed roof 436
glassware 380
global warming 81

globe 1034
globular cluster 12
glossopharyngeal nerve 290
glottis 189
glove 20, 986, 1003, 1004, 1009, 1016, 1020, 1025
glove compartment 807
glove finger 557
glove, back 557
glove, palm 557
gloves 556
glucose 98
gluteal nerve 283
gluteus maximus 254
gnocchi 356
gnomon 905
goal 954, 961, 1011
goal area 954
goal crease 1011
goal judge 1010
goal lights 1011
goal line 960, 1010
goalkeeper 1010
goalkeeper's gloves 956
goalpost 961
goat 219
goat's-milk cheeses 359
goatfish 372
gob hat 545
goggles 1006, 1020
goldfinch 203
golf 1000
golf bag 1002
golf ball 1001
golf cart 1002
golf cart, electric 1002
golf clubs, types 1001
golf glove 1002
golf shoes 1002
Golgi apparatus 84, 159
gondola 1024
gondola car 844
gong 661, 681
goose 210
goose-neck 442
gooseberry 338
gored skirt 578
gorge 49, 50
Gorgonzola 361
gorilla 238
gorilla, morphology 238
Gothic cathedral 694
gouache cakes 644
gouache tube 644
gour 48
government organization 766
grab handle 817
gracilis 254
grade crossing 837
graduated dial 1037
graduated scale 907, 910
grafting knife 152
grain of wheat, section 122
grain terminal 850
grand gallery 684
granitic layer 37
granivorous bird 202
grape 339
grape leaf 324
grape, section 115
grapefruit 343
grapefruit knife 393

UNIVERSE AND EARTH > 2-83; PLANTS AND GARDENING > 84-157; ANIMAL KINGDOM > 158-243; THE HUMAN BEING > 244-311; FOOD AND KITCHEN > 312-429;
HOUSE AND DO-IT-YOURSELF > 430-543; CLOTHING AND PERSONAL ACCESSORIES > 544-643; ARTS AND ARCHITECTURE > 644-695; COMMUNICATIONS AND
OFFICE AUTOMATION > 696-791; TRANSPORTATION > 792-875; SCIENCE AND ENERGY > 876-951; SPORTS AND GAMES > 952-1048

INDEX

1057

graphic equalizer 714
grass 971
grassbox 157
grasshopper 171
grassland 137
grater 397
grating, utensils 396
gravel 440, 455
gravy boat 385
gray matter 285
grease well 417
great green bush-cricket 171
great horned owl 208
great saphenous vein 271
great scallop 368
greater alar cartilage 306
greater covert 198
greater trochanter 257
Greek bread 352
Greek temple 682
green 891, 1000
green alga 91
green bean 335
green cabbage 323
green onion 316
green peas 333
green russula 312
green sweet pepper 327
greenhouse effect 78
greenhouse effect, enhanced 80
greenhouse effect, natural 78
greenhouse gas 79
greenhouse gas concentration 81
Greenland Sea 28
grid system 32
griddle 421
grille 451, 658, 683, 804
grinding, utensils 396
grip 1001
grip handle 519
grip tape 1028
gripping tools 532
grips, types 967
groin 248
groove 394, 1023
ground 465
ground beef 366
ground bond 465
ground connection 464
ground moraine 46
ground pork 367
ground terminal 717
ground wire 464
ground/neutral bus bar 464
grounded receptacle 454
groundhog 213
grow sleepers 595
Gruyère 360
guard 392, 434, 436, 442, 543
guard rail 507, 1028
guardhouse 692
guardrail 862
guava 348
guide 1038
guide bar 154
guide handle 528
guide roller 718
guiding tower 801
guinea fowl 208

guinea pig 212
guitar 665, 666
gulf 34
gum 267, 304
gun 541
gun flap 570
gurnard 373
gusset 634, 640
gusset pocket 581
Gutenberg discontinuity 38
gutta 685
gutter 430
guy line 1030
guy wire 949
guyot 54
gymnastics 974

H

hack 1012
hacksaw 519
haddock 376
hail 72
hair 245, 249, 298, 663
hair clip 617
hair conditioner 620
hair dryer 619
hair follicle 298
hair roller 617
hair roller pin 617
hair stylist 646
hairbrushes 615
haircolor 620
hairdressing 615
hairpin 617
hairspring 904
hakama 991
half bath 436
half handle 392
half-glasses 631
half-pipe 1003
half-slip 589
halfway line 955
halibut 377
hall 436, 864
hallah 354
halo 12
halogen desk lamp 493
halyard 854
ham knife 393
hamate 258
hammer 669, 670
hammer butt 670
hammer felt 670
hammer loop 539
hammer rail 669, 670
hammer shank 670
hammer throw 953
hamster 212
hand 238, 246, 250, 258
hand blender 416
hand brake gear housing 842
hand brake wheel 842
hand brake winding lever 842
hand miter saw 521
hand mixer 414
hand protector 1009
hand rest 753
hand vacuum cleaner 501
hand-warmer pocket 571, 573

handbags 638
handgrip 826, 831, 1038
handheld computer 770
handle 147, 155, 156, 157, 386, 388, 390, 397, 414, 417, 419, 421, 422, 427, 428, 449, 460, 484, 498, 500, 505, 514, 516, 517, 519, 520, 521, 522, 523, 525, 527, 530, 531, 532, 533, 534, 536, 537, 539, 541, 543, 618, 619, 624, 625, 626, 627, 633, 638, 642, 643, 663, 725, 787, 898, 957, 967, 970, 971, 1023
handlebar 145, 993, 1005
handlebar grip 1005
handlebars 833, 1003
handrail 443, 815, 849
handsaw 520
handset 734, 736
handset cord 734
hang-up ring 619
hanger loop 596
hanging basket 139
hanging file 784
hanging glacier 47
hanging pendant 496
hanging stile 445, 479
hapteron 91
harbor 850
hard boot 1021
hard contact lens 632
hard disk drive 760
hard disk drive camcorder 711
hard disk drive, secondary 746
hard palate 304, 306
hard surface 971
hard top gondola 844
hard-shell clam 368
hare 214
harmonica 658
harness 983, 1026
harp 664
harps 661
harpsichord 671
hastate 103
hat switch 753
hatband 546
hatch 24
hatchback 802
hazelnut 341
hazelnut, section 120
head 10, 164, 243, 247, 251, 295, 321, 514, 515, 518, 528, 535, 625, 626, 663, 665, 666, 667, 680, 752, 970, 971, 1001
head and wing 201
head cover 1002
head cushion 996
head linesman 961
head of femur 257
head of frame 444
head of humerus 257
head tube 833
head, bat 243
headbay 935

headboard 484, 486
header 438, 446
headframe 928
headgear 544, 546, 986
heading 696
headland 56
headlight 804, 816, 826, 833, 839, 841
headlight/turn signal 806
headline 696
headphone jack 716, 723
headrail 491
heads, examples 518
headset kit 732
health organization 766
hearing 301
heart 188, 272, 277, 362, 1042
heat deflecting disc 468
heat energy 79
heat loss 79
heat production 941
heat ready indicator 618
heat selector switch 619
heat shield 24
heat sink 747
heat transfer 879
heating 448
heating duct 510
heating element 511, 513
heating equipment 861
heating grille 849
heavy duty boot 554
heavy rain 71
heavy rainfall 68
hedge 139, 431
hedge shears 152
hedgehog 215
heel 246, 250, 392, 520, 530, 552, 565, 598, 663, 665, 957, 1018
heel grip 552
heel rest 414, 498
heel stop 1027
height adjustment 993
height adjustment scale 522
helicopter 874
helix 301, 922
helmet 21, 1003, 1004, 1005, 1009, 1016, 1020, 1023, 1029
helmet ring 21
hemisphere 922
hemispheres 31
hemlath 948
hen 209
hendecagon 921
hepatic vein 269
heptagon 921
herbs 350
heron 206
herring 372
hertz 912
Hertzian wave transmission 700
hexagon 921
hexagon nut 535
hidden pocket 635
high beam warning indicator 828

high card 1043
high chair 488
high clouds 66
high frequency antenna cable 870
high jump 953
high wing 870
high-back overalls 594
high-hat cymbal 678
high-pressure area 69
high-speed exit taxiway 866
high-speed shaft 951
high-speed train 838
high-tension electricity transmission 925, 927
highball glass 381
highland 8, 64
highland climates 64
highway 795
hijiki 314
hiking boot 549
hill 44
hind leg 164
hind leg, butterfly 165
hind leg, honeybee 166
hind limb 184, 186, 241
hind toe 196
hind wing 165
hinge 422, 445, 446, 478, 512, 633, 721, 896, 1022
hip 246, 250
hippopotamus 222
hitch pin 669
hitting area 957
hobo bag 639
hock 216, 225, 367
hockey 1010
hoe 143
hoe-fork 144
hog line 1012
holdback 489
holding 989
holds, examples 989
hole 1000
home antenna 700
home key 749
home user 766
honey cell 168
honeybee 166
honeybee, hind leg 166
honeybee, middle leg 167
honeybee, morphology 166
honeycomb section 168
honeydew melon 344
hood 448, 500, 572, 593, 804, 816, 983, 1017
hoof 217
hook 143, 445, 543, 822, 910, 996, 1018
hoop earrings 602
hopper car 844
hopper ore car 844
horizontal bar 974
horizontal control 756
horizontal end handhold 842
horizontal movement 1047
horizontal stabilizer 869, 875
horizontal-axis wind turbine 950
horn 608, 806, 840

UNIVERSE AND EARTH > 2-83; PLANTS AND GARDENING > 84-157; ANIMAL KINGDOM > 158-243; THE HUMAN BEING > 244-311; FOOD AND KITCHEN > 312-429;
HOUSE AND DO-IT-YOURSELF > 430-543; CLOTHING AND PERSONAL ACCESSORIES > 544-643; ARTS AND ARCHITECTURE > 644-695; COMMUNICATIONS AND
OFFICE AUTOMATION > 696-791; TRANSPORTATION > 792-875; SCIENCE AND ENERGY > 876-951; SPORTS AND GAMES > 952-1048

horned melon 347
hornet 170
horny beak 190
hors d'oeuvre dish 384
horse 216, 219
horse, morphology 216
horsefly 170
horseradish 330
horseshoe 608
horseshoe mount 16
hose 499, 590, 592
hose connector 150
hose nozzle 146
hose trolley 146
hot bus bar 464
hot coolant 941
hot line connector 939
hot pepper 327
hot-air outlet 449
hot-water circuit 453
hot-water riser 453
hot-water supply line 461,
  462, 463
hour angle gear 16
house 649
house drain 462
house dress 576
house furniture 472
house, elevation 432
house, exterior 430
house, foundations 440
house, frame 438
house, structure 432
housing 450, 470, 527, 622,
  718
hovercraft 860
hub 175, 787, 833, 950
Hubble space telescope 18,
  62
Hubble's classification 13
hull 980
human body 244
human denture 268
humerus 201, 256
humid continental-hot
  summer 65
humid continental-warm
  summer 65
humid subtropical 65
humidity 450
hummingbird 203
humpback whale 234
hunting 1041
hunting cap 547
husk 125
hydraulic disc brake 1006
hydraulic resistance 995
hydroelectric complex 934
hydroelectric power plant,
  cross section 936
hydroelectricity 934
hydrofoil boat 857
hydrologic cycle 76
hyena 230
hygiene 614
hygrometer 450
hyperopia 893
hypha 94
hypoglossal nerve 290
hyssop 351

I

ice 77
ice breaker 856
ice cream freezer 427
ice cream scoop 405
ice cube dispenser 379
ice cube tray 506
ice hockey 1010
iceberg lettuce 322
icing syringe 401
ID window 635
identification bracelet 608
identification tag 643
igneous rocks 37
ignition switch 806, 828
iguana 194
ileum 279
iliohypogastric nerve 282
ilium 200, 256
image review button 653
impervious rock 931
impluvium 688
impulse sprinkler 150
in-line skate 1027
in-line skating 1027
inbounds line 960
incident neutron 878
incisors 268
inclination 19
incurrent pore 162
incus 303
index 696
index card cabinet 786
index card drawer 786
index cards 781
Indian chapati bread 353
Indian naan bread 353
Indian Ocean 29
indoor electric grill 420
industrial communications
  702
industry 766
inert gas 468, 469
inferior dental arch 304
inferior nasal concha 306
inferior umbilicus 199
inferior vena cava 269, 271,
  272, 280
infield 958
infiltration 77
infinity 915
inflated carrying tire 848
inflated guiding tire 848
inflator 983, 1033
inflator-deflator 1033
inflorescent vegetables 326
information console 983
information spreading 767
infrared port 769, 770
infrared radiation 79, 890
infraspinatus 255
infundibulum of fallopian tube
  294
injection well 925
ink 645
inkjet printer 758
inlet valve 810
inner boot 1022, 1027
inner circle 1012
inner core 38
inner hearth 448

inner jib 855
inner planets 3
inner table 1045
inner tent 1030
inner toe 197
input devices 748
input lights 716
input selector 716
input tray 758, 759
input/output audio/video
  jacks 717
insectivorous bird 202
insectivorous mammals,
  examples 215
insects 164
insects, examples 169
insert key 749
inside 388
inside-leg snap-fastening 594,
  595
insole 555
instant-read thermometer 399
instep 244, 565
insulated blade 543
insulated handle 420, 542,
  543
insulating material 440, 512
insulating sleeve 467
insulation 947
insulator 938, 939
intake manifold 811
integral 915
integrated circuit 887
intensive farming 80
intensive husbandry 80
interchangeable studs 956
interchanges, examples 796
intercostal nerve 283
interfemoral membrane 243
interior dome shell 17
intermediate booster station
  933
intermediate slope 1024
intermodal car 844
internal ear 302
internal filum terminale 284
internal iliac artery 269, 270,
  280
internal iliac vein 269
internal jugular vein 271
internal modem port 745,
  769
international space station 22
international system of units
  912
Internet 764
Internet service provider 765
Internet user 764
Internet uses 766
internode 96
interrupted projection 33
intersection of two sets 914
intertragic notch 301
interventricular septum 273
intervertebral disk 264
intervertebral foramen 264
intestine 188
intrusive rocks 37
inverted pleat 580
Io 4
ion tail 11
Ionic column 690

Ionic order 686
iris 310
Irish bread 355
Irish moss 314
iron 1001
irregular crystal 73
is an element of 915
is approximately equal to 914
is equivalent to 914
is greater than 915
is greater than or equal to 915
is identical with 914
is included in/is a subset of
  914
is less than 915
is less than or equal to 915
is not an element of 915
is not equal to 914
is not identical with 914
is not parallel to 917
is parallel to 917
ISA expansion connector 747
ischium 200, 257
island 35, 379, 795
island arc 55
isoseismal line 39
ISS 22
isthmus 35
isthmus of fallopian tube 294
isthmus of fauces 304

J

jabot 586
jaboticaba 348
jack 670, 1042
jack spring 670
jacket 571, 573, 575, 762,
  884
jackets 581
jackfruit 347
jaguar 231
jalousie 445
jamb 446, 448
Japanese experiment module
  23
Japanese persimmon 348
Japanese plum 346
Jarlsberg 360
javelin throw 953
jaw 517, 524, 525, 536, 542,
  611
jay 205
jeans 583
jejunum 279
jerboa 212
jersey 1004
Jerusalem artichoke 318
jet tip 627
jewel 904
jewelry 602
Jewish hallah 354
jib 980
jicama 317
jig saw 523
jigger topgallant staysail 854
jigger topmast staysail 854
jiggermast 852
jingle 680
jo 991
John dory 376
joint 998

joint filler 541
joker 1042
joule 912
joystick 753
joysticks 1048
judge 985, 987, 988
judges 974, 975, 979, 1019
judo 988
juice sac 112
juicer 429
juicing 416
jujube 348
jump rope 995
jump, steeplechase hurdle
  952
jumper 577
jumpsuit 583, 593
Jupiter 2, 4
jury platform 1005

K

kale 323
kangaroo 239, 240
kangaroo, morphology 240
karate 990
karate-gi 990
karateka 990
kayak 982
keel 200
keep 693
keeper ring 1038
kelly 931
kelvin 913
kernel 125
kettle 44, 428
kettledrum 679
key 658, 669, 670, 673
key case 637
key finger button 673
key grip 646
key guard 673
key lever 673
key lock 634
keybed 669
keyboard 669, 748, 768
keyboard instruments 668
keyboard port 745
keypad 737
keystone 695
kick pleat 580
kicker 696
kickstand 830
kidney 188, 362
kielbasa sausage 364
killer whale 233
kilogram 913
kilt 578
king 1042, 1047
king's chamber 684
king's side 1046
kingfisher 203
kingpin 818
kiosk 847
kitchen 378, 437, 689
kitchen knife 392
kitchen knives, examples 393
kitchen scale 399
kitchen shears 406
kitchen timer 398
kitchen utensils 392
kiwi 347

knee 217, 225, 244, 248
knee pad 1016, 1029
knee wrap 992
knee-high sock 592
knickers 583
knife 390
knife pleat 563, 580
knight 1047
knit shirt 597
knives, examples 391
knob 477, 530, 957
knob handle 522
knobby tread tire 829
koala 239
kohlrabi 320
kombu 314
Kuiper belt 2
kumquat 342
kung fu 991
kung fu practitioner 991

L

label 720
label holder 786
label maker 781
labia majora 292
labia majorum 294
labia minora 292, 294
labial palp 164
lablab bean 334
laboratory 17
laccolith 42
lace 957, 986, 1018
lacing 1026
lacrimal canal 310
lacrimal caruncle 310
lacrimal gland 311
lactiferous duct 291
ladder 812
ladle 404
Lady chapel 695
ladybug 170
lagomorphs, examples 214
lagoon 57, 58
lake 8, 35, 44, 50
lake acidification 83
lambdoid suture 263
lamina 91
lamp 712
lamp socket, parts 467
lamprey 373
lanceolate 103
land 526
landing 434, 442, 929
landing area 952
landing gear 818
landing gear crank 818, 819
landing light 874
landing net 1040
landing window 874
lane 952, 977, 1014
lane rope 977
lane timekeeper 976
language display button 736
lantern 138, 1034
lap counter 1015
lapel 559
lapiaz 48
lapis lazuli 604
laptop computer 768

laptop computer: front view
768
laptop computer: rear view
769
lapwing 205
larch 134
larding needle 405
large blade 1035
large intestine 279
larger spotted dogfish 371
larva 168
larynx 276
lasagna 357
laser beam 722, 895
laser printer 759
last quarter 11
latch 419
latch bolt 447
lateral bar 994
lateral brush 824
lateral condyle of femur 257
lateral cuneiform 260
lateral filing cabinet 742
lateral incisor 268
lateral line 183, 1012
lateral moraine 47
lateral semicircular canal 303
lateral view of skull 262
lateral-adjustment lever 530
lath 491
lath tilt device 491
latissimus dorsi 254
latrines 689
laundry room 436
lava flow 43
lava layer 43
lawn 139, 431
lawn care 156
lawn edger 142
lawn trimmer 156
leach field 455
leaching 83
lead 698, 1012
lead screw 526
lead-in wire 468, 471
leading bunch 1004
leading edge 869
leading motorcycle 1004
leaf 88, 96, 98, 100, 319
leaf axil 100
leaf lettuce 322
leaf node 96
leaf vegetables 322
leaf, structure 100
leakproof cap 1034
leather end 564
leather goods 633
ledger 438
leech 981
leek 315
left atrium 269, 273
left back 964
left defense 1010
left field 959
left kidney 280
left lung 277
left pulmonary vein 273
left service court 973
left side 632
left ventricle 269, 273
left wing 1011

leg 191, 238, 247, 251, 477,
484, 488, 565, 966
leg curl bar 994
leg extension bar 994
leg-warmer 600
leghold trap 1041
legumes 332
lemon 342
lemon balm 351
lemur 237
length, measure 911
length, measurement 913
lengthwise bulkhead 862
lens 654, 754, 757, 892
lens case 632
lens mount 654
lens system 896
lenses 894
lenticular galaxy 13
lentils 332
leopard 231
leotard 600
lesser covert 198
letter opener 777
letter scale 778
letters to the editor 698
lettuce 322
leucoplast 85
level 929
leveling foot 509, 511, 513
leveling screw 909
lever 421, 533, 611, 880
lever cap 530
lever corkscrew 395
libero 965
library room 436
lichen 86
lichen, structure 86
lichens, examples 87
lid 407, 417, 418, 422, 423,
427, 429, 502, 509, 539,
887
lierne 695
life buoy 857
life cycle of the frog 186
life support system 20
life support system controls
21
lifeboat 853, 863
lift bridge 801
lift chain 458
lift cord 491
lift cord lock 491
lift door 815
lift span 801
ligature 672
light 17, 848
light aircraft 870
light button 729
light rain 71
light ray 892
light sensor 654
light shield 18
lighthouse 851
lighting 467
lighting board operator 704
lighting grid 647
lighting grid access 705
lighting technician 704
lighting/camera control area
704
lightning 74
lightning arrester 937, 939

lightning rod 431, 951
lights 493
lilac 130
lily 107
lily of the valley 107
Lima bean 335
limb 128
lime 342
limousine 803
limpet 369
line judge 961, 974
line map 846
line of latitude 32
line of longitude 32
linear 103
lineman's pliers 542
linen 485
linen chest 480
linesman 955, 965, 968,
972, 1010
lingual tonsil 308
lining 552, 558, 559, 562,
598, 633, 1018
lint filter 508
lint trap 510
lintel 448
lion 230
lip 217, 226
lip makeup 614
lipbrush 614
lipid droplet 84
lipliner 614
lipstick 614
liqueur glass 380
liquid 877, 879
liquid crystal display 653,
713, 728, 732, 733, 905
liquid crystal display (LCD)
television 707
liquid eyeliner 613
liquid foundation 612
liquid mascara 613
liquor cabinet 482
litchi 348
literary supplement 697
lithosphere 38
little finger hook 677
liver 188, 192, 278, 362
livestock car 845
living room 437
lizard 194
llama 220
load 880, 882
loading door 449
loading hopper 825
loafer 548
lobe bronchus 274
lobster 178, 370
lobster, morphology 178
local station 701
location 430
lock 447, 479, 638
lock button 729
lock dial 751
lock-on button 523, 527
locked groove 720
locket 603
locking button 501
locking device 500
locking lever 536, 843
locking pliers 532
locking ring 517

locknut 460
locomotive, diesel-electric
840
loculus 118
lodging 1024
loft 433
log chute 934
log semitrailer 821
loin 246, 250
loin chop 367
long jump 952
long palmaris 252
long service line 968
long track 1014
long-range jet 868
longan 347
longitudinal dunes 59
loofah 621
loop 562, 794
loose curtain 490
loose powder 612
loose powder brush 612
lopping shears 151
lorgnette 630
loudspeaker 724
loudspeaker terminals 717
loudspeakers 714
lounge 864
louse 169
louver 451
lovage 351
love seat 474
low clouds 66
low-pressure area 69
low-speed shaft 951
low-tension distribution line
938
lower blade guard 522
lower bowl 426
lower chord 798
lower confining bed 925
lower eyelid 185, 226, 311
lower fore topsail 855
lower guard retracting lever
522
lower lip 304
lower lobe 275, 276, 277
lower mantle 38
lower mast 853
lower wing 871
lubricant eye drops 632
lubricating system 841
luff 981
lug 680
luggage 642
luggage rack 812, 830
lumbar plexus 282
lumbar vertebra 264, 265
luminous intensity,
measurement 913
lunar eclipse 9
lunar features 8
lunate 258
lung 188, 276, 277
lungs 274
lunula 300
lupine 332
lynx 230
lysosome 159

UNIVERSE AND EARTH > 2-83; PLANTS AND GARDENING > 84-157; ANIMAL KINGDOM > 158-243; THE HUMAN BEING > 244-311; FOOD AND KITCHEN > 312-429;
HOUSE AND DO-IT-YOURSELF > 430-543; CLOTHING AND PERSONAL ACCESSORIES > 544-643; ARTS AND ARCHITECTURE > 644-695; COMMUNICATIONS AND
OFFICE AUTOMATION > 696-791; TRANSPORTATION > 792-875; SCIENCE AND ENERGY > 876-951; SPORTS AND GAMES > 952-1048

M

macadamia nut 340
macaque 236
macaw 211
machicolation 692
machine hall 935, 937
mackerel 373
macronucleus 161
madreporite 163
magazine 697
magenta 891
magma 43, 54
magma chamber 43, 925
magnesium powder 975
magnet 789, 888
magnetic compass 1037
magnetic damping system 907
magnetic field 888
magnetic gasket 507
magnetic lid holder 428
magnetic needle 1037
magnetism 883, 888
magnifier 1035
magnifying glass 897, 898
magpie 204
main breaker 464
main bronchus 274
main circuit vent 452
main cleanout 452
main deck 863
main engine 25
main generator 840
main line 837
main lodge 1024
main lower topgallant sail 855
main power cable 465
main reflex mirror 654
main respiratory organs 276
main rooms 432
main royal sail 855
main sail 855
main scope tube 898
main stand 827
main transformer 838
main upper topgallant sail 855
main upper topsail 855
main vent 43
mainmast 852
mainsail 980
mainsheet 980
maintenance hangar 867
major inner reaping throw 989
major outer reaping throw 989
makeup 612
makeup artist 646
malanga 331
male 916
male ferrule 1038, 1039
male reproductive organs 295
male urethra 296
mallet 514, 678
mallets 680
malleus 303
mammary gland 291
man 244
mandarin 342
mandarin collar 587

mandible 182, 201, 262
mandoline 396
mane 217
maneuvering area 867
maneuvering engine 25
manganese mix 885
mango 349
mangosteen 347
manicure set 610
manned maneuvering unit 21
manrope 800
mantel 448
mantel shelf 448
mantid 171
mantle 177
manual feed slot 759
manway 928
map projections 33
map, physical 34
maple 132
maquis 137
margin 100
marginal shield 191
marine 65
marine mammals 233
marine mammals, examples 233
maritime communications 703
maritime transport 850
marker 645, 1013, 1014
marker light 816, 818, 819
markers 1008
marking tools 538
marmoset 237
marrow 362
Mars 3, 4
marshall 1008
marsupial mammals 240
marsupials, examples 239
marten 229
mascara brush 613
mask 983
mason's trowel 541
masonry drill 526
masonry nail 515
masonry tools 541
mass, measurement 913
massage glove 621
masseter 253
mast 690, 836, 980, 981
mast foot 981
mast sleeve 981
master bedroom 433, 435
master cord 1026
masthead 698, 853
masthead light 859
masting 852
mastoid process 263
mat 988
mat chairperson 987
mathematics 914
matinee-length necklace 603
mating adaptor 23
matter 876
mattress 484, 486, 487, 1033
mattress cover 484
maxilla 182, 201, 262
maxillary bone 267
mean position 889

meander 51
measure of distance 911
measure of length 911
measure of temperature 900
measure of time 903
measure of weight 906
measurement of amount of substance 913
measurement of Celsius temperature 913
measurement of electric charge 912
measurement of electric current 912
measurement of electric potential difference 912
measurement of electric resistance 912
measurement of energy 912
measurement of force 912
measurement of frequency 912
measurement of length 913
measurement of luminous intensity 913
measurement of mass 913
measurement of power 912
measurement of pressure 913
measurement of radioactivity 913
measurement of thermodynamic temperature 913
measuring beaker 398
measuring cup 398
measuring cups 398
measuring devices 900
measuring spoons 398
measuring tools 538
measuring, utensils 398
meat 366
meat grinder 397
meat thermometer 399
mechanical mouse 751
mechanical watch 904
mechanics 881
medial condyle of femur 257
medial moraine 46
median 795
median lingual sulcus 308
median nerve 282
medical team 988
Mediterranean subtropical 65
medium format SLR (6 x 6) 657
medium-tension distribution line 939
medulla oblongata 286
melody strings 659
melon 345
melon baller 405
melons 344
melting 877
meltwater 47
memo pad 776
memory button 716, 728, 735
memory card reader 761
memory card slots 1048
memory cards 655
Memory Stick 655

men's bag 641
men's clothing 558
men's gloves 557
men's headgear 546
men's shoes 552
meninges 285
menu button 713, 727, 728, 729, 730
menu key 733
Mercury 3, 4
mercury 471
mercury bulb 901
merguez sausage 365
méridienne 474
mesa 61
mesh 487, 966
mesh strainer 400
mesocarp 110, 112, 114, 118
mesohyl 162
mesopause 62
mesosphere 62
metacarpal 258
metacarpal, 2nd 242
metacarpal, 3rd 242
metacarpal, 4th 242
metacarpal, 5th 242
metacarpus 201, 259
metal arm 150
metal counterhoop 679
metal frame 669
metal rail 786
metal rod 681
metallic contact grid 946
metamorphic rocks 36
metatarsal 261
metatarsus 261
meteorology 62
meter 913
metering mode 652
metope 685
mezzanine 846
Michigan snowshoe 1026
micro compact car 802
microfilament 159
micronucleus 161
microphone 712, 729, 731, 733, 752, 754, 770
microphone boom 705
microphone jack 731
microscope 897
microscopes 897
microtubule 158
microwave oven 379, 419
microwave relay station 764
microwaves 890
mid-calf length 565
mid-ocean ridge 54
middle clouds 66
middle covert 198
middle ear 302
middle jib 855
middle leg 164
middle leg, honeybee 167
middle lobe 276
middle nasal concha 306
middle panel 446
middle phalange 259, 261
middle phalanx 300
middle piece 295
middle primary covert 198
middle sole 598

middle toe 197
middle torus 687
middy 585
MIDI port 745
midrange pickup 666
midrib 90, 100
midriff band 591
military communications 703
Milky Way 12
millet 124
millet: spike 124
mini shirtdress 584
mini stereo sound system 724
mini-DV camcorder: front view 712
mini-DV camcorder: rear view 713
miniDV cassette 711
minivan 803
mink 228
mint 350
minus/negative 914
minute 917
minute hand 903
mirror 457, 791, 826, 830, 897
miscellaneous articles 787
miscellaneous utensils 405
mist 75
miter box 521
miter latch 521
miter saw, hand 521
miter scale 521
mitochondrion 84, 158
mitral valve 273
mitt 556
mitten 557
mixing 412
mixing bowl 413
mixing bowls 402
mizzen royal brace 854
mizzen royal staysail 854
mizzen sail 854
mizzen topgallant staysail 854
mizzen topmast staysail 854
mizzenmast 852
moat 693
mobile drawer unit 742
mobile filing unit 742
mobile remote servicer 22
mobile unit 701
moccasin 548
mock pocket 573
mode selector 715
modem 764
moderate rain 71
moderator 940
modillion 687
Mohorovicic discontinuity 38
moistener 778
molar, cross section 266
molars 268
molding 441
mole 215, 913
molecule 876
mollusks 368
monarch butterfly 172
mongoose 226
monitor button 729

UNIVERSE AND EARTH > 2-83;   PLANTS AND GARDENING > 84-157;   ANIMAL KINGDOM > 158-243;   THE HUMAN BEING > 244-311;   FOOD AND KITCHEN > 312-429;
HOUSE AND DO-IT-YOURSELF > 430-543;   CLOTHING AND PERSONAL ACCESSORIES > 544-643;   ARTS AND ARCHITECTURE > 644-695;   COMMUNICATIONS AND
OFFICE AUTOMATION > 696-791;   TRANSPORTATION > 792-875;   SCIENCE AND ENERGY > 876-951;   SPORTS AND GAMES > 952-1048

1061

INDEX

monitor lizard 194
monkfish 375
monocle 631
mons pubis 292
Moon 4, 7, 8, 9
Moon's orbit 7, 9
Moon, phases 10
mooring winch 863
moose 221
moped 830
moraine 46
morel 312
morphology of a bat 242
morphology of a bird 196
morphology of a butterfly 164
morphology of a cat 227
morphology of a dog 224
morphology of a frog 184
morphology of a gorilla 238
morphology of a honeybee: worker 166
morphology of a horse 216
morphology of a kangaroo 240
morphology of a lobster 178
morphology of a perch 182
morphology of a shark 180
morphology of a spider 174
morphology of a starfish 163
morphology of a turtle 190
morphology of a venomous snake: head 189
morphology of an octopus 176
mortadella 364
mortar 396
mosaic 688
mosquito 169
moss 88
moss, structure 88
mosses, examples 89
moth 172
motherboard 746
motocross motorcycle 1009
motor 145, 157, 508, 510, 513, 528
motor car 849
motor home 812
motor root 285
motor scooter 830
motor sports 1007
motor truck 839
motor unit 412, 416, 417, 427, 429, 501, 627, 838
motorcycle 826
motorcycle dashboard 1009
motorcycle-mounted camera 1004
motorcycles, examples 829
motorcycling 1008
mouflon 218
mountain 44
mountain bike 834
mountain biking 1006
mountain mass 34
mountain range 8, 34, 37
mountain slope 45
mountain torrent 44
mounting plate 470
mouse pad 752
mouse port 745, 757

mouse, mechanical 751
mouth 185, 245, 304
mouthparts 167
mouthpiece 672, 676, 986
mouthpiece receiver 676
mouthpipe 676
mouthwash 626
movable bridges 800
movable jaw 534, 536, 537
movie set 646
mozzarella 359
mucous membrane 281
mucus 307
mud flap 805, 817, 818, 819
mud injection hose 930
mud pit 931
mud pump 931
muff 640
muffin pan 402
muffler 831
muffler felt 668
muffler pedal 668
mule 218, 548
mullet 374
multigrain bread 355
multiple exposure mode 650
multiple jumps 1008
multiple use key 773
multiplied by 914
multiply key 771
multipurpose solution 632
multipurpose tool 542
mummy 1032
mung bean 335
Munster 358
muntin 445
muscles 252
mushroom 94
mushroom, structure 94
mushrooms 312
music 658
musical instruments, traditional 658
muskmelon 344
muslin 400
mussel 369
mute 677
mutule 685
muzzle 224, 226
mycelium 94
myelin sheath 289
myocardium 273
myopia 893

N

naan bread 353
nacelle 950, 951
nacelle, cross-section 951
nail 515
nail bed 300
nail buffer 611
nail care 610
nail cleaner 611
nail clippers 611
nail file 610
nail matrix 300
nail nick 1035
nail polish 611
nail scissors 610
nail set 514
nail shaper 610

nail whitener pencil 611
nailing tools 514
nails, examples 515
naked strangle 989
nameplate 524, 608, 696
naos 683
nape 197, 246, 250
naris 305
narwhal 235
nasal bone 262, 306
nasal cavity 276
nasal fossae 306
nasopharynx 307
national broadcasting network 700
natural arch 56
natural environment 1000
natural greenhouse effect 78
natural sponge 621
navel 244, 248
navicular 260
navigation key 733
navigation light 860, 869
Nazca Plate 40
Neapolitan coffee maker 424
neck 190, 217, 247, 249, 251, 266, 295, 386, 388, 662, 664, 665, 666, 667
neck end 562
neck of femur 257
neck of urinary bladder 281
neckhole 566
necklaces 603
neckroll 485
neckstrap eyelet 651
necktie 562
nectarine 337
needle 61, 73
negative charge 880
negative contact 946
negative meniscus 894
negative region 946
negative terminal 883, 884
neon lamp 543
neon tester 542
Neptune 2, 5
nerve fiber 298
nerve, olfactory 306
nervous system 282
nervous system, central 284
nervous system, peripheral 282
net 965, 966, 969, 973
net band 973
net judge 973
net stocking 592
net support 966
nettle 324
network port 745
neurons 288
neutral indicator 828
neutral line 888
neutral service wire 465
neutral wire 464
neutral zone 1011
neutron 876
new crescent 10
new moon 10
newborn children's clothing 593
newel post 443

news items 699
newsgroup 767
newspaper 696
newt 187
newton 912
next call 736
next/fast-forward button 727
nictitating membrane 226
nightingale 205
nightshot button 713
nimbostratus 66
nipple 248, 291
nitric acid emission 82
nitrogen oxide emission 82
node 883
node of Ranvier 288
non-add/subtotal 773
nonagon 921
nori 314
normal spiral galaxy 13
normal vision 892
North America 29
North American Plate 40
North celestial pole 19
North Pole 30
north pole 888
Northern Hemisphere 31
Northern leopard frog 187
northern right whale 233
northern saw-whet owl 205
nose 217, 245, 305, 868, 1021, 1029
nose landing gear 868
nose leaf 243
nose leather 226
nose of the quarter 552, 599
nose pad 629
nostril 180, 182, 185, 189, 217
notch 559, 907, 998
notched lapel 568, 569
nozzle 26, 150, 541
nubby tire 1009
nuclear energy 940
nuclear energy, production of electricity 940
nuclear envelope 85, 158
nuclear fission 878
nuclear reactor 945
nucleolus 85, 158, 295
nucleus 10, 12, 85, 158, 160, 289, 295, 876
nucleus splitting 878
number buttons 728
number key 738, 771
number of decimals 773
number plate 1009
numbering machine 780
numeric keyboard 908
numeric keypad 749, 774
numeric lock key 749
numeric pager 730
nut 340, 533, 535, 662, 665, 666, 667
nutcracker 396
nutmeg grater 396
nuts 535
nylon rumba tights 593
nylon yarn 156

O

oak 130
oar 995
oasis 61
oats 126
oats: panicle 126
obi 990, 991
obituaries 699
object 892
objective 897
objective lens 650, 722, 732, 896, 898
oblique fissure 275
oboe 674
oboes 660
observation post 16
observatory 17
obstacles 1008
obturator nerve 282
obtuse angle 917, 918
occipital bone 263
occipitalis 255
ocean 8, 35, 76
ocean floor 54
Oceania 29
oceanic crust 38
octave mechanism 672
octopus 176, 368
octopus, morphology 176
oculomotor nerve 290
odd pinnate 101
off-road motorcycle 829
office building 851
office furniture 740
officials' bench 1011
offshore well 932
Ogen melon 345
ohm 912
oil 930
oil drain plug 810
oil pan 155, 811
oil pastel 644
oil pressure warning indicator 828
oil terminal 851
oil/acrylic paint 645
okapi 220
okra 327
old crescent 11
old-fashioned glass 381
olecranon 257
olfactory bulb 306, 307
olfactory cell 307
olfactory mucosa 306
olfactory nerve 290, 306
olfactory tract 306
olive 327
on-board computer 807
on-deck circle 958
on-off button 427
on-off indicator 618
on-off light 735
on-off switch 423, 425, 494, 499, 500, 501, 618, 619, 622, 627
one 916
one hundred 916
one pair 1043
one thousand 916
one-arm shoulder throw 989
one-bar shoe 550

one-person tent 1031
one-way head 518
onion 315
online game 767
Op-Ed article 698
opal 604
open end wrench 534
open stringer 442
open strings 659
open-air terrace 865
opening 557
opening, utensils 395
opera glasses 631
opera-length necklace 603
operculum 182, 186
opossum 239
opposable thumb 238
optic chiasm 287
optic nerve 290
optical lens 791
optical mouse 751
optical scanner 755
optical sensor 751
optical stage 791
optics 889
oral cavity 276, 278
oral hygiene center 627
oral irrigator 627
orange 342
orange, section 113
orangutan 236
orbicularis of eye 253
orbiculate 102
orbit 201
orbital-action selector 523
orbiter 24, 26
orchestra 660
orchestra pit 648
orchid 106
ordinary die 1044
ore pass 929
oregano 350
oriental cockroach 170
ornamental kale 322
ornamental tree 138
oscillating sprinkler 149
osculum 162
ostrich 207
ottoman 475
outdoor leisure 1030
outer circle 1012
outer core 38
outer jib 855
outer planets 2
outer shell 467
outer table 1045
outer toe 197
outfield fence 959
output devices 756
output jack 666
output tray 758, 759
outside counter 552
outside mirror 804, 813
outside ticket pocket 558
outsole 553, 599
outwash plain 47
oval head 518
ovary 104, 292, 294
ovate 103
oven 378
oven control knob 505
oven thermometer 399

over-blouse 585
overall standings scoreboard 974
overalls 583
overcoat 569, 574
overdrapery 489
overflow 453, 457
overflow protection switch 512
overflow tube 458
overhead connection 938
overhead projector 791
overpass 795, 797
oviduct 192
ovule 104
owl 205, 208
ox 219
oxbow 51
oxford shoe 554
oxygen pressure actuator 21
oxygenated blood 272
oyster 369
oyster fork 387
oyster knife 394
oyster mushroom 313
oystercatcher 204
ozone layer 62

P

Pacific Ocean 28
Pacific Plate 40
Pacific salmon 377
packaged integrated circuit 886, 887
packer body 825
pad arm 629
pad plate 628
padded envelope 779
paddle, double-bladed 982
paddle, single-bladed 982
page down key 749
page up key 749
painting 644
painting, equipment 644
pair 1019
palatine tonsil 308
palatoglossal arch 304
palette knife 645
paling fence 138
palm 557, 957
palm grove 61
palm of a glove 557
palm tree 131
palmar pad 223
palmate 101
palmette 472
pan 906, 907, 909
pan hook 907
panama 547
pancake pan 411
pancetta 363
pancreas 278
pane 445
panel 446, 564, 591, 740, 929
pantograph 838
pantry 379, 437
pants 563, 601, 1009
pants, examples 582
panty corselette 589
panty girdle 591

panty hose 592
papaya 349
paper clip holder 789
paper clips 789
paper fasteners 789
paper feed button 758
paper feed key 773
paper feed light 758
paper guide 739, 759
paper in reserve 743
paper punch 785
paper trays 743
papillary muscle 273
par 5 hole 1000
parabolic dune 59
parallel 32
parallel bars 975
parallel electrical circuit 883
parallel port 745
parallelepiped 923
parallelogram 920
paramecium 161
parapet 797
parapet walk 693
parietal bone 263
parietal pleura 275
paring knife 393
parka 571
parking 836
parking area 867
parking brake lever 807
parking lot 851
Parmesan 360
parsley 351
parsnip 330
partial eclipse 7, 9
partially reflecting mirror 895
partlow chart 818
partridge 211
parts 472, 476, 484
parts of a bicycle 832
parts of a circle 919
parts of a lamp socket 467
parts of a ring 606
parts of a shoe 552
pascal 913
pass 45
passenger cabin 857, 860, 861, 869
passenger car 838, 848
passenger liner 864
passenger seat 829
passenger station 836
passenger terminal 851, 867
passing lane 794
passion fruit 348
passivity zone 987
passport case 637
pasta 356
pasta maker 397
pastern 216
pastry bag and nozzles 401
pastry blender 402
pastry brush 401
pastry cutting wheel 401
patch pocket 558, 572, 594
patella 256
patera 472
path 139
patio 139, 430
patio door 378, 436

patrol and first aid station 1024
pattypan squash 329
pause button 719, 723
pause/break key 749
pause/still button 709, 710
pawl 525
pawn 1047
pay phone 736
PC card slot 768
PCI expansion card 747
PCI expansion connector 747
pea jacket 573
peach 337
peach, section 111
peacock 206
peak 44, 544, 547
peak level meter 719
peaked lapel 558
peanut 332
pear 346
pearl onion 315
peas 333
pecan nut 340
peccary 218
pectoral deck 994
pectoral fin 180, 182
pectoralis major 253
pedal 664, 678, 679, 832, 993
pedal pushers 583
pedal rod 668
pedal with wide platform 1006
pedestal 664
pedestal-type sump pump 454
pedicel 114
pediment 682, 687
pedipalp 174
pedometer 911
peduncle 104, 110, 116, 117, 118
peeler 394
peg 479, 662, 665
peg box 662
pelerine 575
pelican 207
peloton 1004
peltate 103
pelvic fin 181, 182
pen blade 1035
pen holder 633, 635
penalty arc 954
penalty area 954
penalty area marking 954
penalty bench 1011
penalty spot 954
pencil 944
pencil sharpener 790
pendant 603
penguin 207
penholder grip 967
peninsula 35
penis 244, 296
penne 357
penstock 935, 936
pentagon 921
pentaprism 654
penumbra shadow 7, 9
pepino 349

pepper shaker 384
peppered moth 172
pepperoni 364
percent 915
percent key 771
perch 374
perch, morphology 182
percolator 426
percussion instruments 661, 678
perforated pipe 455
perforated toe cap 553
perforation 557
performance tire 808
pergola 139
pericardium 276
pericarp 120
periodontal ligament 266
peripheral nervous system 282
peristome 161
peristyle 683, 689
peritoneum 292, 297
periwinkle 369
peroneus longus 252
peroxisome 158
perpendicular 917
perpetual snows 45
personal accessories 602
personal articles 622
personal communications 703
personal computer 744
personal digital assistant 774
personal radio cassette player 726
pestle 396
petal 105
Peter Pan collar 586
petiole 92, 100
phalanges 201, 259, 261
pharynx 277, 278
phases of the Moon 10
pheasant 210
Philippine Plate 41
Phillips 518
philtrum 305
phosphorescent coating 471
photo credit line 699
photocopier 743
photography 650
photon 895
photoshot button 712
photosphere 6
photosynthesis 98
photovoltaic arrays 22
phyllo dough 353
physical map 34
physician 984
physics 889
pi 917
pia mater 285
piano 661, 668
piccolo 660, 674
pick 143
pickup truck 803
pickups 667
pictograms 748
pie pan 403
pier 797, 798
pierce lever 428

pierced earrings 602
pig 218
pigeon 210
pika 214
pike 374
pike perch 375
pillar 664, 695, 928
pillbox hat 545
pillion footrest 827
pillow 484
pillow protector 484
pillowcase 485
pilot 839, 841
pin 467, 471
pin base 471
pin block 669
pinacocyte 162
pince-nez 630
pinch 468, 471
pine nut 340
pineal gland 286
pineapple 347
pinna 92, 240, 302
pinnacle 693, 694
pinnatifid 101
pins 609
pinto bean 335
pip 113, 115, 119, 1044
pipe 500, 536
pipe clamp 536
pipe wrench 540
pipeline 933
pisiform 258
pistachio nut 340
pistil 105
pistol grip handle 524
pistol nozzle 148
piston 811
piston lever 541
piston release 541
piston skirt 810
pit 189
pita bread 353
pitchfork comb 616
Pitot tube 1007
pituitary gland 287
pivot 542, 624, 880, 1037
placard board 843
placing judge 976
plaice 377
plain 34, 51
plane 530
plane projection 33
plane surfaces 919
planets 4
planets, inner 3
planets, outer 2
planisphere 28
plano-concave lens 894
plano-convex lens 894
plant 96
plant cell 84
plant litter 97
plantain 347
planting tools 140
plants 84
plasma membrane 160, 161
plasma television 707
plasmodesma 85
plastic film capacitor 886

plastic insulator 464
plastron 191
plate 422
plate binding 1021
plate crystal 73
plateau 34, 44
platform 800, 815, 847, 908,
   1028
platform edge 847
platform shelter 836
platform, 10 m 979
platform, 3 m 979
platform, 5 m 979
platform, 7.5 m 979
platter 384
play button 709, 710, 719,
   723
play/pause button 727
players' bench 961, 964,
   1010
playing area 864
playing field 954
playing surface 966
playing surfaces 971
playing window 718
playpen 487
pleasure garden 138
pleats, examples 580
pleural cavity 275
plexus of nerves 267
pliers 532
plug 524, 727
plug adapter 623
plum 337
plumber's snake 540
plumbing 452
plumbing system 452
plumbing tools 540
plunger 424, 540
plus or minus 915
plus/positive 914
Pluto 5
pocket 539, 633, 1002
pocket calculator 771
pocket handkerchief 559
podcasting 767
point 386, 392, 663, 1039,
   1045
pointed tab end 560
pointer 450, 902, 906, 910
poisonous mushroom 95
poker die 1044
polar axis 16
polar bear 232
polar climates 65
polar ice cap 65
polar tundra 65
Polaroid® camera 657
pole 853, 972
pole grip 1025
pole shaft 1025
pole vault 952
pollen basket 166
pollen cell 168
polo collar 587
polo dress 576
polo shirt 585
polygons 920
pome fleshy fruit 118
pome fruits 346
pomegranate 348

pomelo 343
pommel horse 974
poncho 575
pond 138
pons 287
Pont-l'Évêque 358
pontoon 800
pop-up tent 1031
poplar 132
poppy 106
porch 431
porcupine 213
pore 85, 121, 299
pork, cuts 367
porpoise 235
Porro prism 896
port glass 380
port hand 865
portable cellular telephone
   732
portable compact disc player
   726
portable digital audio player
   727
portable radio 725
portable shower head 457
portable sound systems 725
portal frame 798
portal vein 269
porthole 865
position light 839, 875
position marker 665, 666,
   667
positive charge 880
positive contact 946
positive meniscus 894
positive region 946
positive terminal 883, 884
positive/negative junction
   946
possum-belly body semitrailer
   821
post 965, 969
post binder 783
post lantern 495
postage meter 777
posterior horn 285
posterior rugae 246, 250
posterior semicircular canal
   303
posterior view 246, 250, 254,
   257, 294
postmarking module 777
potato 318
potato masher 404
pothole 48
pouch 241
pouch of Douglas 293
poultry shears 406
powder blusher 612
powder puff 612
power adapter port 769
power and backlight button
   770
power button 707, 708, 709,
   715, 716, 723, 729, 744,
   758, 768
power cable 747
power cable plug 745
power car 839

power cord 523, 527, 623,
   717
power indicator 756
power light 758
power mower 157
power plant 935
power plug 770
power source 883
power supply cord 619
power supply fan 745
power supply unit 747
power switch 653, 756, 757
power, measurement 912
power/functions switch 712
practitioner, kung fu 991
prairie 34
precious stones 605
precipitation 71, 76, 77
precision sports 996
prehensile digit 238
premaxilla 182
premolars 268
preset button 728
preset buttons 710
preset tuning button 715
press bar 994
pressed area 722
pressed cheeses 360
pressed powder 612
pressure bar 668
pressure control 627
pressure cooker 408
pressure plate 651
pressure regulator 408, 1034
pressure tube 944, 945
pressure, measurement 913
prevailing wind 68
previous/rewind button 727
prickly pear 349
prickly sphagnum 89
primaries 198
primary covert 198
primary hard disk drive 746
primary mirror 16, 18
primary root 96
primate mammals 238
primates, examples 236
prime focus 17
prime focus observing capsule
   17
prime meridian 32
primrose 109
princess dress 576
princess seaming 589
print cartridge light 758
printed circuit 886
printed circuit board 886
printer 777
printer table 740
printer, ink jet 758
printing calculator 773
printout 908
prism binoculars 896
private broadcasting network
   701
private dressing room 646
probe receptacle 419
proboscis 164
procedure checklist 21
processor 747
producer 647, 704

product code 908
production adviser 704
production control room 704
production designer 646
production of electricity by the
   generator 943
production of electricity from
   geothermal energy 924
production of electricity from
   nuclear energy 940
production of electricity from
   thermal energy 926
production platform 933
production well 924
profile of the Earth's
   atmosphere 62
programmable buttons 753
programmable thermostat
   450
programming control 450
projection device 824
projection head 791
projector 757
promenade deck 864
prominence 6
pronaos 683
propagation 889
propane accessories 1034
propeller 856, 857, 858,
   862, 864
propeller duct 860
propeller shaft 857
property man 647
proscenium 648
prosciutto 363
prostate 297
protect tab 762
protection area 987
protection layer 20
protective cup 986
protective goggles 1006,
   1009
protective helmet 828
protective mat 1013, 1015
protective plate 1009
protective suit 1009
proton 876
proximal phalange 259, 261
pruning knife 153
pruning saw 152
pruning shears 151
pruning tools 151
pseudopod 160
pubis 200, 244, 248
pull strap 643
pulley 810, 882
Pullman case 643
pulmonary artery 270, 273,
   277
pulmonary valve 272
pulmonary vein 271
pulp 113, 266
pulp chamber 266
pulsed ruby laser 895
pulverizer 927
pump 509, 513, 550, 1034
pump motor 454
pumpernickel 354
pumping station 933
pumpkin 329
punch hole 553, 564, 599

UNIVERSE AND EARTH > 2-83;   PLANTS AND GARDENING > 84-157;   ANIMAL KINGDOM > 158-243;   THE HUMAN BEING > 244-311;   FOOD AND KITCHEN > 312-429;
HOUSE AND DO-IT-YOURSELF > 430-543;   CLOTHING AND PERSONAL ACCESSORIES > 544-643;   ARTS AND ARCHITECTURE > 644-695;   COMMUNICATIONS AND
OFFICE AUTOMATION > 696-791;   TRANSPORTATION > 792-875;   SCIENCE AND ENERGY > 876-951;   SPORTS AND GAMES > 952-1048

punching bag 986
pup tent 1031
pupa 168
pupil 226, 310
purfling 662, 665
purse 636
purslane 324
pursuit bicycle 1005
pursuit line 1005
pursuit racer 1005
push button 412, 736
push buttons 734
push-button telephone 737
push-to-talk switch 729, 731
push-up bra 590
push-up stand 995
pusher 397, 429
putter 1001
pygal shield 191
pygostyle 200
pyramid 684, 923
pyramid spot 997
pyramid, entrance 684
python 194

Q

quadrant 919
quadrilateral 920
quail 210
quark 876
quarter 552, 598
quarter window 805
queen 1042, 1047
queen cell 168
queen's chamber 684
queen's side 1046
quiche plate 403
quill 525
quill brush 615
quince 346
quiver 999

R

rabbet bit 529
rabbit 214
raccoon 229
race director 1004
rachis 199
racing suit 1017
rack 407, 418, 502, 505, 512, 998
rack and pinion gear 881
racket sports 966
Raclette 360
raclette with grill 420
radar 857, 858, 861, 865
radar aircraft 873
radar mast 862
radar-absorbent material 873
radial nerve 283
radial passenger loading area 867
radial thread 175
radiation 879
radiation zone 6
radiator 841
radiator grille 816
radiator panel 25
radiators 22
radicchio 322

radicle 96, 129
radio antenna 857, 858, 861, 862, 865, 1007
radio waves 890
radioactive nuclei 878
radioactivity, measurement 913
radish 330
radius 201, 243, 256, 258, 919
rafter 438
raglan 574
raglan sleeve 568, 570, 574, 595
rail 478, 997
railing 433, 434
railroad station 836
rain 72, 74
rain forms 71
rainbow 74
raincoat 568
rainfly 1030
raining, utensils for 400
raised handlebar 1006
rake 143
rake comb 616
RAM module 746
rambutan 348
ramekin 385
ramp 682, 691, 794, 850, 1028
rampart 692
random access memory (RAM) connector 746
random access memory module 746
random orbit sander 527
range hood 378, 504
Ranvier, node 288
rasp 531
raspberry 339
raspberry, section 117
rat 213
ratchet 517, 525
ratchet socket wrench 534
ratchet wheel 904
rattle 188
rattlesnake 193
raven 204
ravioli 357
razor clam 369
reaction direction 880
reactor 941
reactor building 945
reactor vessel 945
read button 730
read/write head 760
reading 630
reading start 722
reamer 416
rear apron 562
rear beam 907
rear brake 832
rear cargo rack 831
rear fender 831
rear foil 857
rear leg 476
rear light 832
rear propeller 856
rear rigid section 815

rear shock absorber 827
rearview mirror 807
récamier 474
receiver 733, 735, 969, 972
receiver volume control 734
receiving tray 738
receptacle 90, 104, 116, 117
receptacle analyzer 543
rechargeable battery pack 713
recharging base 501
record 720
record button 709, 710, 719
record player 714
recording mode 712
recording start/stop button 713
recording tape 708, 718
rectangle 920
rectangular 1032
rectum 192, 279, 293, 297
rectus abdominis 252
rectus femoris 252
red 891, 1045
red alga 91
red cabbage 323
red kidney bean 336
red onion 315
red sweet pepper 327
red whortleberry 338
red-eye reduction 652
red-kneed tarantula 173
redfish 376
reed 672
reel 146, 708
reel seat 1038, 1039
reentrant angle 918
referee 955, 961, 962, 965, 976, 979, 984, 987, 988, 990, 1011, 1014, 1019
reflected solar radiation 78
reflecting cylinder 895
reflector 543, 818, 832
reflex camera, cross section 654
refrigerated semitrailer 818, 821
refrigeration unit 818
refrigerator 379
refrigerator car 845
regular decagon 921
regular dodecagon 921
regular hendecagon 921
regular heptagon 921
regular hexagon 921
regular nonagon 921
regular octagon 921
regular octahedron 923
regular pentagon 921
regulating button 670
regulator first stage 983
regulator second stage 983
relay starting line 953
relay station 700
release lever 533
release of oxygen 98
relieving chamber 684
remote control 710
remote control sensor 707

remote manipulator system 23, 24
remote sensor 757
removable flag pole 1000
removable hard disk 761
removable hard disk drive 761
removable-bottomed pan 403
renal artery 270
renal hilum 280
renal vein 271
reniform 102
repeat button 723
repeater 703
reproductive organs, female 292
reproductive organs, male 295
reptiles, examples 193
repulsion 888
reservoir 423, 935, 936
reservoir-nib pen 645
reset button 744, 759, 903, 911, 1048
reset key 738
resin surface 722
resistance adjustment 993
resistors 886
resonator 681
respiratory organs 276
respiratory system 274
restaurant 861
restaurant review 699
restricted area 963
restricting circle 962
result line 772
resurgence 49
reticle 899
retina 892
retractable handle 634
return 741
reversible reaction 880
reversing switch 516
revolving nosepiece 897
revolving sprinkler 149
rewind button 710, 719
rewritable DVD disc 763
Rhea 5
rhinoceros 222
rhizoid 88
rhizome 92
rhombus 920
rias 58
rib 200, 319, 662, 665
rib joint pliers 533
rib roast 366
ribbing 595, 596
ribosome 84, 159
ribs 256
rice 127
rice: panicle 127
ricotta 359
ridge 44
riegel 46
rifle (rifled bore) 1041
rigatoni 356
rigging 852
right angle 917, 918
right ascension 19
right atrium 269, 272

right attacker 964
right back 964
right defense 1010
right field 959
right kidney 280
right lung 276
right pulmonary vein 272
right service court 973
right side 632
right ventricle 269, 272
right wing 1011
rillettes 363
rim 628, 630, 809, 827, 833
rim flange 809
rim soup bowl 383
rim 75
rinceau 472
rind 113
ring 94, 677, 903, 910, 984
ring binder 783
ring post 984
ring step 985
ring, parts 606
ringing volume control 735
rings 606, 975
ringside 985
rink 1010, 1019
rink corner 1010
rinse-aid dispenser 512
rip fence 522
riser 442
rising warm air 69
river 34, 35, 50, 51
river estuary 35, 57
river otter 229
rivet 392, 532
road bicycle 835
road communications 703
road cycling competition 1004
road racing 1004
road system 792
road transport 792, 851
road, cross section 792
road-racing bicycle 1004
road-racing cyclist 1004
roadway 792
roast 367
roasting pans 409
Roberval's balance 906
robin 203
rock basin 46
rock garden 138
rocking chair 473
rocky desert 60
rocky islet 57
rodents, examples 212
roll film 655
roll structure 1007
roll-up blind 492
roller 492, 617, 751
roller shade 492
rolling pin 402
romaine lettuce 322
Roman amphitheater 690
roman bean 335
Roman house 688
Roman numerals 916
roman shade 492
Romano 360

INDEX

roof 431, 805, 812
rook 1047
room 928
room air conditioner 451
room thermostat 450
rooms, main 432
rooster 209
root 99, 266, 308, 386
root canal 266
root of nail 300
root of nose 305
root system 96
root vegetables 330
root-hair zone 129
rope 603, 882, 985
Roquefort 361
rose 108, 147, 447, 665
rosemary 351
rosette 687
rotary cheese grater 397
rotary file 778
rotary system 931
rotary table 931
rotating dome 17
rotini 356
rotodome 873
rotor 949
rotor blade 875
rotor head 874
rotor hub 874
rough 1000
round brush 615
round head 518
rounding-over bit 529
route sign 813, 814
router 528, 764
routing cardboard 843
row 626
rowing machine 995
royal agaric 312
royal flush 1043
rub rail 819
rubber 554
rubber gasket 460
rubber mat 721
rubber stamp 780
rubber wall 809
rubbing strip 809
ruby 605
ruby cylinder 895
ruching 593
rudder 25, 858, 860, 862,
864, 869, 980
rudder blade 856
ruffled rumba pants 593
ruffled skirt 579
rug and floor brush 500
rule 698
ruler 911, 1035
rump 196
run 442
runner 1045
running shoe 598
Russian module 22
Russian pumpernickel 354
rutabaga 331
rye 124
rye bread 352
rye: spike 124

S

S-Video output 769
sacral plexus 282
sacrum 256, 257, 264
saddlebag 829
safari jacket 581
safety area 988
safety binding 1022
safety handle 157
safety line 847
safety rail 840
safety scissors 611
safety tether 20
safety thermostat 511
safety valve 408, 941
sage 350
sagittal section 292, 296
sail 948
sail cloth 948
sailbar 948
sailboard 981
sailboat 980
sailing 980
sailor collar 586
sails 854
salad bowl 385
salad dish 385
salad fork 387
salad plate 383
salad spinner 400
salamander 187
salami 364
saline lake 61
salivary gland 309
salivary glands 278
salmon, Atlantic 377
salmon, Pacific 377
salsify 330
salt shaker 384
sand bar 53
sand bunker 1000
sand island 57
sand paper 531
sand shoe 818
sandal 549, 550
sandbox 841
sanding disk 527
sanding pad 527
sandy desert 60
saphenous nerve 282
sapodilla 348
sapphire 605
satellite 700
satellite earth station 765
satellite radio receiver 728
satellites 4
Saturn 2, 5
Saturn V 27
saucepan 411
sausage 365
sauté pan 411
savanna 137
savanna climate 64
savory 351
savoy cabbage 323

sawing tools 519
saxhorn 675
saxophone 672
scale 183, 189, 190, 901,
911, 1037
scale leaf 99
scallion 316
scallop 368
scampi 370
Scandinavian cracked bread
354
scaphoid 258
scapula 200, 257
scapular 198
scarlet runner bean 335
scatter cushion 485
schema of circulation 269
school bus 813
Schwann, sheath 289
sciatic nerve 282
scientific air lock 25
scientific calculator 772
scientific instruments 18, 25
scientific symbols 912
scissors 1035
scissors crossing 837
scissors-glasses 631
sclera 311
scoreboard 952, 988
scoreboard, current event
975
scoreboard, overall standings
974
scorekeeper 990
scorer 962, 964
scorers 988
scorpion 173
scotia 686
Scotia Plate 40
screen 622, 707, 936
screen door 812
screen print 595
screw 518, 663
screw base 467
screw earrings 602
screw locking nut 1038, 1039
screwdriver 516, 1035
screwdriver, cordless 516
screwing tools 516
scroll 662
scroll button 729
scroll case 937
scroll foot 472
scroll wheel 750
scrolling lock key 749
scrotum 296
scuba diver 983
scuba diving 983
scuffle hoe 144
sea 8, 35, 51
sea bag 641
sea bass 375
sea bream 372
sea kale 323
sea lettuce 314
sea level 36, 55
sea lion 234
seal 234
sealed cell 168
sealing material 885
sealing plug 884, 885
seam 557

seam pocket 575
seamount 54
search 767
seasons of the year 63
seat 459, 472, 476, 488,
829, 830, 831, 832, 993
seat cover 456, 459
seat post 832
seat stay 832
seat tube 832, 1005
seats 475
seaweed 314
sebaceous gland 298
second 917, 984, 1012
second assistant camera
operator 646
second base 958
second dorsal fin 181
second floor 432, 434
second hand 903
second level of operations
772
second molar 268
second premolar 268
second space 963
second valve slide 676
second violins 661
secondaries 198
secondary hard disk drive 746
secondary mirror 17, 18, 654
secondary root 96
secretarial desk 741
secretary 480
section 697
section of a bulb 99
section of a capsule: poppy
121
section of a follicle: star anise
120
section of a grape 115
section of a hazelnut 120
section of a peach 111
section of a raspberry 117
section of a silique: mustard
121
section of a strawberry 116
section of an apple 119
section of an orange 113
section of the Earth's crust 36
sector 919
Secure Digital card 655
security casing 156
security trigger 155
sedimentary rocks 36
seed 110, 112, 114, 117,
118, 120, 121
seed coat 110, 122
seeder 140
seeding tools 140
seedless cucumber 328
segment 113
seismic wave 39
select button 727, 730
self-adhesive labels 781
self-inflating mattress 1033
self-sealing flap 779
self-stick note 775
semaphore 837
semi-mummy 1032
semicircle 919, 962
semicircular canal, lateral
303

semicircular canal, posterior
303
semicircular canal, superior
303
seminal vesicle 297
semiprecious stones 604
semispinalis capitis 255
semitendinosus 254
semitrailer 820
semitrailers, examples 820
sense organs 298
sensitivity 652
sensor probe 419
sensory root 285
sent document tray 739
sepal 104, 117, 119
separator 862, 885, 924
septal cartilage of nose 306
septic tank 455
septic truck 823
septum 121, 305
septum pellucidum 287
serac 47
serial port 745
server 765, 968, 973
service area 867
service judge 968, 972
service line 972
service provider, Internet 765
service road 866
set 647
set dresser 647
set of bells 681
set of utensils 404
set-in sleeve 560
setting 606
shad 374
shade 493, 494
shade cloth 492
shadow 905
shaft 684, 687, 881, 902,
970, 971, 998, 1001
shake-hands grip 967
shallot 316
shallow root 129, 133
sham 485
shampoo 620
shank 366, 515, 516, 518,
526, 1039
shaping tools 527
shapka 547
shark, morphology 180
sharpening steel 394
sharpening stone 394
shaving 622
shaving brush 623
shaving foam 623
shaving mug 623
shawl collar 586
sheath 100
sheath dress 576
sheath of Schwann 289
sheath skirt 578
sheathing 439, 441
shed 138, 430
sheep 218
sheepskin jacket 571
sheer curtain 489
sheet 854, 1012
sheet film 654
shelf 481, 506, 740
shelf channel 506

INDEX

1066

UNIVERSE AND EARTH > 2-83;   PLANTS AND GARDENING > 84-157;   ANIMAL KINGDOM > 158-243;   THE HUMAN BEING > 244-311;   FOOD AND KITCHEN > 312-429;
HOUSE AND DO-IT-YOURSELF > 430-543;   CLOTHING AND PERSONAL ACCESSORIES > 544-643;   ARTS AND ARCHITECTURE > 644-695;   COMMUNICATIONS AND
OFFICE AUTOMATION > 696-791;   TRANSPORTATION > 792-875;   SCIENCE AND ENERGY > 876-951;   SPORTS AND GAMES > 952-1048

shell 679
shield bug 170
shift key 748
shiitake mushroom 313
shin guard 956, 1016, 1020
ships 856
shirt 560, 593
shirt collar 586
shirttail 560, 584
shirtwaist dress 576
shoe 1004
shoe polish 555
shoe polisher 555
shoe, parts 552
shoebrush 555
shoelace 553, 599
shoes 548
shoes, accessories 555
shoeshine kit 555
shoot 129
shop 688
shopping bag 638
shore 53
shore cliff 58
shorelines, examples 58
short glove 556
short peroneus 254
short service line 969
short sock 592
short track 1013
short track skate 1017
shorts 582, 699, 956, 1004
shot put 952
shotgun (smooth-bore) 1041
shoulder 217, 224, 244, 248,
  535, 664, 792, 971
shoulder bag 641
shoulder blade 246, 250
shoulder bolt 535
shoulder strap 591, 641, 642,
  712, 1002, 1036
shovel 142, 1022, 1025
shower 434
shower and tub fixture 453
shower head 456
shower stall 456
shrew 215
shrimp 370
shroud 852, 980
shuffle play 723
shunt 883
shutoff valve 452, 458, 461,
  462, 463
shutter 444, 762
shutter release button 650
shutter speed 652
shuttlecock, synthetic 970
sickle 153
side 390, 852
side back vent 558
side chair 476
side chapel 694
side compression strap 1036
side door 848
side fairings 1007
side footboard 840
side handrail 849
side hatch 24
side judge 961
side ladder 842
side lane 795

side panel 568
side rail 818
side span 799
side vent 43
sideline 960, 962, 965, 966
sidewalk 431
sidewall 818, 977
siding 837
sieve 400
sifter 401
sight 310, 999, 1037
sighting line 1037
sighting mirror 1037
sigmoid colon 279
signal gantry 836
signal lamp 418, 423, 426,
  428, 498, 505
signal tower 836
signature book 779
signet ring 607
silique, section 121
silk 125
sill 42, 440
sill of frame 445
sill plate 439, 440
sill step 842
silos 850
silverware 386
sima 686
simple leaves 102
simple organisms 158
single chain wheel 1003
single circuit breaker 464
single reed 672
single seat 849
single sprocket 1003
single-bladed paddle 982
single-breasted jacket 559
single-burner camp stove
  1034
single-handle kitchen faucet
  461
single-leaf bascule bridge 801
single-lens reflex (SLR)
  camera 656
single-lens reflex camera 650,
  651
singles sideline 969, 973
singlet 987
sink 378, 457, 461
sinkhole 49
siphon 177
sistrum 681
sitting room 436
skate 371, 1018
skateboard 1029
skateboarder 1029
skateboarding 1028
skater: long track 1017
skater: short track 1016
skeg 981
skeleton 256
skeleton of a bird 200
skerry 56
ski 1022, 1023
ski area 1024
ski boot 1022, 1023
ski glove 1023
ski goggles 1023
ski hat 1025
ski pants 582
ski pole 1023, 1025

ski resort 1024
ski suit 1023, 1025
skid 875
skimmer 404
skin 111, 115, 119, 298
skin surface 299
skip 929, 1012
skirt 573
skirt finger 860
skirts, examples 578
skull 201, 245
skull, lateral view 262
skullcap 547
skunk 229
skylight 431, 433
slat 486
sled 150
sleeper-cab 817
sleepers 595
sleeping bags, examples
  1032
sleet 72, 73
sleeve 558, 559, 874
sleeve strap 570
sleeve strap loop 570
sleeveless jersey 992
slide 513
sliding channel 842
sliding door 456
sliding seat 995
sliding sunroof 805
sliding weight 907
slip 589
slip joint 532
slip joint pliers 532
slip-stitched seam 562
slope 793
sloping cornice 682
slot 386, 421, 518, 635
slow-burning stove 449
slow-motion button 710
slower traffic 794
SLR camera 650, 651
small decanter 381
small intestine 192, 279
small saucepan 411
smartphone 737
smell 304
smelt 372
smock 584
smoke baffle 449
smoked ham 367
smooth hound 371
snail 369
snail dish 406
snail tongs 406
snake 188
snap fastener 557, 571
snap-fastening front 595
snap-fastening tab 571
snap-fastening waist 595
snare 680, 1041
snare drum 661, 678, 680
snare head 680
snare strainer 680
snatch 992
snorkel 983
snout 180, 185, 240
snow 73
snow crystals 72

snow pellet 72
snowblower 824
snowboard 1020
snowboard, alpine 1021
snowboard, freestyle 1021
snowboarder 1020
snowboarding 1020
snowshoe 1026
snowshoe, elliptical 1026
snowshoes 1026
soap dish 457
soccer 954
soccer ball 956
soccer player 956
soccer shoe 956
sock 592, 956
socket 467
socket head 518
socket set 534
socks 565
sofa 474
sofa bed 483
soft binding 1021
soft cheeses 358
soft contact lens 632
soft key 733
soft palate 304, 307
soft pedal 668
soft ray 183
soft-shell clam 368
soil 82
soil profile 97
solar cell 771, 946
solar collector 947
solar eclipse 7
solar energy 98, 946
solar panel 18
solar radiation 76, 78, 946,
  947
solar shield 21
solar system 2
sole 377, 530, 565, 1018,
  1022
soleplate 498
soleus 252
solid 877, 879
solid center auger bit 526
solid line 792
solid rear wheel 1005
solid rocket booster 26
solids 922
solitaire ring 607
sorghum 127
sorghum: panicle 127
sorus 92
soufflé dish 403
sound box 664, 665
sound engineer 647
sound hole 662
sound reproducing system
  714
sound systems, portable 725
soundboard 659, 662, 664,
  665, 669
soup bowl 383
soup spoon 384
soup tureen 385
South America 29
South American Plate 40
South celestial pole 19
South Pole 30
south pole 888

Southern Hemisphere 31
southwester 545
soybean sprouts 336
soybeans 336
space bar 748
space launcher 27
space launchers, examples
  27
space shuttle 24, 62
space shuttle at takeoff 26
space telescope 18, 62
spacelab 25
spacer 944
spacesuit 20
spade 142, 1042
spade bit 526
spading fork 142
spaghetti 357
spaghetti squash 329
spaghetti tongs 406
spaghettini 357
spanker 854
spare tire 812
spareribs 367
spark plug 811
sparkling wine glass 380
sparrow 203
spatial dendrite 73
spatula 404, 645
spatulate 102
speaker 713, 729, 746, 768,
  979
spear 319
specific operations 772
speed ball 986
speed control 413
speed selector 414, 721
speed selector switch 523,
  619
speed skating 1013
speed-increasing gearbox 951
speedometer 828, 993
spencer 581
spent fuel storage bay 945
sperm whale 233
spermatozoon 295
sphenoid bone 262
sphenoidal sinus 307
sphere 922
sphincter muscle of anus 278
spicules 6
spider 174
spider web 175
spider, morphology 174
spillway 934
spillway chute 934
spillway gate 934
spinach 325
spinach tagliatelle 357
spinal column 256, 264, 284
spinal cord 284, 285
spinal cord, structure 285
spinal ganglion 285
spinal nerve 285
spindle 417, 476, 721
spine 163, 1008
spine of scapula 257
spinneret 174
spinning rod 1039
spinous process 265
spiny lobster 370
spiny ray 183

UNIVERSE AND EARTH > 2-83; PLANTS AND GARDENING > 84-157; ANIMAL KINGDOM > 158-243; THE HUMAN BEING > 244-311; FOOD AND KITCHEN > 312-429;
HOUSE AND DO-IT-YOURSELF > 430-543; CLOTHING AND PERSONAL ACCESSORIES > 544-643; ARTS AND ARCHITECTURE > 644-695; COMMUNICATIONS AND
OFFICE AUTOMATION > 696-791; TRANSPORTATION > 792-875; SCIENCE AND ENERGY > 876-951; SPORTS AND GAMES > 952-1048

INDEX

1067

spiracle 165
spiral 517, 720
spiral arm 12
spiral beater 415
spiral binder 783
spiral cloud band 68
spiral nail 515
spiral screwdriver 517
spiral thread 175
spiral-in groove 720
spirit level 538
spirulina 314
spit 57
splat 472
spleen 192
splenius capitis 255
split peas 333
spoiler 868
spoke 833
sponge 162
sponge, anatomy 162
sponge-tipped applicator 613
spongocoel 162
spoon 388
spoons, examples 389
spores 94
sport-utility vehicle 803
sports car 802
sports on wheels 1027
sports, combat 984
sportswear 598
spot 496
spotlight 646
spotlights 649
spout 426, 428
spout assembly 461
spray 498
spray arm 513
spray button 498
spray control 498
spray head 460
spray hose 456, 461
spray nozzle 148
spray skirt 982
sprayer 148
spread collar 561
spreader 141
spring 50, 63, 494, 508, 532
spring balance 910
spring binder 782
springboard, 1 m 979
springboard, 3 m 979
sprinkler hose 147
sprinklers 940
sprinters' line 1005
spruce 135
spur 45, 526, 678
spur gear 881
squamous suture 263
square 920
square movement 1047
square root key 771
square root of 915
square trowel 522
square-headed tip 517
squash 328
squid 368
squirrel 213
stabilizer 999
stabilizer fin 864
stabilizer jack 812
stack 56, 858, 927

stage 897
stage clip 897
stage curtain 648
stage-house 648
stair climber 995
stairs 435, 436, 442, 649, 846
stairwell 434
stairwell skylight 433
stake 139, 141, 1030
stake pocket 819
stalactite 48
stalagmite 48
stalk 88, 111, 115, 119, 320
stalk vegetables 319
stamen 105
stamp pad 780
stamp rack 780
stanchion 1018
stand 408, 413, 493, 618
stand-up collar 587
standard poker hands 1043
standpipe 462
stapes 303
staple remover 790
stapler 790
staples 790
starboard hand 865
starch 122
starch granule 85
starfish, morphology 163
starling 204
start area 1008
start button 903
start judge 1013
start judges 1014
start key 738, 748
start switch 510
starter 145, 157, 976
starter handle 155
starting block 976
starting gate 1008
starting step 443
states of matter 877
station entrance 846
station name 847
station platform 836
station wagon 803
stationary bicycle 993
stationery 771
stay 853
steak 366
steak knife 391
stealth aircraft 873
steam 924
steam control knob 425
steam generator 927
steam iron 498
steam nozzle 425
steam pressure drives turbine 942
steamer 410
steamer basket 410
steel 590
steel casing 885
steeplechase hurdle jump 952
steering wheel 806, 1007
stellar crystal 72
stem 88, 94, 96, 98, 426, 468, 833, 853, 856, 901
stem bulb 859, 865

stem propeller 856
steno book 779
step 817
step chair 475
step groove 443
step setting 911
steppe 65
steps 431, 437
stern 864
sternocleidomastoid 253
sternum 200, 256
stick 663
stick holder 788
stickpin 609
sticks 680
stifle 216
stigma 104, 120
stile 476
stile groove of sash 444
stile tongue of sash 444
still cameras 656
still water level 52
stills photographer 647
Stilton 361
stimulator tip 626
sting 166
stipule 100
stitch 553, 598
stitching 557
stock 659, 663
stock pot 410
stockade 693
stocking 592
stocking cap 544
stomach 188, 192, 278
stomach throw 989
stone 111, 606
stone fleshy fruit 110
stone fruits 337
stone marten 228
stoner 405
stop 224
stop button 155, 709, 710, 719, 723, 903
stopper 620, 1036
stopwatch 903
storage compartment 817
storage door 507
storage furniture 478
stork 207
stormy sky 74
straight 1043
straight flush 1043
straight jaw 533
straight razor 624
straight skirt 579
straight-up ribbed top 565
straightneck squash 329
strainer 416, 429, 1030
strainer body 460
straining, utensils for 400
strait 35
strap 610, 905, 957, 992
strap loop 1036
strap system 667
strapless bra 590
stratocumulus 66
stratopause 62
stratosphere 62
stratum basale 298
stratum corneum 298
stratum granulosum 298

stratum lucidum 298
stratus 66
straw bales 1008
strawberry 339
strawberry, section 116
street sweeper 824
strength sports 992
stretcher 477
string 662, 664, 670
stringed instruments 662
stringing 970, 971
strings 668
strip light 497
stroke judge 976
strokes, types 978
structure 444
structure of a conifer 133
structure of a fern 92
structure of a flower 104
structure of a house 432
structure of a leaf 100
structure of a lichen 86
structure of a moss 88
structure of a mushroom 94
structure of a plant 96
structure of a tree 128
structure of an alga 90
structure of the ear 302
structure of the Earth 38
structure of the spinal cord 285
structure of the Sun 6
strut 439, 679, 857, 873, 949
stud 438, 599
studded tire 808
studio floor 704
studio, television 704
study 433
stump 129
sturgeon 371
style 104, 110, 114, 121
stylobate 682, 686
styloid process 263
stylus 755, 770
stylus cartridge 721
stylus holder 755
subarctic 66
subbase 793
subclavian artery 270
subclavian vein 271
subcutaneous tissue 299
subduction 41
subfloor 439, 441
subgrade 793
subhead 696
sublimation 877
submarine cable 703
submarine canyon 54
submarine line 764
submarine pipeline 933
subsiding cold air 68
subsoil 79
substitute's bench 955
substructure 930
subterranean stream 48
subtract key 771
subtractive color synthesis 891
suburban commuter railroad 836
subway 846

subway map 847, 849
subway station 846
subway train 846, 849
sucker 176
sudoriferous duct 299
sugar bowl 382
suit 573
sulcus terminalis 308
sulfur dioxide emission 82
sulfuric acid emission 82
sum 915
sumi-e brush 645
summer 63
summer solstice 63
summer squash 328
summit 45, 1024
sump 454, 929
Sun 2, 4, 6, 7, 9, 63
sun visor 807
Sun, structure 6
sundae spoon 389
sundeck 865
sundial 905
sundress 577
sunflower 108
sunglasses 631
sunspot 6
supercooling 877
supercross circuit 1008
supercross motorcycle 1009
superficial peroneal nerve 282
superior dental arch 304
superior mesenteric artery 270
superior mesenteric vein 271
superior nasal concha 306
superior semicircular canal 303
superior umbilicus 199
superior vena cava 269, 271, 272
supersonic jetliner 872
supply line 452
supply point 938
supply tube 461
support 468, 476
support thread 175
suprarenal gland 280
sural nerve 283
surface course 792
surface element 504
surface insulation 24
surface of the water 979
surface runoff 77
surface-piercing foils 857
suspended span 797
suspender 799
suspender clip 564
suspenders 564
suspension 848
suspension arm 509
suspension bridge 799
suspension cable 799
suspension truck 838
suture 120
swallow 203
swallow hole 48
sweater vest 597
sweaters 581, 596
sweeping hip throw 989
sweet bay 350

INDEX

sweet peas 333
sweet pepper 327
sweet potato 318
sweetbreads 362
swift 204
swimming 976
swimming pool 977
swimming trunks 600
swimsuit 600
swing bridge 800
Swiss Army knife 1035
Swiss chard 319
switch 454, 466, 507, 528, 837, 883
switch lock 524
switch plate 466
switched outlet 717
swivel 930
swivel base 537
swivel cord 618
swivel lock 537
swivel wall lamp 495
swivel-tilter armchair 741
swiveling nozzle 873
swordfish 372
symbols 1042
sympathetic ganglion 285
symphony orchestra 660
symphysis pubis 292, 296
synapse 288
sync cable 770
synsacrum 200
synthetic shuttlecock 970
synthetic sponge 612
synthetic surface 971
system components 714
system of units 912

T

T-strap shoe 550
tab 568, 634, 635, 781
table 477, 966, 996
table lamp 493
table mixer 413
table tennis 966
table tennis ball 967
table tennis paddle 967
tablespoon 389
tablinum 688
tabloid 697
tabulation key 748
tachometer 828
tack 515, 981
tackle box 1040
tadpole 186
tag 552, 599
tagliatelle 357
tail 178, 188, 191, 216, 225, 227, 241, 243, 295, 869, 1021, 1022, 1026, 1029
tail assembly 869
tail boom 875
tail comb 616
tail feather 196
tail of helix 301
tail skid 875
tail stop 530
tail-out groove 720
taillight 819, 827
tailored collar 573, 586
tailpiece 662

tailrace 937
tajine 408
take-up reel 718
take-up spool 651
takeover zone 952
talk key 733
talus 260
tamarillo 347
tamarin 236
tambourine 680
tamper 425
tandem bicycle 835
tandem tractor trailer 820
tang 390, 392, 531, 541
tank 25, 455, 863, 1034
tank ball 458
tank body 820, 825
tank car 844
tank farm 933
tank lid 459
tank sprayer 147
tank top 601
tank trailer 820
tank truck 825
tanker 851, 862
tap connector 146
tape 538
tape counter 719
tape dispenser 787
tape guide 787
tape measure 538
tape selector 719
tape-guide 718
taproot 128
tarantula 173
target 999
taro 317
tarragon 350
tarsometatarsus 200
tarsus 165, 196, 260
Tasmanian devil 239
tassel 489
taste 304
taste bud 309
taste receptors 309
tasting spoon 405
taxiway 866, 867
taxiway line 867
tea ball 406
team shirt 956
teapot 382
tear-off calendar 776
teaser comb 616
teaspoon 389
technical controller 1019
technical delegates 1019
technical identification band 722
technical producer 704
technical specialist 1019
technical specifications 809
technical terms 110, 112, 114, 118
tectonic plates 40
teddy 588
tee 462, 1001, 1012
tee line 1012
teeing ground 1000
teeth 266, 531
Teflon tape 540
telecommunication antenna 861, 865

telecommunication satellite 765
telecommunications by satellite 702
telephone index 734, 779
telephone line 764
telephone network 702
telephone set 734
telephone, communication 732
teleport 703
teleprompter 706
telescope 16
telescope base 16
telescopic corridor 867
telescopic front fork 826, 829
telescopic sight 898
telescoping antenna 725
telescoping uncoupling rod 842
television 704
television program schedule 699
telltale 980
telson 178
temperate forest 137
temperature 450
temperature control 421, 450, 498
temperature selector 422, 508, 510
temperature, measure 900
temple 245, 629
temporal bone 263
ten 916
tenderloin roast 366
tennis 971
tennis ball 971
tennis racket 971
tennis shoe 548
tenor drum 678
tension adjusting screw 787
tension rod 679, 680
tension screw 678
tent trailer 812
tentacle 176
tents, examples 1030
teres major 255
teres minor 255
terminal 464, 504, 932, 938
terminal arborization 288
terminal bronchiole 274
terminal bud 96
terminal cover 712
terminal moraine 47
terminal railway 851
termite 169
tern 205
terrine 409
tertial 198
testicle 296
Tethys 5
thallus 86, 90
theater 648
thermal energy 926
thermodynamic temperature, measurement 913
thermometer 909
thermopause 62
thermosphere 62
thermostat 418
thermostat control 506

thigh 196, 216, 225, 241, 246, 250, 293, 297
thigh-boot 551
thigh-high stocking 592
third base 958
third floor 432
third valve slide 677
third wheel 904
thistle 109
thong 549
thoracic legs 178
thoracic vertebra 264, 265
thorax 164, 167, 244, 248
thread 518
threaded rod 535
three-blade propeller 870, 871
three-of-a-kind 1043
three-quarter coat 569
threshold 446
throat 197, 971, 1039
throat protector 1016
throttle control 753
thrust 798
thruster 20
thumb 242, 557, 957
thumb hook 676
thumb rest 673
thumb tacks 789
thumbscrew 534
thyme 350
tibia 165, 242, 256, 260
tibial nerve 283
tibiotarsus 200
tick 173
ticket collecting booth 846
tie bar 609
tie beam 438
tie rod 679
tiepin 609
tier 690
tierceron 695
tiger 231
tightening buckle 1036
tightening tools 532
tile 683, 688
tiller 145, 980
tilt-back head 413
timber 683, 689
time card 775
time clock 775
timed outlet 505
timekeeper 962, 985, 990, 1019
timekeepers 988, 1015
timer 418, 993
timing belt 810
timpani 661
tine 145, 386
tip 100, 319, 388, 390, 515, 516, 541, 564, 998, 1022, 1026
tip of nose 305
tip section 1038
tip-ring 1038, 1039
tips, examples 517
tire 804, 808, 817
tire valve 833
tires, examples 808
tissue holder 456
tissues 614

Titan 5
Titan IV 27
Titania 5
toad 187
toaster 421
toe 223, 225, 244, 248, 520, 530, 565
toe hole 1026
toe pick 1018
toenail scissors 611
toggle bolt 516
toggle fastening 572
toilet 435, 456, 458
toilet bowl 459
toilet paper 614
toilet soap 620
toilet tank 456
tom-tom 678
tomatillo 327
tomato 327
tombolo 57
tone arm 721
tone control 666
toner cartridge 759
tongs 406
tongue 278, 304, 306, 362, 552, 564, 599, 1018, 1022
tongue, dorsum 308
tonsil 304
tool belt 539
tool box 539
tool holder 528
tool storage area 499
tool tether 21
tools 499
tools for loosening the earth 142
tools, electricity 542
tooth 180, 189, 520
toothbrush 626, 627
toothbrush shaft 627
toothed jaw 532
toothed wheel 881
toothpaste 626
top 128, 477, 853
top box 829
top cap 884
top coat 574
top flap 1036
top hat 547
top lift 552
top of dam 934
top pocket 997
top rail 476, 478, 487
top rail of sash 445
top road 929
top stitched pleat 580
top stitching 564, 594
topaz 604
topsoil 97
toque 545
toric lens 893
tornado 70
torque converter 508
tortellini 356
tortilla 353
torus 686, 687, 922
total 908
total eclipse 7, 9
tote bag 640, 642
toucan 206
touch 298

UNIVERSE AND EARTH > 2-83; PLANTS AND GARDENING > 84-157; ANIMAL KINGDOM > 158-243; THE HUMAN BEING > 244-311; FOOD AND KITCHEN > 312-429; HOUSE AND DO-IT-YOURSELF > 430-543; CLOTHING AND PERSONAL ACCESSORIES > 544-643; ARTS AND ARCHITECTURE > 644-695; COMMUNICATIONS AND OFFICE AUTOMATION > 696-791; TRANSPORTATION > 792-875; SCIENCE AND ENERGY > 876-951; SPORTS AND GAMES > 952-1048

INDEX

1069

touch line 955
touch pad 768
touch pad button 768
touch screen 770
Toulouse sausage 365
touring bicycle 835
touring motorcycle 829
touring tire 808
tourmaline 604
tow truck 822
towel bar 457
tower 694, 799, 948, 950
tower case 744, 745, 746
tower mill 948
towing device 822
trachea 274, 277
track 846, 952, 1005, 1013
track cycling 1005
track judge 1015
track lighting 496
track search/fast operation
  buttons 709, 723
trackball 752
traditional jacket 991
traditional musical
  instruments 658
traffic circle 796
traffic lane 794
traffic lanes 794
tragus 301
trailer car 849
trailing edge 868
trailing edge flap 868
trainer 963, 984
training wall 934
transceiving parabolic
  antenna 701
transept spire 694
transfer dispensing machine
  847
transfer of heat to water 941
transfer ramp 795
transform plate boundaries 41
transformer 496, 936, 938
transit shed 850
transmission 508
transmission to consumers
  927
transmitter 734
transmitting tower 700
transpiration 77
transporter bridge 800
transverse bulkhead 862
transverse colon 279
transverse dunes 59
transverse flute 674
transverse foramen 265
transverse process 264, 265
trap 453, 459, 460, 648
trapdoor 691
trapeze dress 577
trapezium 258
trapezius 253, 255
trapezoid 258, 920
trash truck 825
traveler 980
traveling crane 937
traverse arch 695
tray 488, 539
tread 442
tread design 809
treble bridge 668

treble keyboard 658
treble pickup 666
treble register 658
treble tone control 667, 716,
  725
tree 128
tree fern 93
tree frog 187
tree, structure 128
trench 55
trench coat 570
triangle 661, 681, 920
triangular fossa 301
triceps bar 994
triceps of arm 254
tricuspid valve 272
trifoliolate 101
trigeminal nerve 290
trigger 753
trigger switch 522, 523, 524,
  527
triglyph 685
trim 643
trim ring 504
trimmer 622
trimming 635
trip lever 150, 458
tripe 362
triple jump 952, 1008
triquetral 258
Triton 5
trochanter 165
trochlear nerve 290
trolley 800
trolley crank 146
trombone 675
trombones 661
Tropic of Cancer 30, 32
Tropic of Capricorn 30, 32
tropical climates 64
tropical cyclone 62
tropical fruits 347
tropical rain forest 64, 137
tropical wet-and-dry
  (savanna) 64
tropopause 62, 78
troposphere 62
trough 52, 889
trout 376
truck 1027, 1029
truck tractor 816, 820
truck trailer 820
trucking 816
trucks, examples 822
truffle 313
trumpet 676
trumpet interchange 796
trumpets 661
trunk 93, 128, 133, 184,
  247, 251, 805
trunks 992
truss structure 22
trussed arch 798
trussing needle 405
tsetse fly 169
tub 139, 509, 513
tub platform 456
tub rim 508
tuba 661, 675
tube foot 163
tube retention clip 470
tuber vegetables 317

tubular bells 661, 681
tubular element 504
tug 856
tulip 106
tuna 375
tundra 137
tuner 714
tungsten filament 469
tungsten-halogen lamp 467,
  469
tunic 585
tunic dress 577
tuning buttons 716
tuning control 715, 725, 728
tuning controls 707
tuning gauge 679
tuning mode 715
tuning peg 664, 666, 667
tuning pin 669
tuning slide 677
tunnel 846
turban 545
turbine 924
turbine shaft turns generator
  942
turbo-alternator unit 927
turbojet engine 869
turbot 377
turkey 209
turn signal 819, 826, 827
turn signal indicator 828
turnbuckle 985
turner 404
turning judges 977
turning wall 977, 978
turnip 331
turnstile 846
turntable 413, 721, 800
turquoise 604
turret 692
turret cap 899
turtle 190
turtle, anatomy 192
turtle, morphology 190
turtleneck 587, 597, 1025
TV mode 710
TV power button 710
TV/video button 710
twig 96, 129
twin-lens reflex camera 657
twin-set 581
twist 526
twist bit 526
twist drill 526
twist handle 753
twist lock 820
two pairs 1043
two-blade propeller 870
two-door sedan 802
two-leaf door 814
two-person tent 1030
two-way collar 570
tympanum 185, 682, 686
type I irregular galaxy 13
type II irregular galaxy 13
types of eclipses 7, 9
types of engines 810
types of golf clubs 1001
types of grips 967
types of movements 1047
types of strokes 978
typist's chair 741

U

u quark 876
U.S. habitation module 23
U.S. laboratory 23
ulna 201, 256, 258
ulnar extensor of wrist 254
ulnar flexor of wrist 254
ulnar nerve 282
ultracompact camera 656
ultraviolet radiation 890
umbra shadow 7, 9
umbrella pine 134
umpire 961, 964, 969, 972,
  1012
under tail covert 196
underarm portfolio 636
underground 691
underground cable network
  702
underground chamber 684
underground flow 77
underground mine 928
underground passage 836
underground stem 99
underpass 797
underwater camera 656
underwear 566, 588
underwire 590
unequal-arm balance 907
uneven parallel bars 974
ungulate mammals, examples
  of 218
unicellulars 160
union of two sets 914
union suit 566
unisex headgear 544
unisex shoes 548
unit price 908
unleavened bread 353
uphaul 981
upholstery nozzle 501
upper 1022
upper blade guard 522
upper bowl 426
upper chord 798
upper confining bed 924
upper deck 813, 868
upper edge 966
upper eyelid 185, 226, 310
upper fore topgallant sail 855
upper fore topsail 855
upper lip 304
upper lobe 275, 276, 277
upper mantle 38
upper shell 192
upper strap 1022
upper tail covert 196
upper wing 871
upright piano 668
upright piano action 670
upright vacuum cleaner 499
upstage 648
Uranus 2, 5
ureter 280, 281
ureteral orifice 281
urethra 280, 281, 292
urinary bladder 280, 281,
  292, 297
urinary system 280
uropod 178

USB connector 762
USB flash drive 762
USB port 745, 769
usual terms 111, 113, 115,
  119
utensils, kitchen 392
utensils, set 404
uterovesical pouch 293
uterus 292, 294
uvula 304, 307

V

V-neck 596
V-neck cardigan 596
vacuole 84, 159
vacuum bottle 1036
vacuum cleaner, cylinder 500
vacuum cleaner, hand 501
vacuum cleaner, upright 499
vacuum coffee maker 426
vacuum diaphragm 811
vagina 293, 294
vagus nerve 290
valance 485
valley 45, 50
valve 121, 676
valve casing 676
valve spring 810
vamp 553, 599
van 815
van body semitrailer 821
vane 199, 510
vanity cabinet 457
vanity mirror 807
vapor 879
variable ejector nozzle 872
variety meat 362
vastus lateralis 254
vault 695
vaulting horse 974, 975
VCR controls 710
VCR mode 710
VCR power button 710
vegetable bowl 384
vegetable brush 405
vegetable garden 430
vegetables 315
vegetables, bulb 315
vegetables, fruit 327
vegetables, inflorescent 326
vegetables, leaf 322
vegetables, root 330
vegetables, stalk 319
vegetables, tuber 317
vegetation regions 136
vein 100
veins 271
velarium 691
Velcro® closure 594
velvet-band choker 603
Venetian blind 491
venom gland 189
venomous snake, anatomy
  188
venomous snake, morphology
  189
vent 451, 807
vent brush 615
vent door 818
ventilating circuit 453

UNIVERSE AND EARTH > 2-83; PLANTS AND GARDENING > 84-157; ANIMAL KINGDOM > 158-243; THE HUMAN BEING > 244-311; FOOD AND KITCHEN > 312-429;
HOUSE AND DO-IT-YOURSELF > 430-543; CLOTHING AND PERSONAL ACCESSORIES > 544-643; ARTS AND ARCHITECTURE > 644-695; COMMUNICATIONS AND
OFFICE AUTOMATION > 696-791; TRANSPORTATION > 792-875; SCIENCE AND ENERGY > 876-951; SPORTS AND GAMES > 952-1048

ventilating fan 841
ventilating grille 500
ventilator 840, 848
Venus 3, 4
vermiform appendix 279
vernal equinox 19, 63
vernier 907
vertebral body 264, 265
vertebral foramen 265
vertebral shield 190
vertical control 756
vertical car lift 498
vertical movement 1047
vertical section 1028
vertical shaft 928
vertical side band 965
vertical take-off and landing aircraft 873
vertical-axis wind turbine 949
vesical trigone 281
vest 581
vestibular nerve 303
vestibule 303, 437, 688
vestibulocochlear nerve 290
vibrating mudscreen 930
vibrato arm 666
vice-skip 1012
video and digital terminals 653
video entertainment system 1048
video monitor 756
video port 745, 769
video switcher technician 704
videocassette 708
videocassette recorder (VCR) 708
videotape operation controls 713
view camera 657
viewfinder 651, 653
vinyl grip sole 595
viola 663
violas 661
violet 107
violin 662, 663
violin family 661, 663
viper 193
visceral pleura 275
vise 537
visible light 890
vision 892
vision defects 893
visor 828
visor hinge 828
visual arts 650
visual display 1048
vocal cord 276
voice recorder button 770
volcanic bomb 43
volcanic island 55
volcano 37, 42
volcano during eruption 42
volleyball 964, 965
volt 912
voltage decrease 927
voltage increase 925, 927, 943
voltage tester 543

volume control 666, 667, 710, 716, 725, 729, 736, 744
volute 472, 686, 687
volva 94
vulture 208
vulva 248, 294

W

waders 1040
wadi 61
wading bird 202
waffle iron 422
wagon tent 1031
waist 246, 250, 552, 662
waist belt 488, 1036
waistband 563, 567, 572
waistband extension 563
wakame 314
walk-in wardrobe 435
walkie-talkie 729
walking leg 174
wall 8, 112
wall cabinet 379
wall cloud 70
wall fitting 495
wall lantern 495
wall side 863
wall stud 440
wall tent 1031
wallaby 239
wallet 637, 771
walnut 132, 341
walrus 234
waning gibbous 11
wardrobe 435, 481
warm air 72
warm temperate climates 65
warm-air baffle 449
warm-up lane 1014
warming plate 423
warning track 959
wash tower 513
washcloth 621
washer 462, 508, 884
washer nozzle 804
wasp-waisted corset 590
Wassily chair 473
waste pipe 459
waste stack 452
waste tee 463
water 925
water bottle clip 833
water bug 171
water carrier 1036
water chestnut 316
water cools the used steam 942
water flow 162
water goblet 381
water hazard 1000
water hose 513
water intake 936
water is pumped back into the steam generator 942
water jets 979
water key 677
water level 423
water meter 452
water pitcher 385
water service pipe 452

water spider 173
water strider 172
water table 49, 83
water tank 425, 627, 841
water turns into steam 941
water-level selector 508
water-level tube 498
water-steam mix 924
water-tank area 871
watercolor cakes 644
watercolor tube 644
watercourse 50, 82
watercress 324
waterfall 49, 50
watering can 147
watering tools 146
watering tube 824
waterline 859
watermelon 345
waterproof pants 594
waterspout 70
watt 912
wave 52, 889
wave base 52
wave clip 617
wave height 52
wave length 52
wavelength 889
wax bean 335
wax crayons 644
wax gourd 328
wax seal 459
waxing gibbous 10
weasel 228
weather strip 446
weatherboard 445
web 184, 957
web frame 863
webbed foot 184
Webcam 754
wedding ring 607
wedge lever 530
weeding hoe 144
weeping willow 131
weighing platform 910
weight 906, 908, 995
weight belt 983
weight machine 994
weight, measure 906
weightlifting 992
weightlifting belt 992
weightlifting shoe 992
weights 994
welt 553
welt pocket 596
West Coast mirror 815, 817
Western Hemisphere 31
Western meridian 32
wet suit 983
wet-weather tire 1007
whale 233, 235
wharf 850
wheat 123
wheat: grain 122
wheat: spike 123
wheel 141, 643, 809, 816, 1004, 1027, 1028
wheel cover 805
wheel mouse 750
wheelchair lift 815
wheelhouse 856

whelk 369
whisk 401
whiskers 226
whistle 428
White 1046
white 891, 1045
white balance 652
white bread 355
white cabbage 323
white matter 285
white onion 315
white square 1046
white tape 964, 966, 969
white wine glass 380
white-tailed deer 220
whitewater, canoe-kayak 982
whiting 376
wholemeal bread 355
widescreen/data code button 713
wild boar 218
winch 822
winch controls 822
wind 83
wind deflector 817
wind instruments 672
wind turbines 949
wind vane 951
windbag 659
windbreaker 572
winder 904
winding adjustment 899
winding mechanism 492
winding shaft 929
winding tower 929
windmill 948
window 419, 435, 444, 502, 505, 805, 812, 848, 868, 981
window accessories 489
window sill 438
window tab 781
windows 635
windshaft 948
windshield 804, 816, 826, 829, 868
windshield wiper 804
wine waiter corkscrew 395
wing 25, 166, 196, 198, 869, 1007
wing covert 197
wing membrane 243
wing nut 535
wing strut 870
wing vein 165
wing, bird 198
winglet 869, 872
wings 243, 648, 871
wings, bat 243
winter 63
winter precipitations 72
winter solstice 63
winter tire 808
winze 928
wiper switch 806
wire 887
wire beater 415
wire brush 680
wire cutter 542
wire stripper 542
wire support 1034

wireless communication 729
wisdom tooth 268
wishbone boom 981
withers 217, 224
wok 407
wok set 407
wolf 232
woman 248
women's clothing 573
women's gloves 556
women's headgear 545
women's shoes 550
wood 1001
wood chip car 844
wood chisel 531
wood ear 313
wood firing 448
wood flooring 441
wood frog 187
woodbox 448
woodpecker 211
woodwind family 660
work furniture 740
worm 824
worm gear 881
wraparound dress 577
wraparound skirt 578
wrapover top 585
wrenches 534
wrestler 987
wrestling 987
wrestling area 987
wrestling shoe 987
wrist 224, 242, 246, 250
wrist strap 1023, 1025
wrist-length glove 556
wristband 992
writing case 637

X

X-rays 890
xD-Picture card 655
xylophone 661, 681

Y

yak 221
yam 318
yard 853
yard line 960
yard-long bean 334
yellow 891
yellow onion 315
yellow sweet pepper 327
yellowjacket 170
yoke 560, 572, 584
yoke skirt 579

Z

zebra 219
zest 113
zester 394
zinc can 884
zinc-electrolyte mix 885
zipper 571, 595, 610, 1030
zither 659
zona pellucida 295
zoom button 712
zoom lens 706, 712
zucchini 328
zygomatic bone 262

UNIVERSE AND EARTH > 2-83; PLANTS AND GARDENING > 84-157; ANIMAL KINGDOM > 158-243; THE HUMAN BEING > 244-311; FOOD AND KITCHEN > 312-429; HOUSE AND DO-IT-YOURSELF > 430-543; CLOTHING AND PERSONAL ACCESSORIES > 544-643; ARTS AND ARCHITECTURE > 644-695; COMMUNICATIONS AND OFFICE AUTOMATION > 696-791; TRANSPORTATION > 792-875; SCIENCE AND ENERGY > 876-951; SPORTS AND GAMES > 952-1048

1071

INDEX